BERNARD PODUSKA

De Anza College

UNDERSTANDING

PSYCHOLOGY AND

DIMENSIONS

OF ADJUSTMENT

McGRAW-HILL BOOK COMPANY

New York   St. Louis   San Francisco   Auckland   Bogotá   Hamburg
Johannesburg   London   Madrid   Mexico   Montreal   New Delhi
Panama   Paris   São Paulo   Singapore   Sydney   Tokyo   Toronto

22⁹⁰

This book was set in Helvetica by Black Dot, Inc. (ECU).
The editors were Elysbeth H. Wyckoff and Natalie M. Talbott Blaney;
the designer was Joan E. O'Connor;
the production supervisor was Charles Hess.
The photo editor was Inge King.
Von Hoffmann Press, Inc., was printer and binder.

UNDERSTANDING PSYCHOLOGY AND
DIMENSIONS OF ADJUSTMENT

1234567890 VHVH 89876543210

See Acknowledgments on pages 531–533.
Copyrights included on this page by reference.

Library of Congress Cataloging in Publication Data

Poduska, Bernard.
Understanding psychology and dimensions of adjustment.

Bibliography: p.
Includes index.
1. Adjustment (Psychology) 2. Personality.
I. Title.
BF335.P62   155.2'4   79-21575
ISBN 0-07-050365-6

CONTENTS

PREFACE

The field of personality and adjustment is one of the most diversified and individualized subjects taught at a college level. One of the main reasons for such diversification is the inherent ambiguity of the terms "adjustment" and "personality." Personality theorists, as well as personality instructors, tend to provide their own definitions for these terms and, consequently, to orient their approaches to psychology toward these particular definitions.

Owing to the resulting proliferation of theoretical biases, the instructor needs to select a text that is *truly* eclectic in that it presents a variety of theoretical points of view with as little bias as is humanly possible; that is, a text designed with the intent of *informing*, rather than *reforming*, the reader. To this end, I have made a sincere effort to present equally the contributions of the psychodynamic theorists, such as Freud, Adler, Rank, Horney, Sullivan, and Fromm; the behaviorists, such as Watson, Dollard, Miller, Skinner, Wolpe, Harlow, and Bandura; and the existential-humanistic theorists, such as Binswanger, Boss, May, Frankl, Allport, Maslow, Rogers, and Perls.

A personality and adjustment text, however, must not only inform the student as to what alternative theories of personality are available, but must also show how they can be applied. I believe that it is the application of these theories that is most characteristic of a course in personality and adjustment. This book has therefore been written to provide a practical means of applying the theoretical information that is presented to the problems of coping with the stresses encountered in everyday life. For example, the book discusses how to distinguish between an acquaintance, a friend, and someone who really cares (Chapter 9), communication techniques that can strengthen parent-child relationships (Chapter 12), when and where to seek psychological counseling (Chapter 15), and ways of enhancing relationships by being more authentic (Chapter 16).

Another important quality to consider when writing or selecting a text is its readability. In my evaluation of a text's readability, I consider not only whether the average student will understand what the author is trying to say, but also whether the style and content of the material presented are interesting and stimulating. With this evaluation of readability firmly in mind, I have attempted to write this text in a style that conveys a sense of "talking with" rather than "lecturing to" the student, and at a pedogogical level suitable to the reading capabilities of the average lower division student.

I have also attempted to emphasize a "back to basics" approach to adjustment; that is, to stress the importance of developing a sense of self-reliance, learning how to cope effectively with stress, assuming personal responsibility for the choices we make, and establishing enduring, meaningful relationships (especially with regard to marriage, family, and parent-child relationships). In addition, to make the material as relevant as possible, topics of special interest, such as human sexuality, vocational selection, drug dependency, self-identity, and personal growth, are thoroughly explored.

In summation, I believe the design of this book provides the following:

1 A reasonable compilation of major personality theories presented in a *readable* format
2 Information on the effect such theories may have on personal development
3 Practical application of such principles
4 Clarification of successful and unsuccessful ways of coping with stress
5 The opportunity for gaining greater understanding of oneself and others
6 Adaptability and flexibility in a variety of individual approaches to teaching courses in personality and adjustment

To enrich the presentation of materials in the text, I have prepared the following supplement for instructors of this course:

Resource Manual and Test File. This supplement offers a source book for expanding text discussions and class activities. For each chapter it provides (1) a detailed outline, (2) a general overview, (3) lecture suggestions, (4) discussion topics, (5) informal meeting suggestions, (6) audio-visual aids, and (7) readings. It also contains approximately 800 objective test items on all important concepts in the text. Answers are provided for all questions.

I would like to acknowledge the foresight shown by Richard Wright concerning the conception of this project, the enthusiasm and editorial expertise demonstrated by Betsy Wyckoff and Natalie Talbott Blaney throughout the development of this text, the assistance of Sheila Cook in helping me meet my deadlines, and the endurance and talents of Blythe Deming, whose typing and proofing of my rough drafts contributed so much to the quality of the final manuscript. I would also like to thank the many reviewers for their helpful suggestions and constructive criticism.

I express my deepest appreciation to Barbara, my wife, whose consideration and "pioneer spirit" encouraged her to lighten my load in many ways; and to Keisha, Tasha, Brandon, Clinton, and Ryan, our children, who were so patient and understanding while "Daddy was working on his book." And I offer special thanks for the many times my prayers were answered when I was in need of guidance, inspiration, and endurance.

Bernard Poduska

PART ONE

THE NATURE OF

HUMAN NATURE

CHAPTER 1

THE NATURE OF

HUMAN ADJUSTMENT

Go placidly amid the noise and the haste,
and remember what peace there may be in silence.

As far as possible without surrender
be on good terms with all persons.
Speak your truth quietly and clearly;
and listen to others, even the dull and ignorant;
they too have their story. . . .

If you compare yourself with others,
you may become vain and bitter; for always
there will be greater and lesser persons than yourself. . . .

Be yourself.
Especially, do not feign affection.
Neither be cynical about love;
for in the face of all aridity and disenchantment
it is as perennial as the grass. . . .

You are a child of the universe,
no less than the trees and the stars;
you have a right to be here.
And whether or not it is clear to you,
no doubt the universe is unfolding as it should.

Therefore be at peace with God,
whatever you conceive Him to be.
And whatever your labors and aspirations,
in the noisy confusion of life
keep peace with your soul.

With all its sham, drudgery and broken dreams,
it is still a beautiful world.

Be cheerful.

Strive to be happy.

Max Ehrmann
Desiderata

THE INDIVIDUAL IN A CHANGING WORLD

It has only been during the last few hundred years that change has been recognized as an inherent characteristic of society and technology, and that an effort has been made to understand its direction and its possible effects on the individual. Crucial to the determination of this direction and its effects are the "adaptability of human nature" and the limits to which the individual can continue to adjust. Will and Ariel Durant, in *The Lessons of History* (1968), concluded that:

> . . . in a developed and complex civilization individuals are more differentiated and unique than in a primitive society, and many situations contain novel circumstances requiring modifications of instinctive response; custom recedes, reasoning spreads; the results are less predictable. There is no certainty that the future will repeat the past. Every year is an adventure. (p. 88)

The term "adventure," by its very nature, implies an undertaking with an uncertain outcome, but a great deal of what is commonly referred to as "sanity" is based, if not on certainty, at least on a reasonable degree of predictability. For instance, when you leave your house in the morning, it is reasonable to predict that it will still be there when you return, and that your loved ones will react in an affectionate and receptive manner. Such constancy tends to place only minimal demands on an individual's capacity to adjust. However, change and dealing with the unpredictable can often strain this capacity. For example, should an individual return to find a note reading:

> Dear Ralph,
>
> It was all a mistake. I've never loved you. So I'm leaving you. I never told you, but the marriage was never legal, so a divorce won't be necessary. It also explains how I was able to sell the house without your signature. You wouldn't have been able to keep up the payments anyway, now that you've lost your job. Not that I suppose it matters with the doctor calling today to inform you of the possibility of your illness being terminal.
>
> I hope you are able to make the proper adjustments in order to cope effectively with these changes.
>
> Adios,
> Maude

As fanciful as this example may seem, the adjustive demands being made on the individual today are almost as great. The moral values learned during childhood are found to be inapplicable to the adult. Many theologians are no longer attempting to prove the existence of God, and instead are debating the "meaning of God in human experience." Even the points at which life begins and ends have become subjects of debate, and the determination of the fate of one's "immortal soul" is no longer as important as the effect of the belief in immortality upon human conduct.

For some, human destiny has been reduced to nothing more than a complicated physicochemical process (materialism). A. N. Whitehead critically notes, "Scientists animated by the purpose of proving that they are purposeless constitute an interesting subject for study." Others find human destiny irretrievably entwined with *transcendency* (that is, going beyond what can be known only through the five senses). They declare that "We look not to the things that are seen but to the things that are unseen; for the things that are seen are transient, but the things that are unseen are eternal" (II Corinthians 4:18). Each point of view, as well as those which fall between these two extremes, demonstrates an attempt at adjustment, an attempt to adapt to environmental demands and change.

In today's world, individuals must adapt both to philosophical changes and to physiological changes in the environment: the destruction and consumption of irreplaceable resources, the pollution of air and water, an ever-increasing population. Some—unable to adjust or unwilling to try— become "mentally ill." Others have only limited adaptive capacity, and their adjustment takes the form of "coping" or enduring. Still others perceive environmental change as an opportunity for creative self-expression. Their adjustment takes the form of a reaffirmation of their being and of the inalienable right to exercise their free will. As long as there are alternatives from which to choose, the adjustment of this latter group is assured.

> In the fell clutch of circumstance
> I have not winced or cried aloud.
> Under the bludgeonings of chance
> My head is bloody, but unbowed.
> It matters not how strait the gate,
> How charged with punishments the scroll,
> I am the master of my fate:
> I am the captain of my soul. (William E. Henley, *Invictus*)

Adapting to Scientific Change

Voltaire, in *Candide* (1759), said, "All is for the best in the best of possible worlds." He later added, "If this is the best of possible worlds, what then are the others?" The American novelist James Cabell, in *The Silver Stallion* (1926), updated Voltaire's observation: "The optimist proclaims that we live in the best of all possible worlds; and the pessimist fears that this is true." During the eighteenth century, *science* was thought to hold the promise of utopia—the best of all possible worlds. However, with technological change came unprecedented affluence, and, for perhaps the first time in history, the average person was presented with the choice between satisfying materialistic needs and satisfying humanistic needs.

THE PROMISE OF SCIENCE   The old idea of the sovereign right of science to pursue abstract intellectual activity in an unrestricted effort to reach the "truth" may be gone forever. Science today tends to direct itself more to the merits of

FIGURE 1.1   Perhaps more than with any other scientific discovery, the peaceful use of nuclear power promised to provide humanity with the Utopia, that perfect world that has persistently eluded all previous efforts to create a world without want. [*Conklin, Monkmeyer Press Photo Service.*]

the "truth-seeking process" than to the eventual attainment of an ultimate truth. As the German author G. E. Lessing (1729–1781) noted, "It is not the truth which a man possesses or thinks he possesses, but the steadfast task to which he has applied himself of striving after truth, [that] is the true worth of man" (Randall, 1940, p. 491).

Science soon came to be perceived as a "new religion," with the laboratory-smocked scientists comprising the priesthood. Truth was no longer an *absolute* to be extracted from the scriptures, but an *abstract* to be independently determined by each individual and prudently qualified by such statements as "Insofar as today's science is able to determine . . ." or "Barring any new scientific breakthroughs. . . ."

In contrast to the intellectual innocence of the prescientific era and its belief in absolutes, today's relativism constantly threatens the individual with "intellectual rape." Giovanni Gentile (1925) said:

> Every force is a moral force, for it is always an expression of will; and whatever be the argument used—preaching or applying blackjacks—its efficacy can be none other than its ability finally to receive the inner support of a man and to persuade him to agree to it. (Randall, 1940, p. 665)

BIOLOGY   The science of biology, assaulting the individual with the theory of evolution, confounded people's sense of identity, jeopardized their sense of dignity, and questioned their sense of worth, importance, and purpose. Charles Darwin's (1809–1882) theory, as presented in his *On the Origin of Species* (1859), suggested that the human race was nothing more than a "favorable variation" in the process of species formation: "I have called this principle, by which each slight variation, *if useful,* is preserved, by the term Natural Selection." The exact cause of such "slight variations" was not entirely understood, but scientific evidence is now pointing to cosmic rays and *chance* mutations of genetic codes. This explanation categorizes the human race as an undignified "cosmic accident" in an evolutionary process that may not even have a goal or purpose.

PHYSIOLOGY   The science of physiology attacked the mysteries of human behavior. Dissecting the anatomy piece by piece, dividing the brain into "specific functions," and thoroughly mapping the complex "wiring" of the nervous system, science looked everywhere, searched every cavity, and found no *scientific* evidence of a soul. As a consequence, humans could be viewed as just another group of organisms that follow the "mechanical laws of the universe."

PSYCHOLOGY   The science of psychology was introduced by Wilhelm Wundt (1832–1920). He used experimental techniques to maintain scientific objectivity while exploring human behavior. John Watson (1878–1958), also an advocate of objectivity, proposed that psychology should not be the study of the mind, as in earlier approaches to psychological research, but rather the study of behavior. Watson, one of the first behaviorists, maintained that:

> Psychology, as the behaviorist views it, is a purely objective, experimental branch of natural science which needs consciousness as little as do the sciences of chemistry and physics. . . . This suggested elimination of states of consciousness as proper objects of investigation in themselves will remove the barrier which exists between psychology and the other sciences. (1914, p. 27)

The concept of free will also came under severe scrutiny when Ivan Pavlov (1832–1920) and other "reflexologists" presented their findings pertaining to *classical conditioning*—the ability to associate an involuntary response with a stimulus that would not normally elicit such a response.

The mechanistic approach to human behavior tended to "equalize" the human race with other species and deny it the dignity of having a free will. The early twentieth-century alternative was Freudian psychoanalytic theory, which tended to perceive the human being first and foremost as an animal; a hapless victim of *instincts* and primitive urges—a neurotic manifestation of repressed *sexuality*. Freud also referred to "free will" as an illusion, believing that one is never free of unconscious influences, but he did not reject the possibility of "limited self-direction"; otherwise, "there would be no point in providing insight to a client if some self-direction were not possible."

As an almost spontaneous reaction to this spiritual vacuum, the existential movement was initiated. Founded on the theology of Kierkegaard and Buber, and the philosophy of Jean-Paul Sartre, existentialism maintained that all human beings possess freedom of choice. Their main problem is being faced with too many alternatives to choose from and not enough information to make the correct choice obvious.

Rollo May (1909–   ), Abraham Maslow (1908–1970), Carl Rogers (1902–   ), and others have attempted to incorporate this philosophical approach into the psychotherapeutic mainstream. They have developed what is now referred to as "humanistic psychology." The main concern of humanistic psychology is to help the individual discover his or her own identity and the meaning of life and existence, as well as to reaffirm the fundamental uniqueness of the individual.

In the Name of Progress

Through continued research, modern science continues to generate challenges to identity and meaning. For example, the exploration of space forces us to ask whether we humans are unique in the universe. The answer to this question is being sought through the use of space probes with messages imprinted on them, the exploration of other planets (particularly Mars), and radio-listening devices searching for extraterrestrial signals.

New thoughts concerning the motivation behind human behavior include Edward Wilson's (1975) *sociogenetic* hypothesis. Wilson holds that all behavior, both individual and group, is genetically motivated, and that its main objective is to ensure genetic survival in the next generation. In addition, biogenetic research continues to make breakthroughs in the area of *cloning*—the reproduction of a "twin" from a single cell of the parent individual without the employment of sexual reproduction. If cloning led to a "favorable variation," one would merely clone as many copies of that individual as was desired.

Science is also making constant advances in the development of body-part replacements and transplants. As a result, the "Frankenstein phenomenon" has become a foreseeable possibility. The Frankenstein phenomenon refers to the identity crisis that could result from the future possibility of performing a brain transplant. In the case of a heart, kidney, or liver transplant, the recipient (Ralph) merely accepts the organ from the donor (George) and is perceived, for example, as being Ralph with George's heart. However, should Ralph accept George's *brain* in a transplant operation (this

FIGURE 1.2

Each of us must determine what price we are willing to pay for changes made "in the name of progress." [*Mimi Forsyte, Monkmeyer Press Photo Service.*]

operation has already been performed successfully between salamanders), then *who would the survivor really be?* What is more, if it is held that the soul departs from the body at the time of death, would the donor's soul (George) be transferred with the brain, or would the brain be without a soul? And if the latter is so, what about the recipient (Ralph) whose body is being kept alive by machines, but whose brain has been removed; what about his soul? With such possibilities, the casual question, "Is that you, Ralph?" takes on new and intriguing meaning.

These are but a few of the many challenges to individual adjustment in the era of scientific "progress." Herbert Spencer (1820–1903), in his *Illusions of Universal Progress,* said of progress:

Whether it be in the development of the Earth, in the development of Life upon its surface, in the development of Society, of Government, of Manufactures, of Commerce, of Language, Literature, Science, Art, this same evolution of the simple into the complex, through successive differentiations, holds throughout. From the earliest traceable cosmical changes, down to the latest results of civilization, we shall find that the transformation of the homogeneous into the heterogeneous, is that in which Progress essentially consists. Progress is not an accident but a necessity. What we call evil and immorality must disappear. It is certain that man must become perfect. . . . The ultimate development of the ideal man is certain—as certain as any conclusion in which we place the most implicit faith. . . . Always towards perfection is the mighty movement—towards a complete development and a more unmixed good. (Randall, 1940, p. 445)

Thus is the state of humanity as it attempts to adjust to the scientific world of the twentieth century. Stripped of the respectability of divine intervention, it is experiencing a reawakening of religious interest. Having had the dignity of free will challenged, it has embraced the doctrine of "do your own thing." The essence of individuality and uniqueness is being threatened, and the questions: Who am I?, What am I?, and Why am I? are being asked with increased urgency.

Adapting to Social Change

In *Sister Carrie* (1900), the American author Theodore Dreiser (1871–1945) wrote: "Our civilization is still in a middle stage, scarcely beast, in that it is no longer wholly guided by instinct; scarcely human, in that it is not yet wholly guided by reason."

In this state of flux, social change appears to be inevitable. Yet when change occurs too rapidly, traditional moral and cultural values can be destroyed. When this occurs, as is often the case in the twentieth century, people are left floundering helplessly. They no longer know how they are supposed to live or by what standards they are to evaluate their conduct.

THE NEED FOR HOPE   One of the more outstanding characteristics of the twentieth century is that people seem to be more effective at providing themselves *with* a living than at providing a *reason* for living. They live in a time in which they are seemingly able to satisfy their physiological needs, thereby acquiring the ability to go on living, but they find it difficult to satisfy their psychological needs, thereby failing to acquire an incentive to go on living.

The reason for living has traditionally been provided by a religious, or spiritual, source, which often included the concept of a "master plan." To complete the plan, it was necessary to fulfill certain behavioral requirements, such as obeying commandments, restricting one's diet, or accomplishing certain tasks. However, many religious master plans have been diluted by social demands, so that they have become vague or contradictory. Purpose has also been acquired through the desire to perpetuate an idea, national identity, or bloodline, establishing a kind of immortality. A growing sense of futility, however, has led to philosophical and political apathy—the thought that "nothing really matters anyway." There seems to be a general lack of incentive. In the twentieth century hope appears to be somewhat elusive.

To illustrate the importance of hope, consider the plight of seamen floating in the North Atlantic after their ship has sunk. Although the expectation of survival in those cold waters is approximately thirty minutes, many seamen are found dead even though rescue teams reach them within ten or fifteen minutes.

The reason for this disparity was determined by behavioral scientists studying the stress of exposure through laboratory techniques.

One phase of their research involved placing a standard strain of domesticated laboratory rats in a high-walled container of ice water and then measuring the length of time they would swim in the frigid water before succumbing to exposure. These results were then compared with the swimming times of a hearty strain of undomesticated Norwegian rats. The results were surprising. In almost all cases, the hardy, well-insulated Norwegian rats would stop swimming shortly after being placed in the icy waters, whereas the relatively fragile, domesticated laboratory rats would continue to swim until they were exhausted. The explanation for the difference was as follows: The laboratory rats, having already undergone the experience of being placed in "undesirable environments" and then being removed from them by the experimenters, had developed "faith" that they would eventually be rescued from their present predicament. The wild Norwegian rats, having had no such experience, sensed the futility of struggling, resigned themselves to their fate, and gave up. As a result of these experiments, special indoctrination and training programs were initiated to instill in the seamen the idea that every effort would be made to rescue them, and that they should never give up, but should maintain the belief that they would survive. Such programs increased the survival rate and raised the overall morale of the seamen by giving them hope.

Unfortunately, with the potential destruction of the entire human race as part of today's reality, many people find it difficult to maintain the belief that they will survive. Moreover, they are not at all sure whether survival would be worthwhile. As General Omar Bradley remarked, "We have grasped the mystery of the atom and rejected the Sermon on the Mount." With the future so uncertain, and the cultural past being obliterated, more and more people see themselves as dehumanized and their lives as having become flat, narrow, and self-limiting. For them, life has no sense of purpose, relevance, or meaning.

THE NEED FOR INDIVIDUAL FULFILLMENT Early twentieth-century psychologists were more concerned with explaining such epidemic depression than with preventing its occurrence. Most early theorists emphasized what could go *wrong* with the individual rather than what could go *right*. They concentrated on how "ill" the individual was rather than on his or her potential for growth. However, during the early sixties, with the introduction of the humanistic approach, a few psychologists began to concentrate their efforts on the expansion of awareness, the enhancement of creativity, and the realization of individual potentials. Eleanor Hoover, speaking of the humanistic approach, stated:

> Where once, under the old Freudian "medical model," Man was seen as either "sick" or "well," he is now seen as having a natural ability to make changes in himself rather quickly, once he sees what needs to be done.

> Where once Man was seen as merely a bundle of responses to stimuli, moldable in

any direction, there is a focus on individuality, the person and the intrinsic complexity, richness and power of mind and consciousness.

Where once "objectivity" meant banishing subjective experience from science, it is now being allowed back in. The belief of humanistic psychologists is that there is no basic contradiction and that a new science can be built which also includes the observer's experience.

Where once purpose or meaning were seen as "religious," each is finding its way back into psychology. (*Los Angeles Times,* April 6, 1975)

The emphasis of this "new psychology" is on perceiving the individual as a whole being—a blend of body, mind, emotions, and even spirit—and on tapping inherent, built-in capacities for growth and development through a wide variety of sensory awareness, encounter, and other therapeutic techniques. Rather than merely attempting to *explain* behavior, the humanistic approach attempts to *inspire* behavior.

In the 1960s, partially due to the influence of humanistic psychology, the idea of individual fulfillment became predominant. The evaluation of one's "trip through life" affected both interpersonal relationships and the individual's dealings with organized institutions. Interpreting the exact meaning of humanistic principles, however, was a personal matter. As a consequence, the establishment of a "meaningful relationship" began to be perceived as an alternative to the institution of marriage rather than as an integral part of such a commitment. "Doing your own thing" became a means of avoiding membership in the "establishment" rather than of developing individual talents and enhancing one's uniqueness. Moreover, the emphasis humanistic psychology placed on subjective experiences was sometimes interpreted as endorsement of the drug scene and free love, experiences which often led to devalued self-images and moral confusion.

THE SEARCH FOR VALUES   In an attempt to escape the loneliness of casual sex and noncommitment, many people turned to the principles of fidelity and interpersonal commitment and a reevaluation of the moral developments of the past few generations. They sought a compromise between the fear of possessiveness that comes from belonging *to* someone and the desire for intimacy that comes from belonging *with* someone.

For some people, however, it is an almost insurmountable task to determine what a satisfactory compromise might be in today's world. Social fragmentation into ethnic, racial, and economic subgroups has made compromise mean that everyone is *giving up* something and not that everyone is *getting* something. In many instances, adopting a set of standards is about as precarious as being a penguin on a melting ice floe—everything seems permanent one moment and is gone the next. Most causes seem to be more dedicated to tearing down what *is* than to building up what *is not.* The founder of French socialism, Claude-Henri de Rouvroy (1760–1825), divided social development into two alternating periods: the "organic" and the "critical":

The law of human development . . . reveals two distinct and alternative states of society: one, the organic, in which all human actions are classed, foreseen, and regulated by a general theory, and the purpose of social activity is clearly defined; the other, the critical, in which all community of thought, all communal action, all coordination have ceased, and the society is only an [indiscriminately formed mass] of separate individuals in conflict with one another.

In the organic ages all basic problems [theological, political, economic, moral] have received at least provisional solutions. But soon the progress achieved by the help of these solutions, and under the protection of the institutions realized through them, rendered them inadequate, and evoked novelties. Critical epochs—periods of debate, protest, . . . and transition, replaced the old mood with doubt, individualism, and indifference to the great problems. . . . In organic periods men are busy building; in critical periods they are busy destroying. (Durant, 1968, p. 89)

It may very well be, applying Rouvroy's construct, that the individual today is faced with adjusting to a critical period in human social development. A desperate effort is being made to *preserve* whatever can be saved from destruction: the environment, the ethnic purity of the ancestral culture, one's genealogical lineage, or "roots," the latest flora or fauna to be threatened with extinction. It is as if there is an empathetic identification with the victims of progress and a realization that the human race could be next.

A DEFINITION OF ADJUSTMENT

Erik Erikson's statement on individual development (1968), *"The ability to accommodate oneself to changing circumstances is a mark of maturity,"* could easily be interpreted as a definition of "adjustment." Although adjustment implies the attainment of a more favorable relationship with one's environment, it does not necessarily mean the attainment of a static condition, contentment, or peace of mind. Nor does being adjusted mean that a person does not feel upset, angry, sad, frustrated, or afraid. Adjustment is the ability to select appropriate and effective measures to meet the demands of the environment while maintaining a healthy attitude toward the circumstances. John Milton (1608–1674), in *Paradise Lost,* noted:

The mind is its own place, and in
    itself
Can make a heaven of hell, a hell of
    heaven.

Biological and Psychological Adjustment

The debate concerning the relative importance of heredity and environment— the ageless nature-nurture conflict—continues unabated in the area of adjustment. Those supporting hereditary determinants propose that the ability to resist stress and adapt to change is genetically determined. Those advocating environmental influences believe that successful adjustment is a result of learning and experience. A popular compromise proposes that individual potential is derived from heredity but is dependent upon environment for its development.

NATURE   Since *Homo sapiens* is a product of evolution, with its physical characteristics genetically determined, there are some who believe that human behavior should also be a product of evolution. Sigmund Freud (1856–1939) was one such theorist. He proposed that each individual human being is born with both a *life instinct* (Eros or libido), which tends to preserve the individual and provide for the survival of the species, and a *death instinct* (Thanatos), which can motivate self-destructive or aggressive behavior. These instincts, as well as other primitive drives, such as hunger-thirst, sex, and the avoidance of pain, are an integral part of the unconscious, wich Freud referred to collectively as the id.

Others believe that an individual can inherit both physiologically determined instincts and experientially determined instincts. In other words, it is possible for a person to inherit certain behavior patterns and also certain thought patterns. René Descartes (1596–1650), famous for his statement "I think, therefore I am," and his discovery of analytical geometry, was one of the first to attempt to prove that certain ideas, such as those concerning theology and mathematics, are innate. Much later, Herbert Spencer (1820–1903), in his *Principles of Psychology* (1855), introduced the concept of "evolutionary associationism," which proposed that "associations which are often repeated in the lifetime of an individual or in the race will be transmitted to the off-spring as an evolutionary instinct."

Carl Jung (1875–1961) took the concept of evolutionary associationism a step further. He proposed that the individual inherits predispositions to have certain experiences, such as the way one relates to the opposite sex or experiences "God." In addition, Jung (1959) believed that the individual also inherits a *collective unconscious,* composed of *universal thought forms* shared with all members of the human race and derived from ancestral experiences.

NURTURE   Those who argue in favor of environmental influence tend to deny the existence of inherited instincts and advocate the theoretical approach proposed by Aristotle (384–322 B.C.)—that of the *tabula rasa,* or blank slate. This theory holds that at birth a person's brain contains no knowledge whatsoever; it is blank, and *all* knowledge is obtained through experience.

John Locke (1632–1704), the founder of British empiricism, noted that "experience supplies our understanding with all the materials of thinking." According to Locke, there are two sources of experience—*sensation* and *reflection.* The experience of sensation is derived from *primary qualities* of perception, such as number, shape, and motion, and *secondary qualities* of perception, such as color, taste, and texture.

The experience of reflection is derived by "observing" one's own intellectual activity, the most essential activity being the formation of complex ideas from the combination of simple ideas. This concept of joining ideas together made Locke a forerunner of *associationism,* which was to become so dominant in the twentieth century.

The concept of associationism gained momentum and greater acceptance through the work of David Hartley (1705–1757). He maintained that associations could occur not only between ideas and sensations but also between body movements and actions. This concept was later to be developed by Ivan Pavlov (1849–1936) through his study of reflexes and the discovery of *classical conditioning.*

It was not until the development of *behaviorism,* however, that associationism became fully established, or that the argument in support of environmental influences was fully substantiated. *Behaviorism* is a psychological approach emphasizing the scientific study of behavior. Researchers study the bond between behavior and its consequences, the role of reinforcement, and the shaping of behavior.

John Watson (1878–1958), considered to be the American founder of behaviorism, summed up the confidence of many behaviorists in the power of environmental manipulation when he said:

> Give me a dozen healthy infants, well-formed, and my own specified world to bring them up in and I'll guarantee to take any one at random and train him to become any type of specialist I might suggest—doctor, lawyer, artist, merchant-chief and, yes, even beggarman and thief, regardless of his talents, penchants, tendencies, abilities, vocations, and the race of his ancestors. (1924, p. 82)

With this power to manipulate and control human behavior, it is necessary to ask *who will control the controllers.* Since "social reinforcement" is capable of modifying attitudes and beliefs as well as conduct, we must also ask who is to determine which set of morals and ethics is to be impressed on which group of people. In addition, since drugs are also used to control behavior, we must decide who is to determine the extent to which thoughts and actions are to be controlled by such methods.

B. F. Skinner (1904–   ), noted for his research with reinforcement, argues that "behavioral manipulation" takes place whether one wishes it to or not; environmental interaction is inevitable. He points out that even in such "nondirective" therapies as the client-centered therapy of Carl Rogers (1902–   ), an important reinforcement for the therapist is the success of manipulating the client's behavior. Therefore, one can only hope for altruistic motives on the part of the manipulator.

Carl Rogers, in a rebuttal to Skinner's position, stated:

> To hope that the power which is being made available by the behavioral sciences will be exercised by the scientists, or by a benevolent group, seems to me to be a hope little supported by either recent or distant history. It seems far more likely that behavioral scientists, holding their present attitudes, will be in the position of the German rocket scientists specializing in guided missiles. . . . If behavioral scientists are concerned solely with advancing their science, it seems most probable that they will serve the purpose of whatever group has the power. (Brecher and Brecher, 1961, p. 87)

The controversy today, therefore, has expanded from whether or not behavior can be modified by the environment to what the purpose of the modification is and who will control it.

Adjusting through Conforming Behavior

Mark Twain once wrote, "A round man cannot be expected to fit in a square hole right away. He must have time to modify his shape" (*More Tramps Abroad,* 1897). The ability to modify one's "shape" is often considered a measure of mental health, and the speed with which one can accommodate change is often seen as a measure of the ability to adjust. In almost all cases of adjustment, there is an ideal that the individual wishes to measure up to. There is a desire to belong to something or with someone, thereby providing the feeling of security and acceptance that comes from fitting in. Living up to the ideal or fitting in sometimes means staying the same; under other circumstances, it requires a decision to change. Neither course is easy, and in many cases the consequences of the decision are irreversible.

THE NEED FOR STABILITY From the moment that an infant first begins to experience the world of visual sensations, the need for stability becomes readily apparent. Much of this stability is derived from *perceptual constancies,* such as *size constancy* and *shape constancy.* Size constancy refers to the phenomenon by which the *perceived size* of an object remains constant regardless of the changes in the size of the retinal image. For example, when someone walks away, you do not normally comment on how fast he or she is dwindling in size. Instead, you are able to correctly perceive the widening distance between yourself and the other person.

Shape constancy deals with the fact that the individual is able to perceptually maintain the "true" shape of an object even though the configuration of a retinal image may progress through an assortment of geometric shapes. This would be the case when you see a coffee table from a particular angle; although the retinal image may be that of a misshapen parallelogram, you are still able to perceive the coffee table as a rectangle. Social stability is supported when everyone in the room, regardless of their vantage points or the actual shape of the images on their retinas, agrees on the rectangular shape of the coffee table. From such elementary beginnings, we can progress to the ability to agree philosophically, affirm each other's experiences, and empathize with another's point of view.

Similarly, anyone undergoing a change, or loss of stability, in lifestyle (geographical, economical, cultural, etc.) experiences stress, sometimes referred to as "culture shock." Many sociologists believe that the perpetuation of a subculture by immigrants, who tend to preserve the old language, customs, and heritage, is a means of maintaining a certain degree of stability and reducing the shock of a new culture. The desire for stability and a growing resistance to change is also shown by the finding of Merrill-Lynch Relocation Management, Inc. In 1978, one-third to one-half of the employees asked to move to a new location objected, whereas a decade ago only about 10 percent refused.

THE NEED FOR CHANGE   The English poet William Cowper (1731–1800) said, "Variety's the very spice of life." Today his statement appears to be especially true with regard to mental life. Most research indicates that the brain requires constant stimulation to maintain a high state of mental efficiency. If an individual is suspended in a tank of water for several hours (Lilly, 1956), or enclosed in a room filled with "white noise," blindfolded, and wrapped in soft material for several days (Vernon, 1963; Hebb, 1961), sensory stimulation is reduced to a minimum, and the individual will begin to experience the effects of *sensory deprivation*. Such research has indicated that when people are subjected to prolonged periods of sensory deprivation, they are no longer able to function normally. Mental efficiency deteriorates, reaction times and coordination suffer, and hallucinations are sometimes experienced. Hebb noted:

> The cognitive, perceptual, and emotional changes associated with and consequent to deprivation leave the subject less competent to meet the adaptational demands of his environment. (Solomon, 1861, p. 237)

Sensory deprivation also increases susceptibility to brainwashing, causes periods of depression, and leads to the development of a general state of apathy.

It appears then that the ability to adjust is heavily reliant upon adequate sensory experiences. It is enhanced by frequent exposure to a variety of stimuli. Research indicates that rats raised in an "enriched" environment—one with a multitude of tactile and visual experiences available—perform better at learning tasks than those raised in a "deprived" environment—one in which sensory experiences were reduced to a minimum (Krech, Rosenziveig, and Bennett, 1962). In addition, the brains of the rats from the enriched environment were found to be larger and heavier than the brains of the deprived rats. This observation is of particular importance when one considers that all brain cell division, and therefore all brain cell production, terminates by the time a child is one year old. Thereafter, all increases in the size of the brain are due to the growth of existing cells and the formation of connections between the brain cells. Research results currently indicate that the more stimulation the brain receives, the more connections that form.

Research findings similar to those in Krech's experiments with rats have also been found in research conducted with infants. Infants receiving a variety of sensory stimulations on an experimental basis displayed motor-skill maturation rates significantly ahead of those infants not receiving such stimulation (White and Held, 1966). In other studies, the incidence of retardation among children raised in "deprived environments," such as can occur in some institutions, was found to be considerably higher than that found in the general population (Dennis, 1960). The effect of enriching the environment was dramatically demonstrated when twenty-five "retarded" children were adopted by families which offered them love and a stimulating environment. The results were an average 29-point *gain* in IQ among the adopted children. A similar group remaining in an institution showed a corresponding *drop* of 26 points (Skeels, 1966).

For many, the preservation of certain cultural links with the past seems to be important for maintaining an awareness of "who we are and where we came from." [*Burk Uzzle, Magnum Photos.*]

FIGURE 1.3

The impoverished environment of a ghetto can also contribute to retarded intellectual development. In an attempt to correct these effects, a community effort referred to as the "Milwaukee Project" was initiated (Herber et al., 1976). In this project, infants were selected at random to attend a special enrichment program. The children attended this program five days a week, twelve months a year, until they entered public schools. At the age of six, the average IQ for the experimental children was 121, and the average IQ for the nonparticipating control group was 87.

Such research has helped to point out the need for enriched environments, as well as the dire consequences of prolonged exposure to unstimulating and depressing environments on adaptive capacity. In studies of impoverished families in rural Appalachia, Polansky et al. (1972) found that a great deal of the retardation encountered was associated with a parental attitude referred to as "apathy-futility." Polansky characterized apathy-futility as a feeling that nothing is worth doing—general pessimism and hopelessness with regard to the possibility of anything ever changing.

The belief in one's power to initiate a change when circumstances are unacceptable seems to be crucial to attaining satisfactory adjustment. Such a belief seems to instill a sense of self-control and enhances feelings of self-determination. With such a belief, actual change may not be necessary.

Belief in the Potential for Growth

Carl Jung called it "individuation," Otto Rank referred to it as the development of the "artist," and Abraham Maslow used the term "self-actualizing." Regardless of the term used, all these theorists were alluding to the *potential for growth* that exists within each individual.

The term "self-realization" is also used with reference to growth potentials, but it tends to emphasize the need of first knowing oneself well before attempting to fulfill specific capabilities and talents. Self-realization is more in keeping with the inscription of the Delphic oracle, "Know thyself." Self-knowledge makes it possible to recognize one's true potentials and also one's real limitations:

> We know what we are, but know
> not what we may be. (Shakespeare, *Hamlet,* Act IV, Sc. 5)

SELF-CONCEPT   A self-concept, like any concept, is a notion, a belief based on judgment. Therefore, a self-concept need not be realistic or accurate, nor is it necessary that it even vaguely resemble reality. As Fritz Perls once said, "The psychotic person *believes* that he is Abraham Lincoln. The neurotic *wishes* he was Abraham Lincoln. Whereas the self-actualizing person *knows* 'I am I.' "

The term "ego" is derived from the Latin word for "I" and is often used in reference to a person's conscious conception of his or her identity. This personal conception of ego is often defined by one's interpretation of the responses, reactions, and evaluations of others as he or she grows up. For example, if a parent is cold and aloof, the child's ego concept may include the belief that "I am unlovable." Social interactions may formulate the belief that "I am a coward." School experiences may generate the belief that "I am stupid." It is important to keep in mind that these ego concepts may have little to do with how lovable, brave, or intelligent the child actually is, but are based primarily on the child's self-perception, which is strongly influenced by the perceptions of others.

The child's *self-esteem* is often based on *self-appraisal,* which usually includes an evaluation of the qualities and accomplishments of others in comparison to his or her own characteristics. The comparison is usually along the lines of "Am I as good as. . . ." It can include such categories as physical appearance, intellectual endowments, talents, and even sexual prowess. This process may involve the use of *self-congratulation,* whereby the individual proclaims that he or she is a great person even if no one else does, or *self-depreciation,* whereby the individual insists that he or she is worthless and everyone else must agree with this perception (Daniels and Horowitz, 1976). In either case, such persons are usually very self-conscious because of their preoccupation with how they think others are perceiving them. They are, therefore, heavily reliant upon maintaining an agreeable "front" for their "critics."

In the normal course of adjustment, *self-appreciation* replaces the immaturity of self-congratulation and self-depreciation, and the well-adjusted adult's self-concept is based on *self-acceptance, self-reliance,* and self-

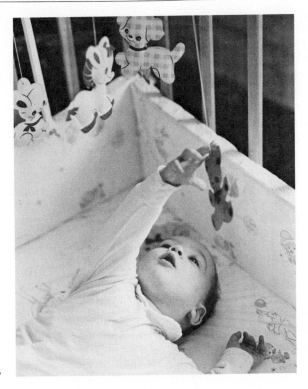

The opportunity to realize one's full potential may not occur until adulthood, but the limits of that potential can often be dramatically affected by what occurs in infancy. [*Arthur Lavine, De Wys.*]

FIGURE 1.4

improvement. Mature individuals know that how others perceive them is out of their control, and therefore they are more involved with maintaining their *self-respect* than their popularity. They are more concerned with *self-competence*—how well they can do something—than with how well someone else can do it. To the well-adjusted individual, it is more important to improve personal performance than merely to surpass someone else's.

In addition, a well-adjusted self-concept will usually include an element of *consistency.* This means that what one thinks and feels matches what one says and does. Beliefs, attitudes, and standards tend to be durable, and there is a close similarity between how the person wants to be and how the person actually is. Above all, however, a well-adjusted self-concept seems to include a *sense of humor:* the ability to laugh at oneself and not to overestimate one's own importance. The possession of a "good" sense of humor also makes it possible to accept criticism from others without becoming overly defensive, to recognize what one really is, and to empathize with the humorous aspects of a frenzied effort to gain control over one's personal destiny.

> This above all: to thine own self be
>   true,
> And it must follow, as the night the
>   day,
> Thou canst not then be false to any
>   man. (Shakespeare, *Hamlet,* Act I, Sc. 3, 75)

CREATIVE ADJUSTMENT For some, adjustment means going backward, returning to the familiar, fearing to risk, and preferring to withdraw from adversity. For others, adjustment means standing still, making as few waves as possible, and doing what one is supposed to do. However, for those who wish to go forward, the choice often includes challenging the unknown, being spontaneous, and developing a part of oneself that has, thus far, existed only as a potential. Such individuals act *upon* their environment by preparing for opportunity and then going after it. Oliver Wendell Holmes (1809–1894) wrote, in *The Autocrat of the Breakfast Table* (1858),

> I find the great thing in this world is not so much where we stand, as in what direction we are moving; to reach the port of heaven, we must sail sometimes with the wind and sometimes against it—but we must sail, and not drift, nor lie at anchor.

Creative adjustment often necessitates the use of novel solutions to common problems, discovering new ways of doing old tasks, and finding new sources of energy to restore one's strength. For example, two parents, deeply concerned about the deterioration of their family unit, decided to try a new and radical approach to their problem. They sold their house, quit their jobs, bought an old fishing boat, trained their teenaged children to be the crew, and started their own excursion boat business between the California coast and the channel islands. The children, who were then using drugs heavily and exhibiting other forms of delinquent behavior, were to try the experiment for one year. If at the end of the year they wanted no more, the parents would return to the mainland and their old way of life. As it turned out, the family grew closer, communication improved, and a sense of "being a family" developed. As a result, at year's end everyone voted to sign on for the "duration."

Creative adjustment often means doing things for the first time, developing new interests, and being autonomous. Rather than merely *wishing* to be able to fly an airplane, play the piano, or speak a foreign language, an adjusted person learns how to *do* these things. Regardless of age, marital status, or economics, a way is found to achieve the desired goal. A person adjusting creatively does not use the phrase "I can't," for this implies a lack of free will and responsibility. Instead the phrase "I won't allow me to . . ." is used. This places the responsibility where it more justly deserves to be. Such a person will tend to deal with preferences rather than with excuses. Rather than saying, "I can't go to Europe because . . . [lack of money, the job, the children, etc.]," the creatively adjusted person is able to say, "I prefer to wait until . . ." or "I prefer to put my money and energy into an education first, and then I'll go to Europe," or "My application for the foreign student exchange program was accepted, and so I'll be studying in England next year!"

Creative adjustment is highly dependent upon a person's originality, creativity, and imagination as means of providing alternatives from which to choose. It is imperative, whenever possible, to avoid reducing conflicts to ultimatums, either/or situations, or forced-choice decisions. Not all alternatives, however, are available to all individuals, and even among the alternatives

FIGURE 1.5

"Good luck" is said to be a result of preparation meeting opportunity. Creative adjustment means being prepared for as many opportunities as possible. [*Joel Gordon.*]

available, not everyone will choose the same ones. Each of us must select for ourselves that which suits our individual needs. Carl Jung, in *Modern Man in Search of a Soul* (1933), wrote: "The shoe that fits one person pinches another; there is no recipe for living that suits all cases. Each of us carries his (or her) own life-form—an indeterminable form which cannot be superseded by any other."

SUMMARY

In this chapter we have discussed the difficulties involved in trying to adjust to a world of change. Special emphasis was given to the problems generated by the world of science. Attention was focused on biology and the impact of Darwin's theory of evolution on today's thinking. Advances in physiology and psychology were also dealt with.

In addition, the problems of adjusting to the social changes that are taking place in today's world were examined. It was shown that hope and individual fulfillment are vital to attaining satisfactory adjustment. In this connection, we also investigated the difficulty of establishing values and standards in today's world, along with the difficulty in finding meaning and relevance.

The definition of adjustment was also treated. With reference to biological and psychological adjustment, the great debate regarding the influence of heredity and environment on human behavior (nature versus nurture) was presented. The individual's ability to accommodate or resist change was scrutinized from the standpoint of attaining a balance between the need for stability and the need for change. Today's psychologists stress the potential for growth that is believed to exist in each individual. The formation of a self-concept is based on one's level of self-esteem, self-acceptance, and self-confidence. Creative adjustment can play an important role in the development of a well-adjusted personality.

DISCUSSION QUESTIONS

1 Do you believe that science has actually improved the quality of life, or do you believe that life was more satisfying before it was "corrupted" by modern science?

2 Do you believe that the "mind" should be studied separately from the body, or is the brain merely another organ?

3 Do you believe people today have more or less hope for the future than people may have had twenty-five years ago? fifty years ago?

4 Will Durant believes that "in organic periods men are busy building; in critical periods they are busy destroying." Do you believe that you are living in an organic or critical period?

5 Do you believe that some aspects of your personality were genetically determined while other characteristics were produced by environmental influences? Which characteristics would you attribute to which influence?

6 Do you agree with Carl Rogers when he suggests that we should be vitally concerned about "who is controlling the controllers" in reference to the modification of a people's morals, ethics, and attitudes? If so, in what way should they be controlled, and by whom?

7 Do you think of yourself as a person who adapts to change easily or one who prefers the familiarity of a stable environment?

8 What elements do you believe are essential to the creation of an enriched environment that would provide an optimum opportunity for child development?

9 Whose opinion of you has the greatest effect on your sense of esteem? Parents? Spouse? Friends? Children? Employers? Teachers?

10 Can you think of an example of creative adjustment in which someone has used a novel, untraditional, or unconventional approach to coping with a problem?

EXPERIENTIAL EXERCISES

1 Many of the advantages of modern science are dependent upon an abundant supply of energy. Imagine how your world might change if there were no electricity and no petroleum products available. What would be some of the first steps you would take in an attempt to adjust?

2 Conduct a survey of your fellow students. As part of the survey, ask them if they believe life will be of a higher quality or of a lower quality than it is today by the year 2000? In what way do they believe the role of science will affect the quality of life in the future?

3 Try to imagine two worlds of extremes. In one world there will be total conformity in that everyone will wear the same or a similar uniform, live in the same type of dwelling, belong to the same political party, etc. In the other world total nonconformity will prevail: no one will obey laws unless they wish to; no one will pay any attention to any schedules; there will be no need to fulfill certain requirements to obtain degrees in education; there will be no need to serve an apprenticeship to become a journeyman, nor to obtain a license to practice medicine or fly an airplane.

CHAPTER 2

MODELS OF

HUMAN NATURE

Now, for the first time in his history, man can perceive that the idea of the unity of the human race and the conquest of nature for the sake of man is no longer a dream but a realistic possibility

Yet modern man feels uneasy and more and more bewildered. He works and strives, but he is dimly aware of a sense of futility with regard to his activities. While his power over matter grows, he feels powerless in his individual life and in society. While creating new and better means for mastering nature, he has become enmeshed in a network of those means and has lost the vision of the end which alone give them significance—*man himself*. While becoming the master of nature, he has become the slave of the machine which his own hands built. With all his knowledge about matter, he is ignorant with regard to the most important and fundamental questions of human existence: what man is, how he ought to live, and how the tremendous energies *within* man can be released and used productively.

Erich Fromm

Man for Himself

MODELS OF HUMAN NATURE

For centuries, great thinkers have been challenged by the question "What is the true character of human nature?" Hippocrates (460–377 B.C.) believed that the characteristics of an individual's personality were primarily determined by the balance attained between four "humors"—blood (courage), phlegm (listlessness), black bile (depression), and yellow bile (irritability). Hippocrates also noted constitutional influences on individual patterns of behavior and made a distinction between the personalities of obese and lean individuals.

Rather than concentrating on physical characteristics, Gordon Allport (1897–1967) attempted to explain human variation through behavioral attributes and the classification of certain common, cardinal, and central *traits,* which he thought characterized the individuality of each person. Sigmund Freud and Erik Erikson both stressed the continuity of human development and the influence of past experiences on personality formation and variation. Still other models of human nature were proposed by *learning* theorists such as John Dollard, Neal Miller, and B. F. Skinner, who emphasized the importance of training, reinforcement, and cultural conditioning on the shaping of individual nature. In contrast to the learning theorists' focus on the influence of the external environment, the *existentialists* and *humanists,* such as Viktor Frankl, Rollo May, and Abraham Maslow, believe that an understanding of human nature can come only through the satisfaction of our transcendental needs for meaning, spiritual identity, and self-realization.

Each of these theorists has presented his own point of view as to the basic causes of variations in personality and human nature; each has presented his particular model of human nature with which others can agree or disagree. However, most would seem to agree with William Shakespeare's Hamlet, who exclaimed, "What a piece of work is a man! . . . the paragon of animals!"

Comparing Animal Nature with Human Nature

Initially, the idea that humans were animals, even "the paragon of animals," was difficult for many to accept. For some, the concept is still repulsive. However, once humanity was able to adjust to the impact of Darwin's theory of evolution, it became possible to establish a new level of empathetic affiliation with other animals. The realization became clear that by increasing our understanding of other animals, it was possible to increase our understanding of ourselves. Comparative psychology attempts to do just that by studying the similarities and differences in the behavior of different species and then, where it is appropriate, by comparing animal nature with human nature.

WAYS WE ARE ALIKE   It has been known for a long time that the *primary drives* of animals (hunger, thirst, pain avoidance, sex, etc.) and those of human beings have a great deal in common. However, with regard to the sex drive, although the nature of the drive seems to be similar, there appear to be major differences in what provokes its expression. Carl Jung noted in his *Psychology of the Unconscious* (1953):

> The erotic instinct is something questionable. . . . It belongs, on the one hand, to the original animal nature of man, which will exist as long as man has an animal body. On the other hand, it is connected with the highest forms of the spirit. But it blooms only when spirit and instinct are in true harmony. If one or the other aspect is missing, then an injury occurs, or at least there is a one-sided lack of balance which easily slips into the pathological. Too much of the animal disfigures the civilized human being, too much culture makes a sick animal. (p. 28)

It was not until recently that the sociobiologists were able to point out that there are also similarities between the *secondary drives,* or social drives, of animals and humans, such as affiliation, aggression, and cooperation. With regard to affiliation, sociability is one of the most distinguishing characteristics of all primates, both human and nonhuman, for they are seldom found living totally isolated from others (Ehrlich, 1976). The organizational forms by which various social groups are established differ, however, from species to species. The organizational basis of the lower animals is primarily that of survival, while affiliation needs, affection, and convenience seem to be major influences behind the organization of human groups.

This is not to say that lower animals do not develop affectional relationships as well. For example, chimpanzees will often embrace each other after being apart, various kinds of monkeys will intertwine their tails as a sign of affection, and social grooming occurs among a great many varieties of animals. Another outstanding example of affection and friendship among

FIGURE 2.1   The many similarities between the social drives of humans and nonhuman animals, including affection and cooperation. [*George Rodger, Magnum Photos.*]

animals is the social play among the very young members of a group. Perhaps the strongest affectional bond, however, is to be found between a mother and her offspring and between siblings, where close, intimate contact is maintained over a relatively long period of time. This type of maternal affection was noted by Jane Goodall (1965) while studying chimpanzees in Tanzania. She observed that orphaned infants were "adopted" by adult brothers and sisters. Just as humans demonstrate mutual affection when they attempt to rescue another, dolphins will often come to the aid of an injured member of their group by coordinating efforts to lift the victim to the surface in order for it to breathe. Another example of mutual regard and affection can be observed in the cooperation within a group of wild dogs, who regurgitate food in order to feed those of the pack who were unable to join the hunt. Perhaps the greatest group cooperation, however, is to be found among members of the insect world, such as the honey bees, termites, and ants.

As with humans one can also find quarreling, intraspecies killing, and wars among many of these same groups. Konrad Lorenz, in his book *On Aggression* (1966), and Robert Ardrey, in *The Territorial Imperative* (1966), proposed that aggression is *instinctive* and closely associated with survival and the need of both humans and nonhumans to protect their space. Behaviorists disagree with this point of view and maintain that aggression is learned, a result of conditioning. Erich Fromm (1975), on the other hand, is opposed to both views. He believes that aggression "is a *reaction* to the threatening of vital interests of the animal or of a man." All, however, seem to agree that both humans and animals are capable of being aggressive, although animals tend to ritualize their encounters more and are therefore frequently able to avoid a direct confrontation in which someone may be injured. Humans have yet to fully master this state of the art of communication.

THE UNIQUE QUALITIES OF BEING HUMAN   One of the last vestiges of human pride, one of the last bastions of our superiority over other animals, has been the belief that we are unique in possessing the ability to communicate through a language. For a long time, language was thought to be an *acquired* skill made possible by the superiority of the human brain. Noam Chomsky, a linguist at the Massachusetts Institute of Technology, disagreed with this premise. He suggested that human beings possess "*innate* language-generating faculties" (Alexander, 1970). In support of Chomsky's premise, findings derived from research conducted throughout the world by anthropologists, speech therapists, and linguists have indicated that all normal children master their particular native tongue and learn the basic grammatical principles associated with it in a universal order. This sequence begins when the child is eighteen months old with a "first word," which is generally a noun or proper name. Around two years of age, the child begins to put two words together. By the time the child reaches the age of six, an understanding of 8,000 words and the use of 4,000 words are common (Slobin, 1971).

In order to explore the possibility that language may not be as unique to humans as we would like to think, Keith and Cathy Hayes of the Xerkes Laboratory of Primate Biology took a baby chimpanzee named Viki into their home and raised it as a member of the family for six years. Viki, after intensive training, was able to learn only four words during this period: mama, papa, cup, and up (Hayes, 1951).

It was thought that Viki attained such a minimal vocabulary because of the inability of chimpanzees to manipulate their tongue and vocal cords in the same way as humans. In order to get around this handicap, Allen and Beatrice Gardner (1969) conducted an experiment in which they taught a chimpanzee named Washoe to communicate through the use of American Sign Language (ASL or Ameslan). Washoe's vocabulary reached approximately 200 words, and he used them in combinations of up to six words.

An even more elaborate study of the acquisition and use of language among chimpanzees was conducted by David Premack (1972), who taught Sarah, a seven-year-old chimpanzee, how to communicate through the use of symbols. Using plastic symbols to represent words, Sarah was able to develop an understanding of syntax. According to Premack, she "was able to think of the word not as its literal form but as the thing it represents."

Such mental manipulations are thought by some to be indications that language may no longer be considered unique to humans, and that abstract thought may be shared with other members of the animal world. Erich Fromm (1975), however, maintains that "man is the unique case in nature in which life is aware of itself—completely in opposition to the animal." Fromm also believes that "man is the only animal that is conscious of himself: of his inhibition before others, of his importance, of the future and of death." It is this ability to anticipate the future that the English essayist William Hazlitt (1778–1830) referred to when he wrote, "Man is the only animal that laughs and weeps; for he is the only animal that is struck with the difference between what things are, and what they ought to be."

THE DIFFERENT MODELS OF HUMAN NATURE

Oscar Wilde (1854–1900) said, "The only thing that one really knows about human nature is that it changes. Change is the one quality we can predicate on it" (1895). Abraham Lincoln (1809–1865) said:

> Human nature will not change. In any future great national trial, compared with the men of this period, we shall have as weak and as strong, as silly and as wise, as bad and as good. (Reply to Missouri Committee of Seventy, 1864)

Whether or not one agrees with these statements, the fact remains that our perception of ourselves, our subjective belief in what we are like, strongly influences how we perceive other individuals. From these observations we arrogantly attempt to generalize the nature of the whole human race.

In an effort to create models of human nature, schools of psychology adopt a specific view of human nature from which all personality appraisals, theories of motivation, and diagnostic evaluations are formulated. For example, the *negative* view of human nature held by Sigmund Freud, the founder of the psychoanalytic school, may be exemplified by his statement: "In the depths of my heart I can't help being convinced that my dear fellow men, with a few exceptions, are worthless" (Jones, 1955, p. 182).

The *neutral* view of human nature is reflected in this statement by B. F. Skinner, a strong proponent of the behavioristic school:

> Autonomous man serves to explain only the things we are not yet able to explain in other ways. His existence depends upon our ignorance, and he naturally loses status as we come to know more about behavior. . . . We do not need to discover what personalities, states of mind, feelings, traits of character, or the other prerequisites of autonomous man really are in order to get on with a scientific analysis of behavior. (1971, pp. 12–13)

The *positive* view of human nature, advocated by supporters of the humanistic and existential schools, appears in the words of Abraham Maslow (1971):

> All the evidence that we have indicates that it is reasonable to assume in practically every human being, and certainly in almost every newborn baby, that there is an active will toward health, and impulse toward growth, or toward the actualization of human potentialities. (p. 25)

These three points of view, however, are merely variations on a theme that has been challenging the minds of great thinkers for centuries: "What is the true character of human nature?"

The Psychoanalytic Model

Seldom has the thinking of one person had so great an impact on the human race's perception of itself as have the thoughts of Sigmund Freud, founder of the psychoanalytic school of psychology. Some evaluate Freud's impact to be that of a pornographic curse, claiming that he overemphasized the role of sex in the development of our personalities. Others appraise Freud's contribution to be that of inspired genius, maintaining that he provided the first comprehensive explanation of personality development and pathological behavior. Such extremes in assessments are traditional where Freud's work is concerned; few have been able to remain neutral. Regardless of the position one takes, however, it is generally recognized that Freud's contributions are among the most important ever made to the field of psychology. If for no other reason, this is true because Freud's theory challenged others to develop additional theories in opposition to, or in support of, his psychoanalytic concept. As an evaluation of his life, Freud stated:

> I am not really a man of science, not an observer, not an experimenter, and not a thinker. I am nothing but by temperament a conquistador—an adventurer, if you want to translate the word—with the curiosity, the boldness, and the tenacity that belongs to that type of being. (Levin, 1978, pp. 448–449)

SIGMUND FREUD Sigmund Freud (1856–1939), a Viennese neurologist, encountered numerous cases of hysteria. Hysteria involves the appearance of symptoms of organic illness in the absence of any related organic pathology. Individuals suffering from hysteria would demonstrate symptoms such as blindness, deafness, anesthesia, and paralysis without an apparent neurological or organic cause. In order to learn more about the treatment of hysteria, Freud went to Paris to study under the famous Jean Charcot. Charcot had been employing a new treatment of hysteria and had discovered that he could induce and/or remove the symptoms of hysteria through the use of hypnosis. Freud was not a very good hypnotist and had difficulty hypnotizing many of his patients. As a consequence, he would often have his patients converse without the advantage of hypnosis.

Another Viennese physician, Josef Breuer, had also been working on a treatment for hysteria that induced patients to talk about their symptoms. Even though Breuer's "talking cure" was emotionally disturbing for them, patients often showed marked improvement after undergoing it.

Freud also found this process effective. In 1895, he and Breuer jointly published *Studies of Hysteria.* Freud continued the theoretical development of his concepts based upon his experiences with his patients and self-analysis. In 1900, he published his *Interpretation of Dreams,* and in 1901, *The Psychopathology of Everyday Life.*

THE ID Freud believed that sexuality is generated through a fundamental drive called the "libido." The libido was considered to be a primitive source of energy that motivated pleasure-seeking and goal-seeking behavior. Freud believed that this energy source functioned primarily at an *unconscious* level, which he referred to as the "id." The id is considered to be a product of evolution and is therefore innate rather than learned. There are no values of rightness and wrongness associated with the id, only survival and the primitive urges of fear, rage, and lust.

Fear is our reaction to threat, either external or internal. Most external threats are of a physical nature, while most internal threats are of a psychological nature. According to Freud, internal threats originate from the id's rage and lust urges. Since the id functions only in order to maintain physical and psychological survival, it is not concerned with social and moral consequences and therefore tends to act rather impulsively.

THE SUPEREGO According to Freud, the superego, or conscience, constitutes both our basic value system concerning right and wrong and our concept of an "ideal self." This value system is not innate, but is taught to us by our society and is therefore culturally bound. The principal teachers of these values are our parents. In fact, for the first few years of our lives, our parents act as our external conscience. Our parents attempt to control our behavior by showing their approval or disapproval with such statements as, "I really appreciate your picking up after yourself. That really helps me out a lot," or "Let me put it to you this way, Dennis. You want to be six some day, don't you? Sure, you do. Well, the way you get to be six is to never, ever push the needle across Daddy's record like that again." Gradually, however, such parental control is internalized and is expressed as self-control.

Freud believed that the superego is actually the internalization of our parents' consciences. He also theorized that, along with their concepts of right and wrong, we internalize their concept of how we should *ideally* be when we grow up. This "perfect" self-image is referred to as the "ego ideal."

THE EGO IDEAL Ideally the conceptualized ideal self will tend to be realistically similar to the actual parental model. This similarity between how we would ideally like to be and a real human being increases our chances of actually living up to that ideal.

Should we lack an acceptable parental model to identify with, or to use as a basic example for the development of our ideal self, we will usually create our

For most children, self-esteem is
merely the reflection of the
esteem seen in a parent's eyes.
[*Ed Lettau, Photo Researchers.*]

FIGURE 2.2

own image of an ideal self from a composite of models. Unfortunately, it is often
impossible to live up to such compositions because they are usually made up
only of the "good" qualities perceived. Symptomatic of such a creative
endeavor are statements like, "When I grow up, I'm going to be as rich as Mr.
Harrison, and popular like Mr. Falcon, and have all the girls after me like they
are with Scott . . . and if anybody gets in my way, I'll treat them just the
way. . . ."

Repeated disappointment and self-vilification is the destiny of individuals
whose behavior fails to correspond favorably with their highly idealized beliefs
about how they should behave. Such an individual will often lament, "Oh, if I'd
only said that when it happened. If I'd only thought of it then. But no, klutz just
stood there looking dumb. Someday. . . . Someday, I'm going to be so
smooth."

THE EGO   The ego is the part of an individual's makeup that acts on the *reality
principle*. It is the part of a person that relates to the demands of the real world.
It is the mediator between the impulsiveness of the id and the prudishness of
the superego. In one of his lectures, Freud (1933) described the plight of the
ego:

The poor ego has a still harder time of it; it has to serve three harsh masters, and has to do its best to reconcile the claims and demands of all three. . . . The three tyrants are the external world, the superego, and the id. (Lecture 31, p. 77)

Freud (1933) believed that in order to develop a healthy personality, there must be harmony between these three psychological entities, with the ego being dominant—*"Where id was, there shall ego be."* A personality possessing such a balance is said to be "task-oriented"; that is, able to discriminate between a "task," a job that needs to be done, and a "threat," something that endangers the ego. In contrast, an "ego-oriented" personality is one wherein such a balance has not been achieved. Almost everything and everyone are seen as personal threats. The ego-oriented person will see a broken date as proof that "you can't trust anyone," that members of the opposite sex are "all alike." The task-oriented person will see the same situation as one in which another date has to be found.

The Psychosexual Stages

The degree of harmony developed between one's id, superego, and ego depends primarily upon how successfully an individual passes through what Freud refers to as the "psychosexual stages." The term "psychosexual" refers to a "tension-release" sequence, and the stages are labeled in accordance with the source of the tension and the manner by which this tension is released. For example, in the "oral" stage, tension may be generated by hunger, thirst, or curiosity, and the release of that tension is achieved orally by the ingestion of food, drink, or exploration of an object with the mouth.

According to Freud, a person can *resolve* a stage, *fixate* at a stage, or *regress* to a former stage. In order to resolve a stage, a person must satisfactorily complete a stage by achieving a balance between the major personality characteristics of that stage. For example, in resolving the "anal" stage, a person will achieve a balance between being compulsively neat and hopelessly disorganized, and yet will still be able to preserve his or her individuality.

Freud believed that no one resolves a stage perfectly, because no one has perfect parents by whom to be guided through that stage. Failure to be properly guided through a particular stage may result in "fixation." When a person fixates at a particular stage, it means that he or she will no longer continue to mature emotionally. The individual's personality will be dominated by exaggerated forms of the characteristics of that particular stage, and, as a consequence, at thirty-five the individual will tend to have the emotional maturity and world-view of a six-year-old. Sometimes, however, emotional immaturity can be the result of *regression*. Whenever a stage appears to be too threatening, an individual may attempt to avoid dealing with it by regressing, or going back, to an earlier stage of development. Such is often the case when a four-year-old threatened by a new sibling regresses to bed-wetting and thumb-sucking after having already "grown out" of such behavior.

Whether or not a person resolves, fixates, or regresses to a stage is highly dependent upon (1) inherited predispositions and (2) parental attitudes. "Inherited predispositions" include maturation rates, such as how early or late one begins to walk and talk, and becomes "potty-trained"; physical characteristics, such as size, "sex role conformity," and general attractiveness; and intellectual capabilities, such as IQ, creativeness, and learning speed. "Parental attitudes" refers to the dominant theme upon which the parents' childrearing practices are based, such as being overprotective, rejecting, or perfectionistic. (See Chapter 12, Parents and Children.)

THE ORAL STAGE   The oral stage of psychosexual development spans the period from birth to around the age of one and one-half to two. Fixation at this stage can become manifest in either the *oral-receptive* or *oral-aggressive* types of personality.

The oral-receptive personality often develops as a result of poor health or a slow rate of maturation. These can lead to the child's attaining mobilization and verbalization later than would normally be expected. Such children, unable to fend for themselves, will become more dependent upon others for need satisfcation.

The alcoholic personality is considered by some to be an exaggerated form of oral-receptivity. This type of individual is usually unable to tolerate stress or anxiety well, and will attempt to reduce the anxiety orally through the ingestion of alcohol, drugs, or food.

In contrast to the dependency of the oral-receptive type of personality, the *oral-aggressive* personality often exaggerates the need for independence, power, and control over others. The oral-aggressive type of person usually has a fast maturation rate, which enables the child to attain early mobility and verbalization, and, hence, "control" over the environment. Later in life, such control will often take the form of political, economic, or social power. In both periods, however, the power of words is the oral-aggressive person's primary tool. There can, therefore, develop a tendency to manipulate others verbally by selling, seducing, or "slaughtering" as the need arises.

THE ANAL STAGE   The anal stage occurs roughly between the ages of two and four. Fixation at this stage may result in an *anal-retentive* or an *anal-expulsive* type of personality.

It is during this period that the parents attempt to enculturate the child. Symbolic of this enculturation is their teaching the child the appropriate times and places for relieving oneself. Since such enculturation attempts are seen as a direct threat to their individuality, most children will tend to resist such attempts by refusing to cooperate. The anal-retentive person assumes the attitude of "You can't make me," whereas the anal-expulsive individual takes on an attitude of "You can't stop me."

The anal-retentive person tends to hold back in an attempt to demonstrate self-control. If the child's parents are "perfectionistic," then this self-control will tend to please them, and such restraint would be praised. As a consequence, the child soon learns to control not only his or her bodily functions, but thinking and emotions as well. The thinking becomes conservative, disciplined, and

FIGURE 2.3   The oral-aggressive type of personality tends to rely primarily on the power of words as a means of manipulating or controlling the behavior of others. [*The Bettmann Archive, Inc.*]

well organized; the emotions are repressed or are expressed only with restraint. This holding back of emotions may also be perceived as providing the additional advantage of "emotional invulnerability," the attitude that "You can't hurt me. I always remain calm and under control."

The anal-expulsive personality, in contrast, is characterized as being impulsive, self-indulgent, and irresponsible. Usually this type of person has been raised under "permissive" child-rearing practices, and therefore tends to be intolerant of social restrictions and rebellious toward rules and regulations. The "you-can't-stop-me" attitude may also mean, "I can't stop me," a denial of responsibility for one's actions or a lack of self-control. This seems to be especially true with regard to a lack of emotional control—the individual may fly into a rage over the simplest irritant, go into a deep depression as a result of the slightest disappointment, or fall madly in love at first sight. As a consequence of such behavioral spontaneity and emotional impulsiveness, the anal-expulsive person tends to live in an erratic, disorganized world of confusion consisting of misplaced items, forgotten appointments, and unstable relationships.

THE PHALLIC STAGE   The phallic stage, usually occurring between the ages of five and seven, was considered by Freud to be one of the most important of the psychosexual stages. Its name is derived from the term "phallus," referring to the male genitals. The reason for this reference is that the male tends to experience far greater difficulty in resolving this stage than the female. The purpose of the phallic stage is to establish identification with the parental model of the same sex. Resolution of this stage for the male is accomplished through *transferring* identification from the mother figure to the male parental model. Resolution of this stage for the female is accomplished through *maintaining* identification with the female model. In both cases, male and female, identification until this stage has been with the mother figure. She has been perceived as being almost godlike, so why not want to be like her when one grows up? For the daughter, the realization of these desires will not present any insurmountable problems. However, to be just like his mother is quite another matter for the son. The mother, among other things, has given birth to children, and this the son will never do. Hence, in order for the son to achieve his identity goals, it is necessary for him to transfer his identification to the male parental model.

THE LATENCY STAGE   The latency stage occurs between the ages of eight and twelve. It is a period that seems to allow a person's physical maturation. It is the play period, the tomboy period, the period in which a person can just be a child. As such, the danger associated with this period is not so much that of fixation, but of regression. That is, should an individual fail to fully resolve this stage, there is a strong tendency to regress or return to this stage later on in life.

Most regressions are due to having missed, or bypassed, this stage, usually because of having to grow up too fast—for example, the child who is forced to go to work or to help raise siblings. In either situation, the child is prevented from satisfying the need to play, to just "be." As a consequence, when adult pressures of job and/or family are generated later in life, the person who has missed the latency stage will have a tendency to regress by having a "fling," going on a spending spree, or having an affair as a means of satisfying the need to play that was denied as a child.

THE GENITAL STAGE   The genital stage begins at the onset of puberty and runs to adulthood. This stage has two phases: the *homosexual* phase and the *heterosexual* phase. The first phase is often referred to as the "best-friend" phase. Deep emotional relationships are established with members of the same sex on a nonsexual basis. The heterosexual phase normally follows the homosexual phase. Now the friendships are established with members of the opposite sex, and the supplemental dimension of sexual expression of affection is added.

Failure to pass through the "best-friend" period satisfactorily—that is, leaping directly from the latency stage into heterosexual relationships—can cause a devaluation of an individual's self-esteem as well as a devaluation of one's opinion of the opposite sex. For example, for the female, entering into sexual relationships before she is emotionally and socially mature enough to cope with such intimacies can contribute to feelings of inferiority and an overdependence on males for companionship. Not having learned how to express her emotions in a nonsexual manner, she will tend to use sex and to blame sex for most of her problems, viewing males as the cause of her grief.

The male who enters into heterosexual relationships while still emotionally immature will often do so in an attempt to "prove" his masculinity. As a result, in subsequent relationships, females are often perceived only as "prizes," and thought of only in terms of conquests, tallies on a score sheet, or trophies. Furthermore, because of not having learned how to express emotions in other ways, there is a tendency for such males to generalize sex as an expression of all emotions. Depression, boredom, anger, or whatever, are all expressed indiscriminately through sexual intercourse.

As can readily be seen, one's chances of passing unscathed through all the psychosexual stages appear to be minimal. According to Freud, everyone emerges from childhood somewhat "scarred." This scarring was perceived by Freud as the source of most mental, physical, and social suffering later on in life, and it was to the investigation and alleviation of such suffering that he dedicated his life. Freud once commented:

> In my youth I felt an overpowering need to understand something of the riddles of the world in which we live and perhaps even to contribute something to their solution. (Roazen, p. 67)

Today there is little doubt that Freud did indeed "contribute something to their solution"; exactly what his contributions were is still a subject of controversy. Freud was all too familiar with this controversy:

> My innovations in psychology had estranged me from my contemporaries, and especially from the older among them: often enough when I approached some man whom I had honored from a distance, I found myself repelled, as it were, by his lack of understanding for what had become my whole life to me. (Roazen, p. 86)

The Behavioristic Model

Unlike the psychoanalytic school, the behavioristic school cannot point at the efforts of one solitary person as the motivating force behind its creation. Proponents of elementism, reductionism, associationism, and scientific materialism were all predecessors of behaviorism.

In *A Plea for Psychology as a Natural Science* (1892), William James presented his aspirations for psychology when he stated, "I wished, by treating psychology *like* a natural science, to help her become one." And, as if in an attempt to realize James's aspirations, behaviorists from Watson to Skinner have been dedicated to establishing the discipline of psychology as a science. Watson (1913) argued that the subject matter of psychology was the understanding, prediction, and control of human and animal behavior. He maintained that "the Behaviorist, in his efforts to get a unitary scheme of animal responses, recognizes no dividing line between man and brute" (p. 158).

Today behaviorism is considered to be one of the most powerful schools of psychology. A great deal of the behavioral school's acceptance is due to its tenacious adherence to the experimental methods of scientific research and to its development and application of *classical* and *operant conditioning* techniques.

CLASSICAL CONDITIONING The process of classical conditioning is based on the principles of association, the interaction between a stimulus and a response. In this case, the interaction involves a *reflex* and the creation of an *involuntary response* to a once *neutral stimulus*.

A reflexive response to a stimulus, such as blinking when a puff of air hits the eye, is an innate response that is *elicited,* or involuntarily drawn out, from an organism by something in the environment. Ivan Pavlov discovered that if a stimulus which does not normally cause a reflexive response is *paired* repeatedly with one that does, then the reflexive response becomes associated with the "neutral" stimulus. Once this is achieved, either stimulus is then capable of causing the response. With the creation of such an association, the organism is said to be "classically conditioned."

According to the behaviorist school, *all* emotional reactions are the result of classical conditioning. Although the capacity to feel emotions is innate, the determination of what will activate an emotional response is learned. A fear response to pain, for instance, is automatic, but if pain becomes associated with having been bitten by a German shepherd, then a fear response will most likely become an automatic consequence of any future exposure to German shepherds, even if the person is never again bitten.

Conditioning does not necessarily occur, however, only with undesirable stimuli. Being *rescued* by a German shepherd can generate feelings of affection just as automatically. Having a friend repeatedly bail you out of difficulties can lead to automatic feelings of affection being experienced whenever that friend appears. Experiencing a certain aromatic scent that is worn *only* at times when love-making takes place can become an automatic "turn-on" in future encounters.

GENERALIZATION Through classical conditioning, fear, affection, sexual arousal, and any other emotional response can be involuntarily drawn out of an individual merely by presenting the appropriate stimulus. An important side-effect of this phenomenon, however, is the fact that the individual will respond not only to the stimulus for which conditioning has occurred, but to all *similar* stimuli. This phenomenon is referred to as "generalization." In reference to the preceding examples, a person who had been bitten would probably, through generalization, fear *all* dogs, not just a single, particular German shepherd. The rescued individual would love all dogs. The "bailed-out"

FIGURE 2.4 Those emotional responses and attitudes that are established in childhood are often very difficult to change later on in life. [*Erika Stone.*]

individual would tend to like all people who are similar to the friend. The "turned-on" individuals would find themselves becoming sexually aroused by any aroma similar to the special scent.

Generalization to stimuli that are *physically* similar to the conditioned stimulus, such as in the situations with the dogs, is referred to as *primary* generalization. However, when generalization takes place with stimuli that are *not* physically similar, but mean the same or are *synonomous,* then it is referred to as *secondary* generalization. Such would be the case when a person had been jilted repeatedly after having been assured of love. The words "I love you," through the process of secondary generalization, become synonomous with being rejected. As a consequence, the person may automatically feel defensive, suspicious, and even angry upon hearing these words.

Generalization is also a behavioristic means of explaining the "love- or hate-at-first-sight" phenomenon. This is the type of situation which occurs when a student walks into a classroom for the first time and immediately takes a dislike to the instructor. It is also exemplified by the stomach-flipping, hand-sweating, mind-blanking feelings one experiences upon first spotting "the perfect one" at a party, or the development of a prejudice toward an entire race or ethnic group, based upon the behavior of one or two of its members.

DISCRIMINATION Unlike generalization, which occurs automatically, it is necessary to teach discrimination, the process whereby an individual responds to the original conditioned stimulus but *not* to similar stimuli. In order to teach discrimination, it is necessary to have pairing occur *only* with the original conditioned stimulus and *never* with similar stimuli. For the person bitten by the German shepherd who generalizes fear to all dogs, discrimination comes only through repeated exposure to nonbiting dogs and the realization that not all dogs, not even all German shepherds, bite.

The behaviorists believe that the development of a keen sense of discrimination is essential to the development of a healthy personality. Broad generalization tends to inhibit social and emotional maturation. For example, it would be maladaptive for a youngster, due to one or two disappointing experiences, to generalize that *all* men or *all* women are alike. The same would be true of a fear of *all* authority figures, being sexually attracted to *all* members of the opposite sex, or developing a mistrust of *everyone* over thirty.

EXTINCTION AND SPONTANEOUS RECOVERY The process of extinction is based on the fact that if a response to a stimulus is not reinforced, the ability of that stimulus to generate a response will disappear. This disappearance of a response is called "extinction." Extinction is a major premise of behaviorism, for it demonstrates that what can be learned can also be unlearned.

The unlearning, however, does not necessarily take place all at once, nor does the "extinct" behavior necessarily disappear forever. Often, after a period of time has passed during which there were no exposures to the previously conditioned stimuli, the sudden reappearance of the stimuli can evoke a reappearance of the conditioned response. This phenomenon is referred to as "spontaneous recovery." Being aware of spontaneous recovery is especially important when initiating interpersonal contacts. For example, a person who has remarried may promise to never again get angry at the mention of the name of a former spouse. Through repeated exposure, the response to the name has become extinct. A period passes without mention of the name. Then, unexpectedly, the name comes up in a conversation, and the person instantly responds with anger. When this occurs, the new spouse often becomes righteously indignant and may make statements like, "You promised me you'd never get angry about that name again. You promised me. How can I believe you any more? How can I ever trust you again?" Trust can easily be restored once it is understood that the breaking of the promise was unintentional and due to spontaneous recovery.

OPERANT CONDITIONING Operant conditioning differs from classical conditioning in several important ways. First, in classical conditioning, the response is elicited or *drawn out* of the individual, whereas with operant conditioning, the response is emitted or *sent out* by the individual. Second, the classically conditioned response is involuntary, and the operantly conditioned response is voluntary. Finally, in classical conditioning, the *stimulus occurs first,* followed by the response; however, in operant conditioning, the *response occurs first,* followed by a *stimulus reinforcer,* or consequence.

B. F. SKINNER   B. F. Skinner (1938) took the approach that reinforcement is *anything* that changes the probability of the preceding response occurring again. In Skinner's approach to reinforcement, it is imperative that the *desired* response occur first—before the reinforcement occurs—because the reinforcement will automatically strengthen whatever response occurs immediately prior to the presentation of the reinforcing stimulus. To illustrate the importance of this premise, imagine a parent picking up a child who has just thrown a temper tantrum and attempting to soothe the child with hugs, kisses, and candy. The hugs, kisses, and candy would most likely qualify as reinforcement. By definition, reinforcement will increase the probability of the preceding response occurring again. Unfortunately, since the preceding response, in the example, was a temper tantrum, the parent can expect an increase in the frequency of temper tantrums.

Skinner (1963) points out that anything that does *not* change the probability of a response is *not* reinforcement. Therefore no change in behavior or learning can be expected unless its use is terminated and a replacement is found. If spanking does not change the probability of lying, stop the spanking; if money doesn't increase the frequency of good grades, stop the money; if criticizing doesn't increase a person's feeling of self-worth, stop the criticism.

POSITIVE REINFORCEMENT   One of the most effective means of modifying behavior is the employment of positive reinforcement, or reward. There are several ways of looking at positive reinforcement. One definition states that positive reinforcement is anything that *increases* the probability, the frequency, or the magnitude of the preceding response. For example, when a person is completely out of money and is making a number of searching responses, such as looking in pockets, jackets, glove compartments, and under seats, and unexpectedly finds a dollar under the seat, there will be an increase in the probability of that person looking under car seats in search of money in the future.

Another definition of positive reinforcement concentrates more on the "when" aspect of the situation than on the outcome or consequences. Using this definition, reinforcement is considered positive if it occurs *immediately after desired behavior.* For instance, in many mental institutions, desired behavior, such as the patient's dressing, grooming, or eating without assistance, is immediately rewarded so as to increase the probability of that type of behavior being repeated.

A third definition of positive reinforcement deals with the *presentation* of a desired stimulus that had previously been absent from the environment. The reinforcement is presented after a particular response has been made. This would be the case where a child who lacks attention makes a response that leads to trouble with the authorities and, as a result, receives all sorts of attention. More delinquent behavior can be expected as a result of such circumstances.

In the world of the neurotic, it is often difficult to obtain positive reinforcement on a regular basis. Although positive reinforcement may be available, the neurotic individual, due to having learned maladaptive behavior patterns, feels that the price, the amount of effort required in responding, is often too great. A person who habitually criticizes and belittles the efforts of others may find that there are very few instances in which his or her own efforts are praised. Due to this lack of encouragement, such an individual may consider long-term goals, such as obtaining a college degree, as too costly and unrealistic.

NEGATIVE REINFORCEMENT   When a noxious stimulus, such as an electric shock, loud noise, or bright light, is presented, and then is withdrawn because a particular response has been made, the removal of the unpleasant stimulus would be considered negative reinforcement. In other words, the removal, avoidance, or escape from a noxious stimulus would negatively reinforce whatever response accomplished that feat. For instance, the response of developing a psychosomatic illness may provide the means of leaving a dull party; being on time for work may make it possible to avoid getting fired; and hanging up on someone who is disliked conveniently removes that person's voice from the environment.

Negative reinforcement, however, is not synonymous with punishment. Negative reinforcement involves the avoidance or removal of an undesired stimulus. Punishment often involves the presentation of an undesired stimulus, such as inflicting pain, humiliation, and rejection, or the *withholding* of a desired stimulus, such as affection, possessions, or freedom.

Generally speaking, punishment should be used only to *stop* ongoing, undesired behavior, and positive reinforcement (reward) should be used to *initiate* or *maintain* desired behavior. In other words, the behaviorists recommend praising a child who eats properly rather than spanking one who does not eat properly. According to the logic behind this reasoning, it is far more effective to have a person behave in a certain way out of a desire to please than out of a fear of punishment.

INCENTIVE VERSUS BRIBE   Many people, when first exposed to behavior modification techniques, object to the use of rewards to get others to behave in a desired manner. Many parents will insist that their child should naturally want to behave properly. Since such behavior is expected, it need not be rewarded. The behaviorists, however, think otherwise. One of their most fundamental premises is that no one does anything for nothing; there is always reinforcement involved with a given response.

When the reinforcement is innately reinforcing, usually satisfying some survival need, it is referred to as "primary" reinforcement. When the reinforcement satisfies a social need, it is referred to as "secondary" reinforcement. Since people are not born with a value for secondary reinforcements, such as money, gifts, praise, and appreciation, they must learn to value them. An infant, for example, will not distinguish between a $100 bill and a piece of notebook paper. Through experience and reinforcement, however, the infant will gradually come to discriminate between their relative values.

The behaviorists tend to make no moral judgments with regard to the use of materialistic reinforcers like sweets, gifts, or money, and aesthetic reinforcers, such as hugs, praise, and inner feelings of well-being and pride. Their only concern is with bringing about the desired behavior; the morality and ethics involved are considered to be more appropriately the concern of philosophers and theologians.

Basically, if the intent of the reinforcement is to bring about ethical behavior, it is considered an *incentive,* whereas if the reinforcement is intended to bring about unethical behavior, it is considered a *bribe.* For example, free transportation may be provided as an incentive to get people to go to the polls and vote, and free liquor may be provided as a bribe to get unqualified voters to stuff the ballot box.

SHAPING AND MAINTAINING BEHAVIOR   Since a desired response must first occur before it can be properly reinforced, it is imperative to have some method of bringing about this response for the first time. The procedure for bringing about the initial response is called "shaping." Shaping involves reinforcing successive approximations of the desired behavior. For example, suppose that the desired behavior is to have a child clean his or her own room. Reinforcement should occur after such approximations of the desired behavior as picking up one sock, then picking up two socks, then only after three or four items have been picked up, and so on, until reinforcement occurs only after the room is completely cleaned up. Such a procedure would be referred to as "shaping in" desired behavior. A similar procedure would be used in "shaping out" undesired behavior.

During the shaping procedure, continuous reinforcement is used to attain the final behavioral goal. However, once a response has been established, partial reinforcement must be used in order to maintain a relatively high level of performance. Partial, or intermittent, schedules of reinforcement do not allow reinforcement to occur after every response, but rather on the basis of different ratios of response to reinforcement or on the basis of different intervals of time between a response and when the reinforcement occurs. For instance, piecework represents a fixed ratio schedule of reinforcement; gambling is based on a variable ratio of responses to reinforcement; superstitious behavior is often a result of a fixed interval schedule; and social recognition often reflects a variable interval schedule or reinforcement.

All these schedules are capable of maintaining a high level of performance over a long period of time with only a minimal need for sustaining reinforcement. The most resistant response to extinction is the variable interval schedule. This schedule is also one of the most widely used techniques employed in child-rearing. As a consequence, what children learn in youth will often stay with them throughout their lives. Dorothy Law Nolte, in her poem "Children Learn What They Live," reflects this behavioristic attitude toward child development:

> If a child lives with criticism, he learns to condemn.
> If a child lives with hostility, he learns to fight.
> If a child lives with ridicule, he learns to be shy.
> If a child lives with shame, he learns to feel guilty.

If a child lives with tolerance, he learns to be patient.
If a child lives with encouragement, he learns confidence.
If a child lives with praise, he learns to appreciate.
If a child lives with fairness, he learns justice.
If a child lives with security, he learns to have faith.
If a child lives with approval, he learns to like himself.
If a child lives with acceptance and friendship,
He learns to find love in the world.

The Existential Model

In contrast to the behavioristic endeavor to analyze behavior, the purpose of existentialism is to analyze the nature of human existence, to encourage individuals to assume personal responsibility for their existence, and to pursue the task of finding meaning in that existence.

Existentialism stresses self-awareness and the realization that the way a personality is formed depends upon the choices the individual makes in the process of living. All choices are predicated on one's own perceptions: how individuals see themselves, how they see the world. Based on these perceptions, one attempts to discern whether he or she has any control over the outcome of a particular situation. Control over the lives of others is considered to be mostly illusionary, whereas self-control is always considered to be a viable option. Therefore, one's efforts can be much more effective when directed toward *self-direction, self-reliance,* and perhaps most important of all, *self-acceptance.*

SØREN KIERKEGAARD   Although the elements of existentialism have appeared periodically throughout history, the unorthodox teachings of the Danish theologian and philosopher Søren Kierkegaard (1813–1855) are considered by many to be the genesis of the modern existential movement. Kierkegaard emphasized the importance of the individual. He stated that "The individual is the category through which . . . this age, all history, the human race as a whole, must pass" (1939). His teachings also emphasized the need of each individual for a sense of identity, for self-awareness, and, through this awareness, for constant striving to become more *authentic.* In *Concluding Unscientific Postscript* (1944), Kierkegaard wrote:

> The principle that the existing subjective thinker is constantly occupied in striving, does not mean that he has . . . a goal toward which he strives, and that he would be finished when he had reached this goal. No, he strives infinitely, is constantly in process of becoming. (p. 84)

Kierkegaard believed that "to be human is not a fact, but a task." Kierkegaard, however, was first a theologian and then a philosopher. His teachings were directed primarily at enabling individuals to better realize the full meaning of being Christian rather than the meaning of being human.

FRIEDRICH NIETZSCHE   The spiritual intentions of Kierkegaard were dealt a bitter blow by the German philosopher Friedrich Nietzsche (1844–1900), who

FIGURE 2.5 The way you respond to the world depends a great deal on how you see the world, including how you see yourself and how successfully you seem to fit into the scheme of things. [*Charles Gatewood.*]

reasoned that an individual, in order to achieve authenticity, must become *responsible* for himself or herself. Further, to assume such responsibility, one must be *free* to make personal choices which might affect the nature and quality of one's existence. However, Nietzsche reasoned, freedom would not be complete unless one were not only able to choose *between* good and evil, but to choose *beyond* good and evil. This, according to Nietzsche, could be accomplished only if "God is dead." With God dead, Nietzsche believed, individuals could experience a freedom of being that would be impossible under what he considered to be the oppressiveness of Christianity. He metaphorically expressed this concept in *Joyful Wisdom* (1960):

> . . . our ships can at last put out to sea in face of every danger; every hazard is again permitted to the discerner; the sea, *our* sea, again lies open before us; perhaps never before did such an "open sea" exist. . . . (p. 276)

The atheistic approach to existentialism expounded by Nietzsche was later modified to allow for the inclusion of a belief in God. If one were to be as free to choose as Nietzsche proposed, this freedom would necessarily have to include the right to accept or reject a belief in God.

Nietzsche (1960) did recognize, however, that with new freedom came new responsibility. For instance, things in and of themselves do not possess value or significance; the individual is responsible for attributing significance to the world:

> Whatever has *value* in the present world, has not it in itself, by its nature—nature is always worthless—but a value was once given to it, bestowed upon it and it was *we* who gave and bestowed! We only have created the world which is of any account to man! (pp. 235–236)

The inevitable outcome of such reasoning was that one's own significance must also be self-imposed.

JEAN-PAUL SARTRE   The dehumanizing experience of World War II and the depersonalizing effects of massive industrialization rekindled an interest in the question of personal significance. The French philosopher Jean-Paul Sartre (1947) concluded that one's existence is "everything." In his statement that *"existence precedes essence,"* Sartre asserts that only through the affirmation of our own existence do we have any essence at all—"We *are* our choices."

Sartre (1971) placed a great deal of importance not only on personal responsibility, as Nietzsche did, but on *self-reliance* as well:

> Man can will nothing unless he has first understood that he must count on no one but himself; that he is alone, abandoned on earth in the midst of his infinite responsibilities, without help, with no other aim than the one he sets himself, with no other destiny than the one he forges for himself on this earth. (p. 205)

Existential Analysis

Sartre's emphasis on self-reliance was to have a major impact on the psychotherapeutic approaches of existential psychology. Two Swiss psychiatrists, Ludwig Binswanger (1881–1966) and Medard Boss (1903–   ), had developed a form of "existential analysis" during the 1920s, but existentialism did not receive full recognition as a therapeutic approach until its introduction to America through a book edited by Rollo May, called *Existence: A New Dimension in Psychiatry and Psychology* (1958).

The free will philosophy of existentialism found itself in direct conflict with the determinism of American behaviorism. It was realized that all forms of conditioning would naturally interfere with the manifestation of free will—there could be no conditioning without interference with free will. Rollo May (1967) attempted to defend the existential position in *Existential Psychology,* when he wrote:

> The Existentialism emphasis in psychology does not, therefore, deny the validity of the approaches based on conditioning, the formulation of drives, the study of discrete mechanisms, and so on. It only holds that you can never explain or understand any *living* human being on that basis. And the harm arises when the image of man, the presuppositions about man himself are exclusively based on such methods. There seems to be the following "law" at work: the more accurately and comprehensively you can describe a given mechanism, the more you lose the

existing person. *The more absolutely and completely you formulate the forces or drives, the more you are talking about abstractions and not the existing, living human being. . . .* The distinction is whether the "person has meaning in terms of the mechanism" or the "mechanism has meaning in terms of the person." The Existential emphasis is firmly on the latter. (pp. 17–18)

PERSONAL RESPONSIBILITY   In the existentialist way of thinking, how a person turns out as a human being is primarily the result of the choices he or she has made, given the unique assortment of alternatives available during a human lifetime. The individual is never the *victim* of the environment, but rather an *interpreter* of that environment. Based on their personal interpretations, individuals will choose how to interact with the environment—how to "be" in the environment. Rollo May (1967, p. 17) maintains that "there is no such thing as truth or reality for a living human being except as he participates in it, is conscious of it, has some relationship to it."

All people are responsible for their own participation in relationships. Rather than being overly concerned about what our partners are doing or feeling in a relationship, it is recommended that we should each concentrate on our own personal actions and feelings and how they might be contributing to the success or failure of the relationship.

EFFECTIVE WORRY VERSUS INEFFECTIVE WORRY   Existentially, it is essential to differentiate between ineffective and effective worry. For instance, an aspiring runner cannot do anything about the possibility of rain on the day of the track team tryouts, and excessive worry about the weather is an example of ineffective worry. However, our budding athlete can do something about the quality of his or her diet, the amount of rest obtained, and the amount of practice that precedes the tryouts.

Ineffective worry, however, is most often expended on concern about the feelings and welfare of others and the exaggerated belief that one can *make* another person feel or "be" a certain way. From an existential point of view, one person cannot make another person *anything*. One person cannot *make* another lose weight, fall in love, or be happy. And those who assume the burden and responsibility for someone else's happiness, for example, are then held accountable should the other person ever end up unhappy or miserable. The "victims" of such broken promises will often cry out accusingly, "It's all your fault. I'd never be in the mess I'm in today if it weren't for you. You've ruined my life."

There is nothing wrong, of course, with trying to influence and encourage someone to choose to be happy. But there are also no guarantees that the behavior will be either understood or appreciated. The only person who knows for certain the true intentions behind any action is the one who performs it. Therefore if the person performing the action feels good about it, that is sufficient reason for doing it, no matter how it is received.

BEING RESPONSIBLY SELFISH   Once one is free from the illusion that it is possible to *make* another person happy, it is no longer necessary to feel responsible for another person's happiness. Each individual is responsible for his or her own happiness.

According to existentialists, in order to become happy, it is necessary to consider your own feelings first. For many, the concept of considering one's own feelings first seems selfish. It is—but the negative connotations often associated with selfishness need not apply if one is being *responsibly selfish*.

The existentialists believe that everyone does everything for selfish reasons: people are charitable because it gives them a good feeling; people love each other because they personally enjoy experiencing the feeling associated with loving. Unfortunately, many people do not wish to assume the responsibility for their selfishness. As a consequence, they will go to great lengths attempting to prove that they are not really being considerate of themselves. Some of the most typical statements made by such individuals are: "I'm doing this for your own good"; "I'm only thinking of you"; and "I didn't want to hurt your feelings." In most cases, however, if one were to get right down to it, these people really are doing it "for their own good." In reality, they are thinking of themselves, and it is usually their feelings they are uncomfortable with, not the other person's.

Lying, faking, or putting up a phony front in the name of trying to protect someone else's feelings is *irresponsibly selfish*. Being responsibly selfish, and considering one's own feelings first, provides the opportunity to know what these feelings are and the potential to *share* these feelings with another.

In addition, someone who begins by considering how he or she really feels will probably be able to communicate these feelings more effectively. Most important of all, this person will be able to be honest with the other person by telling that person how he or she *really* feels.

Such honesty, however, should not be misconstrued as carte blanche to go about announcing one's true feelings regardless of the consequences. For example, the principle of honest expression is not intended to enable someone to say things like "You know, I have been noticing you in class. I mean, you're hard to *not* notice. I mean, I've seen 'ugly' in my day, but, wow, man! You have got to be the ugliest person I've ever seen!" By considering one's own feelings first and being responsibly selfish, what would one feel about himself or herself should such thoughts be expressed to another person—shame, disgust, revulsion? In contrast, what would a person feel if such thoughts were left unexpressed—self-respect, relief, empathy?

SELF-ACCEPTANCE   An important part of considering one's own feelings is the process of becoming aware of what these feelings really are. Self-awareness also includes growing to understand one's *thoughts*. It includes growing to understand the nature of one's own *memories* and how they may be inaccurate, incomplete, and distorted by fantasy and fabrication. It includes becoming aware of one's own *experiencing* of life and the fact that no one else can experience the emotions, perceptions, or sensations of someone else. Self-awareness also includes the realization that *expectations* and *anticipations* are one's own and not those of one's parents, peers, or society. It is not for others that one strives so hard to "be," but for oneself.

Existentialism proposes that individuals should first attempt to accept themselves as they are, as they have chosen to be. This does not necessarily mean that a person will *like* what he or she has chosen to be, but merely that one must acknowledge the fact that this is the way one *is.*

Existentialism asks us to accept our uniqueness, our potentials and limitations, our humanness. Once we have accomplished this, we can try to change from a position we have already accepted, not from an unacceptable position that has further degraded as a result of failure to accept it. And should we perceive that we have failed, we can choose to try again. Therein lies the power of the existential theory—a person is always free to choose: "We *are* our choices."

The Humanistic Model

The humanistic approach to psychology evolved out of existentialism, and it is considered to be an integral part of the "third force" in psychology today. One of its "improvements" over existentialism is its *positive* view of human nature. Existentialism takes a negative to neutral view of human nature. Where the existentialists propose that each individual should exercise the option to "be" oneself, the humanistic psychologists suggest that each individual should strive to be the *best* person he or she is capable of becoming.

Another difference between the two approaches is the total freedom of choice in existentialism. In the existentialist scheme, one can choose digression as well as progression—to become neurotic or psychotic or to commit suicide if desired. The freedom of choice in humanistic psychology, however, is *directional.* This means that people have an innate tendency to want to grow and thereby realize their full potential. This potential can be realized, however, only if a person *chooses* to grow. Just how much growth an individual is to experience is up to the individual.

CARL ROGERS   The seeds of Carl Rogers's (1902–   ) *Self Theory,* from which his nondirective, or *client-centered,* therapy (1951) was to develop, are to be found in the contributions of other personality theorists, such as Otto Rank and Erich Fromm.

In his self theory, Rogers stresses that the basis for an individual's personality is the desire to realize his or her potentialities. Full realization is accomplished when the person's "real self" reflects a close approximation of the person's "ideal self." Speaking of this realization in *Client-Centered Therapy* (1951, p. 513) Rogers stated: "We may say that freedom from inner tension, or psychological adjustment, exists when the concept of self is at least roughly *congruent* with all the experiences of the organism."

Rogers believed that, in order to accomplish this degree of integration, a person must be able to satisfy his or her "need for *positive regard.*" For Rogers (1959), "positive regard is defined as including such attitudes as warmth, liking, respect, sympathy, [and] acceptance" (p. 208). *Unconditional positive regard* will be experienced when individuals are valued, respected, and loved just for what they are. Unfortunately, infants are often the only ones to

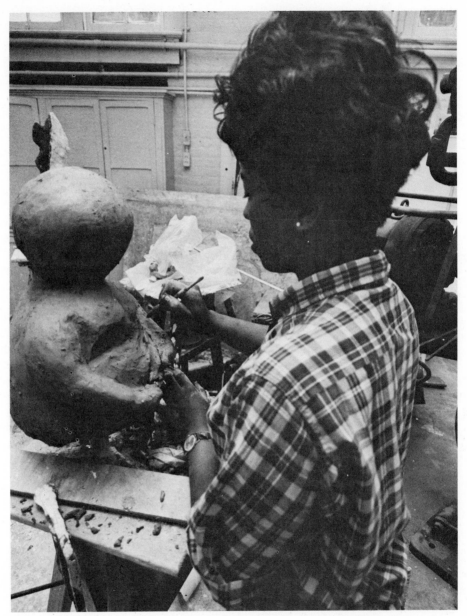

FIGURE 2.6 The humanists advocate personal growth as a means of achieving a healthy personality. Included in the concept of growth is the need to acquire a means of self-expression. [*Ken Heyman.*]

experience such unqualified acceptance. Most human beings must cope with *conditional positive regard,* wherein only some of their qualities and behaviors are approved of.

According to Rogers (1959), a mature person is able to realistically perceive that it is not possible to please everyone, and "accepts the responsibility of being different from others, accepts responsibility for his [or her] own behavior . . . " (p. 207). Someone who is able to achieve an exceptionally high level of maturity is defined by Rogers as a *fully functioning person*. Rogers stated in *Psychology: A Study of a Science* (1959):

> It should be evident that the term "fully functioning person" is synonymous with optimal psychological adjustment, optimal psychological maturity, complete congruence, complete openness to experience, complete extensionality. . . . The fully functioning person would be a person-in-process, a person continually changing. (p. 235)

ABRAHAM MASLOW   The fully functioning person described by Rogers is quite similar to Abraham Maslow's (1908–1970) *self-actualizing* person. Though both theorists advocate personal growth as a prerequisite for achieving a healthy personality, their concepts of the motivational forces governing such striving are somewhat different. Rogers's theory emphasizes a relatively uncomplicated need for self-acceptance, a need for positive regard. Maslow's theory encompasses an entire "hierarchy of needs" ranging from the more basic physiological needs to the more transcending need to be self-actualizing.

Maslow (1970) proposed that self-actualizing is achieved by passing through a sequence of need levels. One must achieve a state of sufficiency, or reasonable satisfaction, in each of the lower levels before aspiring to a higher level. In this process, each person must determine what is required in order to satisfy the needs of a particular level. There are no set amounts—sufficiency is relative to the individual. However, as was mentioned before, the needs of the lower levels must be satisfied prior to attempting to become seriously involved with a higher level. In addition, the sequence of the hierarchy must be adhered to. The levels of Maslow's hierarchy of needs, arranged in an ascending order, are (1) physiological needs, (2) safety needs, (3) love and belonging needs, (4) esteem needs, and (5) self-actualizing needs.

SUMMARY

In this chapter a variety of perspectives concerning human nature and the basic causes of variations in personality were discussed. The similarities and differences between human nature and the behavioral characteristics of animals were compared, with emphasis on methods of communication and the acquisition of sign language among chimpanzees.

Three major schools of psychology were presented: the psychoanalytic, the behavioristic, and the existential-humanistic approaches.

The psychoanalytic school, founded and developed by Freud, was outlined through a descriptive overview of the Freudian theoretical model pertaining to the id, ego, and superego. Freud's psychosexual stages were also presented, including some of the ramifications of fixating, resolving, and regressing.

The behavioristic model was investigated from a historical standpoint, with special consideration being given to the development and application of classical and operant conditioning.

The existential approach to psychology was also dealt with historically, including such contributors as Kierkegaard, Nietzsche, and Sartre. Some of its major premises, such as personal responsibility, perception, effective worry, being responsibly selfish, and self-acceptance, were also discussed.

Finally, the chapter presented the humanistic model, as developed by Carl Rogers and Abraham Maslow. Emphasis was given to Maslow's hierarchy of needs and the characteristics of a self-actualizing person.

DISCUSSION QUESTIONS

1 In what way do you believe humans are like other animals? In what way do we differ?
2 What do you think is the primary cause of aggressive behavior in today's society?
3 Do you believe human nature can change, or will it always be the same?
4 What do you believe was Sigmund Freud's greatest contribution to the field of psychology?
5 What person do you think has had the greatest influence on the creation of your concept of an ideal self?
6 Do you think that your parents used positive reinforcement or negative reinforcement as the primary means of modifying your behavior while you were growing up?
7 Can you think of a particular stimulus, such as a particular person, place, symbol, or word, that causes an automatic and instantaneous emotional response in you?
8 Do you agree with the existential premise that people have "freedom of choice" and do not "have to" do anything they do not choose to do?
9 Do you believe that you can make others happy, angry, or sad if they don't choose to feel that way?
10 Carl Rogers talks of a "fully functioning" person as being well-adjusted, mature, and open. Can you think of some examples of people with these characteristics?

EXPERIENTIAL EXERCISES

1 Many theorists suggest that humans are very similar to other animals. If you were to have a choice, which member of the animal kingdom would you choose to be? Have each member of a group carefully select an animal that he or she would like to be. In addition, have them name the kind of animal they think would best represent their personality now. Have them describe the characteristics of each selection and explain why they made the selection they did.
2 In advertising, "product appeal" is often generated by using behavioral modification techniques. For example, a great deal of pairings, or associations, are made between a particular product and a "basic" emotional response in the consumer, such as sex appeal, insecurity, and pride. Select ten advertisements from a magazine and ten television commercials. What emotion is appealed to the most often?
3 Existentialism is based on "freedom of choice." Have each member of a group make a list of the past five *major* choices he or she has made (college, marriage, job, address, etc.). Then have the individuals reflect on how their lives would have changed had they made a choice that was just the opposite of the one they actually made.

CHAPTER 3

SELF-IMAGE AND

ADJUSTMENT

And a man said, Speak to us of Self
Knowledge.
And he answered, saying:
Your hearts know in silence the secrets
of the days and the nights.
But your ears thirst for the sound of
your heart's knowledge.
You would know in words that which
you have always known in thought.
You would touch with your fingers the
naked body of your dreams.

And it is well you should.
The hidden well-spring of your soul must
needs rise and run murmuring to the sea;
And the treasure of your infinite depths
would be revealed to your eyes.
But let there be no scales to weigh your
unknown treasure;
And seek not the depths of your knowledge with staff or sounding line.
For self is a sea boundless and measure-
less.

Kahlil Gibran
The Prophet

ASPECTS OF THE SELF

From the time of the ancient Greeks and the statement "Know thyself,"
self-knowledge and self-awareness have been generally encouraged. Although the actual accomplishment of this superficially simple task has
remained consistently difficult, its achievement has almost always resulted in
great personal satisfaction. The English poet Alfred Tennyson (1809–1892), in
his *Oenone* (1832), wrote:

Self-reverence, self-knowledge, self-
control,
These three alone lead life to sovereign
power.

However, self-reverence is not possible without self-respect, which is most often generated through self-love and pride. Similarly, self-knowledge is not possible without self-examination, but in order to be successful, such an evaluation must be done with as much sincerity and objectivity as possible. Finally, self-control is not possible without a certain degree of self-confidence and the development of a realistic self-image, for otherwise one may tend to merely live out "self-fulfilling prophesies," such as "I'm lazy," "I'm no good," or "I'm nothing but trouble."

The elements that influence the development of a self-image arise from both external and internal sources. A self-image is formed by the way others act and react toward one's physical, mental, and personality characteristics, as well as by one's own perceptions and appraisals of these events. This image can be unstructured and fragmented, as is often the case with psychotics. It may be distorted, as in the case of neurotics. Or it may be realistic, as it most often is for well-adjusted persons.

Psychologists of various schools of thought have applied various terms to this self-image, such as "self," "ego," "persona," and the "I," "me," and "mine" quality of an individual. There is as much disagreement as agreement among psychologists regarding how to go about evaluating self-images or, for that matter, determining what actually constitutes a self-image. Perhaps it would be wise to start with the view that William James once expressed in a letter to his wife (1878):

> I have often thought that the best way to define a man's character would be to seek out the particular mental or moral attitude in which, when it came upon him, he felt himself most deeply and intensely active and alive. At such moments there is a voice inside which speaks and says: "This is the real me!" (Vol. 1, p. 199)

Physical Appearance

The human body, perhaps more than any other aspect of the self, represents each of us to the world. The body's physical characteristics and proportions have a profound effect both on how others perceive and react to us and upon our own self-perceptions. The consequences of being too tall or too small, obese or thin, strong or fragile, attractive or homely, can, and often do, affect a person's entire life. For instance, physical appearance can affect one's emotional interactions with parents and siblings, especially in the case of a child who is sickly, the runt of the litter, the prettiest, or the smartest. Physical attributes can also affect the quality and characteristics of the pool of individuals from whom a mate is selected. Peter Blau wrote that people end up with the partners they deserve. He believed that the more desirable a person is, the more desirable a suitor has to be in order to win. Physical characteristics can also affect the nature of the occupational opportunities available to an individual—especially such characteristics as sex, stature, and physical or mental handicaps. Most important, however, is the effect physical appearance can have on an individual's feelings of adequacy, self-confidence, and relative worth. This effect is highly dependent upon how one feels when comparing oneself with others.

NORMS AND ATTITUDES Every society, whatever its cultural standards, will have an ideal concept of physical attractiveness. Sometimes women are supposed to be flat-chested (1920s), and at other times, well-endowed (1940s). Sometimes beards are "in" (late 1960s and early 1970s), and sometimes mustaches are "in" (1890s). During each period, each individual must deal with a new set of expectations. Fads are generally liked by people whose physical characteristics lend themselves easily to the "in" look. For example, having hair that won't take a curl is great when the "straight-hair" look is popular. And the wide acceptance of the "ugly-is-in" look deriving from various rock groups during the 1960s allowed an often-excluded element of society to participate equally in a world that is often dominated by the "beautiful people."

One might anticipate that those whose physical characteristics do not easily adapt to certain social norms would feel uncomfortable and perhaps even alienated. One might also expect that people who are too tall or short, too fat or thin, or too old or young, would develop poor self-concepts and have low self-esteem. However, there could be other factors in these people's lives that could compensate for such deficiencies. In order to determine just how important an individual's attitude toward his or her body is in the formation of a self-concept, the July 1972 issue of *Psychology Today* offered its readers a 109-item questionnaire concerning "body image." Over 62,000 readers responded. A sample was extracted from these responses consisting of an equal number of males and females. Forty-five percent of the sample were under twenty-four years of age, 25 percent were between twenty-five and forty-four, and 30 percent were forty-five and older (Berscheid, 1973).

With regard to attitudes toward overall body appearance, only 7 percent of the women and 4 percent of the men were quite or extremely dissatisfied. In contrast, 45 percent of the women and 55 percent of the men indicated that they were quite or extremely satisfied with the appearance of their bodies. This attitude persisted regardless of the age of the respondent. An even greater percentage of older, rather than younger, men were found to be satisfied with their bodily appearance.

Generally, those who had a positive body image considered themselves to be more likeable, assertive, conscientious, and intelligent than the "average person." They also seemed to enjoy sex more and to get along with others more easily. These results contrast with the responses of those who had a negative body image and low self-esteem. Only 11 percent of these respondents considered themselves to be above average.

It is important to note, however, that despite the efforts of the women's movement, many women still value physical attractiveness in relation to their primary goals of getting married and having children. As a consequence, most women see their bodies as vehicles for achieving their career goals, status in the community, and success. This is in contrast with most men, who find their intellect, rather than their bodies, being of greater importance in achieving success in a career and acquiring status among their peers. In today's society, except for the professional athlete, it is usually only the lower-status jobs that require a man's bodily strength. As a result of such attitudes, women tend to consider their bodies to be more important to them than do the men. However, both sexes tend to place about equal emphasis on the importance of a person's face. The respondents to the *Psychology Today* survey considered the face to be the most important factor in the development of self-confidence. Some 89 percent of the women were satisfied with their faces, and 92 percent of the men were satisfied.

Breasts were not nearly as important as the surveyors had anticipated. Only about 25 percent of the women were dissatisfied with the size of their breasts. However, what did seem to be of primary concern was weight. Forty-nine percent of the women were dissatisfied with the size of their hips, and 36 percent of the men were dissatisfied with their stomachs. In this survey, twice as many women as men indicated that they were *very* dissatisfied with their weight.

Over 30 percent of the population is currently overweight, but only about 5 percent of all weight problems are due to a physically malfunctioning body. (For an estimate of what one *should* weigh see Table 3.1 [Whitney, 1977].) As to why so many are overweight, there seem to be a multitude of reasons, such as childhood training, poor eating habits, lack of exercise, and emotional factors. In a survey conducted by Richard Stuart (1974) of the University of Michigan, for instance, it was found that some husbands encouraged their wives to become overweight in an attempt to make them less sexually attractive—to the husbands as well as to potential lovers. It seems that in some cases, the husbands had lost their sexual desire, which in turn threatened their image of being masculine, so they arranged for their wives to gain weight and then used their obesity as an excuse for not being sexually aroused. In addition, some husbands were found to use their wife's obesity as a means of winning arguments, finding that references to weight would often result in the wife's withdrawing from the confrontation.

It has also been found that obesity is the most frequent cause of childhood taunting. Regardless of the physical changes that might transpire as the person grows up, the "ugly duckling" effect tends to persist. Cruel statements such as "Beauty is only skin deep, but ugly goes clear to the bone" can have an enduring influence and affect a person's attitude years after the actual incident. As a result of such incidents, many individuals will develop "faulty" self-images—that is, they become people who have rejected or lost touch with their true and unique selves and continue to respond to an imaginary distortion of their real potential. Carl Rogers (1959) refers to this situation as being "incongruent." A person is said to be experiencing incongruency when an experience is perceived as being inconsistent with one's self-concept, such as when a person has adopted a facade and is merely "playing a role."

According to Rogers (1959), a person whose lifestyle and self-concept are incongruent lives in a constant state of intimidation and is "potentially vulnerable to anxiety, threat, and disorganization."

TABLE 3.1 IDEAL WEIGHTS DERIVED FROM LIFE INSURANCE STATISTICS

*Desirable Weights for Women Aged 25 and Over**

HEIGHT WITH SHOES, 2-INCH HEELS		SMALL FRAME	MEDIUM FRAME	LARGE FRAME
FEET	INCHES			
4	10	92–98	96–107	104–119
4	11	94–101	98–110	106–122
5	0	96–104	101–113	109–125
5	1	99–107	104–116	112–128
5	2	102–110	107–119	115–131
5	3	105–113	110–122	118–134
5	4	108–116	113–126	121–138
5	5	111–119	116–130	125–142
5	6	114–123	120–135	129–146
5	7	118–127	124–139	133–150
5	8	122–131	128–143	137–154
5	9	126–135	132–147	141–158
5	10	130–140	136–151	145–163
5	11	134–144	140–155	149–168
6	0	138–148	144–159	153–173

Desirable Weights for Men Aged 25 and Over†

HEIGHT WITH SHOES, 1-INCH HEELS		SMALL FRAME	MEDIUM FRAME	LARGE FRAME
FEET	INCHES			
5	2	112–120	118–129	126–141
5	3	115–123	121–133	129–144
5	4	118–126	124–136	132–148
5	5	121–129	127–139	135–152
5	6	124–133	130–143	138–156
5	7	128–137	134–147	142–161
5	8	132–141	138–152	147–166
5	9	136–145	142–156	151–170
5	10	140–150	146–160	155–174
5	11	144–154	150–165	159–179
6	0	148–158	154–170	164–184
6	1	152–162	158–175	168–189
6	2	156–167	162–180	173–194
6	3	160–171	167–185	178–199
6	4	164–175	172–190	182–204

*For nude weight, deduct 2 to 4 pounds.
†For nude weight, deduct 5 to 7 pounds.
Source: Prepared by Metropolitan Life Insurance Company. Derived primarily from data of the Build and Blood Pressure Study, 1959, Society of Actuaries.

Such a sense of vulnerability can often be incorporated into a person's attitude toward his or her body. Individuals who regard their bodies as weak and fragile will behave less boldly than those who perceive their bodies as well defended. In general, body image research has indicated that the average

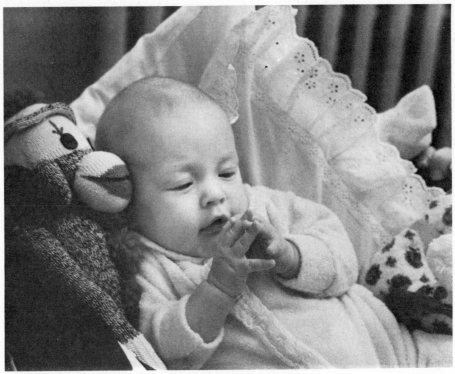

FIGURE 3.1   The search for the answers to such questions as "Who am I?" and "What am I?" may start with the initial discovery of your own body. [*Erika Stone.*]

man is *less* secure and more disturbed about his body than is the average woman. For example, men hospitalized for surgery experience greater anxiety about the body-threatening implications of the situation than women placed in similar situations.

SELF-CONCEPT AND BODY IMAGE   The formation of a body image concerning our physical characteristics begins around the age of three or four months, when we first discover our fingers and toes. From that point on, body awareness will continue to expand through the processes of feeling, mouthing, moving, watching, and experiencing such body sensations as warmth, cold, and pain. These experiences all contribute to the development of a mental image of "my body." Preliminary recognition of one's own body appears to be possible after a child has reached an age of about ten months. G. G. Gallup (1968), investigating this self-recognition ability, found that chimpanzees also had it and would exhibit *self-directed* behavior toward a mirror image, seeming to recognize the image as a reflection of themselves rather than a view of another chimpanzee behind a glass. Lower-order animals, children younger than ten months, and older mental defectives usually exhibit *other-directed* behavior in response to mirror images.

Although the ability to recognize ourselves in the mirror, under normal circumstances, remains relatively constant throughout our lives, our judgment concerning size and proportion with regard to our body and various body parts is usually inaccurate. For example, we usually tend to think of ourselves as being slimmer, taller, and younger looking than we really are. We also have a tendency to overestimate or underestimate the size of our arms, head, waist, etc. In experiments conducted by Leo Schneiderman, subjects were confronted with a distorted mirror image caused by manipulating the movable, mirrored panels that made up the full-length mirror. However, when the subjects were asked to correct the distortions, many of them made numerous errors and most were amazed at how vague their image of themselves really was.

Similar vagueness has been encountered when subjects have been asked to comment on the personal qualities of a series of shadow-profile pictures in which their own silhouette was included without their knowledge. Rarely would the subjects recognize their own silhouette, but, in most instances, the subjects would attribute more favorable qualities to their own profile than to the profiles of others (Fisher, 1972).

Such favoritism seems to be generated, at least in part, by self-protecting defenses designed to avoid or reduce loss of esteem. Such research techniques as described above are among a number of methods used in attempts at evaluating an individual's self-concept. In addition to these methods, the word association test and sentence completion test are used. The draw-a-person test (Machover, 1949) is also used. In this test a child is asked to draw a person, then to draw another person of the opposite sex. The test is based on the assumption that the first drawing is a self-portrait and the second is representative of the child's concept of the opposite sex.

In order to gain a more comprehensive personality assessment of an individual, Stephenson (1953) developed a method called the "Q-sort" technique. This method calls for a list of descriptive statements to be placed on cards. A test subject is then asked to sort the cards into a given set of piles in accordance with their personal applicability. There is no one list or one given set of piles to be used with the Q-sort technique. These may vary with the situation and the intended use of the information gained, such as in appraisals of an employee's need to achieve, screening of personnel, or diagnostic evaluation of clients and patients.

Butler and Haigh (1954) used the Q-sort technique in order to measure a person's self-concept. They used a list of statements describing certain personal qualities, such as "is well-liked," "evades responsibility," and "works diligently." These statements were to be sorted into nine piles in accordance with how self-descriptive the subject believed they were. The particular distribution of the cards thus provided a representative illustration of how a person perceived himself or herself. A subject using the Q-sort method can also be instructed to sort the cards in order to describe an "ideal self." The two self-concepts resulting from the two sortings—the current self and the ideal self—can then be compared and used as a means of measuring psychotherapeutic progress.

Not all therapists, however, approve of the use of such testing techniques. Carl Rogers (1946), for instance, maintains:

The counseling process is furthered if the counselor drops all effort to evaluate and diagnose and concentrates solely on creating the psychological setting in which the client feels he is deeply understood and free to be himself. It is unimportant that the counselor know about the client. It is highly important that the client be able to learn himself. (Not to learn *about* himself, but to learn and accept his own self.) (p. 140)

For those therapists who do incorporate such testing, however, there is general agreement that when there is a great deal of difference between an individual's "real" self-concept and an "ideal" self-concept, the individual tends to enhance the real self-concept through the overuse of defense mechanisms. For instance students of average intellectual ability may attempt to enhance their self-image by convincing themselves that they would have made the dean's list if they had not had to work, gone out for the team, or became so emotionally involved with someone else.

In moderation, such self-enhancing distortion of one's body image seems to be a fairly universal trait and tends to produce a fairly consistent lag between actual occurrence of a change in the body and incorporation of that change into one's body image. This lag is most often associated with such changes as those accompanying aging, weight gains or losses, and disfigurement.

DISFIGUREMENT   R. G. Barker and B. A. Wright (1954) conducted extensive research dealing with the problems of rehabilitation. They conceived the term "somatopsychology" to describe the investigation and treatment of the psychological effects of prolonged physical illness and disability. Findings from their (and similar) research seem to indicate that just how successfully a person adapts to "new" physical limitations depends a great deal upon (1) the age of the person when the trauma takes place, (2) the nature and "visibility" of the disfigurement, and, perhaps most importantly, (3) the reaction of those persons closest to the victim.

With regard to the effects of age on adjusting to disfigurement, it is usually easier to adjust to congenital birth deformities and defects acquired while still young than to disfigurement that occurs later in life (Schilder, 1950). In most of these cases, the child merely incorporates the deformity into a "normal" body image, and will often remain unaware of the deformity as such until later in life, when the reactions of others draws it to his or her attention. Adaptation to blindness seems to follow a similar pattern, although the person's body image tends to remain fixed at the age at which the blindness occurs. Consequently, the body image of a person who goes blind at the age of sixteen will tend to remain that of a sixteen-year-old regardless of the true age or physical changes that might transpire with aging.

Age also seems to be an important factor in accepting the effects of radical surgery, such as a mastectomy (breast removal). Women who are older, married, and have already had children seem to be able to make the adjustment more easily than younger, single women.

Mastectomies are also a representative example of the second factor in adjustment—"the nature and visibility of the disfigurement." Partially due to the tremendous emphasis placed on breasts in today's society, many women avoid breast examinations out of a fear of cancer detection which might result in such radical surgery. Many women are willing to sacrifice their lives in order to maintain an image of femininity.

Sexuality also seems to be an important concern for the psychological adjustment of many amputees. Fears of being only "half a human being" are often coupled with a conviction of loathsomeness. This combination can often lead to severe depression, chronic agitation, and feelings of self-punishment. In some instances, the individual will deny the loss of the limb and resist the use of prosthetic devices, such as artificial arms or legs. However, even with conscious acceptance of the loss of a limb, in 98 percent of the cases, the individual will experience a *phantom limb* (Noyes and Kolb, 1963). The phantom limb phenomenon is the sensation that the missing limb is still there. It is an impressive illustration of just how powerful and persistent a person's body image can be.

The most important factor in the adjustment to disfigurement, however, seems to be the reaction of those closest to the victim. Whether the disfigurement be a birth deformity that the child will live with throughout life, the residual effects of surgery, or the traumatic effects of accident or war, the attitude taken by the immediate family and loved ones will have a profound effect on the ultimate level of successful adjustment achieved. It seems especially important for those involved to accept the reality of the situation and not to attempt to conceal the facts by being overprotective or oversolicitous. It is also important to recognize that *everyone* needs a period of time to get used to the defect or disfigurement, not just the victim. The family and loved ones can also be important in providing love, care, and encouragement, particularly with regard to the development and acquisition of skills and abilities that will help compensate for the current disabilities.

Social Appearance

Although our physical appearance has a great deal to do with how others see us, there are other, often more subtle, factors that can also have a strong influence on how we are perceived by others and how we perceive ourselves. For instance, many times, our cultural, educational, and economic backgrounds can have an almost imperceptible effect on our images, as can our occupation, position in the community, and religious affiliations. These images are seldom static and isolated. Rather, they are dynamic, forming a kaleidoscope of symbolic representations of who we really are.

The course of human development is complex. It is seldom either ideal or linear, and is often imperfect and multilinear. According to Andras Angyal in *Foundations for a Science of Personality* (1941), each person is composed of many "selves," individuated systems of action—a repertoire of familiar roles to be called upon to perform on cue. During the course of normal development, according to Angyal, these differentiated "selves" are progressively organized into a "symbolic self." Individual personality "parts" become integrated into a functional whole. Angyal further proposed that during the course of abnormal development, or under severe stress, a person can experience "regression" and the differentiation and disintegration of these various "parts" and roles. In consequence, a "fragmented" personality may develop.

Prescott Lecky, in his book *Self-Consistency: A Theory of Personality* (1945), also emphasizes the need for integration. He stresses "self-consistency" as the most important unifying element in the development of a self-concept. Lecky explains that people will tend to resist experiences that are not consistent with their value structure in order to maintain personal integrity. For example, a person with strong religious convictions would resist overtures by others to attend a pornographic movie; a person who is proud of being stubborn would tend to be as obstinate at home as at the office; and a person who attempts to live by principles rather than circumstances would tend to apply the principles to himself or herself as well as to others.

One of the primary purposes of achieving a stable and realistic self-concept, and maintaining consistency within one's lifestyle, is to establish a sense of *personal identity*. The concept of personal identity refers not only to our subjective perceptions and feelings about ourselves, but also to how this self-evaluation relates to the world around us, and to the evaluations of ourselves by others. William James said, in *The Principles of Psychology* (1890):

> In its widest possible sense, however, a man's Self is the sum total of all that he can call his, not only his body and his psychic powers, but his clothes and his house, his wife and children, his ancestors and friends, his reputation and works, his lands and horses, and yacht and bank account. All these things give him the same emotions. If they wax and prosper, he feels triumphant; if they dwindle and die away, he feels cast down. (James, 1952, p. 188)

The relative frequency and intensity of feelings of triumph and dejection can often provide estimations of the relative success one has had in adjusting to society. Such estimations are usually based on the current values of that society, and they are often organized into role expectations. Role expectations are presumptions which anticipate the function and behavior of an individual in a given position within a particular society. As examples, we might suggest the function of a person in a parental position and how that person is to act, or the function of a person who is a friend, and how his or her behavior is to differ from that of someone who is merely an acquaintance.

When role expectations are not too rigid, they can act as guidelines which help to inform us how to *most effectively participate* in a given social setting. However, when role expectations become too rigid and inflexible, the uniqueness of the individual can often be stifled, leading to frustration and low self-esteem.

Often such values and role expectations can provide the nucleus in the formation of an ideal self, or "how we would like to see ourselves." Such images usually incorporate idealized concepts of how one *should* be, especially with regard to one's masculinity, femininity, or sexual prowess. As a consequence, when we fail to live up to such expectations—when our real

FIGURE 3.2   For many, personal worth often depends upon comparison with others. [*Burt Glinn, Magnum Photos.*]

selves or how we actually see ourselves turns out to be what we might initially view as mediocre or average—we often find the image difficult to accept. We may then avoid "finalizing" our self-image until we grow up. In such a situation, we often attempt to avoid growing up for as long as possible.

Our evaluation of ourselves also includes our public self, or "how we think others see us." Our public selves often depend on a specific, familiar environment, so that prerehearsed lines, gestures, responses, and counterresponses can be carried out before a well-known audience. However, when the environment changes abruptly, one's public self may become inappropriate, ineffective, and even insufficient with regard to the challenge of the new coping task. Such might be the case when a person raised in a small farming community moves to a large city, when an adolescent goes away to college or the military, or when an only child marries into a large family.

In such transient situations, as habitual responses are discarded and new responses are experimented with, many people will undergo some degree of personal deterioration. Under these circumstances, a person may attempt to portray an ideal public self, or "how we wish to be seen by others." As a consequence, we often create a phony for the benefit of our new reference group. A reference group is that group of people against whom one competes and/or compares himself or herself (Festinger, 1942, 1954). For example, a stock car racer's reference group would be other stock car racers in the same class, and not grand prix or midget auto racers. Football players compare with and compete against other football players rather than with golfers or tennis pros. College students tend to compete against a reference group made up of other college students, and not against high school students or college graduates (Festinger, 1942).

Another important function of the reference group is that of serving as a source of a reflected self, or "how others actually see us." Through their comments, criticisms, and candor, we are often able to piece together a realistic image of how we are actually being seen by those around us. Such information can be invaluable in attempts to correct, modify, or reappraise our original self-concepts. As the American columnist Donald Marquis (1878–1937) wrote in his short satirical work entitled *Pride:* (1935):

> too many creatures
> both insects and humans
> estimate their own value
> by the amount of minor irritation
> they are able to cause
> to greater personalities than themselves (p. 171)

DEVELOPMENT OF THE SELF

We all come into the world restricted and enhanced by genetic endowments which will influence our physical, mental, and emotional development. Given these basic characteristics of similarities and uniquenesses, we are then shaped and molded by our environment until we conform as nearly as possible to the expectations of our society. Yet in spite of these external pressures, we tenaciously cling to our uniqueness, endeavoring to retain some semblance of individuality. Each of us, it seems, wants in some way to be different from everyone else. William James, in *The Will to Believe* (1956), wrote, "There is very little difference between one man and another; but what little there is, is very important. This distinction seems to me to go to the root of the matter."

External Influences

From the moment of birth, our senses are bombarded with an infinite variety of stimuli. Some of these we attend to with great interest, others we all but ignore. It is from this selectivity that we determine how great an impact a particular stimulus might have on the development of our personalities.

Factors such as the perceived importance of events and other people can have a profound influence on how significant an effect events and people have on our self-concept. The attitudes, responses, and actions of significant others, such as parents, teachers, and close friends, can have a greater impact on an individual than would those from others whose involvement is more casual. In addition, values associated with experiences which involve those we consider important are most likely to be internalized—that is, incorporated into our personalities and adopted as part of our own set of standards.

PARENTS AND SOCIETY   One of the few things that has found general agreement among the various personality theorists is the influence of parents on the development of a child's self-concept. A theorist who tends to place a greater emphasis than most on such parental influence is Harry Stack Sullivan (1892–1949). Sullivan's "interpersonal theory" of personality development is an approach based on the importance of interactions with other people. The most important of these interactions are those involving one's parents. Sullivan contended, in his book *Schizophrenia as a Human Process* (1962), that the self:

> . . . is built up of all the factors of experience that we have in which significant other people "respond" to us. In other words, our self is made up of the reflections of our personality that we have encountered mirrored in those with whom we deal. (pp. 249–250)

Sullivan (1953) believed that the process of becoming a human being is equivalent to the process of becoming socialized. He maintained that no individual truly has freedom of choice in regard to behavior because no one is ever completely free from the demands or effects of others. According to Sullivan, even when alone, a person still carries a private selection of "significant others." By this Sullivan meant that we all carry internalized images, or "personifications," of those who have been personally important to us.

Personification results from some of our earliest attempts to pattern our experiences. It is seen as a means of categorizing others, things, and oneself into easily distinguishable reference groups. For example, others can be personified as being "good mothers" or "bad fathers." Things are personified when a ship becomes a "she," or a nation becomes the "fatherland." And, in Sullivan's theory (1953), one's self can be personified as being the "good me," which involves behavior that brings feelings of euphoria, the "bad me," which reflects behavior that damages self-esteem; and the "not me," which denotes behavior that is unacceptable and uncontrollable.

As children, people learn to think of themselves in terms of the "good me," "bad me," and "not me" as a consequence of interactions with their parents. Generally, the child will see the parents as being "good," and behavior which is like that of the parents, or is approved of by the parents, is also seen as good. Thus, such behavior should be performed by the "good me." Subsequently, the child will often pretend to be a parent. This pretending gradually turns into role playing as the child grows up. In the normal process of child development, the child will gradually become the personification of the parents and will come to be recognized as an acceptable member of society.

It is also from these personifications and the internalization of roles and standards that concepts such as "society" and "culture" become manifest. Edward· Sapir (1884–1939), in the *Journal of Social Psychology* (1934), proposed that what we refer to as culture "exists" only in the minds of the individuals whose culture we are discussing. Culture can, therefore, be understood only in terms of the actions, feelings, and ideas of those individuals who make up a particular society. In this manner, a culture, along with its prevailing national character, can often become self-perpetuating.

Margaret Mead (1901–1978), the noted anthropologist, was one of the principal theoreticians to do research dealing with national character. She assumed that to achieve a certain degree of stability within a social system, groups of people will tend to display similar mental characteristics, or psychological regularities (Mead, 1963). Such psychological regularities as the belief in certain myths and traditions tend to regulate cultural attitudes toward such things as personal space, the function of time, and interpersonal relationships. In most cases, the individual character of the members of a particular culture will tend to reflect those attitudes.

TEACHERS AND PEERS   Next to the parents, teachers are often considered to be the most important people in a child's development. The social development that Sullivan emphasizes continues to progress within the classroom.

From the age of five or six on, a child's world includes social institutions and peers as well as parents and home. Comparisons of capabilities and performance tend to become more critical and more crucial in the development of one's self-concept and social recognition.

Erik Erikson (1963) feels that the elementary school ages from six to eleven are especially critical in the child's psychosocial development with regard to a sense of *industry* or *inferiority*. Erikson believes that during this period, if a child's curiosity, enthusiasm, and exploratory activities, both mental and physical, are encouraged, the child will develop a strong sense of industry and feelings of self-confidence. Such encouragement occurs when building projects are praised, art projects are admired, and/or scholastic achievements are rewarded. Unfortunately, no child can excel in all things. In some cases, a child may really have to struggle just to maintain, let alone excel. As a consequence, children are often exposed to harsh criticism, ridicule, and even humiliation, and this can generate feelings of inferiority. For example, projects may be seen as "making a mess," learning difficulties may be seen as "laziness," and lack of coordination may be seen as the gestures of a "buffoon." Such ridicule and rejection carry a great deal of emotional impact when they come from a parent or a teacher. They can be especially painful when they come from a peer group.

R. J. Havinghurst, in *Human Development and Education* (1953), defines a peer group as "an aggregation of people of approximately the same age who *feel* and *act* together." Typically in childhood, peer groups are made up of gangs—groups of children who have formed their own society which is separate from, but not necessarily in opposition to, the authority of the adult society. The need to be accepted by such groups becomes progressively more important as the child grows older. Rejection by such groups can be traumatic and can lead to low self-esteem and a devalued self-image. Chronic rejection can often lead to isolationism, delinquency, and, in some cases, mental illness. As an indication of the tremendous inhibiting influence social

FIGURE 3.3 Some of the most influential, most imitated, and most remembered people are the teachers and friends we encounter during childhood. [*Burt Glinn, Magnum Photos.*]

rejection has had, observe how ostracism, exile, and excommunication have historically been used to maintain conformity.

Internal Influences

As powerful as the external pressures of society may be, they often seem insignificant when compared to the strength of the forces generated from internal resources. For example, many parents have thrown up their hands in desperation, completely frustrated in their attempts to mold a child's behavior through the use of physical punishment and restriction. Similarly, heads of penal institutions have often wondered at the persistence of hardened criminals who continue to break out of prisons knowing that they will ultimately be captured and returned to serve additional time.

In both situations, external pressures appear to be ineffectual. However, should an adolescent become infatuated with a new boyfriend or girlfriend, the parents may witness an almost overnight transformation in behavior.

Throughout the ages, individuals have insisted that "walls do not a prison make," but that we all build our own personal prisons with our fears, expectations, and guilt. Nathaniel Hawthorne (1804–1864), in *The House of the Seven Gables* (1851), exclaimed: "What other dungeon is so dark as one's own heart! What jailer so inexorable as one's self!"

SELF-IMAGE AND INDIVIDUALITY   C. H. Cooley, in *Human Nature and the Social Order* (1902), defined the self as "that which is designated in common speech by the pronouns of the first person singular, 'I,' 'me,' 'my,' 'mine,' and 'myself.' " According to Cooley, an individual's self-image is based on the way he or she is perceived by others, a concept referred to as the "looking-glass self."

Such a concept, however, tends to place the responsibility for one's self-image on the perceptions of others and may lead to defensive measures should the impressions threaten the adequacy and worth of the individual. The black American author W. E. B. Du Bois (1868–1963) illustrated this point in *The Souls of Black Folk* (1961):

> It is a peculiar sensation, this double-consciousness, this sense of always looking at one's self through the eyes of others . . . One feels his two-ness—an American, a Negro; two souls, two thoughts, two unreconciled strivings; two warring ideals in one dark body, whose dogged strength alone keeps it from being torn asunder. (p. 3)

The American philosopher and proponent of "social behaviorism," George Mead (1934), also held that a person's self-image arises from social interactions and our concern for how others react to us. Mead believed that we gradually learn to perceive the world as others do in order to anticipate other people's reactions. For Mead, each individual has a different "self" for each social role. By incorporating estimates of how the generalized other would react in a given situation, a person is able to formulate impressions of various social roles. Accordingly, it is the uniqueness of our particular interpretation of these roles, along with the exclusiveness of our personal formula, that provides us with our individuality.

However, this very diversification prompted Sullivan (1962) to include in his definition of personality the statement that "personality is conceived as the *hypothetical entity* which manifests itself in interpersonal relations" (p. 302). It also induced Sullivan to refer to personal individuality as an illusion. In *The Fusion of Psychiatry and Social Science* (1964), he wrote:

> For all I know every human being has as many personalities as he has interpersonal relations; and as a great many of our interpersonal relations are actual operations with imaginary people—that is, in-no-sense-materially-embodied people—and as they may have the same or greater validity and importance in life as have our operations with many materially-embodied people like the clerks in the corner store, you can see that even though "the illusion of personal Individuality" sounds quite lunatic when first heard, there is at least food for thought in it. (p. 221)

One might argue the existence of individuality by employing René Descartes's (1596–1650) "methodical doubt," by which he discovered the certainty of his own existence: *"I think, therefore I am."* And, continuing this line of reasoning, "I think differently from others, therefore I am different from others." Perhaps it is this difference that constitutes individuality. Henry David Thoreau (1817–1862) publicized the differences between various people, and the importance of individuality, in *Walden* (1854), where he wrote: "If a man does not keep pace with his companions, perhaps it is because he hears a different drummer. Let him step to the music which he hears, however measured or far away."

THE QUEST FOR IDENTITY   According to the existentialists, one of the greatest challenges a person will ever face in life is that of finding himself or herself—the "quest for identity." In reference to the difficulty of this challenge, Dag Hammarskjöld (1905–1961), who served as secretary-general of the United Nations, wrote in *Markings* (1964, p. 78):

> The longest journey
> Is the journey inwards
> Of him who has chosen his destiny,
> Who has started upon his quest
> For the source of his being
> (Is there a source?)

Karen Horney (1885–1952), a neo-Freudian and the first female psychoanalyst, approached the problem of discovering identity from the standpoint that the self-concept of each individual is made up of an *ideal self* and a *real self* (1937). The ideal self represents the self we would like to be and often includes the concept of being perfect. The expectations of this ideal self are constantly being compared with actual achievements or the performances of the real self. Horney believed that the healthy person will attempt to "actualize" the real self—that is, direct his or her energy toward realizing the self's greatest potential. In the process, a person will gradually outgrow undesirable tendencies and ultimately achieve a high degree of resemblance between the ideal self and the real self. In this case, identity is based on an *awareness* of what one wants to be and an *acceptance* of what one is—and achieving a balance and harmony between the two.

The neurotic person, on the other hand, will *reject* the real self and "become" the ideal self. This assumption of a faulty self-image creates a perpetual conflict between the real self and the ideal self, a constant battle between the "despised self" and how a person thinks he or she *should* be. Horney, in *New Ways in Psychoanalysis* (1939), referred to this conflict when she said:

> . . . the neurotic struggles to reconcile: his tendencies toward aggressiveness and his tendencies toward yielding; his excessive demands and his fears of never getting anything; his striving toward self-aggrandizement and his feeling of personal helplessness. (Goldenson, 1970, p. 561)

Rather than attempting to actualize the real self, which has been abandoned, neurotics will attempt to actualize the ideal self. This process would, of course, include the achievement of grandiose goals, the attainment of godlike perfection and supremacy over all others. Such a person's identity is, therefore, based on delusions of grandeur and neurotic pride.

The resolution of the disparity between real self and ideal self seems to be essential to the attainment of a sense of personal identity. With such integration, a person is able to achieve an element of consistency in lifestyle. In consequence, one's memories of what one used to be are not incompatible with what one has become. Nor are the anticipations of what one hopes to be incongruent with what one is.

FUNCTIONS OF THE SELF

Often when we refer to a person as having a strong ego, or when we compliment someone for having a good personality, what we are really implying is that the person's self is functioning effectively. In other words, we are saying that those elements which make up an individual's personality are capable of (1) maintaining interpersonal security by achieving a balance between conflicting forces; (2) maintaining self-esteem by enhancing the individual's feelings of worth and adequacy; while (3) maintaining effective contact with reality by continuously updating his or her appraisal of the world based on new perceptions.

Maintaining Interpersonal Security

In order to maintain interpersonal security, we must be free from apprehension, anxiety, and self-doubt. We must be able to feel self-confident and have the assurance that we are capable of coping with situations regardless of the circumstances. In order to achieve such a state of being, we must feel safe from both *internal* as well as *external* sources of danger and threat.

INTERNAL THREATS AND CONFLICTS   One of the primary means of attaining a secure self is to achieve a state of balance and harmony between opposing internal forces, and to neutralize the energy arising from such conflicts. Almost all major personality theories contain the element of internal conflict as an important contributor to the development of mental illness. For Freud, it was the conflict between the impulses of the id and the practicality of the ego. In one of his lectures, *The Anatomy of the Mental Personality* (1933), Freud drew an analogy between the ego and the id and a rider and a horse:

> One might compare the relation of the ego to the id with that between a rider and his horse. The horse provides the locomotor energy, and the rider has the prerogative of determining the goal and of guiding the movements of his powerful mount towards it. But all too often in the relations between the ego and the id we find a picture of the less ideal situation in which the rider is obliged to guide his horse in the direction in which it itself wants to go. (p. 77)

As previously noted, Karen Horney believed that the conflict is primarily between real self and ideal self. For Carl Jung, the conflict is often between the individual's *persona,* or social mask, and the *shadow,* or the more unacceptable part of one's personality. In addition, Jung held that within each person there is a conflict with opposite-sex qualities—the feminine "anima" in the male and the masculine "animus" in the female. For Otto Rank, the conflict is primarily between "life fear," or a person's fear of a loss of individuality through conforming, and "death fear," or the fear of being separate and alone.

For each of these theorists, and others, mental health is achieved primarily through the resolution of these conflicts. Once this peace is attained, the energy which once existed in the form of anxiety and depression can then be diverted to self-realization and growth.

EXTERNAL THREATS AND NEEDS   Most often, when one thinks in terms of external threats, the mind conjures up thoughts of physical injury, being without food or water, or being ravaged by the elements. Perhaps in a less extreme frame of mind, one might also think of external threats from the standpoint of possibly losing a job, flunking a course, or having a car or stereo repossessed. In either case, the external threat is related to being denied the ability to satisfy a particular need. Erich Fromm (1955) speaks of four basic human needs that are subject to external threats: the needs for *relatedness, transcendence, rootedness,* and *identity*.

The need for relatedness refers to the need to establish positive relationships with other people, primarily in the form of love relationships. However, while attempting to satisfy this need, a person is under the constant threat of rejection, which can often lead to loneliness and isolation.

The need for transcendence refers to the need to be creative, to be productive, and to go beyond merely sustaining one's life. Unfortunately, the creativity of many people is often stifled by the monotony of the assembly line. Others find themselves engaged in what seems to be an endless succession of meaningless work. Still others must devote the entirety of their days to merely staying alive.

The need for rootedness refers not only to the need for ties to one's immediate surroundings, but also to one's past and future. Feelings of rootedness include feelings of nationalism and of racial and ethnic brotherhood, as well as a sense of being part of a community. However, in a highly mobile society which tends to value "new" more than "old," heritage, ancestry, and the preservation of yesteryear are often forsaken for individual accomplishment, personal identity, and living in the "here and now."

The need for identity refers to the need for recognition, respect, and self-esteem. However, recognition often takes the form of hero worship, respect is often confused with an admiration for power, and self-esteem is often measured by how closely one imitates the latest styles of dress and behavior. It often appears as if the image we project to others is more important than the image we have of ourselves. Perhaps the counsel of Plato (427–347 B.C.) is still applicable today: "Shall we not, then, as we have lots of time, retrace our steps a little, and examine ourselves calmly and earnestly, in order to see what these images in us are?" (Murphy, 1949, p. 225).

Maintaining Self-Esteem

Maintaining self-esteem is one of the most important functions of the self. One of the primary means by which this is accomplished is through the *control of*

FIGURE 3.4   The level of stress associated with some forms of external threat often builds gradually. This is often the case when a student has enrolled in a relatively difficult course; the first day is not too bad, but the stress has a way of building. [*Ginger Chih, Peter Arnold.*]

awareness (Sullivan, 1956). By controlling awareness (that is, by carefully sorting and selecting information in such a way as to reject from conscious awareness those items which might threaten self-esteem), a person may systematically distort his or her self-concept so as to reflect the best of all possible images.

SELECTIVE INATTENTION   One means by which self-image can be enhanced is by just not paying attention to those things which might jeopardize feelings of self-esteem. Sullivan (1956) referred to this process as "selective inattention." Through this process an individual may "notice" something, yet remain *consciously unaware* of the experience. For example, we may "notice" that we have not been able to date a particular individual for some time, but are completely unaware that this other person has been doing everything possible, save turning the dogs loose, to reject us.

Such selective inattention also tends to control internal self-awareness. It may exclude from awareness knowledge of unacceptable desires, beliefs, and attitudes. For example, one may be consciously unaware of having sexual desires for a particular person and insist that the relationship is purely platonic. Or someone may adamantly deny being prejudiced, prejudgmental, or negative toward a particular group of people. (This type of individual will insist that mixed marriages won't work "from a practical point of view.")

Selective inattention is also incorporated into the perception of one's physical and social appearance. For instance, people tend not to pay attention to new wrinkles, extra pounds, graying hairs, shortness of breath, etc., in order to avoid a lowering of their self-esteem. Similarly, they tend not to notice that they interrupt others, talk too loud, have an unusual way of laughing, or are a little too pushy, because such an awareness might cause them embarrassment and require a reappraisal of their self-image.

PROPRIATE STRIVING   Maintaining one's self-esteem is not, however, solely a defensive process, for it also includes the need for growth and self-realization, a process that Gordon Allport (1961) called "propriate striving." Propriate striving refers to the total dedication of the self to the attainment of goals; to the motivation to selectively *increase tension* rather than decrease it.

Allport believed that propriate striving begins to emerge at about the time a person enters adolescence. From that time on, the individual begins to develop a personal orientation toward the future. Propriate striving includes such goals as the selection and attainment of a vocation, a mate, and a particular lifestyle. It also includes the desire for adventure, emotional involvement, and exposure to new and interesting challenges. The successful attainment of such goals or the experiencing of meaningful encounters with adventure and challenge tends to enhance and sustain feelings of adequacy and self-esteem.

Assimilating the Data of Experience

E. R. Hilgard, in an address to the American Psychological Association (1949), mentioned that the "continuity of motivational patterns"—the tendency for people to regard themselves as essentially the same people despite superficial changes—is vital to the development of a stable personality.

Providing a sense of continuity to experiences, thoughts, and perceptions seems to be absolutely essential to the maintenance of good mental health. Without continuity a person's world soon becomes fragmented. In such cases people tend to become dissociated from their behavior, and events quickly become disorganized and unrelated.

THE EXPERIENCE OF TIME   One of the most outstanding distinctions between humans and other animals is the extent of our foresight—the human capability to relate to the future, the ability to establish cause and effect relationships that may span years, decades, or even lifetimes. Research has indicated that lower animals are also capable of foresight (Fersler and Hammer, 1965), but on a much more limited basis. For example, O. H. Mowrer and A. D. Ullman (1945) were able to establish a three-second waiting period between the time a hungry rat was presented a food pellet and the time it could be safely consumed. This waiting period was attained by administering an electric shock to the rat if it attempted to eat the pellet before the three-second waiting period had transpired. However, Mowrer and Ullman were unable to establish such "self-control" among rats whose waiting period was twelve seconds. Apparently, the rats were simply unable to get the connection between having eaten the food pellet early and getting a shock sometime later; the cause and effect relationship was, seemingly, too broad.

Behavior reflecting self-control has also been demonstrated among pigeons. Fantino (1966) was able to teach pigeons to restrain themselves from obtaining immediate satisfaction when a greater satisfaction was soon to follow. Similar results were found among sixth-graders. The brighter students were able to delay satisfaction more readily than were the less bright students. However, although all the sixth-graders were able to wait a day in order to get a large candy bar rather than receive a small candy bar immediately, only about half of them were willing to wait a full month for the larger bar (Mischel and Metzner, 1962).

Waiting for anything will tend to make the experience of time seem longer. Albert Einstein (1879–1955) is quoted as having jokingly explained, "When you sit with a nice girl for two hours, it seems like two minutes; when you sit on a hot stove for two minutes, it seems like two hours. That's relativity" (Ornstein, 1977, p. 105).

Generally, time periods filled with exciting, enjoyable activities will seem to pass more quickly than will comparable periods of time filled with boring activities or inactivity. Such minor distortions of the experience of time are common, and merely give rise to some of the perceptual differences between children, adults, and the elderly. Gross distortion of time experiences or loss of time orientation as to the day, month, or year, however, is usually considered to be one of the primary symptoms of mental illness. Such symptoms can also be artificially induced by the use of certain drugs, such as LSD, marijuana, and amphetamines, which are all capable of distorting one's perception of time. Unfortunately, for some individuals, such time distortion can become permanent due to the misuse of such drugs.

For some people, the distortion between real time and perceived time is held to an absolute minimum. Such people seem to possess an incredible gift for being able to judge the passage of time accurately—a talent which enables them to wake up at a given time, "guess" the approximate time of day, and appraise the duration of an event quite accurately. Other, less fortunate individuals seem to be doomed to be late for almost everything, faced perpetually with having no idea what time it is, and destined to be completely oblivious of how much time has passed. Scientists often attempt to explain such differences by referring to what is commonly known as our "biological clock."

Thus far, there does not appear to be any specific organ or a specific set of receptors sensitive to the detection of time. Our physiological functions tend to follow a rythmical pattern of wakefulness and sleep, hunger and digestion, as well as alertness and lethargy, and many believe that these functions may provide subtle cues to the passage of time. In fact, it has been found that altering the rates of certain metabolic processes can alter a person's perception of time. For example, the higher one's fever becomes, the faster the passage of time will be perceived (Hoagland, 1932).

Although the exact manner in which the human brain perceives, calculates, and evaluates time is not completely understood, there is evidence that the left hemisphere of the cortex, which processes the functions of language and mathematics, seems to deal with time in a linear, sequential fashion. It has been found, for instance, that damage to the left hemisphere tends to interfere with perception of sequence, while right-hemisphere damage does not (Curmon and Nachshon, 1971). The right hemisphere appears to process information *holistically,* that is, simultaneously coordinating a variety of sensory inputs in order to arrive at a total picture of a particular situation. These total pictures, rather than the more confusing, error-prone memories based on a sequential orientation, are often transformed into permanent memories. It is upon these memories that much of an individual's self-image is based. They are also the foundation for one's use and appraisal of allotted time, and the basis for one's anticipation of the future.

CHOICES BASED ON EXPERIENCE   Even though most children are not able to utilize properly the past, present, and future tenses until they reach the age of four, most have already begun verbalizing the "when-I-grow-up . . . " concept. This concept will usually incorporate an "I-want-to-be-a . . . " commitment. Although the specifics of this commitment may change over the years, the choices being made will gradually form into a generalized concept of one's life cycle.

The life cycles of all people include perceptions of the sequential process of birth, life, and death. However, each person's formulation of the specifics of this process, as well as the schedule of events or time of this cycle, is unique. Many people are not consciously aware of having created such a schedule. However, most will, at one time or another, become aware of being "ahead of," "on," or "behind" schedule with regard to their careers, marriages, and the achievement of particular goals by a particular age. In many cases, perceiving oneself as being hopelessly behind can lead to severe depression, feelings of inadequacy and worthlessness, and an overwhelming feeling of guilt for having failed others who were depending on one's boisterous promises of how "someday" things would be different.

Staying on schedule is usually a result of having made the "right choices." The correctness of a choice, however, can be evaluated only in retrospect, after a decision has been made. Many people, unfortunately, are reluctant to accept this precept, wanting to determine which is the "right" decision prior to making a commitment. Such people tend to seek the proverbial "guarantee" in life, and such a guarantee just does not exist. As a consequence, these individuals are inclined to be overly cautious, to vacillate between alternatives, and to be prone to indecision. William James, in *The Principles of Psychology* (1890), expressed his belief that "There is no more miserable human being than one in whom nothing is habitual but indecision."

PERSONAL RESPONSIBILITY AND CHOICE   From a practical viewpoint, many of our more prudent decisions are primarily made after cautious interpretation of past experiences, painstaking scrutiny of what is happening in our life at the present, and careful consideration of the possible consequences in the future. Having taken such precautions, an individual must then assume the responsibility for dealing with the outcome of the decision. By making responsible choices, a person is able to avoid or reduce anxiety, for anxiety is often symptomatic of irresponsible behavior. For example, if a student chooses to

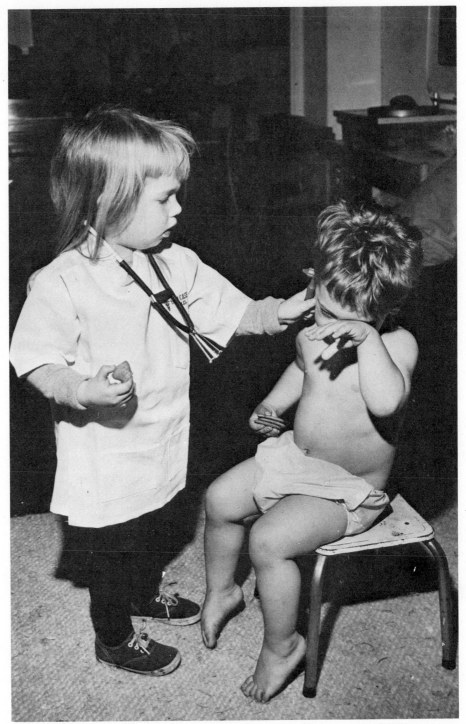

FIGURE 3.5   Part of knowing who you are is knowing who you want to be. [*Ray Shaw, Photo Trends*.]

watch TV rather than study for an exam, then that student is most likely going to feel a high degree of anxiety as a consequence of behaving in an irresponsible manner. In contrast, a more responsible student, who chooses to study for the exam, will tend to remain relatively calm and relaxed.

This same kind of anxiety will prevail whenever we try to lie our way out of a situation rather than assume responsibility for what has happened. A person will also experience anxiety when engaged in stealing or involved with illegal drugs, or after deliberately falsifying a legal document. The same would be true for someone who deviates from an accepted code of conduct, set of morals, or ethical values. In all such cases, the individual doesn't want to get caught— that is, the person wants to engage in a certain activity, but does not wish to assume the responsibility for such behavior, or to accept the consequences that may be associated with it.

There are, of course, other reasons why an individual may feel anxiety over making a decision. A common source of anxiety is ego involvement, or concern for how one might be perceived by others as a result of having made a particular decision. No one wishes to appear a fool. Nathaniel Hawthorne (1804–1864) spoke of this dilemma in *The Blithedale Romance* (1958), when he noted:

> The greatest obstacle to being heroic is the doubt whether one may not be going to prove one's self a fool; the truest heroism is, to resist the doubt; and the profoundest wisdom, to know when it ought to be resisted, and when to be obeyed. (p. 38)

SUMMARY

In this chapter, we explored the importance of self-knowledge with regard to the development of a self-image, along with the effects of physical and social appearance on one's attitude toward oneself and others. Physical appearance was considered in relationship to norms and public opinion, with special emphasis on the problems of disfigurement. Social appearance was discussed with concern for the variety of roles each person develops for various social situations and how these different selves affect a person's overall concept of a self. Included in this section was a discussion of the relative importance of goals, aspirations, and achievements on one's maintenance of a self-image.

In addition, the problems and difficulties involved in the development of a self were examined. Separate consideration was given to external influences, such as parents, society, teachers, and peers, and to internal influences, such as the need for individuality and the quest for identity.

The various functions of the self were also explored from the standpoint of various theorists' proposals regarding the source of conflicts and the means by which self-esteem is maintained by controlling one's conscious awareness of both external and internal threats. We also investigated the function of the self as a source of motivation for self-improvement and for self-realization of such needs as those for relatedness, transcendence, rootedness, and identity.

The role of experience in modifying one's self-image was also included in this chapter, especially in regard to the perception of time, the formulation of one's concept of his or her life cycle, and the importance of assuming personal responsibility for the choices one makes in life.

DISCUSSION QUESTIONS

1   How important do you think physical appearance is with regard to personality development?

2   Are you satisfied with your overall body appearance? What aspects of your appearance do you think are your strongest points? Your weakest?

3   What form of disfigurement do you think would be the most difficult for you to adjust to?

4   Do you believe there is a great discrepancy between how we think others see us and how others actually see us, or are the two images usually fairly close?

5   According to Sullivan, "significant others" are people who tend to have a great deal of influence on the development of our personality. Who do you consider to be "significant others" in your life?

6   Personality theorists talk of internal conflicts, such as between being dependent and being independent or being real and being phony. In your opinion, what are some of the other common conflicts most people must cope with?

7   How have you habitually dealt with being rejected? For example, have you tried to insulate yourself from being hurt, rejected back, become deeply depressed or angry, rebounded to someone else, etc.?

8   Allport believes that "propriate striving" includes the desire for adventure, emotional involvement, and new challenges. In what way are you incorporating "propriate striving" into your lifestyle?

9   Do you believe that you are able to judge the passage of time fairly accurately? When does time seem to pass quickly for you? Slowly?

10   Do you consider yourself to be ahead of, on, or behind schedule with regard to your life plan?

EXPERIENTIAL EXERCISES

1   Without using their names, occupations, or educational status, have each member of a group answer the question, "Who are you?"

2   Arrange for each member of a group to experience the disadvantages of life in a wheelchair. Borrow or rent a wheelchair and have each member attempt to carry on his or her daily routine without getting out of the chair. Allow two to four hours for each member's turn in the wheelchair. At the conclusion of the exercise, have the members of the group share their experiences and reactions.

3   A great deal of our identity, or who we are, is associated with our names. However, there is a growing tendency toward identifying people by associating them with numbers, such as drivers license numbers, credit card numbers, and Social Security numbers. For one week, have the members of a group (including the instructor when possible) identify each other only through the use of the last four digits of their social security numbers. Have the members discuss how they felt being referred to by a number. Were there any reactions that were unexpected? Did any of the members come to "identify" with their number?

CHAPTER 4

MOTIVATION

AND LEARNING

What can I wish to the youth of my country who devote themselves to science?

Firstly, *gradualness*. About this most important condition of fruitful scientific work I never can speak without emotion. Gradualness, gradualness and gradualness. From the very beginning of your work, school yourselves to sever gradualness in the accumulation of knowledge.

Learn the ABC of science before you try to ascend to its summit.

Learn, compare, collect the facts!

Secondly, *modesty*. Never think that you already know all. However highly you are appraised, always have the courage to say to yourself—I am ignorant.

Thirdly, *passion*. Remember that science claims a man's whole life. Had he two lives they would not suffice. Science demands an undivided allegiance from its followers. In your work and in your research there must always be passion.

Ivan Petrovich Pavlov
Bequest to the Academic Youth of Soviet Russia (1936)

MOTIVATION

The noted British philosopher and mathematician Alfred Whitehead (1861–1947) is quoted as having said (*Dialogues of Alfred North Whitehead,* 1953, p. 276): "No period of history has ever been great or ever can be that does not act on some sort of high, idealistic motives, and idealism in our time has been shoved aside, and we are paying the penalty for it."

The importance Whitehead places on "idealistic motives" emphasizes the significance of *intent*. When we judge a period in history, the achievements of a nation, or the actions of an individual, it is more often the intent behind the behavior rather than merely the behavior itself that determines our estimation of its character.

When we use the term "intent," we are usually referring to the ultimate *purpose* of the behavior, the *incentive* prompting the behavior, or the *design* predicating a particular plan of action—in other words, the *reason why* someone does something. This reason is called the "motive." The energy activating the behavior is referred to as the "motivation."

The Nature of Motivation

Behavior may be motivated or unmotivated. *Motivated behavior* has both action and direction. *Unmotivated* forms of *behavior,* such as random behavior, may have action but they lack direction. When we say that motivated behavior has direction, we mean that it has a specific purpose. The hypochondriac, the murderer, and the swindler are all aware of this principle, as are the therapist, the minister, and the student. There is always a specific purpose behind motivated behavior.

NEEDS   In order for something to be able to act as an inducement (or incentive) to behavior, there must first exist a *need*. A need is usually created through *deprivation*. *Physiological needs,* for example, can be generated by depriving a person of food, drink, or warmth, thus creating a biological deficit, or imbalance. A physiological need can also be created by inflicting pain or administering a shock, whereby a need to avoid or escape a situation is created.

On the other hand, *psychological needs* tend to be generated through *perception,* and with perception the need can be either real or imagined. For instance, we may have a real need to reduce anxiety, but may have only an imagined need for protection from people who are "out to get" us. Psychological needs also rely heavily upon stimuli from the environment, or social cues, as an initiating source. For example, the need for achievement may be initiated by having compared one's own performance with that of another. Similarly, a need for dominance may be generated as a consequence of having experienced oppressive behavior from others; while the need for prestige may be generated from having been treated as an inferior by a particular social group.

The terms "need" and "want" provide a means of distinguishing between physiological needs and psychological needs. Physiological, survival-oriented needs are referred to as "needs." Psychological, socially oriented needs are referred to as "wants." An individual *needs* to eat in order to live. However, a person does not really need a newer car, better job, or bigger house. We may *want* these things, but would be quite capable of surviving without them.

Generally, most advertisements attempt to develop a desire for something so that the consumer will want the product regardless of need. In addition, many advertisers attempt to exploit what they refer to as the "hidden needs" of the consumer—needs the average consumer is not consciously aware of—a premise which is vividly pointed out by Vance Packard in *The Hidden Persuaders* (1957). According to Packard, advertising often stresses hidden needs, such as the consumer's need for emotional security, reassurance of worth, ego gratification, creative outlets, a sense of power, and a sense of immortality. All of these needs rely heavily on what the consumer has been taught to value through exposure to previous advertising campaigns, social experiences, and vicarious associations.

MOTIVES AS DRIVES   The term "drive" usually refers to the desire, or *state of arousal,* a person (or animal) experiences after having been deprived of something desired or wanted. The drive is the motivating force behind a behavior. For a person deprived of food, the state of arousal is experienced as being hungry, and his or her actions are motivated by hunger, just as being deprived of drink leads to actions motivated by thirst. Such drives are *innate* and tend to rely on internal cues for activation. However, some drives are

FIGURE 4.1 In order to make a consumer-oriented society truly effective, the consumer must be told what to consume. [*Ken Heyman.*]

learned and tend to exist in a dormant state until aroused by external stimuli. These drives are sometimes referred to as *latent drives*. For an illustration of how easily latent drives can be transformed from a dormant to an aroused state, consider the experiences of smelling the fresh pastries while walking past a bakery, seeing the latest model of a powerful sports car, or hearing that the company will help pay the cost of further education for those employees who wish to return to school. In all these cases, a sudden transformation from tranquil contentment to frenzied obsession can take place.

Drives are sometimes thought of as *energizers*. They are the energy force that can cause a person to take action. Without an innate or learned drive, deprivation alone would be meaningless. For example, denying a koala bear access to sauerkraut would not be likely to lead to a high state of arousal. Should the koala bear be deprived of eucalyptus leaves, however, a strong hunger drive would be generated.

STRENGTH OF DRIVES   When attempting to assess motivation, it is important to keep in mind that we can *never* observe motives. Only behavior can be observed—motives must be inferred. A single type of behavior can express several different motives. For example, consider buying a bouquet of roses. This action may be motivated by sympathy for someone's bad fortune, by empathy for someone who is ill, by pride in someone's accomplishments, or by revenge against someone who is allergic to roses. Similar possibilities apply when trying to determine the motive behind a compliment, a thoughtful deed, or a kind gesture.

These same limitations exist with regard to the assessment of a motive's strength. The relative strength of the motivation must be inferred from the behavior. One means of determining this strength is by estimating the amount of effort put forth in an attempt to satisfy a drive. For example, counting the frequency of the responses can reflect the amount of effort put forth. One might count the number of phone calls made, the number of letters written, or the number of trips made. Another measure of effort might be the magnitude of the response. The magnitude is often reflected in the amount of time, money, or other resources an individual is willing to devote toward the attainment of a particular goal.

Frequency and magnitude might also be included as a part of the *general activity* level. This can also be an indication of the strength of the motivation. A person's general activity level is often represented by such behavior as pacing, wakefulness, and increased smoking or drinking. These measures can be incorporated with an estimate of how great an obstacle the individual is willing to overcome in order to attain a goal. For instance, how many years of study is the person willing to endure, what is a person willing to undergo to escape from an oppressive environment, or how many times will a person be told "no" and yet keep on trying? Sometimes the price becomes too high, and the person may abandon one goal in favor of another.

Having someone make a choice between two or more goals is another means by which the strength of a drive can be measured, especially in a "forced-choice" situation. In a forced-choice situation, it is necessary to choose between the alternatives given. Selecting one automatically rejects the others. A common example of such a situation is when a person chooses to go back to school rather than to accept a tempting job.

Motivational strength can also be reflected by the degree of *compulsiveness* associated with a particular behavior. Dollard and Miller (1950) speak of a drive as being a "stimulus which impels action." When a stimulus is frequently associated with a particular response, they refer to such "stimulus-response regularity" as a "habit." Examples of habits include drumming one's fingers when impatient and going back home when feeling insecure. Habits generally have a low degree of compulsiveness associated with them. That is, stopping the behavior, or being prevented from carrying out the behavior, does not usually place the individual under too much duress. However, certain habits, such as the frequent use of marihuana, nicotine, or amphetamines, can often lead to a psychological dependence. A fairly high degree of compulsion is associated with the consumption of such drugs. Once a person has become addicted to certain narcotics, stopping the use of the addictive drug is almost impossible without professional treatment.

Primary Drive: Survival and Development

The classification of motives has traditionally followed a nature-nurture trend of categorization. That is, a distinction is made between motives that are innate, or inborn, and those that are acquired, or learned. Drives which are innate are called "primary drives." They deal with (1) the survival of the individual (hunger, thirst, temperature, sleep, avoidance of shock and pain); (2) the optimal development of the individual (physical contact, sensory stimulation and variety, manipulation); and (3) the survival of the species (predispositions toward sexual and maternal behaviors).

HOMEOSTASIS   The key to understanding the function of primary drives is the term "homeostasis," which is derived from the Greek words for "same status." The American physiologist Walter Cannon (1871–1945) introduced the term as a reference to the regulatory nature of the body's internal environment. In his book *The Wisdom of the Body* (1930), Cannon described how homeostasis—a state of balance—is maintained with regard to the body's nutritional needs, temperature needs, and water content. Such self-regulation seems to be accomplished through a complex process of monitoring crucial variations in internal stimuli, such as the levels of acidity, salinity, or sugar in the blood, and then reflexively correcting for deviations outside the normal ranges. Should one of these variables fluctuate outside a particular limit, internal adjustive changes take place in an attempt to correct this deviation. These internal changes are experienced as a primary drive. For example, when the sugar level in a person's blood is detected as being below a normal range, the adjustive reaction is experienced as hunger. Detection of a state of dehydration is experienced as thirst. A drop in body temperature is experienced as being cold.

SPECIFIC HUNGERS   Under the influence of such a regulatory system, the detection of some deficiencies can become very exact. Thus the primary drive which is activated can be specific to the precise nutritional needs of the individual. These narrowly defined drives are referred to as "specific hungers." They represent a need for such dietary components as vitamins, calcium, phosphorus, and salt.

A vivid example of eating habits being governed by a specific hunger was demonstrated by an infant who was one year old when he began to favor salty foods. His eating habits included licking soda crackers, chewing salty foods and then spitting the bulk out, and sucking on saltshakers. At eighteen months, one of his first words was "salt." By age three, his diet emphasized pretzels, mackerel, and teaspoons of pure salt. Eventually, the child began to show other physical symptoms and was hospitalized. As a consequence of being placed on a strict saltless diet, the boy died within a week due to a loss of salt from his system. The cause of this deficiency was an insufficiency of his adrenal glands (Wilkins and Richter, 1940).

Laboratory experiments with rats have shown that a rat whose adrenal glands have been removed will survive only a few days on a regular diet.

However, such a rat can live indefinitely when provided with unlimited access to salt (Denton, 1967). Similarly, rats who have had their parathyroid glands removed will reduce their intake of foods containing phosphorus since the body tends to retain phosphorus without the parathyroids (Richter and Helfreck, 1943). Simultaneously they will increase their intake of calcium-rich foods, since the parathyroid glands aid in the body's use of calcium (Lewis, 1964).

Such food selection experiments are often based on "cafeteria feeding." In this technique, the subjects of the experiment are offered unlimited access to a variety of foods from which they are free to choose the kind and amount of food desired. One of the first experiments using cafeteria feeding was conducted by Clara Davis in 1928. In this experiment, infants between the ages of six and twelve months were allowed to choose from a selection of twelve to twenty different kinds of food. At the end of six weeks, they had all "voluntarily" maintained a well-balanced diet and had a growth rate equal to that of infants being fed on a preselected, healthy diet. In one such experiment, an infant cured itself of rickets by drinking large amounts of cod liver oil (vitamin D) until the condition was corrected.

FEEDING DISTURBANCES   The satisfying of specific hungers appears to rely heavily on the ability of our taste buds to detect the needed nutrients. When satisfying these needs, a person is inclined to say that the food tastes "good." However, the desirability of food can also be influenced by sight, smell, and texture, as well as by social customs, such as eating times, eating taboos, and familiarity with a culture's "delicacies" (snails, insects, snakes, etc.).

The emotions can also influence eating habits, as many a parent has witnessed after severely scolding a child for not "cleaning" his or her plate. In most cases, the more the parent shouts the less the child feels like eating. Worry can also influence a person's appetite. Many people tend to worry themselves "fat" due to "nervous eating," compulsive nibbling, and, according to Freud, generalized attempts to reduce their anxiety orally. In extreme cases, emotional disturbances can lead to such psychoneurotic reactions as bulimia (pathological overeating) or anorexia nervosa (the inability or refusal to eat). According to some psychoanalysts, obesity caused by emotional disturbances, or bulimia, is often the result of an unresolved oral stage. It may stem from an unconscious desire for affection, a hostility toward the mother, or even an unconscious connection between eating and becoming pregnant. Other therapists look more at the "payoffs" which are acquired as a consequence of being overweight, such as remaining sexually unattractive, getting attention, or testing the genuineness of another person's love.

H. Bruch (1957) believes that there are three major categories of obesity. First, there is overeating due to the normal excesses practiced by a particular ethnic group or family, or due to the mere presence of other people. Most people who live alone tend to eat more sparingly and to maintain a diet that is generally less adequate than those who live among others. In addition, most people will eat more than usual in the presence of others. Animals demonstrate similar patterns, as shown in research conducted by Bayer (1929). His findings indicated that hens in groups of three or more would eat twice as much as they would eat when they were alone.

Second, obesity can be due to acute emotional stress, such as a death in the family, severe marital problems, or the birth of a sibling. In such cases, eating is often associated with the expression of love and therefore may act as a pacifier, or a means of reducing anxiety.

Third, there is overeating due to excessive feeding by a parent as a means of compensating for severe marital disturbances between the parents. As a result of such *stress-feeding* sequences, the child will often learn to deal with stress by overeating and thus will tend to maintain a state of obesity throughout life.

It is generally accepted that obesity may also result from a failure to take metabolic rate into account. The metabolic rate is the rate at which an individual burns up calories in conjunction with the amount of activity performed. Since some of us have higher metabolic rates than others, some of us require more food than others without becoming overweight. Similarly, physically active people require a greater food intake than do individuals who are relatively sedate. Although sedate people tend to eat as much as active people, they fail to burn off the extra calories. The extra calories are stored as fat, and the individual becomes overweight. It seems that a minimal amount of exercise is needed in order to keep the body's weight-controlling mechanisms functioning normally (Mayer et al., 1954, 1956). In other words, exercising is not as effective in losing extra weight as it is in the prevention of gaining extra weight.

In contrast to the obesity resulting from bulimia, a person suffering from anorexia nervosa often becomes emaciated. In 5 to 15 percent of the cases, the loss of weight is so extreme that the individual dies of malnutrition. Anorexia nervosa occurs nine times more frequently among women than it does among men, with its onset most typically occurring among teenage girls and young women. Many of these women have had a history of obesity (Crisp, 1970). In one case reported by Bliss and Branch (1960), the woman's weight had dropped from 180 to 60 pounds. Although anorexia nervosa is usually difficult to treat, due to the patient's tendency to regurgitate what little food is consumed, some degree of success has been experienced with behavior modification techniques (Backrach, Erwin, and Mohr, 1965).

THE NEED FOR SLEEP   The need for sleep also appears to be under the control of an internal regulatory system. Consequently, there is a range of variation in the amount of sleep people need. Julius Segal (1977) of the National Institute of Mental Health reported that a survey conducted in Scotland indicated that 8 percent of the sample required five or fewer hours of sleep nightly; 15 percent needed five to six hours of sleep; over 13 percent required ten or more hours; and the remainder of the population slept seven to nine hours. Segal felt that such variations may be influenced more by heredity than environment, since individualized sleep patterns tend to appear early in infancy. Some laboratory studies have shown sleeping variations among newborn infants to range from as few as ten hours to as many as twenty-three hours per day. Because of such inborn variations, Segal suggests that parents should consider the individual sleep needs of their children when attempting to impose an arbitrary bedtime.

Although there appears to be no specific amount of sleep that can be considered normal for all people, a phenomenon referred to as "hypersomnia," or oversleeping, can often occur among individuals who are under stress, especially among teenagers. For some individuals, sleep is seen as a means of escaping or retreating from anxiety or depression. For others, anxiety or depression can lead to *insomnia,* or the inability to sleep adequately.

It is estimated that up to 25 percent of the United States population have problems with sleeping. In 1973, these people spent over $1½ billion on sleep-inducing drugs. Unfortunately, many "sleep-facilitating" drugs can actually cause more problems than they solve. For example, through the use of such drugs, sleep patterns and rhythms can be distorted, and the all-important REM (rapid eye movement) period, or dreaming phase (Dement and Kleitman, 1957) of sleep, is often reduced or eliminated. The loss or reduction of these dream periods is especially critical because it seems that we are motivated to sleep as much by a *psychological need to dream* as a *physiological need to rest* (Dement, 1960).

APPROACH AND AVOIDANCE   The primary drives of hunger, thirst, sleep, and the need for warmth are all considered to be approach-oriented drives. This classification is primarily due to the fact that deprivation will lead to approach, or acquisition-oriented, behavior in order to satisfy one's needs. In addition, all four of these drives have their control center located in the forebrain area called the "hypothalamus." Some interaction, therefore, between these drives can be expected, such as changes in a person's appetite due to taking sleeping pills, having sleeping difficulties because of diet pills, or having one's eating habits affected by temperature (Hamilton, 1967).

Avoidance reactions range from simple innate reflexes, such as jerking away when burned, to more complex escape or avoidance behavior. Such behavior is learned from having experienced an *aversive stimulus,* and either (1) making some response that removes the aversive stimulus (escape behavior: Campbell, 1956) or (2) making some response that prevents the aversive stimulus from being experienced again (avoidance behavior: Turner and Solomon, 1962). Some examples of escape behavior would be when a person comes home to a hot apartment and turns on the air conditioner or when a person has a headache and takes an aspirin. Avoidance behavior in such cases would be to turn on the air conditioner before leaving the apartment or to stop drinking early the night before.

The most common primary drives that are avoidance-oriented are extreme heat or cold, electric shock, and pain. However, unlike the others, one's tolerance of pain or one's reaction to pain is strongly influenced by experience and training. For the most part, our reactions to pain are learned from our interactions with our parents during childhood. Children who have overprotective parents tend to be more sensitive to pain as adults. Tolerance of pain can also be affected by the presence or absence of others. A greater tolerance of pain is possible when we believe that the pain is shared with others (Seidman et al., 1957).

Emotions and beliefs can exaggerate the effects of pain, as in anticipation of a dentist's drill. They may also deemphasize the effects, as in the case where a soldier is engaged in combat and fails to notice a wound.

THE NEED FOR STIMULATION   Investigators have been aware of the effects of long-term isolation and reduced sensory stimulation for quite some time. Before scientific experimentation began in the early fifties, however, much of their information was provided by reports made by Arctic explorers, shipwreck survivors, and victims of solitary confinement. With a high degree of consistency, these reports would include descriptions of inability to concentrate, irritability, loss of coordination, and frequent incidents of hallucination and delusion.

In 1951, D. O. Hebb of McGill University in Montreal was asked by the Canadian government to conduct extensive scientific research into the field of sensory deprivation. The purpose of this investigation was to determine whether soldiers who were isolated in boring environments [primarily the technicians on the distant early warning (DEW) line of radar stations in northern Canada] would become more susceptible to propaganda.

Hebb offered students $20 a day to remain in a soundproof room, wearing gloves and goggles, and listening to nothing but "white" noise. That is, they were confined to an environment in which they were deprived of the senses of vision, hearing, and touch. Although most subjects entered the experiment enthusiastically with thoughts of easy money, few were able to endure this deprived state for more than a few days. The main reason for this surprisingly short period was that many of the subjects began to experience the same symptoms of sensory deprivation that had been reported by other victims of prolonged isolation—confusion, disorientation, and hallucinations (D. O. Hebb in Heron, 1957, and in Solomon, 1961). The findings derived from such sensory deprivation research have provided strong evidence that the brain requires constant and varied stimulation to maintain mental health and to function at an optimum state of efficiency.

In Hebb's experiments, some subjects were given the opportunity to listen to boring stock market reports. It was found that these dull reports would be listened to repeatedly just for the novelty that they introduced into the environment. A similar need for novelty has been observed in monkeys who were placed in closed boxes with nothing but a little door available to relieve the monotony. In such cases, the monkeys would repeatedly open the doors with no reward offered other than a chance to look outside the box (Butler and Alexander, 1955).

On the basis of such findings, many developmental psychologists contend that curiosity is inborn and can be observed even among infants as young as one month (Bayley, 1933; Fantz, 1965; Rheingold, 1970). Infants will normally progress through three methods of satisfying their curiosity: (1) tasting, smelling, touching, observing, and listening to everything in the

When you know very little about the world, there is a tendency to be curious about everything. It's only when a person "knows it all" that interest in exploring the unknown tends to disappear. [*Erika Stone.*]

FIGURE 4.2

immediate environment (sensory exploration); (2) feeling, moving, and traveling to various objects (motor manipulation); and (3) asking questions about things in the environment. Such exploration methods seem to be attempts to satisfy what might be referred to as a "stimulus hunger." They have led many psychologists to talk of an inborn "curiosity drive." Other psychologists, however, believe that such behavior is merely the result of a need for activity.

Research conducted by Kagan and Berkun (1954) tends to support the activity drive theory. They found that rats would press a lever in order to unlock a running wheel, the only reward for such behavior being an opportunity to run in the wheel for twenty seconds. Related research indicated that depriving a rat of the opportunity to run for a period of time caused heightened activity when it was finally allowed to run again (Skinner, 1933).

Continuing research along the need-for-activity theme, a number of researchers (Kretch et al., 1962; Rosenzweig et al., 1972) began to explore the effects of activity on development. Typically, they would raise one group of rats in an enriched environment filled with a variety of rat toys to climb on and manipulate. A second group of rats would then be raised in a deprived environment consisting of a small, unstimulating cage. When two groups were later compared, it was found that, with regard to learning tasks, the rats raised in the enriched environment consistently outperformed those raised in the deprived environment. Also the brains of the rats from the enriched environment were larger and heavier than those of their less fortunate counterparts.

Similar intellectual enhancements have been observed among infants who have been exposed to stimulating environments from birth (colorful mobiles over their cribs, patterned linens, opportunities to observe the world outside the crib). Due to this increased stimulation, infants reached developmental coordination goals four to six weeks ahead of infants exposed to a normal environment (White and Held, 1966). The implications of such findings are especially important with regard to the possible effects of being raised in an impoverished environment, such as is often found in the inner cities. However, the broader implications can affect both children and parents, for most frequently it is the child's parents who will determine the amount of stimulation a child will receive.

Most of this stimulation is provided through the parent's everyday expressions of affection and concern for the child, usually in the form of talking, laughing, touching, feeding, and bathing. Just how essential such affectionate stimulation can be was pointed out by Bakwin (1942), when he noted that many infants in hospitals would waste away when isolated from human contact. R. A. Spitz (1946) coined the term "anaclitic depression" to describe the mental, emotional, and physiological state of infants deprived of sufficient mothering. Such children were consistently found to show signs of retardation in the areas of social, perceptual, and manipulative development (Spitz, 1949).

Early investigations concerning maternal deprivation were conducted primarily with institutionalized children. However, Sears et al. (1957) and Prugh and Harlow (1962) extended their investigations to the home. They found that children of unaffectionate mothers had more feeding, sleeping, and training problems than did children of affectionate mothers. These findings did not suprise Harlow, who had been conducting research concerning affection for some time. The most famous of these studies was conducted with what Harlow refers to as the "terry cloth mothers." The terry cloth mothers, made of wire mesh tubes covered with terry cloth, were the only "mothers" some infant monkeys ever knew. The most important finding of these experiments was that the contact comfort provided by the terry cloth mother was more influential to the development of a bond of affection than was the nutritional comfort (milk formula) which could be provided by an uncovered wire mesh mother (Harlow and Zimmerman, 1958). In other words, contact comfort seems to be a basic need which is essential to the normal developmental process, and affection appears to be primarily affected by physical contact.

Using Harlow's research as a basis, it was found that by increasing the amount of physical manipulation and human contact experienced by institutionalized infants, one could increase their developmental rates. As a result, the deleterious effects of institutionalization were reduced or eliminated (Casler, 1965).

SURVIVAL OF THE SPECIES   As can be seen from the results of investigations conducted with regard to maternal deprivation, as well as from the almost daily reports of child abuse, not all children are born into a world of love and maternal care. Maternal instinct apparently is not as instinctive as might be commonly believed. In fact, most researchers agree that the term "instinct" is inappropriate in reference to maternal behavior (Wiesner and Sheard, 1933). The inappropriateness of the term stems from the wide variation in maternal behavior observed among different species, as well as within a particular species.

It has been found that most mammals will demonstrate four types of maternal activity: nest building, birth behavior, retrieval of young, and nursing. However, nest-building behavior has been introduced in nonpregnant rats by removing the rats' thyroid or merely by placing newborn pups inside their cages (Koller, 1952, 1956). Birth-related behavior, such as licking the newborn, can also be interfered with by external stimuli (Birch, 1956), and retrieval behavior seems to depend heavily upon whether or not the young are still nursing.

What seems to exist, then, is a propensity, or predisposition, toward maternal behavior rather than an instinct. For instance, mothers will nurse because they "want to" and not because they "have to." Similarly, mutual bonding will occur as a result of the close interaction of the mother and child, not because of an instinctive love (Mead, 1962). Obviously, mutual bonding has an adaptive advantage for the survival of the species. Therefore, survival will be more likely when infant and mother both possess an innate sensitivity to stimuli associated with attachment (Ainsworth, 1969). According to Judith Bardwick, in a paper submitted to the *Journal of Social Issues* in 1974:

> What one inherits is the capacity to develop a behavioral system. The nature and the form of the developed behavioral system will be a joint function of the inherent capacity to develop and the particular environment in which development takes place. . . . behavioral systems which are characteristic of a species have a biological function which aids in the survival of that species and have, through natural selection, become part of the genetic code of that species. (Fitzgerald, 1977, p. 30)

Another aspect of human nature which is closely associated with the survival of the species is the concept that we inherit not only the ability to reproduce, but also the need to reproduce. Such a need is thought to exist in both men and women. It can be strongly influenced by social values, such as the importance placed on carrying on the family lineage, the esteem placed on goals which are consistent with parenting, and cultural attitudes with regard to what constitutes a true sense of personal fulfillment.

In today's world, attempts to control population growth, increasing economic demands, and the social pressures associated with the women's movement present a considerable challenge to traditional parental values. Social change is being encouraged, and for those who can neither accept the traditional role nor completely reject it for some of the alternate lifestyles currently offered, conflict and feelings of stress are not uncommon. Many find it extremely difficult to accept a new set of values based not on the challenge of forming closely knit family ties but upon the competitiveness of career achievements. These new roles and goals are often substitutive and ultimately unfulfilling, leaving many individuals wondering what they will have to accomplish to feel satisfied with themselves. For much of humanity, parent-hood has been the primary means of achieving such self-satisfaction—the most accessible means by which to express creativity, share the potential to love, and ensure a way by which to achieve "immortality." However, a social policy now seems to be developing which tends to restrict parenthood to a selected few. For instance, in 1976, almost one-third of couples with wives aged fifteen to forty-four were physically unable to have children due to surgical sterility. The psychological ramifications of such a trend are as yet unknown. Nor is it known just how successful individuals will be at learning to substitute other forms of love for parental love. Will people learn to be satisfied with the pride of "possessor-thing" relationships or "career-peer" relationships rather than the pride of parent-child relationships? Perhaps the married couple of the future will have to limit their parental pride to statements like: "That's right. We've had three Buicks since we got married. We were planning on a fourth, but with the cost of living going up, we're just not sure we could afford another right now."

Secondary Drives—Social Survival and Values

In addition to the behavior of a compulsory nature that is generated by primary drives, humans also appear to demonstrate purposeful striving, as well as self-generated autonomous behavior, motivated by secondary drives.

Though the primary drives are considered to be inherited, there is some disagreement about the origin of secondary drives. Most theorists agree that secondary drives are acquired.

SOCIAL NEEDS   One of the most thorough investigations into the field of secondary or social needs was conducted by Henry Murray (1938), who developed "personology," a psychological approach to "the scientific study of the total person." Through this approach, Murray attempted to gain an understanding of the "totality of motivational forces" which influence human behavior. In so doing, he divided needs into two major classes: *viscerogenic*, or primary, needs, and *psychogenic*, or secondary, needs.

Murray concentrated his research efforts in the area of psychogenic needs. These, he felt, were qualities of an individual's personality that could be strongly influenced by social pressures. He referred to such external pressures as "presses." A press is anything that does something to a person or for a person.

Murray believed that external pressures, or presses, activate needs within the individual. The specific nature of the need activated depends upon the state of the individual plus the nature of the stimulus. Murray refers to this need-press combination as a "thema." For example, a need-press combination of poverty (need) plus an offer of an athletic scholarship (press) may activate a person's need for achievement.

THE NEED FOR ACHIEVEMENT   The need for achievement, or the desire to meet some internalized standard of excellence, is but one category in Murray's list of psychogenic needs (see Table 4.1). However, the achievement drive has received more attention from researchers than perhaps any other secondary drive. D. C. McClelland (1955), for instance, has devoted almost his entire scientific career to the investigation of the achievement drive. Much of his research has centered on the development of a means of measuring the relative strength of such a drive.

One of the techniques he developed in an attempt to measure the need to achieve (nAch) was a projective test using four cards (two from the thematic apperception test). The cards have pictures of men working, a father and son, a boy at a desk, and a boy daydreaming. After having been shown one of these cards, the subject would be asked to tell a story based on the content of the picture. The relative strength of a person's need to achieve could be ascertained from an analysis of the stories (McClelland et al., 1953). Based on research using McClelland's techniques, it has been found that students with a high need to achieve make higher grades than those with a low need to achieve (Morgan, 1951). In addition, research conducted by French and Tomas (1958) demonstrated that subjects with a high need to achieve worked, on the average, twice as long as the others on complex insight problems.

Need to achieve, however, does not always reflect actual performance. The strength of this need in an individual may be more closely related to level of aspiration (Ricciuti and Schultz, 1958) than to actual ability. Furthermore, since a person's true ability can often be influenced by such factors as opportunity, experience, and personal adjustment, it is important to distinguish between the need to achieve (nAch) and the desire for achievement (vAch). The need to achieve is associated with striving for effectiveness and is self-directed. The desire for achievement is associated with conformity and impressing people and is, therefore, other-directed (DeCharms et al., in McClelland, 1955).

FEAR OF FAILURE Often associated with a desire to achieve is the fear of failure. McClelland and Liberman (1949) found that those rated in the middle of the scale for need for achievement seem to have the greatest fear of failure. The fear of failure seems to be closely related to primary drive reduction, when failure to obtain food or drink can mean death or physical pain. With regard to secondary drives, failure to obtain a goal can mean disappointment, frustration, and emotional pain. Therefore, the fear of physical or mental pain, can motivate strong avoidance responses. This is not, however, the same as the motive to "approach failure" implied by Freud, in which some individuals derive unconscious gratification from failing (Tresemer, 1974). Far from being a source of unconscious gratification, the sense of having failed to realize one's full potential is often a source of great anxiety, conflict, and stress.

THE NEED TO BELONG William McDougall (1871–1938), a British psychologist who taught at both Harvard and Duke Universities, proposed that social life stems from natural *instincts*. In his book *An Introduction to Social Psychology* (1908), he described how nonspecific instincts, such as fear, curiosity, and gregariousness, would gradually become specific through repeated exposure

TABLE 4.1 TYPICAL THEMAS

NEED	THEMAS
Abasement	To submit passively to a motherlike person. To accept blame readily from a superior. To confess wrong-doing to anyone who will listen.
Achievement	To strive to earn a large income. To attain honors and awards through outstanding achievements. To rival and surpass associates.
Affiliation	To have a close friend. To please many people. To work closely with another, or on a team.
Aggression	To overcome the opposition of another who is perceived as a threat. To cause another to submit: to control, to obligate others. To demonstrate superiority over others by hurting them.
Autonomy	To resist any form of restraint or coercion from parents. To quit deliberately activities which are required by authorities. To express needs relating to desired objects freely and impulsively. To seek exemptions from rules.
Counteraction	To strive anew in the face of failure. To overcome humiliation by taking strong positive action. To seek constantly to overcome weaknesses in oneself. To seek obstacles and difficulties to surmount.
Defendance	To defend the self against any criticism from anyone. To conceal quickly or justify a misdeed or humiliation in relationships with one perceived as an inferior. To be vindictive toward anyone who interferes with strivings.
Deference	To admire and support an older sibling, parent, friend. To praise, honor, or eulogize a boss, teacher, hero. To yield eagerly to the influence of a friend, partner, parent. To imitate the example of a model such as one's boss.
Dominance	To control one's environment by making things suit one's plan. To influence or direct the behavior of friends, classmates, parents. To take charge of situations: leader, boss, director, persuader. To persuade, to restrain, to direct, to control others.

Source: Nicholas Di Caprio, *Personality Theories: Guides to Living,* Saunders, Philadelphia, 1974.

to specific situations. With regard to the instinct of gregariousness, for example, the nonspecific need to associate with, or be in the presence of, others would become a specific need to be with one's family, close friends, or ethnic group through repeated association with these individuals.

Freud also believed in instincts. However, he did not believe in the existence of a social instinct, nor did he accept it as the reason for people wanting to be with one another. For Freud, primitive sexual urges were the reason for gregarious behavior. Such feelings, of course, would be disguised. Many of them appear as "the affectionate relations between parents and children, which were originally fully sexual, feelings of friendship, and the emotional ties in marriage which had their origin in sexual attraction" (Murray, 1964, p. 85).

TABLE 4.1 TYPICAL THEMAS

NEED	THEMAS
Exhibition	To make an impression on members of the opposite sex. To fascinate, shock, entertain, intrigue people perceived as significant. To draw attention to oneself through appearance and behavior.
Harm avoidance	To avoid taking risks by a conservative approach to life. To take precautionary measures in any threatening situation. To worry excessively about the uncertainties of life.
Infavoidance	To maintain a high level of pride in relationships with others. To avoid failure in undertakings. To be especially sensitive to belittlement, scorn, and indifference of others.
Nurturance	To be attracted to babies, small animals, and helpless creatures. To rally for the underdog. To enjoy matchmaking, directing young people, giving support. To sympathize with, console, comfort one who is afflicted.
Order	To organize and plan a trip or program. To produce a balance or orderly arrangement. To work out a system in the midst of confusion.
Play	To enjoy pleasure-making through sports. To enjoy laughing and making jokes in company with others.
Rejection	To respond to some people with an air of superiority. To deliberately snub or exclude certain people.
Sentience	To need activities and people that promote sensual pleasures. To seek unusual experiences as a means of changing moods.
Sex	To be attracted to many sexual partners. To be preoccupied with erotic concerns. To be attracted by an older man or woman.
Succorance	To respond dependently to a motherlike person. To cling to any authority figure who demonstrates concern. To seek to be counseled, advised, consoled by a sympathetic friend.
Understanding	To ask questions of a knowledgeable person. To speculate about unknowns. To attempt to idenfity the causes of things and events.

Freud believed that all social behavior was the by-product of the defense mechanism of *sublimation*—the conversion of unacceptable urges into socially acceptable behavior. For example, through the process of sublimation, sadistic impulses can be converted into the admired skills of a talented surgeon, and frustrated desires can be channeled into artistic expression. As a consequence of this premise, Freud perceived group relationships as variations on the family theme. Leader-member relationships mimic father-son relationships, and the relationships between group members imitate sibling relationships.

The instinct theories proposed by McDougall and Freud are opposed by Allport, Dollard and Miller, and others. These psychologists maintain that gregariousness is acquired. Allport, for instance, believes that the need for physical comfort from the mother will later lead to a need for social companionship. Dollard and Miller, on the other hand, perceive the mother-child relationship as merely a specific source of reinforcement. This bond, they say, will later be generalized to other individuals who may act as similar sources of reinforcement.

Abraham Maslow (1908–1962) disagreed with the behaviorists and their specific reinforcement theory. Maslow preferred to view the individual as an integrated whole. He rejects the behavioristic approach because in his view it deals with separate units of behavior but ignores the total person. In *Motivation and Personality* (1970) Maslow states:

> In good theory there is no such entity as a need of the stomach or mouth, or a genital need. There is only a need of the individual. It is John Smith who wants food, not John Smith's stomach. Furthermore, satisfaction comes to the whole individual and not just to a part of him. Food satisfies John Smith's hunger and not his stomach's hunger . . . when John Smith is hungry, he is hungry all over. (pp. 19–20)

Maslow, however, did agree, in principle, with McDougall's premise that social instincts influence behavior. Maslow proposed that human motivations are innate and arranged in an ascending hierarchy of priority and potency: physiological, safety, belongingness, self-esteem, and self-actualizing. Within this proposed hierarchy, each of the preceding (lower) needs must be satisfied before a higher need can be satisfied. With regard to the need for belonging-ness, for example, Maslow felt that one could successfully endeavor to satisfy this need only after having achieved a state of sufficiency in the physiological and safety needs.

The need to belong, however, involves more than merely being in the presence of others. It involves a need for evidence that one is accepted and approved of by the group, and it requires that the individual adjust to the habits and standards of the group. Furthermore, the need to belong requires conviction—a firm belief in what full membership in the group represents, such as the belief in the principle of fidelity that accompanies the sense of belonging experienced within a marriage, the belief in the importance of heritage and neighborliness upon becoming a member of an established community, or the belief in confidentiality and prudent conduct when accepting membership into an elite organization.

THE NEED TO BE LOVED   Closely allied to the need to belong is the need to be loved. However, while the need to belong can often be satisfied through the expression of interest, concern, respect, and appreciation, the need to be loved requires the additional experiences of caring and devotion.

The need to be loved is the need to know that someone else is interested in our dreams and ambitions as well as in our problems and frustrations. It is our need to have another person show concern for our welfare, and appreciation for the effort we put forth in our struggles. The need to be loved is the need for understanding from someone who cares. When such sympathy and tenderness are forthcoming, we are often convinced that we are loved.

It is often difficult to maintain the delicate balance between being similar enough to be accepted yet different enough to remain unique. [*Bill Price, Photo Researchers.*]

FIGURE 4.3

Deeply integrated with the concept of love is the premise that one not only needs *to be loved* but needs *to love.* We have a need to give as well as a need to receive. Generally, people reserve such emotional giving for those who have contributed to their need for security or have provided a source of aesthetic beauty. However, in many instances, the need to love is generated from the charity which someone has demonstrated toward another.

THE NEED TO BE IMPORTANT   We also have a need to feel significant, to have a sense of importance, to think that we are "somebody." This need is often a by-product of having achieved a sense of belonging and having satisfied the need to love and be loved.

The need to be important reflects the desire for recognition. We need to receive recognition for whatever quality, talent, or skill we may possess, and/or for the time, emotions, or energy that we may expend. The need to be important encompasses the concept of relevancy and the knowledge that what one does, says, feels, or stands for is neither futile nor wasted.

This need stimulates the development of such traits as ambition, industriousness, and perseverance. Without it much of what tempts our interests and imaginations would never be accomplished. Our inventiveness, creativeness, and curiosity about the unknown, unexplored, and unconquered would never reach fruition. However, equally important to the actual achievement is experiencing the appreciation expressed by others. Without this admiration—without empathy and understanding, and the esteem that can be derived from the achievement—the accomplishment will often be experienced as a shallow victory, irrelevant and unimportant. This is why the opinions and estimations of those nearest to us are so vital. How important we seem in the eyes of our children, spouses, parents, and others we love will often outweigh any national recognition or public acclaim. Whenever such value and recognition is lacking, as is often the case with undiscovered artists, unloved delinquents, and alienated and rootless youth, there is a tendency to turn to nonconformity, immorality, and lawlessness as a means of gaining recognition or "getting back" at the source of these feelings of rejection.

LEARNING TO MEET OUR NEEDS

The goal of most therapists is to have the *dependent* become the *independent*. This goal is shared by most parents and most teachers. In one form or another, the object is to engender a sense of *self-reliance,* and to develop the individual's ability to meet his or her own needs. Therapists, teachers, and parents all act as experienced guides. The ultimate decision to follow their example or to learn from their counsel, however, is up to the individual. As Galileo once said, "You cannot teach a man anything; you can only help him to find it within himself."

One definition of learning is "a change in behavior due to some experience." The change in behavior referred to can be a change in the probability of the behavior occurring again. For example, if a small child says the word "nanny" to his or her grandparent, and the resulting experience is being given a piece of candy, the probability of the child using the word "nanny" again has most likely increased.

Another observable change in behavior is that of magnitude. A change in the magnitude of a response might be illustrated by the extra effort put forth by some students after they have been told that the first ten students to hand in their term papers will receive extra points.

A change in the frequency, or rate, of a response can also be an indication that learning has taken place. For instance, after a "friend" finds out that a particular person is a "soft touch," the frequency of approaching that person for loans may increase.

Learning, then, is a change in performance—a change in the probability, magnitude, or frequency of behavior. The process of change can be brought about through association, reinforcement, or example.

Learning by Association

In what is considered to be a historic model of the effects of classical conditioning, Watson and Rayner (1920) conditioned a child named Albert to have a fear of rats. Before the conditioning took place, Albert demonstrated no

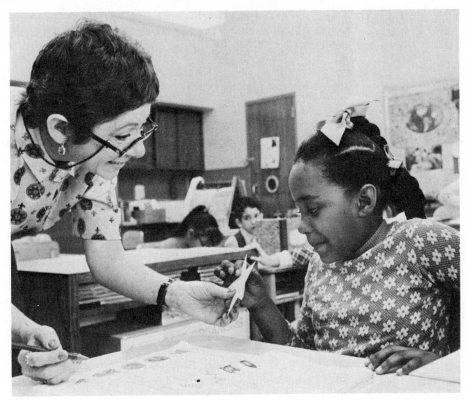

FIGURE 4.4   Whether it is a Nobel prize or a gold star, the recognition and appreciation of our efforts by others can be a powerful reinforcer. [*Raimondo Borea, Editorial Photocolor Archives.*]

fear of the rat and would attempt to play with it. During the conditioning process, a steel bar was struck with a hammer whenever Albert even reached for the rat. This event automatically generated a fear response. After a few associations of the loud noise with the rat, Albert would elicit a fear response toward the rat even in the absence of the loud noise.

Perhaps even more pertinent to the importance of the role that association plays in the process of learning is the fact that Albert's fear became generalized. In addition to being afraid of rats, Albert was also afraid of rabbits, dogs, fur coats, and anything else that was similar to the rat.

The principle of generalization dictates that once a conditioned response to a particular stimulus has been established, similar stimuli will also cause the response to occur. If the stimulus is physically similar, as in the case of Albert and furry things, it is called a "primary generalization." If, however, the stimulus is only *synonymous* to the conditioned stimulus, it is called "secondary generalization." In the case of secondary generalization, radically different stimuli are capable of evoking similar responses. For example, through such statements as, "Have your fun now, because once you grow up and get married, that's the end of it," or "Enjoy yourself while you can, because once you have children, your life is over," a person can be conditioned as a child to believe that his or her life ends as soon as marriage and children become a reality. Through the process of secondary generalization, a marriage proposal or the thought of having children could become synonymous with the threat of dying.

Learning by Reinforcement

One of the main differences between learning through classical conditioning and learning by operant conditioning pertains to the learner's role. In classical conditioning, the individual is passive and merely responds to the environment. In operant conditioning, the individual takes an active role in learning by acting on the environment and then responding to the consequences of such action, which often come in the form of reinforcement. For example, fear of a bully may occur as a result of pairing the pain of being hit with the presence of the bully who is doing the hitting (classical conditioning). However, discovering that when the bully is punched in the stomach (act) he folds up like an accordion (consequence) can be very reinforcing, and it will usually lead to more belly blows being thrown (operant conditioning).

Reinforcement is anything that changes the probability of a response occurring again. Reinforcement is considered to be positive if, when it is presented, it tends to strengthen the behavior that preceded it. Reinforcement is considered to be negative when the removal of the reinforcing stimulus strengthens the response that takes it away. Such would be the case when you put on a coat (response), and thus remove the undesirable feeling of being cold (reinforcement), or when you take off your shoes because they pinch.

Learning by Modeling

Everyone who reads this text has learned by example. From your first attempt at tying shoe laces to your first driving lesson or your first college registration week, you learned from a model.

The relative importance of what a model (the person being observed) *does* versus what a model *says,* with respect to the subsequent imitative behavior demonstrated by an observer, was studied by James Bryan (1969). As part of the investigation, Bryan had fourth- and fifth-grade children bowl for prizes which were one-cent gift certificates. Each child unknowingly bowled with an adult confederate. Some children would bowl with a confederate who talked about the virtues of generosity and also acted generously by donating some of his certificates to the poor. Other confederates talked of greed and selfishness, but acted generously. In both of these situations, the children were more likely to donate to the poor after having observed charitable behavior, regardless of what the model had talked about. Children who were exposed to confederates who talked of generosity, but did not act generously (did not make a donation), as well as children whose confederates talked of greed and selfishness and did not donate, were less likely to act generously. Actions do seem to speak louder than words. In further analysis of the research findings, it was found that although verbal exhortations tend to influence the way a person thinks, it is behavior that has the greatest influence on the way a person acts.

Albert Bandura (1967) referred to the influence of a model's behavior on an observer's behavior as "observational learning." This concept includes such matching behavior as imitation and identification. Sometimes called "no-trial learning," the method permits an observer to watch how the model performs and then to copy that behavior. Such imitative behavior can lead to the acquisition of new responses, such as learning which fork or spoon to use at a formal dinner by merely observing the behavior of the host or hostess. It can also strengthen or weaken inhibitory responses, such as booing a politician after hearing others in the crowd do so, or becoming less fearful of the water upon watching other children splashing and playing.

Just how great an influence a model's behavior can have on an observer depends, to some extent, on how much prestige, competence, and/or power the model possesses (Bandura and Walters, 1963). In one experiment, a family situation was created. In some instances, the male adult had the power to control who got treats, who could play games, and who would be rewarded. In other instances, the female adult had that power. The results of the experiment indicated that, regardless of the sex of the children participating in the family, or the sex of the adult in power, the children would imitate the adult in power more frequently than the other adult (Bandura et al., 1963). This tendency to identify with powerful models is also found among adults. An extreme example of such identification was found among World War II prisoners, who often imitated the Gestapo guards as a reaction to severe stress (Bettelheim, 1958).

However, being the victim as well as the observer of a contemptible model's behavior can lead to the adoption of behavior which is the *opposite* of that which was observed. For example, being mistreated by a bully may cause a person to be considerate to the weak and helpless. This may not be the most desirable way to learn, but it is often very effective. Kahlil Gibran, in *Sand and Foam* (1926), wrote: "I have learned silence from the talkative, toleration from the intolerant, and kindness from the unkind; yet strange, I am ungrateful to these teachers."

Another important factor in modeling influence is the degree of nurturance associated with the model. Boys who perceive their fathers as being warm and understanding tend to be more like their fathers (Payne and Mussen, 1956). Similarly, girls who receive love and attention from their mothers tend to be more like their mothers (Mussen and Parker, 1965). Unfortunately, due to the high incidence of divorce and separation, children do not always have both parents available as modeling sources. Nor do many parents, in today's mobile society, have the modeling advantages of an extended family to draw upon. As a consequence, many individuals have been forced to turn to experts in the field of child-rearing rather than being able to rely upon the intuition, knowledge, and experience of close relatives.

The availability of a real model, however, is not absolutely necessary for the development of imitative behavior. Imitative behavior can also take place as a result of being exposed to symbolic models, such as are found in books, magazines, movies, and television.

The fact that what is seen on television can influence behavior (Murray, 1973) has been a major concern of parents, educators, law enforcement

FIGURE 4.5 Imitation, or the copying of the behavior we observe in others, can have a powerful influence on personality development in children; therefore, parents need to be especially mindful of the example they set. [*Ken Heyman.*]

officials, and even heads of state for years. The amount of violence being portrayed is the main concern. In 1972, the Surgeon General reported to Congress: "The overwhelming consensus [is] that televised violence does have an adverse effect on certain members of society." Robert Liebert (1973), one of the Surgeon General's investigators, believed that the amount of TV violence a child is exposed to by the age of nine is more influential than home life, school performance, and family background in determining how aggressive an adult the child will be.

In an attempt to counter this trend in programming, many civic organizations, such as Action for Children's Television and the Committee on Children's Television, Inc., have proposed guidelines for children's television. The guidelines pertain to audience appeal, racism, sexism, social issues, appropriate portrayal of ideals, and constructive play (see Table 4.2).

The issue of violence on television has also become a concern in other countries. Many foreign leaders object to the cultural excesses portrayed in exported American programs. They fear that the real-life crime statistics of their own countries will begin to resemble those of the United States due to the modeling influence of American TV. (As a comparison, there are more murders in Manhattan, population 1.5 million, than in the entire United Kingdom, population 60 million. On the average, someone is killed or wounded in the United States every four minutes by gunfire, and every three minutes, someone is robbed at gunpoint.) In addition, there is a growing concern about the cultural influence American programming has on local traditions, customs, and values. One source of worry is the increasing Westernization of other cultures due to the modeling influence of magazines, films, and television provided by American industries. As to the seriousness of this type of situation, the American social scientist Thorstein Veblen (1857–1929) stated in *The Theory of the Leisure Class* (1899): "With the exception of the instinct of self-preservation, the propensity for emulation is probably the strongest and most alert and persistent of the economic motives."

INTERRELATIONSHIP OF MOTIVATION AND LEARNING

In this chapter we have seen how important motivation is in both a biological and a social context. We have also discussed some of the ways in which learning takes place. While learning often occurs through association, reinforcement, and modeling, the exact nature of what is learned depends a great deal on the unique interests and environment of each individual.

Motivation of such primary needs as food and sleep begins at birth, when the neonate first learns that sucking from the mother's breast or a bottle will supply food. The social needs for love, belonging, achievement, and importance take on more complex forms as we grow older. For instance, our physical and neurological limitations, along with our social competence and emotional stability, can often play as important a role in the development of our personal interests as the nature of the stimulation in the environment, the age at which intellectual challenging began, or the quality of the education we have received.

Most people know of someone who plodded through school and later became a famous figure or a financial success. Winston Churchill's grades were a continual disappointment to his family, and yet he provided outstanding leadership for his country during one of the worst wars in modern history. The person sitting next to you in class may be an "A" student although IQ tests indicates only average intelligence. Motivations provide such people with a tool that allows them to surpass their normal ability or projected potential.

Perhaps even more familiar are the individuals who are not achieving their potential. "You can do better" and "Learn to apply yourself" are frequent refrains many young students hear. This failure to achieve can result from a poorly developed self-image, unrealistic expectations, or simply a faulty priority system. For example using study time to work on your campaign for class office would be an example of faulty priorities.

Many parents and teachers tend to *underestimate* the importance of a child's emotional involvement with a learning experience. Often adults will make such statements as "Oh, you're just a little upset about your first day at school. You get over it," or "You may not like it now, but you'll grow to love it." In

TABLE 4.2 GENERAL GUIDELINES FOR SELECTING TELEVISION PROGRAMMING FOR CHILDREN

1 Does the program appeal to the audience for whom intended? (A program for 12-year-olds should be different from a program for 6-year-olds.)

2 Does the program present racial groups positively and does it show them in situations that enhance the Third World child's self-image? (Who has the lead roles? Who is the professional or leader and who is the villain?)

3 Does the program present gender roles and adult roles positively? (Are the men either super-heroes or incompetents? Are the women flighty and disposed to chicanery? Are teenagers portrayed with adult characteristics?)

4 Does the program present social issues that are appropriate for the child viewer and perhaps are something a child can act on at a child's level? (Litter versus atomic fallout, or pet care versus saving wolves.)

5 Does the program encourage worthwhile ideals, values and beliefs?

6 Does the program present conflict that a child can understand and does it demonstrate positive techniques for resolving the conflict?

7 Does the program stimulate constructive activities and does it enhance the quality of a child's play?

8 Does the program separate fact from fantasy? Does it separate advertisements from program content?

9 Does the program present humor at a child's level? (Or is it adult sarcasm, ridicule or an adult remembering what he thought was funny from his childhood?)

10 Does the program have a pace that allows the child to absorb and contemplate the material presented?

11 Does the program have artistic qualities?

12 Has your child seen an appropriate amount of television for the day? (Or is it time to turn off the set?)

Source: San Francisco's Committee On Children's Television, Inc., 1511 Masonic Avenue, San Francisco, California, 94117, 1975.

reality, many children never do "get over" a particular childhood trauma. Most children are good judges of how they feel, and some may grow to hate what their parents expected them to "love." Children who do not like school initially and are told that they will learn to like it may come to dislike the entire academic experience. There are many reasons for this: perhaps the child began at too young an age, received an undue amount of ridicule, or was handicapped by social incompetence.

As a result of such negative attitudes, many children become *underachievers*. They fail to perform as well as those with similar abilities and backgrounds. Their level of achievement may be average, or even above average, but they accomplish less than would be expected. They are often labeled "lazy" because of what appears to be a lack of motivation. For many of these children, however, the lack of motivation could more accurately be described as an inability to find a reinforcer that would develop a desire to study, a reason to want to learn.

This seems especially true among the brighter students, who tend to underachieve more often than others, primarily because they have more "room" to underachieve. It is generally assumed that good academic performance requires an above-average IQ, but a high IQ does not necessarily assure good performance in school. In most cases, schools are set up for the average student, and the bright student can often do fairly well without really trying. However, in many instances, it is socially unwise to do too well in school. As a result, students who are capable of getting high grades may deliberately set out to get poor ones in order to be accepted by their peers.

Although underachieving is often deliberate, in some situations it is unavoidable, particularly among those who attend school in lower-income areas. In such schools, many teachers attempt to escape the poor academic environment as soon as possible and see their students as incapable of learning. The students often accept this negative view of their abilities as true and subsequently do not do well (Rosenthal and Jacobson, 1968). Children from such environments typically have a higher dropout rate than those from higher-income groups. The interrelationship between motivation and learning was cogently summed up by Thomas Ringness, in *Mental Health in the Schools* (1969):

> In the homes of many such children there is no father; . . . home life is disorganized, with no regular mealtime and therefore no family interaction at the table or, indeed, at any other place. Language skills are not practiced, and there is cumulative loss in the child's language development, which militates against school learning. Furthermore, most school textbooks and other materials tend to emphasize a kind of life that is not typical for these children, with consequent disinterest, frustration, and inability of the pupil to identify with the material presented. Add to these problems the attitude of many teachers toward these children—low expectations concerning their abilities and motivations—and one can see that the dropout is essentially a culturally caused problem. (p. 154)

Thus we see that there is a very special relationship between motivation and learning. Learning is dependent upon motivation in one form or another throughout the lifetime of the individual. The more aware one is of self and others and of how society operates, the better prepared one will be to use motivation and learning for setting effective personal goals.

SUMMARY

This chapter has dealt primarily with the issues of motivation and learning. With regard to motivation, the concept of primary and secondary needs was explored—how these drives are generated and how their relative strengths can be measured.

Primary drives were discussed from the standpoint of the body's need to maintain a biological balance, or homeostasis. Discussion of the hunger drive included the effects of specific hungers and cafeteria feeding, as well as disturbances in eating habits, which can lead to obesity or emaciation. The need for sleep and the effects of too much sleep and too little sleep were also examined, along with our need for stimulation and the effects of stimulus deprivation. The innate drives associated with reproduction were also investigated, with emphasis on just how instinctual the maternal instinct really is.

Secondary drives were explored from the standpoint of social needs, such as the need for achievement cited by Henry Murray and researched by David McClelland. The fear of failure and the fear of success were also explored in conjunction with Freudian and humanistic theory.The need to belong and the need to be loved were presented, with emphasis on social instincts, and the importance of caring and devotion. These needs were found to be closely affiliated with the need to feel important and to experience recognition for one's efforts.

The learning processes were examined. The processes of learning by association, by reinforcement, and by modeling were particularly emphasized. Included in this examination were the effects on behavior of classical and operant conditioning, generalization and desensitization, reward and punishment, and real and symbolic modeling.

The chapter concluded with a discussion of the interrelationship between motivation and learning, centering on the importance of learning what really motivates us.

DISCUSSION QUESTIONS

1 How many of the things that you are now striving for are actually wants rather than needs?
2 Can you think of anything for which you have developed a psychological dependence—for example, nicotine, marijuana, alcohol, barbiturates, amphetamines, caffeine, etc.?
3 Do you think that you eat more or less as a consequence of being anxious? depressed?
4 For many, stimulus deprivation can be very disturbing. In what ways do you attempt to maintain a relatively constant source of stimulation (for example, turning on a stereo, radio, or TV; making sure you are with someone at all times; or working on a hobby)?
5 In what ways do you feel you are important? Who do you believe thinks you are important to their lives?
6 Is there anything, or anyone, that you have been classically conditioned to fear?
7 Who are some of the people who have acted as models which may have had an influence on the development of your personality?
8 Do you hope to turn out more like your father or your mother? Both? Neither?
9 Do you consider yourself a fast or slow learner? Do you base this belief mostly on academic performance or on the opinion of others?
10 Do you believe that there should be special academic programs for the gifted or retarded child or should such children be taught in the same program as the other students?

EXPERIENTIAL EXERCISES

1 In order to explore the consequences of being denied something for which a psychological dependence has developed, have each member of a group voluntarily deprive themselves of such an item for seventy-two hours. Some typical examples might be cigarettes, alcohol, drinks with caffeine, nonprescriptive drugs, or even certain rituals such as watching TV. After the deprivation period is over, have each member discuss his or her reactions, behaviors, and emotional states. Were there any that were unable to go the full seventy-two hours?

2 Table 4.1 is composed of a list of some of Murray's needs. Have each member of the class or of a group list these needs in descending order of importance as they might apply to themselves. What are some of the most important needs? The least important?

3 As a means of quantifying the amount of violence on TV, have the members of a group prepare a count of all acts of violence that they observe while watching a typical week of television. What effect do the members think these acts of violence may have on the development of personalities in America?

PART TWO

PROBLEMS OF

ADJUSTMENT

CHAPTER 5

STRESS

After months of therapy, Deborah began to learn that there were many reasons why the world was horrifying to her. The shadow of the grandfather dynast was still dark over all the houses of the family. She went back often again, hearing grandfather's familiar voice saying, "Second in the class is not enough; you must be the first." "If you are hurt, never cry, but laugh. You must never let them know that they are hurting you." It was all directed against the smiling sharers of the secret joke. Pride must be the ability to die in agony as if you did it every day, gracefully. Even his pride in her was anger. "You're smart—you'll show them all!"

Hannah Green
I Never Promised You a Rose Garden

DEFINITION OF STRESS

The very fact that survival can never be fully guaranteed from one moment to the next is one of the most fundamental sources of stress. From the simplest organisms to complex human beings, the challenge of survival, in one form or another, requires vigilance, endurance, and adaptability.

Biological survival usually takes precedence over claims to a mate or to territory or to dominance within a group. However, surviving in the labor market, the business world, or the world of academia can often expose a person to as much stress as some of the most primitive forms of tribal warfare. Similarly, the efforts needed to be a friend or keep a friend, to do your part in keeping the family experience pleasant, or to form a political organization can often strain the adaptive abilities of even the most stable of individuals. The emotional strain of being an inadequately prepared parent, being trapped within a disastrous relationship, or perceiving yourself as a failure can be as destructive as the physical strain of being seriously ill or experiencing the trials of a natural catastrophe.

In many cases, the stress associated with assuring the survival of one's *reasons* to go on living—spiritual beliefs, hope in the future, or self-esteem—can be more difficult than attempting to assure the survival of one's *means* to go on living—job, home, or food supply. The absence of such reasons, in itself, can be a source of great stress and often creates a feeling of emptiness within the individual. Rollo May, in *Man's Search for Himself* (1953 p. 14), observed: "The chief problem of people in the middle decade of the twentieth century is *emptiness*. By that I mean not only that many people do not know what they want; they often do not have any clear idea of what they feel."

Stress, then, is associated not only with literal survival, but with *symbolic survival*. It results from physical as well as psychological demands. It is caused by internal conditions as well as external conditions. *Stress is a response to anything that imposes a demand for adjustment.*

Physiological Demands

The disastrous physiological effects of prolonged exposure to the elements, severe malnutrition, or chronic illness have long been recognized. Such physical deterioration is usually due to the body's inability to maintain its functions within certain limits—that is, its inability to sustain a homeostatic, or balanced, biological state. For example, when a person is exposed to extreme cold for a prolonged period, the rate at which the body loses heat may exceed its ability to generate heat. As a consequence, the body's normal temperature range cannot be maintained, and the person may die of hypothermia.

Stress, however, need not have a physical source to generate physical demands on the body. Any situation that is capable of generating an emotional reaction is capable of placing physiological demands on the body's adaptive resources.

Hans Selye (1907–   ), an Austrian physician, noted that cases of physical distress often display similar symptoms even though the causes may may have been quite diverse. In *Stress without Distress* (1974), Selye points out:

> In 1926, as a second-year medical student, I first came across this problem of a stereotyped response to any exacting demand made upon the body. I began to wonder why patients suffering from the most diverse diseases that threaten homeostasis have so many signs and symptoms in common. Whether a man suffers from a severe loss of blood, an infectious disease, or advanced cancer, he loses his appetite, his muscular strength, and his ambition to accomplish anything; usually, the patient also loses weight, and even his facial expression betrays that he is ill. (pp. 35–36)

Selye referred to this phenomenon as the "syndrome of just being sick." In 1936, while conducting research with rats, he encountered an experimental replica of this syndrome. Selye once again noted that the physical symptoms of distress were quite similar regardless of whether the rat had been subjected to the stress of extreme temperatures, bacterial infection, the injection of toxic agents, or emotional trauma. Selye eventually came to refer to this phenomenon as the "general adaptation syndrome" (GAS).

Selye believes that the similarity of distress symptoms occurs because the body, when confronted with a stressful situation, undergoes a total mobilization of its adaptive resources. This adaptive process has three distinct stages—the *alarm-reaction stage,* the *resistance stage,* and the *exhaustion stage.*

The alarm-reaction stage is characterized by physiological changes designed to help counter a physical threat. An example would be the physiological changes that usually take place when a car begins skidding out of control. The alarm-reaction stage also deals with the physiological changes designed to correct a homeostatic imbalance, such as when adapting to hunger. Selye thought of these changes as a "generalized call to arms of the defensive forces in the organism" (Selye, 1956, p. 311). With regard to psychological stress, this "call to arms" tends to produce a state of emotional arousal, tension, and feelings of insecurity (anxiety).

During the resistance stage, the individual's adaptive resources attempt to (1) repair any damage to the body; (2) overcome any deficiencies, such as the need for food, drink, or warmth; or (3) in the case of psychological stress, incorporate needed defense mechanisms, such as denial, rationalization, and repression, in order to maintain self-esteem and/or self-control.

In the final stage, the exhaustion stage, natural adaptive resources are depleted due to deficiencies having remained uncorrected or grown worse. As a result, the individual may succumb to degeneration or disease. Selye, in *The Stress of Life* (1956), proposed that "diseases of adaptation," such as ulcers, asthma, and high blood pressure, are the result of the body's inability to successfully continue resistance. Similarly, the exhaustion of one's psychological resources would tend to render an individual susceptible to psychoneurotic or psychotic reactions.

Psychological Demands

One of the features that distinguishes psychological demands from physiological demands is the limited distinction between real and imagined danger in a psychological demand. As Freud (1926) noted, normal anxiety is evoked by "real danger . . . which threatens from some external object" (p. 51). Neurotic anxiety can be viewed as fear in the absence of real danger, often the result of inadequate defenses against unacceptable thoughts or desires. For example, people who have been told that they may have cancer will often undergo severe psychological stress and exhibit *normal anxiety*. However, individuals who are incapacitated due to a fear of contracting a disease (pathophobia), although otherwise in good health and living in a healthy environment, would most likely be exhibiting *neurotic anxiety*.

AWARENESS OF THREAT   *Awareness* of a potentially dangerous or undesirable situation is crucial to the manifestation of psychological stress. Alfred Hitchcock, the famous director of suspense films, stated in an educational television series called "The Men Who Made the Movies":

> The essential fact is . . . to get real suspense, you must let the audience have information. Now let's take the old-fashioned "bomb theory." You and I are sitting talking, say about baseball. . . . We're talking for five minutes. Suddenly, the bomb goes off. The audience has a ten-second terrible shock.

> Now, let's take the same situation. Tell the audience at the beginning that under the table—and show it to them—there's a bomb and it's gonna go off in five minutes. And we talk baseball. What is the audience doing? They're saying, "Don't talk about baseball! There's a bomb under there! Get rid of it!"

> They'd help, but they can't jump out of their seats and up on to the screen to grab hold of it, and throw it out.

The mental uncertainty and helplessness that Hitchcock refers to are not only a basis for suspense, but also the basis of stress.

Awareness of an external threat depends primarily on receiving information, such as being given notice of probationary status in school, seeing cracks form on the face of a dam, or hearing about the death of a friend. The intensity of the stress resulting from exposure to such information varies. It is influenced by such factors as (1) the personality predisposition of the individual, (2) the individual's physical state (fatigue, illness, etc.), and (3) the opportunity for action and defense (Freud, 1926; Fenichel, 1945). For example, for one person, the awareness of the death of a friend may result in a sense of loss followed by an "appropriate" period of grief. The same information may stimulate another person, overwhelmed by the sense of loss, to attempt suicide.

NEUROTIC ANXIETY AND PANIC   A disproportionate emotional reaction to "mild" stress often indicates that certain external cues have somehow been linked with an "internal danger." The cumulative effect threatens to overwhelm the individual's ego defenses. As a consequence, the individual may feel unable to exercise control over unacceptable, and therefore repressed, impulses, desires, or thoughts.

A. T. Simeons, in his book *Man's Presumptuous Brain* (1961), proposes that human beings repress "primitive" impulses because of *socialization*. Thus, if allowed to react freely, as do other animals, people would merely carry out their natural responses to "fight or flight." Simeons believes that we are now taught to "reason" with enemies instead of to fight, to endure quietly instead of protesting, and to remain "cool, calm, and collected" in the face of adversity instead of fleeing. As a consequence, we must suffer the anxiety of being civilized.

The stress resulting from such "unnatural" behavior is often experienced as *free-floating anxiety*. This means that the individual experiences a sense of dread and foreboding, but is unable to specify the exact cause of the anxiety. Free-floating anxiety, however, can increase in intensity to such a level as to create a *state of panic*. At this level, a person is overwhelmed by fear and may be incapable of rational thought. Freud cited three conditions which are most likely to induce a state of panic: (1) signs of impending danger that cannot be avoided, (2) lack of time or opportunity to act effectively during the crisis, and (3) loss of emotional ties, support, or reassurance from loved ones or leaders (Freud, 1921; Anna Freud, 1937).

Investigations by Irving Janis, a pioneer in stress reactions, place special emphasis on Freud's second condition—dealing with the ability to take effective action. Janis sees one of the essential elements for the inducement of panic as being the *potential for entrapment* (Janis et al., 1955). Some of the most notable examples of such panic are the reactions of large groups of people when a fire breaks out in a crowded theater or nightclub that has only a limited number of exits.

The amount of ego involvement associated with an event also contributes to whether an individual perceives the source of stress as being a mild inconvenience or a major threat to one's sense of security. For example, receiving a failing grade on an exam may merely serve as the deciding factor in one student's attempt to select a major, though for another student the score represents the student's entire sense of worth, parental rejection, hopes for the future, and a sense of complete failure.

GUILT   Often closely associated with a sense of failure is the additional stress of the psychological demands created by feelings of shame or guilt. Usually, the feeling of shame is more "other-directed," and the feeling of guilt is more "inner-directed."

Irving Janis, in his book *Stress and Frustration* (1971), refers to this inner-directedness as "reflective guilt." This kind of guilt is a feeling that is "usually aroused whenever we become aware of a personal wish, intention, or plan that we regard as morally wrong or unethical." According to Janis, people struggling with reflective guilt will often seek reassurance from others that what they are about to do will be approved of. Such reassurance is often sought in order to support their own efforts at self-scrutiny. Under these circumstances, new information can often have a substantial effect on the decision to act or not and can influence the intensity of the guilt feelings associated with the decision.

Since neurotic guilt is relatively unresponsive to new information, Janis regards the degree of responsiveness to new information as a major distinguishing factor between reflective guilt and "neurotic guilt." For example, imagine the drop in the level of guilt experienced by an employer who has just been presented with the new information that the worker who was scheduled to be terminated was caught stealing from the company. The intensity of the reflective guilt experienced in such a situation can be compared to the lack of response to new information shown by a person experiencing neurotic guilt. Consider, for example, the case of someone suffering from a neurotic depressive reaction who learns it is human and natural to feel bad after breaking off a close relationship, and that everyone, at one time or another, has had such an experience. Despite this new information, the individual with neurotic guilt insists on maintaining a self-image based on self-condemnation and self-castigation because of the hurt the other person experiences as a result of being rejected.

SHAME   Janis believes that *reflective shame* is stimulated by anticipated or actual signs of social disapproval. Thus, shame involves an awareness by others of an individual's transgressions. When we are children, before we have internalized external values, social disapproval often takes the form of "instructive discipline." Once we are "old enough to know better," social disapproval will often take the form of humiliating accusations, such as "Shame on you," "You're acting like a sissy." Some situations stimulate the institution of even more severe penalities, such as the silent treatment or being banished. The threat of such penalties tends to have a powerful inhibiting influence. This

FIGURE 5.1   In many instances, the selection of a vocation can be complicated by the existence of certain paradoxes involving sex-role expectations. For example, as a child, a boy may be ridiculed if he prefers learning to cook or play the piano to engaging in sports activity. Yet this same person may be praised and held in high esteem as an adult who has become an accomplished chef or pianist. [*Dan Budnik, Woodfin Camp and Associates.*]

is often exemplified by the conduct of combat soldiers who are afraid to let the others down (Smith, 1949; Glass, 1953).

Continued emphasis on living up to social expectations is highly influential in the establishment of moral values and ethics and an awareness of the importance of cultural roles and traditions. Sex roles and social status are of particular cultural importance. They are usually learned through modeling, verbal admonitions, and formal training. Children will experience various degrees of stress as they attempt to conform to or rebel against the enculturation process. For example, cross-cultural surveys have indicated that the more reliant an economy is on physical strength, the greater the emphasis on sex differences, with the greatest prestige going to the males (Barry, Bacon, and Child, 1957). Children become aware of the greater freedom, authority, and power held by males and generally prefer the male role (J. Kagan, 1964). Females who do not perceive their social role as being equal will often attempt to be more masculine. This often results in social disapproval, ostracism by both sexes, and, quite frequently, rejection by possible spouses.

Males who fail to acquire masculine mannerisms, interests, and characteristics are also subject to tremendous social pressures. Male peers will often ridicule the effeminate individual. Adult males, including fathers, will often exaggerate their disappointment and disapproval. Generally, males in our society are taught that their vocational role and achievement are of primary importance, and that the roles of spouse and parent are secondary (D'Andrade, 1966). As a result, low-status vocations, unemployment, and underachievement can create high-stress situations for the male. In contrast, females in our society are raised to be nurturing and responsible. The role of spouse and parent is primary—vocation is considered secondary (D'Andrade, 1966). Thus, being unmarried, divorced, infertile, or neglectful of children will most likely create high-stress situations for women in our society.

As in most stress situations, reassurance from members of the opposite sex is of tremendous value, and, therefore, reassurance of one's masculinity or femininity receives a great deal of attention. In this regard, Carl Jung, in *Contributions to Analytical Psychology* (1928), wrote:

> The woman is increasingly aware that love alone can give her her full stature, just as the man begins to discern that spirit alone can endow his life with its highest meaning. Fundamentally, therefore, both seek a psychic relation one to the other, because love needs the spirit, and the spirit love, for their fulfillment. (p. 185)

CAUSES OF STRESS

Although the period in which we live today is often referred to as the "age of anxiety," the levels of anxiety in the twentieth century are probably neither higher nor lower than those during any other period of history. Mental hospital records, for instance, indicate that the admissions rate of patients under fifty years of age is approximately the same today as in 1840 (Goldhamer and Marshall, 1949; Page and Landis, 1943; Dunham, 1966).

The specific nature of the threats may vary from one time to another or from one society to another—for example, in modern-day America we do not fear being run over by a horse and carriage but may fear being run over by an automobile, and we do not believe our thoughts are being controlled by an evil spirit or a medicine man but may fear they could be controlled by a computer. No one culture seems to produce any greater or lesser number of reasons for hospitalization than any other (Field, 1960; Toker, 1966; Page, 1965; Elsarrag, 1968). The basic cause of stress seems to remain the same—*deprivation, frustration, conflict,* and *pressure.*

Deprivation

Whenever the means of gratifying one's needs are withheld or denied, a state of deprivation exists. Whether the needs are as basic as the need for food and drink, or as abstract as the need for dignity and justice, when a person's needs remain unsatisfied, the inevitable result is stress.

Although deprivation can be an objective facet of reality—for instance, when a person faces starvation, dehydration, or freezing—it can also be a subjective experience based on the acquisition of new information—such as finding out that other workers received a raise but you did not. Deprivation can also be based on cognitive evaluation of one's present situation compared with one's past situation, or through a comparison of another's situation with one's own. The level of stress experienced is often directly proportionate to the difference perceived between how things should be, will be, or used to be, and how things actually are.

PHYSICAL LONELINESS   Deprivation may exist early in a person's life, as when a child is deprived of paternal care and affection, or late in life, when an elderly person is deprived of social respect and dignity by a youth-oriented society. The stress that is a result of being deprived of physical companionship, however, can often be more easily tolerated than the pain associated with being denied the intimacy of emotional and intellectual companionship. Without physical companionship, one experiences being alone. Without emotional and intellectual companionship, one is more likely to experience being lonely. This does not necessarily mean that the stress created by physical rejection is not painful. Both physical and emotional rejection can threaten our appraisals of our own "lovability." It merely points out that when a companion is physically absent, there are fewer cues to remind the lonely person of the one who is gone and fewer opportunities to deal with the distance.

Physical loneliness can also be the result of separation from a place, group, or institution. The American Indians, for example, experienced a sense of loneliness after having been deprived of the lands of their ancestors. Immigrants have experienced loneliness while waiting to be assimilated into their new environment. New graduates will often experience loneliness upon leaving the familiar friends, faculty, and facilities associated with their high school or college.

EMOTIONAL LONELINESS AND ALIENATION   Distance need not be physical, however, in order to develop the stress of separation. Corporate executives, military commanders, and political leaders often talk of the "loneliness at the top." By this they mean the separateness they feel between themselves and the "people." A similar sensation of loneliness has often been expressed by parents with regard to their children. Ira Tanner, in *Loneliness; the Fear of Love* (1973), talks of the loneliness experienced by many teenagers:

> 40 percent of the young adults between eighteen and twenty-two, and 31 percent of those between fifteen and seventeen feel they do not have a single friend that they can rely on. In the words of several who have experimented with drugs: "Drugs give me a warm feeling, a sort of substitute warm feeling that I would get from having a close friend." "Experimenting with drugs has put me in a new place; given me a new set of friends . . . even if they are drug users." (p. 18)

Some parents will attempt to close the distance between their teenaged children and themselves by setting up contrived situations for the purpose of having the teenager "open up" and somehow bridge the gap between them. In most cases, the teenagers perceive such plans as another example of parental manipulation and as a violation of their *personhood* and sense of dignity. As a consequence of such manipulative efforts, the added stress of being misunderstood tends to compound the feelings of separateness.

Whenever people are deprived of their personal dignity, through the denial

Loneliness is often felt most intensely when one is near others but not with others. [*Ed Lettau, Photo Researchers, Inc.*]

FIGURE 5.2

of individual rights, civil rights, or human rights, they will tend to feel alienated and will undergo some degree of stress. Whenever people are denied the privilege of expressing how they really think or feel, or the opportunity to vote, protest, or have access to due process, or the opportunity to life, liberty, and equality, they will experience the stress associated with a denial of freedom. This is a stress that often results in an attempt to sever the bond between the oppressed and the oppressor, whether it be through passive withdrawal of support or active involvement in an insurrection.

THE NEED TO WORK   Often included among human rights is the opportunity to work and acquire property. Pope Pius XII (1876–1958), in a 1944 radio broadcast, stated:

> If a worker is deprived of hope to acquire some personal property, what other natural stimulus can be offered him that will inspire him to hard work, labor, saving and sobriety today, when so many nations and men have lost everything and all they have left is their capacity for work.

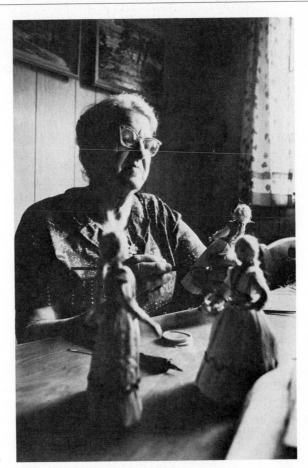

For many, work is seen as an opportunity to make a contribution, and through this contribution a sense of dignity and worth is derived. The need to work is often closely associated with the need to find meaning and purpose in life. [*Bruce Roberts, Rapho/Photo Researchers, Inc.*]

FIGURE 5.3

The capacity to work seems to hold a special meaning for those who have been forced to quit working. This is especially noticeable among the elderly. Mandatory retirement and being denied the opportunity to retain their positions as functional members of society can represent a direct attack on their self-esteem (Buhler, 1969; Beauvoir, 1972). With over half of all those over 65 and living alone having an annual income that falls below the official government poverty index (Kahn, 1974), it is easy to understand why the elderly rate financial insecurity as their number one concern (Kogan and Shelton, 1962).

Being denied the opportunity to work, and the resulting financial insecurity, can also cause severe stress among the unemployed, especially during a recession or depression. However, when an undesirable situation is widespread, individuals will tend to complain less or not feel quite so unfortunate, especially after having compared their misfortune with that of people who are considered to be in the same boat (Stouffer et al., 1949; *Working America*, 1973). Janis (1971) refers to this evaluation of gain or loss through a comparison with others as "relative deprivation."

Such relativism can play a particularly important role in the lives of the handicapped, the chronically ill, and the elderly. When people have been deprived of the use of one eye, one leg, or one arm, comparing their situation with the lives of those who have been deprived of the use of *both* will often reduce the intensity of stress. This reduction in tension is due in part to the attitude that things could be worse.

Frustration

Frustration occurs whenever goal-directed behavior is blocked. When people have been motivated toward achieving a particular goal and, for whatever reason, are unable to achieve it, they will experience the stress associated with being frustrated.

Frustration may occur as a result of *physical obstacles,* such as being a victim of job discrimination, *physical deficiences,* such as being too short to play on the basketball team, or *psychological deficiencies,* such as being functionally illiterate. Regardless of the specific cause, the result is always the same—the person will undergo some degree of stress.

PHYSICAL OBSTACLES   The number of physical obstacles that can thwart the simplest of objectives seems almost infinite: locked doors, jammed windows, clogged drains, crowded freeways, rusted bolts, etc. Their preponderance may even prompt a belief in divine intervention—the conviction that "someone up there doesn't like me." Yet it is often just such elementary causes of frustration that compel individuals to invent, create, and modify so as to improve the world around them. In this vein, one might be able to evaluate progress as nothing more than the reduction, prevention, or elimination of frustrations.

Since the beginning, the elements have been a constant source of physical obstacles. In some cases, the deserts have been too dry; in others the snow drifts have been too high. Rivers have been too deep, winds too strong, and the fog too thick. Crops have been destroyed by hail and drought, ships have been sunk by hurricanes and tides, and people and property have been destroyed by tornadoes and earthquakes. In such cases, the individual experiences both the stress associated with the actual catastrophe and then the additional frustration of having to start all over again (Schanche, 1974).

Geographical barriers are a traditional source of physical obstacles. Mountain ranges, for example, present formidable barriers to people attempting to migrate, as do vast deserts and oceans. More frequently, however, geographical factors contribute to feelings of frustration through the barrier of distance—keeping loved ones apart, making medical help inaccessible, limiting employment or educational opportunities, etc.

SOCIAL OBSTACLES   Overcoming the most formidable physical barriers can sometimes be relatively simple compared with overcoming certain social obstacles. As an illustration, one need only recall the civil rights struggle emanating from the Supreme Court's 1954 decision in *Brown v. Board of Education.* This decision ended school segregation and culminated in the passage of the Civil Rights Acts of 1964 and 1965, and the Voting Rights Act of 1965.

Frustration can also be experienced because of socioeconomic barriers that tend to prevent upward mobility. Most research indicates that there has been little change in socioeconomic mobility patterns in the United States since the time of the nation's founding (Lipset and Bendix, 1959). Approximately 95 percent of the business elite have been sons of successful business executives, while only about 3 percent of such business leaders come from the lower classes (Keller, 1953; Bendex and Howton, 1959). Closely keyed to occupational mobility is educational opportunity. A study conducted by William Sewell (1971) revealed that individuals from the upper class have four times the chance of attending college as individuals from the lower class. They have a six times greater chance of graduating and a nine times greater chance of obtaining a postgraduate degree. Occupational disadvantages have also been a source of frustration among American women. In the American labor force, women have traditionally been paid less then their male counterparts and have held a disproportionately high percentage of low-status jobs (Galenson, 1973; Amundsen, 1971; Suelzle, 1972).

Social stresses need not be a product of mass actions, however. Frustration can, and often does, result from the efforts of the individual. Consider, for example, the frustration experienced after an unsuccessful attempt at trying to impress someone or trying to get someone to appreciate your sacrifices, or when one learns that "being oneself" is not going to be enough to hold a relationship together.

PHYSICAL DEFICIENCIES Although most people are reasonably satisfied with their physical characteristics, many suffer the stress associated with not conforming to the social ideal. They find that they are too tall or too short, too fat or too thin, too busty or too flat-chested, etc. In most cases, we adapt to such deviations from the norm and reduce what stress is experienced through the use of defense mechanisms like rationalization and compensation. However, for some people, physical deficiencies can become the source of major frustration and stress, for example, wishing to become a member of a police or fire-fighting force, but being unable to pass the physical or wishing to become a fashion model, but lacking the minimum height.

Physical weakness can also be of concern to someone who is chronically ill, malnourished, or physically handicapped. However, physical deficiencies will often cause the greatest concern among the middle-aged and elderly. These individuals tend to experience the frustration that comes from comparing the physical prowess of their youth with their current physical abilities (Norwak, 1977).

Closely associated with concern about our physical prowess are our perceptions of our sexual prowess. Perhaps in no other area will a sense of physical inadequacy be a greater source of stress than in sexuality. The stress associated with sexual dysfunctioning and maladjustment is fairly widespread,

Most children learn early in life to accept physical limitations such as visual, hearing, or speech impairments. It is the lack of social acceptance that is difficult to cope with. [*Jean Shapiro.*]

FIGURE 5.4

occurring in some 50 percent of all American marriages (Lehrman, 1970; Masters and Johnson, 1970). Experiences with sexual dysfunctions will often lead to a fear of failure, which, in turn, can lead to a fear of rejection. As a consequence, the intensity of sexual frustration and the accompanying stress can become extreme.

PSYCHOLOGICAL DEFICIENCIES   The frustrations associated with psychological deficiencies will usually stem from deficiencies in the areas of (1) *cognition,* (2) *emotions,* or (3) *self-esteem.*

One of the most prevalent deficiencies in the area of cognition is that of mental retardation. According to most estimates (Gardner, Tarjan, and Richmond, 1965; Presidential Panel on Mental Retardation, 1962; President's Committee 1967, 1969), an estimated *3 percent* of the population is considered to be mentally retarded (IQ below 70). Unfortunately, due to their limited ability to solve problems, many people who are mentally retarded find failure and frustration an all-too-familiar facet of life.

Garfield (1963) hypothesized that the high incidence of emotional disturbance observed among the mentally retarded is due to a more frequent exposure to failure, frustration, and ridicule. Although it is often difficult to adequately evaluate the effects of failure, it appears that failure can have a greater effect on normal children in some instances than on the retarded. For example, in experiments conducted by Gardner (1958), normal children with a history of success were more severely affected by failure than were the retarded children, who had a history of failure.

This is not to say that the mentally retarded do not experience the stress and frustration associated with failure. Much of the aggressive behavior associated with mental retardation is believed to be the result of frustration (Talkington, Hall, and Altman, 1971). However, since a certain level of intelligence is required in order to comprehend that one has indeed failed, or that there are goals that are unobtainable, the relationship between low intelligence and frustration is not a simple one. Dollard et al. (1939) noted:

> Not only would low intelligence seem likely to increase the amount of frustration experienced by an individual; it would also be expected to diminish the effectiveness of socializing forces in that it would imply a lowered capacity to appreciate the consequences of specific acts. (p. 116)

The emotional disturbances due to frustration that are experienced by the mentally retarded, however, are not unlike those experienced by individuals who lack adequate education or professional training. The anger, disappointment, depression, and apathy associated with being unable to solve problems is a universal phenomenon. However, those who lack emotional support can often become overwhelmed by such stresses. The emotions of affection and love seem to provide the greatest amount of reassurance. The need for affiliation in order to have access to these emotions seems to be the greatest during the periods of our lives in which we are the most vulnerable—during our youth and old age (Bates, 1972).

The periods of youth and old age are also critical with regard to self-esteem. According to Erikson (1968), during the period of adolescence, a time when abilities are relatively limited, achievement becomes highly critical. As a consequence, the individual experiences an "identity crisis":

> Adolescence is the last stage of childhood. The adolescent process, however, is conclusively complete only when the individual has subordinated his childhood identifications to a new kind of identification, achieved in absorbing sociability, and in competitive apprecenticeship with and among his age mates. (p. 155)

During the period of early adulthood and middle age, most people tend to maintain some degree of optimism with regard to how they are doing, or will do, in life. Generally they have a sense of self-control and confidence (Vaillant, 1977). However, sometime during middle age, there comes the realization that one's own life is finite (Gutmann, 1975). Now some of the self-confidence and the feeling of being able to direct the outcome of one's life begins to diminish. Although it is usually in the latter part of life that personal reflection becomes most significant, reflection can be a constant source of self-appraisal. As a result, reflection can also have a tremendous influence on self-esteem.

Maslow (1970) divides *esteem needs* into two categories: self-esteem and other-esteem. The first relies on estimations of self-respect and self-regard. The latter represents reputation, status, or socioeconomic successes. The process by which one maintains a balance between self-esteem and other-esteem can often be a major source of stress. For example, being dared by one's peer group to steal the biology midterm exam makes it necessary to choose between immorality and perceived cowardice.

Another esteem-related source of stress is our comparison between what we are and (1) "what we could be" (our expectations), and (2) "what we should be" (our social standards) (Epstein, 1973). Similarly, Rosalind Gould (1939) noted that a rather accurate picture of an individual's struggle between status and an acceptable self is portrayed through the constant shifting of aspiration levels. Through this shifting, the level of aspiration is set neither too high, leaving the individual in a perpetual state of frustration, nor too low, leaving the person empty of any feelings of accomplishment.

Conflict

Whenever we confront a situation that requires a decision between two mutually exclusive alternatives, we will undergo the stress associated with conflict. Sometimes, the conflict can be compounded by having too many alternatives to choose from. In fact, this is a basic premise of the existential school. The existentialists make the supposition that the primary problem an individual faces today is not a lack of freedom, but rather too much freedom. As a consequence, many individuals are threatened with being overwhelmed by alternatives. They are "condemned to freedom" and yet are unable to choose effectively (Sartre, 1957).

Others complain that it is the apparent lack of alternatives that creates stress. Life, they say, is a continuous series of ultimatums—of either-or, take-it-or-leave-it choices. They point out that even deciding not to decide is a decision. Kierkegaard (1941) attended to this dilemma when he pointed out that choosing is an internal event and, therefore, is not dependent upon an external change in the state of affairs. Choice involves a commitment, a movement within the personality. Thus "The real action is not the external act, but an internal decision in which the individual puts an end to the mere possibility and identifies himself with the content of his thought in order to exist in it" (1941, p. 302).

KURT LEWIN'S VALANCE THEORY Kurt Lewin (1890–1947), the founder of field theory in psychology (1935), viewed the "internal changes" that Kierkegaard spoke of as merely changes in the "psychological motion" within defined regions of a person's life space. Life space, according to Lewin, is the total psychological environment that each person experiences subjectively. It is our perception of our internal and external world. For example, if a goal is attractive, it is considered to have approach-motivating characteristics. If the goal is undesirable, it is considered to have avoidance-motivating qualities. Conflicts are indicated by combinations of these characteristics. There are approach-approach conflicts, when both goals are desirable; approach-avoidance conflicts, when a goal has both desirable and undesirable characteristics; and avoidance-avoidance conflicts, when the conflict is between two undesirable choices. It is important to note, however, that the valance of any event, object, or person is a subjective quality added by the perceiver, not an innate quality of the stimulus causing the reaction.

APPROACH-APPROACH   We are confronted with an approach-approach conflict and the accompanying stress whenever we must make a choice between two desirable alternatives, the familiar dilemma of wanting to eat your cake and have it too. Often the conflict is generated by the need to decide which of two colleges to attend. Each of the colleges may have admirable qualities, but the goal of going to college will remain blocked until a decision is made, and the frustration, stress, and anxiety will often continue to increase in intensity as the deadline for registration nears. In many cases, the ultimate decision is likely to be made more out of a desire for relief than out of a logical process of elimination.

Fortunately, most approach-approach conflicts are usually less intense and normally involve decisions between favorite desserts (vanilla or chocolate) or vacation spots (Hawaii or Europe). Being in a position where one wins either way is often considered to be a low-stress conflict, although the level of stress can be considerably intensified by external pressure from significant others, such as parents or spouses, to "hurry up and make up your mind."

Similarly, if the pathways to these desired goals are blocked, the intensity of the stress will also tend to increase. In such a situation, there is often a tendency, in Lewin's (1936) terms, to "go out of the field," withdrawing into daydreams and fantasy. For example, a teenager who is offered an opportunity to go on a vacation with friends of the family and also to go on an expedition with an explorers' club may find both alternatives highly desirable. Thus the youth may have some difficulty making a decision. All too often, however, the parents in this situation will insensitively press for a decision now or "you're not going on either one."

APPROACH-AVOIDANCE CONFLICTS   The approach-avoidance conflict is perhaps a bit more prevalent than the approach-approach type in this not-so-perfect world. This conflict deals with the weighing of the desirable against the undesirable—as when an individual contemplates obtaining a college degree, but wishes to avoid the years of lectures, books, and exams. Possible gains are weighed against possible losses—as when a person wants to make a lot of money quickly, but also wishes to avoid high financial risks. Put in different terms, the "good" is weighed against the "evil."

The approach-avoidance conflict also deals with the weighing of the decision's potential for pleasure against its potential for pain. The teachings of Descartes and Hobbes support the concept of *hedonism* (the hypothesis that the primary motivating force behind human behavior is the seeking of pleasure and the avoidance of pain). They provide a partial explanation for the ambivalence often associated with an approach-avoidance conflict. However, the stress and anxiety accompanying such a decision-making process do not necessarily constitute a simple hedonistic relationship. Kierkegaard, for instance, asserts that "anxiety is a desire for what one dreads, a sympathetic antipathy. Anxiety is an alien power that lays hold of an individual and yet one cannot tear oneself away, nor has a will to do so; for one fears, but what one fears one desires" (1944, p. xii).

In the dilemma Kierkegaard describes, the anxious person is caught between two possibilities, neither of which can be willingly abandoned. As a consequence, the person is paralyzed in his or her own freedom.

Fromm (1970) also expands on the implied hedonism of the approach-avoidance conflict. He advocates a modification in the definition of what constitutes pleasure—a differentiation between satisfaction, joy, and happiness. He points out (1947) the difference between the satisfaction obtained through psychological growth and satisfying one's neurotic cravings. There is a difference between the motives of a person who joins the navy to see the world and of one who joins to get away from the constant fighting at home.

In most instances, the approach-avoidance conflict is relativistic, based on our individual predispositions, past experiences, and levels of aspiration. Each person weighs the advantages of choosing a particular alternative against the disadvantages. In cases where *each* alternative has both desirable and undesirable characteristics, the conflict is referred to as a "double approach-avoidance conflict." This would be the case where a student is attempting to choose between a class that satisfies a requirement (approach) but is supposedly very boring (avoidance) and a class that is supposed to be very interesting (approach) but does not satisfy any of the requirements for a particular degree (avoidance).

AVOIDANCE-AVOIDANCE CONFLICTS   Most of us can think back to some time in our lives when we remarked, "Huh, some choice!" Such a remark is usually directed to an avoidance-avoidance conflict—a conflict in which *both* alternatives are undesirable. A typical example is when a parent asks a child to choose the means by which punishment is to be administered, and the choice entails staying home from either the championship game or the rock concert. In more serious incidents, the conflict might be presented by a judge: "Thirty days or three hundred dollars." Under less severe circumstances, the conflict might be between living with a toothache and going to the dentist, between washing or drying the dishes, or the inevitable moment of truth, when one is offered the alternatives, "Are you going to tell the coach or am I?"

The avoidance-avoidance type of conflict usually presents the greatest amount of frustration and stress. For this reason, it is often associated with a higher level of anxiety than the other types of conflicts. The ability to resolve an avoidance-avoidance conflict is closely related to one's degree of maturity and selfhood. The immature and the neurotic will often attempt to evade such decisions. They will procrastinate or, if at all possible, get someone else to decide. The mature individual, on the other hand, will usually accept the responsibility for the decision and confront the inevitable with the necessary courage.

Pressure

In today's world, it is not uncommon for people to complain that there are too many demands being made on them. They find it difficult to bear the burdens associated with trying to keep pace with social and economic changes. In general, it is often hard for them to endure the pressures of living in modern society.

In an effort to overcome these pressures, many people drive themselves too hard, aspiring to ever higher levels of achievement. Others attempt to escape through the use of drugs, alcohol, or sex. Still others attempt to confront these pressures with reason. Erich Fromm, in *Man for Himself* (1966), notes:

> For the first time in his history, man can perceive that the idea of the unity of the human race and the conquest of nature for the sake of man is no longer a dream but a realistic possibility. . . . Yet modern man feels uneasy and more and more bewildered. He works and strives, but he is dimly aware of a sense of futility with regard to his activities. While his power over matter grows, he feels powerless in his individual life and in society. . . . While becoming the master of nature, he has become the slave of the machine which his own hands built. (p. 4)

POPULATION   In today's world, one of the greatest and most pervasive sources of pressure is that of population. Historically, due to a favorable proportion of resources to people, overpopulation tended to act only as a temporary source of stress. People needing, or wanting, more room merely migrated to less populated areas. For example, during the time of Christ, the world population was only 300 million, and its growth rate (less than 1 percent) was such that it would take 14,400 years for the population to double. However, this is not the case today. By the end of the twentieth century, the population will be between 7 and 8 *billion,* and the average growth rate (1.8 percent) is capable of doubling the population every thirty-nine years (U.S. Census Bureau, 1976).

As a means of studying the effects of overcrowding, John Calhoun (1962) allowed a group of rats to reproduce without restriction within a confined space. The inevitable overcrowding that resulted produced what Calhoun refers to as a "behavioral sink," that is, a condition where there is a high incidence of pathological behavior due to the inherent pressures of overpopulation. For example, some members of the group became highly, and often indiscriminately, aggressive. Others exhibited pathological withdrawal. Abnormal sex patterns also emerged, such as hypersexuality, bisexuality, and homosexuality. In addition, offspring were often neglected, abused, or abandoned altogether. Although a direct comparison with human behavior cannot be made, it is evident that many of these same symptoms can be found in many of our overcrowded urban communities.

In the Calhoun experiment, the population grew rapidly from the original two rats to over eighty living in a space designed for not more than fifty. As a consequence, access to nest building material, territory, and food quickly

FIGURE 5.5 The stresses brought about by an ever-increasing population are associated not only with overcrowding but also with the consequences of a depletion in natural resources, a reduction in food supplies, and an increase in pollution. [*J. R. Laffont/Sygma.*]

developed into formidable problems. A rapid rate of population growth tends to place a great deal of economic pressure on our society as well. This is especially true among the underdeveloped nations, where rapid growth usually means an increase in the number of infants and children. Consequently, in some areas of the world, over 40 percent of the population is under fifteen years of age. And, since children tend to consume more than they produce, more of the economic resources of these areas are used for maintenance than for expansion and growth. Such a state of affairs, unfortunately, will usually result in economic stagnation.

As a means of combating this trend, many nations are attempting to alleviate population pressures through the use of voluntary and, in some cases, mandatory birth control measures. According to research conducted by Ansley Coale and Edgar Hoover (1958), a 50 percent reduction in fertility over a twenty-five-year period would result in a 40 percent increase in per capita income. Considering that perhaps hundreds of millions of people are chronically malnourished and millions die of starvation (Eberstadt, 1976), the need to limit the size of a population becomes quite evident. However, population size is not necessarily the sole, or even the primary, reason that so many face the stress of being undernourished. In *Myths of the Food Crisis* (1976), Nick Eberstadt points out that one of the main causes of hunger in the world today is international inequality, class distinction, and prejudice: "There is no . . . justification for hunger of any kind anywhere; enough food is produced each year to feed everyone on earth comfortably. It is inequality and inequality alone that can be blamed for hunger today" (p. 34).

PREJUDICE The inequality that Ebersadt refers to, however, is not an inherent characteristic, but rather a socially or economically acquired distinction. The inequality may be based on any number of factors, such as race, religion, nationality, region of birth, ancestry, economic achievement, or social class. Injustices, discrimination, and social degradation are perpetuated by the almost universal phenomenon of prejudice (an attitude of prejudgment toward a group). Prejudiced beliefs can become manifest in many ways. As extreme examples we might mention Hitler's methodical attempt to exterminate the Jews; the caste system of India, in which social status was, and is, determined by the caste of one's birth (the lowest social group, the pariahs, or untouchables, were completely dependent upon the high castes for their livelihood); and the discrimination against various racial, religious and ethnic minority groups in the United States.

The pressures and stresses experienced by victims of prejudice and discrimination often arise from the concept of *accommodation.* Under this method, role and status are sharply defined, and members of minority groups are expected to know their "place." In many instances, rules of etiquette are strictly enforced, and the punishment for transgressions can range from being lynched to being socially ostracized.

Segregation tends to emphasize inequality and often adds the additional stress of humiliation. The victim of prejudice is denied access to housing, educational facilities, or hotels and restaurants which have been reserved for the dominant group. However, even when such restrictions are removed, economic discrimination may tend to perpetuate such injustices. This might be illustrated by the unemployment statistics among blacks in general, which range between 11 and 15 percent, rising as high as 35 to 40 percent among black teenagers (Bureau of Labor Statistics, 1978).

Similarly, the American Indians—of whom 400,000 of a total Indian population of 5,500,000 live on reservations—must often dwell in poverty and substandard housing, and they have a life expectancy of only 43.5 years. The average Indian completes only about 5 years of schooling versus an 11.2-year average for other Americans (Morgan, 1972). This condition tends to aggravate and perpetuate feelings of helplessness. In such cases, the choice is often limited—conform to the lifestyle of the dominant group or continue to live under the pressures of prejudicial attitudes, social discrimination, and poverty.

CRIME AND VIOLENCE According to FBI statistics, the index of crimes increased by 39 percent between 1970 and 1975 and by 240 percent since 1960. Robbery, burglary, larceny, and auto theft rates have doubled or tripled since 1960. In addition, rural communities, once sought after as a haven from urban crime, are no longer as crime-free as they once were. Although the rate of crime in the city is still three times that in the country, the *rate of increase* in crime is rising faster in suburban communities than in any other areas (Uniform Crime Report, U.S. Census Bureau, 1976).

Faced with a major crime rate of 6110 per 100,000 population in metropolitan areas, many people have had to change their lifestyles as a defense against crime and violence. For example, many people no longer venture out at night; they carry as little cash as possible; they shop in groups; and they install elaborate locks and burglar alarms to reduce the incidence of crime. Unfortunately, such precautions seldom provide a true sense of security, and many, especially the elderly, live in constant fear of becoming victims of crimes of violence. In fact, in some respects, violence often seems to seek out specifically those who go out of their way to espouse or support positions of nonviolence.

R. E. Lane, in his book *Political Ideology* (1962), describes what he refers to as a fear of intimacy within our society that is founded on a "fear of equality." According to Lane, our society in general, and politicians in particular, do not really want to have to deal with the true concepts of liberty and equality for fear that the system would no longer function in its traditional fashion. Because of this, a state of stress is created whenever the status quo is threatened with the institutionalization of true equality. Lane points out that, historically, violence has often been resorted to as a means of protesting egalitarian advances, especially when these advances have been accomplished through nonviolent means.

In support of his position, Lane notes that Jesus Christ, who advocated brotherly love, was mobbed and crucified. He also contends that Abraham Lincoln was assassinated because of his generous plans for equality and peace rather than because of his conduct during the Civil War. Similarly, John F. Kennedy and Robert F. Kennedy both espoused greater cooperation and personal involvement between people and government, and both were assassinated. According to Lane, the examples are numerous—Dr. Martin Luther King, Jr., Malcolm X, as well as other civil rights workers, to name just a few. It is his belief that this attitude tends to perpetuate a sense of separateness within our society and with it the continuation of feelings of alienation.

ALIENATION As a population continues to increase, recognition of the importance of the individual tends to decrease. The individual becomes part of a group or organization. One's influence, as well as one's importance, often becomes a function of group identification rather than of individuality. For many, however, effective association with others is difficult, if not impossible, to achieve. For such individuals, the stress of remaining outside the group can be especially depressing. Individuals of mixed blood, such as the mulatto (negroid and caucasian) or the half-breed (Indian and caucasian), have often found it particularly difficult to gain acceptance. Many members of mixed marriages have also found themselves to be "marginal" individuals—persons who stand on the boundary between two different groups, uncertain of their acceptance into either.

Feelings of alienation need not stem solely from such tangibles as bloodline, ethnic background, or socioeconomic status. Such feelings can arise merely as a result of the distance between oneself and the government, between management and labor, or what Karl Marx (1964) described as the separation of workers from the means of production. According to Marx, a worker who no longer owns the tools he or she works with, and who is employed by others rather than self-employed, will have little or no identification with the product produced. As a result, the worker will experience some degree of alienation.

Often, as a result of such alienation, workers develop a sense of futility. Their lives seem meaningless, and a complacent acceptance of their own insignificance begins to dominate their perception. Erich Fromm, in a 1966 address to the American Orthopsychiatric Association, noted that in today's society:

> A man sits in front of a bad television program and does not know he is bored; he reads of Vietcong casualties in the newspaper and does not recall the teachings of religion; he learns of the dangers of nuclear holocaust and does not feel fear; he joins the rat race of commerce, where personal worth is measured in terms of market values, and is not aware of his anxiety. . . . If enough people become aware of their shared misery, they will probably effect changes. Anger may often be less sick than adjustment. (p. 30)

REACTION TO STRESS

We have all, at one time or another, felt our hearts pound, our mouths go dry, or the sensation of butterflies in our stomachs. In addition, many of us have experienced uncontrollable trembling, mind-splitting headaches, or the pain associated with ulcers. Some of us have even experienced increased irritability, confusion, and delusions and hallucinations. All these symptoms, as well as a variety of others, are typical reactions to stress.

The severity of the reaction depends, to some extent, upon the nature and severity of the stress. The stress to which we are reacting may be a natural catastrophe, such as an earthquake, flood, or fire; an act of human violence, such as assault, riot, or war; socioeconomic pressure, such as discrimination, unemployment, or increased incidence of crime; or a personal loss or devaluation resulting from divorce, incrimination, or repressed fears. The severity of the reaction, however, is also dependent upon the particular characteristics of the individual, including previous experiences of successful coping, level of self-confidence, and availability of external support.

Our perceptions of stress are subjective, as are our reactions to stress. For some, the reaction is mild—a shrug of the shoulders and the decision to start all over again. For others, the reaction is more neurotic, often converting anxiety into psychosomatic illness, phobias, or depression. For still others, the adjustment may take the form of a psychosis. As Oliver Wendell Holmes (1809–1894), noted in *The Autocrat of the Breakfast Table* (1858), "Insanity is often the logic of an accurate mind overtaxed."

FIGURE 5.6   Part of the shock experienced after a natural disaster is due to the mind's inability to comprehend, or refusal to accept, the enormity of what has happened. [*Pictorial Parade, EPA.*]

Individual Differences

One person may find stress invigorating and challenging, while another may find the same stressful situation depressing and threatening. Individual tolerances for stress vary widely. According to some researchers, many people are predisposed to react to stress through the development of physical illnesses (Dunbar, 1954; Sheldrake et al., 1975). Other people seem to fall into a category or type of personality more susceptible to neurosis (Eyesenck, 1961; Rosenberg, 1967) or psychosis (Kantor and Herron, 1966; Mednick and Schulsinger, 1968, 1973). The differences between people provide a variety of strengths and weaknesses. Each human being has a unique set of resources and unique limits of tolerance. Martin Buber espoused this position, when he said:

> Every person born into this world represents something new, something that never existed before, something original and unique. It is the duty of every person to know that there has never been anyone like him in the world, for if there had been someone like him, there would have been no need for him to be in the world. (Buber, quoted in Severin, 1965, p. 46)

According to Hans Selye (1974), "Complete freedom from stress is death." Until that time, each person will experience some degree of stress. The stress can range from a pleasant experience to an unpleasant experience—for example, from the exuberance of a wedding day to the grief a funeral. It can be due to overstimulation or to understimulation—for instance, the chaos of a thousand phone calls at the office or the agony while waiting for the doctor to return a call. Stress can range from deprivation to excess, but whatever the conditions, the greater the extreme, the greater the stress. Only when there is indifference is there absence of stress.

This does not necessarily mean that *all* stress is undesirable. In tolerable amounts, stress can be quite beneficial. Stress can intensify desire, strengthen determination, and even enhance learning ability. Yerkes and Dodson (1908) determined, from their experimentation with rats performing discrimination tasks, that mild shock acted as an aid to learning the easier tasks but interfered with the learning of the more difficult tasks. This correlation between stress and performance is now referred to as the "Yerkes-Dodson law." It seems to hold true in a variety of stress-performance situations. For example, stress might help a soldier learn how to reload a rifle quickly, yet might interfere with the difficult task of disarming an unexploded bomb. Unfortunately, however, it has also been determined that the efficiency level of our ability to perform tasks tends to go down under severe stress, and so, it appears, does our resistance to illness .

Physiological Reaction to Stress

Our nervous system is organized in such a manner as to ensure the survival of the individual. Under normal, nonstressful circumstances, a portion of the nervous system called the "parasympathetic division" operates to conserve energy and resources so as to maintain minimal levels of functioning throughout the body. However, under conditions of stress, an individual's parasympathetic system tends to shut down. The "sympathetic division" cuts in, preparing the entire organism for "flight or fight." The process is analogous to "flooring" the gas pedal of a car. Under such conditions, the body, or the engine, gives its all. How long either can sustain such abuse is merely a matter of time and the durability of the weakest link in the system.

STRESS AND DISEASE   Several researchers have attempted to investigate the apparent correlation between exposure to stress and the incidence of illness. Among them have been Holmes, Rahe, and Masuda, who, in 1967, published the results of a fifteen-year study of thousands of cases of patients with tuberculosis. From this investigation, they found a high correlation between the occurrence of a "life crisis" and the onset of the disease. Subsequent to their observations, a similar correlation was discovered between clusters of life events requiring adjustment and other physical illnesses, such as heart disease and skin ailments. Holmes and Masuda concluded that "clusters of life events do help cause illness. The life-change events can be considered *necessary* to the occurrence of disease but not *sufficient,* all by themselves, to cause disease" (*Psychology Today,* 1972).

Using a questionnaire, the two researchers asked 394 people to rate the amount of social adjustment required for each of forty-three different life events. The results of their survey provided them with a "social readjustment

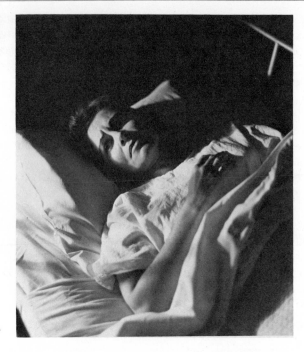

In many cases, a patient's attitude toward an illness, faith in the effectiveness of the treatment, and overall desire to get well seem to have a considerable influence on the course an illness takes. [*Suzanne Szasz.*]

FIGURE 5.7

rating scale." The scale ranged from the most stressful event (death of spouse), having a value of 100 *life change units* (lcu's), to the least stressful event (minor violations of the law), having a rating of 11 lcu's (see Table 5.1).

When the occurrences of the events on the social readjustment rating scale were compared with the incidence of illnesses, it was found that, among individuals who had accumulated between 150 and 199 lcu's (mild life crises), about 37 percent would experience some illness within two years. Among those scoring between 200 and 299 (moderate life crises), the incidence of ill health rose to 51 percent, and it reached 79 percent for those with 300 or more life change units (severe life crises). In addition, it was found that those who experienced the more severe forms of life crises (death of spouse, divorce, marital separation, jail terms) were more likely to experience the more severe forms of illnesses (cancer, heart disease, schizophrenia, etc.).

PERSONALITY TYPE AND DISEASE   Helen F. Dunbar (1955) suggested that there is a high correlation between personality type and certain diseases. For example, Dunbar believed that people with strong dependency needs and a tendency to repress their feelings of anger and frustration are prone to get ulcers, perfectionistic people are likely to get migraine headaches, and those with a fear of separation from their mothers are subject to asthma attacks.

Dunbar also proposed that people who are demanding, hard-working, and usually dissatisfied with themselves are likely to have coronaries.

Meyer Friedman and Ray Rosenman, authors of *Type A Behavior and Your Heart* (1974), also recognized a relationship between personality type and coronaries, as well as hypertension and other cardiovascular disorders. They noticed that patients who were high achievers, aggressive, and impatient—"Type A" personalities—also had a high serum cholesterol count. Type B's "felt no sense of time urgency, exhibited no excessive competitive drive or

TABLE 5.1 SOCIAL READJUSTMENT RATING SCALE

RANK	LIFE EVENT	MEAN VALUE
1	Death of spouse	100
2	Divorce	73
3	Marital separation	65
4	Jail term	63
5	Death of close family member	63
6	Personal injury or illness	53
7	Marriage	50
8	Fired at work	47
9	Marital reconciliation	45
10	Retirement	45
11	Change in health of family member	44
12	Pregnancy	40
13	Sex difficulties	39
14	Gain of new family member	39
15	Business readjustment	39
16	Change in financial state	38
17	Death of close friend	37
18	Change to different line of work	36
19	Change in number of arguments with spouse	35
20	Mortgage over $10,000	31
21	Foreclosure of mortgage or loan	30
22	Change in responsibilities at work	29
23	Son or daughter leaving home	29
24	Trouble with in-laws	29
25	Outstanding personal achievement	28
26	Wife begins or stops work	26
27	Begin or end school	26
28	Change in living conditions	25
29	Revision of personal habits	24
30	Trouble with boss	23
31	Change in work hours or conditions	20
32	Change in residence	20
33	Change in schools	20
34	Change in recreation	19
35	Change in church activities	19
36	Change in social activities	19
37	Mortgage loan less than $10,000	17
38	Change in sleeping habits	16
39	Change in number of family get-togethers	15
40	Change in eating habits	15
41	Vacation	13
42	Christmas	12
43	Minor violations of the law	11

Source: Holmes and Rahe (1967, p. 215).

free-floating hostility" and tended to have low serum cholesterol counts. Friedman and Rosenman found that "if a subject exhibited this [Type A behavior] pattern, . . . he was almost three times more likely than a Type B man to get coronary heart disease" (p. 63). In fact, in one pilot study, where eighty Type A subjects were compared with eighty Type B subjects, the Type A subjects had *seven times* as much coronary heart disease as the Type B subjects. In addition, the high incidence of coronary disease among Type A versus Type B individuals appeared to be independent of such factors as smoking or diet.

PERSONALITY AND RESISTANCE TO DISEASE   Friedman and Rosenman are not the only ones who believe that a person's behavior could be used to predict the type and incidence of future illnesses. Samuel Silverman, author of *How Will You Feel Tomorrow?* (1975), also maintains that the onset and nature of an illness can be predicted by taking into consideration such factors as a person's ability to discharge severe tensions. Silverman contends that if psychological stresses, such as guilt or anger, are repressed, they will manifest themselves at the body's weakest point, the target organ, in the form of a disease or other somatic complication.

Hans Selye, during the development of his theory of the general adaptation syndrome (GAS), also noted:

> Any kind of activity sets our stress mechanism in motion, though it will largely depend upon the accidental conditioning factors whether the heart, kidney, gastrointestinal tract, or brain will suffer most. In the body, as in a chain, the weakest link breaks down under stress although all parts are equally exposed to it. (1974, pp. 45–46)

In his research, however, Selye distinguishes between *direct* and *indirect* pathogens. Direct pathogens cause damage or disease irrespective of the body's reaction—for example, in the case of the administration of a strong acid or poison. On the other hand, many indirect pathogens, such as allergens (elements that cause allergic reactions), bacteria, and viruses, appear to cause extensive damage only when the body's resistance to their intrusion weakens or fails.

Lowered resistance and personality predispositions are also becoming subjects of considerable interest among investigators into the causes of cancer. Although there are approximately 110 forms of cancer found in humans, and such factors as genetics, chemicals, and radiation appear to be contributing factors in the development of the disease, William Schofield of the University of Minnesota points out that "there is pretty good evidence that susceptibility to cancer may be influenced in part by psychological and emotional traits" (Young, 1976).

Evidence tending to support such statements can be found in research such as that conducted by Lawrence Le Shan (1966). Le Shan found, after having interviewed nearly 500 cancer patients, that 72 percent of them had suffered from childhood traumas, such as desertion or parental alienation. As a consequence, deep feelings of guilt and inadequacy seemed to have developed. Yet these same individuals attempted to present an outward impression of being tolerant, considerate, and confident. In a control group of noncancerous patients, only 10 percent had experienced similar traumas or developed the same type of personality characteristics.

It is important to keep in mind, however, that the idea of a psychosomatic relationship with cancer is still highly controversial. Both sides of the issue have strong proponents. As Arthur Holleb of the American Cancer Society points out, "At the moment there is no scientific evidence that psychological factors are involved in the cause of cancer" (Young, 1976). However, Charles Garfield of the University of California Cancer Research Institute responds, "On the other hand, there is so much evidence in the direction of a psychosomatic link, it would be a grave error to ignore the possibility" (Young, 1976).

Psychological Reaction to Stress

According to the *Dictionary of Psychology* (Warren, 1962), *intelligence* is the "ability to meet new situations quickly and successfully." The evolutionists believe that it is our superiority in this area that has allowed the otherwise fragile *homo sapiens* to successfully cope with danger and other changes in the environment. However, when such dangers or changes threaten to overwhelm our adaptive resources, our emotional stability may be jeopardized. As a result, a neurosis will develop, or, in some cases, a psychosis. R. D. Laing (1964) points out, while describing one form of psychosis, that when subjected to severe stress, a person will often resort to "a special sort of strategy that a person invents in order to live in an unlivable situation" (1964, p. 187).

DISASTER SYNDROME. Disorders resulting from the severe stress of financial failure, social disgrace, or natural disaster were once classified by the American Psychiatric Association (1952) as "gross stress reactions." According to the *Diagnostic and Statistical Manual of Mental Disorders,* second edition (DSM II), 1968, their classification has changed. The *Manual* says:

307 Transient situational disturbances
This major category is reserved for more or less transient disorders of any severity (including those of psychotic proportions) that occur in individuals without any apparent underlying mental disorders and that represent an acute reaction to overwhelming environmental stress. (pp. 48–49)

Individuals suffering from this reaction, more commonly referred to as a "disaster syndrome," will typically pass through three stages: the "shock stage," the "suggestible stage," and the "recovery stage" (Raker et al., 1956; Wallace, 1956, 1957).

During the *shock stage,* the victim appears dazed and apathetic and is often unaware of the extent of any injuries which may occurred. Many individuals become disoriented, wander aimlessly, and may have no recollection of the traumatic event. Others become stuperous and may stare continuously, moving little or not at all. For example, following the destruction of an apartment building due to the explosion of a broken gas main, an individual who lived across the street from the apartment house commented:

> I just stand here all day long looking across the street, I don't know why. I can't get over it. To think that they could be so alive the night before, playing cards, talking to us. Then all of a sudden, for no reason, they are wiped out. A big house is there one minute and the next minute nothing is left of it at all. I just can't understand it. (Janis, 1965, p. 217)

The *suggestible stage* is characterized by passive compliance with any directions or commands that might be given. Victims will often show a great deal of concern for the welfare of others, but most of their efforts to give assistance are highly inefficient, as are their attempts to carry out routine tasks.

During the *recovery stage,* victims are able to pull themselves together somewhat, and they regain some semblance of self-control. However, a good deal of anxiety will tend to persist. Many victims have recurrent nightmares, suffer from insomnia, and display a compulsive need to talk about the traumatic event.

In some cases, the symptoms associated with the recovery stage may reappear days or even weeks after the crisis has passed. In addition to these symptoms, many individuals will also suffer from uncontrollable trembling, irritability, and restlessness.

In such cases, the individuals are said to be suffering from a "posttraumatic syndrome." This syndrome may be intensified by feelings of grief over the loss of a loved one or guilt related to what the survivor could have done.

HELPLESSNESS   The feeling of hopelessness that accompanies the perception of having lost control over the conditions of one's life, or the feeling of helplessness that is associated with defenselessness, can often affect the strength of one's determination, the zeal in one's motivation, and even the will in one's desire to go on living. In the extreme, this loss of will may very well explain the phenomenon of voodoo deaths, wherein individuals who have been "cursed" die despite the absence of any obvious organic cause (Cannon, 1942).

Feelings of helplessness are also a frequent experience of prisoners of war, as well as those individuals actively involved in combat. Grinker and Spiegel, acting as clinical investigators for the U.S. Army, found that such feelings were a major contributing factor among psychiatric casualties (1945a). Critical to the development of a breakdown seemed to be a loss of self-confidence in one's invulnerability. Typically, a change will occur in a person's attitude from "nothing terrible will happen to me," to "something terrible is bound to happen to me." Such a change was found to be quite common among airmen during the extended bombing raids over Europe in World War II. It would result in a decrease in efficiency and morale and a corresponding increase in anxiety and somatic complaints (Grinker and Spiegel, 1945b).

Scientific investigation into the area of helplessness has been conducted by many researchers (Richter, 1957; Ramey, 1972; Hiroto, 1974); however, some of the most outstanding research in this area has been conducted by M. Seligman and S. Maier (1967, 1968). According to Seligman, coping successfully with stress is a matter of learning and practice. People who have not learned successful coping methods, and who repeatedly find that nothing changes regardless of what they do, will often develop an attitude of helplessness, becoming extremely apathetic. To support this premise, Overmier and Seligman (1967) conducted an experiment in which dogs were first restrained in hammocks while noninjurious electric shocks were administered. They then placed the same animals in a shuttlebox. A shuttlebox is a boxlike device with an electric gridwork in the floor on one side of a low barrier and an insulated floor on the other side. Normally, animals given a shock on the electrified portion will quickly learn to escape the shock by leaping over the barrier to the insulated portion of the shuttlebox. The test animals, however, did not react in this fashion, but endured the shocks with resolute whimpering. It seemed that they had learned from their previous experiences with the hammocks that there was nothing that could be done to escape the shocks.

Similar results were obtained with humans using a loud noise rather than shock. Subjects who had learned that there was no way of avoiding the loud noise became apathetic and passively endured the noxious stimulation (Hiroto, 1974). Their reaction was found to be quite similar to the fatalistic attitude exhibited by people who have learned that it is futile to struggle against the establishment, the fates, or the poverty that surrounds them.

In such cases, there is typically an absence of fear. Emotions are seemingly replaced by intellectual resignation. Spinoza, in an attempt to explain this lack of affect, believed that fear existed only when accompanied by hope—"Fear cannot be without hope, nor hope without fear" (1910). This lack of emotional affect appears to be symptomatic of people who are overwhelmed by feelings of helplessness, who believe that they have no control over their destiny, or who are subject to the whims of their oppressors. An extreme example would be the "walking corpses" referred to by Bettelheim (1960), when he described the inmates of the Nazi concentration camps.

DEPRESSION Perhaps the most appropriate description of any emotional affect associated with reactions to stress and helplessness would be *depression*. A. T. Beck (1967, 1969) proposes that depression is a behavioral response to hopelessness. People become depressed because they have lost hope. This position, however, is in opposition to that of most theorists. They maintain that hopelessness is usually a by-product, if not a direct result, of being depressed, and that it is because of depression that a person is likely to lose hope. The discouragement of the depressed and the fatalism of the helpless was vividly described by Ernest Hemingway (1899–1961), in his *A Farewell to Arms* (1929):

If people bring so much courage to this world the world has to kill them to break them, so of course it kills them. The world breaks everyone and afterward many are strong at the broken places. But those that will not break it kills. It kills the very good and the very gentle and the very brave impartially. If you are none of these you can be sure that it will kill you too but there will be no special hurry. (p. 249)

According to the National Institute of Mental Health, more than 125,000 Americans are hospitalized for depression. Another 200,000 are being treated at clinics, and possibly as many as 4 to 8 million need therapeutic support due to depression. Thus, it is no wonder that there is a growing concern with the role stress plays in the development of depression.

When depression is thought to be the result of exposure to external stress, it is referred to as *exogenous depression,* or sometimes as reactive depression. Typically, exogenous depression is associated with the loss of a loved one. The symptoms include a tendency to oversleep and overeat, emotional detachment, apathy, and a sense of dejection (Kiloh and Garside, 1963).

Depression resulting from internal sources is referred to as *endogenous depression,* or sometimes as psychotic depression. The symptoms of this type of depression are often a loss of appetite, apathy, and low self-esteem. The distinction between these two forms of depression is not always clear, however. Some therapists believe that the two forms of depression are actually merely differences in the degree of severity along a continuum, with internal biochemical factors being aggravated by external sources of stress (Kendell, 1968).

One of the most frequent sources of stress to precede the onset of depression appears to be the loss, or perceived loss, of a loved one. This loss can be due to emotional withdrawal, physical separation, or death. In the case of emotional withdrawal, spousal alienation is perhaps the most common. Emotional withdrawal can take the form of the silent treatment, where one spouse refuses to speak or verbally respond to the other. It may also be manifested in a lack of interest in, or total abstinence from, sex, or a complete indifference to the physical, mental, and emotional well-being of the partner.

Although most depression resulting from separation is due to long-term, and often involuntary, separation, depression can also occur even when separations are voluntary and brief. This seems to be especially true of children separated from their mothers. Studies conducted by Robertson (1958) and Bowlby (1960) indicate that when separated, a child will typically pass through three phases of grief. During phase one, the *protest* period, a two- to four-year-old will cry almost continuously, interrupted only occasionally by calls for the mother. Even after quieting somewhat, the child will remain vigilant for the mother's return, and will reject the overtures or demands made by a substitute mother.

Phase two, the period of *despair,* is characterized by moaning, suppressed weeping, and looks of sadness and despair. The child no longer remains vigilant, and is relatively unresponsive to stimuli that might signal the return of the mother. Finally, about a week after the separation occurs, the child will enter phase three, the period of *detachment.* During this phase, the child's apathy deepens, and the child becomes less responsive to all stimuli in the environment. In addition, the child will usually begin verbalizing a lack of caring, and even an open hostility, for the absent mother.

The depression experienced by a child during separation is often quite similar to the feelings of grief experienced during a time of bereavement. Although some grief is to be expected following the death of a loved one, Edith Jacobson (1957) makes a distinction between *pathological depressive reactions* and *normal mourning.*

In cases where pathological depression develops following the death of a loved one, there is usually a history of emotional instability, as well as feelings of repressed hostility toward the deceased. The feelings of hostility will often generate strong feelings of guilt and self-condemnation, accompanied by a sense of worthlessness. As a result, the individual will frequently attempt to avoid friends, neglect social responsibilities, and, should such a trend continue, contemplate suicide.

Such feelings can be contrasted with those of a bereaved person going through a period of normal mourning. Typically, there is an absence of guilt and self-condemnation. This is not to say that such a person will not mentally review the activities leading up to the death, but at least there is not an obsession with thoughts of what could have been. The period of grief is also shorter than it is in pathological depression. The bereaved person gradually accepts the reality of the situation, though without necessarily fully comprehending the true significance of what has happened. Victor Frankl, in *The Doctor and the Soul* (1965), captures the spirit of this kind of dilemma, when he admonishes such people "to be courageous and patient: courageous in leaving the problem unresolved for the time being, and patient in not giving up the struggle for a solution" (p. 374).

SUMMARY

In this chapter, the concept of stress was explored. Included in this treatment was a discussion, from the standpoint of Hans Selye's general adaptive syndrome, of the physiological demands associated with stress. The psychological demands of stress were also discussed, and the effects of anxiety, guilt, and shame were particularly emphasized.

In addition, some of the causes of stress were examined. The causes were grouped into four major categories: (1) deprivation, covering such factors as physical and emotional loneliness, alienation, and the need to be productive; (2) frustration, including physical and social obstacles, as well as physical and psychological deficiencies; (3) conflicts, considering especially Kurt Lewin's valance theory and approach-avoidance ambivalence; and (4) pressure, dealing with such factors as population, prejudice, crime, violence, and social distance.

The various reactions to stress, and the wide variety of effects stress can have due to individual differences and tolerances, were also investigated. These differences were of particular concern with regard to physiological reactions to stress and the possible effects personality type may have on one's physical and mental health. The discussion focused on resistance to such diseases as coronaries and cancer, in particular. Individual differences in psychological reactions were also investigated, especially the disaster syndrome, and transient situational disturbances, as well as the resultant feelings of helplessness and depression that are often associated with stress.

DISCUSSION QUESTIONS

1 What role do you think a patient's attitude plays in the ultimate outcome of an illness?

2 Would ygu prefer to know ahead of time that something terrible *might* happen or would you rather deal with the situation if and when it actually happens?

3 What are some of the advantages afd disadvantages of feeling guilt? Shame?

4 Ofe of the causes of stress is said to be deprivation. Of what do you feel most deprived?

5 What is one of the greatest or most frequent sources of frustration in your life?

6 Since "nobody's perfect," do you believe that your deficiencies are more physical or psychological?

7 Can you think of an approach-approach conflict that you have faced recently? Approach-avoidance? Avoidance-avoidance?

8 In your opinion, how could governments attempt to reduce feelings of alienation among members of an ever-increasing population?

9 According to Holmes's social readjustment rating scale, about how many points do you think you have accumulated in the past year?

10 What has traditionally caused you to feel depressed, and how have you coped with these periods?

EXPERIENTIAL EXERCISES

1 Air traffic controllers, policemen, and firemen are considered to have the most stressful vocations. Arrange to have a member of one of these professions appear as a guest of the class or group. Have your guest discuss some of the most stressful aspects of the job and how he or she has learned to cope with such stress.

2 In order to better appreciate the social obstacles that many members of minority groups must face, have the members of a group discuss their personal experiences with prejudice. Have the members discuss how they believe their parents would react if they were to marry into a different race, nationality, religion, or ethnic group. Compare the parental attitudes with those of the group members.

3 In order to better understand the effects of stress, make arrangements for a group of students to visit stress-oriented locations, such as a prison, or jail, mental institution, hospital emergency room, or unemployment office. Name the physical and psychological sources of stress observed. What were some of the symptoms of stress observed among the people present at these locations?

CHAPTER 6

COPING WITH STRESS

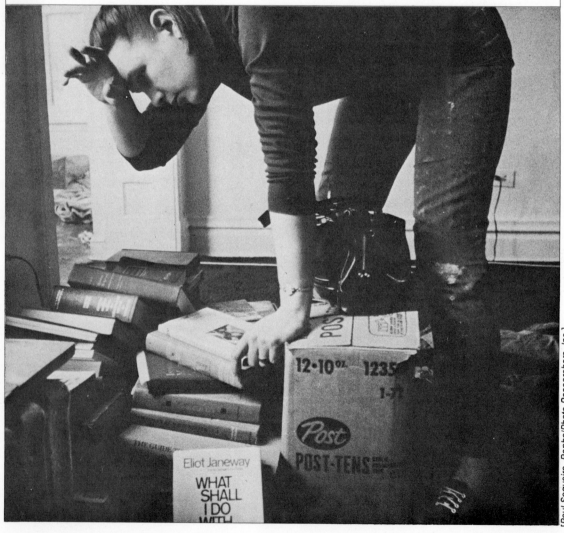

Man's search for meaning is a primary force in his life and not a "secondary rationalization" of instinctual drives. This meaning is unique and specific in that it must and can be fulfilled by him alone; only then does it achieve a significance which will satisfy his own *will* to meaning. There are some authors who contend that meanings and values are "nothing but defense mechanisms, reaction formations and sublimations." But as for myself, I would not be willing to live merely for the sake of my "defense mechanisms," nor would I be ready to die merely for the sake of my "reaction formations." Man, however, is able to live and even to die for the sake of his ideals and values!

Viktor Frankl
Man's Search for Meaning

COPING WITH STRESS

There are probably as many differences in the ways people cope with stress as there are differences in individual personalities. Some attempt to run away, and others tend to attack the source of the stress. Some consent to endure stress, and others refuse to ever surrender. For some, coping with stress ends with a nervous breakdown; still others appear to grow stronger with each episode.

Such individual differences in the way people react to stress have been noted by professionals and nonprofessionals alike. For instance, throughout academic history, instructors who have practiced the sadistic art of giving unannounced quizzes have had the opportunity to observe students employing a variety of coping methods. For example, once the instructor has announced, "There is going to be a pop quiz today," the student reaction is usually a reflexive "Oh, no! Not today!" followed by groaning, fake seizures, morning sickness, recurring bouts with malaria, or, occasionally, the "weak heart" that is not to be subjected to unnecessary strain. Some students will give "kill" commands to imaginary attack dogs while pointing at the instructor; some of the less imaginative may merely make a break for the door or an open window. However, in time, an air of calmness and dignity will gradually return to the classroom as many students realize that they are actually prepared for the quiz—that they will be able to cope with whatever does happen, or that nothing in life really matters anyway, and that all is lost.

Our bodies are structurally designed to react to stress in an automatic, or reflexive, manner. However, many stressful situations are far too complex to be successfully dealt with at the relatively simplistic reflex level. Therefore, more sophisticated coping patterns must be developed as a part of the process of growing up. These more complex methods of coping are usually learned through experience and by observing effective coping techniques being used by others. However, should an individual be denied sufficient opportunity to exercise his or her coping capabilities, such as when parents are overly protective, or should an individual be exposed primarily to examples of ineffective coping methods, such as when members of the family are alcoholic, antisocial, or severely neurotic, then reactions to stress often remain undeveloped and often maladaptive.

Infantile Reactions

The emotional reactions to stress expressed by infants or extremely immature individuals are basically *irresponsible*. They reflect little or no consideration of the possible consequences of the reactions. Infantile reactions are often "maximum responses" in that the intensity of the reactions seldom varies from that of total involvement. Infantile persons are seldom a little upset—they will typically throw temper tantrums or become hysterical or severely withdrawn when faced with even the mildest degree of stress.

Immature Reactions

In most cases, the reactions to stress exhibited by children or relatively immature people are ineffective and irresponsible. This is primarily because such people tend to concentrate more on themselves than on the source of the stress. For example, after losing a job, an immature person may concentrate on maintaining the image of still being employed rather than on attempts to find a new job.

Such people are ego-oriented and tend to interpret stressful situations in terms of personal threat. As a consequence, they tend to rely heavily on ego-oriented coping methods, such as the overuse of defense mechanisms. Blaming others for personal failures, displacing aggression, and venting emotions inappropriately would be typical examples of immature, or ego-oriented, reactions to stress.

Mature Reactions

One of the major characteristics of mature reactions to stress is the assumption of personal responsibility for dealing not only with the source of the stress, but with the possible consequences of the reactions. Mature reactions to stress tend to deal directly with the source of the stress and attempt to prevent, correct, or adjust to it. People who tend to deal directly with the problem at hand are said to be using task-oriented methods. For example, even a relatively small fire at home can create a substantial amount of stress. A mature reaction to this stress situation would be to concentrate on putting the fire out. This is in contrast with a relatively immature reaction in which an individual's primary concern is with being blamed for the fire. Dealing directly with people in authority or with those who may be responsible for creating a stressful situation, taking precautionary measures in order to avoid unnecessary stress in the future, and being willing to accept defeat or failure gracefully would be typical examples of mature, or task-oriented, reactions to stress.

Hans Selye, in his book *Stress without Distress* (1974), defines stress as "the nonspecific response of the body to *any* demand made upon it" (p. 27). With regard to the need to cope with stress, Selye points out: "No matter what you do or what happens to you, there arises a demand for the necessary energy required to maintain life, to resist aggression, and to adapt to constantly changing external (or internal) influences" (p. 32). Selye proposes, in other words, that stress is unavoidable. It follows from this that the process of coping with stress is—from the moment of our birth to the time we die—an integral, and inevitable, part of living.

Some people seem to learn quickly how to cope efficiently and effectively as they are growing up. To such individuals, stress is a fact of life, a *task* to be worked through. In fact, many deliberately seek out ways of increasing the level of stress in their lives. They often feel bored and restless in its absence. Such individuals tend to enjoy high-risk sports, such as skiing or scuba diving, as well as the adventure of the business world or trying something new or different. William James (1897) acknowledged the existence of such lifestyles. He claimed that "need and struggle are what excite and inspire us; our hour of triumph is what brings the void." However, for many other people, stress is seen as a perpetual burden to be struggled with, avoided, or, at the very least, endured. The coping abilities of such individuals are often limited or maladaptive, and their level of tolerance to stress is minimal.

Precautionary Measures

According to Richard Lazarus (1966), the way we react to stress is dependent upon the way in which we appraise the element of threat. Lazarus refers to this initial analysis as the "primary appraisal." This appraisal can be strongly influenced by such factors as individual needs, personal beliefs, and awareness of the number of alternative courses of action available. In other words, the perception of stress-producing factors is subjective. What may be perceived as an extreme threat by one person, thereby resulting in a state of panic, may be seen as inconsequential by another, and be all but ignored.

Our appraisal of the effectiveness or ineffectiveness of our coping behavior is what Lazarus calls our "secondary appraisal." This appraisal is, in turn, highly dependent upon how realistically we perceive the threat, how objectively we see our coping abilities, and how precisely we have anticipated the need to cope with a given situation.

Richard Lazarus, in his book *Psychological Stress and the Coping Process* (1966), emphasizes the importance of the "anticipation of harmful events." He describes this period as one "in which cues about what is to follow and what can be done to cope with it are sought and evaluated" (p. 31). It is the stress resulting from anticipation that is often used to distinguish physiological stress from psychological stress. Physiological stress is usually a consequence of harm which has already occurred (what *has* happened). Psychological stress, on the other hand, is often a result of one's expectations of harm

Although effective coping patterns can be learned through practice, as in fire drills, under the severe stress of an actual emergency pathological behavior can determine what actions are actually taken. [*Bruce Anspach/EPA Newsphoto.*]

FIGURE 6.1

harm that is yet to occur (what *might* happen). According to Lazarus, the "degree of threat is a function primarily of amount, imminence, and likelihood of the anticipated harm" (p. 43).

The general patterns of emotional response to psychological stress are classified by Irving Janis (1971) into three categories: high, moderate, or low anticipatory fear patterns. Individuals classified as experiencing *high anticipatory fear* are likely to undergo "extreme feelings of vulnerability" before the threatening event occurs and are "more likely than others to be anxiety-ridden" after the event occurs. People who have a *moderate anticipatory fear* tend to see themselves as being "somewhat vulnerable" but are optimistic about their abilities to cope with an impending threat. Such people also tend to be "much less likely than others to display emotional disturbances" following the traumatic event. In contrast, those demonstrating *low anticipatory fear* reactions often perceive themselves as having "almost complete invulnerability" preceding the actual occurrence of the threat. Afterward, however, they tend to be "more likely than others to display anger and resentment."

These anticipatory fear patterns tend to support Lazarus's belief (1966) that although effective coping patterns are learned, the overall effectiveness is strongly influenced by the severity of the stress. According to Lazarus, "More adaptive and reality-oriented forms of coping are most likely when the threat is comparatively mild; under severe threat, pathological extremes become more prominent'' (p. 162). In accord with Lazarus' premise, the low anticipatory fear pattern would not necessarily reflect a "reality-oriented" form of coping, but rather a denial of one's vulnerability and a repression of one's true feelings of anxiety.

Aggressive Measures

For a great many people, *aggression* is synonymous with such terms as violence, assault, attack, and destruction. As a result of these negative connotations, there is a tendency to avoid aggressiveness whenever possible or to feel guilty about having lost control over one's aggressive tendencies. This can be especially true when aggressiveness is motivated by anger. In such instances, aggression can become a source of great anxiety for those to whom it is directed, as well as for those who are merely bystanders. Such hostility is usually equated with rejection and/or injury and sometimes with feelings of unworthiness, inadequacy, or inferiority.

The use of aggressive measures as a means of coping with stress, however, can be extremely effective and can just as easily be associated with such feelings as pride, determination, and self-respect. Such feelings are often generated as a result of having used aggressive measures in attempts at overcoming obstacles, correcting deficiencies, or asserting one's human rights.

In addition, the use of aggressive measures need not necessarily be expressed destructively. For example, aggressiveness is one of the key elements behind such things as medical research, social reform, and scientific investigation. It can also be an essential ingredient in the process of realizing one's full potential, maintaining one's sense of dignity, or achieving one's impossible dreams.

AGGRESSIVE BEHAVIOR   Sigmund Freud believed that aggression is *inborn,* the outward manifestation of the death instinct (Thanatos) (Ostow, 1958). John Dollard and Neal Miller propose that aggression is closely associated with *frustration* (Miller, 1941), and Albert Bandura states that aggression is *socially learned* (1970). Regardless of which of these theories is accepted, there appears to be a general agreement that aggression is an integral part of human behavior. There is much less agreement, however, in discussions on the manner in which aggression is expressed, and therefore this is a frequent source of anxiety.

For some, the aggressive feelings generated by rejection and alienation are transformed into a defense against future encounters with intimacy (Fairbairn, 1954). For others, aggression is often a disguised plea for love that is, unfortunately, hidden beneath the anger that stems from feelings of having never been loved (Janov, 1970). In either of these situations, the aggression tends to be self-defeating, maladaptive, and usually socially unacceptable.

A socially acceptable expression of aggression is one in which the expression of aggressive feelings is channeled directly at the source of

FIGURE 6.2   Children learn through loving relationships with responsible parents. [*Erika Stone.*]

frustration or threat, while emotional restraint and behavior controlled by reason are displayed in other areas. But it is often very difficult to develop an emotional outlet for aggression that satisfies such social expectations and still retains its emotional effectiveness. This difficulty is usually due to the unreasonableness of the social limitations placed on individuals—limitations that tend to suppress the overt expression of aggression. As a result of such social restrictions, Konrad Lorenz (1966) believes, "present-day civilized man suffers from an insufficient discharge of his aggressive drives" (p. 243).

Traditionally, games, sports, and other competitive events, along with the drama of the stage or novel, provided a vicarious means by which both the need for an aggressive outlet and the need for socially acceptable behavior could be satisfied. Today, such vicarious means of aggressive release have become national institutions centered around such events as the World Series, Super Bowl, and professional boxing, while television provides an infinite number of opportunities for vicarious adventure, emotional diversion, and aggressive identification.

Humor, it is believed, is also used as a socially acceptable outlet for feelings of hostility or aggression (Freud, 1960). For example, the punch line of a joke can be used to introduce the element of surprise or ridicule, and an individual can be made to appear stupid, illogical, or merely the fool. However, such demeaning behavior is often considered to be socially acceptable because the victim has usually consented to the telling of the joke beforehand,

Konrad Lorenz not only made the study of aggression his life's work, but also demonstrated a socially acceptable means of expressing aggression by being scientifically aggressive. [*Pictorial Parade, Inc.*]

FIGURE 6.3

with the implicit understanding that he or she may very well bear the brunt of it. In other situations, one group may tacitly agree to have other groups customarily be the victim of their humor, as in the case where jokes are habitually directed toward a particular nationality, religion, or sex. This, of course, does not mean that *all* humor is necessarily based on hostility, only that humor often provides a convenient attack outlet for such feelings, and minimizes exposure to the stress of a counterattack.

Such is not usually the case, however, when aggressive feelings are expressed openly without the protection of the disguised intent that humor allows. For instance, one can generally expect some reciprocation in any attempt at talking things out. Such direct confrontations, however, are generally thought to be one of the healthiest forms of aggressive behavior. Carl Rogers (1951) believes that only through the *acceptance* of our own feelings of hostility, and those of another, can we grow to a point where such feelings can be expressed without fear of rejection or ridicule. Rogers emphasized the importance of this premise with regard to interpersonal relationships:

> We can love a person only to the extent that we are not threatened by him; we can love him only if his reactions to us, or to those things which affect us, are understandable to us and are clearly related to those basic motivations within us

all which tend to bring us closer to compatible and meaningful relations with other people and the world. If . . . I can see this person's hostility as an understandable component of the person's defense against feeling the need for closeness to people, I can then react with love towards this person. (1951, p. 161)

George Bach and Peter Wyden have expanded on Rogers's position. They maintain that verbal fighting is an "art" that needs to be learned and practiced in order to perfect the technique of "fighting fairly." In their book *The Intimate Enemy* (1969), they present their belief that people who are able to achieve satisfaction through the verbal expression of their aggressive needs are less likely to have a need to express these feelings physically. Such a belief is based on their conviction:

. . . that people who master the fine art of fair verbal fighting and conflict resolution will be disinclined to commit physical violence. . . . The more values of realistic and aggressive intimacy pervade a culture, the more people commit themselves to constructive verbal fighting, the more safely sated will be man's appalling appetite for lethal violence. (p. 328)

ASSERTIVE BEHAVIOR *Assertiveness* has been defined as "standing up for personal rights and expressing thoughts, feelings, and beliefs in direct, honest, and appropriate ways" (Lange and Jakubowski, 1976, p. 7). This is in contrast

FIGURE 6.4 Being able to "talk things out" as a form of aggressive behavior can often prevent less desirable expressions such as physical violence or overt rejection. [*Sybil Shelton, Peter Arnold, Inc.*]

with *aggressiveness,* which may not always include an appropriate respect for the personal rights of others.

Assertiveness was first developed by Andrew Salter (1949) as a counter-conditioning technique. Today, this technique is commonly referred to as *assertiveness training,* and it emphasizes desensitizing the fear that prevents a person from standing up for his or her rights.

Manuel Smith, author of *When I Say No I Feel Guilty* (1975), believes that *"Our assertive rights are a basic framework for each individual's healthy participation in any human relationship"* (p. 27). As a means of dramatizing the importance of these principles, Smith developed a Bill of Assertive Rights:

I   You have the right to judge your own behavior, thoughts, and emotions, and to take the responsibility for their initiation and consequences upon yourself (p. 28).

II   You have the right to offer no reasons or excuses to justify your behavior (p. 45).

III   You have the right to judge whether you are responsible for finding solutions to other people's problems (p. 47).

IV   You have the right to change your mind. (p. 50).

V   You have the right to make mistakes—and be responsible for them (p. 51).

VI   You have the right to say, "I don't know" (p. 53).

VII   You have the right to be independent of the goodwill of others before coping with them (p. 55).

VIII   You have the right to be illogical in making decisions (p. 58).

IX   You have the right to say, "I don't understand" (p. 60).

X   You have the right to say, "I don't care" (p. 63).

According to Smith, there is a tendency for people to cling to the belief that *everyone* should want to improve by correcting every personality flaw, overcoming all deficiencies, and, in whatever way possible, striving for "perfection." In an attempt to counter this tendency, Smith proposes that individuals decide for themselves whether or not they wish to improve themselves and not rely on the expectations of others. In other words, it is all right to accept oneself as is, rather than to strive for the new, improved version others may want. As a means of emphasizing one's commitment to self-judgment, Smith recommends the use of such terms as "I prefer to" or "I want to," rather than "I have to" or "I should."

Adjustive Measures

Arthur Jensen (1969) pointed out—embarrassing as it might be from a scientific point of view—that it is far easier to measure intelligence than it is to define it. However, a function that is often included in definitions of intelligence is *adaptability.* Adaptability also seems to play an important role in distinguishing the task-oriented individual from the ego-oriented individual. This does not mean that task-oriented persons are necessarily more intelligent. They are merely more flexible and therefore able to adapt to new situations more easily.

Ego-oriented individuals, on the other hand, often become preoccupied, if not obsessed, with protecting their self-image. As a consequence, they tend to adopt rigid behavior patterns. Such rigidity limits the number of alternatives available when seeking a solution to problems, and, as a result, these individuals are likely to experience the stress of frustration more frequently than do the more adaptable task-oriented personalities.

Due to the flexible nature of task-oriented people, they are more likely to use evasive measures to provide themselves more time to collect their resources, readjust their levels of aspiration, develop alternative means of achieving their original goals, and, if necessary, select a completely new set of goals.

WITHDRAWAL   Professional gamblers often cite the ability to know when to quit as one of the principal characteristics of a winner. The same can often be said of a person in the field of business where the decision to close a store, cancel a program, or take a particular product off the market can be vital.

The ability to determine when it is appropriate to withdraw is also an essential characteristic of interpersonal relationships. Typically, ego-oriented individuals are unable, or at least unwilling, to make the decision to get out of a relationship that has become mutually destructive. Such individuals are often willing to endure physical and mental abuse, public humiliation, and repeated episodes of rejection and neglect. Yet, these same people will often defend their martyrdom by exaggerating the merits of being tenacious and their hope of preserving what is worthwhile in the relationship. In most cases, however, there has never really been anything in the relationship worth preserving. Hans Selye (1974) cautioned:

Man . . . is especially vulnerable to psychic insults, and there are various little tricks to minimize these . . . a few that I have found useful:

Whatever situation you meet in life, consider first whether it is really worth fighting for.

Even if you systematically want to hoard love, don't waste your time trying to befriend a mad dog. (p. 134)

The process of withdrawal involves the element of escape, not only as it pertains to destructive relationships, but also to such things as dead-end jobs, poverty, boredom, and the ghetto. Furthermore, escape alone is not always enough; prolonged evasion or avoidance is frequently required in order to prevent reinvolvement. Task-oriented individuals are usually well aware of their limitations and weakness and therefore tend to avoid temptation, as in the case of a reformed alcoholic deciding not to take that first drink, the person who is prone to having affairs turning down a luncheon date, or the compulsive buyer staying out of department stores.

Escape should not be confused with running away to avoid responsibility, as might be the case with an ego-oriented solution to stress. In many instances, escape is essential to the physical and/or psychological welfare of the individual. It often affords an opportunity to regroup, to think things out under less pressure, or to refurbish one's resources in order to fight yet another day.

Nor should avoidance be confused with the ego-oriented person's tendency to procrastinate. Careful avoidance of unnecessary stress can be a demonstration of both wisdom and good common sense, whereas procrastination is often used in an attempt to avoid responsibilities, delay the inevitable, or distort reality in order to create the illusion that the problem no longer exists. Hans Selye (1974) advises:

> When faced with a task which is very painful yet indispensable to achieve your aim, don't procrastinate; cut right into an abscess to eliminate the pain, instead of prolonging it by gently rubbing the surface. (p. 135)

ADJUSTING LEVELS OF ASPIRATION   The importance of flexibility in an individual's personality has already been pointed out. Flexibility enables a person to use withdrawal as a means of coping with stress. Another important coping characteristic is presented by Duane Schultz in his book *Growth Psychology* (1977):

> Another quality of emotional security is what Allport called "frustration tolerance." This indicates how a person reacts to stress and to the thwarting of wants and desires. Healthy persons tolerate these setbacks; they do not resign themselves to frustration but instead are capable of devising different, less frustrating, ways of reaching the same or substitute goals. Frustrations are not crippling to healthy personalities as they often are to neurotics. (p. 18)

Allport emphasized that frustration is not crippling to the healthy personality. For many people, frustration is not even undesirable. For the task-oriented person, *too little* frustration can lead to apathy and a general lack of motivation. *Too much* frustration, however, can lead to anger, anxiety, and a tendency toward blind, repetitive behavior. A *moderate* level of frustration, however, can be highly motivating and perceived as a respectable challenge. As a result, task-oriented individuals tend to set up lifestyles that confine the experience of frustration to moderate levels. They accomplish this by (1) being able to adjust their levels of aspiration, (2) selecting alternate means of achieving their goals, and (3) being able to select alternative, or substitute, goals when necessary.

EGO-ORIENTED METHODS

Sigmund Freud envisioned the ego as a component of the personality that is not present at birth but emerges from the id. Freud saw the ego as "the organized portion of the id" (1959). The ego is molded and shaped by contact with the external world. In Freud's view, "the ego stands for reason and good sense while the id stands for the untamed passions" (1964). As such, a person's ego is never far from the influence of the primitive demands made by the id—demands for immediate satisfaction, regardless of the consequences.

FIGURE 6.5

Task-oriented individuals tend to set up lifestyles that confine frustrating experiences to moderate levels. A runner will initially set a goal of *completing* the 26-mile marathon rather than winning it. [*Dan Brinzac, Peter Arnold, Inc.*]

For people with a task-oriented personality, such demands for satisfaction are considered a part of their humanness, and the task of the ego is merely to develop a socially acceptable means of expressing the urges of the id. For example, a relatively guilt-free means of satisfying sexual desires is provided by getting married. However, for people with ego-oriented personalities, these primitive urges are a source of constant threat, and such people often live in perpetual fear of losing control over the "uncivilized" part of their makeup. This might be the case where an individual avoids dating because of the sexual implications involved. As a consequence, such a person must continuously employ defense mechanisms to ward off what can be referred to as *internal threats*.

Task-oriented people meet external demands through the realistic application of their personal resources. The realistic application is possible because of the ability of task-oriented people to accurately evaluate their capabilities and limitations. Ego-oriented people, unfortunately, base their self-images on ideals which are usually unrealistic fantasies of what it would be like to be perfect. As a consequence, anything that may threaten the image of oneself as ideal is perceived as a threat, and one's ego must constantly be defended against any weakening of this delusion. The task-oriented personality balances the demands of the id and the pressures of the ideal image of the superego. Put in other words, it balances the ability to discriminate between a task—a job to be done—and a threat—an ego that needs to be defended. The ego-oriented personality is one in which such a balance has never been achieved.

Defense Mechanisms

The ego-oriented individual tends to be almost totally dependent upon defense mechanisms as a means of coping with stress. The task-oriented person, on the other hand, will make only minimal use of defense mechanisms. It is important to keep in mind that the use of defense mechanisms is normal. Everyone makes some use of defense mechanisms. It is only the overuse of defense mechanisms that is considered to be mentally unhealthy.

Defense mechanisms are an unconscious adjustive reaction to a possible loss of self-esteem, a congitive reaction to the dissonance between innocence and guilt, and/or a protective effort to reduce anxiety. Defense mechanisms protect the ego from unwarranted or unjust criticism by the superego (conscience) and from the unacceptable impulses of the id. They are not innate, but learned. Therefore, the degree of skill in the use of defense mechanisms varies from individual to individual. The greater the skill, the more highly defended a person's ego will be, and the less likely the person will experience episodes of high anxiety.

However, no defense mechanism is perfect, and there will always be a certain degree of leakage around the edges. These leaks manifest themselves as anxiety. The more defense mechanisms being used, the more leaks there are to contend with. These, in turn, require the use of more defense mechanisms to reduce the ever-increasing anxiety. In addition, the mainte-nance of these defense mechanisms requires energy. Consequently, the more of them a person is maintaining, the less energy will be available for other endeavors, such as developing potentials, coping with "real" problems, and allowing oneself to love and be loved.

REPRESSION According to Freud, *repression* is one of the fundamental psychic mechanisms of psychoanalytic theory (Blum, 1953). Repression is a defense by which a person automatically buries unacceptable thoughts or desires in the realm of the unconscious awareness. The existence of what is unacceptable is as real as ever, though, and keeping it unconscious requires a great deal of energy. Therefore, repressing a large amount of material for a long period of time can lead to emotional exhaustion. When this happens, a person is unable to adequately defend the ego, and repressed feelings may begin to come to the surface in the form of *emotional overreactions*. The overreaction is the dam bursting, draining the reservoir of unexpressed emotions. For example, when parents of battered children vent their feelings on a child, the real motivation behind such an outburst may stem from repressed feelings of hostility toward their own parents—feelings generated from childhood abuses experienced years before the current outburst.

REACTION FORMATION   Another defense against becoming consciously aware of repressed material is the defense mechanism referred to as a *reaction formation.* When reaction formation is used as a defense, the individual acts out the opposite of the unconscious thoughts or desires that are unacceptable. For example, in the case of the Oedipus complex, a son may grow up unconsciously hating women. However, since hating women is unmasculine, the person suffering from such a complex may defend his ego by acting out the opposite; that is, by being overly nice to women.

PROJECTION   Another reason for not becoming too dedicated to analyzing the motives behind the actions of other people lies in the defense mechanism called *projection.* Projection is the defense mechanism through which the ego is defended from unacceptable thoughts or desires by the person's attributing them to others.

Some of the more common examples of projection might be exhibited through such statements as "I'm not the kind of girl (guy) you think I am" and "Everyone is out to get the other guy; thank goodness I'm not like that." Similarly, when someone points an accusing finger and says "I know what you're thinking," the finger pointer, in reality, is about to express what he or she is actually thinking.

FIXATION   Freud believed that in the process of growing up, it is necessary for a person to pass through various stages of development before reaching adulthood. For some, however, adulthood may become too great a threat, and this leads to a halting of the maturation process. This is often the result of the defense mechanism called *fixation.* Through this process a person's emotional maturation stops at a particular level of development. Such a person will tend to respond to the stresses of adulthood from the vantage point of a child. *Evasion of growth,* or the refusal to grow up, is often a manifestation of this defense. In such cases, bosses are seen as fathers, wives as mothers, and peers as being much older.

REGRESSION   Whenever defense mechanisms weaken, or fail completely, there is a tendency, especially for the neurotic, to regress or to resort to more primitive defenses. Regression can entail a return to an earlier stage of development—a period in which the present conflict did not exist. A typical example of this form of regression is illustrated when a four-year-old child, threatened by the arrival of a new sibling, regresses to an earlier, less stressful time, a time before the demands of toilet training. Such a regression might manifest itself in the form of bed-wetting.

Regression involving the use of more primitive defenses can usually be viewed as a tactical retreat. If intellectualization fails, one falls back upon rationalization. If that fails, one may resort to apathy, and so on. It is not

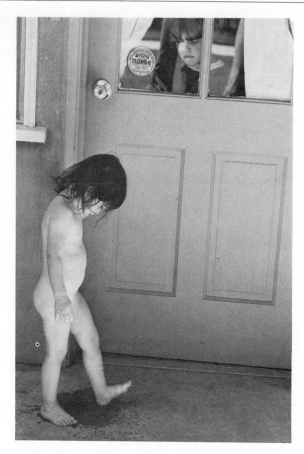

FIGURE 6.6

The defense mechanism of regression can involve a return to an earlier, less stressful stage of development—for example, a return to the time before toilet training. [*Hella Hammid, Photo Researchers, Inc.*]

uncommon, for example, for regression to be used by a person undergoing therapy. For instance, a client of this type might say to the therapist, "I've been reading up on the symptoms of various forms of personality disorders, and I've come to the conclusion that I have a hysterical personality (intellectualization)." The therapist may reply, "I find your conclusion interesting, but how do you account for your lack of symptoms as presented in this diagnostic manual?" "So maybe I'm in the early stages, or something (rationalization). Who cares anyway (apathy)?"

Psychological Escape

One of the primary uses of defense mechanisms is to protect the ego. *Flight* is one of the most common methods of achieving such protection. If a person is challenged by an external threat, physically running away often provides a relatively simple means of escape. However, one cannot run away from internal threats quite as easily. Escape from internal threat requires psychological flight through the use of such defense mechanisms as apathy, displacement, fantasy, and denial.

NOMADISM   A defense mechanism through which people attempt to physically escape a threatening situation is called *nomadism.* In the use of this defense, people attempt to reduce anxiety by physically removing themselves from the source of the stress. For example, should an undesirable work assignment be scheduled for the next day, then one merely avoids going to work (illness is often used as an excuse). Should an interpersonal relationship threaten to become too involved, then one merely breaks off the relationship and avoids seeing the other person. Should the people in one town begin to discover what is behind the phony mask, one merely leaves that town and goes to another. Some people, through the use of nomadism, establish a lifestyle in which they perpetually drift from job to job, from school to school, and from relationship to relationship.

APATHY   Unlike nomadism, the use of *apathy,* or withdrawal, as a defense mechanism removes people psychologically, rather than physically. Apathy is a defense mechanism by which people emotionally withdraw from the perceived threat. It is often accompanied by loss of appetite, lethargy, and emotional blunting. A general lack of enthusiasm, an attitude of not caring, and a tendency to rechannel energies and interests are also symptomatic of apathy. These attitudes are typically expressed through such statements as "It doesn't matter anymore," "Do whatever you want," "I just don't care what happens," or, "I think I'll take up fishing again. At least I don't have to think about anything, and things are simple."

DISPLACEMENT   Another defense mechanism that serves to protect people from experiencing uncomfortable emotions is called *displacement.* Displacement is the defense mechanism by which people release pent-up emotions in the direction of a source other than the original cause of the emotion. This displaced source is usually considered to be a safe target.

A frustrated mother venting her feelings of hostility on her children, when they would more appropriately be directed toward an insensitive husband, is an example of displacement. Other examples of displacement include kicking the car door after being turned down on a date, yelling at your spouse because your boss has been on your back all day, or throwing a rock at a dog because of being upset with your parents. In each case, a relatively safe target is chosen for the pent-up feelings.

In addition, the manner in which the feelings are expressed may not always resemble the original impulse. For example, an employee may feel like slugging the boss, but *yells* at the spouse instead. A child may feel like yelling at a parent, but ends up kicking the wall.

FANTASY   When it is not possible to use sublimation as an emotional outlet, or when other avenues for satisfaction in the real world are unavailable, it is not uncommon to turn to the use of *fantasy* as a means of reducing anxiety or bolstering the ego. The use of fantasy in moderation, or in conjunction with productive endeavors, often helps to reduce the stress associated with delayed gratification. For instance, a person just entering medical school may occasionally fantasize about what it will be like after the medical degree is received.

Unfortunately, the overuse of fantasy can lead to a "dreamer" type of lifestyle, that is, the person who daydreams constantly and talks incessantly about some day being rich and famous. This sort of person rarely puts forth any real effort toward actually trying to achieve the goal in question.

DENIAL   While rationalization is used to distort reality, the defense mechanism of denial is used to avoid reality. *Denial* is a defense by which a person attempts to escape reality by either (1) refusing to consciously process information, or (2) invalidating threatening information that has been processed.

Research psychologists, studying the areas of sensation and perception, have demonstrated the phenomenon by which a person refuses to consciously process information in a number of experimental situations. For example, under laboratory conditions, a tachistoscope can be used to flash neutral words or taboo words on a screen. When neutral words, such as "barn," "door," and "ball," are flashed, subjects perceive them correctly at relatively short exposure times. However, when taboo words, such as "spit" or "whore," are flashed on the screen, the exposure times must be lengthened considerably before subjects are able to consciously perceive them (Bruner and Postman, 1947; McGuinnies, 1949).

Outside the laboratory, awareness of a person's refusal to process information is most likely to show up in such statements as "Can't she see what he's up to? For crying out loud, she'd have to be blind not to know what's going on." Or, "I never suspected that she was an alcoholic. Yet, when I look back, the clues . . . the symptoms . . . they were everywhere. Why wasn't I able to see them before this?"

Should this first line of defense fail, and the information enter conscious awareness, then the second aspect of denial, invalidation, will often come into play. The threatening information is merely declared invalid, inaccurate, false, or prefabricated. For example, parents, when first informed of their child's involvement with drugs, sex, or stealing, may protect themselves with denial and make such statements as "There must be some mistake, officer. Our child would never get mixed up with something like that."

Defensive Compromise

Sometimes internal conflicts cannot be completely resolved. As a result, some degree of anxiety tends to persist despite the manipulative efforts of the individual. In such cases, *defensive compromise* can offer some relief. It enables the individual to achieve a further reduction in the level of anxiety by either explaining away the conflict or settling for something less than perfection.

COMPENSATION   The defense mechanism of *compensation* requires the deemphasizing of areas in which a person feels inferior and the accentuation of areas in which the person excels. For example, people who think that they are homely may tend to detract from this characteristic by emphasizing their athletic abilities, musical talents, or some other favorable aspect of personality. Similarly, a person who feels sexually inadequate may attempt to compensate through the acquisition of large sums of money or political power, and a child who feels unlovable may try to gain approval through intellectual achievements, being good, or being helpful or productive.

INTELLECTUALIZATION   Compared to many of the other defense mechanisms, *intellectualization* is fairly sophisticated. It is more commonly found among those who are fairly intelligent or well educated. Through this defense mechanism, people try to remove uncomfortable emotional overtones through cognitive processes. They make an attempt to remove the emotional discomfort by thinking rather than feeling. This often is referred to as "head tripping."

A typical example of intellectualization would be an attempt to analyze what is "really" bothering someone rather than accept the explanation the person gives for being emotionally upset. The intellectualizer might say something like, "You think that you're mad at me for being late, but I believe the real reason lies with your repressed hostility for your father. You tend to see me as a representation of his authority, and therefore. . . ."

EMOTIONAL INSULATION   In contrast to intellectualization, which attempts to remove the emotion after the fact, *emotional insulation* attempts to prevent the emotion from ever occurring in the first place. Emotional insulation is a defense mechanism through which people attempt to avoid feelings. The general premise of this mechanism is that people cannot get hurt if they do not become emotionally involved. Often this premise is taught by parents through statements like "Now don't get your hopes up. You may be disappointed," "Don't get too excited," or "The worst thing you can do is to let people know how you really feel before they have committed themselves."

As a result of such teachings, people will often become afraid of extremes in emotions and will seek to avoid situations that have the potential of becoming emotionally uncomfortable. By the use of this defense mechanism, they reduce life's emotional ups and downs to mere ripples. Unfortunately, such people are prevented from experiencing emotions like love, caring, and appreciation as well as anger, resentment, and disappointment.

SUBSTITUTION   The defense mechanism of *substitution* is similar to displacement in that they both involve the release of pent-up emotions toward a source other than the cause. However, there are two main differences between them. One difference is that the alternate outlet for the emotions, when substitution is used, may not be any safer than the original target would have been. For example, a child who has been rejected by his or her real parent may reach out to a substitute parent to love, even though there is a real possibility that the child may be rejected again.

The second difference is in the manner in which the emotions are expressed. In the case of displacement, the final means of expression may be quite different from the original reaction, as when one feels sexually aroused but ends up working out at the gym. However, in the case of substitution, the ultimate means of expression is often quite similar to the original impulse—feeling like you want to slug the boss, but joining a boxing team instead.

SUBLIMATION   Freud proposed that much of the motivation behind paintings, sculptures, and other art forms is basically generated from redirected sexual desires. The rechanneling of unconscious sexual desire is called *sublimation.* Freud emphasized the expression of sexual desires in a nonsexual, socially acceptable manner as being the prime function of sublimation, but the concept of this defense mechanism has been expanded to include the transformation of all energies associated with desires that cannot be realized. This transformation is usually constructive, and the redirection is generally useful and/or socially acceptable. For example, some people may become teachers because they have no children of their own. Similarly, aggressive, socially unacceptable tendencies may be acceptably redirected by joining the military, taking up the art of meat cutting, or even by becoming a surgeon.

DEFENSIVE IDENTIFICATION   Sometimes, as a supplement to fantasy, individuals will attempt to carry out their dreams vicariously by identifying with those who are actually engaged in the activity they only dream about. Such vicarious living would be a form of *defensive identification,* wherein people attempt to increase their own sense of self-worth by identifying with another person—for example, imitating the characteristics of a famous entertainer, television personality, or movie star.

   Defensive identification can also be used in an attempt to increase one's worth through affiliation or association. A very common example of such usage is the practice of name dropping: "Guess who I saw today?" "Of course, today I'll be having lunch with *the* Mr. Stewart; we seem to be seeing so much of each other these days!" "Senators, representatives . . . why *all* the *important* people stay at this hotel when they come here."

   Similarly, membership in, or association with, a prestigious group or organization can be used to bolster one's sense of importance. For instance, a person may feel relatively inferior before joining a particular fraternity, country club, or gang, and then feel quite superior upon becoming a member.

   Association with an institution or even a geographical location can also be used for ego enhancement. Some examples of such usage might be illustrated by such statements as "I attended Yale (Harvard, Vassar, Stanford, etc.)" or "I'm from Texas (Vermont, uptown, the city, etc.)."

RATIONALIZATION   *Rationalization* is a defense mechanism by which individuals attempt to justify their actions to themselves or others. Many people learn quite early in life that punishment or severe criticism can often be avoided if they are able to provide sufficient justification for their actions. For example, a child may justify having been in a fight by explaining that another child had called the parents a bad name. This may cause the parents to consider the otherwise punishable activity justifiable, and punishment is avoided.

Rationalization is also frequently used as a means to redeem one's actions while simultaneously protecting one's ego. Generally, there are two basic principles employed in this redemption process—they are the principles .of "sour grapes" and "sweet lemons." The sour grapes principle is employed by someone who, after several attempts, quits trying. Since being a quitter is regarded as an unacceptable quality in our society, rationalization is used to protect one's self-image. For example, people who apply for a job but are turned down repeatedly may stop trying and rationalize this behavior with comments such as "They won't hire me because I'm———— (oriental, Turkish, female, Catholic, young, etc.). Anyway, who would want to work for a bunch of bigots?"

The sweet lemons principle is generally used after one has behaved foolishly. By this means the individual attempts to sweeten an otherwise sour situation. For example, someone might have bought a car that breaks down continuously. In order to save face, the individual will rationalize the predicament with such statements as "I'm gaining a tremendous amount of knowledge from owning this car. I've learned how to repair transmissions, rear ends, water pumps, carburetors. . . ."

UNDOING   Sometimes, the evidence pointing toward a person's wrongful behavior becomes so blatant that the defense mechanism of denial is overwhelmed. Individuals in this situation then come face to face with the consequences of their actions. In some cases, the guilt and shame experienced can completely undermine the sense of self-esteem. In such cases, individuals will often turn to the use of the defense mechanism called *undoing*. The mechanism involves symbolic acts, or rituals, designed to abolish or atone for the misadventures of the past. One example of undoing might be a remorseful "rip-off" merchant contributing large sums of money to the poor. Others would be a repentant sinner administering some form of self-punishment, such as enduring severe discomfort or engaging in extreme forms of fasting, and a regretful father who neglected his own son and then becomes a Scout leader or a Big Brother.

COPING WITH STRESS EFFECTIVELY

Gordon Allport (1961) proposes that during the normal process of growing up, each individual passes through a series of developmental stages. Allport refers to these stages as "self-experiences." They are periods in which personal involvement is centered on a particular facet of the personality, such as self-identity, self-esteem, or self-image. Allport refers to one of the most important of these self-experience stages as the period in which individuals come to perceive themselves as rational copers.

It is during this period of development (six to twelve years of age) that individuals first come to fully comprehend the extent of their abilities to solve problems. During this period the promise of full autonomy is first experienced, and a sense of confidence is derived from the realization that some day one will be able to experience the freedom and independence that comes from self-reliance.

As individuals continue to mature, they develop special talents and skills that increase their ability to cope. They also acquire the knowledge, information, and experience that enable them to work out a variety of problem-solving approaches and alternative courses of action, and the ability to rule out those alternatives that are unworkable. By having learned how to cope with stress effectively, these individuals tend to acquire an air of self-confidence and self-assurance. Rational copers appear to know where they are going, how they intend to get there, and how long it is going to take.

The exact means by which mature people cope with stress may vary from individual to individual. The approaches may range from existential transcendency to behavior modification, or from self-actualization to psychoanalysis. Each in its own way provides a means of coping effectively with stress. Each is based on a set of principles, explicit or implied, that are designed to provide guidance and direction during the coping process.

Rewards of Successfully Coping with Stress

William James (1842–1910), in his book *The Will to Believe* (1897), admonished:

> Be not afraid of life. Believe that life is worth living and your belief will help create the fact. (p. 62)

This statement by James seems to be especially true with regard to the rewards of having successfully coped with stress. Perhaps at no other time does life seem so "worth living" as it does after one has surmounted the insurmountable. After having successfully coped with stress, we experience pride, a feeling of self-confidence, and a sense of independence that comes from being self-reliant.

There is also a feeling of relief, a reevaluation of our limitations and capacities, and, in many cases, a redirecting of our resources toward growing rather than merely maintaining. It is the availability of this rechanneled energy that often allows us to become more creative, more inquisitive, and more demonstrative than ever before. As a consequence, life does indeed become worth living.

Increasing Tolerance

The ability to tolerate stress is considered to be a major criterion for evaluating a person's mental health. Every time we experience a sense of accomplishment for having successfully coped with stress, our level of stress tolerance is likely to increase. With each successful experience, we gain a greater awareness of what we can deal with and, in addition, we are better able to reduce, or minimize, the stress stemming from the fear of being overwhelmed.

Such an increase in self-awareness, however, requires exposure to stress as well as practice in meeting stress. Unfortunately, many parents attempt to protect their children from the experiences of disappointment, frustration, and pressure. In so doing, they deny their children the opportunity and rewards of developing a tolerance for stress. In contrast, parents who permit their children to be exposed to the stresses of life in manageable doses, while simultaneously providing encouragement and affection, will aid in the development of their children's self-esteem and self-confidence.

The development of a high tolerance for stress also tends to minimize the importance of the numerous everyday irritants and frustrations. As our tolerance for stress increases, we come to realize that we are able to live with many of the things that needed to be changed or dealt with before. For example, little idiosyncrasies in another individual's personality may have been a source of great irritation at one time. Having gained increased tolerance, however, we consider such differences inconsequential. For instance, a husband might comment to his wife, "You know, for years it would drive me right up the wall when you'd pour milk on your cake; now, it just seems to make you all the more special . . . and lovable."

People with high stress tolerances often appear to be tension-free. This image is the result of their not getting upset over little things. They often appear to be in harmony with their environment—possessing a balanced personality. However, the truly healthy personality is not necessarily a tension-free personality, nor has the person necessarily achieved a state of psychological equilibrium. According to Frankl (1962):

> Mental health is based on a certain degree of tension, the tension between what one has already achieved and what one still ought to accomplish, or the gap between what one is and what one should become. Such a tension is inherent in the human being and therefore is indispensable to mental well-being. We should not, then, be hesitant about challenging man with a potential meaning for him to fulfill. It is only thus that we evoke his will to meaning from its state of latency. I consider it a dangerous misconception of mental hygiene to assume that what man needs in the first place is equilibrium or, as it is called in biology, "homeostasis," i.e., a tensionless state. (pp. 106–107)

Setting More Effective Goals

A great deal of the stress in people's lives is due to the frustration of having achieved goals which were substitutes for what they really wanted. Faced with the emptiness of their achievements, many people become despondent and pessimistic. Life ceases to have meaning. Without meaning, it ceases to have value. In contrast, the optimism of a person who has developed successful means of coping with stress tends to reflect Nietzsche's sentiment that "He who has a *why* for living can bear with almost any *how*."

Such optimism usually results from having sought after meaningful goals. It is the offshoot of having pursued goals that one really wanted, rather than substitutes—such goals as meaningful relationships, love, and friendship, rather than casual sex, possessions, and the development of relationships with those who might be useful.

Similarly, the successful attainment of goals in the past often creates a foundation for having hope for the future. In addition, the anticipation of fulfillment associated with hope tends to reduce anxiety and helps us to avoid the onset of despair (Korner, 1970). However, the successful individual develops faith as well as hope. This faith helps the individual to integrate experiences, making sense out of a seemingly chaotic world. The development of faith in oneself, and what one is doing, is sometimes referred to as "spirituality." Gerald Corey (1978) maintains:

> In order to keep ourselves from dying spiritually, we need to allow ourselves to imagine new ways of being, to invent new goals to live for, to search for new and more fulfilling meanings, to acquire new identities, and to reinvent our relationships with others. In essence, we need to allow parts of ourselves to die in order to experience the rebirth that is necessary for growth. (p. 299)

This type of personal growth takes courage—the courage to define goals, to actually attempt to achieve them, and to persevere under unfavorable circumstances, Rollo May, in *Man's Search for Himself* (1953), defines such courage as:

> . . . the capacity to meet the anxiety which arises as one achieves freedom. It is the willingness to differentiate, to move from the protecting realms of parental dependence to new levels of freedom and integration. The need for courage arises not only at those stages when breaks with parental protection are most obvious—such as at the birth of self-awareness, at going off to school, at adolescence, in crises of love, marriage, and the facing of ultimate death—but at every step in between as one moves from the familiar sourroundings over frontiers into the unfamiliar. (p. 224)

SUMMARY

In this chapter, the relative merits of various approaches to coping with stress were discussed. The first approach explored was the task-oriented method. This involves the measures one can take to deal with stress: (1) precautionary measures, (2) aggressive measures, and (3) adjustive measures.

The precautionary measures include the importance of anticipating what might happen, overcoming deficiencies and inadequacies before the resources are actually needed, and the need to develop a sense of responsibility.

Aggressive measures include the choice of being constructively aggressive in an effective, but socially acceptable, manner. The need to be assertive was discussed with special emphasis on Manuel Smith's bill of assertive rights.

The area of adjustive measures was approached from the perspective that it is just as important to know when to get uninvolved as it is to know when to get involved. Similarly, one must be able to objectively recognize one's limitations as well as one's capabilities, and remain flexible to change and open to reassessment.

The second approach to coping with stress is the ego-oriented method. This method emphasizes the need for protecting one's self-image rather than dealing directly with the causes of the stress. Paramount to this defense is the use of defense mechanisms, and therefore the characteristics of eighteen commonly used defense mechanisms were presented.

Finally, the importance of coping with stress effectively was investigated, with special emphasis on the need for increasing one's tolerance for stress and setting up realistic, attainable goals.

DISCUSSION QUESTIONS

1 What physical symptoms of stress do you exhibit while anxiously waiting to give a talk before a class (perspiring, dry mouth, stomach uneasiness, trembling, voice irregularities, etc.)?

2 Do you agree with the premise that humor is merely a socially acceptable way of expressing hostility?

3 Under what circumstances do you believe you are most assertive and tend to stand up for your rights?

4 What are some of the indications that a person may be involved in a mutually destructive relationship?

5 Which of the following defense mechanisms are you most likely to use with regard to taking a test that you are not prepared for: rationalization (excuses), nomadism (being absent), or apathy (not caring).

6 Which of the following defense mechanisms are you most likely to use with regard to breaking off a meaningful relationship; emotional insulation (avoiding feelings or getting involved again), substitution (rebounding to someone else), or intellectualization (thinking through the situation)?

7 Why do you believe it is so difficult for a person to adjust his or her level of aspiration downward?

8 What is your typical reaction to overly aggressive people?

9 The task-oriented person typically knows his or her limits and therefore tends to avoid excessive behavior (drinking, buying, working, etc.). Do you usually stay within your limits? When are you most likely to exceed your limits?

10 What are some of the ways in which a person can increase tolerance to stress?

EXPERIENTIAL EXERCISES

1 One of the more effective ways of coping with stress is by taking precautions against possible disasters. Arrange for a group of students to visit a local disaster control center. Have the students report on the precautions taken to avoid panic and to provide medical assistance. Report on any plans involving supportive therapy for members of a community following a disaster.

2 Have the members of a group share their vocational aspirations. Include in the discussion childhood dreams, present career ambitions, disappointments, and any adjusting of their levels of aspiration over time. What are some of the major influences which effect a person's level of aspiration?

3 People who are physically disabled or handicapped have found it necessary to cope with stress. Arrange to have a handicapped person or physical therapist appear as a guest speaker in order to share his or her experiences with stress and coping.

CHAPTER 7

INEFFECTIVE

COPING BEHAVIOR

[Nancy Hayes, Monkmeyer Press Photo Service.]

We should not try to "get rid" of a neurosis, but rather to experience what it means, what it has to teach, what its purpose is. We should even be thankful for it, otherwise we pass it by and miss the opportunity of getting to know ourselves as we really are. A neurosis is truly removed only when it has removed the false attitudes of the ego. We do not cure it—it cures us. A man is ill, but the illness is nature's attempt to heal him.

Carl Jung
Civilization in Transition

INTRODUCTION

Long before taking a course in psychology, most individuals are aware that some people are relatively hard to get along with because of certain personality characteristics, such as continuously putting off things that need to be taken care of (like bills). Sometimes the lack of compatibility stems from what seems to be a cruel streak in people who show little or no remorse for what they have done. Relationships with these people are often confusing, sordid, or exploitive, and are almost always destructive. Many such relationships involve people who could be classified as having a *character disorder*.

People with character disorders have a tendency to distort the real world by attempting to manipulate other people and situations to their own advantage. For instance, they may find it necessary to lie, cheat, or even double-cross a few people in order to get what they want, but in their minds the end usually justifies the means. For the most part, the thinking of such people is relatively narrow and egocentric. They usually think only of themselves and tend to be excessively selfish. In addition, there is usually a lack of emotional and moral maturity.

As maladapted as people with character disorders may be, they still tend to maintain contact with reality. Their reality is often grossly distorted, but they at least tend to get involved. It is different with people who could be classified as *neurotic*. The neurotic not only tends to distort reality but also attempts to avoid ever getting involved in the first place. This is done primarily because of fear: fear of being overwhelmed, fear of losing control, or merely fear of the feelings that are an integral part of life. As a consequence, out of a fear of making a mistake, neurotics avoid trying anything new, and out of a fear of getting hurt, they tend to avoid intimate relationships. Neurotics also tend to be afraid of responsibility. When things go wrong, they are likely to blame others, to justify their own behavior, or in some way to manipulate the situation to avoid blame.

For some people, even after a dedicated effort at avoiding life, interaction with other people and contact with the frustrations and stress of the real world seem inevitable. Where avoidance has failed, escape becomes necessary. Attempts to escape from what is perceived as an unacceptable world can be through such means as alcohol, psychoactive drugs, and, in many instances, psychosis. People who resort to such means tend to distort reality with delusions of grandeur or persecution. In some cases, they completely lose contact with reality and replace it with a fragmented world of hallucinations. In general, the less contact there is with reality, the less effective the coping methods will be, whether this reduction in contact is due to distorting, avoiding, or completely escaping the real world.

The exact category of coping effectiveness in which an individual might be placed can often become a matter of on which there is some disagreement. Some therapists prefer not to label people at all. However, as a guide to diagnosing behavior disorders, the American Psychiatric Association has published the *Diagnostic and Statistical Manual of Mental Disorders.* The first edition appeared in 1952 (DSM-I). A revised edition was published in 1968 (DSM-II), and a third revision appeared in 1978 (DSM-III).

DSM-III was developed to bring about a higher level of reliability in specific diagnosis. Preliminary studies indicate that greater consistency in diagnosis is achieved with the procedures presented in DSM-III than with those in DSM-II (Spitzer, Endicott, and Robins, 1975). Rather than merely placing people into broad categories (paranoia, depressive neurosis, etc.) or into subgroups (catatonic or hebephrenic-type schizophrenia, etc.), as was often true of DSM-II, the DSM-III offers an evaluation of the individual along five axes:

1 *Clinical psychiatric syndrome(s),* such as organic mental disorders, drug-use disorders, schizophrenic disorders, paranoid disorders, anxiety disorders, dissociative disorders, and psychosexual disorders
2 *Personality disorders* (adults) and *specific development disorders* (children and adolescents), such as paranoid, introverted, antisocial, dependent, compulsive, and passive-aggressive disorders
3 *Physical disorders:* clinical problems of a nonmental nature that could contribute to the mental condition, such as neurological damage, diabetes, and malnutrition
4 *Severity of psychosocial stressors:* rating of the intensity of environmental stress, such as mild (argument with a neighbor), severe (bankruptcy), catastrophic (internment in a concentration camp)
5 *Highest level of adaptive functioning in past year:* an estimation of adaptive functioning in social relations, occupation, and use of leisure, along a continuum including designations as grossly impaired, poor, fair, good, very good, and superior

Because DSM-II has been the accepted standard since 1968, however, the majority of references and terms currently appearing in psychological literature, as well as in communications between most psychologists and physicians, are based on the criteria set forth in that manual. Therefore, for the sake of familiarity, and in order to facilitate understanding, the terminology and classifications in this chapter will be based on DSM-II.

DISTORTING REALITY

Crucial to the development of effective coping behavior is the ability to perceive reality accurately. An individual must be able to distinguish between the real and the imagined, and also between what is consciously motivated and what is unconsciously motivated. People who are unable to distinguish between reality and fantasy are said to be *psychotic*. People who are driven by anxieties and compulsions for which they have no logical explanation are often considered to be *neurotic*. In the first situation, the individual has completely lost contact with reality. In the second situation, the individual is merely avoiding reality by repressing it. In either case, such ineffective coping behaviors tend to be inappropriate and self-defeating.

There are, however, those persons whose maladaptive behavior is not so much self-defeating as it is *other-defeating*. In other words, such people are likely to cause more difficulties for others than for themselves. People who persistently victimize others are sometimes referred to as having *personality disorders*.

Personality Disorders

Personality disorders tend to distort reality to fit a need. Consequently, other people who happen to come in contact with someone who has a personality disorder are likely to become the victims of a lifelong pattern of social maladjustment. Unlike the neurotic, who is often caught up with internal conflicts, anxiety, and guilt, the individual with a personality disorder usually remains relatively free of such symptoms, while simultaneously creating numerous problems for others.

Another important factor that distinguishes personality disorders from neurosis and psychosis is that personality disorders are primarily the result of *faulty personality development*. Neurotic reactions, on the other hand, are often the result of attempts to adapt to environmental stress. In contrast to individuals who have learned to repress undesirable thoughts and impulses, individuals with a personality disorder have learned to act out such conflicts.

According to the *Diagnostic and Statistical Manual of Mental Disorders*, second edition (DSM II, 1968), "This group of disorders is characterized by maladaptive patterns of behavior," and "generally, these are lifelong patterns, often recognizable by the time of adolescence . . . " (p. 41). Typically, such behavior patterns tend to interfere with interpersonal relationships much more than with school or job performance, although these areas too can often be affected because of the inability to interact effectively with others.

Since the range of behavior exhibited in personality disorders is quite extensive, the entire repertoire of classification will not be presented here. Some of the most frequently encountered personality disorders are discussed in the following sections.

Passive-Aggressive Personality

One of the most outstanding characteristics of the passive-aggressive personality is the tendency to *procrastinate*. Procrastination provides an effective means of expressing hostility in a covert manner. In other words, the individual has found that people are less likely to express anger or criticism over what has not been done than over what has been done. This is especially true when the person appears outwardly sincere, charming, and agreeable, as the passive-aggressive individual often does. For example, a husband may put off doing the chores around the house (fixing the sink, painting a door, or repairing an appliance). As a result, the wife accuses him of being lazy and reminds him of how he is always "going to get to it someday." The husband apologizes profusely, is very understanding of the wife's needs, and renews his promise to take care of his responsibilities. He then continues to procrastinate. This behavior is extremely frustrating for the wife, often creating a severely stressful situation. Of course, not every husband who puts off repairing a sticking door is a passive-aggressive personality. However, when such behavior is an integral part of a person's lifestyle, unconscious hostility can be suspected.

Passive-aggressive personalities are generally uncooperative, negative, and contrary. Such obstructionism is characteristic of their attempts to thwart the efforts or ambitions of others. This type of person will typically remain uninvolved—the nonviolent nonoffender who "accidentally" breaks something of value, "forgets" to take care of responsibilities, or is consistently late. For example, the passive-aggressive person may "accidentally" break a string on someone else's guitar while trying to tune it, may "forget" to relay an important message to a roommate, or may be "unavoidably" late to pick up a friend on the day of an exam.

Usually, after prolonged exposure to such exasperating manipulations, the victims will begin to present ultimatums, stating that they don't want to hear any more excuses, that they want to see a change in the person's reliability or the relationship will be ended. Such a threat can be very upsetting to passive-aggressive individuals, for they are usually very dependent and are unable to effectively cope with rejection. Many times, the person threatened with rejection will attempt to placate the complainer with explanations, such as "I'm doing the best I can," while continuing to be slow and inefficient. When friends suggest ways in which the individual's performance might be improved, he or she will often become stubborn and sullen and will often withdraw and sulk over the lack of appreciation being displayed.

Paranoid Personality

One of the most outstanding characteristics of persons with paranoid personalities is their tendency to be *insanely jealous*. This unfounded jealousy is usually directed toward members of the opposite sex and expressed verbally through threatening statements like "Don't you ever let me catch you with another man/woman, or so help me, I'll. . . ." Nonverbal threats are usually made through the use of limited physical abuse, such as grabbing, restraining, or slapping, the implication being that such abuse is only a sample of what could happen.

Such jealousy is based on unwarranted suspicions and a general distrust of everyone (Million, 1969). Individuals with a paranoid personality will often manipulate the direction of a conversation in an attempt to trap the victim in a lie or contradiction. For example, such an individual may ask, "Did you come straight home today?" The victim may answer, "Yes, dear." The trap is sprung with "Then why is that bag of groceries on the table? You lied about coming straight home, didn't you? Where else did you go before you decided to come home?"

It is not uncommon for an individual with a paranoid personality to become involved with minute details, needing to know another's every move. This person may habitually check the odometer of the car and make elapsed-time runs from one location to another to monitor the movements of the victim. As a consequence, interpersonal relationships with a paranoid-type personality tend to be restrictive and often suffocating.

Since the person with a paranoid personality is usually very attentive, many people are initially flattered by this need "to know all about you." As time passes, this exaggerated attention is seen more and more to be invasion of privacy, a stifling possessiveness. Consequently, the victims of a paranoid personality will often attempt to assert their independence in order to get some breathing room. Having an inflated feeling of self-importance, however, paranoid personalities are extremely sensitive to any slights. They may become highly emotional, explaining that only love and concern are behind the actions. The paranoid will usually apologize for being overly protective and promise to control that jealousy in the future, but usually within a short period of time the suspicion returns.

Obsessive-Compulsive Personality

Obsessive-compulsive personalities are characterized by a tendency toward rigid conformity, orderliness, and a strict adherence to the dictates of their conscience. An individual with this type of personality is perfectionistic and often obsessed with cleanliness and hygiene. Everything must be neat and orderly. A great deal of energy is devoted to petty details.

This commitment to detail often interferes with the establishment of close, enduring relationships. The person with an obsessive-compulsive personality tends to be intolerant of those who are less meticulous. As a result, many people find themselves feeling frustrated over what they perceive as unwarranted pettiness. For example, an obsessive-compulsive roommate may complain about somebody having moved one of the pencils on his or her desk, may disturb others by periodically "disinfecting" the air with an aerosol spray, or may get on the nerves of others by continuously arranging the books in the room according to size.

This intolerance, along with a general lack of flexibility and adaptability and a tendency to adhere strictly to rules, procedures, and rigid schedules, usually makes the person with an obsessive-compulsive personality unsuitable for jobs in a supervisory position. Although such a person is usually reliable and efficient, those who work under this type of person are seldom capable of living up to the unreasonable expectations demanded of them. In addition, interpersonal relationships often lack warmth and are usually maintained at an informal level—proper, objective, and socially correct.

Antisocial Personality

For the person who has developed a reasonably mature set of values, i.e., a strong conscience, and who has been able to adjust to the social demands of civilization, the lifestyle of the antisocial personality may appear incomprehensible. Commonly referred to as a sociopathic personality, this type of person has failed to achieve a "normal" level of moral, ethical, or social development and represents a generalized threat to society. As defined by the DSM II (1968), the term "antisocial personality":

> . . . is reserved for individuals who are basically unsocialized and whose behavior pattern brings them repeatedly into conflict with society. They are incapable of significant loyalty to individuals, groups, or social values. They are grossly selfish, callous, irresponsible, impulsive, and unable to feel guilt or to learn from experience and punishment. Frustration tolerance is low. They tend to blame others or offer plausible rationalizations for their behavior. (p. 43)

The sociopath is apparently unable to control impulses, regardless of their nature. As a consequence, aggressive or sexual impulses require *immediate* gratification with little regard for the consequences of such a discharge. Should such gratification involve breaking the law or some other deviant behavior, which results in the sociopath's arrest, there is little or no feeling of remorse. Similarly, punishment seems to have no effect on preventing the person from repeating the criminal activity.

Although people with antisocial personalities often engage in activities that are against the law, they are usually not successful at being professional criminals because of the impulsive, unplanned nature of most of the crimes committed. "Normal" criminals often have a goal to work toward, exhibit rational behavior, and avoid being caught whenever possible (Cleckley, 1964). In contrast, sociopaths often have no goal in mind other than to satisfy the current urge, often lie even when telling the truth would be easier, and steal things for which they have no use, displaying little or no concern over possible apprehension.

This lack of concern, along with the absence of anxiety over the consequences of their behavior, tends to be present in all aspects of sociopaths' lives. Other people are seen as convenient sources of gratification, to be exploited whenever possible. Having no scruples, sociopaths are chronic liars, and they will use any means of deception possible if it will satisfy their immediate needs—"conning" seems to come naturally.

Perhaps this trait has developed over years of practice, for most individuals with antisocial personalities begin exhibiting such tendencies early in life. In fact, the severity of antisocial behavior during childhood is one of the most reliable predictors of adult sociopathy (Robins, 1966). Typically, these individuals were unwanted children, were neglected as they grew, received little or no structuring, and had few if any limits placed on their behavior. Delinquency, truancy, and excessive use of alcohol or drugs comes early. Deviant sexual behavior, such as rape, and wanton destructiveness, including

Caution is an example of how
one can cope with fear gradually
to keep from being
overwhelmed. [*Erika Stone.*]

FIGURE 7.1

arson, is also relatively common. Interpersonal relationships tend to be
exploitive, fidelity is nonexistent, and divorce, separation, or abandonment is
the most frequent outcome of marriage. Close association with a sociopath for
any extended length of time usually means getting "ripped off" in some form or
another—double-crossed, deceived, becoming a victim of theft, or just being
"played for a sucker."

AVOIDING REALITY

Perhaps everyone, at one time or another, has wished that the weighty
problems of life would simply go away. If we could, we would like to just put a
box over our problems and never have to deal with them again—literally
believing in that old saying, "Out of sight, out of mind." In the real world,
however, most of us come to realize that the problems don't really go away,

and that attempts to cover them up merely postpone the time when we will ultimately have to deal with them.

However, there are some individuals who seem to be unable to deal with certain problems at any time in their lives. Being unable to effectively cope with persistent problems can lead to a wide range of maladaptive behavior patterns, most of which tend to be self-defeating and emotionally disabling. Coupled with the constant fear of being overwhelmed by what seem to be unsolvable problems, many of these individuals develop feelings of insecurity, inadequacy, and inferiority. A cycle of personal failure followed by self-criticism often leads to a lifestyle of self-fulfilling prophecies. The very problem these individuals wish to avoid becomes the dominating factor in their everyday lives, as when a person who fears rejection consistently behaves in a way that literally invites rejection. In a sense, due to a preoccupation with trying to avoid that which really bothers them, these people become their own worst enemies. Sir Thomas Browne (1605–1682) once said: "But how shall we expect charity towards others, when we are uncharitable to ourselves? *Charity begins at home,* is the voice of the world; yet is every man his greatest enemy, and, as it were, his own executioner."

Psychophysiological Illness

Most of us have experienced a close call while driving, narrowly avoiding an accident—that frightening moment when the heart pounds, the muscles tense, the stomach flips, and the adrenalin goes shooting through the bloodstream. At that moment, we are experiencing our physiological reactions to stress, a defensive reaction that is directed by the brain through the autonomic nervous system.

Such reactions are in themselves stressful, and the muscles, blood vessels, and organs affected can tolerate this degree of activation for only short periods of time. When stress persists over long periods of time, biological systems may begin to break down. This often results in the development of psychosomatic illnesses. In other words, the adage is true—a person can literally be worried sick.

It is important to realize that psychosomatic illnesses (from the Greek words *psyche* meaning "mind," and *soma* meaning "body") are *real* illnesses. They are not to be confused with *hypochondriacal neurosis,* which is a condition characterized by a preoccupation with, or fear of, diseases despite good physical health. According to the DSM II, psychophysiological disorders are a:

> . . . group of disorders characterized by physical symptoms that are caused by emotional factors and involve a single organ system, usually under autonomic nervous system innervation. The physiological changes involved are those that normally accompany certain emotional states, but in these disorders the changes are more intense and sustained. The individual may not be consciously aware of his emotional state. (p. 46)

Similarly, psychophysiological reactions are not to be confused with *conversion reactions,* wherein anxiety is converted into physical symptoms such as blindness, deafness, anesthesia, and paralysis. James Butcher (1971) differentiates between these reactions by making the following distinctions:

PSYCHOPHYSIOLOGIC REACTIONS	NEUROTIC CONVERSION REACTIONS
1 Involve organs and viscera innervated by the autonomic nervous system, which is *not* under full voluntary control of the patient.	1 Can involve any system or organ. Almost any disease can be simulated.
2 Symptoms are physiological and involve actual physical or structural problems that can threaten life.	2 Symptoms are frequently symbolic and involve no physiological basis.
3 Symptoms fail to alleviate anxiety and can lead to increased anxiety.	3 Symptoms dissipate anxiety, and the patient can be described as having *la belle indifférence.*
4 Treatment deals with the physical problem (for example, surgery for ulcers) *and* psychotherapy.	4 Treatment is entirely psychological.

Source: James Butcher (1971, p. 37).

The American Psychiatric Association (1968) subclassifies the psychophysiological disorders in accordance with the specific organ or system which is predominantly affected. For instance, ailments classified under *skin disorders* include neurodermatitis, psoriasis, eczema, and hives. *Musculoskeletal disorders* include rheumatoid arthritis, backaches, and muscle cramps. *Respiratory* disorders refer to ailments such as bronchial asthma, hyperventilation, and persistent hiccups. *Gastrointestinal disorders* include peptic and duodenal ulcers, colitis, anorexia nervosa (loss of appetite), and diarrhea or constipation. *Cardiovascular disorders* cover ailments such as hypertension (high blood pressure), vascular spasms, Reynold's syndrome (poor circulation), and migraines. It is important to keep in mind, however, that although illnesses in these systems *can be* psychosomatic, or emotionally generated, they can also be, and often are, the result of disease or other biological causes.

Why one particular organ or system is affected and not another is not fully understood. Some investigators believe that biological predispositions provide for individual differences in emotional response patterns, such as blood pressure (Hodapp et al., 1975) or heart rates (Lacey, 1967). Others maintain that organ susceptibility is a result of prior infections (Rees, 1964). Another theoretical position proposes that individual personality characteristics might influence the specific nature of the psychosomatic illness. For example, a person who suffers from ulcers is likely to feel deprived and revengeful, a person with hypertension usually feels threatened and apprehensive, asthma-prone individuals often feel alienated, and those with severe acne usually feel persecuted (Graham et al., 1962).

Neurotic Reactions

Although the term "neurotic reaction" refers to a wide range of maladaptive behavior patterns, there is one identifying characteristic that permeates all levels of neurotic coping—the element of *fear*. However, since the fear exists in the absence of real danger, it is referred to as *anxiety*. The anxiety experienced in most neurotic reactions is of a free-floating nature. It is not consciously attached to any one specific source.

For the most part, the maladaptive behavior patterns of neurosis are designed to reduce this anxiety and to protect the individual's ego, or self-image, from further devaluation. Characteristically, neurotics tend to maintain a relatively poor appraisal of their worth. There is usually a lack of self-confidence and an excessive need for approval from others. In a sense, the neurotic is saying, "I know I'm a failure, what I do is insignificant, and I'm unworthy of affection, but would you please love me anyway?"

This quest for approval and affection is approached in a universal, no-exceptions-made attitude. As a consequence, rejecting someone or being rejected by someone is to be avoided at all costs. The usual result of such an approach is inability to cope with, or to adequately express, feelings of hostility. Subsequently, such feelings are often displaced, resulting in poor or erratic work patterns and in difficulties with social or interpersonal relationships.

The neurotic, although severely handicapped, is usually not completely disabled. The person who is neurotic exists more on the level of the walking wounded. Unlike the psychotic, the neurotic experiences no gross distortions of reality, no hallucinations or delusions, and no severe personality disintegration. However, the neurotic does lack ego strength, is highly vulnerable to stress, and is generally unable to cope effectively with inner conflicts. Although neurotics may have some insight as to the inappropriateness of their behavior, they also display a persistent generalized feeling of helplessness about being able to change familiar coping patterns. In order to present a few of the more specific behavior patterns exhibited in neurotic reactions, some of the most common types of neurosis are discussed in the following sections.

ANXIETY NEUROSIS   Although anxiety plays an important part in all forms of neurosis, nowhere is it so evident, so dominant, as it is in the case of an anxiety neurosis. The anxiety is usually chronic in that it has been present for a long period of time, often for years. In such cases, the individual will usually have developed the habit of finding excuses for being so anxious, so worried, or so constantly on edge. For example, a student experiencing an anxiety neurosis might attempt to excuse the anxiety as being a natural consequence of an impending exam. However, after taking the exam, the student is then worried about the score; after receiving the score, the student is worried about how the score will affect the final grade; after getting the grade, the student is concerned about the grade point average and its effect on graduate school; and so on, ad infinitum.

However, the excuses, by definition, are not the true source of the anxiety.

This factor helps to explain why the anxiety persists even though the perceived threat no longer exists. One of the earliest explanations of the true reasons for such anxiety was presented by Pavlov (1928). He was conducting research in the area of classical conditioning and discrimination, wherein dogs learned to salivate when a circle was presented, but not to salivate when an ellipse was presented. In order to test the limits of the ability of dogs to discriminate, the shape of the ellipse was gradually distorted to more closely resemble a circle. As the ellipse was made more and more circular, a point was reached at which the dogs could no longer discriminate between the two stimuli. At this point, the dogs became emotionally upset and demonstrated what is referred to as "experimental neurosis." Similar results were demonstrated by H. S. Liddell (1944) and W. H. Gantt (1944). It is believed that humans experience a similar form of emotional stress when they are expected to perform a discrimination task that is too fine. One of the most common examples of such a task occurs when a person is presented with a form of double-binding, or "multiple-message" communication. For example, when a child puts his or her arms around a parent only to feel the parent stiffen, the child reacts by pulling back, and the parent then criticizes the insincerity of the aborted hug with such statements as "That wasn't much of a hug. Why don't you give me a real hug?" The child is then faced with trying to discriminate between the nonverbal message, "Don't hug me," and the parent's verbal message, "Hug me." In such cases, the discrimination task may be too fine, resulting in the creation of high anxiety.

Some propose that anxiety is not a matter of conditioning and discrimination problems, but is learned from observing the stress reactions of others (Bandura, 1969). Others point at intrapsychic conflicts—disharmony between the super ego and the id—as the primary source of anxiety (Freud, 1963). Regardless of the theoretical cause, however, the victim of anxiety is faced with living with an almost constant feeling of foreboding and dread. The tension associated with such stress can often lead to somatic complaints, such as muscle aches, indigestion, and insomnia. When the level of anxiety increases dramatically, the victim can experience what is called an "acute anxiety attack," or a state of panic. An attack of this nature can incapacitate an individual to such a degree that normal responsibilities alone are overwhelming. Symptomatic of such a state is a pounding heart, trembling, profuse sweating, and an inability to concentrate, followed by a feeling of utter exhaustion when the attack is over.

PHOBIC REACTION   As in the case of an anxiety neurosis, there is also an element of intense anxiety present in the *phobic neurosis*. In both cases, the anxiety is experienced in the absence of real danger. Unlike the free-floating, nonspecific nature of the anxiety experienced in an anxiety neurosis, the fear in a phobic neurosis, is specific to a particular stimulus or situation. Due to the specific nature of the fear, phobias are often defined by a specific term, such as "claustrophobia" (fear of small, closed places), "agoraphobia" (fear of open places), "acrophobia" (fear of high places), "mysophobia" (fear of germs), "nyctophobia" (fear of darkness), and "ochlophobia" (fear of crowds).

Generally speaking, "phobia" can refer to a fear of anything as long as that fear is intense enough to interfere with a person's everyday functioning. However, some restrict the use of the term to those fears which are (1) irrational, (2) displaced, and (3) based on shame or guilt. According to these criteria, it would not be irrational to have a fear of guns after being shot with one, but it would be considered irrational to have a fear of brass doorknobs, at least if you had never been harmed by one. Similarly, having a fear of guns would not be a displaced fear, for it is the gun that is feared, whereas the fear of remembering something terrible that happened in a room that had brass doorknobs would be an example of displacement. In addition, one would not necessarily associate guilt or shame with having been shot, but if a person had been sexually abused as a child, there is a high probability that feelings of shame or guilt would be associated with such an experience.

Most theories dealing with the cause of phobias lean toward an acceptance of the fact that a phobia represents a displacement of anxiety from its real source to some symbolic substitute. The actual dynamics of this displacement, however, vary with the theory. For instance, in 1909, Freud described the classic case of a five-year-old boy called "Little Hans" who was unable to leave the house because of a phobic fear of horses. Freud proposed that Little Hans's fear of horses was actually a displaced fear of castration, which was unconsciously associated with his father.

Disagreeing with the Freudian approach, Watson and Rayner (1920), in another historic case, demonstrated how phobic reactions are apparently the result of classical conditioning and the phenomenon of generalization. During the course of their research, a small child called "Little Albert" was classically conditioned to fear a white rabbit by pairing the rabbit with a loud, frightening noise. Because of the process of generalization, Little Albert came to have a phobic fear of anything white and furry. As a result of these findings, Watson and Rayner concluded that the same kind of learning process is involved in the development of father-phobic reactions.

It has been found that most phobic reactions respond quite favorably to *counterconditioning,* a procedure based on the belief in the learning theory approach to the development of phobias. Counterconditioning involves the replacement of the old fear response with a new, more desirable response through the process of associating the old anxiety-evoking stimulus with something positive. For example, speaking before a group of people (once feared) may be associated with approval, fame, and fortune.

Equally effective in ridding people of phobias is the process of *desensitization.* In this process the old fear response becomes extinct as the person learns to relax while gradually progressing through a hierarchy of anxiety-evoking stimuli. For example, a person might eliminate a fear of snakes by learning to remain relaxed while looking at a picture of a snake, then while watching a snake in a cage across the room, then on a table with the cover on, then with the cover off, then putting a hand on the glass, and finally touching the snake.

OBSESSIVE-COMPULSIVE NEUROSIS   The anxiety experienced by people who manifest the symptoms of an obsessive-compulsive neurosis is generally thought to stem from their fear that they would either start thinking some unacceptable thought if they were not preoccupied with the obsessive thought or would be doing something unacceptable if not constantly engaged in some form of compulsive behavior.

The obsessive thoughts are usually spontaneously recurring words, ideas, or impulses that persist in dominating a person's thinking. On a minor scale, almost everyone has experienced the irritation of having a particularly catchy tune repeatedly come to mind or of finding it almost impossible to stop thinking about some "dumb jingle" from a radio or television commercial. However, unlike people with pathological obsessions, most of us are eventually able to put such thoughts out of our minds and to continue with our daily routines. For the obsessive-compulsive, however, there is no such relief. Their mental activities are dominated by thoughts of hitting someone, of deviant sexual acts, or dwelling on death.

Similarly, most of us have experienced the need to wash our hands, stick to a schedule, or perform some good luck ritual before engaging in certain activities. However, for obsessive-compulsive individuals, the compulsion to wash is usually seen as the *only* way to reduce anxiety. Rather than merely sticking to a routine, they are overwhelmed by uncontrollable urges to perform certain acts in a specific sequential pattern, accompanied by a feeling that something terrible would happen should any portion of the sequence be omitted. In addition, certain rituals, such as dressing and undressing, arranging items in a room, or continuously checking to see if the windows and doors are locked often take on a magical quality and must be carried out in order to ward off evil or bad luck.

DEPRESSIVE NEUROSIS   As long as the intensity and duration of the emotional experience are appropriate to the situation and expressed within certain limits, there is nothing inherently wrong with being depressed, any more than there is anything wrong with being angry or disappointed. The appropriateness and limitations set on expressions of depression are usually established by the individual's particular society or subculture, thereby providing outlets for the grief, sadness, and remorse that follow severe personal losses. A person experiencing a depressive neurosis usually exceeds these arbitrary limits. For example, it is considered appropriate to feel sad and disappointed for a short period of time after receiving a poor report card, but to remain deeply depressed throughout the entire summer could be considered excessive and thus symptomatic of a depressive neurosis.

Some forms of stress, such as a personal failure, financial loss, or the death of someone close, will usually precipitate the onset of a depressive reaction. In such cases, the individual tends to feel overwhelmed by the circumstances, personally responsible for the disaster, and helpless to do anything about it. In fact, the sense of helplessness appears to be an important factor in the development of a depressive neurosis. Klein and Seligman (1976) found that depressed individuals demonstrated the same degree of helplessness and acceptance of the inevitable as did a group of subjects who had learned helplessness by being exposed to unsolvable escape problems.

One of the most frequently encountered causes of depressive neurosis is a breakup, separation, or divorce between two individuals who had formerly

Depressive reactions often appear to be a consequence of inability to control the intensity and duration of one's experience of grief. [*Elias Baitel, Rapho/Photo Researchers, Inc.*]

FIGURE 7.2

been involved in a significant relationship. At first, there is usually a period of protest and denial, which is often expressed by such statements as "This can't be happening," or "This can't be happening to *me!*" Frequently, a period of despondency follows, usually accompanied by grief of a greater intensity than would normally be expected. The individual seems unable to overcome strong feelings of dejection and apathy. Feelings of guilt, self-deprecation, and self-reproach soon follow, expressed by statements like "It's all my fault," "No one could ever put up with me for long," or "I'm no good for anybody or anything." Along with a general loss of interest, restricted thinking, and withdrawal from friends and family, suicidal thoughts and behavior will often appear during this period. Attempts at suicide are often interpreted as attempts to reaffirm a belief that someone cares whether or not the person lives or dies. However, in many cases, there is apparently a complete loss of the will to go on living; suicide is merely seen as a means of ending an otherwise hopeless situation (Leonard, 1974).

Suicide

Rollo May (1958) quoted a person undergoing therapy as saying, "I know only two things—one, that I will be dead someday, two, that I am not dead now. The only question is what shall I do between those two points" (p. 90). The meaninglessness of life which is implied in that statement illustrates the alienation, aimlessness, and boredom many people are faced with in today's society. Similarly, Maddi (1967) talks of an epidemic of "existential neurosis," wherein people continue to go through the motions of living aimlessly without experiencing any sense of purpose or significance. For many, as life loses its meaning and becomes more unlivable, the only alternative seemingly available is escape from life itself—suicide.

Although suicide is not necessarily associated with neurotic or psychotic depression, those who have been diagnosed as such have a suicide rate that is thirty-six times as great as the general population (Pokorny, 1964). Similar research has shown that among those who committed suicide, 80 percent had been depressed prior to the fatal act (Baraclough et al., 1969). In another investigation, 94 percent had episodes of serious depression prior to the suicide (Robins et al., 1959). Strange as it may seem, most suicides occur during the period of improvement immediately following a depression (the first three months)—a period during which a person may appear to have recovered from the depression. It seems that it is during this period that depressed people are able to generate enough energy to carry out their suicidal intentions.

With over 30,000 people committing suicide each year, suicide is ranked among the top ten causes of death in the United States. Among people between the ages of fifteen and twenty-four, it is ranked second, surpassed only by death from automobile accidents. However, the suicide rate among teenagers is only about 5 per 100,000 for females and 10 per 100,000 for males. The rate among those over seventy years of age is approximately 23 per 100,000 for females, and 60 per 100,000 for males (Green, 1973). Some researchers suggest that the reasons for the rate increase with age seem to be linked to greater opportunities to be exposed to (1) loneliness, loss of loved ones, and breakup of important relationships; (2) health problems; (3) failure; and (4) bitterness and the need for revenge (Farberow and McEroy, 1966; Colson, 1973).

The first suicide prevention center in the United States was founded in Los Angeles in 1958, by Edwin Shneidman and Norman Farberow. They attempt (1970) to classify people who commit suicide in four categories. The categories are based on the type of reasoning which occurs prior to the suicide. One type of thinking is referred to as "catalogic" thinking. This is characterized by extreme depression, feelings of despair, and hopelessness. The individual is usually lonely, fearful, and pessimistic and may have recently suffered a loss of prestige through the loss of a job or a loss of affection through the loss of a loved one.

A second type of suicidal thinking is called the "logical" type. It is often associated with someone facing a terminal illness, severe disability, or great physical pain. Usually, the person displaying this type of thinking does not wish to be a burden on others or to undergo the psychological or physiological deterioration that appears to be inevitable.

A third type of suicidal thinking is associated with strong religious or cultural beliefs. It is referred to by Shneidman as "contaminated" thinking. The person displaying this thinking preceives death as a transition to another life or spiritual level or as a means of saving face.

The fourth type of thinking is called "paleologic." It is generally used only in reference to those who are psychotic. Due to hallucinations and/or delusions, such individuals are often compelled to end their lives as a means of atonement for imaginary misdeeds or inherent evil.

ESCAPING FROM REALITY

Although our coping patterns and techniques are usually acquired early in life, the relative effectiveness of these coping methods is often not fully recognized until adolescence. As the individual reaches puberty, the dreams of childhood begin to fade and the fantasies of adulthood beckon from a future that is still somewhat distant. Achieving self-acceptance during this period seems essential in developing a healthy self-image and achieving full emotional maturity.

Those of us who are mature will usually accept that we are all less than we would like to be. Many people, however, find themselves unable to accept a self-image that is short of perfection. This lack of acceptance often results in a wholesale rejection of what they *are* in preference to a fictional ideal of what they *should be*. This difference between what might be and what is often leads to a lifestyle based on self-deception, restricted thinking, and uncontrollable impulses—a lifestyle based on escapism.

In some cases, the escape involves a physical running away. For many, however, the escape involves the use of drugs as a means of avoiding the inevitable pain and frustration that is so much a part of life. Others escape into madness, which R. D. Laing defines as "a special sort of strategy that a person invents in order to live in an unlivable situation" (1964, p. 187).

Alcoholism

In the United States, 66 percent of the population over fifteen years of age drink alcoholic beverages on certain occasions, 58 percent drink at least once a month, and 10 percent drink more than one ounce of absolute alcohol per day—that is, the equivalent of two mixed drinks or two glasses of wine or two cans of beer every day (U.S. DHEW, 1974). Eighty percent of the men and 60 percent of the women over twenty-one drink alcoholic beverages, or approximately 100 million adults (Channing, 1971). This makes alcohol one of the most heavily used and abused drugs in our society. One in ten users, or approximately 10 million people, become alcoholics.

DEFINING ALCOHOLISM   The exact number of alcoholics in the United States varies with what is accepted as a definition of alcoholism. If one defines an alcoholic as anyone who has a problem with drinking, then the number jumps to about one-third of the drinkers, or over 35 million. According to the National

Institute on Alcohol Abuse and Alcoholism (1974), a problem drinker is someone who exhibits one or more of the following characteristics:

1 Must drink in order to cope with life.
2 Frequently drinks to intoxication.
3 Goes to work intoxicated or drinks on the job.
4 Drives while intoxicated.
5 Get injured as a result of being intoxicated.
6 Is out of character while intoxicated.

Some investigators of alcoholism distinguish between problem drinkers and alcoholics. They tend to rely on the definition of alcoholism presented in the *Diagnostic and Statistical Manual of Mental Disorders* (1968), which provides the following categorization:

303 Alcoholism

This category is for patients whose alcohol intake is great enough to damage their physical health, or their personal or social functioning, or when it has become a prerequisite to normal functioning.

303.0 Episodic excessive drinking. If alcoholism is present and the individual becomes intoxicated as frequently as four times a year. . . . Intoxication is defined as a state in which the individual's coordination or speech is definitely impaired or his behavior is clearly altered.

303.1 Habitual excessive drinking. This diagnosis is given to persons who are alcoholic and who either become intoxicated more than 12 times a year or are recognizably under the influence of alcohol more than once a week, even though not intoxicated.

303.2 Alcohol addiction. This condition should be diagnosed when there is direct or strong presumptive evidence that the patient is dependent on alcohol. If available, the best direct evidence of such dependence is the appearance of withdrawal symptoms. The inability of the patient to go one day without drinking is presumptive evidence. When heavy drinking continues for three months or more it is reasonable to presume addiction to alcohol has been established. (p. 45)

One of the simplest definitions of alcoholism is provided by Alcoholics Anonymous (AA). According to AA, alcoholics are people who are "powerless over alcohol" and, as a result of drinking, have found their lives "unmanageable." As a means of checking whether or not a person may have a drinking problem, AA (1954) has compiled a list of twelve questions concerning drinking habits and their effect on one's daily life. The experience of AA indicates that anyone who answers "yes" to four or more of these twelve questions has definite alcoholic tendencies:

1 Have you ever tried to stop drinking for a week (or longer), only to fall short of your goal?
2 Do you resent the advice of others who try to get you to stop drinking?
3 Have you ever tried to control your drinking by switching from one alcoholic beverage to another?

4 Have you taken a morning drink during the past year?
5 Do you envy people who can drink without getting into trouble?
6 Has your drinking problem become progressively more serious during the past year?
7 Has your drinking created problems at home?
8 At social affairs where drinking is limited, do you try to obtain "extra" drinks?
9 Despite evidence to the contrary, have you continued to assert that you can stop drinking "on your own" whenever you wish?
10 During the past, have you missed time from work as a result of drinking?
11 Have you ever "blacked out" during your drinking?
12 Have you ever felt you could do more with your life if you did not drink?

TEENAGERS AND ALCOHOL   Most people envision the typical alcoholic as a "skid row bum." In reality, however, only about 3 to 5 percent of alcoholics live such a lifestyle. In fact, it is this very misperception that allows so many cases of alcoholism to pass as social drinking.

The truth is that alcoholism strikes people from all walks of life, regardless of age, sex, socioeconomic level, race, or nationality. In contrast to the image of the old drunk, alcoholism has become a major problem among the teenagers in today's society. Alcohol has become the drug of choice among adolescents (Hartford, 1975). About half of all young people have tried alcohol by the time they are fourteen; 80 to 85 percent have tried it by the time they are eighteen, and approximately 5 percent drink until they are intoxicated at least once a month (Hornick and Myles, 1975). The alcohol abuse problem, however, does not necessarily begin with teenagers. Reports of ten- to twelve-year-old elementary-school children having drinking problems are becoming commonplace. Current investigations indicate that the present generation is starting earlier and drinking more than the previous one (Ottenberg, 1975).

Although there are numerous reasons why young people drink, the reason most frequently given is *peer pressure* and the desire to conform. Due to immaturity, the young also tend to accept all challenges and take advantage of any opportunity to show off. This practice has often resulted in the death of participants engaging in "chug-a-lug" and other drinking contests. In addition, since drinking alcoholic beverages is usually perceived as something adults do, some teenagers will drink in order to enhance their self-image, feel grown up and important, or strengthen the impression of their own masculinity or femininity. Drinking is also seen by many teenagers as a means of expressing rebelliousness toward the dictates of adults in general, and their parents in particular. Paradoxically, many parents express relief that their son or daughter is *only* drinking alcohol and is not involved in drugs.

Aside from the physical, intellectual, and social problems it causes, teenage drinking is also the number-one killer of our youth. Over 8000 people between fifteen and twenty-five years of age die each year in alcohol-related accidents. Nationwide, half of all highway deaths involve alcohol, and it is estimated that drivers who have chronic drinking problems are responsible for two-thirds of these deaths. In addition, half of all homicides and one-third of all suicides can be linked with alcohol abuse (National Institute on Alcohol Abuse, 1974).

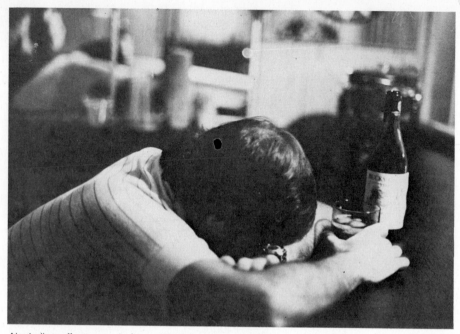

FIGURE 7.3   Alcoholism affects people from all walks of life, regardless of age, sex, socioeconomic level, race, or nationality. It is indiscriminately destructive. [*Rita Freed, Nancy Palmer Photo Agency.*]

PHASES OF ALCOHOLISM   The lethal aspects of alcohol abuse, however, are associated not only with so-called violent death, but also with death from disease. After heart disease and cancer, alcoholism is America's biggest health problem. The average life span of an alcoholic is twelve years shorter than that of the nondrinker (*Time,* 1974). Cirrhosis of the liver and other circulatory problems are a major cause of premature death among alcoholics.

In view of such deleterious effects, one might assume that individuals would control or stop drinking before it became a problem. Unfortunately, potential alcoholics are usually unable to detect the point at which they stop drinking alcoholic beverages as beverages and start drinking them as drugs. In other words, alcoholics are almost always the last to realize that they have become alcoholics. In a study of over 2000 alcoholics, Jellinik (1971) concluded that all alcoholics tend to pass through the same developmental sequence in their transition from social drinking to chronic alcoholism.

The first phase, or *prealcoholic phase,* is characterized by the use of alcohol as a means of reducing the tensions of everyday life. This phase can last from a few months to five or ten years, and can provide social drinkers with a false sense of confidence regarding their ability to control the pattern and quantity of their drinking. It is important to note that 90 percent of alcoholics begin their excessive drinking in social settings rather than alone.

During this phase many individuals learn how to "hold their liquor," and thereby compensate for the perceptual distortions and decreased motor coordination that normally accompany the consumption of alcohol. However, it might be wise to recall the admonition of the Greek philosopher Epictetus, who pointed out that "He is a drunkard who takes more than three glasses, though he be not drunk."

The second, or *prodromal, phase,* is distinguished by the periodic occurrence of blackouts. A blackout is a period of time in which drinkers behave in a fairly normal manner, yet have no memory of the experience after sobering up. Following such an episode, individuals will usually feel uncomfortable and tend to avoid any reference to the night before because of the existence of certain blank spots, such as how they got to bed, how the lamp got broken, or exactly *when* the Harrisons left.

This discomfort tends to spread to include all aspects of drinking. As a consequence, people in this phase will begin sneaking drinks by mixing their own drinks somewhat stronger than the others, spiking nonalcoholic drinks, and maintaining a secret supply in order to get a little boost while in the garage or basement. By the time these drinking patterns are established, they are feeling quite guilty about their drinking habits, and they will usually become very defensive or angry if someone shows any concern or is critical about their drinking.

The *crucial phase* is entered when the individual loses control over drinking. This phase often begins one or two years after the first occurrence of blackouts. At this point, once the individual begins to drink, there is no stopping short of becoming intoxicated. For example, if one student invites another to have a beer after class, the nonalcoholic student will do just that—have a beer or two and then proceed to some other activity, such as studying or working. The alcoholic student, on the other hand, will tend to hang around the pub drinking with other students who happen to drop in. This person will say goodbye to one group only to continue drinking with that group's replacement, and finally will again reach the state of being "totally smashed."

Hangovers now become a problem, and some work loss due to drinking is experienced. As a result, there is a tendency to swear off for short periods of time, but the old drinking patterns soon return. Excuses for drinking are sought in an attempt to rationalize the excessive drinking. At first, the excuses center around special occasions or other reasons to celebrate. However, as the holidays run out, the alcoholic begins to blame excessive drinking on the job, the spouse, the children, or some other outside factor.

Attempts to regain control over the drinking often include switching to other forms of alcohol, such as changing from vodka to wine, or from mixed drinks to beer. In fact, one of the most common misconceptions about alcoholism is that those who drink only beer won't get as drunk as they would on mixed drinks or won't become alcoholics. Contrary to popular belief, one can of beer is the alcoholic equivalent of one mixed drink, and moving up to malt liquors is like graduating to doubles.

Another common attempt at controlling one's drinking is by setting certain times of day before which drinking is not allowed—such as before noon or before five. However, special occasions, such as being on a camping trip or vacation, will often afford the opportunity to make an exception to the rule. Eventually, morning drinking will begin as a means of getting started, or as a means of combating the effects of a hangover.

As these efforts at control continue to fail, the individual will usually be overcome with remorse, will renew promises, and will make new resolutions. Some individuals will begin moving from place to place—changing jobs, avoiding old friends, and even beginning to neglect their families. Gradually, the level of tolerance for alcohol decreases. Now even a small amount of alcohol can cause intoxication. The individual now enters the *chronic phase* of alcoholism.

The chronic phase is characterized by benders that last several days. Prior to this phase, drinking sprees were usually planned for the weekends or holidays. During this phase, however, such binges occur spontaneously. The individual becomes preoccupied with drinking and will often drink anything that contains alcohol. Job, family, and friends are usually lost, and associations are limited to other alcoholics in a misery-loves-company sort of lifestyle.

Although the time it takes to progress through these phases may vary from a few months to ten or fifteen years, the sequence is usually the same, as aptly put in this Japanese proverb:

> First the man takes a drink,
> Then the drink takes a drink
> Then the drink takes the man!

Drug Abuse

The phrase "use only as directed" is clearly printed on the labels of even the mildest of medications. So it would seem that such instructions would receive particular emphasis in cases where *psychoactive* drugs are involved, that is, drugs capable of altering a person's mood, emotional state, or thinking processes. However, in a drug-oriented society, such as we have in the United States, such precautionary instructions are not even associated with drugs like alcohol, nicotine, and caffeine. With regard to prescription durgs, such as barbiturates and amphetamines, and some narcotics, such as morphine and codeine, the instructions to use only as directed are often ignored or blatantly and deliberately disobeyed. In either case, the consequence is an ever-increasing problem with drug abuse.

Due to its vagueness, the term "drug abuse" is subject to a broad range of interpretations. Most interpretations, however, will usually include such words as "addiction" and "dependence." The term "addiction" is defined by the World Health Organization (WHO) as:

> . . . a state of periodic or chronic intoxication detrimental to the individual and to society, produced by the repeated consumption of a drug (natural or synthetic). Its characteristics include: (1) an overpowering desire or need (compulsion) to continue taking the drug and to obtain it by any means, (2) a tendency to increase the dosage, and (3) a psychic (psychological) and sometimes physical dependence on the effects of the drug. (1965, p. 722)

FIGURE 7.4   Once a person develops a preference for the drug-induced state (being "high"), "normal" activities such as working, sports, and learning often become secondary to obtaining the drug. [*Charles Gatewood.*]

The definition's reference to the need to "increase the dosage" refers to the fact that a tolerance for a drug can be acquired with continued use, and this requires the user to increase the dosage in order to obtain the usual effects, or to maintain. An increased tolerance reflects the development of a *physiological dependence* on a drug. This dependence can result in severe withdrawal symptoms should the user ever be deprived of the drug. Physiological dependence and withdrawal symptoms are most often experienced by those who are addicted to alcohol, barbiturates, or narcotics.

Drug dependence, however, is not necessarily synonymous with addiction, for the term is often used in reference to a *psychological dependence* as well. A psychological dependence results when the user has developed a preference for the drug-induced state (being "high") over the way he or she feels while not under the influence of the drug. As a consequence, the user develops a habitual use of the drug. Typical examples of such dependence would be the habitual use of marijuana in order to enjoy a party, engage in sexual activities, or just relax.

Psychoactive Drugs

Psychoactive drugs are commonly divided into four main classifications. The *hallucinogens* include drugs such as marijuana, hashish, peyote, and LSD (lysergic acid diethylamide). The *stimulants* include cocaine and amphetamines. The *depressants* are made up primarily of barbiturates. The *opiates* comprise opium and its derivatives—heroin, morphine, and codeine.

People have been using, and misusing, psychoactive drugs for centuries. Marijuana, for instance, was well known to the Chinese almost 5000 years ago. Egyptian, Persian, and Greek physicians were using opium for medicinal purposes 3000 years ago, and peyote and coca leaves (from which cocaine is derived) have been used by the Indians of South and Central America for untold centuries. However, it has only been during the past 100 years that the physical, mental, and social impact of these drugs has been fully appreciated in the United States.

HALLUCINOGENS   Hallucinogenic drugs are capable of interfering with the brain's ability to process sensory information. Through the use of such drugs, visual experiences can undergo gross distortions, and swirling patterns of color can be generated spontaneously. In addition, the sense impressions of touch and sound can be interfered with so as to make it difficult to orient oneself in space. Time becomes distorted. The ability to distinguish between reality and fantasy may be lost completely.

There are several hallucinogens sold on the illegal drug market, such as PCP (an animal tranquilizer), THC (the active ingredient in marijuana), and LSD (lysergic acid diethylamide). However, LSD tends to be the most popular of the so-called psychodelics, or mind-expanding drugs. The term "mind-expanding" refers to the drug's ability to allow a person to become consciously aware of repressed material. However, if a person is not psychologically prepared to handle such material, the thoughts, emotions, and imagery resulting from this exposure can be terrifying. In such cases, the individual is said to experience a "bad trip."

In some instances, especially where there has been a psychotic predisposition, the individual may not "return" from a bad trip and may remain psychotic or require extensive therapeutic assistance for an extended period (Frosch et al., 1965). In addition, many individuals may spontaneously reexperience the horrifying hallucinations of a bad trip without warning. Such spontaneous experiences may occur months after all use of LSD has been terminated.

The much milder hallucinogenic drugs, such as marijuana and hashish, are often thought of as "harmless" drugs. This is because prolonged use does not lead to physiological dependence, there are no withdrawal symptoms when use is interrupted or terminated, and there is no scientific proof that the periodic use of these drugs has any serious long-term effects. However, their use is still illegal. Moreover, just as in most victimless crimes, there are often undesirable consequences, as well as a number of indirect victims, as a result of transgressions.

Aside from the bribery, corruption, and homicide that are often associated with multimillion-dollar drug smuggling efforts, there are the more subtle consequences of preferring to supplement the natural experience of living with artificially induced experiences by use of drugs. Many families have been severely disrupted or fragmented due to persistent use of drugs by teenagers. In this regard, only preference for alcohol over the welfare of the family is so destructive. In addition, there is often a psychological dependence which results in a loss of interest in activities that do not include drugs. Many heavy users tend to drop out of school early, have difficulty keeping a steady job, and have numerous conflicts with the law.

However, even with these kinds of consequences, it is estimated that over 50 percent of college students have at least tried marijuana. The National Commission on Marijuana and Drug Abuse (1972) found that curiosity and the desire to share a social experience with peers were the primary motives for smoking marijuana among those who smoked less than once a month. For those who smoked two to ten times per month, the social aspect of the activity was more important. Special emphasis was placed on the opportunity to develop close social relationships. Among those who smoked more than ten times a month to as often as several times per day, the motivation centered more on the relief of anxiety and boredom than on the social aspects of drug use.

The average user apparently smokes marijuana in order to reduce the tensions of everyday life, much as the average drinker uses alcohol. For alienated youth, however, there is often the additional element of separating themselves from what they perceive as a sick society (Suchman, 1970). In addition to this counterculture facet, there is a less hostile youth culture, which is motivated by a desire for new and different phenomenological experiences (Marin and Cohen, 1971). As is the case with many alcoholics, however, a small number of users employ marijuana as a means of escaping from neurotic anxiety, depression, or frustration stemming from what seem to be unsolvable problems (Bloomquist, 1968).

STIMULANTS In contrast with the relaxed state so commonly sought through the use of marijuana, a state of invigoration is what the user of stimulants is anxious to attain. *Cocaine,* a natural stimulant derived from the coca plant, was one of the first stimulant drugs to achieve general acceptance among drug users. The coca plant is native to the Andes mountains of South America. Natives of this region have traditionally chewed the leaf of this plant as a means of combating the rigors of living and working at high altitudes.

In 1884, Freud began investigating the medicinal advantages of cocaine, especially its ability to relieve depression. (Karl Koller was to discover that cocaine acts as a local anesthetic in eye surgery as a result of a paper Freud wrote on the subject [Reik, 1955].) By 1896, cocaine was also to find its way into the commercial world as the main stimulating ingredient of a drink called Coca-Cola, and it continued to be the drink's primary ingredient until it was replaced by caffeine in 1906. Today, this relatively expensive drug is illicitly used by members of the middle and upper socioeconomic classes, primarily to obtain a feeling of euphoria, self-confidence, and omnipotence.

Much less expensive, and much more readily available, are the stimulants called amphetamines ("uppers"). Some of the most commonly used amphetamines are Benzedrine (bennies), Dexedrine (dexies), and Methedrine (speed). Next in popularity to marijuana, these stimulants (pep pills) are widely used as a means of getting high. Although amphetamines are not addictive, users develop a tolerance and must continually increase the dosage to get the same effects. Prolonged use can lead to psychosis, with hallucinations and paranoid delusions. Although these drugs are usually taken orally, Methedrine is sometimes injected directly into the veins, resulting in extreme emotional, social, and behavioral patterns characterized by excessive compulsiveness, aggressiveness, and belligerence. After such an injection, the person is said to "freak out." Habitual users are often referred to as "speed freaks."

DEPRESSANTS   The opposites of uppers, of course, are "downers," a classification of drugs called "depressants." Dominant in this category of drugs are the powerful sedatives known as *barbiturates*. Some of the most commonly used barbiturates are Seconal (red devils), Amytal (blue heavens), and Nembutal (yellow jackets). These drugs are normally prescribed by physicians as sleeping pills. They are, therefore, readily available, and are frequently chosen as a means of committing suicide. Approximately 3000 people a year die due to an overdose of barbiturates (Bayh, 1971).

In addition to the dangers of an overdose, these drugs are highly addictive, creating both a physiological and a psychological dependence. Withdrawal symptoms are severe, resembling the delirium tremens (DTs) associated with chronic alcoholism, the hallucinations and delusions of a psychosis, and seizures similar to the grand mal seizures of an individual with epilepsy. Without medical supervision, withdrawal from the heavy, habitual use of barbiturates can result in death.

OPIATES   Only the opiates, or "hard drugs," are as addictive as the barbiturates and have as severe a set of withdrawal symptoms. Although all derivatives of opium (codeine, morphine, and heroin) are addictive, heroin is by far the drug of choice among narcotics users. There are an estimated 600,000 to 700,000 heroin addicts in the United States. Most of them live in the large metropolitan areas on the east and west coasts (Richards and Carroll, 1970). Most addicts are between the ages of fifteen and twenty-five; males outnumber females eight to one (Du Pont and Greene, 1973).

Initially, the user of *heroin* experiences a rush of "high." However, with prolonged use, these feelings tend to disappear, and the main objective of continued use of heroin becomes the avoidance of withdrawal symptoms. The "junkie," as the heroin addict is commonly called, becomes obsessed with keeping appointments with a "fence," to get money for stolen merchandise, or a "pusher," to get a new supply, or "bag." The addict is constantly on the lookout for (1) a way to get more money, (2) a means of securing a source of heroin, and (3) a safe place to take the drug. "Kicking the habit" is extremely difficult due to the severity of the withdrawal symptoms. However, some optimism is being shown with regard to the use of *methadone* as a substitute for heroin. An individual who undergoes methadone treatment will gradually develop a tolerance for methadone similar to that for heroin. As a result, the individual would suffer withdrawal symptoms should treatment be terminated. However, while taking methadone, the individual experiences no craving for heroin, nor would any of the desired effects be experienced should heroin be injected. As a result, the individual's need to obtain large amounts of money is eliminated. Thus the user's criminal activities are reduced, and energies can be directed toward more productive endeavors.

Psychosis

Generally speaking, when lay people use the terms "mentally ill," "crazy," or "insane," they are referring to the condition designated by the diagnostic term "psychosis." Many psychological professionals object to the common lay terms, especially the implication of illness. Ullman and Krasner (1975) protest that people who are labeled as mentally ill will most likely act "sick" in order to gain whatever social or interpersonal advantages are available to the sick. Furthermore, since being sick implies having been infected by a disease, there is often an unspoken understanding that there is nothing the sick person can do in order to get well; recovery is then up to the treatment.

"Crazy" and "insane" connote illogicality, maladaptiveness, or irresponsibility, but according to many theorists, the psychotic break may be the most logical means of dealing with an otherwise illogical situation. This means of coping actually allows the individual to work through an otherwise unsolvable dilemma (Laing, 1964; Scheff, 1970; Mosher, 1974).

In an attempt to minimize the effects of the implications and connotations associated with labeling, the American Psychiatric Association (1968) limits its definitions to the types of symptoms displayed, proposing that the term "psychosis" should refer to those patients whose:

> . . . mental functioning is sufficiently impaired to interfere grossly with their capacity to meet the ordinary demands of life. The impairment may result from a serious distortion in their capacity to recognize reality. Hallucinations and delusions may distort their perceptions. Alterations of mood may be so profound that the patient's capacity to respond appropriately is grossly impaired. Deficits in perception, language and memory may be so severe that the patient's capacity for mental grasp of his situation is effectively lost. (p. 23)

NEUROSIS VERSUS PSYCHOSIS Many neurotics worry about getting worse and some day becoming psychotic. However, there is a saying that "the best defense against a psychosis is a neurosis." Many in the field of psychology tend to make a definite distinction between the two coping patterns. Murray Banks, in one of his lectures, quipped that the difference between a neurotic and a psychotic is that the neurotic builds dream castles in the air, the psychotic moves in, and the psychiatrist collects the rent!

E. B. McNeil (1970), however, presents a more serious approach to the problem of distinguishing between neurosis and psychosis. McNeil points out that the personality of the neurotic person undergoes mild decompensation (a breakdown of organized functioning), but the psychotic undergoes severe decompensation. For example, it may take a close friend to notice that a coworker is unduly depressed or anxious (neurotic reaction), but even a stranger could recognize the abnormality of an individual who sits in a corner, rocking back and forth, while babbling about the need to stop the invaders.

In addition, the neurotic tends to maintain good contact with reality. Neurotics are able to react to and act upon the environment in an appropriate fashion, whereas psychotics often experience a complete loss of contact with reality. For example, a neurotic knows who, what, when, where, and why he or she "is," but a psychotic may believe he or she is Napoleon, the Emperor of France, exiled on St. Helena.

Perhaps the most outstanding distinction between neurosis and psychosis, however, is that delusions and hallucinations are *absent* in neurosis and almost always present in psychosis. Delusions are false beliefs. Psychotics with delusions of grandeur believe they are famous; those with delusions of persecution believe they are being plotted against; and those with delusions of influence believe their thoughts or actions are being controlled by others. Hallucinations, on the other hand, are sensory experiences in the absence of adequate stimuli. For example, voices are heard when no one is talking, poisons are tasted in perfectly nutritious food, or people or things are seen that are not actually there.

Another distinction between neurosis and psychosis is that neurosis is generally thought to be a maladaptive reaction to stress, while psychosis may have organic causes. An *organic psychosis* can be caused by such factors as the effects of alcohol, lead poisoning, carbon monoxide, brain trauma, high fever, arteriosclerosis, stroke, encephalitis, meningitis, and syphillis, or as a reaction to surgery or childbirth. This does not mean that these factors *always cause a psychosis, however, only that they can cause a psychosis.*

In contrast, psychoses for which there is no apparent organic, or biological, cause are considered to be *functional psychoses.* Currently, there is strong evidence that a biochemical, genetic, or metabolic factor will eventually be linked to the development of what are currently referred to as functional psychoses.

SCHIZOPHRENIA   The most commonly diagnosed type of psychosis is *schizophrenia.* It is estimated that at least 1 percent of the American population (over 2 million people) is schizophrenic (Dohrenwend and Dohrenwend, 1974). Schizophrenics constitute 20 percent of all first admissions to mental hospitals and 50 percent of the hospital population in the United States. The highest incidence is among those in their early twenties. There is no noticeable difference between the sexes in the rate of schizophrenia.

The primary symptoms of schizophrenia are (1) *affective disturbances,* such as inadequate emotional responses, emotional blunting, indifference or apathy, and/or inappropriate crying, giggling, or laughing; (2) *thought disturbances,* involving bizarre ideas, unusual use of language, inability to think abstractly, random associations, and/or inflexible attitudes; and (3) *autistic behavior,* characterized by attending to internally generated stimuli, fantasy, delusions, and/or hallucinations. Due to certain distinguishing symptoms among certain types of schizophrenia, the *Diagnostic and Statistical Manual of Mental Disorders* (1968, pp. 33–34) divides this psychosis into several subcategories. The most common of those are:

> *Simple schizophrenia.*   Typified by a diminished interest and a steady withdrawal from reality, a history of inadequate social adjustment, emotional blunting, a preoccupation with fantasy, and in contrast to the other types, there is often an absence of delusions and hallucinations.

Hebephrenic schizophrenia. Characterized by bizarre socially unconventional behavior, accompanied by spontaneous giggling, unusual gestures and mannerisms, strange word combinations and "secret codes," and a tendency towards assaultive or destructive behavior.

Catatonic schizophrenia. The catatonic stupor state is characterized by extreme withdrawal, mutism, and the assumption of a rigid body position. The catatonic excitement state is often characterized by violent destructive behavior, in which the individual is usually assaultive and often dangerous.

Paranoid schizophrenia. Characterized by pronounced delusions of grandeur and persectuion, most often accompanied by auditory hallucinations.

Process schizophrenia develops during adolescence, in the absence of any severe stress and without any overt signs of tension or anxiety. It is considered to have a poor prognosis for recovery. In contrast, *reactive schizophrenia* occurs suddenly, usually following a severe stress or trauma, in an individual whose earlier development was normal. It has a good prognosis for recovery (Kantor and Herron, 1966). As a matter of some interest, many recent cases of schizophrenia among adolescents and young adults have remained undiagnosed due to the peer group's assumption that the person's unconventional behavior, emotional inappropriateness, or bizarre thought patterns were merely the side effects of drug use.

AFFECTIVE PSYCHOSES The most distinctive symptom associated with *affective psychoses* is the experiencing of extreme moods—either great elation or deep depression. The elated mood is referred to as the "manic" state. The despondent mood is referred to as the "depressive" state.

A *manic-depressive* reaction is characterized by spontaneously occurring mood disturbances. There are three variations of this reaction: the manic type, the depressive type, and the circular type. The *manic* type is characterized by extreme feelings of euphoria, hyperactivity, and grandiose ideas. Manic individuals become impulsive and are likely to phone or visit people at all hours of the day or night, go on spending sprees, or indulge in ill-advised business ventures. Their speech becomes accelerated, and sentences are often left incomplete as they shift from topic to topic.

The *depressive* type of reaction is characterized by feelings of hopelessness, guilt, and sadness. In this type of reaction, the individual's thinking is slowed and motor reactions are retarded. The individual usually has a low level of self-esteem, often due to feelings of shame over imaginary misdeeds. As might be expected, this type of individual is highly suicidal.

The *circular* type of reaction is marked by alternate attacks of both manic episodes and depressive episodes, followed by periods of remission. The intervals between episodes range from six months to ten years, and the manic phases are usually of a shorter duration (averaging about three months) than the depressive episodes (averaging about six months).

PARANOID REACTIONS The paranoid reactions are relatively rare, and account for only about 1 percent of hospital admissions. However, the actual incidence of this reaction could be much higher. Paranoid individuals are often very skilled at not drawing any undue attention to themselves. The primary symptoms of this reaction are delusions of grandeur and delusions of persecution. According to Norman Cameron (1959), the delusions of persecution result from the paranoid's desperate attempt to justify distrust and suspicion of others, account for personal failures, or explain persecution by others.

One of the distinguishing factors of this classification of psychoses is that the paranoia usually affects only one area of the person's life. Most often this area has to do with sexual infidelity, although it can center around real or imaginary inventions, business dealings, or government interference.

If the organization of the delusions is not well structured and some aspects are viewed as illogical, the reaction is usually diagnosed as the milder *paranoid state*. However, should the delusions be highly organized and supported by plausible explanations, then the individual may have developed *paranoia*.

Usually, the paranoid individual becomes a threat to others only if the delusions develop to the point where it is necessary to get "them" before "they" get him or her. As a result of having taken certain defensive maneuvers, such as attempting to kill the persecutors, the paranoid individual is often hospitalized. The prognosis for recovery, however, is extremely poor.

SUMMARY

In this chapter, the various consequences of ineffective coping behavior were explored. It was pointed out how those who consistently distort reality to suit their own needs often develop some degree of personality characteristic disorders. Among these are the passive-aggressive, paranoid, obsessive-compulsive, and antisocial personality disorders.

Psychosomatic illnesses, and the psychophysiological consequences of not dealing with internal or external stress directly, were also discussed, as was the development of neuroses, such as the anxiety, phobic, obsessive-compulsive, and depressive reactions. Special consideration being given to the effects of depression and the role it plays in attempts at suicide.

The chapter also treated the problems associated with alcoholism and drug abuse with regard to escaping from reality. Escaping from reality through psychosis was also investigated. The distinction between neuroses and psychoses was emphasized.

DISCUSSION QUESTIONS

1 The passive-aggressive personality has a tendency toward procrastination to the point where there is interference with interpersonal relationships. Do you think you have known a person with this trait?

2 Have you ever been involved with an "insanely jealous" person who thought he or she owned you? How did you react to this person's suspicious nature?

3   What are some of the things you might look for as indications that an illness may be psychosomatic?

4   A few of the more common phobic fears involve heights, closed-in places, darkness, and crowds. Do you have a phobic fear of anything?

5   There appears to be an increase in the number of suicides among teenagers. What do you think would be some of the reasons for such an increase?

6   Included in this chapter are AA's twelve questions concerning drinking habits. Do you know of someone, including yourself, who would answer yes to four or more of these questions?

7   Do you believe that you have developed a psychological dependence for a particular drug (nicotine, caffeine, alcohol, marijuana, etc.)? If so, which one?

8   When you hear that someone has had a nervous breakdown, do you think of the person as being neurotic, psychotic, or neither?

9   How do you believe the lives of today's teenagers would change if *all* drugs not legitimately prescribed by a physician were suddenly made unavailable?

10 How do you account for the increase in teenage alcoholism?

EXPERIENTIAL EXERCISES

1   Many communities maintain some form of crisis center concerned with suicide, drug abuse, runaways, child or wife abuse, etc. Such centers often rely heavily on the support of volunteers. Arrange to have several members of the class commit themselves to such organizations and provide reports of their experiences to the rest of the class.

2   To become more familiar with the dynamics of mental health programs, invite representatives from Alcoholics Anonymous or from suicide prevention or community mental health centers to appear as guest speakers. Ask them to discuss some of the changes in community attitudes toward their programs.

3   For a better understanding of the world of the mentally ill, have a number of students present book reports on such books as:

H. Green, *I Never Promised You a Rose Garden,* 1964. (Schizophrenia.)
B. Kaplan, *The Inner World of Mental Illness: A Series of First-Person Accounts of What It Was Like,* 1964.
F. R. Schreiber, *Sybil,* 1974. (Multiple personalities.)
C. C. Sizemore and E. S. Pittello, *I'm Eve,* 1977. (Multiple personalities.)

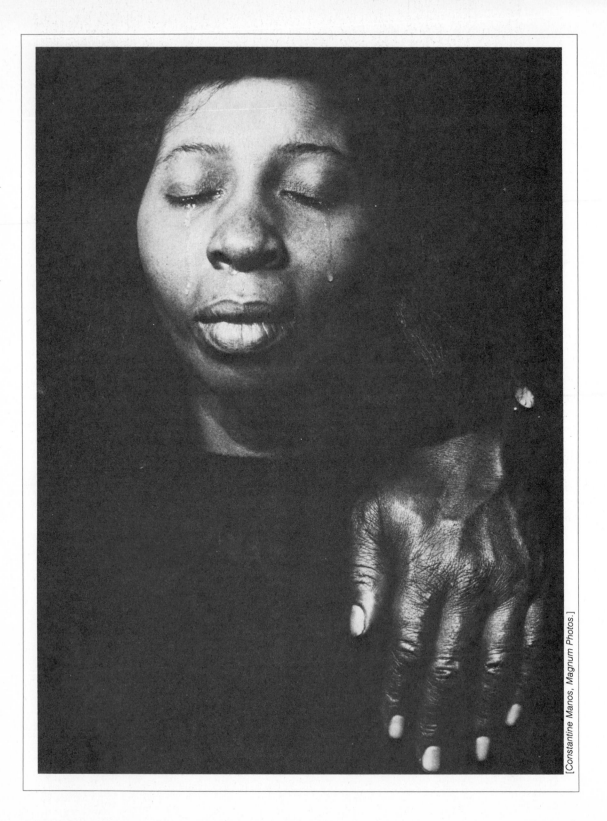

PART THREE

THE INDIVIDUAL

AS A SOCIAL BEING

CHAPTER 8

THE INDIVIDUAL

AS A GROUP MEMBER

No man is an island, entire of itself; every man is a piece of the continent, a part of the main; if a clod be washed away by the sea, Europe is the less, as well as if a promontory were, as well as if a manor of thy friends or of thine own were; any man's death diminishes me, because I am involved in mankind; and therefore never send to know for whom the bell tolls; it tolls for thee.

John Donne
Devotions

A SENSE OF BELONGING

Achieving a sense of belonging is one of our most basic needs. It is a means by which we are able to satisfy our need for security, our need for extended identity, and our need for affiliation. In other words, we need each other. We might be *able* to survive without each other, but it is questionable whether or not we would *want* to survive without each other. Aristotle (384–322 B.C.) believed that "Without friends no one would choose to live, though he had all other goods."

As a result of such needs, we have historically joined together into groups, and from these groups we have formed our societies. "He who is unable to live in society, or who has no need because he is sufficient for himself, must be either a beast or a God" (Aristotle, *Politics*, 1963, p. 385).

Forming a Group

A group is formed by an association between two or more people. The actual size of a group may vary, and with it, the type of social interaction that will take place. One is more likely to experience a sense of intimacy as a member of a group of only two people than if the group were larger. Similarly, a person is more likely to experience a sense of security as a member of a well-organized and highly disciplined group than as a member of a large, unorganized mob. An individual, however, is capable of experiencing a sense of power and protective anonymity in either situation. Therefore, in attempting to assess the behavior of a person who is a member of a group or the behavior of the group itself, it is often just as important to determine the size of the group as it is to determine the nature of the group.

DYADS, TRIADS, AND GROUPS When there are only two members forming a group, the group is referred to as a "dyad." A dyad is a relatively stable group which usually has a positive attitude and characteristically develops an atmosphere of cooperation, compromise, and mutual consideration. Interaction between the two often takes the form of a *social exchange* in which feelings of superiority and inferiority are manipulated. However, well-matched

FIGURE 8.1   You don't have to be alone to feel lonely. [*Randy Matusow.*]

partners often work efficiently together, play spontaneously, and tend to think creatively. These characteristics will, in most cases, all but disappear, however, with the introduction of a third member into the group.

When there are three members in a group, the group is called a "triad." Triads are notoriously unstable groups with an almost instinctual tendency to form into a dyad plus one outsider. Such a tendency often creates severe tension within the group. Intense competition is also created among the members while attempting to form a partnership, and thereby avoid becoming the outsider. One of the most frequent examples of the dynamics of a triad is to be found when the group consists of a married couple and a lover; sooner or later, one of the three will usually get left out.

When the group size increases to more than three, a *social hierarchy* will usually form, thereby establishing lines of communication and levels of authority. Many studies have indicated that the optimum size of a group is about five (Seashore, 1954; Hare, 1952; Slater, 1958). The relative success of the five-member-group concept of organization prompted the U. S. Army to form what was referred to as the "pentomic army," wherein there were five platoons to a company, five companies to a battalion, five battalions to a regiment, etc. When the membership of a group exceeds five, efficiency diminishes, communication becomes less effective, and participation often drops off. Smaller groups also seem to experience a greater sense of cohesiveness, and thus a greater sense of belongingness.

Dignity is based on a belief in one's excellence. [*Hugh Rogers, Monkmeyer.*]

FIGURE 8.2

FORMAL AND INFORMAL GROUPS   A *formal group* or organization is one in which the positions and titles of the various members are specified, the lines of authority are clearly defined, and the official channels of communication are well established. The particular arrangement agreed upon is often dependent upon the objectives of the organization and exactly what the organization wishes to accomplish. For example, the organization of a formal group, such as a religion, might be quite different from that of a corporation, political institution, or branch of the military.

Formal organizations tend to be highly efficient and durable, and to provide an optimum level of *mutual predictability*. Mutual predictability is the ability of each member of the group to predict, with a high degree of accuracy, how other members of the group will behave. Each member is aware of individual responsibilities and their limits. Such might be the case in a large manufacturing concern, where a supervisor clarifies his position by saying "I'm sorry, but those units are not my responsibility. Models H33 through H59 are handled by Section 12. My section deals with models H10 through H24 only."

One of the greatest disadvantages of the formal group is the threat of *dehumanization*. The position, or title, sometimes becomes more important than the *person* filling the position. Emotions like empathy and compassion are often inhibited because of the need to go through channels. There is also a tendency to develop perceptual orientations of inferiority and superiority based on what a person *does* rather than who the person *is*.

Should the formal organization of a group prove to be inefficient, or if it should fail to satisfy the needs of the individual members, then *informal groups* will usually form in order to continue to accomplish the group's goals or to provide greater benefit to its members. The informal groups may take the form of cliques, "grapevines," or friendships.

Some of the advantages of an informal organization are that it allows for spontaneity, role flexibility, and the ability to bypass bureaucratic red tape. For example, a newly hired employee might be informed: "You must always get the supervisor's signature before getting replacement tools. But if you've got a rush job and need something in a hurry, just explain the situation to Harry at the service desk, and he'll lend you one of the spares until you get around to replacing it officially."

Some of the disadvantages of an informal organization are lack of coordination, fluctuation in levels of dependability, and a reluctance to assume responsibility, as for instance, when a problem arises after an attempt to bypass the formal group organization. "Yes, I know I'm supposed to get your signature before getting a replacement tool, but I was in a hurry, and Ralph told me that I could go to Harry and. . . . Just a minute, I'll get Ralph to explain it to you." Ralph's explanation will often go something like, "Gee, Boss, the new guy must have misunderstood me. I've always been told that you have to get your supervisor's signature before replacing a tool." In other words, what is said "off the record," or "unofficially," within an informal group will usually remain off the record and unofficial.

Compulsory, Circumstantial, and Voluntary Membership

In order to become a member of a group, all we have to do is introduce ourselves to another person, and presto—a group is formed. Even without formal introductions, however, we can still become members of a group. In fact, we often become members of a group even when we don't want to, as when we find our names on an advertiser's mailing list, gain too much weight, or turn sixty-five. We *inherit* some group memberships, such as being a member of a particular race, nationality, or family ancestry. Other memberships are *earned,* such as being a member of a college's alumni; *bestowed,* such as being included among those having received the Nobel prize; or *chosen,* such as when one decides to join a particular political party.

COMPULSORY MEMBERSHIP   Membership in a group is one of the first things an individual inherits. In fact, membership can actually begin even before birth by being included among those fetuses whose mothers are in the first or second trimester of pregnancy, by being included among those with chromosomal abnormalities, or by being included among those who are born prematurely. However, once we are born, we *automatically* become a member of an incredible number of groups. For instance, our physical and mental characteristics are partially determined through inheritance; among these are weight, height, strength, physical attractiveness, and intellectual competence. All these characteristics have the ability to provide compulsory membership within a particular group, such as being included among those people who are overweight, winners of beauty contests, or students in classes for the gifted or for the educationally handicapped.

Unfortunately, certain inherited characteristics, such as race, skin color, and national origin, can also be used to *exclude* certain people from group membership. Racist attitudes are founded on the belief that the people of one group are not equal to the people of another group (Van den Berghe, 1967). Inequality usually implies gain for one group at the expense of another, and most systems based on such a belief will inevitably generate protest.

Many countries have made attempts to reduce the intensity of such protests by trying to create a sense of equality and sameness among their people, notably Yugoslavia, Israel, and the United States. Franklin Roosevelt (1882–1945) once said, in a Boston campaign speech, "All of our people all over the country except the pure-blooded Indians are immigrants or descendents of immigrants, including even those who came over here on the *Mayflower*." Most attempts, however, at achieving such social blending appear to have fallen short of the ideal objectives. In fact, in today's world, there appears to be an attempt to achieve just the opposite. There appears to be a wave of ethnic-inspired dissonance occurring throughout the world in which ethnic groups, and other minorities, are now *asserting* their distinctiveness and developing a movement that favors a return to *ascribed* characteristics of a natural distinctiveness rather than *achieved* characteristics as determinants of social stratification. An ever-increasing number of people are now experiencing greater pride in their tribal affiliations, immigrant heritage, or the fact that they are blacks or Chicanos. Such pride, however, requires that the people who are identified with minority groups be granted (1) full civil rights, (2) equal opportunity, and (3) equal participation in the social, economic, and political facets of the community.

Being identified with a particular group due to color need not be limited to skin. The color of their eyes can qualify individuals for membership in a particular group. The same is true for the color of their hair, or, for that matter, the length of the hair, the texture of the hair, or even the presence or absence of hair. In other words, no matter what physical characteristics people have or don't have, those characteristics can make them candidates for membership in a group, regardless of whether or not they want to be members.

VOLUNTARY MEMBERSHIP   A people's freedom of choice is usually limited only by the alternatives provided them and the creativeness of their own imaginations. Depending upon the circumstances in which people find themselves, there may exist a great number of alternatives from which to choose (an enriched environment) or there may exist only a few alternatives from which to choose (a deprived environment). Regardless of the number of choices available, the existentialist believes that a choice *always* exists.

A person may choose to band together with others of the same *philosophical* orientation, such as being liberal or conservative, materialistic or spiritualistic, or deceitful or candid. Often, a person's philosophical beliefs will form the basis for one's *political* beliefs, and as a result, an individual may choose to be a member of a revolutionary organization or a recognized political party or, by choosing not to be interested in politics, an individual may be grouped among those who are nonparticipants.

The kind of interests a person chooses to have can also be very influential in the determination of group membership. For example, the type of music a person prefers can draw people together in order to experience a "happening" at Woodstock, the classics at Carnegie Hall, or the polkas of Lawrence Welk. A person's particular taste in any of the arts will often tend to alienate some and simultaneously attract others.

A person's intellectual interests also have the power to form bonds of understanding, as well as islands of misinterpretation. Ham operators and CB buffs often form large groups with strong feelings of mutuality. Those who live in the binary world of computers must often satisfy their affiliation needs through small groups of two or three.

Most individuals are aware of such shortcomings even before they choose their vocations. As with the selection of any vocation, there exists the possibility of immediate group acceptance among one's coworkers, as well as immediate ostracism by others; "Glad to have you with us" and "You're making a big mistake. You're throwing your whole life away."

When choosing a vocation, one must also consider the supplemental group demands that may be made. For example, union membership may be compulsory, additional credentialing may be expected, or an individual may be required to become a member of particular clubs or organizations. During the process of satisfying such group demands, many individuals may find themselves joining groups whose members live in the suburbs, own two cars, commute, and are developing a drinking problem. Should the demands become too great, some may choose to join a group of individuals who are looking more closely at the *quality* in their lives, rather than just at the *quantity* in their lives.

SOCIALIZATION

Through the influences of modeling and reinforcement of behavior patterns which are acceptable to society, the norms and values of one generation are transmitted to another. This process is called "socialization." Will and Ariel Durant, in their book *The Lessons of History,* noted:

> Evolution in man during recorded time has been social rather than biological: it has proceeded not by heritable variations in the species, but mostly by economic, political, intellectual, and moral innovation transmitted to individuals and generations by imitation, custom, or education. (1968, p. 34)

In order to accomplish this purpose, a child must learn (1) what *behavior* is socially acceptable, (2) what *social roles* are expected, and (3) which *social attitudes* will receive support and which will be opposed.

The early years of a child's life are the most crucial with regard to the process of socialization. It is during these years that the influence of the immediate family will have the greatest effect. Studies have shown that social maturation progresses more rapidly in larger families (six or more children) than in small families (one or two children), with children coming from medium-sized families (three to five children) demonstrating the most rapid

For the rapidly changing
adolescent, the search for
identity can seem endless.
[*Charles Harbutt, Magnum.*]

FIGURE 8.3

advances in social adjustment (Boll, 1957; Koch, 1960). One proposed explanation for such variations in progress is that the larger family helps to establish a greater number of interaction systems between members. According to a formula developed by Bossard and Boll (1960), a family of three has five systems, whereas a family of four has eleven, a family of five has twenty-six, and a family of six (two parents and four children) has fifty-seven interaction systems.

The exact nature of such interactions has been studied by many noted psychologists. B. F. Skinner, for instance, believes that the socialization process is a function of the shaping and reinforcement of behavior. Albert Bandura, on the other hand, advocates the hypothesis that socialization is merely the result of imitation and mimicry. Finally, Erik Erikson (1950), through his theory of ego psychology, represents one of the more successful attempts to combine the effects of psychological insight with sociological influences into one theme of psychosocial development.

The Eight Ages of Life

Although Erikson is associated with the psychodynamic theorists, such as Freud, he disagrees with Freud's emphasis on sex and prefers to believe that our social view of ourselves is more important than our sexual urges. Erikson believes that human development must be viewed in terms of its dependence on our interactions with each other. As a consequence, he is primarily concerned with psychosocial development and the role that society and interpersonal relationships play in the socialization process.

Like Freud, Erikson developed an elaborate stage theory as a means of explaining individual development. Freud, however, believed that individual development is completed by the time a person reaches late adolescence or early adulthood. In contrast, Erikson believed that the developmental process *continues throughout life,* and that personal growth results from successfully coping with the confrontation between one's individual needs and the demands of society. Erikson referred to such a confrontation as an "identity crisis." He believed that certain types of crises were more critical during one period of a person's life than during another. Erikson formulated this belief into eight stages of development. The resolution of a stage permits continued psychosocial development and mental health; failure to resolve a crisis stage could result in the development of psychological disorders. (See Table 8.1.)

Erikson's final stage of development involves the conflict between ego integrity and despair. With ego integrity, an individual is able to reflect on life with the wisdom that comes from a long life and not feel a sense of having been cheated. Death is not welcomed, but it is not feared either, for there exists the knowledge that life will go on through the efforts of the next generation. In contrast, those who fail to achieve ego integrity will often experience a feeling of despair, futility, and purposelessness. Their realization that it is too late to start over again often generates a feeling of helplessness, bitterness, and remorse.

How Groups Influence Us

Most theories of personality development and adjustment acknowledge that individual development and behavior can be influenced by others (Langer, 1969). The magnitude and nature of this influence is dependent upon such factors as the size of the group, the sex of the participants, the perceived importance of the others, prior expectations, cultural background, and perhaps even the language involved in the interaction.

TABLE 8.1 ERIKSON'S STAGES OF DEVELOPMENT

STAGE	REFERENCE	PSYCHOSOCIAL CONFLICT	AGE PERIOD
8	Mature age	Ego integrity vs. despair	Mid-50s to death
7	Adulthood	Generativity vs. stagnation	Mid-30s to mid-50s
6	Young adulthood	Intimacy vs. isolation	Early 20s to early 30s
6	Adolescence	Identity vs. role diffusion	12 to 20
5	Middle childhood	Industry vs. inferiority	6 to 11
4	Early childhood	Initiative vs. guilt	4 to 5
3	Late infancy	Autonomy vs. shame	1 to 3
2	Early infancy	Trust vs. mistrust	0 to 1

Source: Erikson (1950, p. 273).

SOCIAL FACILITATION AND INTERFERENCE At times, having others around tends to bolster our feelings and increase our energy output. In such instances, *social facilitation* is said to take place. A typical example of social facilitation might be an old-fashioned barn raising. However, social facilitation can occur in almost any situation involving a group effort. Social facilitation can also occur while people are working independently in the presence of others doing a similar task. Under such circumstances, people will tend to produce more than when they are isolated.

There are times, however, during which the presence of others interferes with our performance. The occurrence of such a phenomenon is referred to as "social interference." The stage fright experienced by an amateur entertainer when first called upon to perform before a large audience would be a common example of social interference. On a more personal basis, shyness can be said to be a product of social interference. Although the incidence of shyness varies from culture to culture (a relatively low incidence among Jewish people compared with non-Jewish Americans, and a relatively high incidence of shyness present in those raised in a traditional Japanese culture) (Zimbardo, et al., 1975), there appears to be a direct correlation between the amount of emphasis a culture places on competition, individual success, and personal responsibility for failure, and the incidence of shyness among its people (Zimbardo, Pilkonis, and Norwood, 1975).

Generally speaking, social facilitation usually will occur when an individual is performing a familiar, well-learned task, whereas social interference tends to occur when an individual is attempting to perform a new, or unfamiliar, task.

The positive or negative connotations associated with the terms "social facilitation" and "social interference" tend to break down when crowd behavior is involved. Social facilitation can lead to the spiraling of a crowd's level of excitement during a crisis situation. Such a spiraling effect can lead to mass hysteria in the case of a fire in a theater or nightclub, such as the Cocoanut Grove fire in Boston, 1942 (Newcomb, Turner, and Converse, 1965). A similar intensification of passions can occur when a "lynch mob" atmosphere becomes all-pervasive. However, the presence of others can just as effectively inhibit individual behavior, as when a person is tempted to take something, say something, or do something that would not be approved of by others.

This facilitating and inhibiting effect, or *social control,* need not be solely dependent upon the physical presence of the *controlling agents,* such as parents, peers, or police. Often, merely being associated with the standards adhered to by a group is sufficient to affect a person's behavior. For example, special units in the military whose members are expected to perform in independent actions often rely on the affects of absentee social facilitation. In contrast, many religious sects rely heavily on absentee social interference in order to inhibit undesirable behavior among their members.

BEHAVIOR IN CROWDS John Calhoun (1962) conducted an experiment on the effects of overcrowding. Calhoun allowed rats to reproduce at an unrestricted rate within a confined space. Overcrowding was the end result, with the population reaching eighty in a cage designed to hold only fifty. To make

The importance of the individual
is often one of the first things to
be lost in a crowd. [*Cornell
Capa, Magnum.*]

FIGURE 8.4

matters worse, two dominant males set up their territories and harems at each end of the cage, thereby forcing the remaining sixty or so rats to occupy the small middle area of the cage. The result? Social and individual pathology. Mothers abandoned their offspring, infant mortality soared, and the rate of pregnancy decreased. Abnormal sexual behavior also appeared, such as homosexuality, bisexuality, hypersexuality, and sexual abstinence. Indiscriminate and unprovoked aggression was rampant; some animals attacked themselves.

Although the results of Calhoun's experiment cannot be directly linked to the startling similarity of types of behavior found among humans in some crowded urban areas, the need to investigate the psychological and sociological stresses generated through overcrowding becomes readily apparent.

When referring to crowding, however, it is sometimes important to distinguish between *spatial density* and *social density*. When the *number of subjects remains constant,* but the space is varied, the crowding is due to a change in spatial density. If the *space remains constant,* but the number of subjects confined in that space is varied, then the crowding would be due to a change in social density.

Some experiments in spatial-density research were conducted by Chalsa

Loo, who first observed groups of four- and five-year-old children at play in a 90-square-foot room, and then in a 265-square-foot room. Research in which the space remains the same, but more and more children are placed in the room (Hutt and Vaizey, 1966), would be an example of social-density research. According to Loo, "When the number of people remains constant while space decreases, members do not see each other as causes of their discomfort; rather they may perceive that they are all pawns to something greater than themselves, their physical environment." However, when space remains constant while people increase, the new members are often seen as the cause of the discomfort.

Although the density of a crowd can affect our behavior, the polarization of the crowd is also an important factor. The polarization of a crowd refers to the degree of attention the crowd focuses on any one person, event, or idea. For example, a lynch mob will usually concentrate its attention, the release of its aggression, on one or more persons in the form of a vindictive hanging. Aggressive mobs will often release their hostility indiscriminately in the form of destructive rioting or looting. Expressive mobs will usually be nonaggressive and concentrate their attention on getting a point across or merely having a good time, such as at a revival meeting or the Mardi Gras.

SOCIAL ROLES

The English philosopher Thomas Hobbes (1588–1679) believed that if human beings were to exist in their natural state, there would be "no arts; no letters; no society; and which is worst of all, continual fear and danger of violent death; the life of man [would be] solitary, poor, nasty, brutish, and short." In order to escape the dangers of the anarchy described by Hobbes, we have organized social systems. These systems are made up of members who have agreed to behave in a manner that conforms to the expectations of the community. For each status, or position, within the community, there exists a standard of expected conduct, attitudes, and beliefs. These standards of performance for the typical occupant of a given position constitute a *social role*.

The degree of success we experience in living up to role expectations will often affect the value that we place on our self-image. Each member of a society must therefore achieve a balance between maintaining independence and uniqueness (rebelling) and simultaneously sustaining a role within the community (conforming).

Conformity

A person who yields to group pressure to behave or believe in accordance with group expectations is demonstrating *conformity*. One of the classic experiments in the study of conformity and group pressure was conducted by Solomon Asch (1955). Groups of college students were asked to identify which line, chosen from a group of three appearing on a card, matched the length of a standard line appearing on another card. In this experiment, only one subject in each test group was actually naive. The other members of the group had been instructed to unanimously select an incorrect line. Even though there actually was a line on the card that was identical to the standard line, the results of Asch's experiment indicated that almost 37 percent of the naive subjects yielded to group pressure and went along with the majority's incorrect selection.

When the subjects were interviewed after the experiment, some of them explained their behavior by saying that they went along with the rest of the group just for the sake of not appearing different. Individuals who conform merely for the sake of propriety—that is, outwardly going along with the group while inwardly continuing to disagree with it—are said to be demonstrating expedient conformity. This is in contrast to true conformity, in which agreeing with the group poses no conflict between behavior and belief.

Although most instances of conforming involve action, conformity can also be shown through inaction. The members of a group may refuse to participate or get involved, as in the situation where bystanders refuse to go to the aid of someone in need of help. However, in all incidents of conformity, there will exist a conflict between one's internal standards of conduct and the external pressures emanating from the group.

The organization and expected range of behavior associated with various social roles tend to define the distinctive nature of each social system. Thus, the appropriateness or inappropriateness of an individual's behavior must be judged in accordance with the norms and values of the culture within which the behavior takes place. This consideration is the basis for the principle of *cultural relativity*. To illustrate the principle, note, for instance, that unchaperoned dating might be quite acceptable in one culture and considered to be moral behavior, though in another culture such unmonitored behavior would be considered indecent and immoral.

Cultural relativity becomes especially significant if an individual is considered to be a *marginal person*. A marginal person is "one whom fate has condemned to live in two societies and in two, not merely different, but antagonistic cultures" (Stonequist, 1937). The most common examples of a marginal person can be found among those of mixed blood, children of immigrants, and those in transition from one socioeconomic class to another. Such individuals will often experience a greater frequency of *intrarole conflict* than the nonmarginal person.

An intrarole conflict is one in which a *single role* may be fulfilled by more than one form of behavior. For example, in the "old country," wives were treated as inferiors never to be consulted in important matters. In the "new country," however, wives are considered to be equals and are included in all decision-making processes. The married son in this situation will most likely experience intrarole conflict as he simultaneously tries to live up to the expectations of how a husband should act held by his parents and the social expectations of the "new" culture in which he has been raised.

Similarly, an individual can experience *interrole conflict* while attempting to satisfy *two roles* which are incompatible. The fulfilling of the expectations of one role means the rejection of the expectations of the other. This may occur, for example, when a person is faced with the dilemma of living up to the roles of being parent-*provider,*working at two jobs in order to provide a decent living for the children, and being parent-*companion,* in which more time would be devoted to being with the children.

Often an interrole conflict is a matter of obedience. In such conflicts people must ethically determine the limits of their responsibility. Perhaps the most dramatic experiment in the study of obedience was conducted by Stanley Milgram (1965). In this experiment, average people were instructed to electrocute other people. In actuality, Milgram wished to determine why average people had obeyed the dictates of Hitler and participated in the atrocities committed agains the Jews by the Third Reich. In order to investigate this phenomenon, Milgram constructed a "shock machine" with fake switches bearing labels ranging from 15 to 450 volts. An ad in the newspaper asked for volunteers for an educational experiment in which the participants would be paid $4.50 per hour. Those answering the ad were instructed to "teach" a "learner" a series of word pairs by administering a "shock" each time the learner made a mistake. The magnitude of the shock was to be progressively increased after each mistake. The learner was actually an accomplice, acting the part of a suffering victim, and the experimenter instructed the naive teacher to "please continue" when there were protests of "I don't want to kill the man." Milgram found that 65 percent of the people participating as teachers obeyed the experimenter and continued to administer the shocks all the way to the 450-volt level, and 100 percent went beyond the 300-volt level before disobeying. This experiment indicated that most people faced with the interrole conflict between obeying the relevant ruling authority and following the dictates of their conscience will tend to obey the external authority. In other words, Nazism could just as likely occur here in America as it did in Germany.

Cooperation and Competition

Studies of cooperation and competition have indicated that cooperative groups are usually more effective than competitive groups, provide a higher degree of membership satisfaction, and produce a higher-quality product. Nonetheless, competition is still a fact of life. The drive to do better, or be better, than someone else seems to be the very essence of competition. Aristotle, in his *Politics,* said, "Inferiors revolt in order that they may be equal, and equals that they may be superior. Such is the state of mind which creates revolutions."

COOPERATION One of the most important factors influencing the degree of cooperation to be developed within a group is how the various group members perceive the amount of dedication and expenditure of effort being put forth by the other members toward the attainment of the group goal. Much of the outcome will be based on whether or not the group effort is perceived as being one-sided or two-sided cooperation.

One-sided cooperation occurs when the efforts of the group are directed toward the benefit of only *one* member. Such a situation can often be exploitive, as in the case where a group of people is forced to make extortion payments. However, one-sided cooperation can also be voluntary, as in the case where family members all participate in the care and nurturing of a newborn infant. All infants are involved in one-sided cooperative relationships until they reach the age of about two and a half to three years. From then on, children will rapidly develop two-sided cooperative relationships, with team play appearing at about six or seven years of age.

Two-sided cooperation involves a mutually beneficial relationship in which all group members receive some gratification. An example of two-sided cooperation would be that experienced between members of a mountain-climbing expedition who are tied together. Unfortunately, two-sided cooperation can also be the basis for pork-barrel politics, corporate and political bribery, and industrial price-fixing as a means of reducing competition.

Another possible manifestation of too much cooperation is the phenomenon referred to as "groupthink" by Irving Janis in his study of foreign policy decision making. Janis defines groupthink as "a deterioration of mental efficiency, reality testing and moral judgment that results from ingroup pressures." Janis believes that under certain situations, group loyalty can develop to such an extent that regardless of how wrong a member may feel the course being taken by the group might be, members are prohibited from raising controversial issues which may detract from the group's uniformity, unanimity, and cohesiveness. Janis also believes that some of the most dramatic examples of the fiascoes which can result from groupthink are such incidents as the Bay of Pigs invasion, the failure to prepare for the attack on Pearl Harbor, the invasion of North Korea, and the escalation of the Vietnam war.

COMPETITION Economic, political, and sexual competition seems to have been in existence long before recorded history began. For a time, competition in human beings was thought to be instinctual. However, today, except for the psychodynamic school and the sociobiologists, most theorists adhere to the proposition that competition is learned. The psychodynamic school supports the traditional Darwinian approach to evolution and the concept that those who are better adapted to their environment are more likely to survive and reproduce. In this view, competition is considered to be an integral part of the process of natural selection.

The sociobiological approach is also founded on the concept of evolution. However, rather than dealing with the process of natural selection at a species or group level, this approach advocates that such competitiveness is genetically based. Harvard zoologist Edward Wilson (1975) presented the theory that social behavior is genetically determined in his book *Sociobiology: The New Synthesis*. According to this theory, molecular replication, or self-duplication, began to take place millions of years ago in a primal "soup" of molecular building blocks. As the number of replicators increased, the competition for building blocks increased. Some replicators acquired the ability to break down other molecules in order to use the building blocks of the disassembled molecules for their own replication processes. These replicating molecules were the first predators. In order to protect themselves from these predators, some molecules developed protective shells within which genetic existence could continue. Richard Dawkins (1976), in his book *The Selfish Gene,* describes the evolutionary culmination of this process as one in which the sole purpose for existence, and the prime motivational force behind behavior, is to ensure the preservation and perpetuation of one's genes. The original protective shells have evolved into the complex organisms of today. Dawkins writes:

> Now they swarm in huge colonies, safe inside gigantic lumbering robots, sealed off from the outside world. . . . They are in you and in me; they created us, body and mind; and their preservation is the ultimate rationale for our existence. . . . we are their survival machines. (1976, p. 21)

The sociobiological theory, however, is highly controversial. Most sociologists and psychologists continue to believe that competitiveness is learned.

Support for this position is provided by the existence of wide variations in the degree of competition found from culture to culture. In some cultures, competition is virtually nonexistent, such as among the Zuni, Hopi, and Pueblo Indians, where cooperation predominates. In contrast, there are other cultures, such as the Kwakiutl of Vancover Island, in which competition is all-pervasive. Kwakiutl tribesmen use gifts as competitive weapons, whereby each man attempts to outgive the other until one goes bankrupt and, in some instances, even commits suicide (Benedict, 1934).

One need not go outside American society, especially the middle-class portion of American society, in order to find examples of competition, however. Due to self-generated social pressures and effective advertising, middle-class Americans are among the most competitive-minded groups in our society. Those considered to be members of the upper classes have already satisfied most of their needs and can therefore maintain a noncompetitive or a relatively low competitive profile. A similar profile of noncompetitiveness can also be found among members of the lower classes, who have learned to avoid competitive situations, such as tests and social climbing, because of prior experiences with failure and rejection. Besides, they often have a greater need for mutual cooperation in order to survive more efficiently. However, for those in the middle class, early upbringing has often been dominated by praise for *winning* rather than *participating,* for being *better* than someone else rather than for *self-improvement,* and for being the *best* rather than for overcoming a handicap.

This is not to say that all competition is bad. Competition can increase an individual's alertness, provide a challenge to do well, create an opportunity to test one's abilities, and can often add zest to what would otherwise be a boring or undesirable task. It is only when competition prompts an individual to behave unscrupulously in order to win, results in the person's participating *only* to win, or becomes the basis for an individual's self-image that competition becomes a deleterious motivating force.

Feelings of inferiority in one area prompt some people to compensate by developing other areas in which they can excel. [*Charles Gatewood.*]

FIGURE 8.5

ALFRED ADLER   The important role that competition plays in people's lives was well appreciated by Alfred Adler (1870–1937). Adler began as a disciple of Freud but eventually broke away from pure psychoanalytic theory to form what he referred to as "individual psychology." One of the basic premises of Adlerian psychology is the belief that human beings possess an innate aggressive drive. Adler called this drive a "will to power" (1927). He believed that people are not driven to establish homeostasis or equilibrium, but to attain power and superiority.

Adler based this premise on the belief that all children feel inferior and wish to overcome this feeling. According to Adler, children feel inferior because they are inferior in relation to their parents, their older siblings, and new challenges and situations. Individuals who feel *highly* inadequate are said to have an *inferiority complex*. As a consequence of these feelings of inferiority, people develop individual lifestyles that provide a means of compensating for their real or imagined inadequacies. *Compensation* is an attempt to make up for, or cover over, some weakness.

Adler believed that birth order is an important factor in the determination of a sense of inadequacy, and that children will often develop certain goal orientations as an attempt to compensate for such inadequacies. For example, first-born children are likely to perceive their younger siblings as being treated more leniently and are likely to compensate by exaggerating their own authority as the eldest. Later in life, such individuals will tend to be great respecters of authority and will compete heavily in order to obtain as much authority over others as possible.

According to Adler, the second-born child is in a very competitive position and will often be jealous of the elder sibling's adeptness at most skills and possession of special privileges because of age. In order to compensate, the second-born is likely to be overly ambitious and often predatory, that is, almost amoral with regard to getting to the top.

Last-born and only children are likely to be treated as continual babies, and they will tend to expect others to do things for them. As a result, they become very competitive for the attention and affection of others. This need to be in the spotlight is just one manifestation of the *sibling rivalry* experienced by children from multiple-child families, who must compete constantly for parental attention.

Adler believed that such rivalries and feelings of inferiority cause many individuals to develop maladaptive lifestyles in which they can perpetuate a state of needless competition. By maintaining such a state, an individual can vicariously get back at a brother, outdo a sister, or put one over on a parent.

In Adler's view one of the most disturbing manifestations of such needless perpetuation of competition occurs between the sexes. Adler refers to this competition between the sexes as "masculine protest." He defined it as "a needless domineering attitude toward the opposite sex." Adler considered the "macho man" syndrome to be a demonstration of male "masculine protest," in which the female is perceived as inferior or as a "silly little plaything." An example of female masculine protest in its extreme would be lesbianism. However, it most frequently appears in the form of the sweet little tyrant, a wife who "rules the roost of a hen-pecked husband." In either case, the striving for superiority will usually result in both partners experiencing a loss of esteem and devalued self-images.

Adler believed that cooperation is possible only when individuals cease to perceive others as the competition. Identification can take place only when individuals no longer need to see others in terms of superiority and inferiority. A marriage can be successful only when both partners become more interested in promoting the happiness of the other than in securing their own gratification.

Nonconformity

Each culture establishes its own social institutions, moral values, and social norms. Social institutions include economic, governmental, educational, and religious systems. Moral values encompass social ideas of right and wrong that respond to internal control. Social norms are the standards of behavior which have been developed by the group, and which its members are expected to follow. Those who behave in accordance with the group's expectations are said to be "conformists." Those who are not affected one way or the other by such expectations are said to be "independent." Those who act in opposition to such expectations are said to be "nonconformists."

In a simple society whose members all accept a single set of norms, deviation is fairly easy to define. However, in a complex society that has a wide variety of competing norms, it may be extremely difficult to arrive at a consensus definition of deviation.

Because no two members of a society are identical, perfect conformity to the norms is usually not expected. Some latitude is permitted for individual interpretation and expression. The more heterogeneous the group, the more liberal the latitude. However, when behavior is considered to be beyond the accepted limits for individual variance, the behavior is considered to be *deviant.*

If the nonconforming behavior is being expressed by only one person in the community, it is referred to as *individual deviation.* This would include such instances as an individual becomimg a hermit, developing a shoe fetish, or becoming a juvenile delinquent in an otherwise law-abiding community. If the nonconforming behavior is being expressed by an individual who is conforming to the norms of a group which behaves in the same nonconforming manner, the group is considered to be a *deviant subculture,* and the individual is participating in *group deviation.* Examples of group deviation would be when an individual becomes a juvenile delinquent in a ghetto by joining a street gang, drops out of society in order to become a "hippie," or migrates to a community in order to more easily associate with other homosexuals.

It is important to keep in mind that such deviant subcultures have their own separate norms which are often adhered to very closely. For instance, the group will often have its own manner of dress, its own private language, stylized greetings and acknowledgments, taboos, and moral values, all of which are often based on a strong belief in a particular ideology or religion. Once such norms become "formalized" and accepted by a relatively large membership, the group can be referred to as a "counterculture." The hippie movement would be considered a counterculture. According to Theodore Roszak, in his book *The Making of a Counterculture,* it is "a culture so radically disaffiliated from the mainstream assumptions of our society that it scarcely looks to many as a culture at all, but takes on the alarming appearance of a barbaric intrusion."

Another example of counterculture would be the aggressive black groups who seek to use "black pride" to destroy the myth of the passive black who is content with his or her place in society. The "red power," "gray power," and "Chicano" movements could also be considered countercultures. Whether the dominant society approves or disapproves of a counterculture is often dependent upon whether the deviation is perceived as enhancing or detracting from the society's desired image. For example, setting up a rural commune, referred to as a "kibbutz," is approved of by the urban society in Israel. However, attempts to establish rural communes in the United States have met with considerable disapproval.

The path each member of a society follows must ultimately be chosen as a matter of conscience and of reaching an acceptable balance between one's personal integrity and one's responsibility to the group. The English poet Sir Fulke Greville (1554–1628) once noted: "It is not enough that you can form, nay, and follow, the most excellent rules for conducting yourself in the world. You must also know when to deviate from them, and where lies the exception."

Prejudice

Prejudice has been defined as "an unfavorable attitude toward an object (idea, or people), which tends to be highly stereotyped, emotionally charged, and not easily changed by contrary information" (Krech et al., 1962). Prejudices are not instinctive, but solely the result of *learning*. Prejudicial attitudes are usually unjustified overgeneralizations acquired from the observation of models, or people who are admired and accepted as authorities. Prejudice is usually learned through *teaching* rather than actual contact or experience. What contacts do occur merely serve to maintain the prejudice through occasional reinforcements.

Although the acquisition of prejudice is not inevitable, it is, in one form or another, almost a universal phenomenon. Anatole France pointed this out in his book *The Crime of Sylvestre Bonnard,* when he wrote, "He flattered himself on being a man without any prejudices; and this pretension itself is a very great prejudice."

RACISM   *Racism* is the attitude that one race of people is superior to another and is therefore entitled to certain rights and privileges that the other is not entitled to. Very often the racist person will attempt to enforce the discriminatory privileges that are a consequence of this attitude. With regard to the expression of racist attitudes, Stokely Carmichael and Charles Hamilton, in their book *Black Power: The Politics of Liberation in America,* distinguish between what they refer to as "individual racism" and "institutional racism."

Individual racism is usually expressed on a personal, one-to-one basis with the intent of humiliating or injuring its victims or denying them the use of their property. Examples would be the black person forced to step off the sidewalk by a white person when they meet on the street, the beating up of an Indian who enters a segregated bar, or the confiscation of Jewish property by the Nazis.

Institutional racism is usually expressed on a community level. In such instances, prejudicial attitudes have been codified, legalized, and ingrained in tradition. Examples include state prohibitions against minority voting privileges, segregation of schools, and taboos against interracial sexual encounters.

The reasons for maintaining racist attitudes vary with the culture, group, or individual. One of the most common reasons is for the purpose of *scapegoating*. Scapegoating is the practice of displacing aggression or blame onto a particular person or minority group. Often such aggressive feelings are a result of political, social, or economical frustration. An example of political scapegoating might be the McCarthy hearings of the fifties. The plight of the

Okies in the thirties would be an example of social scapegoating. The lynching of blacks in the South and the killing of Jews in Nazi Germany would be examples of economic scapegoating.

Another reason racial attitudes are maintained is for the purpose of sustaining social ideals and myths. For instance, the belief that another race is less intelligent, irresponsible, and shiftless tends to support an attitude of paternalism toward that race. In addition, double standards can be allowed, according to which it is considered improper to cheat or lie to members of one's own race, but quite acceptable when directed toward another race.

The limitation of membership in select groups is also a reason for some people to support racism. Feelings of superiority can often be artificially sustained by denying membership in the group to those who are "unworthy." In an attempt to measure the intensity of the racial attitudes held by individuals, E. L. Bogardus (1925) developed a "social distance scale." The use of this scale involves asking the subjects if they would accept members of a specific race or nationality into the following relationships: (1) close kinship by marriage; (2) in my club as personal chums; (3) on my street as neighbors; (4) in my occupation; (5) as citizens in my country; (6) as visitors in my country; or (7) would exclude my country. The subsequent application of this social distance scale tended to support the proposition that prejudice is often a matter of degree.

Studies have shown that not only groups of people but also individuals often need to maintain a sense of superiority. It has also been shown that a person who feels inadequate will often develop prejudicial attitudes toward another race to compensate for this feeling. For example, studies conducted by Bettelheim and Janowitz (1950) indicated that returning World War II veterans who did not obtain jobs as good as the ones they left were more anti-Semitic and antiblack than those who obtained similar or better jobs than those they left.

Other individuals seem to possess a predisposition toward having an authoritarian personality, which often results in the development of prejudicial attitudes. Because such individuals are usually oversubmissive to strong authority, they often need to release pent-up feelings towards a nonthreatening group, usually a minority group. In addition to the authoritarian personality, people who have paranoid tendencies will often direct their suspicions toward a particular group or race as being the source of their persecution. Although such individuals are few in number, the real danger from such people lies in their attaining positions of leadership, wherein their paranoid attitudes can become contagious.

SEXISM The propensity for one group of people to find a reason for being prejudiced against another group seems almost infinite. Many prejudices are based on acquired characteristics. Others are based on inherited characteristics. Some prejudicial attitudes are transient, but others take on a historical or traditional quality. One of the most enduring prejudices, however, is that which seems to exist between the sexes: *sexism.* In actual practice sexism usually

FIGURE 8.6 The reasons for maintaining racist attitudes varies with the culture, group, or individual; however, they almost always include feelings of insecurity. [*Gerhard E. Gscheidle, Peter Arnold.*]

refers to the sexist attitudes which maintain that women are inferior. Sexists attempt to impose second-class citizenship upon the female half of the population.

Sexism, like racism, results in stereotyping, discrimination, and devalued self-images. Until recently, women were supposed to merely accept their genetic lot in life: be pretty, get married, and raise children. The image of what being female in American society meant was divided (primarily by advertising efforts) between being the "sex symbol," who was capable of buying her way to the marriage altar, and the fertile hausfrau, who swapped her sexuality for a clean laundry. Germaine Greer, in *The Female Eunuch* (1971), states: "Because she is the *emblem* of spending ability and the chief spender, she is also the most effective seller of this world's goods. Every survey has shown that the image of an attractive woman is the most effective advertising gimmick." Although women may represent the ideal spender, they certainly have not achieved the status of the ideal earner.

Even though the Equal Pay Act of 1963 outlawed pay discrimination because of sex, the practice of paying women less than men doing the same job, while their qualifications are otherwise equal, tends to persist. A government survey indicated that as of 1972, *two-thirds* of all full-time working women earned *less* than $7000, while during the same year *three-fourths* of all full-time working men earned *more* than $7000. These statistics are representative of the disparity between incomes found in other surveys. For example, according to statistics published by the U. S. Department of Labor, the median income of full-time women workers in 1968 was $4457, while the income of full-time male workers was almost $7500. As an indication of the trend that is developing with regard to such disparities, in 1955 the median income of working women was 64 percent of the median for men; by 1968, the median for women was down to 58 percent of the male median.

For decades, the stereotyping of women workers as merely "earning pin money" or "wanting to do something a little more interesting in their lives" provided fragile justification for providing them with low pay for lowly jobs. Women were often denied access to the better jobs because they would "just get married or pregnant anyway." However, this image of the female worker is no longer valid, if indeed it ever was. In 1973, almost two-thirds of all American working women were either heads of households (single, widowed, or divorced) or married to men whose incomes were below the poverty level.

The 1964 Civil Rights Act forbids job discrimination due to sex. However, social expectations tend to maintain a great deal of job discrimination by default. A 1965 survey of 2000 executives indicated that two-thirds of the men and one-fifth of the women would not want to work for a woman. A survey conducted by Joan Crowley et al. (1973) revealed the effect of such expectations. Crowley's survey indicated that 64 percent of the men wanted to be promoted, but only 48 percent of the women wanted to be promoted. On the surface, such results would indicate a lack of aggressiveness in women. However, a follow-up survey showed that one of the main reasons for such apathy among females was that most of the jobs they held were dead ends. For the women, therefore, promotion did not mean moving closer to the top. It merely meant the assumption of a lot more responsibility for only a little more pay.

In 1973 *Fortune* magazine reported on the ten highest-ranking women in big business. Eight of the ten made it to the top because of family connections, marriage, or the fact that they helped create the business that they presided over, not by working their way up through the corporate hierarchy. In addition, fewer than 1 percent of all working women in America were doing work considered to be "professional." This is in contrast with the situation in the Soviet Union, where one-third of the engineers and three-fourths of the physicians are women.

The question of equal opportunity and equal pay becomes more salient every year. In 1953 only 26 percent of all married women held jobs, whereas by 1973, over 42 percent of all wives were working outside the home. If one considers only those wives with children between the ages of six and seventeen, the figure jumps to 50.1 percent. For most women the problems arising from being victims of discrimination on the job are compounded by the fact that they are expected to work *in addition to* taking care of the house and children.

According to studies being conducted by Marcia Guttentag (1976) of Harvard University, the stresses associated with sexist stereotyping, occupational discrimination, and being delegated to a position of social inferiority may be contributing to the rise of mental illness among women. Figures provided by the National Institute of Mental Health indicate that *twice* as many women as men are diagnosed as suffering from depression. The highest rates occur among women between the ages of twenty-one and forty-four. This is not to say that men do not experience depression as well, only that most surveys show that no matter how one defines mental illness, American women tend to appear less healthy than American men.

PROSOCIAL BEHAVIOR

It was the great Dutch philosopher Benedict Spinoza (1632–1677) who stated that "Man is a social animal," but it was the famous German genius Johann von Goethe (1749–1832) who said, "Kindness is the golden chain by which society is bound together." Many today fear that this chain has fallen into disrepair and that people are becoming more and more reluctant to help a stranger or become involved with each other. However, the words of the English philosopher Francis Bacon (1561–1626) are as true today as they were almost four centuries ago: "If a man be gracious and courteous to strangers, it shows he is a citizen of the world, and that his heart is no island cut off from other lands, but a continent that joins to them."

In a society that values independence and self-reliance, the question may often arise, "Am I my brother's keeper?" (Genesis 4:9). Under what circumstances is it more appropriate to allow others to cope with their own problems, and at what point does one step in and render aid? The decision to intervene or not is often a difficult one. A person facing such a dilemma must consider such factors as (1) "What if my efforts to help are rejected, and I end up looking like a fool?"; (2) "What if I try to help and, as a result, someone gets hurt?"; (3) "What if I don't try to help and, as a result, someone gets hurt?"; or (4) "What if I try to help and *I* get hurt?"

Each of us must resolve within ourselves the moral conflict between being egoistic, with personal safety and self-regard taking first priority, and being altruistic, with the well-being and best interests of others considered to be the greater good. In the words of Immanuel Kant (*Critique of Pure Reason,* 1781), "Morality is not the doctrine of how we may make ourselves happy, but how we make ourselves *worthy* of happiness."

Who Will Be a Good Samaritan?

In 1964, Kitty Genovese was murdered in Queens, New York, while thirty-eight neighbors looked on. The stabbing attack lasted for over half an hour, and the assailant was frightened away two separate times when people turned their lights on in order to investigate the screaming. But since no one came to the victim's aid or even called the police, the assailant was able to return a third time and kill Miss Genovese. Later, when the assailant was questioned by the police about his boldness in returning three different times after all the screaming, he answered, "I knew they wouldn't do anything. People never do." When the witnesses were questioned, most of them justified their behavior by saying that they thought someone else would do something or call the police.

This event shocked many Americans. It seemed to epitomize the social indifference and alienation that is thought to exist in today's society. In 1965, in what some thought was an attempt to legislate morality, California became the first state to pass a "Good Samaritan" law. This law was enacted in order to provide a means for compensating private citizens for injuries suffered while trying to prevent a crime, catch a criminal, or render aid in an emergency. By 1976, fourteen different states had passed similar laws. In 1968, Vermont enacted a law making it a criminal offense *not* to go to the aid of another person who is in danger, thus becoming the first state to follow the legal precedent set by most European countries. Sociologists, however, knew that legislation alone would not answer why some people fail to help others during an emergency. As a consequence, many sociologists began independent studies in the area of *prosocial behavior*.

Research findings indicated that we are more likely to come to the aid of another person if we are *alone* with the person in need of help (Latané and Darley, 1968; Latané and Rodin, 1969). It was also found that when there are other people present, as in the case of Kitty Genovese's murder, a *diffusion of responsibility* tends to take place. Personal responsibility is spread from one individual to everyone who is present. Such diffusion seems to be reduced somewhat when the members of the group are able to communicate with each other and thereby delegate authority or organize a plan.

How others are reacting to the situation also seems to have an influence on whether or not a person decides to intervene. Latané and Darley (1968) performed an experiment in which smoke was allowed to enter a room containing two confederates and one naive subject. The confederates were instructed to ignore the smoke and present an air of indifference. With the confederates reacting to the situation casually, only 10 percent of the naive subjects (who were college students) reported the smoke to authorities. In contrast, 75 percent of the naive subjects reported the smoke when they were in the room alone, and 38 percent when all three individuals in the room were naive. Bryan and Test (1967) also found that the way others react has an effect on whether or not a bystander will intervene. By having a desired behavior demonstrated, or *modeled,* first, the researchers found that the frequency of bystander intervention would often *double*. These findings resulted from observing the frequency with which passing motorists stopped to assist a woman with a flat tire. In one experimental situation, the woman's car with the flat tire was the only car by the road. In a second situation, a second car at which a motorist had stopped to help change a flat tire was placed nearby in order to provide a model.

The *sex* of the participants and the degree of *dependency* also appear to be important factors in determining whether or not a person will give assistance to another. Research conducted by Scholer and Bateson (1965) indicated that females would help a highly dependent female more than they would a less dependent female, whereas males tended to help a less dependent male more than they would a highly dependent male. Further research along this line by Gruder and Cook (1971) indicated that such results were more heavily influenced by the sex of the beneficiary than by the sex of the helper. These differences seem to follow social role expectancies. The female is perceived as weaker and more helpless, so it is socially acceptable to help females. The males in our society are generally seen as being more aggressive and competitive, and, therefore, it is less acceptable to give assistance to those who have failed to live up to their roles. Such findings may explain why males tend to render assistance in an emergency more often than females. They are expected to do so, and their more frequent involvement may often be a matter of maintaining an image rather than of greater courage.

What Is a Good Samaritan?

The correctness or incorrectness of a decision is fully realized only after the fact—in retrospect. So it seems to be with regard to rendering assistance to others in times of need. Only in retrospect can one truly evaluate the balance between the rewards and costs associated with having helped others.

The ethics involved with helping others is often founded in *intent.* It is not enough to provide for others if the intent behind the giving of those provisions is to create indebtedness, an opportunity to call due a favor owed at some future date. Nor is it enough to help only those who are capable of helping back, while forsaking those who are unable to reciprocate, such as the old, the poor, and the handicapped. In many instances, the price of assistance is dependence. Some people never learn self-reliance because things are always done for them by someone else. In such cases, the most effective help is often rendered by withdrawing one's help completely.

The ability to accurately perceive the appropriateness of one's action or inaction develops as a by-product of social maturation and the development of moral reasoning. Lawrence Kohlberg (1963, 1969) has proposed a theory on the development of moral reasoning. Kohlberg's theory is based on the belief that moral reasoning develops through a progressive hierarchy containing six stages.

The first two stages constitute what Kohlberg refers to as the "premoral" level. At this point the individual's moral values are based on physical acts and needs rather than social standards. During *stage one,* the moral values of children or adults are based on *personal fear* and the desire to *avoid punishment*—"Might makes right." In *stage two,* moral values have a more *egocentric* motive behind them. If an act contributes in some way to satisfying one's personal needs, it is "good." If an act interferes with self-satisfaction, it is considered "bad."

The second two stages of moral development are referred to by Kohlberg as the "conventional" level. Now the primary concern is to live up to the expectations of others and maintain social order. The conventional level is made up of stage three and stage four. In *stage three,* the values of others are *internalized.* At this stage, individuals attempt to think and behave in accordance with how they believe their parents or peers would think or behave in a given situation. *Stage four* takes this type of reasoning a step further, and the person begins to think and behave in accordance with the dictates of established authority. Moral reasoning is often very rigid and inflexible at this stage. This attitude is frequently represented by such statements as "Because that's the law," "I don't make the rules, I just obey them," or "Because I said so."

The *third level* in the process of developing moral reasoning is called the "principle" level. Moral values are now based on relatively abstract principles and standards of a universal nature. Like the previous levels, level three is made up of two stages, stage five and stage six. People in *stage five* will base their moral values on a more flexible interpretation of rules, regulations, and standards. Judgment is more relative than absolute, and consideration is given to extenuating circumstances. An individual reasoning at this stage would be likely to say something like "You may win by using such methods, but it would be a shallow victory." People whose moral reasoning has developed to *stage six* will be basing their moral values on universal principles that have been internalized and are thought to be an integral part of one's sense of integrity and an identification with the dignity and worth of others. Their values are based on mutual trust and respect, and are founded on one of the oldest, yet simplest, moral principles of all, the Golden Rule: "Do unto others as you would have them do unto you." Unfortunately, Kohlberg admits, most people operate at the conventional level of morality, and many operate at the premoral level throughout their lives.

SUMMARY

This chapter has explored group dynamics as revealed in groups of two (dyads), three (triads), or more members. We found that groups can be *formal,* with well-established positions, titles, and lines of communication, or *informal,* with friendship as the basis and with communication often via a grapevine.

It was pointed out that people belong to more groups than they may realize. This results from the phenomena known as *compulsory, circumstantial,* and *voluntary* membership.

The process of socialization was investigated Erik Erikson's eight-stage theory of psychosocial development was presented. The effects of socialization on perception, language, and behavior, when others are present or absent, was also looked into.

Social roles, and the costs and rewards associated with *conforming, cooperating,* and *competing* with the norms set by a culture, were discussed, with particular emphasis on Alfred Adler's theory on feelings of inferiority.

The origin and consequences of such antisocial behaviors as *aggression, prejudice,* and *social deviation* were also considered. The discussion concluded with a treatment of *prosocial* behavior and one's personal and social responsibilities.

DISCUSSION QUESTIONS

1 Make a list of the number of groups you actually belong to. Which of these groups represent voluntary membership, and which represent involuntary membership?

2 Are there particular groups you would like to belong to but find it difficult or impossible to join? For what reasons?

3 Do you belong to any groups that you would prefer not to be included in? What can you do about such membership?

4 Do you agree or disagree with Erikson's premise that individual development continues beyond adolescence into old age?

5 Do you work better in the company of others or when alone?

6 What group of people seems to have the greatest influence on how you behave—how you think (parents, peers, ethnic group, etc.)?

7 In what areas do you try to maintain your uniqueness and in what areas do you find yourself conforming?

8 Do you believe that your birth order has had an affect on your personality development as Adler proposes?

9 In what ways have you been a victim of prejudice? In what ways are you prejudiced?

10 Do you believe that people are becoming less concerned about the welfare of others or more fearful of their own welfare? Is this a reason for becoming less involved with the plight of others?

EXPERIENTIAL EXERCISES

1 Try to imagine what your life might be like if your group memberships were to change radically, for example, if you belonged to a different race, sex, nationality, economic group, etc.

2 The next time you are at a popular sporting event, watch the reactions of the crowd as the game progresses—winning, losing, referee decisions, etc. What are the cues that allow you to infer the mood of the crowd?

3 Using Erik Erikson's eight stages of development as a guide, list the crucial factor from each stage (trust versus mistrust, autonomy versus shame, initiative versus guilt, etc.) that seem to be most representative of your own personality.

CHAPTER 9

INTERPERSONAL

RELATIONSHIPS

[James Carroll, Editorial Photocolor Archives.]

This awareness of himself as a separate entity, the awareness of his own short life span, of the fact that without his will he is born and against his will he dies, that he will die before those whom he loves, or they before him, awareness of his aloneness and separateness, of his helplessness before the forces of nature and of society, all this makes his separate, disunited existence an unbearable prision. He would become insane could he not liberate himself from this prison and reach out, unite himself in some form or other with men, with the world outside.

Erich Fromm
The Art of Loving

RELATING TO OTHERS

One of the most powerful statements on interpersonal relationships was made almost 2000 years ago: "Greater love hath no man than this, that a man lay down his life for his friends" (John 15:13). Although one may not be called upon to make such a sacrifice except in the most dire of circumstances, the statement tends to exemplify the extent to which interpersonal relationships can develop.

Due to our potential for developing intense emotional involvements, it is often necessary to be selective in (1) choosing with whom we are to become involved, (2) determining what the nature of the involvement will be, and (3) deciding to what degree of intensity the involvement will be allowed to progress.

Our selection of the people we are to become involved with is often based on our *perceptions* of them. For example, do we see them as being attractive, considerate, or useful? Our determination of the nature of the relationship is often based upon *social influences*. For instance, is the person we are interested in married, a close relation, or of a particular socioeconomic class? The degree of intensity to which the relationship is allowed to progress is often determined by how *vulnerable* we allow ourselves to be.

Judging Others

The way we relate to others is greatly influenced by our perceptions of them. Our perceptions need not necessarily concur with the perceptions of others, however. It is commonplace to hear such statements as: "I don't know what you see in him." "You've got to be kidding. That's the one you've been raving about?" "I know he's your friend, but I just don't trust him." "I know most people think that she just uses people, but once you get to know her. . . ."

These differences of opinion come from the fact that the person observed merely provides the stimuli from which our sensations can be formed and our perception interprets these sensations.

As an illustration, consider the words "add," "subtract," "increase," and "multiply," and determine which one does not belong in the group.

Many will perceive the words "add," "subtract," and "multiply" as mathematically oriented. Therefore, "increase" is perceived as not belonging to the group. Others, however, may perceive the words "add," "increase," and "multiply" as implying quantities that are all growing larger and, therefore, they perceive that "subtract" does not belong to the group.

There is no right or wrong answer. Each of us is free to choose either interpretation, just as we are free to interpret the variety of physical, intellectual, and aesthetic qualities of each individual we encounter.

THE PROCESS OF PERCEPTION   The Gestalt school of psychology concentrates most of its efforts on increasing our understanding of the process of perception. Its theme, "The whole is greater than the sum of the parts," emphasizes that one cannot merely quantify the physical measurements of a person's face to arrive at a definition of beauty, or list the various deeds an individual has performed in order to define love. The reason this cannot be done is because we always add a little something of ourselves to each situation we perceive. Vital to the formation of our perception of the world around us, and the people in it, is what we bring with us—our past experiences, our values, and our needs.

Another important factor influencing perception is the effect of the circumstances surrounding the event when it is experienced. For example, events occurring in close proximity to each other tend to be perceived as related. People who appear similar to other people tend to be perceived as being alike, as are people who are perceived as being part of a particular group. Individuals who surround themselves with weak followers may appear important. However, the same individuals, when surrounded by strong leaders, may seem unimportant. Our perceptions of people can also be influenced by our perceptions of the badness or goodness of their behavior. Meeting a police officer issuing a traffic ticket can create quite a different impression than meeting an officer who has just saved a child's life.

FIRST IMPRESSIONS   Kurt Lewin (1890–1947) developed the concept of "life space," which takes into consideration a person's external and internal environments as they are perceived at any given moment. Lewin believed that our behavior is influenced by the way that we see the world, not by the way the world is, and that our interpretation of the world is subject to distortion, delusion, and deception.

One of the most common sources of error when forming an opinion of another person is making a *judgment at first sight*. First impressions have a tremendous influence on the way we interpret any additional future information about that person. In addition, there is often a strong tendency to perceive others in terms of simple stereotypes, or prejudices, thereby perceiving someone who has just been introduced as a "typical female," "another racist," or "obviously sexist."

Often, irrelevant characteristics are taken into consideration and generalized to form an overall impression of an individual. This phenomenon is referred to as the "halo effect." For example, physically attractive people are often perceived as being more intelligent, witty, and honest than those who are considered less attractive. A study by Karen Dion (1972) indicated that teachers tend to be more lenient with attractive children when disciplining for misconduct. Other studies have reported that teachers' expectations of performance, assumptions of intelligence, and predictions of future success are often higher for attractive students than for those they consider unattractive.

One's attitudes can also affect interpersonal perceptions. Fritz Heider (1957) talks of two people achieving a state of "balance" or "imbalance" in establishing a relationship. If the two people like each other and both like sailing, or if they like each other and both dislike sailing, then a balance exists, and the relationship is likely to flourish. However, if the two like each other, but one likes sailing and the other dislikes sailing, then a state of imbalance exists, and the relationship will experience a certain degree of stress. A state of imbalance also exists if the two dislike each other but both like sailing.

COGNITIVE DISSONANCE   One's attitudes and beliefs can also introduce stress into a relationship through what is referred to as "cognitive dissonance." Cognitive dissonance is said to occur when one attempts to accept simultaneously two ideas that are incompatible. In this situation the acceptance of one idea requires the rejection of the other, such as when one believes that justice is blind but also believes that the rich go free and the poor go to jail. Cognitive dissonance also occurs when one's behavior is incompatible with one's beliefs, such as when an individual believes that candy is fattening, but cannot seem to resist taking just one more piece of chocolate.

This incompatibility between the way we think and the way we act attracted the interest of Leon Festinger (1957). Festinger developed a concept of cognitive dissonance that advocated that this incompatability between thought and action can cause a great deal of discomfort. In order to reduce this discomfort, it is necessary for us to either change our *beliefs* or change our *behavior*.

Festinger successfully tested his hypothesis in an experiment in which students were asked to carry out a very boring task. After they had completed this task, each student was asked to try to persuade another student to do the task by lying about how interesting the task was. One group of students was paid $1 for lying and another group was paid $20 dollars for lying. Festinger found that those who were paid only $1 had changed their attitude toward the task and believed that the task was actually interesting. Those students who were paid $20 still believed the task was boring. This was exactly what Festinger had predicted, anticipating that the students paid only $1 would experience cognitive dissonance between their belief that it is wrong to lie for a paltry $1 and the fact that they had done just that. As a result, they were

FIGURE 9.1 The need to relate to others seems to be one of the most basic needs. [*Oliver R. Pierce, Photo Researchers.*]

motivated to change their belief that the task was boring. Therefore, when they told others how interesting the task was, they would not be lying. This type of mental shifting is often required with regard to maintaining relationships.

For example, it is not uncommon for people to experience cognitive dissonance between their sexual morals and their sexual conduct. If one believes that it is wrong to have sexual relationships before marriage, but nevertheless becomes sexually involved, then it is often necessary to convince oneself that it is *not* wrong to become sexually involved before marriage. One might argue, "How else are you going to find out if the two of you are sexually compatible?" "You can't really get to know someone without going to bed together." The alternative to changing one's belief is to change one's behavior.

The Need to Relate

The need to affiliate with others seems to be one of the most basic of human needs. We need to relate to others to attain greater security, to sustain ourselves as a race, and to perpetuate our ideas and accumulate knowledge. However, our greatest need for relating to others is our need to *escape from loneliness.* Erich Fromm, in his book *The Art of Loving* (1970), states:

> This awareness of himself as a separate entity, the awareness of his own short life span, of the fact that without his will he is born and against his will he dies, that he will die before those whom he loves, or they before him, the awareness of his aloneness and separateness, of his helplessness before the forces of nature and of society, all this makes his separate, disunited existence an unbearable prison. He would become insane could he not liberate himself from this prison and reach out, unite himself in some form or other with men, with the world outside. (pp.6–7)

According to Fromm (1947), we are primarily social beings, and we can fully understand ourselves only in terms of our relationship with others. For Fromm, individual psychology is really social psychology, since he believes that our individual character traits are developed from our experiences with others. Fromm believes that one's character represents one's habitual ways of acting, thinking, and feeling, and that character types take on either a *nonproductive* or a *productive* orientation. According to Fromm, a nonproductive personality is one which lacks individuality, creativeness, and a desire to contribute to the general welfare. A nonproductive personality type's basic orientation to relationships with others is "What's in it for me?" Individuals adhering to such an orientation can fall into four categories: (1) receiving type, (2) exploiting type, (3) hoarding type, and (4) marketing type.

A person with a *receiving type* of orientation often has a "the-world-owes-me-a-living" attitude. Such a person has not learned that one must *earn* what one wants, and, therefore, this person will often expect others to provide what is desired upon request. As a consequence, such an individual becomes highly dependent on others and will often establish "submissive" or "master-slave" relationships. Receptive people often feel inadequate ("I'm no good, all good things are external") and insecure ("What if people stopped giving the good things to me?"). As a result, they usually require constant reassurance and repeated demonstrations of affection from their provider.

Unlike the receptively oriented individual, people who have an *exploitive type* of orientation do not *wait* to be given what is wanted; they usually just *take* what they want. To such a person, waiting for someone else to provide leads to frustration. It is much faster to act for oneself. Other people are evaluated in accordance with their perceived usefulness. As a consequence, the exploitive individual will usually establish a parasitic relationship. When the host is no longer of any use, that person is discarded. The exploitive individual has not developed a capacity for empathy or compassion and tends to see the world as one in which "everyone is out to get everyone else." In order to avoid getting taken, exploitive individuals will find themselves in a constant state of competition for the *dominant* position within a relationship.

An individual with a *hoarding type* of orientation is one who tends to be overly conservative. Such an individual is often suspicious of anything new or different and will, therefore, usually appear obstinate when confronted with change. Hoarding people prefer things to remain the way they are and are often compulsive in their need for orderliness. Because of this compulsiveness, they often lack spontaneity, originality, and creativity. Such individuals also tend to mistrust other people. Consequently, they tend to keep their thoughts, opinions, and feelings to themselves.

People who have a *marketing type* of orientation toward life tend to see the world as a marketplace in which they personally are both the product and the seller. Such individuals will read the market and then attempt to meet the demand. This attitude prevails in choosing their careers, selecting their mates, and deciding which friends to associate with. They allow their standards of value to be set by others and will then make chameleonlike efforts to satisfy these standards. Since such individuals value themselves as a commodity, they usually sell themselves to the highest bidder. In other words, they tend to stay within a relationship only as long as no one comes along with a better offer.

In contrast to the nonproductive personality types just described, Fromm (1947) also believes that we have the potential to develop *productive types* of personality dedicated to the attainment of knowledge and love. The productive personality seeks to develop its full potential, so as to experience a sense of worth and significance through self-expression, rather than solely through the acquisition of material goods. Productive personalities attain a sense of pride through creating and doing, and are able to identify with the products and activities with which they become involved. The productive personality is also able to identify with the efforts of others, thereby attaining a feeling of empathy, compassion, or caring.

Establishing an Understanding within a Relationship

The success or failure of almost any type of relationship depends a great deal upon (1) the degree of effectiveness maintained in communication and (2) the degree of compatibility arrived at between that which is *expected* from the relationship and that which is *provided*. Misinterpretations of what one person is trying to communicate to another, or misunderstandings arising from having failed to satisfy certain expectations, can often create unnecessary tensions within a relationship. All too often, such misperceptions will actually destroy an otherwise viable relationship and cause needless emotional pain and loneliness. Therefore, it is imperative that these factors be considered whenever two or more people attempt to relate to one another. It doesn't matter whether the relationship is between employer-employee, teacher-student, husband-wife, friend-friend, or stranger-stranger; what does matter is that they *understand* each other.

BERNE'S EGO STATES   Eric Berne (1964), in his book *Games People Play*, describes some of the factors that contribute to ineffective communication and incompatibility within a relationship. According to Berne, one of the most important factors to consider in communication patterns within a relationship is the *ego state* of the individuals involved. The term "ego state" refers to a particular set of feelings that are associated with the way one behaves when in a certain state of mind. For example, the ego state of an individual while being reprimanded by a policeman might reflect embarrassment or shame and be quite different from the ego state of that same individual while discussing a project with an employee and experiencing anger or disappointment.

Berne believes that the ego states of each individual fall into one of three categories "(1) ego states which resemble those of parental figures; (2) ego states which are autonomously directed toward objective appraisal of reality; and (3) those which represent archaic relics, still-active ego states which were fixated in early childhood." (1964, p. 23). These three ego states are commonly referred to as one's Parent, Adult, and Child, respectively.

A person's parent ego state is based on an internalization of one's perception of one's parents. That is, each of us carries an image of what we think our parents were like. When people are under the direct influence of this parental image, they will tend to respond as parents ("Don't give me any excuses, just do it!"). When under the indirect influence of this parental image, people will respond the way their parents would have wanted ("Now, that's what I call performance."). A person's parent state serves two main functions. First, it provides an ego state suitable for raising children. Secondly, it enables people to respond quickly and effectively to certain situations which require someone to provide supervision.

Our adult ego state refers to our ability to be objective and businesslike while making decisions. The adult ego state represents a state of maturity and the ability to maintain control, act dispassionately, and respond appropriately. Our adult state is the one that calculates the "probabilities which are essential for dealing effectively with the outside world."

The child ego state refers to the image people have internalized of their childhood qualities. The child state is thought to be "childlike," rather than "childish," to distinguish between behaving spontaneously or creatively and merely behaving immaturely. The child state can exist in two forms: the *adapted* or the *natural* child. The adapted child reflects the ego state of people who continuously attempt to modify, or adapt, their behavior to comply with the expectations of their parents. In contrast, the natural child is reflected in spontaneous expressions of creativity or rebelliousness.

Berne calls communication between people a "transaction." The initiating event is referred to as a "transactional stimulus," and the subsequent reaction to this event is a "transactional response." Transactions are considered *complementary* if they are appropriate and follow a natural order in a healthy relationship. For example, communication between two adult ego states would be a complementary transaction, as would transactions between parent and parent states (critical evaluation), two child states (playing), and parent and child states (teaching).

Transactions are considered to be *crossed transactions* when the ego state of one person attempts to communicate with the complementary ego state of another (for example, adult to adult, or parent to parent), but evokes instead a "crossed" response from an inappropriate ego state (such as child to parent) and communication breaks down. For instance, the adult ego state of one person may attempt a complementary transaction with the adult ego state of another: "Well, we've got a long, hard drive ahead of us, so we'd best just stick to soft drinks tonight." However, the other person may create a crossed transaction with a child-motivated response, such as "Speak for yourself, good buddy. I can drink all the booze I want and still get us there on time." In such cases, the people involved are attempting to communicate through different ego states. Understanding, as well as the relationship, will tend to suffer because of this differentiation. In a sense, the two are "just not communicating at the same level."

LEVELS OF COMMUNICATION One of the most common sources of error in communication is in determining which level an individual is communicating on. For example, if a loved one is communicating at an intimate level in an attempt to express how important remembering one's birthday really is, and another person is operating at a much more superficial level, talking about how cheap the gift is, then, most likely, their attempts to communicate will end in failure. Bernard and Huckins (1975) discuss "five levels of discourse," or levels of communication, at which people will attempt to relate to one another. Each level has its own combination of content, meaning, and emotional involvement, as well as its advantages and disadvantages.

Level V is the *least intimate* level of discourse and is most commonly used during casual encounters. The conversation is often cliché-ridden, full of social chitchat, and often meaningless beyond maintaining a defensive facade. This level of communication is generally thought of as an "I-It" level, rather than an "I-Thou" level of discourse. Martin Buber (1970) believed that another person should not be treated as an "It," a thing "to be used or experienced, nor as an object of interest or fascination" (1970, p. 11). Buber's concern was that each individual be perceived as a "Thou," someone unique and irreplaceable. For Buber, "every being I encounter is seen to be essential" (1970, p. 46).

Level V is also thought of as friendly dialogue, however, and can be useful in preparation for more meaningful dialogue in the future.

Level IV is primarily informative and is used to transmit facts, directions, or knowledge. Dialogue at this level will often take on the characteristics of a lecture, which may or may not be appropriate to the situation. For example, communicating at Level IV is absolutely necessary in a teacher-student, guide-tourist, or journeyman-apprentice situation. However, communication at Level IV between equals will often carry derogatory overtones, and the recipient may feel humiliated or resentful at being lectured to.

Level III is the first level at which an individual's *true* feelings are introduced and a sense of an "I-Thou" attitude begins to appear. The feelings introduced at this level of communication are usually feelings about one's perceptions of the external environment. For instance, an individual might say something like "I really don't like the way the election turned out," "I'm sure glad to see them fixing up that part of town," or "I think this is one of the most beautiful views in the world."

Level II is similar to Level III in that an attempt to express one's feelings is being made. However, in this level of communication, the feelings that are expressed are about what is going on inside the person rather than what is going on outside. A person attempting to communicate at Level II is much more vulnerable to criticism and therefore much more cautious in the selection of a listener. At this level, a person might make such statements as "I'm really frightened. I need to have someone hold me," "I really felt hurt when you said that to me," or "I love you."

Level I is the *most intimate* level of communication. In order to achieve communication at this level, it is usually necessary to have established a "meaningful relationship." In contrast to the other four levels, Level I is most often *nonverbal*. In fact, due to the emotional intensity involved, it is often impossible to relate the true meaning of what is being experienced in a verbal form. Level I communication will often occur at a time that is special or during what Maslow (1970) refers to as a "peak experience"—for instance, in the looks exchanged between parents of a newborn child, the embrace between lovers about to be separated, or the gentle, knowing touch between an elderly couple when death is near.

EXPECTATIONS WITHIN A RELATIONSHIP   Most of the relationships that fail have been built on promises that could not be kept and expectations that could not be met. In most such cases, the individuals involved overestimated their power to make another person happy and underestimated their demands for compliance with their expectations.

The existentialist believes that no one can *make* others stay when they want to leave, love when they want to hate, or be happy when they want to be sad. For instance, people cannot make others love them merely by being nice. The others may choose to view the behavior with contempt and the person doing the "nicing" as a sucker. According to the existentialist, people are sad, mad, or glad because they have *chosen* to feel that way and not because someone else has *made* them feel that way. This premise is especially significant with regard to happiness. No one can *make* another person happy, so don't promise to do so. When we make such a promise, we assume full responsibility for another person's happiness, and if that person is not happy, then it is our fault. To illustrate this premise, imagine a newly married husband who wants to make his bride happy by sending her a bouquet of carnations and does not know that (1) her ex-husband used to send her carnations whenever he was having an affair, (2) someone close to her has always died soon after she has received a bouquet of carnations, and (3) she is allergic to carnations. The existentialists are not advocating that we not send flowers or do nice things for others, but rather that we do these things because *doing them makes us happy,* and that we deal separately with how the behavior is received. Since each of us has grown up with slightly different expectations, it is rare that an individual lives up to the expectations of others. As a consequence, it is often necessary for individuals to compromise in order to maintain a relationship. Each individual is faced with assessing the *cost* of maintaining a relationship, weighing both its positive and negative aspects.

Our responsibility within a relationship is *primarily* for ourself. Each of us must monitor our own depth of commitment, degree of vulnerability, and intensity of feelings toward the other. In communicating, both are responsible for what they "send" to each other and for interpreting what they receive from each other, not for how the other receives what was sent.

Most relationships that succeed are sustained through mutual consent. An individual can consent to be *useful,* that is, to be of use to another when it is convenient. An example would be volunteering to help put up a fence for a neighbor when there is nothing else to do. An individual can also consent to be *used,* that is, to be used by another when it is not convenient. An example would be when a person says, "Remember now, if you ever get in trouble again or need some help, no matter what time of the day it is, you call me." However, a person does not wish to be exploited, that is, to be used without consent, as when someone borrows your car to visit his girl friend and you learn later that she lives in another state. Consenting to be useful or used within a relationship is part of the privilege inherent to that relationship. Abuse of the privilege will usually result in the termination of the relationship.

PERSONAL RESPONSIBILITY FOR SELF AND OTHERS

Inherent in the formation of any relationship is the potential for conflict. Disputes may arise from struggles to maintain separate identities, from invasions of "territory," or merely from misunderstandings. As a result, most relationships are in a constant state of motion, wherein the people involved are moving *toward* each other, *against* each other, or *away* from each other. Karen Horney believes:

> From the point of view of the normal person there is no reason why the three attitudes (directions of movement) should be mutually exclusive. One should be capable of giving in to others, of fighting, and of keeping to oneself. The three can complement each other and make for a harmonious whole. (*Our Inner Conflicts,* 1945, p. 45)

Rank's Life Fear versus Death Fear

The problem of how one goes about moving toward others and joining in a relationship while simultaneously moving away to maintain a sense of uniqueness and individuality has been dealt with by many personality theorists. One of the most noted of these is Otto Rank (1952).

Rank proposed that one of the major conflicts within us is between our *life fear* and our *death fear.* Our life fear can be defined as a fear of separateness, being alone, or not having a sense of belonging. Our death fear can be defined as a fear of losing individuality, identity, or uniqueness.

According to Rank, each person attempts to resolve the conflict between wanting to be a part of the group (thereby nullifying the life fear) and wanting to be a unique individual (thereby nullifying the death fear) by identifying with one of three levels of adjustment. These levels of adjustment are the level of the *average man,* the *neurotic,* and the *artist.*

THE AVERAGE MAN   Rank's first level of adjustment, which he considered to be the lowest level of adjustment, is referred to as the level of the "average man." The average man has a very intense life fear and is fearful of not being a member of the group. Therefore, if people identify with this level, they will attempt to dissipate any guilt they might have for not appreciating the values of the group (parents, society, peers, etc.) by internalizing these values as their own. They will often rationalize their taste with a statement like "I thought I'd look silly wearing this new style, but now that I've tried it on, I don't look half bad." At the average man level, they will tend to believe that what the group wants *is* what they want. If their peers in the group want to own campers, they will become convinced that they also want to own a camper.

An average man is also easily swayed by advertising. If the advertisement says: "What do people think of you as you drive down the freeway in the car you now own? Well, they won't think that way if you're driving the car that the smart people are buying," then the average man is often convinced that he or she really wants that car.

As an average man, one has a relatively moderate death fear. People are therefore often able to placate the desire to be individuals and to stand out from the crowd by placing their "signatures" on mass-produced possessions. "Hi, there. Boy, would you believe how crowded these campgrounds are? I've never seen so many campers. Which one's yours?" "Mine's the one with the smiling buzzard painted on the back." "Hey, that's really clever. That buzzard really makes yours stand out."

THE NEUROTIC   Rank's second level of adjustment is referred to as the level of the "neurotic." As a neurotic, a person has a very intense death fear. Unlike the average man, the neurotic abhors conformity more than loneliness and, therefore, is constantly trying to avoid both. The fact that such a person continues to struggle is one of the reasons that Rank considers the neurotic to be a higher level of adjustment than the average man.

The neurotic perceives the average man as having sold himself out. Although neurotics have not resolved the conflict between the fear of being separate and the fear of losing identity, they vow never to give in to either one. Such individuals may not know yet who they do want to be, but they know fairly well who they don't want to be—they don't want to be like everyone else. "No nine-to-five commuter job for me. I don't intend to go through life like Dad did. Believe me, this job is only temporary." The neurotics will also express how they "have taken about as much as they intend to take," but, above all, they will remind others that "they will never settle for mediocrity." As a consequence of this attitude, they often face a situation where they outwardly "play the game," to obtain the approval of others, and inwardly despise the people who play them, to retain their sense of individuality. They will tolerate the silly rules and petty regulations, but they will never allow themselves to believe that the "establishment" way is the right way. They will never lower themselves to that level and become "one of them." "Okay, okay, I'll do it by the book. They've got me again. I want that promotion, and if I have to go by their stupid regulations to get it, then I guess I'll have to. What idiot made up these dumb qualifications anyway?"

Horney (1937) refers to this feeling of helplessness as "basic anxiety"— "an insidiously increasing, all-pervading feeling of being lonely and helpless in a hostile world," a feeling that is inseparable from repressed feelings of hostility. Horney (1945) believes that the need for security is an integral part of our being, but that we are often torn between moving against, toward, or away from something in order to achieve it. Neurosis is often the result of one of these directions becoming the pervasive organizational principle of an individual's personality.

Rank generally agrees, believing that on the neurotic level, we manipulate others in order to get without having to give, in order to be appreciated without having to appreciate, and in order to be loved without having to love. On the average man level, we manipulate in order to preserve the illusion that what we have is what we really want.

THE ARTIST   Rank's third and highest level of adjustment, the "artist," does not need to manipulate. Artists resolve the conflict between life fear and death fear

FIGURE 9.2 Rank's highest level of adjustment is the artist. This individual has a sense of individuality, as well as a sense of belonging. [*Martha Swope.*]

by accepting the reality of their separateness and by acknowledging that each of us is indeed unique. At the same time, we recognize that our distinctiveness can continue to exist within the group. As artists, we have a sense of individuality as well as a sense of union, such as when we volunteer to help, but stress the importance of being allowed to help in our own way.

As artists, we have accepted that we are born alone and will die alone, and that even in a group we are still alone, still a separate part of that group. As artists, we have realized that even if we devoted all our energies toward conforming, we would still be unique. Therefore, since our separateness and uniqueness are indisputable realities, we prefer to devote our energies toward sharing our separateness when possible, and toward enhancing our individuality in order to realize our full potential.

Self-Destructive Behavior

Most of us, at one time or another, have questioned the motivation of someone who stays in a relationship that appears to be a source of perpetual misery. We might have asked "Why does she keep going back to him? Doesn't she realize what a rotten person he is?" or "I don't see how he puts up with her. I would have bailed out long ago." On the surface, such masochistic behavior may appear purposeless, but most theories of personality assure us that there is usually a reason behind such self-destructive behavior.

THE BEHAVIORIST EXPLANATION   The behaviorists will often point out that the people staying in such relationships are doing so because they are receiving some kind of *reinforcement*. This reinforcement is sometimes referred to as the "secondary payoff," or the *real* reason behind the actions. For example, in some relationships, fighting can be a source of emotional involvement in what would otherwise be a stagnant world of indifference. The real reason for the fighting, the secondary payoff, is that *some* emotional involvement is better than *no* emotional involvement at all.

THE EXISTENTIALIST EXPLANATION   The existentialists propose that people often remain in unhappy relationships because they *want* to. Maybe they are not supposed to want to, but according to existential theory, we all have "freedom of choice." Therefore, if some people remain in bad situations, it is because they *choose* to remain in them. The choice is often because of *familiarity*. One's childhood or other past experiences may have made unhappiness a familiar state. Such relationships are miserable, but the people have coped with being miserable so frequently or for such a long time that the only situation in which they are truly comfortable is an unhappy one. Such a person might comment, "I know it's no bed of roses, but then when has it ever been any different?"

THE PSYCHOANALYTIC EXPLANATION   The psychoanalytic theorists believe that our conscience is actually the internalization of our parents and their concepts of right and wrong, of justice, and of having the punishment fit the crime. As we internalize these values, we acquire an awareness that punishment is an integral and vital part of an episode involving wrongdoing. Punishment is often seen as necessary in order to complete the episode. Punishment puts an end to the anxiety and fear associated with having done something or thought something that was considered wrong. It puts an end to wondering whether or when one will be caught; and if one is caught, punishment puts an end to the worry about what form and how severe the punishment will be. Imagine suffering the anguish of such a statement as, "I'm not sure what your punishment will be. I'll need a few days to think about it, but I'm telling you now, it's going to be something that you'll not soon forget." In just a matter of a few days, most people would probably be pleading to be punished. Since punishment can eliminate such emotional anguish, Freud proposed that as a crucial part of the forming of our super ego, or conscience, we actually develop a *need to be punished*.

Freud believed that we would experience a need to be punished should we transgress our values of right and wrong or fail to live up to our "ego ideal"—the image of the self we wanted to be when we were growing up. With such a concept internalized, each time we fail to live up to our moral expectations, fail to sustain our standards of justice, or fail to fulfill our image of

FIGURE 9.3   For some, a miserable relationship is preferred to no relationship at all. [*Sybil Shelton, Peter Arnold.*]

perfection, we will unconsciously believe that we *deserve* to be punished. As a consequence, some people will unconsciously seek out others to administer the punishment. This will result in a *sadomasochistic* relationship. In such a relationship, the individuals are often convinced that they don't deserve any of the good life. They feel that they deserve every rotten thing that happens to them and don't deserve to be happy.

Trouble Getting the Message Across

The English poet Oliver Goldsmith (1728–1774) noted that "Friendship is a disinterested commerce between equals; love, an abject intercourse between tyrants and slaves." Whether Goldsmith's observations are entirely accurate or not is debatable, although his statement does tend to exemplify the potential for "message distortion" inherent in communication between people who are emotionally involved with each other.

It would probably be difficult for many of us to recall all the times we have found ourselves engaged in a vital, emotion-filled discussion when someone has thrown up his hands and sighed in frustration, "We're just not communicating." Actually, such a statement is only partially true. Although its implication that the individuals are not understanding each other is probably accurate, the insinuation that *no* communication is taking place is probably not. According to

Watzlawick, Beavin, and Jackson (1967), people cannot help but communicate, even their *silence* is saying something. As a consequence, we may often find that people are communicating even when they don't want to communicate.

VERBAL COMMUNICATION   One of the most frequent sources of verbal misunderstanding is confusion between the *denotative* meaning and the *connotative* meaning of a word. The denotative meaning of a word is the dictionary definition of the word. For example, the word "airplane" is defined as "an aircraft, heavier than air, . . . with fixed wings and driven by propellers or jet propulsion." The connotative meaning of a word involves the "emotional overtones" or "personal meaning" that the word implies to a particular individual. For example, the word "airplane" may carry with it intense feelings of anger, hate, and grief for those who suffered through the London blitz and lost their entire families in the bombing raids.

The meaning of a word can also vary between the sexes. For instance, when the words "bow," "file," and "nail" were presented to a male audience, the definitions given were generally associated with arrow, rasp, and hammer. When the same words were presented to a female audience, the definitions were generally associated with dress or hair, manicure, and polish (Goodenough, 1942). With such divergent meanings arising from these relatively neutral words, it is not too surprising that misunderstandings often occur between the sexes with regard to such terms as "love," "meaningful relationship," and "being friends."

NONVERBAL COMMUNICATION   Through the process of communication we attempt to bridge our separateness and come to know each other. It is currently believed that our *nonverbal* means of communication reveal more about us than perhaps any other means. Some investigators estimate that up to 93 percent of all human communication can be considered to be nonverbal (Mehrabian, 1968; Harrison, 1972). Nonverbal communication includes such factors as silence, gestures, the manner of standing, sitting, and walking, physical position in relation to others, facial expressions, and touching or not touching.

In many large hospitals and orphanages with "institutionalized" children, it has all too often been noted that emotional, physical, maturational, and intellectual retardation can result from "insufficient touching." These effects can be especially harmful among children under one year of age. In many cases, the child may actually die from *marasmus,* a "wasting away" despite adequate physical care. As late as 1919, about *half* the mortality among institutionalized infants under one year was attributed to marasmus. To counter this affliction, many hospitals hired extra help and organized "volunteer touchers" to provide their infants with adequate handling and tactile stimulation. Today, cases of marasmus are rare, but the need to be touched is something no one fully outgrows.

Most children who are raised outside an institution receive sufficient

The way we sit, walk, and move can tell more about us than words. [*Chester Higgins, Jr., Rapho/Photo Researchers.*]

FIGURE 9.4

touching and with it assurance that they are loved. In turn, the children learn to touch back in order to express their love. However, in most American families, girl babies are generally touched more than boy babies. This tradition of touching, hugging, and caressing the girl, while only occasionally giving the boy a playful punch, often continues into adolescence. As a result, many males in our society are believed to be "tactilely starved." Many times this need to be touched can be confused with a need for sex, and in the area of sexual communication, where nonverbal communication is of the essence, many American males are at a loss as to how to express their feelings.

The analysis of the expression and interpretation of nonverbal communication is referred to as "kinesics" when dealing with body posture and movement (Birdwhistell, 1970), and "proxemics" when dealing with relative position and distance between people (Hall, 1963). An interesting and popularized view of these fields was written by Julius Fast in *Body Language* (1970). In this book, Fast explores such subjects as the way we stake out our "territory" and how we react when someone "invades" this space (try sitting on top of someone else's desk, and see how the person reacts); the ways we attempt to mask our true thoughts and feelings (the "that's-all-right" smile we give to a stranger who has just stepped on our foot); and the various positions, postures, and gestures we use to assert or defend ourselves (people with their arms folded across their chests are saying "Convince me"). However, it is important to keep in mind that the "science" of interpreting body language is still developing. As Birdwhistell warns, "No body position or movement, in and of itself, has a precise meaning." The meaning can vary from culture to culture and from individual to individual.

THE DOUBLE BIND   The question of precise meaning that Birdwhistell refers to becomes especially pertinent with regard to messages that carry more than one meaning. Communication containing two opposing meanings is called a "double bind." The double bind presents a "damned-if-you-do, damned-if-you-don't" situation. It is a no-win situation; no matter which message a person chooses to respond to, the response will be wrong. For example, a teenager may ask a parent, "Is it okay if I stay over at a friend's house on Friday night?" The parent replies, "Sure, go on. Stay with your friend. You never want to be home with us anyway." The teenager hesitates, trying to interpret the parent's comment and discriminate between the two messages, then answers, "Well, I don't have to stay over. I can come home if you want me to." "No. If you and your friend have already made arrangements, then. . . ." "Okay, I'll stay overnight then." Whereupon the parent gloats, "What did I tell you? You never want to be home with us."

Double-binding can be accomplished by sending one message through verbal content and a second message by tone of voice. It can also result from sending the message in words which can have dual meanings, or double entendre; and by sending one message verbally and a second message nonverbally. However, in all cases of double-binding, the burden of interpretation lies with the recipient of the message. This burden can create tremendous amounts of emotional stress. Research has indicated that persistent use of double-binding between parent and child may be a contributing factor in the later development of schizophrenia (Bateson, 1960; Haley, 1959; Laing and Esterson, 1964). For most of us, however, double-binding is primarily a contributing factor in the development of conflict and stress within a relationship.

SUCCESSFUL INTERPERSONAL RELATIONSHIPS

The American novelist Willa Cather (1876–1947) expressed how tremendously significant interpersonal relationships can be when she wrote, "Only solitary men know the full joys of friendship. Others have their family; but to a solitary and an exile his friends are everything" (*Shadow On the Rock,* 1931). Perhaps it is because relationships can be so significant to our lives that we place so much importance on their success or failure. Successful relationships can transcend the trials of time and separation, fill the heart with hope and joy, and provide a sense of communion. The failure of a relationship, however, can often result in emotional wounds that will not heal, ever-deepening depression, and loneliness.

One of the most important factors contributing to the success of interpersonal relationships is being able to keep them in *perspective*. This means being able to see the relationship for what it really is.

The emotional demands of a relationship, any relationship, can vary from polite recognition ("Excuse me while I go over and say hello to Ralph") to intense feelings of identification ("Oh, you can't imagine the horrible things that went through my mind when they told me you had been in an accident. I don't know which one of us has suffered the most"). It would be humanly impossible to achieve intense feelings of identification in *every* relationship. Besides, most relationships do not warrant that degree of commitment. Therefore, it is necessary to be able to allocate an amount of emotional involvement that is appropriate to the particular relationship, reserving the most intense emotions for the most intimate relationships.

By keeping interpersonal relationships in perspective, a person can be more selective with the degree of commitment inherent in each type of relationship and not demand more from a relationship than it warrants. Failure to keep a relationship in proper perspective can lead to conflict and misunderstandings, accompanied by such statements as "Hey, I thought you were my friend" or "I thought what we had together meant more to you than just . . . " or "I thought you really loved me."

Everett Shostrom, author of *Man the Manipulator* (1972), proposes that the degree of commitment within a relationship follows a gradual progression through "dimensions of emotions." The dimensions of emotion begin with interest and move to concern, then appreciation, then caring, and, finally, to love. It is proposed that by using these levels of emotional involvement as a guide, one can establish a hierarchy of interpersonal relationships and a more realistic perspective of their levels and the degree of commitment appropriate for each level.

Acquaintanceships

In the normal course of an average day each person is presented with numerous opportunities to initiate new relationships. Such opportunities may occur at work, school, church, or just about anywhere. Though most of these opportunities are disregarded, from time to time a particular person will seem to stand out from the crowd. Our curiosity is aroused and we become *interested* in that person.

Interest in another person is a *passive* involvement. For example, a student might eat lunch in a crowded cafeteria almost every day. Each day there are the same long lines, institutionalized food, and a lack of space at the tables. Occasionally, however, a randomly selected tablemate's individuality stands out, thus promoting a series of "student" questions like "What's your major?" "What year are you in?", "Have you taken so and so yet?" During the course of the conversation, the student might find that the other person has been accepted into graduate school but is finding it difficult to obtain the needed tuition. Since the first student is, at this point in the relationship, only *interested* in the welfare of the other, the relationship warrants only a passive involvement. Therefore, the first student may merely respond with something like, "Let me know how it turns out" or "Send up a flare if you get a loan." However, should the two students continue to meet, the initial relationship may grow to include not only interest, but *concern* as well.

The emotion of concern requires an *active* involvement within the relationship. With concern, there exists a desire to participate and contribute to the welfare of the other. In the previous example, the first student might write letters to foundations which offer scholarships, make a few phone calls, or introduce the needy student to certain people who may be able to help out financially. When a person experiences concern, what happens to someone else really matters. By choosing to be concerned, a person is choosing to be assertive and to *act* rather than merely *react* to the situation. There may be various motivations behind the concern, however. The intent of the concern may be exploitive: "Maybe if I get this student a loan, I'll get a percentage." The intent may be for convenience: "Things will work out better for both of us." The intent of the concern may be for self-satisfaction: "Boy, I sure get a kick out of helping someone."

When an individual experiences both interest and concern, the relationship has progressed to the level of an *acquaintanceship*. The individuals are not friends or lovers yet, but acquaintances, and therefore not yet deserving of the privileges associated with more intimate relationships. Acquaintanceships are often conditional arrangements in which a mutual exchange is continued only as long as certain conditions are maintained. One of the more common conditions is that the limitations of the relationship be respected. For instance, the relationship usually does not include the privilege of borrowing substantial amounts of money. "Hi again. I've noticed that we use the Xerox machine about the same time every day. I thought I was going to be a little late today though. Transmission fell out on the way to work. Say, could you loan me? . . ."

When the conditions within an acquaintanceship become unacceptable, the relationship is relatively easy to terminate. Most often, this is accomplished merely by physically avoiding the other individual. Residual feelings are seldom greater than annoyance, mild resentment, and perhaps some thoughts of what might have been.

Friendships

From among an individual's many acquaintances there will often arise a few in whom is perceived a form of *excellence*. With the perception of excellence, the feeling of *appreciation* is added to the feelings of interest and concern, and the relationship evolves into a *friendship*. The perceived excellence may be attributed to the other's personality, intellect, talents, or physical attractiveness. However, it is important to keep in mind that the excellence is *perceived,* and

FIGURE 9.5

When you're among friends, more than any other time, you can be yourself . . . guard down, open, and trusting. [*Erika Stone, Peter Arnold.*]

may or may not actually exist. Appreciation is generated primarily through the recognition of another person's specialness, quality, and significance.

The commitment within such a relationship is often toward the *preservation* or *enhancement* of the excellence, with the awareness that should this excellence be lost, so too would be the feelings of appreciation, and the friendship could come to an end. For example, one might grow to appreciate the kindness and consideration a fellow employee demonstrates to the patients in a hospital. Because of this perceived excellence, a friendship develops. Later, the friendship is threatened because of this person's involvement with drugs and the way this involvement affects the manner in which the patients are being treated. As a friend, one is willing to commit enormous amounts of time, energy, and emotion in an attempt to alleviate the drug problem and reestablish the excellent qualities once perceived.

Behavior that threatens a friendship will often arouse feelings of anger if the behavior was unintentional. "Hey, I'm sorry I didn't pick you up on time, but I had trouble borrowing some money to get my transmission fixed." However, if the behavior was intentional, then feelings of hurt often result. "Quite frankly, the reason I didn't pick you up on time is because I had this thing going at the Xerox machine and it seemed more important than you." Experiencing the feeling of hurt repeatedly is a good indication that the relationship is *not* a friendship, for such a relationship would lack a type of love the Greeks referred to as *philos*—brotherly love.

Philos is a type of love used to express one's love for humanity. It is based on one's ability to identify with others and, through this identification, to feel compassion and empathy. *Philos* is the basis for a deep friendship and is frequently the motivation behind attempts to rescue another in spite of great personal risk.

In most cases, *philos* is a nonpossessive, undemanding type of love, based on the assumption that one can possess only things, not people. No one can possess another, unless, through freedom of choice, that person relinquishes self-determination to another. A person can be unwillingly oppressed or suppressed, but not possessed. This recognition, and respect, for another's freedom is especially important if the relationship is to continue to grow and, perhaps, become even more meaningful.

Meaningful Relationships

Occasionally, as a friendship deepens, the feeling of caring for another person develops. The emotion of caring is founded on identification, empathy, compassion, and the recognition that the other person is *as important as oneself*. Feelings of empathy are based on having been in the other person's situation. Compassion results from the ability to identify with human frailty and vulnerability. With the addition of the feeling of caring, a friendship evolves into what is often referred to as a "meaningful relationship."

Caring often provides us with a sense of relevance, a feeling that what happens to us matters to someone else. Caring, therefore, can transcend both distance and time. Being separated does not necessarily diminish the intensity of the caring experienced. Caring can often remove the feeling of being alone and unsupported. An individual may be alone in a room but, when there is caring, may know he or she is not alone in the world. Caring is an acknowledgment of a person's irreplaceability and the fact that he or she has made an impact—that the life of the person who cares will never be quite the same because of the relationship.

After a relationship has evolved to this level, sexual loving is often introduced. Other forms of sexual contact, however, can be and often are introduced earlier in a relationship (prostitution at an acquaintanceship level, for instance).

Love Relationships

A meaningful relationship evolves into a love relationship with the addition of *devotion*. With devotion, there emerges a dedication to the welfare of the other individual and a consecration of the sanctity of the relationship. Many fear that if they allow themselves to expand their emotional commitment to include love they might lose their identity. They fear that they would be engulfed by the relationship, that they would exist only through and for the loved one. A true love relationship supplements and enhances one's individuality and identity, for the one who is loved has been selected above all others.

Since one grows to love another, the selection of individuals to be included within a love relationship would be limited. The growth process from interest to concern to appreciation and caring can be emotionally demanding, and the more intimate the relationship, the more intense the emotions. Many, however, attempt to bypass this evolutionary process. As a result, they sometimes confuse *need* for love. Such individuals will tend to experience a greater and greater need for someone, rather than a greater and greater love for someone. For example, one roommate may ask the other, "Are you *interested* in what Ralph does when he's not with you?" "Look, Ralph and I have what you might call an open relationship; what he does on his own time is up to him." "Aren't you *concerned* about what might happen to him?" "Concerned about Ralph? He can take care of himself." "What is it you appreciate the most about Ralph?" "Well, Ralph's a little too self-centered for me to appreciate much of anything about him right now. but I'll shape him up someday." "Don't you *care* about him?" "I told you before, Ralph can take care of himself. He doesn't have to lean on others for support." "Tell me honestly, do you *love* Ralph?" "Love him! Of course, I love him. I'm going to marry him, aren't I?" Far too often, the other kinds of relationships are neglected through the illusion that only a love relationship is worthwhile. Acquaintanceships, friendships, and meaningful relationships are important. They have tremendous worth and are of major significance in our attempts to attain emotional maturity.

SUMMARY

In this chapter, we have discussed the role of perception in our evaluations of others and the influence of first impressions. We also looked at what happens when we perceive our behavior as incompatible with our beliefs. The discussion then proceeded to what Festinger calls "cognitive dissonance," and to Erich Fromm's theory of nonproductive and productive personality types, the receiving, exploiting, hoarding, and marketing types.

The problems of communicating effectively were explored, and we saw how communication takes place at different levels and through both verbal and nonverbal means. The problems encountered from having promised to make someone else happy were also dealt with.

Otto Rank's concepts of the average man, the neurotic, and the artist were presented as possible explanations for why people conform or not. Theories of the behaviorists, existentialists, and psychoanalysts were presented to explain why some people need to be miserable and why they might believe that happiness is evil. In addition, explanations for some of the most common problems of verbal and nonverbal communication were also presented.

In the last section of this chapter, we considered some of the factors that contribute to successful relationships, such as being able to establish a hierarchy of relationships. We start with an acquaintanceship and grow to a friendship, a meaningful relationship, and finally, a love relationship.

DISCUSSION QUESTIONS

1 What is the first thing you usually notice about a person? What is it about a person that tends to impress you the most?

2 In your opinion, do any of your friends or acquaintances represent Fromm's nonproductive personality types: receiving, exploitive, hoarding, or marketing? Do you consider yourself to be among these types?

3 How many relationships do you have in which you are able to communicate at Level I, the most intimate and often nonverbal level?

4 Do you think you are influenced more by what Rank referred to as "life fear" (fear of separateness) or "death fear" (fear of loss of individuality)?

5 Do you consider yourself to be an "average man," a neurotic, or an artist?

6 Do you become uneasy if things go "too well for too long"? Do you believe that a person has to "pay" for his or her good times?

7 How frequently does double-binding (two contradictory messages occurring simultaneously) become a part of your communication patterns?

8 Based on Shostrom's definition of friendships and acquaintanceships, how many real friends do you have? How many "meaningful relationships"?

9 Under what kind of circumstances do you feel that you are most authentic?

10 Do you tend to "assume" rather than check "reality"? Do you tend to find yourself in uncomfortable situations as a result?

EXPERIENTIAL EXERCISES

1 Make a list of the ways in which you would judge a person if you were to become blind. How influential are these characteristics in your appraisals now?

2 Take some time to evaluate the *real* reason you are involved in your present relationship or why you were involved in a previous relationship (dependence, security, convenience, sexual gratification, emotional commitment, etc.).

3 Explore with a group of friends the many ways in which double-binding messages can be communicated (for instance, through the tone of voice, subtle use of words, facial expression, body position, gestures, etc.).

CHAPTER 10

HUMAN SEXUALITY

*This arises
That becomes.*

. . . Speak to us of Love.
And with a great voice he said:

When love beckons to you, follow him,
Though his ways are hard and steep.

And when his wings enfold you yield to him,
Though the sword hidden among his
pinions may wound you.

Love gives naught but itself and takes
naught but from itself.

Love possesses not nor would it be
possessed;
For love is sufficient unto love.

When you love you should not say,
"God is in my heart," but rather, "I am
in the heart of God."

And think not you can direct the course
of love, for love, if it finds you worthy,
Directs your course.

Love has no other desire but to fulfill
itself.
But if you love and must needs have
desires, let these be your desires:

To melt and be like a running brook
that sings its melody to the night.

To know the pain of too much tenderness.

To be wounded by your own understanding of love;
And to bleed willingly and joyfully.

To wake at dawn with a winged heart
and give thanks for another day of loving;

To rest at the noon hour and meditate
love's ecstasy;

To return home at eventide with gratitude;

And then to sleep with a prayer for the
beloved in your heart and a song of praise
upon your lips.

                                  Kahlil Gibran
                                  The Prophet

Alphonse Karr (1808–1890) once remarked, "The more things change, the more they remain the same." So it seems regarding our current attitudes toward sex. Each new generation threatens to abandon the preceding generation's antiquated concepts toward sexual morality in favor of the more liberated views of the latest "sexual revolution." However, as the ripples subside and the wave of change moves on to the next generation, our basic attitudes, morals, and concepts of normality seem to remain pretty much the same. This is not to say that some change does not take place, only that the most pessimistic fears of the older generation and the most optimistic fantasies of the younger generation are seldom realized.

Sexual practices and mores have undergone a variety of changes throughout history and will undoubtedly continue to do so. Except for a relatively rapid change in sexual attitudes following World War I (Kinsey, 1969), such changes have taken place gradually and have been in keeping with other changes in the culture's value systems.

Recreation versus Procreation

Two of the most controversial areas with regard to attitudes toward human sexuality are (1) deciding on the purpose of human sexual behavior, and (2) determining the proper circumstances under which such behavior is to occur.

Historically, the most widely accepted purpose of sex has been to bear children (procreation), and marriage has provided the *only* proper circumstances in which sexual relationships could occur. Although some may view this as a rather restrictive approach to sex, it has, at times in the past, been even more restrictive. For example, during medieval times, directives from the Catholic Church forbade married couples to have intercourse on Sundays, Wednesdays, and Fridays, as well as for forty days before Christmas and Easter. Intercourse was also forbidden from the time of conception to forty days after the birth of the child. Prior to the twentieth century, sexual restraint and complete abstinence were often encouraged, celibacy being considered the ideal according to the teachings of St. Paul.

Martin Luther (1483–1546) did not think that complete abstinence was all that ideal and, during the sixteenth-century Protestant movement, he proposed that sexual relationships within the sanctity of marriage need not be considered sinful, but could be both natural and spiritual events.

The naturalness of the sexual act was to gain support with the introduction of the theory of evolution. However, unlike other mammals, humans do not appear to be under the influence of an estrus cycle. Among the other mammals, the estrus cycle is determined by hormonal changes, and sexual intercourse is permitted only during estrus, a period in which the animal is said to be "in heat," or fertile, and conception is most likely to take place. Humans, on the other hand, often engage in intercourse when conception is *least* likely to occur. When one considers that the average person will engage in sexual

VD is for everybody.
If you need help, see a doctor.

A Public Service of
Transit Advertising &
The Advertising Council

American
Social Health
Association

FIGURE 10.1   The common belief that "It couldn't happen to me," among those who engage in casual sex, tends to perpetuate the epidemic venereal diseases. [*The Advertising Council.*]

intercourse over 5000 times during a lifetime (Kinsey, 1948; Collier, 1973), this is probably to our advantage with regard to controlling the size of our population.

The frequency with which we engage in sexual behavior is often considered to be one of the distinguishing factors which separate *homo sapiens* from the other animals. No other animal appears to be even remotely as preoccupied with sex as we are. The average frequency of intercourse for a couple in their thirties is about three times per week, whereas, in the case of many of the larger mammals, a frequency of once a year is not uncommon.

In order to reduce the number of pregnancies that would be expected to occur with such a high frequency of copulation, some form of birth control has frequently been employed. However, around the turn of the century, interest in limiting the size of the family gained momentum, and reformers began to advocate the use of contraception by the general population. The use of contraception, however, implied having intercourse purely for the inherent pleasure involved, and this was a direct challenge to the procreation principle. As medical advances made contraception more effective and less encumbering, the concept of "sex for fun" or recreation became more acceptable and more realistic, for with the proper employment of modern contraceptive methods, the "pregnancy price" for having intercourse could be drastically reduced.

It is important to note, however, that although the price was reduced, sexual intimacy was still not "free." For many, the "free love" of the late sixties and early seventies turned out to be a cruel deception resulting in feelings of emotional desolation, devalued self-images, unwanted pregnancies, and/or the contraction of venereal diseases, which have reached epidemic proportions.

THE NEW MORALITY   Many surveys of current sexual attitudes indicate that the double standard still exists, with both adults and high school students approving of males engaging in petting and coitus more than females (Reiss, 1960). The social status of males is still strongly influenced by their virility as is the status of females by their virginity, but with a much greater tolerance for any deviations from these norms. According to a 1977 survey, 33 percent of the men still want to marry a virgin (Pietropinto). However, a 1973 survey conducted by Zuckerman (1976) revealed that 63 percent of college-age females between the ages of eighteen and twenty-two had engaged in premarital intercourse.

Although 63 percent of those interviewed in a 1977 survey indicated that premarital sex relations were wrong (Yankelovich, Skelly, and White), down from 75 percent in 1970 (Swift). In 1976, 55 percent of the unmarried women and 85 percent of the unmarried men had had intercourse by the time they were twenty. In contrast, Kinsey's 1953 report disclosed that only 23 percent of the twenty-year-old women had had intercourse prior to marriage. It is significant to note that, although the percentage of male teenagers having premarital relationships has not changed substantially since the Kinsey report, the number of female teenagers engaging in premarital intercourse has more than doubled, and both sexes have indicated an increase in the number of different partners being experienced prior to marriage (Verner and Stewart, 1977).

The consequences of such activity can be seen in the tremendous increase in teenage pregnancies, abortions, births of illegitimate children, and venereal disease. Figures now indicate that one in ten teenaged girls will become pregnant before she marries. Teenage pregnancies are occurring at the rate of between 1 and 2 million per year (Stern and Price, 1977). It is estimated that well over 500,000 abortions a year are performed on unwed, teenaged girls, and that over 250,000 give birth out of wedlock, about 15 percent of these children being given up for adoption. The number of illegitimate births per 1000 teenagers has risen from 8.3 in 1940 to 22.9 in 1973 (Reiss, 1976). Another 250,000 or more will get married, and over half of these marriages will fail within three to five years. Unfortunately, many of these unwed mothers end up on welfare, where the suicide rate is seven times that of their peers.

As severe as these consequences are, an additional consequence has appeared among sexually active youth—an epidemic of venereal disease. At present, VD ranks second to the common cold in incidence of infectious diseases. In 1975 there were 925,000 cases of gonorrhea and 26,000 cases of syphillis, and an estimated 300,000 cases of the currently incurable herpes II.

In attempts to explain the increase in sexual behavior among the youth, some psychologists have pointed to the decline in the quality of the American family, resulting in the need for the youth to seek affection outside the family, often substituting sex for love. Others have pointed to the use of drugs as having provided a precedent for defying the rules of the establishment; once one had broken one rule, breaking the rules governing sexual conduct was merely another small step toward attaining total autonomy. Still others believe that the present level of sexual behavior is nothing more than a surrendering to the hedonistic principles of seeking pleasure and avoiding pain. For many, however, the phenomenon of "doing it more, but enjoying it less" appears to be taking precedence. For these individuals, casual sex lacks depth or meaning.

In addition to these factors, many believe that the various sociological movements intent upon gaining equality for women and/or liberating them have had a significant influence on the increase in sexual activity among teenaged girls. Men have been burdened with the sociological pressure of "proving" themselves for generations, and now, perhaps as a sign of having attained the desired "equality," many women are also finding themselves under pressure to prove themselves. It is no longer just a matter of "Will she or won't she," but a question of "Can she or can't she," referring to her ability to achieve an orgasm, multiple orgasms, or simultaneous orgasms (Kaplan, 1974).

CONTRACEPTION As an attempt to explain the increased incidence of premarital pregnancies and venereal disease, many sociologists, psychologists, and physicians blame the advances in contraceptive methods (Table 10.1). Paradoxically, the medical advances in contraception that were designed to *decrease* the number of pregnancies may have inadvertently contributed to their *increase*. It seems that with the advent of "the pill" and IUDs (intrauterine devices), the responsibility for birth control was shifted from the male and the use of the condom or withdrawal to the female and the less cumbersome modern methods. (The reduction in the use of the condom is also believed to be contributing to the increase in the incidence of VD, for which it provides at least partial protection.) Recent surveys, however, indicate that 75 percent of the girls interviewed never or only occasionally used contraceptives (Zelnik and Kanter, 1971). It is important to point out that although these contraceptive methods exist, they are not necessarily available to the preadult youth, nor, in many cases, is adequate knowledge of these methods always available. Even when such methods are available, many teenaged girls refuse to use them because to do so would imply a premeditated intent to engage in sexual intercourse, whereas a greater perception of virtue can be preserved if they are "unexpectedly carried away by the passion of the moment." The poet Alexander Pope (1688–1744) wrote:

> The ruling passion, be it what it will,
> The ruling passion conquers reason still.

How to talk to your teenager about something that's not easy to talk about.

When it comes to sex, you probably didn't know at 19 what your teenager knows at 14.

Yet now you do know more.

You also know that a long talk about the facts of life could avoid some of the many problems you may have had while you were growing up.

But what do you say? And how do you say it?

That's where our booklet could help. It's free. It's got authoritative facts.

And it can help make a tough subject just a little bit easier.

Planned Parenthood
Dept. F, 810 Seventh Ave., New York, N.Y. 10019

NAME _____

ADDRESS _____

CITY _____

STATE _____ ZIP _____

A Public Service of This Magazine & The Advertising Council

Ad Council

FIGURE 10.2   Planning when to have children begins long before a person gets married. [*The Advertising Council.*]

In cases where couples are cohabiting but unmarried, the moral dilemma of premeditation is not as great a problem, and conventional methods of contraception are employed with a frequency approaching that of many married couples. In most cases of living together, the individuals are primarily concerned with having a closer relationship or taking advantage of the economics of such an arrangement, rather than having a family. Although 52 percent of the people in one interview did not think it was morally wrong for couples to live together, 70 percent disapproved of their having children under such circumstances (Yankelovich et al., 1977). During the sixties, many cohabitational arrangements were considered "open" arrangements, in which each partner retained the right to experience sexual partners outside the arrangement if desired. By the mid-seventies, however, the incidence of open arrangements began to decline in preference to "faithful" relationships, in

TABLE 10.1 COMPARING CONTRACEPTIVE METHODS

METHOD	EFFECTIVENESS	COST	ACTION REQUIRED AT TIME OF COITUS	REDUCED OPPORTUNITY FOR COITUS
Tubal ligation	Virtually 100%	Varies across the country. Expenses involve physician's services and hospital	None	None
Vasectomy	Virtually 100%	Varies. Cost of office visit plus minor surgical procedure	None	None
Oral contraceptive (The Pill)	Almost 100% if taken as directed	Approximately $2 per month with prescription	None	None
Oral contraceptive (Mini-Pill)	Highly effective if taken daily	Approximately $2 per month with prescription	None	None
Injectable	Almost 100%	Cost of office visit every three months plus cost of drug	None	None
Intrauterine devices (IUDs)	Highly effective	Cost of office visit plus $3–$10 depending on device used	None	None
Diaphragm with jelly or cream	Highly effective if used correctly	Cost of office visit plus $5–$10 for diaphragm and price of jelly or cream (about $2 monthly)	May be inserted up to 12 hours before coitus	None
Condoms	Highly effective if used correctly	Approximately $1.50 per package of three	Interruption of foreplay	None
Temperature rhythm	Highly effective if used correctly	Initial cost of thermometer to record basal body temperature	None	Coitus limited to about 10 days per menstrual cycle
Calendar rhythm	Moderately effective	None	None	Coitus limited to 5-15 days, depending on menstrual cycle

Source: John Gagnon, *Human Sexuality in Today's World,* Boston: Little Brown and Company, 1977, pp 126-127. Reprinted from February 1974 issue of *Good Housekeeping,* Hearst Corporation.

NEED FOR MEDICAL SERVICES	UNSUITABILITY FOR SOME WOMEN	COMMON EARLY SIDE EFFECTS	GENERAL RISK FACTOR	RARE BUT POTEN-TIALLY DANGEROUS SIDE EFFECTS
Yes, office surgery or hospitalization	Not reversible	Several days recuperation needed	Risk associated with any surgical procedure	Surgical complications
Yes, minor surgery	(Not reversible in men)	Temporary scrotal swelling; soreness or discomfort	Risk associated with any surgical procedure	Surgical complications
Yes, examination and prescription. Tegimen instruction. Regular checkups	Medical reasons determined by doctor	Irregular bleeding, spotting, nausea, vomiting, weight gain, breast engorgement	Abnormal sugar metabolism, liver function, changes in blood chemistry, high blood pressure	Thrombo-embolic disorders, incuding stroke and blood clots in lung or heart
Yes, examination and prescription. Annual checkups	Medical reasons determined by doctor	Irregular bleeding, spotting, weight gain	Less than "Pill." Some changes in blood chemistry	None yet identified
Yes, examination and injection every three months	Not to be prescribed for women who can use other methods	Irregular or excessive bleeding, absence of menstruation, weight gain	Chance of post-treatment infertility; long-term effects uncertain	Excessive uterine bleeding
Yes, examination and insertion. Annual checkup	Medical reasons determined by doctor	Irregular bleeding, spotting, cramps, discomfort	No effects on system in pregnancy, highest incidence of spontaneous abortion	Pelvic inflammatory disease (infection), perforation of uterus
Yes, examination and fitting. Instruction to learn technique of insertion	Infrequent medical reasons determined by doctor	None	None	None
No	No	None	None	None
Instruction to learn interpretation of temperature chart	Cannot use if woman has grossly irregular menstruation	None	None	None
Instruction to learn computation of safe and unsafe days	Cannot use if woman has grossly irregular menstruation	None	None	None

TABLE 10.1 *(Continued)*

METHOD	EFFECTIVENESS	COST	ACTION REQUIRED AT TIME OF COITUS	REDUCED OPPORTUNITY FOR COITUS
Cervical-mucus rhythm	Highly effective if used correctly	None	None	Coitus limited to about 10 days per menstrual cycle
Chemical contraceptives (foams, creams, jellies suppositories and foam tablets)	Moderately effective. Foams highest, foam tablets and suppositories lowest	Ranges from approximately $1.50–$3 per month	Insertion not more than one hour before coitus. Suppositories and foam tablets require waiting period	None
Withdrawal	Moderately effective	None	Interruption before ejaculation	None
Douche	Least effective	Initial cost of equipment	Do immediately after ejaculation	None

which the couple declared total commitment to each other to give the relationship a "better chance."

COPING WITH AN UNWANTED PREGNANCY   Being unmarried and sexually active can be a source of constant anxiety, not only from a standpoint of morality, but also from a biological standpoint. In many cases, the onset of each menstrual period is received with gratifying relief, each late period with preoccupying concern, and a missed period with mortifying disbelief. Once conception has been confirmed, however, the question of what to do next becomes imperative. Depending on the circumstances and the expectant mother's personal beliefs, the choice may be made to have the baby and keep it, to have the baby and arrange for an adoption or foster home, or to have an abortion.

One of the most controversial issues with regard to the various methods of contraception available is that of abortion. A 1977 survey disclosed that 47 percent of the women questioned said that having an abortion was "morally wrong," and 44 percent of the women said that it was not (Yankelovich). The abortion issue has quickly expanded beyond morality into a matter of civil rights, where 64 percent believe that a woman has the right to have an abortion, into a matter of economics and whether or not state and federal governments should finance abortions, into a sociological matter concerning the general welfare of the unwanted child, and into a matter of the legal rights of both the expectant mother and the child.

Nevertheless, the question of the morality of abortion often has the greatest psychological impact on the person involved. The moral dilemma is

NEED FOR MEDICAL SERVICES	UNSUITABILITY FOR SOME WOMEN	COMMON EARLY SIDE EFFECTS	GENERAL RISK FACTOR	RARE BUT POTEN-TIALLY DANGEROUS SIDE EFFECTS
Careful instruction needed	Should not be used in presence of infection or if drugs are being taken for other medical reasons	None	None	None
No	No	None	None	None
No	If husband cannot control ejaculation	None	None	None
No	No	None	None	None

often founded in the person's particular religious convictions and philosophical ideas associated with the existence of a soul. The dilemma seems to center on *when,* or even *if,* the unborn gains a soul and what the consequences of the abortion would have, physically and spiritually. Does the unborn have a soul at the moment of conception, as an embryo, as a fetus, when it becomes viable, at birth, or never? Obviously, the question is one of personal belief, and therefore the responsibility for arriving at an acceptable answer lies with each individual concerned. It is not surprising that in a world in which it often takes a committee to determine whether or not a person is really dead, when life-support machines should be withdrawn, or even who is to be allowed to have the advantage of such machines, it can be equally confusing and tormenting to determine when life begins.

The Importance of Sex

In spite of the fact that Americans in general are said to be preoccupied and inundated with sex, many surveys indicate that we do cherish other values as well. In 1977, Croseley Surveys Inc. reported that over one-third of all men believed *love* to be the most important thing in life, an additional 30 percent said love was essential for good sex, and that most men valued a woman's self-confidence and intelligence over her beauty. In a 1970 college survey, women responding to the question "What qualities do you value most highly in a spouse" did not even list sex appeal among their highest valued qualities, which were love, honesty, compatibility, understanding, loyalty, intelligence, sense of humor, and responsibility (Saxton, 1972).

FIGURE 10.3 *(Left)* For some, the abortion issue has expanded beyond morality into civil rights. [*Mimi Forsyth, Monkmeyer Press Photo Service.*] *(Right)* For many, the abortion issue is a matter of morality based on the doctrine of "Thou shalt not kill," which is an extension of human rights. [*Paul Conklin, Monkmeyer Press Photo Service.*]

Although sex isn't everything, it still appears to be a vital ingredient in the attainment of a successful marriage. In one survey, wives who rated their marriage as "very good" also reported that they had intercourse more often than those whose marriages were rated as less satisfactory (Lobsenz et al., 1974). The problem with such results is that it is difficult to determine whether happier marriages lead to more sex, more sex leads to happier marriages, or both.

SEXUAL INFLATION   As if in an attempt to stay in step with the times, the incidence of sexual behavior has been increasing more each year. We have already noted the increase in the incidence of premarital sex, and a similar increase in the frequency of sexual intercourse has also been observed among married couples. In the past twenty-five years, there has been a 25 to 50 percent increase in the average weekly incidence of marital intercourse (Hunt, 1974). However, even with this increase, nearly one-third of the women in the

1974 Lobsenz survey indicated that intercourse occurred "too infrequently." With the average couple engaging in intercourse about two to three times per week, and with 70 percent of the men in the Pietropinto survey saying that they wanted sex three times a week or more, it would appear that many men also believe that intercourse occurs "too infrequently."

Many believe that the increase in frequency of intercourse is a direct result of having "brought sex out into the open." Couples today are better informed, more tolerant, and more willing to experiment than ever before. For example, Kinsey's research in the early fifties indicated that oral-genital contact was experienced by 60 percent of the college-educated couples, 20 percent of those with a high school education, and 10 percent of those who had not gone beyond grade school. In contrast, most recent surveys indicate that about 80 percent of all couples today have experienced oral-genital contact.

Along with the increases in frequency already mentioned, there has also been an increase in the frequency of *extramarital* relationships. The greatest increase has been among women under twenty-five, where it is now estimated to be nearly 50 percent, a figure that is almost equal to the incidence of infidelity among married men. Kinsey's 1953 report revealed that about one-fourth of American women had had extramarital intercourse by the time they were forty, whereas the recent survey (Levins, 1975) indicated that over 38 percent of the wives under forty had had such experiences. Some sociologists predict that if the present trend continues, by the end of the decade the incidence of extramarital relationships for both women and men will exceed 50 percent.

Several possible explanations for this increase have been proposed. Among them is the rise in the number of women in the job market, where there is greater opportunity to meet other men. The increase in premarital sex among teenagers has also played a part (statistically, women who have had premarital sex are more inclined to have extramarital sex, and the probability increases the younger the woman was when she had her first sexual experience). Perhaps most important has been the demand of women for liberation and greater sexual satisfaction. However, as great as these demands have been, and with the incidence of frequency having increased in almost every category of sexuality in the past two decades, only about one-third of the women report that they initiate sex more than half the time. Moreover, the *frequency of the incidence of orgasm appears to have remained virtually the same* (Lobsenz, 1974; Levin, 1973; Pietropinto, 1977; Kinsey, 1948).

THE EMPHASIS ON PERFORMANCE How long can you delay climax? How many times can you make love in one night? How many orgasms can you have? How good are you in bed? The evaluation of one's sexual performance seems to be becoming one of the dominant factors in human sexuality today. The importance of developing a sense of togetherness, experiencing a sense of emotional communion, and the expression of one's most intimate feelings are being threatened by the need to be technically correct, statistically within the norm, and sexually superior to the competition.

The demand for better performance seems to emanate from both external and internal sources. Movies, television, and magazines bombard us with standards of sexual perfection. We are told how we should look, sound, feel, and smell in order to radiate the proper degree of sex appeal. We are told what to drive, wear, and buy in order to enhance our images of masculinity or femininity. We are told where we are to live, take our vacations, and go to school in order that we might increase our chances of having a sexual encounter. The bookshelves are overflowing with a proliferation of "how-to" books and sex manuals, and the great majority of the population that may experience an occasional sexual dysfunction can turn to any number of "sex clinics" in order to get properly adjusted.

Since 99 percent of all sexual dysfunctions, such as impotency, premature ejaculation, vaginismus (closing of the vagina due to involuntary contraction of vaginal muscles), and failure to attain orgasm, are psychologically caused by anxiety, repressed hostility, and/or negative learning experiences, it is not too suprising to find an increase in their occurrence with the increased orientation toward performance. As one new client at a sex clinic stated, "I didn't know I had a problem with premature ejaculation until I read that if your wife doesn't have coital orgasm at least 50 percent of the time, your climax is premature." Based on this standard, the client could delay his climax for two hours and, if his wife did not have an orgasm, he would still have a "problem" with premature ejaculation. Current studies indicate that 85 percent of the men are making an effort to prolong intercourse by delaying their climax, and many of the women are attempting to have their orgasms sooner or faking it, so as not to disappoint their partners. Attempts at record setting and deception for the sake of performance tend to make sex mechanistic and dehumanizing and inevitably defeat the individuals' quest to become more sensitive, experience greater empathy, and allow for greater vulnerability. Perhaps the greatest tragedy resulting from such compulsive competition is that it often prevents the individual from experiencing self-acceptance and the realization that it is all right to be oneself—that it is all right just to "be."

SEXUAL IDENTIFICATION

By the time most children begin school, their sex role development is well under way. *Sexual identity*—one's sense of oneself as male or female—is usually established before the age of three. During their early years of schooling, children also learn the sex role standards of the culture in which they are growing up, establish a sex role identity, and acquire a set of sex-typed behaviors that will tend to persist into adulthood (Kagan and Moss, 1962). *Sex role standards* are the culture's standards of masculinity or femininity—the stereotyped expectations for how men and women ought to behave. Standards of masculinity and femininity are pervasive and widely accepted within any culture. Except when challenged by such movements as the women's movement of the sixties and seventies, they are usually taken for granted. Studies have shown that the concepts of sex role standards held by most children tend to be quite traditional, even when the children grow up in families where the parents do not hold traditional views of masculinity and femininity.

There are a number of theoretical views which attempt to explain how sexual identity is actually achieved. However, foremost among the pioneers in this field is Sigmund Freud. This is not to say that his theory is more "correct" than the others, but his was the first, and his work has prompted the development of other theories of sexual identification in opposition to his hypothesis or in its support.

Freud's Theory of Identification

The issue of sexuality was to plague Freud and his theory into modern times. If it had not appeared to hold such a fundamental involvement in the formation of neurosis, Freud too may have set it aside if for no other reason than to reduce some of the criticism. However, as Freud continued his investigation, the importance of sexuality persisted. Perhaps even more important was his disclosure that he believed that sexuality did not begin with puberty, but with infancy.

PSYCHOSEXUAL STAGES   What Freud (1917) referred to as "infantile sexuality" was not the same orgasmic phenomenon experienced by adults, but rather a more generalized erotic experience associated with a "tension-release" sequence. The tension Freud referred to was generated by primitive drives, and the release of this tension was achieved through the satisfaction of these drives. During the development of his theory, Freud observed that this tension-release sequence seemed related to different parts of the body at different ages, and that certain personality characteristics could be linked with this association. Freud began to refer to these periods of association as "psychosexual stages," and he named these stages of development after the particular part of the body involved. The five basic stages are the oral, anal, phallic, latency, and genital stages.

The "oral" stage, occurring between the ages of birth and two, refers to the fact that the tensions in the infant's world are primarily generated by such drives as hunger, thirst, and curiosity. The release of these tensions is accomplished orally by the ingestion of food, drink, or objects. The personality characteristics associated with this stage are referred to as "oral-receptive" or "oral-aggressive."

The "anal" stage occurs from about the age of one and one-half to around four. In this stage, the tension derives from attempts at toilet training, which is symbolic of the process of becoming an acceptable member of society. The release of this tension is achieved through proper selection of time and place to satisfy one's toilet needs. Personality characteristics associated with this stage are referred to as "anal-retentive" or "anal-expulsive."

Both of these stages are considered to be important phases in the development of our personality. However, Freud believed that the degree of success attained in the development of a healthy personality depends primarily on the degree of sexual identity we attain in our passage through the phallic stage. In fact, Freud even went so far as to claim that *all* neuroses could be traced to failure to successfully pass through this stage.

PHALLIC STAGE   According to Freud, the answers to such questions as, "Who am I?" and "What am I?" are to be found in our sexuality. Freud believed that achieving proper sexual identification and developing an acceptable means of sexual expression were paramount to developing a healthy personality. Although the process of sexual discrimination begins earlier, for the most part sexual identification is to be achieved during our passage through the phallic stage of psychosexual development.

The phallic stage derived its name from the term "phallus," which refers to the erect penis or clitoris and is not meant to include the entire genital area.

PENIS ENVY   Although a child's actual awareness of the physical difference between males and females is often observed at an earlier age, the real implications of this difference do not seem to manifest themselves until the phallic stage of psychosexual development. According to Freud, the real implications of this difference are: (1) if the child is female, she may ask, "Why don't I have a penis?"—the implication being that she is somehow inadequate due to the absence thereof; and (2) if the child is male, he may wonder, "Will I lose my penis too?"—the implication being that he could do something that would result in the loss of his penis. The real implications, in other words, involve the physical representations of one's maleness or femaleness, one's sexual identity and sense of adequacy. Tension in this stage stems from the phallus and sexual identification, whereas the release of this tension takes place through achieving identification with a parental model of the same sex.

This perception of inferiority originates in what Freud (1961) refers to as "penis envy." Penis envy is the phenomenon by which the female child, upon becoming aware of her physical lack of a penis, somehow associates the male possession of a penis with the perceived power and dominance of the male.

Karen Horney (1922, 1967), the world's first female psychoanalyst, disagreed with Freud's concept of penis envy (as do most other theorists). She had noted that many men seemed to envy the procreative abilities of women, and she commented, "I know just as many men with womb envy as women with penis envy."

INTERNALIZING YOUR PARENT   Establishing identification with the appropriate parental model turns out to be more difficult than one might initially imagine. Freud believed that the process is especially difficult for the male child. This is due to the fact that in order to successfully complete this stage, the male child must stop his identification with his mother and transfer this identification to his father. Later in life, the process might be comparable to an individual changing his citizenship. The process is not quite as difficult for the female child, but still challenging. All she is required to do is to maintain her identification with her mother and resist the temptation to transfer her identity to her father. In either

FIGURE 10.4   Freud considers the establishing of identification with the appropriate parental model to be vital to the development of a healthy personality. [*Ken Heyman.*]

case, until this stage, both male and female children have been identifying with their mother. Prior to this stage, they may have exhibited behavior identifiable with the father, but for the most part, such behavior has been merely imitative. The *real* power in the world has been associated with the mother figure. She has been the source of food, comfort, and safety. Therefore, it seems only logical to want to be just like her when one grows up. This goal is reasonable for the female child, but for the male child, it is often doomed to frustration. For one thing, the mother has given birth to children, and this the male child could never do. A more reasonable alternative for the male child would be to want to be just like his father when he grows up. The identification itself is achieved through the process of *internalization,* which involves the psychological incorporation of the father. During this process, the child begins to take on the mannerisms, expressions, values, and attitudes of the individual with whom he is identifying. The acquisition of the father's "power" is especially important to the male child. Freud believed that during the phallic stage the male child both feared and envied the power of the father. By becoming more like his father through identification, the child would acquire a greater degree of safety.

RESOLVING THE PHALLIC STAGE   Freud was also acutely aware of the importance of parental attitudes and the effect that they might have on how successfully a child resolves the psychosexual stages.

Resolution of the phallic stage occurs when the male child *transfers* his identity to a male parental model, or when the female child manages to *maintain* her identity with a female parental model. The phallic stage is basically resolved when the child has internalized the concept of "I want to be like you when I grow up." Initially, one would think that the most important factor influencing this identification process would be the example set by the parent of the same sex. However, Freud believed that in most cases, the most influential factor appeared to be the attitude the parent of the opposite sex demonstrated toward the parent of the same sex. Typically, a positive attitude of love and admiration toward the partner is highly conducive to the resolution of the phallic stage, whereas a negative attitude of hate and contempt will usually result in some degree of fixation at the phallic stage. For instance, a child is more likely going to want to identify with a parent if the child hears statements like "Oh, now wasn't that thoughtful. Look what your father did while we were gone. Let me tell you, there aren't too many wives as lucky as your mother," or "You know, the more I get to know about your mother, the more I love her. She never ceases to amaze me."

Seeing such attitudes demonstrated, the male child is encouraged to identify with his father and to try to become more like him. This encouragement is important because, according to Freud, the male child enters into a form of sexual competition with his father during the phallic stage, and the inherent anxiety associated with such competition is reduced through identification.

THE INCEST TABOO Freud's concern with the phallic stage is more understandable when one considers the anger the child experiences toward the parent of the same sex, the competitor, while experiencing intense attraction for, and possessiveness toward, the parent of the opposite sex. As we shall see in the following section, in such a situation, the potential for generating a high level of anxiety as well as frustration is very great. Freudian theory suggests that the primary sources of fear and anxiety during the phallic stage are associated with the "incest taboo" and the "fear of castration."

Freud believed the incest taboo, the prohibition of sexual intimacy among members of the immediate family, was a universal phenomenon. Although the anthropologist Margaret Mead did discover a few exceptions in primitive societies, and royalty has often been exempt from this taboo, for most practical purposes, one can consider the incest taboo to be universal. It is believed that such a taboo is required in order to provide a stable family relationship. Without such a taboo, it is believed the sexual relationships, the overt competition for partners, and the undesired consequences of resulting pregnancies would completely disrupt the family unit.

Even with such a taboo, the frequency with which incest occurs is far greater than statistics indicate. This frequency of occurrence is indicative of the implication that we don't need a taboo to inhibit us from doing something we have no desire to do, but rather that a taboo is needed to discourage us from doing something we do desire to do. Such reasoning lends support to Freud's description of the dynamic forces which are active during the phallic stage.

THE FEAR OF CASTRATION   The form and direction these forces take are largely dependent upon the attitudes the parents manifest toward them. If the parents are insecure and threatened by these forces, then the phallic stage can become a very difficult and traumatic time for the child, and resolution of this stage may not be achieved. For example, the father may be the type who is jealous of any attention shown to his wife by *any* male, and this would include his son. He would see the situation between himself and his son as one of competition. The son would be perceived as the enemy, and the father would be faced with removing him from the competition. One way of removing him from the competition would be by emasculating him. The father would not literally castrate the son but he would most certainly make an attempt to castrate him figuratively with such remarks as "Now what's the matter with our sissy? Is Momma's little boy gonna cry again?" Such verbal attacks can be devastating, and the son may very well remove himself from the competition because of his fear of being castrated figuratively.

In such a situation, Freud believes that the attitude of the mother is crucial. If her attitude toward men in general, and her husband in particular, is negative, then she most likely will perceive the father as being insensitive and brutish. The mother may react by becoming overly protective of the son, saying things like "There, there. Everything will be okay. Your father just doesn't understand things the way we do. Does he?" The mother's use of the pronoun *we* is symptomatic of the unconscious alliance often developed between the mother and son against the father.

Typically, the mother in this type of situation will attempt to emasculate the father in order to diminish his power and influence. She will often use sarcasm as a weapon, making statements that are designed to humiliate or degrade the father. She may say things like "Sure, you're a big man when you're yelling at a little boy, but you're not so tough when it's someone your own size. Someone like your new foreman. Then it's 'Yes, Mr. Wilson. Whatever you say, Mr. Wilson.' "

In time, under a continuous barrage of such remarks, the father can be effectively castrated. However, it is important to note that Freudian theorists believe that no person actually castrates another person. Castration is always self-inflicted. The victim merely uses someone else as a tool. In the example above, the father, if he allows such ridicule to go unabated, would be allowing his emasculation to occur, using the mother as the implement.

MATERNAL SEDUCTION   According to Freud, the successful castration of the father satisfies several needs of the mother. For one, the mother has been able to express her unconscious hostility toward men. She has also been able to establish herself as the undisputed power within the family unit. Unfortunately, she now finds herself married to a eunuch, and this threatens her ideal image of her femininity. In order to reaffirm her femininity, she needs to confirm her attractiveness to males. This confirmation presents a problem, because she doesn't like men in general. For a solution to this problem, the mother will often turn her attentions to a nonthreatening male—her son. He is unconsciously seen as the ideal solution. He has not yet developed some of the more objectionable habits other males have acquired. He isn't going to leave her or be unfaithful, and, perhaps most important, he has already declared his love and devotion for her. Once this selection has been made, the mother's attitude is no longer merely one of overprotection, but one which also includes overpossessiveness and seduction.

These elements of castration and seduction place the male child in a particularly stressful situation. For although he perceived the father as his competitor during the phallic stage, the father was also seen as the protector. In other words, as long as the father was there and effective, he could prevent any manifestation of what Freud refers to as "instinctual" impulses associated with the mother. This prevention included the prevention of any reciprocating responses by the mother to the love overtures of the child.

It is important to keep in mind that the child perceives the mother as very powerful and capable of having anything she wants, anytime she wants, and that includes any sexual interest she might have for her son. Such an interest is automatically perceived because of the egocentric type of thinking that is typical of this age group. Now, having castrated the father, the mother is viewed as being even more powerful than before, and she has no reason to inhibit her seduction of the son. Therefore, one of the unconscious fears the child has is that the mother would assert herself sexually toward him, and that he really wouldn't want to defend himself even though he is supposed to because of the incest taboo. A typical dream around this age that illustrates these unconscious fears would be of a witch chasing the son, who is attempting to run away but is up to his hips in mud.

REJECTING THE FATHER MODEL   In order to reduce his association with maleness, the male child will usually decide not to identify with the father. After all, the mother views the father with contempt, so there would be no advantage gained by being like him. In fact, having seen what the mother does with males like his father, there appears to be some definite disadvantages to being like him. Often the mother will encourage such a decision with such statements as "Promise me you'll never turn out like your father," or "I don't know what I would do if you ever turned out like your father." Once the decision is made not to transfer identity to the father, resolution of the phallic stage is virtually doomed, and fixation will most likely occur.

DEFEMINIZATION   A similar situation can occur between the female child and the parents. In this case, the most important factor is the father's attitude toward the mother. If his attitude toward women in general, and his wife in particular, is negative, then the daughter may decide to stop identifying with her mother and transfer identity to her father. She is also likely to have developed a tendency to perceive women as being somewhat inferior already, and the father's attitude merely reaffirms her suspicions.

In a family in which mutual respect is demonstrated between the parents, the children tend to perceive the sexual roles of the parents as being equal, there merely being differences in the areas of responsibility and decision making. However, in families where this respect is lacking, the illusion of power and superiority is usually shifted to the dominant parental figure. In the case of the daughter whose mother is held up to ridicule and viewed with contempt, the power is perceived to exist with the father in particular, and with men in general. For example, if the father makes statements like "What idiot wrote a check for eleven dollars and didn't subtract it from the account? I'll bet it was your mother again. I tell you, if that woman had a brain, she'd have to be registered." "What's your excuse this time? It certainly can't be because you're tired. All you women do all day is sit around and yak at each other over the telephone."

Under continuous attack, the mother is effectively defeminized, seen as a failure as a wife, and therefore appears as an unacceptable model with whom to identify. In such a situation, the female child will usually attempt to fill the vacuum created by the mother's perceived failure as a wife and woman by attempting to usurp the mother's weakened position.

THE ROLE OF MISTRESS   Initially, the daughter will assume the role of the "other woman." This is a role that is unconsciously presented to her by the father, who will often turn to the daughter as a sounding board for how his wife doesn't understand him, love him, or satisfy his basic needs. The daughter is often enraptured by this attention and will begin to idolize the father.

Bolstered by the feeling of maturity experienced with this increased attention paid her, the daughter will often go to the mother with statements like "Dad's really a wonderful person. If you would only try to talk to him instead of yelling . . . if you would only try to understand him. . . ." Such statements tend to infuriate the mother. She will often retaliate with comments like "Who do you think you are, telling me how to treat my husband? Wait till you're older. You'll find out that it's not so easy to live with a man." These exchanges tend to further alienate mother and daughter, and to increase the alliance between father and daughter. The daughter's relationship with the father will slowly evolve from one of being his "mistress" to one of being his "wife." Simultaneously, an ever-increasing identification with the father and masculinity will occur, along with an ever-increasing alienation toward the mother and femininity.

THE OEDIPAL COMPLEX   Freud thought that the inherent difficulties in resolving the phallic stage were of such a nature as to maximize the probability that the stage would *not* be resolved. Should the phallic stage not be resolved, Freud believed that the result would be the formation of an *Oedipal complex* (from the Greek tragedy *Oedipus Rex*). In his view, the Oedipal complex was the *nuclear* complex of every neurosis.

Freud used "Oedipal complex" to refer to the neurotic manifestations of both males and females, but later the female syndrome was to be referred to as the "Electra complex" (even though Freud specifically rejected this term), after another Greek myth.

The formation of the Oedipal complex begins when the male child refuses to *transfer* his identity to the father, preferring to maintain his identity with the mother, or when the female child refuses to *maintain* her identity with the mother, preferring to transfer her identity to the father.

THE EMOTIONAL MARRIAGE   In the case of the male child, his identification with a female model is only the beginning of an identity crisis. The crisis continues to develop as the intensity of the maternal seduction begins to increase. This maternal seduction is partly the result of the mother's doubts about her own femininity. In order to reaffirm her attractiveness, the mother will unconsciously attempt to make her son her "little sweetheart." The son will usually reciprocate by acting the part of the "little man." Through a constant reciprocity of mutual affection, the mother and son will often come to the realization that emotionally they don't need anyone else. In their emotional immaturity, they grow to believe that they could never love another or be loved by another the way they love each other. Such an emotional commitment of faithfulness usually develops into what can be referred to as an "emotional marriage."

Neither the mother nor the son is necessarily conscious of making this emotional pact. Thus, neither is consciously aware of the hidden intent behind such questions as "What do you think of my new dress? Do you think I look pretty? Pretty enough to take out on a date?" Such questions are often supported by the two going out for dinner or movies together as "dates." It is important to note that such statements and activities are not in themselves damaging—it is the unconscious motivation to preserve the emotional marriage that is destructive to personality development.

ROLE REVERSAL   Freudian therapists believe that it is this emotional marriage that contributes to the third of the crises the male child faces with identity. The third crisis is that of "role reversal."

Role reversal occurs as the emotional marriage continues to become more established. In dealing with the realities of life, the mother is often faced with going out and making a living. She will work all day, come home, and complain about the high cost of living. In general, she assumes the set role normally assumed by the husband.

The male child, in an attempt to demonstrate his appreciation and affection, will attempt to ease her burden. He may begin by straightening up the house, doing some of the washing, or maybe even cooking a few meals. In short, he assumes the sex role normally considered to be that of the wife. A role reversal takes place, and fixation at the phallic stage is almost assured.

It is important to keep in mind that the usual roles of "wife" and "husband" are generally prescribed by the culture in order to provide a mutually beneficial balance within marital relationships. In recent times, many mature individuals have consciously chosen to reverse these roles—the female assuming the husband's role and the male assuming the wife's. However, this arrangement still provides a mutually beneficial balance within the relationship. The problems arising from the Oedipal complex form of role reversal most often occur when the male child grows up and enters into a legal marriage and *both* partners want to be *wife*. Such an arrangement can often lead to constant bickering as to how the house should be run, how the children should be raised, and who should be out working. The possibility of role incompatibility being the cause of marital discord may be especially high if constant

Freud did not believe that a person was born homosexual, but that this sexual preference was an outgrowth of failing to resolve the phallic stage of psychosexual development. [*Barbara J. Ellis, Peter Arnold.*]

FIGURE 10.5

comparisons to the male's mother and her high qualifications are contributing factors.

LATENT HOMOSEXUAL FEARS Another defense mechanism that is often employed in order to prevent the conscious realization of threatening material is *projection*. Projection is the mechanism by which unacceptable thoughts or desires are attributed to others. In cases where the unacceptable material is associated with the Oedipal complex, the projection is usually directed toward a girl friend or wife. The content of the projection usually concerns her alleged interest in another male. For instance, the defensive male may make a statement like "Come on, why don't you admit it? You'd like to go to bed with Ralph, wouldn't you?" In reality, it is the projecting male who unconsciously wants to "go to bed with Ralph," but such desires would be unacceptable, so they are attributed to the girl friend. In a sense he is saying, "It's you, not me, who is sexually interested in another male."

Many Freudian psychologists believe that such unconscious feelings, along with severe doubts about one's own masculinity, often develop into a type of free-floating anxiety referred to as "latent homosexual fears." Failure to realize that unconscious homosexual fears are the source of jealousy can lead to a chronic state of suspicion in every relationship. This, however, does *not* mean that all jealousy is derived from latent homosexual fears.

In the situation just described concerning the jealous boy friend, it is important to note that the boy friend is not homosexual, but merely afraid that he might be homosexual. Such fears can lead to the use of another defense mechanism called "reaction formation." A reaction formation is a mechanism by which an individual acts out the opposite of his unacceptable desires. In this case, the unacceptable desire is to have sexual relationships with a male due to his sexual identification with a female model. Using reaction formation as a defense, he would act out the opposite. That is, he would demonstrate obsessive interest in having sexual relationships with females. This male promiscuity is considered to be an unconscious attempt to prove one's masculinity and is referred to as a "Don Juan syndrome."

One can see that a fixation at the phallic stage can manifest itself in a variety of rather subtle forms whereas some of the more obvious ramifications, such as sexual dysfunction and sexual preference for partners of the same sex, are often much more readily apparent and will be dealt with later in this text (see Sex Therapies, Chapter 15).

The Behaviorist Theory of Identification

Those advocating the behavioristic approach to personality disagree with Freud's explanation of how identification is achieved. They criticize the Freudian explanation as being too subjective and unnecessarily complicated. The behaviorists prefer a much more objective and simpler explanation for the process of identification. Their primary concern is with the prediction and control of behavior and the role reinforcement plays in accomplishing these goals. The question, for the behaviorist, is not so much one of the "goodness" and "badness" of the behavior, but one of how appropriate or inappropriate the behavior might be. Often the question is reduced even further to merely whether or not the behavior is *desired* or *undesired*.

REWARD AND PUNISHMENT In order to control desired and undesired behavior, the behaviorists (Skinner 1953, 1971) use reward and punishment. *Reward* is said to be reinforcement which occurs immediately after desired behavior and increases the probability of the behavior occurring again, as when a child is paid after finishing a chore: "I'll tell you what I'm going to do. Since you did such a fantastic job raking up the leaves, I'm going to give you a big hug and a piggyback ride to the park." One of the definitions of punishment is that it is reinforcement which occurs immediately after undesired behavior and decreases the probability of the behavior occurring again, such as when a small child has gone out into the street: "And if I ever catch you out in the street again, I'll give you another spanking." Generally, reward is used in order to acquire or maintain desired behavior, whereas punishment is used to stop or prevent undesired behavior. However, it is important to realize that punishment only supresses behavior and will not prevent it unless the punishment continues. The behaviorists believe that any person can learn to behave in an appropriate or socially acceptable manner through the judicious and prudent administration of these policies.

Just how successfully these policies are administered is dependent primarily upon parental attitudes. Unfortunately, some parents improperly administer these policies and ineffectual lifestyles result. One such attitude is referred to as a "perfectionistic" attitude.

PERFECTIONISTIC PARENTS   Parents with a perfectionistic attitude attempt to bring about desired behavior by relying heavily on punishment. In other words, they concentrate on what the child does wrong rather than on what the child does right. A typical example might be when the boy brings home a report card, and his father critically remarks, "Four As and a B. What seems to be the trouble with history? You're probably just not concentrating. If you can get As in your other subjects, you can get an A in history. Now, I want to see you apply yourself a little more this next semester. How are you ever going to amount to something if you don't apply yourself?"

A child raised with this attitude will seldom experience a feeling of success; there will always appear to be room for improvement. No matter how well the child performs, the reinforcement will be directed toward the negative aspects of the performance, rather than the positive aspects. As a result, the child may tend to avoid paternal associations, and failure to identify with the parent may occur.

Another example of a perfectionistic parental attitude might be as follows: "So this is the tree fort you wanted me to see. A little small, isn't it? Looks more like a cabin than a fort. Is that the only window? Doesn't seem like a very smart place to put a window. If you had put the window on the other side, you would be able to see the road. Bet you didn't think of that. Probably in too much of a hurry again. You've got to learn to take your time on a project. You've got to learn to think things out, and not just haphazardly slap things together the way you have here. It doesn't even look safe." As a result of such criticism, the child will usually acquire a sense of guilt for having disappointed his parents and a sense of inadequacy for having failed to live up to expectations.

UNREALISTICALLY MORAL PARENTS   A parental attitude that can be equally devastating to the child's personality development is "unrealistic moral standards." By "unrealistic," the behaviorists are referring to standards which call forth severe punishment for *any* infraction of the rules and leave perfect adherence unrewarded. Such an attitude seems to operate under an "all-or-nothing" principle; one is either a saint or a sinner. For example, a daughter may be doing homework, when her mother asks, "Where did you get this ruler? I don't remember your having one like this." "It's Bonnie's. I'm just borrowing it." "It's a very nice one. I'm surprised she let you borrow it." "Well, actually, she had already gone, and she'd just left it on top of her desk. So, I just . . ." "So, you just stole it. You stole this ruler, didn't you? Why, you little thief!"

As a result of such inflexibility, the daughter will often develop an attitude of self-condemnation, avoid association with her mother, and thereby fail to identify with her.

Children raised under this attitude are also likely to develop a certain degree of resentment toward their parents. This resentment arises because they are often punished when they haven't behaved inappropriately. In other words, they are often punished for something they have not done. For example, they may be guilty merely by association. "I just found out that your friends Marlene and Ted *have* to get married! It seems that she's pregnant. Are you pregnant too? I told you something like this would happen if you associated with the likes of those two. I'll make an appointment with the doctor for as soon as possible. For the present, you are not to leave this house, or even to talk to another boy." The fact that the girl is still a virgin seems to have little effect.

In the application of both of these parental attitudes, the punishment occurs independent of the child's behavior. As a consequence, the punishment soon loses its potential for inhibiting the behavior. When this occurs, the positive aspects of the forbidden response may override the negative aspects, and the child will begin to behave in just the opposite manner to the way the parents had wanted the child to behave. If a child is constantly punished for lying in spite of the fact that he is telling the truth, then the child will often begin to lie. Since the punishment occurs regardless of the child's response, there is no advantage in telling the truth and no disadvantage in lying. In other words, there no longer exists a conflict between telling the truth and lying. The absence of such conflicts can lead to promiscuity, sexual deviancy, or other forms of sociopathic behavior.

Bandura's Theory of Identification

Bandura (1963) proposes that Freud's concept of the identification process is nothing more than a form of *observational learning*. Observational learning is based on Bandura's premise that all human behavior is learned and is the result of how we *perceived* past social-learning events. It is apparent from such a premise that Bandura is not a pure behaviorist in that he acknowledges the existence of internal influences, which Skinner does not take into consideration.

Bandura and behaviorists also disagree on the significance of reinforcement. Bandura agrees with Skinner that learning does take place as a consequence of reinforcement, but he further advocates that learning can also occur in the absence of reinforcement or through vicarious reinforcement. In other words, Bandura believes that learning can take place merely through observation.

In order to support this position, Bandura conducted numerous experimental investigations of imitative behavior. The results of these investigations indicated that learning does appear to take place through observation alone. (Perhaps the most famous of these were his experiments of aggressive behavior involving the use of a plastic "Bobo" doll; Bandura found that children behaved more aggressively after observing adult models demonstrating aggressive behavior toward the doll.) Bandura also found that the degree to which the imitative behavior occurred could be influenced by the consequences of the observed behavior, that is, whether or not the behavior was rewarded, punished, or ignored, with rewarded behavior being imitated the most.

However, Bandura also found that the degree of imitative behavior which

Children learn values and
behavior patterns by identifying
with models. [*Erika Stone.*]

FIGURE 10.6

occurred was highly dependent upon the degree of similarity between the
subject and the model being observed. The greater the similarity, the greater
the influence on imitative behavior. Such factors as age, sex, and perceived
competence seem to have an exceptionally strong influence as to whether or
not the model is imitated. Bandura, therefore, was not surprised to find that
most children resemble their parents. He found that children with aggressive
parents were more aggressive and those with less aggressive parents were
more dependent.

On the basis of such findings, Bandura concluded that the process of
identification encompasses nothing more than the child observing the behavior
of the parents and then imitating that behavior. In regard to sexual identification, Bandura noted that the child would tend to identify more with the parent of
the *same* sex because of closer similarities and because imitating appropriate
sex role behavior would more likely be rewarded (Bandura, Ross, and Ross,
1963).

Getting rewarded or punished as a consequence of imitating behavior,
emotional responses, and/or attitudes was part of what Bandura referred to as
the "incentive and motivational process." In other words, he believes that there
has to be a reason for deciding to imitate, or not to imitate, a particular
behavioral model. One must be able to anticipate being rewarded or punished
for behaving a certain way, so that one has some incentive to imitate.

When we inflict such rewards and punishments on ourselves, it is referred
to as "self-administered reinforcement." Bandura believes that we administer
such reinforcement in accordance with how successful we are at achieving
certain standards of conduct. These standards are based on the perceived
levels of conduct that we have observed in others, primarily in our parents. We
feel pride when our attempts to imitate closely approximate our ideal model
and guilt when our attempts fall short of our ideal model. Unfortunately, our

ideal model is not always a healthy model. In other words, the child will reflect the values and coping techniques of the models he is exposed to, regardless of how detrimental the effects might be in the long run. This seems to be of particular significance with regard to child abuse, where studies have shown that most parents who have abused their own children were themselves the victims of child abuse (McConnell, 1977). Observational learning may also be a factor with regard to alcoholism, which also tends to run in families. For example, it has been found that children taken from alcoholic parents and raised in foster homes have no greater incidence of alcoholism as adults than does the general population (Roe et al., 1945). Far too often, the child will admire parental behavior, regardless of its qualitative nature, and consequently will begin to incorporate undesired as well as desired characteristics early in life.

SEX AND LOVE

Sex is not love and love is not sex; the two can, and often do, exist as separate entities. Sex can be purely physical and love can be purely spiritual. It is the unique ability to combine these two elements into a physical expression of love that can make a sexual relationship so much more fulfilling than either an emotional or a physical relationship alone.

Each individual must generate his or her own understanding of the meaning of sex. However, in most cases, a sexual relationship which is entered into with maturity and a sense of commitment and responsibility will often result in a mutual sense of fulfillment, high self-esteem, and an enduring sense of happiness. A sexual relationship that is entered into with the intent of exploiting or conquering will usually result in feelings of degradation and a loss of self-esteem.

Although variations in the level of hormones appear to have a major influence on the intensity of the sexual drive among the lower animals, a corresponding fluctuation in the intensity of sex drives among humans does not seem to exist (Luttge, 1971). Experience, habits, and attitudes seem to play a much more important part in the sex drives of humans and other primates (Harlow, 1962). As a consequence, sex need not be experienced as a basic need that demands to be satiated. It is not so much a *need* generated from a *lack* of something physical as it is a *desire* generated from an *abundance* of something emotional. Peter Koestenbaum, in his book *Existential Sexuality* (1974), sustains this position when he maintains:

> One of the pillars of existential sex is the clear knowledge that sex is a luxury, not a necessity. Sex is a value that can be freely chosen and not an essence that must be fulfilled. It is a genuine option, not an inevitable obligation; an opportunity, not a duty.

> Sex seen as a choice, not a need, frees us from the tyranny of "experts"—moral and medical—returning our bodies and the life of our bodies to the rightful owner: the inwardness residing within each of us. (p. 45)

FIGURE 10.7   The ability to share both sex and love with another individual is unique to the human race. [*Laimute E. Druskis.*]

The Need to Love

Humanistic psychologists believe that the key to satisfying one's sexual needs is to satisfy one's love needs. One of the most important factors in satisfying these needs lies in an individual's ability to be *vulnerable* in association with another person. This key centers on the ability to experience a high degree of risk with no guarantees. In other words, it is far more important *to* love than *to be* loved. It is far more important to *give* of oneself sexually than to sexually *take* from another.

Unfortunately, many believe that what they really want is merely to be loved rather than to love. To illustrate the fallacy of this belief, consider the situation when Mary Lou complains, "Nobody loves me. I wish someone would love me." Ralph replies, "I love you, Mary Lou. I've always loved you." "Oh, Ralph, I know you love me. That's not what I mean." In this example, Mary Lou is expounding that what she really wants is *to be loved*. Ralph reemphasizes that he does love her, and she tells him that's not what she means. Many humanists propose that what she means is that she doesn't love him, and what she really wants is someone *to* love. Of course, this is not to negate the fact that it is great to be loved back too!

If a person does not become personally and emotionally involved with another person, the relationship and any sexual involvement will often lack meaning. The lack of meaning may plague an individual's entire life. It flows from the lack of involvement. This in turn is caused by constantly being on guard and protecting oneself against possible hurt and by the tendency to avoid getting too close to someone, too attached to something, or too obsessed with or desirious of some goal. An individual with these traits tends to repress feelings of love. If people and things get old, wear out, or lose their usefulness, this individual believes they can easily be replaced as they have no particular, intrinsic value or meaning and no real significance. Such individuals often fail to realize that the lack of significance is a product of their subjective evaluations.

Self-actualizing individuals, however, realize that the meaning and significance of others depend on their own willingness to impart meaning and significance to the relationship (Maslow, 1970). Such persons are aware that they alone determine the relative value of their relationships. Exactly how much value we assess in such situations is directly proportionate to how much of ourselves we are willing to commit, how vulnerable we are willing to be, and how great a risk we are willing to take. By self-actualizing, we will tend to *express* our love rather than *repress* it and to express our sexuality rather than deny it.

The Need to Express

Love, like other emotions, is intended to be expressed, not repressed. Whenever an emotion is repressed, the energy is merely contained, not neutralized. Since such containment is usually only partially successful, in many cases this energy is diverted to other outlets. For instance, repressed anger at an employer may be displaced onto a spouse. Repressed love can also be displaced onto a substitute for what one originally wished to love. Individuals who have been rejected by the original objects of their love may substitute a nonthreatening object like money or develop a sexual fetish for something inanimate like a shoe.

Repressing emotions can also result in an overreaction when they are finally released. A person who represses anger may overreact to a "small" irritant. This is referred to as "venting," and it is an important contributing factor to marital discord. A person who represses love is likely to overreact to any casual indications or symbols of affection. This is usually referred to as being infatuated, or "falling" in love, and is often an important contributing factor to marital infidelity.

Expressing love sexually, however, can result in the development of a more meaningful relationship. Sexual loving is seen as an opportunity, not an obligation. Although there exists a deep emotional investment, sexual loving is a contribution, not a sacrifice. Sexual loving comes from the recognition that someone is as important as oneself, and it can provide a durable emotional bond between two individuals. By loving someone and having another love back, there is no loneliness.

SUMMARY

In this chapter, we have seen that although our moral concepts of human sexuality are changing somewhat, they are not necessarily degenerating at the rate many fear they are. The main areas of concern seem to be increased premarital sex, extramarital sex, venereal disease, and abortion, as well as increased demand for greater sexual performance.

The process of sexual identification is a complex one which starts very early in life and, according to Freud, becomes critical during what the "phallic stage" of psychosexual development. During the phallic stage the child acquires sex role identification by internalizing the characteristics of the parent of the same sex. According to the behaviorists, identification takes place through the process of reward and punishment. Bandura, however, believes that such identification is acquired through observational learning and imitation of the parents.

This chapter also dealt with the tremendous amount of stress that can be generated by conflicts between internal desires and external restrictions, such as the conflict proposed by Freud between parent and child for the affection of the parent of the opposite sex, the incest taboo, and the fear of being castrated.

Just how critical the resolution of the phallic stage is to successful sex role identification became evident through consideration of the ramifications of fixating at this stage and the development of an Oedipal complex. According to Freud, the development of an Oedipal complex can often lead to sex role confusion or role reversal. This chapter also included the existential-humanistic view on sexual loving.

DISCUSSION QUESTIONS

1   Do you consider present changes in the attitudes toward sexual morality to be an indication of moral decay, a temporary swing of the pendulum, or a moral advancement?
2   Do you believe the double standard is still in effect?
3   What is you opinion of premarital sex? Of casual sex?
4   Why do you believe that in spite of an increased availability and knowledge of contraception, teenage pregnancies are on the increase?
5   Do you believe that in today's world there is a greater emphasis on sexual performance than there is on intimacy and emotional expression?
6   How important do you believe sex role identification is with regard to personality development?
7   Do you recognize in yourself any of the personality characteristics Freud associated with the oral stage, the anal stage, or the phallic stage?
8   Can you recall a person who represented a model for you to imitate as a child or someone you idolized as a teenager?
9   Do you agree or disagree with the premise that homosexuality is a sexual preference rather than a psychiatric disorder?
10   Do you believe that the new sex therapies tend to dehumanize the clients?

EXPERIENTIAL EXERCISES

1   Ask your grandparents or others from that generation what sexual mores were dominant when they were teenagers.
2   Visit your community family planning clinic, or some district office that provides a similar service, and obtain information representative of the problems associated with premarital sex, such as pregnancies, abortions, venereal diseases, etc.
3   Select a student, or neighbor, who is from another country, and ask that person to discuss how the sexual attitudes of his or her native country differ or how they are similar to those of the United States.

CHAPTER 11

MARRIAGE AND FAMILY

IN TRANSITION

[Suzanne Szasz.]

Love cannot be expected to last forever unless it is continually fed with portions of love, the manifestation of esteem and admiration, the expressions of gratitude, and the consideration of unselfishness. . . .Marriage is not a legal coverall. Rather, it means sacrifice, sharing, and even a reduction of some personal liberties. It means children who bring with the financial burdens, service burdens, care and worry burdens; but also it means [feeling] the deepest and sweetest emotions of all.

Spencer W. Kimball
Marriage and Divorce

THE CHANGING ROLE OF MARRIAGE AND THE FAMILY

For many, change in and by itself is threatening, and proposals of change within the institutions of marriage and family can be especially threatening. In such cases, fear can influence people's perception to such an extent that the past is altered to correspond to how they want to remember it, the present is transformed into being the way they want to see it, and the future becomes a figment of what they want to imagine it will be.

Coping with the Trend

It was not too long ago that the notion that there was an eternal quality associated with marriage and the family was almost universal. Each and every member of the community was expected to grow up, get married, have children, and "live happily ever after." Respectable people were not supposed to even talk about things like divorce. Marriage was literally "for better or worse . . . 'til death do you part." Children were not "planned" with any real degree of certainty, and the childless marriage was to be pitied. The extended family was not that uncommon; grandparents could be found sharing the same home with their children and grandchildren. Each member of the family contributed to the general welfare of the entire family. Maintaining and preserving the honor and reputation of the family was the personal responsibility of every member so as not to disgrace the family name or bring shame upon the family within the community.

Today, with one out of three young people having come from families that were broken up by divorce or separation, it is not uncommon to hear statements like "I've decided that I'm never going to get married," "We've decided not to have any children." Frequently, people will ask each other questions like "Do you realize that almost everyone we know is divorced or planning on getting one?" "Are the children yours, or are they from a previous marriage?"

Many people, especially some parents, may find such statements and

FIGURE 11.1   The extended family represents a unique and effective means of providing each member with emotional support, physical resources, and a sense of social and individual identity. [*Mimi Forsyth, Monkmeyer Press Photo Service.*]

questions difficult to deal with. Since many were raised with the traditions and customs of a former generation, it is understandable that they might be somewhat reluctant to accept them as part of a trend toward "individual awareness" and "freedom to be." An example of such reluctance might be as follows: "What do you mean you're going to get married, but she's not going to take on our family name?" "Well, you see, Dad, she's an individual, and . . ." "Individual my eye! If she marries my son, she's family, and everybody who's a member of this family is gonna use the same name!"

This is not to say that it is only the older generation that is having difficulty coping with the trend. The current generation too finds itself struggling with the responsibility of choice. Today, perhaps more than ever before, a lack of consensus is placing the responsibility for the "correctness" of a choice more directly on the individual making the choice than it does on social mores.

MARRIAGE AND DIVORCE: BOTH HIGH AND RISING   Since 97 percent of the women and 96 percent of the men in the United States will eventually get married (Bernard, 1973), personal concern for the future of the American concept of marriage and family is valid. Faced with the fact that in California for every 100 marriages today there are 50 divorces, one's concern can easily turn to dread. Based on the present trend, predictions of 63 divorces for every 100 marriages by 1990, compared to 9 per 100 marriages in 1910, can turn dread into a feeling of hopelessness.

In the face of such statistics, it is not uncommon to hear ominous cries of "decline," "decay," and "disintegration" in reference to the institutions of marriage and the family. Yet a recent survey by the Institute of Life Insurance (1975) found that 87 percent of the respondents over age twenty-nine stated that achieving a "happy family life" was the most important goal in their lives. Hope springs eternal even among the divorced, for one in three of our population will divorce and remarry a second time. What's more, other studies have shown that married people reported higher feelings of satisfaction and general well-being than unmarried people (Campbell, Converse, and Rogers, 1975), and statistical evidence indicates that more people are getting married today than ever before.

On the surface, there appears to be some incongruity between having an increase in the divorce rate and having a greater number of people say that they are happier married. Such incongruity suggests a general belief that "happiness" is to be achieved through marriage, and if it is not achieved (usually within three years), a divorce will occur, followed by a second attempt through remarriage. This is not to suggest that today's attitude toward marriage and divorce can be compared to shopping in an ice cream store which carries a variety of flavors, a situation where the person behind the counter yells, "Next!" and the reply is "Let's see, this time I think I'd like to try. . . ." However, sociologists have now begun to investigate a form of polygamy that they refer to as "serial polygamy," in which an individual will experience more than one wife or husband sequentially rather than simultaneously.

THE NEW ROLE OF DIVORCE   It appears that the social taboos against divorce have all but disappeared, and that attitudes toward divorce and remarriage can be likened to attitudes once held exclusively for the widowed of our society. In the past, life expectancies were much shorter than they are today, and the early death of a spouse was not at all unusual. In such cases, remarriage was considered an economic necessity. Oaths of "until death do us part" did not necessarily mean for a long time. For example, in 1900, the average life expectancy was forty-seven years, whereas in 1977 it was seventy-two years (*World Almanac,* 1978). Today, however, with a much longer life expectancy, some sociologists propose that divorce is merely serving as an emotional safety valve, limiting the duration of the relationship much as death once did. Many sociologists are therefore viewing divorce not necessarily as an index of instability but perhaps as representative of a more mature outlook toward marriage. This outlook emphasizes the importance of the emotional basis of marriage and the unwillingness of people to remain in a relationship which is psychologically or emotionally destructive. Other sociologists, however, are fearful that a growing proportion of the people in today's society are afraid to establish or sustain a lasting relationship. In such cases, divorce may be being used as a means of escaping the anxiety that develops when such an individual is threatened with intimacy. Kangas and Solomon

(1975) equate the fear of intimacy with the fear of dependency, the fear of entrapment, the fear of rejection, and the fear of being exploited.

THE NEW ROLE OF MARRIAGE   Meeting the personal and emotional needs of family members has become almost a requirement for maintaining a marriage relationship today. This emphasis is representative of a growing attitude that marriage is primarily a personal rather than a religious or civil event. Until the latter part of the nineteenth century, marriage was primarily a sacred event closely tied to the church and religious orthodoxy. During the latter part of the nineteenth century, it became predominantly a civil matter and was primarily a concern of estate and the legalities of the union. However, twentieth-century attitudes toward marriage have shifted to perceive it as something personal. Marriage is now perceived by many as a means of achieving personal fulfillment, erotic experience, and authenticity through a love relationship. Marriage and the family today are often seen as a refuge from the outside world, a world which is progressively more often seen as being phony, dishonest, and hypocritical. Such a role, however, places an additional burden on the marriage, and when game playing and hypocrisy penetrate the marital barrier, the marriage often fails.

IS THERE A FUTURE FOR MARRIAGE AND FAMILY?   The emphasis on what function marriage and the family serve has changed and will continue to change, but our need for marriage and family does not seem to have diminished; nor, according to many, is it likely to. In order to ensure the survival of the human race, some accommodation between the sexes must be maintained. This relationship must be enduring enough to provide for the protection and reasonable care of the offspring. Regardless of what faults the institution of marriage might have, it is still the most successful means by which to satisfy these needs.

The institutions of marriage and family do not appear to be breaking down as much as they appear to be in *transition* and in the process of *redirection*. The trend is away from lifelong, monogamous relationships and toward later first marriages, more divorce, and more remarriages with fewer children making up the family unit (U.S. Department of Commerce, 1970). There is also a tendency to experiment with alternatives to marriage, such as open marriages, group marriages, marriage contracts, and "living together," which will all be dealt with in greater detail at the end of this chapter. It is important to keep in mind that such trends and alternatives are not necessarily bringing about beneficial social changes, merely that they are bringing about changes. Many authorities contend that the present increases in delinquency, male and female prostitution, and drug abuse are traceable to an increase in family instability.

Historical Parent-Child Relationships

As a psychological defense against our dissatisfaction with the world we find ourselves in today, there exists a tendency to reminisce longingly for the days of yesteryear. As a consequence, we often tend to cling to fond memories of the past and create a nostalgic desire to return to the "good old days." We often forget, or choose to ignore, that those good old days often included smallpox epidemics, debtors' prisons, and outhouses.

WHEN FAMILY NEEDS COME BEFORE INDIVIDUAL NEEDS   During the process of tracing the historical origins of the family, it soon becomes evident that the primary function of the family was *survival*. In order to ensure the survival of the family unit, however, the needs of the family were to take precedence over the needs of the individual. This is in sharp contrast to today's family where meeting the needs of the individual often takes precedence over the preservation of the family unit. This might be the case when parents explain to their children that "We're getting a divorce because we believe that, under the present circumstances, we just don't seem to be able to grow as individuals. We seem to be holding each other back from achieving our full potentials." In their book *Open Marriage* (1972), Nena and George O'Neill describe such a marriage as one which lacked *synergy*. They define synergy as the combined, cooperative action of two individuals working in concert; when one person grows, the other person is stimulated to grow as well.

In the past, the family was customarily organized into an economic cooperative with the labor being distributed among all members of the family, regardless of age. The defense of the family was also mutually shared, with each member assuming the responsibility for the protection of each of the other members. During times of stress, the family united in order to present a solid front. Today's family still tends to look first to other members of the family in times of stress, but there tends to be a far greater emphasis on the demonstration of strong individualism and "going it alone."

One of the reasons for such contrasts is that most family units evolved in order to meet the needs of a nonindustrialized society. The family was an efficient means of functioning within an agrarian society and provided an effective means of preserving and transmitting title and property. The present form of the family did not appear until the advent of the Industrial Revolution and the subsequent perception of offspring as children rather than as little adults. Because of this new perception, children began to be set apart from adults. They were provided with a special position in the family unit.

WHEN CHILDREN WERE SEEN AS LITTLE ADULTS   For centuries, children were not necessarily loved by their parents, nor were they expected to love their parents. They were, more or less, considered to be little adults, and like any adult, some were liked or loved and others were not. During the Middle Ages, and through the seventeenth century, families did not necessarily provide children with primary affection, education, or even socialization. These functions, when provided at all, were usually carried out by the community as a whole. In this respect, the families were much more "open" than families of today. Child rearing was shared with servants, hirelings, care centers, and wet nurses. It was not unusual, especially among the more affluent, to have most of

In past centuries, childhood as we know it today was brief or nonexistent. Life was short and preparation for adult responsibilities had to begin at an early age. [*Culver Pictures.*]

FIGURE 11.2

the child's rearing performed by people other than the parents. "Of 21,000 children born in Paris in 1780, 17,000 were sent to the country to be wet-nursed, 3,000 were placed in nursery homes, 700 were wet-nursed at home, and only 700 were nursed by their own mothers" (De Mause, 1975). When such practices are combined with the fact that most children were sent out for apprenticeship training, or service, by the age of seven, it becomes obvious that there was little time left for the parents to become involved with child rearing.

These practices, of course, were reserved for those children who were fortunate enough to survive infancy, for infant mortality used to be tremendously high. For example, even as late as 1900, the infant mortality rate was 162.4 per 1000, compared to 20 per 1000 in 1975. Much of the mortality rate was attributable to poor medical care and hygiene. A large portion of the infant deaths, however, were a direct result of neglect, if not outright abuse. Beatings were common, and during earlier periods of history, infanticide was widespread. In many families, often no more than one female child was permitted to survive. Infanticide was also practiced when the child had any defects or was illegitimate.

These practices are, for the most part, no longer employed, and there appears to have been an evolutionary progression toward a more humane treatment of children. Lloyd De Mause (1975) has categorized the major historical modes of parent-child relationships, ranging from infanticide to assistance in self-actualizing.

1   *Infanticidal Mode (Antiquity).*   The killing of unwanted children at birth, and/or the abusing of those who survived.
2   *Abandonment Mode (Medieval).*   The child-rearing was primarily given over to wet nurses, foster homes, nunneries, or servants.
3   *Ambivalent Mode (Renaissance).*   The beginning of a greater emotional involvement on the part of the parent towards the child. Usually of a love-hate fashion.
4   *Intrusive Mode (Eighteenth Century).*   The disciplining and training of the child became primarily the responsibility of the parents, and closer identification with the child became possible.
5   *Socializing Mode (Nineteenth Century to Present).*   The parents see the child as someone who requires training and guidance in order to become fully socialized. Positive as well as negative manipulation is introduced.
6   *Helping Mode (Just Beginning).*   The parent recognizes that the child is the best judge of what his needs might be at any particular stage. Through the establishment of good communication, the parents are able to help the child achieve personal fulfillment.

Since all these modes of parent-child relationships are still practiced to some degree within today's families, some psychiatrists use this evolutionary scale in order to judge the emotional and psychological health of the individuals involved.

Today's View of Marriage

Throughout history there has always seemed to be a certain degree of anxiety and trepidation associated with taking the marriage vows and assuming the responsibilities and restrictions connected with being married. However, with today's emphasis on individuality and personal freedom to realize one's full potential, marriage is being seen as a form of prison—a furry prison, but nonetheless a prison, one into which most of us clamor to get, one we believe to be cuddly, warm, and safe. As Montaigne said, "Marriage happens as with cages: the birds without . . . despair to get in, and those within despair of getting out."

BEING "FORCED" INTO MARRIAGE   The statement "We had to get married" once referred exclusively to premarital pregnancy, but today it has taken on new social and sometimes even pathological implications. Although couples are still getting married because of pregnancy [about 80 percent of those who get married while still in high school (Udry, 1966) and about 33 percent of all brides are pregnant at the time they are married (*In the News,* 1970)], many now seem to be getting married out of desperation.

For some, the desperation stems from finding themselves unable to live up to the perfectionistic demands of their parents or, equally frustrating, unable to satisfy the insatiable emotional demands of their parents. In some cases, the marriage is not so much an escape as a timely shove on the part of the parents. "It's about time you gave some serious thought to settling down. You're not getting any younger, you know." Such pressure does not originate solely with parents, however. Peer pressure can also be very influential. "You two have been going together a long time now. I guess it won't be long before you get married." "Well, we really haven't talked about it much." "Hey, come on, man, we've known all along that the two of you are going to get married some day." Such expectations are representative of the expectations of society in general. Although our society has become much more tolerant of the single person, it still expects everyone to get married. It is still widely believed that there is something wrong with a person who doesn't want to get married. Consequently, many will get married primarily as a means of gaining social approval. Margaret Mead said, "It's very, very difficult to lead a life unless you're married. So everybody gets married—and unmarried—and married, but they're all married to somebody most of the time."

This hunger for approval can also be part of a deep-seated personal need. In our highly competitive society, some children raised by achievement-oriented parents are expected to master certain skills before they are "ready." As a result, they may experience the world as one of perpetual failure filled with disappointed parents (McClelland, 1961). They often perceive themselves as ugly, stupid, and innately unlovable. As a consequence, marriage may be seen as a means of declaring to themselves and to others that "someone approves of me." Such feelings of inadequacy can also lead to neurotic identification as the motivating factor behind getting married, the belief being that the admired qualities of the partner will somehow become a jointly owned resource and will therefore be shared with the less gifted partner. For example, a person who was overly shy might comment, "I'm sure glad I married Ralph. He's so outgoing and friendly. If it were left up to me, we wouldn't know anyone." A person from the wrong side of the tracks, meanwhile, might declare, "I used to be treated like a nobody in this town until I married Thelma. You better believe they treat me with respect now."

One of the most pervasive motivating reasons behind getting married out of desperation seems to be a fear of loneliness. A 1973 Harris survey indicated that the number of people who felt a sense of alienation, powerlessness, and futility had doubled since 1966, and that today well over half the people in the United States experience such feelings. Although the causes of loneliness vary, some contributing factors seem to be social mobility, competition, the quest for power and independence, and weakened family ties (Slater, 1970).

THE STRUGGLE FOR FREEDOM   Since the beginning of the twentieth century, attaining and securing personal freedoms has been increasingly emphasized. Whether it be the freedom to vote, the freedom to obtain an education, or the freedom to work, all have contributed to the principle of the freedom "to be."

The emergence of subcultures and movements attesting to this principle

FIGURE 11.3   Perceiving themselves to be victims of sexism, women have begun to organize into movements designed to eliminate sexual discrimination. [*Constantine Manos, Magnum.*]

began in the late fifties and early sixties. The emergence of the protesters, the use of drugs, the creation of a separate teen culture, as well as the freedom marches and the women's liberation movement, have brought about dramatic changes in our social values and traditions. Many of these changes have had a major impact on the attitudes we hold toward marriage and family.

The Industrial Revolution shifted the wife-mother from a position of economic cooperation to housekeeping and child care. This placed the wife-mother in a special position and the husband-father in another special position within the family unit. The agrarian cooperation once experienced between husband and wife in growing and canning was displaced by the industrial coexistence of management and labor. The husband was expected to assume the role of management and provide the capital needed to run the family, and the wife was expected to assume the role of labor and provide the work force.

Since the advent of the women's liberation movement, there has been an effort to free women from the rigid expectations associated with these roles and to restore an atmosphere of cooperation within the family unit. As an indication of the effect of such movements, as well as recognition of a growing economic necessity, 41 percent of the American work force is now made up of women. It has yet to be fully determined what effect this migration from home to factory will have on the emotional, mental, or social health of the children being raised within such families. Thirty-four percent of all mothers with preschool children are now working at outside jobs. Similar changes are being experienced in attitudes toward sex, morals, and social behavior. Since the masculine and feminine roles are interdependent, there can be no major change in one without a corresponding change in the other. We can therefore anticipate reciprocating change for some time to come. Perhaps Margaret Mead (1971) expressed this current trend in attitude best when she said:

> By dint of telling women that their major job was to be wives and mothers, we told most men their major job was to be breadwinners and very much limited the number of men who could do the things they wanted to do most. We always talk about career women, and the wonderful careers they would have had, if they hadn't had those five children. But nobody looks at fathers and thinks what a life he'd have had if he hadn't had those five children. (p. 53)

THE DATING AND MATING PROCESS

Although much of the motivation behind today's experimentation with marriage seems to be an effort to "be sure before taking the plunge," no sure way of selecting a mate has yet been devised. For centuries, the process of selecting a mate was considered to be a function of the parents. The decision was often a practical one based on economics and politics. This is in direct contrast with today's mate selection, which is often an emotional decision based on romantic love and affairs of the heart. Julie de Lespinasse (1732–1776) wrote, in one of her letters, "The logic of the heart is absurd." Many a marriage counselor and divorce court judge might agree with that statement.

Finding the Right Mate

Historically, the problem of finding the right mate was the exclusive responsibility of the parents, the assumption being that because they were older and more experienced, they would be more capable of making a wise decision. Their wisdom was often supplemented by family, community elders, and/or, in some instances, a marriage broker. The mutual intent of all involved in making the selection was to produce the best arrangement possible for the good of the community and family, as well as the couple involved. One of the most important factors to be considered when making such an arrangement was the *perpetuation of the group's identity*. In order to better ensure this, certain restrictions were usually imposed on the selection process. The most prevalent restrictions were *endogamy*, which required or encouraged marriage within a particular group, and *exogamy*, which required or encouraged marriage outside a particular group.

ENDOGAMOUS AND EXOGAMOUS RESTRICTIONS Endogamous restrictions are usually designed to ensure that mates will be selected from the same race, religion, or ethnic group. "Mixed marriages" have generally been discouraged

The added difficulty of adjusting
to cultural differences as well as
individual differences places an
extra burden on the "mixed
marriage." [*Suzanne Szasz,
Photo Researchers.*]

FIGURE 11.4

and thought to threaten the purity of the original group. Gradually, many
endogamous restrictions are being lifted within the United States, especially
regarding religious and ethnic considerations. However, in spite of the fact that
the Supereme Court ruled antimiscegenation laws unconstitutional in 1967,
strong endogamous restrictions seem to persist with concern to interracial
marriages. The 1970 census revealed that only 23,566 white men were married
to black wives (a decline of almost 2500 from the 1960 census), and that only
2.1 percent of married blacks had white wives. A survey conducted by the
Roper Organization, Inc., for the Virginia Slims Company indicated that 76
percent of the people polled would not be in favor of a member of their family
marrying someone of another race.

Exogamous restrictions, unlike some of the endogamous restrictions, are,
in general, less likely to be eased. The exogamous restrictions are usually
designed to prevent marriage between close relatives and are often closely
aligned with incest taboos. In support of exogamy, we have created state laws
forbidding marriages between parents and children, between brothers and
sisters, and even, depending on the state, between first cousins.

HOMOGAMY AND HETEROGAMY   In addition to the restrictions already mentioned, the parents would also consider such factors as socioeconomic
position, education, and personality characteristics. A homogamous attitude
toward these considerations meant that the parents believed that the individuals getting married should have similar backgrounds and interests. Heterogamy is the belief that opposites attract or that a marriage is more likely to

succeed if the individuals complement each other. Such a belief advocates that a dominant person should marry someone who is submissive, a person who likes to take care of people should marry someone who wants to be taken care of, or, in many unfortunate cases, a sadist should marry a masochist.

THE INTRODUCTION OF DATING   It was not until World War I and the Roaring Twenties that the institution of prearranged marriages was successfully challenged. With surprising swiftness, the age-old tradition was abandoned and quickly replaced by dating as the primary means of selecting a mate. Dating differs from prior courtship rituals in several important ways: (1) formal introductions by a member of the family are not considered necessary; (2) no chaperon is necessary; (3) no commitment to continue the relationship beyond the date itself is required; (4) the date is arranged by the participants rather than by the parents; (5) physical intimacies are often expected rather than forbidden (Mead, 1959, p. xv).

For the first time in history, the arduous task of choosing a mate has been turned over to the two individuals most directly involved, the young, the impressionable, and the inexperienced. Perhaps the French dramatist Pierre

FIGURE 11.5

More than ever before, mate selection has become an informal, personal decision rather than a formal, family consideration. [*Chester Higgins, Rapho/Photo Researchers.*]

Corneille (1604–1684) summed up the plight of prospective dates when he said, "Guess if you can. Choose if you dare."

What You Bring with You into a Relationship

Just as the marriage selections our parents once made were heavily influenced by personal biases, attitudes, and prejudice, so too are the selections made by the youth of today. Most of these predispositions are developed in childhood and adolescence, and an individual may not necessarily be aware of their continued influence. As a consequence, much of the motivation behind the selection of a particular mate may be of an unconscious nature.

THE BEHAVIORISTS AND MATE SELECTION   Like the psychoanalysts (Freudian school), the behaviorists also believe that many of the characteristics we desire in a mate are determined in childhood. The similarity ends there. According to the behaviorists, our emotional responses to certain characteristics perceived in others are a result of *classical conditioning*. Classical conditioning is the process by which a connection is established between a stimulus (your physical or aesthetic characteristic) and a response (your emotional reaction to the characteristic). The connection is through an involuntary reflex, and therefore, the emotional response is involuntary. A child, for example, who has been classically conditioned to the physical characteristics of his or her father need only to have the father "presented," as in the case of his returning from a trip, and the child will automatically experience a love response, "Daddy's home!"

An important consideration to keep in mind with regard to classical conditioning, however, is that a person will respond not only to the *original* stimulus, but to all stimuli which are similar. For example, Dad, whom Phyllis loved very much, was graying at the temples when she was about five or six years old. Today, twenty years later, Dad's hair is completely white, but Phyllis still admires and is attracted to men who are graying at the temples. This phenomenon, referred to as "generalization," is put forth by the behaviorists to explain why we are able to "instantly fall in love." Each of us has been conditioned to automatically respond to a particular set of characteristics in others. Whenever we encounter someone with a set of characteristics that is similar to the one we have been conditioned to, we will automatically experience an emotional response. Such a conditioned encounter could conceivably go like this: "I had met about twenty or thirty people at the party, but none of them really turned me on. I was getting discouraged and was about to leave, when (he/she) walked in. The moment I saw (him/her) I knew I was in love." Others in the room will experience a variety of emotional responses to the person's entrance depending on how they have been conditioned; instant hate, envy, like, indifference, etc.

The behaviorist's explanation also accounts for such anomalies as, "I know he's irresponsible but I can't help loving him," "I thought that after all this time I would be completely over feeling anything for her, but the moment I heard her voice on the phone, my stomach did a complete flip." It also helps to explain how an individual is capable of consistently selecting "losers," and ends up making statements like "I swear I don't know how you find such neat friends. The ones I choose end up running off with my roommate, ripping off my stereo, or running up my phone bill."

THE EXISTENTIALISTS AND MATE SELECTION The existentialists do not agree with the behaviorist belief that we cannot help but feel the way we do toward certain people. The existentialists believe that we *deliberately* and freely select the people we choose as mates. It doesn't really matter whether we are consciously aware of the reasons behind our selection or not, we are still responsible for our selection. It is of little avail, in existential thinking, to whine and complain after the fact that we thought our spouse would change after we were married, or that we didn't think the heavy drinking would turn into alcoholism. Consciously or unconsciously, we deliberately select the mate that we really want, even if the reason is that we really want to be unhappy or really want to marry someone who does not love us.

Mate selection, as with many of our choices, will usually take one of three paths; the *familiar* path, the path we are *supposed* to take, and the path of the *unknown*. By choosing to take the familiar, we may come from an unhappy home life full of fighting and verbal abuse and, incredible as it may seem to others, go right out and choose to marry someone with whom we can fight and from whom we can take verbal abuse. It was miserable before, and it is miserable again, but it's a familiar misery, and one can get used to it by deciding to resign oneself to one's fate. Fortunately, a person who comes from a family full of love and happiness will also tend to choose the familiar and will usually select someone with whom such joy can be perpetuated. Several surveys have indicated that happy marriages tend to run in certain families (Popenoe and Wicks, 1937; Terman, 1938; Burgess and Wallin, 1953).

Choosing what we are supposed to choose is usually based more on reason than passion. More often than not, one who chooses this way is primarily concerned with pleasing others. The person merely goes around with a shopping list of qualities one is supposed to want in a mate. The mate must be of a certain race, nationality, or religion; belong to a certain social or economic group; attend a particular college, etc., etc. Should someone meet such criteria, who could possibly object to such a choice? Unfortunately, practical does not always mean happy. Besides, such an individual is highly dependent upon the opinions of others and therefore must constantly keep checking with the others to update criteria for selection.

Choosing the unknown is often the most realistic basis for making a selection. After all, what will be happening twenty years from now, what direction the growth of each spouse will take, or what major events will take place, are all unknowns. The future is an unknown quality. However, the present is a known quantity, and therefore the selection is based on the present, the way the person is perceived today. In choosing the unknown, one is acknowledging a lack of control over life, and simultaneously an ability to cope with whatever *does* happen, not what *might* happen.

In existential selecting, one is more aware of what one has control over (one's own emotions and happiness), and what one has no control over (another person's emotions and happiness). "The pleasure of love is in loving. We are happier in the passion we feel than in that we arouse" (La Rochefoucauld, 1665). The choice that is made should be based on the qualities perceived in the prospective spouse at the time the decision is made, not on the partner's perceived potential and the belief that the partner can be changed. "What you see is what you get."

What Are the Chances for a Successful Marriage?

After being exposed to reports that 1 of every 3 marriages ends in divorce, or that 50 divorces occur per 100 marriages in California, one might begin to get pretty discouraged about the chances of having a successful marriage. The important thing to keep in mind while reading such statistics is that they are usually *divorce* statistics rather than *successful marriage* statistics. If the above statistics are reversed, they then state that two out of three marriages succeed; the California statistics include those who are getting divorced for the third, fourth, or nth time. So actually, even today, the chance of having a successful marriage is still quite good.

INCREASING THE CHANCES   The chances increase the more both partners have in common, if both have had a relatively happy childhood, and if both their parents' marriages were happy ones. A lack of conflict between the prospective partners and their parents also seems to increase the likelihood of having a good marriage.

The chances are also good the second time around, for many remarriages appear to be more satisfying and enduring than many first marriages. Being of the same race, religion, ethnic background, and social level seems to have a high correlation with successful marriage. One's chances also continue to increase with the length of the courtship. Joseph Addison (1672–1714), in one of his essays, noted that "Those marriages generally abound most with love and constancy that are preceded by a long courtship. The passion should strike root and gather strength before marriage be grafted on it." Time is also in one's favor with regard to age. Those marrying before they are eighteen have three times the divorces of those who marry after eighteen, and those marrying before they are twenty have twice the divorce rate of those over twenty (Glick, 1957; Carter and Glick, 1970). Time can also be a factor when considering education. High educational achievement and high economic achievement both increase the chances of achieving success in marriage.

DECREASING THE CHANCES   The younger the couple is at marriage the poorer their chances are of having a successful marriage. A divorce is three times as likely to occur in a marriage where the bride is under eighteen years of age than where she is between twenty-two and twenty-four. Divorce is twice as likely in a marriage where the groom is under twenty-two and the bride is under twenty than in those where the groom is over twenty-two and the bride is over twenty (Carter and Glick, 1970). The chances also decrease if the bride is pregnant at the time of her marriage (over 50 percent end in divorce), if either the husband or wife has a markedly higher degree of education than the other, or if the partners have been married more than twice before.

Perhaps much of the anxiety being felt about the chances of having a successful marriage is merely bad publicity. There seems to be plenty of talk and statistics about the rate of divorce. Therefore, it is not unusual to hear "Ralph and Mary Lou are getting a divorce. That's another one that didn't make it." However, one will seldom hear "George and Irma are having a successful marriage. That's another one that's making it," even though their numbers are greater.

MARRIAGE AND FAMILY: WHAT IT MEANS— ITS SUCCESS, ITS FAILURE

Over 2300 years ago, the Greek poet Menander said, "Marriage, if one will face the truth, is an evil, but a necessary evil." The institution seems to be as needed today as it was in ancient Greece. Marriage is necessary in order to assure social stability, in that the family is the major social unit in our society and allows for the perpetuation of traditions, customs, and mores. Marriage is necessary in order to provide for a lifelong relationship which can be mutually supportive and offer enduring companionship. Marriage is necessary to provide exclusive, or in some cultures at least preferential, sexual privileges for the partners. Marriage, however, is also necessary to provide a basis for creating a family and legitimating the children.

What It Means to Be Married

One of the most universal ceremonies celebrated by the human race is the wedding ceremony. The procedure, ritual, and wording of the ceremony may vary (see Figure 11.6), but the intent is always the same: to set apart the couple being married from all others. After the ceremony is completed, the couple is seen as an exclusive union, entitled to special privileges and trusts not to be enjoyed by any other.

Any relationship between a man and woman short of marriage is a limited relationship. It is limited by the state and by the legal rights the partners may be denied, such as legitimating the offspring, inheritance rights, medical consent powers, insurance benefits, and any economic claims or rights to pensions. It is limited by the couple's religion too. Carnal relationships lacking the sanction of marriage are considered sinful; in some religions, failing to get married prevents a couple from attaining a higher level of religious exaltation, such as being sealed in the temple for Mormons or receiving the sacrament of marriage for Catholics.

The nonmarital relationship is also limited by society because the consequences of such arrangements often challenge the foundation upon which the society is based: who is to be responsible for whose children, what property belongs to whom, and what rights, privileges, or obligations do

OUR MARRIAGE CEREMONY

We are gathered here in the presence of these witnesses to join this man and this woman in the Bonds of Holy Matrimony.

Let me admonish both of you to always remember that Love and Loyalty are the foundation of a happy and enduring marriage; that marriage is a relationship in which the independence of the parties is equal, the dependence is mutual, and the obligations are reciprocal. If the Vows you are about to take are kept inviolate, then your lives will be contented and peaceful, and the relationship which you are establishing will survive all adversity.

BERNARD

do you take

BARBARA

to be your wedded wife, to love her, to protect her, to provide for her, and do you promise to always be unto her a dutiful and faithful husband?

BARBARA, DO YOU TAKE BERNARD

to be your wedded husband, to love him, to inspire him with courage and true thoughts and do you promise to always be unto him a dutiful and faithful wife?

Place your ring on the third finger of your bride's left hand, and repeat after me the following statement:

"WITH THIS RING – I THEE WED, AND WITH MY HEART'S DEEPEST AFFECTION – I DO THEE ENDOW."

The ring that you have presented to your bride is emblematic of the beauty and sincerity of your love and affection toward each other, and should serve as a constant reminder to each of you of the solemn and sincere promises and vows you have exchanged. NOW,

BERNARD AND BARBARA,

having exchanged their Marriage Vows, and having pledged their love and affection each for the other, and having evidenced the same by the giving and receiving of a ring.

THEREFORE, BY VIRTUE OF THE AUTHORITY VESTED IN ME AS COMMISSIONER OF CIVIL MARRIAGES FOR WASHOE COUNTY, NEVADA, I PRONOUNCE YOU,

BERNARD, AND YOU, BARBARA,

HUSBAND AND WIFE.

H. K. BROWN, COMMISSIONER

Carl J. Burmeister

By_____

Deputy

FIGURE 11.6 The procedure, ritual, and wording of the ceremony often vary; many couples choose to write their own words rather than rely on a standard set of vows.

individuals have to each other? Finally, such lesser relationships are limited by the individuals themselves in that the very nature of the arrangement is a declaration of a limited commitment, such as when an individual states, "We'll stay together for as long as it's cool. When it's not cool any more, we'll split," or "I'm willing to sleep with you, but I don't want you to be the mother/father of my children," or "I want you to be one of my friends, not one of my family."

Through marriage, a couple may
enjoy an exclusive union not to
be enjoyed by any others. [*Ray
Ellis, Photo Researchers.*]

FIGURE 11.7

To be married is to declare a *total* commitment to one another, "to cleave unto each other while forsaking all others." It is a declaration of *intent* to share the rest of their lives with each other, both the good times and the bad. It is a declaration that, given all others, the couple has selected each other to be the mother and father of their children and the means by which their genetic lineage will be perpetuated.

BECOMING PART OF A NEW FAMILY   Most of us have vicariously, or personally, experienced the postceremonial commotion of greetings and farewells that accompany a wedding. Everyone seems to be hugging everyone else, and with kisses, tears, and sincerity, the words "Welcome to the family" are repeated over and over. At first, it may be difficult to comprehend all that these four words may imply or the sense of belonging and community that they can bestow. A survey in Detroit of 728 homes found that 67 percent of the families saw other members of the family at least once a week, 20 percent said that they saw each other several times a week, and 13 percent said that they saw each other less than once a week (Goode, 1966). Being accepted as a member of a family can mean an additional sense of security in that the emotional, physical, and economic resources of the family can now be made available when needed. As a member of the family, an individual is entitled to be included when decisions are made that may affect other members of the family. One is entrusted with the confidential affairs of the family. The family member is also entitled to all rights, privileges, and properties of inheritance, and to share in the dignity, honor, and prestige awarded the family through the efforts of preceding generations.

Of course, not all of us will marry into a family of means or prestige. Nor will we necessarily hold all members of the new family in high esteem. Many will accept the new relatives with reluctance or under protest or, sometimes, will merely tolerate them. Oscar Wilde said of relatives, "Relations are simply a tedious pack of people, who haven't got the remotest knowledge of how to live, nor the smallest instinct about when to die."

STYLES OF MARRIAGE Human beings seem to be gregarious by nature and therefore need to be with others in order to live life to its fullest. Apparently they also need a permanent, paired relationship to attain a sense of completion and a means of validating their lives. As an indication of the importance of having a companion, married people seem to live longer, maintain better physical and mental health, and have a lower incidence of suicide. Our more specific need for companionship is most often satisfied through marriage.

However, since each of us is unique, we often form relationships that have a distinctive style or quality about them. Vance Packard, in his book *The Sexual Wilderness* (1968), categorized such relationships in accordance with their style and their quality:

Relationships Distinguished by Style

Fun marriage. Preoccupation with having a good time—planning outings and holidays. A high premium is placed on pleasure. Stability and security are not a primary concern.

Colleague marriage. Both spouses have outside careers. Each recognizes and respects the other's competencies, and views the other as an equal. Jobs or professional interests are usually related which can often restrict the couple's mobility.

Nestling marriage. Characterized by participants' need for emotional warmth and psychological support—nurturing for the male, protection and economic security for the female. A theme of "togetherness" and mutual dependency is established.

Relationships Distinguished by Quality

High companionship. Spouses are best friends and enjoy sharing confidences and physical intimacies. They tend to gain their ecstacy in doing things together, and find little satisfaction in doing something alone or with someone other than the mate.

Minimal interaction. Stay together out of familiarity, economic convenience, or the necessity of caring for the children. Communication deals mainly with the essentials of the family arrangement. Spouses tend to live in parallel grooves.

Peripheral husband. The man's role in the total picture is minimized. His function is that of a providing bystander. The basic units of house, children, and family are considered to be the province of the "mother," as the "wife" role is minimized.

FORMS OF MARRIAGE   Consider for a moment the statements "I love you because I need you" and "I need you because I love you." What do you believe to be the critical differences between these statements? Eric Fromm, in his book *The Art of Loving* (1970), distinguishes between the statements by pointing out that the first statement, "I love you because I need you," is an expression of *infantile* love, which is primarily a "taking" type of love. The person is saying that "because you satisfy my needs for security, companionship, sex, etc., I love you." The second statement, "I need you because I love you," is an expression of *mature* love, which is primarily a "giving" type of love. This person is saying that "because I love you, I need you as a recipient of my love." Almost all of us get married because we are in "love." However, the true meaning of the word, and the form in which its meaning becomes manifest in a husband-wife relationship, can vary. John Cuber and Peggy Harroff, in their book *Sex and the Significant Americans* (1965), have classified some of the forms marriage relationships might take:

Conflict-habituated.   A relationship associated with high tension and controlled conflicts. The couple tend to nag at each other, quarrel perpetually, and maintain resentment by bringing up the past. Verbal barbs are frequent, and the habitual fighting can last for their entire lives.

Devitalized.   A marriage relationship which has undergone a transition from "deep in love" during the early years to "marital duty" in middle age. The relationship is often efficient, but operates in an emotional void as the pair become apathetic and lifeless.

Passive-congenial.   A marriage relationship characterized by a passivity from the beginning. The marriage is an arrangement that is "comfortably adequate," and an economic and social convenience. Primary investments of emotions and energy are devoted to interests outside of the marriage, such as careers or artistic endeavors.

Vital.   In this kind of relationship, the couple is intensely bound together by psychological needs. The presence of the spouse is indispensable to the attainment of full satisfaction from an activity. "Togetherness" is everything, but individual identity is maintained. Conflicts are settled quickly.

Total.   In this kind of relationship, "life" exists only within the relationship, and there are few private experiences. A sense of oneness prevails, and conflicts are resolved with unity and the preservation of the relationship being the primary concern rather than the determination of who is right or wrong. This kind of relationship is relatively rare.

Marriage: Its Success or Failure

The selection of a spouse is perhaps the most important personal decision anyone will ever make. The intensity and quality of the love a couple share at the beginning of their married lives often provide a time filled with an overwhelming sense of fulfillment. The possibility that one has made the wrong choice or that the love felt in those early days will not last forever seems remote. The possibility that the relationship could end in divorce is inconceivable. Yet, for many, such impossibilities will unfortunately become realities. Often the couple fail to realize early that the state of matrimony is dynamic rather than static, and that the honeymoon, or any other period, cannot be expected to last forever. Spencer W. Kimball, in his book *Marriage and Divorce* (1976), admonishes:

> Love cannot be expected to last forever unless it is continually fed with portions of love, the manifestation of esteem and admiration, the expressions of gratitude, and the consideration of unselfishness. (p. 8)
>
> Marriage is not a legal coverall. Rather, it means sacrifice, sharing, and even a reduction of some personal liberties. It means children who bring with them financial burdens, service burdens, care and worry burdens; but also it means [feeling] the deepest and sweetest emotions of all. (p. 20)

MARRIAGE AS AN OPPORTUNITY TO LOVE ONE ANOTHER   One of the most appealing qualities of marriage and family is that they provide an almost infinite number of opportunities for giving and receiving love. The concept of marriage and family embodies the potential for a countless variety of ways to express concern, appreciation, and care for another. Often, however, concern turns into indifference, appreciation turns into contempt, and care turns into bitter sacrifice. In most cases, such unfortunate transitions are the result of irresponsible selfishness and the inability to maintain effective communication.

In order to maintain concern, one must remain actively involved with the other and not allow the interaction to deteriorate into one of passive interest. Active involvement includes a personal commitment of one's time, emotions, and resources in an attempt to enhance the life of the other or at least to lighten the other's burden.

One's appreciation is based on *perceived* excellence in the other. It is a subjective experience which is dependent upon how one *chooses* to see the other, and it is up to both individuals to choose whether or not they will continue to perceive beauty in spite of the passage of time, to perceive success in spite of innumerable setbacks, or to perceive courage in spite of the wrinkled brows and worried looks.

To continue to care is to continue to think of the other as being as important as oneself, to think of the other's thoughts as being as profound as one's own, to consider the other's feelings as being as valid as one's own, and to hold the attainment of the other's goals as being as urgent as the attainment of one's own goals. To continue to care is to have each person's thoughts governed by the theme "One day at a time . . . with you in mind."

THE TRANSITION FROM SINGLE LIFE TO MARRIED LIFE   The transition from being single to being married is a major and often difficult one to make. The realization that much of the autonomy experienced as a single person must now be replaced with a sense of togetherness may produce a moment of indignant defiance. Gradually, most people come to understand that together-ness does not necessarily mean becoming inseparable, or that the individual is to lose all personal identity. It merely means that both individuals must *voluntarily* reduce their personal liberties, and thoughtfully consider what possible consequences actions might have upon the partner. For example, as a single person, an individual can sell the house on impulse and move to a new location. However, this is not recommended when one is married. What would happen if one spouse greeted the other with "Hi, dear! Guess what? I sold the house today, and I'm taking a job as a camel driver in Mauritania!"

Of course, sometimes in the marriage major decisions will have to be made, and, at such times, the positions of dominance and submission may change depending on the issues. The questions usually associated with this conclusion are: "Who will make the decision?" "Who will be dominant?" "Who will be submissive?" The issue of dominance and submission is one of the most misunderstood concepts associated with marriage. All too often, dominance-submission is misinterpreted to mean master-slave and the subsequent relinquishing of one's freedom. In its intended sense, the dominance-submission issue is one of consent and responsibility. The person who accepts the dominant position has *consented* to be *responsible* for considering the desires, values, and feelings of the person who has *consented* to the domination. The person in the submissive position will continue to consent only as long as the other fairly considers his or her feelings. Should the dominant partner become oppressive rather than dominating, then consent would be withdrawn immediately. Among emotionally mature individuals, the concepts of dominance and submission are not synonymous with superiority and inferiority, but are merely different positions of responsibility. These positions can be alternated between partners as they deem appropriate. For example, it would not be uncommon for a mature person to say, "I just don't feel competent to make a decision in a situation like this. You've had some experience in this area. I'd prefer to leave the decision up to you. Whatever you decide, I'll go along with it 100 percent." The experiences stemming from such situations allow each of the partners to develop confidence and trust in the other and a mutual realization that "When *I* decide what *we* will do, it affects both of *us*."

TO BE RESPONSIVE TO EACH OTHER, NOT RESPONSIBLE FOR EACH OTHER
Many people enter into a marriage under the illusion that they have the power to make their spouse happy. In fact, according to the existentialists, no one has the power to make anyone be anything. The existentialists believe that the spouse *chooses* to be happy, sad, or mad based on perceptions of the world. Unfortunately, the illusion that one has power over the feelings of others often persists and, most often, manifests itself in the bedroom. Many interpersonal conflicts originate in the area of sex. More often than not, the conflict is brought about because one or both of the spouses has assumed responsibility for the sexual feelings of the other. One partner cannot be responsible for the sexual attitudes, feelings, or satisfaction experienced by the other. One cannot *make* the other have an orgasm, an erection, or even a

good time unless the partner chooses to allow such an experience. It is masochistic and futile for one partner to decry, "If I were any kind of a man, I'd make you feel like a woman should," while the other partner sighs, "If I were more of a woman, I would make you feel like more of a man." That's like saying, "If I were more of an orangutan, I'd make you feel more of a giraffe." Neither partner is responsible for the other's feelings of inadequacy. However, as a considerate spouse, one can be responsive to the other's feelings of inadequacy, personal doubts, or fear of being rejected. As an empathetic spouse, one can be responsive to the partner's need for greater intimacy, sensuality, and closeness. Rather than blame oneself for not "turning on" the partner ("It's all my fault that you're not sexually satisfied"), one can share his or her own feelings of satisfaction or dissatisfaction. It is rather insensitive to reject the partner's sexual overtures outright—"Good grief! Not again! You're insatiable!"—and then feel responsible for the partner's depression. One can reject an overture while being responsive to the partner's need to be reassured of love. "I really appreciate your offer, dear, and I want you to know that I love you, but the way I feel tonight, I think it would be disappointing for both of us." What is true for sex is also true for other areas of a relationship. One partner cannot be responsible for *any* attitude, feeling, or degree of satisfaction experienced by the other.

FIGHTING FAIR   It is important to keep in mind that to be effectively responsive to another person, one must be able to empathize with the other's perception of the world. Each of us perceives the world differently. This does not mean that the way one person sees the world is right and the other's view is wrong. It merely means that there is room for independent interpretation.

Unfortunately, many spouses will attempt to assume responsibility for the accuracy of the other's perceptions. This will usually result in an endless series of arguments intended to show that one spouse is wrong and the other is right. A much more effective means of communicating would be to use the opposing points of view as an opportunity to *share* each other's perceptions, so that each spouse can be more responsive to the motivations of the other. It is very difficult to sustain an argument based on a statement like "You seem to be a little edgy tonight. Is something bothering you, or am I misperceiving the distance that I sense between us?" However, the argument can go on for endless, futile hours based on such statements as "Now don't try to lie to me, you're upset about something. Is it something that I said? I must have done something to make you so distant. And don't tell me that I'm just imagining it."

The premise that conflicting opinions between spouses need not be dealt with in a destructive manner is also advocated by Everett Shostrom in his book, *Man, the Manipulator.* Shostrom proposes that fights between husband and wife are either destructive, which produces an increased accumulation of the unforgivable and unforgettable, or constructive, which leads to mutually beneficial solutions to problems and a greater sense of closeness between the couple. A summary of Shostrom's destructive and constructive fight styles follows:

Destructive Fight Styles

1   Apologizing prematurely.
2   Refusing to take the fight seriously.
3   Withdrawing; evading "toe-to-toe confrontation"; walking out; falling asleep; applying the "silent treatment."
4   Using intimate knowledge of partner to hit "below the belt," playing the humiliator.
5   Chain-reacting—throwing in the kitchen sink from left field, bringing in unrelated issues to pyramid the attack.
6   Being a "pseudo-accommodator"—pretending to go along with partner's point of view for momentary peace, but hoarding doubts, secret contempt, resentments, private reservations.
7   Attacking indirectly (against some person, idea, activity, value, or object which the partner loves or stands for)—"Carom fighting."
8   Being a "double binder"—setting up expectations but making no attempt to fulfill them; giving a rebuke instead of a reward.
9   "Character analysis"—explaining what the other person's feelings are.
10 Demanding more—"Gimmee"—nothing is ever enough.
11 Withholding—affection, approval, recognition, material things, privileges—anything which would give pleasure or make life easier for the partner.
12 Undermining—deliberately arousing or intensifying emotional insecurities, anxiety, or depression; keeping partner on edge; threatening disaster.
13 Being a "Benedict Arnold"—not only failing to defend the partner, but encouraging attacks from outsiders. (1972, pp. 132–133)

Constructive Fight Styles

1   Program fights at special times to avoid wear and tear on innocent bystanders. Leave plenty of time to handle feelings.
2   Each partner gives full expression to his own positive feelings.
3   Each partner gives full expression to his own negative feelings.
4   Each one replays partner's argument in his *own* words, to be sure he understands it.
5   Entertain the "feedback" of the other person's evaluation of your behavior. This means "chewing over" evaluations of yourself before accepting or rejecting them.
6   Define clearly what the fight is about.
7   Discover where the two positions coincide as well as differ.
8   Each partner defines his "out-of-bounds" areas of vulnerability.
9   Determine how deeply each partner feels about his stake in the fight. This enables each to decide how much he can yield.
10 Offer correctional critiques of conduct—this means for both to develop positive suggestions for improvement in each other.
11 Decide how each can help the other relative to the problem.
12 Recognize the Yablonsky (spontaneous explosion without reason) and wait for it to subside; don't "hook in."
13 Try to score the fight by comparing the learning yield of the fight against the injury. Winners are those who learn more than they get hurt.
14 Fight—after thinking. Compare your opinions with each other after the leftovers, evasions, and unsettled issues, if any.

15 Declare a fight holiday, a truce, a period of time in which no fight engagements are to be made. This provides the conditions for exercising the fine art of making up and enjoying its benefits, such as warm body contact, good sex, etc.

16 Be prepared for the next fight. Intimate fighting is more or less continuous, and paradoxically if it is accepted and expected, the quality of fighting is less vicious, the fights less long, the injury less, and the learning of new aspects more. (1972, pp. 133–134)

ONLY YOU CAN DESTROY YOUR MARRIAGE   A couple that is breaking up will present many excuses to explain what caused their marriage to fail. When the reasons are analyzed carefully, however, the responsibility almost always rests with the two individuals making up the marriage. In an address at Brigham Young University, Spencer W. Kimball stated:

> When a couple have commenced a marriage based upon reasonable standards, no combination of power can destroy that marriage except the power within either or both of the spouses themselves; and they must assume the responsibility. . . .

Often the destructive elements have developed in the individual prior to the wedding and are already a major personality characteristic. These elements often take the form of undesirable habits, such as heavy drinking, propensity for drugs, excessive gambling, or impulsive buying. None of these habits can make a positive contribution to the welfare of the marriage or family.

On the contrary, in many cases, these habits will often lead to such abuses as paternal neglect, abandonment, or the physical beating of the spouse and/or children. The use of physical violence is cited as a major contributing factor to divorce. In one study, 23 percent of the middle-class couples and 40 percent of the working-class couples filing for divorce gave "physical abuse" as a major complaint (Levinger and O'Brien, 1974). These statistics may not be all that surprising when one considers that a survey conducted by the National Commission of Causes and Prevention of Violence revealed that *one out of four men* and *one out of six women* approve of a husband slapping a wife under certain conditions. (Twenty-six percent of the men and 19 percent of the women approved of a wife slapping a husband.) Studies by the University of New Hampshire indicate that about 56 percent of the couples surveyed had used physical force on each other at some time in their marriage.

Physical violence within a marriage, however, is not always a contributing factor to the failure of a marriage. If one were to consolidate most of the reasons given for failed marriages, such as being a poor provider, poor housekeeper, inadequate lover, inept parent, etc., the most prevalent would be having *failed to live up to expectations.* Expectations brought to a marriage are soon converted into demands. Expecting your spouse to treat you in a certain way soon becomes a demand to be treated that way. Expectations of how a role is to be carried out within the marriage soon become demands that a particular role be fulfilled, regardless of how inappropriate the demand might be or how incompatible the role might be with the spouse's personality. One of

Divorce is often merely the public declaration that a marriage has failed; privately, the couple has known for a long time that the marriage was over. [*Jan Lukas, Photo Researchers.*]

FIGURE 11.8

the most destructive elements to assault a marriage is the belief that the purpose of one spouse is to live up to the expectations of the other. Perhaps a poem by Fredrick Perls (1969) says it best:

I do my thing,
And you do your thing,
I am not in this world,
To live up to your expectations,
And you are not in this world,
To live up to mine.

You are you,
And I am I,
And if by chance, we find each other
It's beautiful
And if not
It can't be helped.

Desertion, Divorce, and Death

It is all but universal for a couple to enter into marriage with the expectation that it will last forever. Desertion, divorce, or even death is something that happens to someone else, not to us. There is a tendency to believe that if a couple diligently maintains togetherness, sharing, and good communicating, as in Cuber and Harroff's "total" relationships, this will ward off divorce. On the other hand, one would naturally expect a marriage filled with "quarreling, tension, and resentment," as in Cuber and Harroff's "conflict habituated" relationship, to end in divorce. Yet the evidence seems to indicate that the chances of either type of marriage relationship ending in divorce are about equal. For the congenial couple, the stress of *any* discord may be just too much for the marriage to sustain. For the quarreling couple, there may exist that final blow from which their marriage cannot recover. However, far from becoming discouraged over such evidence, many believe that people today are not getting divorced because they are disillusioned about marriage, but because they expect so much from it.

THE RATE OF MARRIAGE FAILURES PAST AND PRESENT   Although the number of marriage failures appears to be at an all-time high, sociologists like Talcott Parsons believe that if one were to include "unrecorded" desertions and separations, as well as recorded annulments, in the divorce statistics of the past, the *rate* of divorce in the United States would really not have gone up over the years. In the past, divorce was often very difficult, if not impossible, to obtain, and desertion and separation were used as viable alternatives. In other words, it is believed that many people would have gotten divorces if they could have obtained them as easily as today. There is some statistical evidence to support this notion. Whenever a state or country liberalizes its divorce laws, there is an immediate upsurge of divorces followed by a gradual leveling off. The initial surge seems to represent a backlog of all those who had wanted a divorce before the laws were changed but couldn't get one. The plateau would be more representative of the true rate of marriage failure.

DESERTION   Desertion is a practice that has always been condemned both publicly and privately. It is nevertheless a practice that has persisted through generations. It used to be considered a "poor man's divorce" or the mark of a scoundrel, and it was almost always considered to be a man's prerogative. However, this no longer appears to be the case. According to the records kept by Ed Goldfader of Tracers Company of America, Inc., a missing-persons-locating firm in New York, the firm sought 300 runaway husbands for every wife who ran away in the early sixties. In 1973, the ratio of husbands to wives had narrowed to one to one, and, in 1974, the firm was hired to locate 147 more missing wives than husbands. The exact cause for such a dramatic increase is not yet known, although some suspect that the women's liberation movement has had an influence. Others blame the economic necessitites of having the wife out in the working world, where she is more likely to become attracted to other men. Still others believe that women have merely become fed up with being housewives.

Desertion often exacts an exceptionally heavy emotional and economical toll from those persons left behind. The suddenness of the departure usually does not allow the others affected to adequately prepare themselves for the event. There is often the additional anguish of not knowing whether or not the spouse is dead or alive. This ignorance can be especially difficult if attempts are made to resume dating or remarry. The economic burden is often overwhelming in situations where the deserter was also the sole breadwinner. In most cases of desertion, spousal and child support are sporadic, insufficient, or nonexistent.

SEPARATION   Physical desertion is often difficult to deal with, but "emotional desertion" can often be equally devasting. Emotional desertion occurs when one spouse emotionally "leaves" the relationship by withdrawing any and all affection that might have existed for the other. The resulting void can often be suffocating, and is therefore sometimes replaced with anger and conflict. The expression of anger is often preferred over having no emotion expressed at all. A divorce may as yet seem too final, so, to avoid the continuous accumulation of hurt and to get some breathing room, the couple may agree to a *separation*.

The most common form of separation is a separation which is mutually agreed upon due to *marital discord*. Reconciliation is the primary purpose behind the separation. The couple usually sees the separation as a means of allowing each of them to cool off, thereby avoiding any further escalation of violence. Such precautionary measures are not at all unwarranted, according to police records, which show that *family members* constitute the largest single category of murder victims in the United States, and that there are more police calls for family violence than all the other incidences of crime combined. Such a mutually agreed upon separation has no legal limitations or qualifications whatsoever, and the couple are considered to be as legally married as when cohabiting.

In many cases, however, the expressed intent of the separation is to get a divorce. Often the court will grant an *interlocutory* decision, which stipulates provisional obligations and restrictions the couple must adhere to until the final divorce decree is obtained. An interlocutory decision will usually outline the financial responsibilities, visitation restrictions, and property rights of each individual.

Only a few choose to obtain a *legal separation,* about 2 to 3 percent. A legal separation provides for all the responsibilities of marriage but none of the gratifications. The marriage is *not* terminated by a legal separation. It merely restricts the privileges of each partner. Neither, for instance, can remarry or cohabit, and the husband is still financially responsible for the separate maintenance of the wife. Usually a legal separation is obtained for political, social, or professional advantages or when divorce is forbidden for religious reasons.

DIVORCE   In some Islamic countries, in order to initiate a divorce, a husband need only say "I divorce thee" three times to his wife, and the marriage is terminated. In most other countries, a divorce is much more difficult, if not impossible, to obtain. For example, until 1972, it was impossible to obtain a divorce in Italy. Today, in Italy as in most countries, it is getting easier to obtain a divorce, although divorce laws have traditionally experienced a cultural lag with respect to changes in social attitudes.

Historically, divorce was often limited to the politically powerful and the wealthy. However, divorce now occurs with greater frequency among the poor than among the rich. It is believed that concern for the poor motivated a change in the laws. During the Victorian era, women and children of the lower class were often seen as defenseless victims of abuse from drunken husbands, and virtuous wives as prey to all sorts of immoral sexual demands. Mercy and decency demanded that an escape be provided for such individuals. As a result divorce laws began to ease. This trend has continued into today's courts, where grounds such as adultery and cruelty have given way to terms like "incompatibility" and "irreconcilable differences."

A divorce is a legal termination of a marriage. The grounds for granting a divorce, as well as how the property is divided, vary from state to state (Table 11.1). In one way or another, however, the divorce terminates the couple's right to cohabit, places specific limits on the legal and financial obligations of both parties, and grants each the right to remarry.

In the past, one spouse would have to sue the other for divorce and had, therefore, to prove that there were sufficient grounds for granting the divorce. Today, all but five states (Illinois, Massachusetts, Mississippi, Pennsylvania, and South Dakota) have some form of no-fault divorce or dissolution. With 95 percent of the divorces uncontested and an equitable division of property enforced in thirty-six states, much of the unpleasantness associated with divorce is being reduced or avoided altogether. However, even under the most amiable circumstances, a certain amount of emotional trauma can be expected when dealing with such issues as physical custody, legal custody, visitation rights, and support payments. Alimony, almost unknown outside Europe and the United States, is often another highly emotional area, for it too is capable of having long-term effects on both individuals. Although most states can legally grant alimony to either spouse, it is still rare for the husband to be granted spousal support. Since the financial obligations on the husband can often be considerable, many will "desert" after the divorce in order to avoid payment.

COPING WITH THE DEATH OF A SPOUSE   Although the words " 'til death do you part" are often included in the wedding ceremony, few if any ever attempt to grasp their full meaning. Yet, should nothing else disrupt the marriage, ultimately death will. Because men are usually two to three years older than their wives and tend to have a shorter life span than women, widows outnumber widowers about four to one.

The whole issue of death tends to be considered an uncomfortable topic of discussion in today's society. During the Victorian era, one avoided talking

TABLE 11.1   WHAT THE DIVORCE LAWS SAY COAST TO COAST

	Grounds for Divorce					Division of Property			Alimony		
	BREAKDOWN OF MARRIAGE	STANDARD FAULT GROUNDS	INCOMPATABILITY	SEPARATION	ALCOHOLISM OR DRUG USE	COURT CANNOT MAKE A DISTRIBUTION	COURT EMPOWERED TO DISTRIBUTE	COMMUNITY PROPERTY —JOINT OWNERSHIP	TO EITHER SPOUSE	TO WIFE ONLY	NO ALIMONY
Alabama	●	●		●	●	●				●	
Alaska		●	●		●		●		●		
Arizona	●							●	●		
Arkansas		●		●	●		●			●	
California	●							●	●		
Colorado	●						●		●		
Connecticut	●	●		●	●		●		●		
Delaware	●						●		●		
Dist. of Columbia		●		●			●			●	
Florida	●					●			●		
Georgia	●	●			●	●				●	
Hawaii	●	●				●			●		
Idaho	●	●	●					●		●	
Illinois		●			●		●			●	
Indiana	●	●					●		●		
Iowa	●						●		●		
Kansas		●	●		●		●		●		
Kentucky	●						●		●		
Louisiana		●		●	●			●			●*
Maine	●	●					●		●		
Maryland		●		●		●				●	

Notes: Standard fault grounds include adultery, cruelty, desertion. Separation means living apart with normal financial support provided in division of property, when court cannot make a distribution, property goes to husband or wife depending on who has legal title.
*Louisiana limits alimony to ⅓ of the husband's income.
Source: Business Week, Feb. 10, 1975.

TABLE 11.1 *(continued)*

	Grounds for Divorce					Division of Property			Alimony		
	BREAKDOWN OF MARRIAGE	STANDARD FAULT GROUNDS	INCOMPATIBILITY	SEPARATION	ALCOHOLISM OR DRUG USE	COURT CANNOT MAKE A DISTRIBUTION	COURT EMPOWERED TO DISTRIBUTE	COMMUNITY PROPERTY—JOINT OWNERSHIP	TO EITHER SPOUSE	TO WIFE ONLY	NO ALIMONY
Massachusetts		●			●	●			●		
Michigan	●						●		●		
Minnesota	●						●		●		
Mississippi		●			●	●				●	
Missouri	●						●		●		
Montana	●	●					●		●		
Nebraska	●						●		●		
Nevada		●	●		●			●		●	
New Hampshire	●	●		●	●		●		●†		
New Jersey	●			●			●		●		
New Mexico		●	●					●		●	
New York		●		●		●				●	
North Carolina		●		●		●					●‡
North Dakota		●	●		●		●		●		
Ohio		●		●	●	●			●		
Oklahoma		●	●		●		●		●		
Oregon	●						●		●		
Pennsylvania		●				●					●
Rhode Island		●		●	●	●				●	
South Carolina		●		●	●	●				●	
South Dakota		●			●		●			●	
Tennessee		●		●	●		●			●	
Texas		●		●				●			●

†New Hampshire limits alimony to a term of three years (subject to renewal).
‡North Carolina provides for alimony only if the spouse is unable to work.

TABLE 11.1 *(continued)*

	Grounds for Divorce					Division of Property			Alimony		
	BREAKDOWN OF MARRIAGE	STANDARD FAULT GROUNDS	INCOMPATABILITY	SEPARATION	ALCOHOLISM OR DRUG USE	COURT CANNOT MAKE A DISTRIBUTION	COURT EMPOWERED TO DISTRIBUTE	COMMUNITY PROPERTY—JOINT OWNERSHIP	TO EITHER SPOUSE	TO WIFE ONLY	NO ALIMONY
Utah		●		●	●		●		●		
Vermont		●		●			●		●		
Virginia		●		●		●				●	
Washington	●							●	●		
West Virginia		●		●	●		●		●		
Wisconsin		●		●	●		●			●	
Wyoming		●		●	●		●			●	

about sex. Today, we avoid talking about death. Kübler-Ross has attempted to open up the area of death. In her book *Death and Dying,* she discusses the five stages that dying patients and their families will usually pass through while dealing with the crisis. Although a person may not experience each stage in the order given, usually the first stage is *denial,* wherein the certainty of death is rejected. The second stage is *anger*—the patient and family ask "Why me?" and "Why us?" The third stage is *bargaining*—a trade is attempted in order to avoid the inevitable. The fourth stage is *depression*—the sadness of losing a loved one is dealt with by the family, and the sadness of losing everyone is dealt with by the patient. The fifth stage is *acceptance*—the patient and family become more receptive to the idea of death. This does not mean that the family will understand death, but merely that they accept it. Even such great minds as Kierkegaard's did not fully comprehend death; he admitted: "In spite of this extraordinary knowledge or facility in knowledge, I can by no means regard death as something I have understood."

Alternatives in Marriage and Alternatives to Marriage

As the twentieth century progressed at an ever-increasing rate of change, the institutions of marriage and family were faced with an ever-increasing insistence to modernize. Some people became socially dissatisfied and felt that the traditional concepts of the conventional marriage and nuclear family needed to be challenged. As a consequence, a small minority of the population began to experiment with alternative styles within marriage as well as with forms of relationships that might offer an alternative to the very concept of marriage.

THE NEED FOR LIMITS WITHIN A RELATIONSHIP   With today's society placing so much emphasis on self-realization and fulfilling one's potential, the average individual is faced with seeking intimacy while simultaneously maintaining enough distance to develop personal potentials. In an attempt to achieve a satisfactory balance between the two, some have turned to such alternatives as the open marriage, swinging, marriage contracts, and group marriages. Each of these alternatives has some advantages and some disadvantages making such arrangements suitable for some and totally unacceptable for others.

THE OPEN MARRIAGE   One attempt to modernize the institution of marriage is put forth by Nena and George O'Neill, in their book *Open Marriage; A New Lifestyle For Couples* (1972). According to the O'Neills, an open marriage is one in which the partners are committed to personal growth within a flexible relationship. The couple is expected to live in the here and now, rather than to dwell on the past or to anticipate the future. The privacy of the partner is to be considered inviolate. There is to be "role flexibility" to allow for changes in economic or social circumstances. Open and honest communication is to be maintained in order to avoid "game playing." Open companionship is also to be included in the marriage, and this companionship encompasses the opposite sex. The maintaining of open companionships, however, does not necessarily include sexual involvement, although it is considered to be an open option.

An extension of the open companionship concept might be what is referred to as "swinging." Swinging is the practice of one spouse sexually sharing the spouse of another by mutual consent. "Swinging parties" are often arranged through referrals or through advertising in avant-garde newspapers. The percentage of couples actively participating in open marriages or swinging is extremely small, but both concepts found a great deal of at least vicarious appeal in the late sixties and early seventies. The main problem with such arrangements is one of achieving *equality* in the area of enthusiasm. It seems to be rare that both partners can agree on just how "open" they want the marriage to be, or just how committed each partner is to having multiple sex partners.

THE MARRIAGE CONTRACT   The marriage contract has historically been used as an addendum to a legal marriage and would more accurately be called a premaritial contract. In such cases, each person's rights, privileges, and responsibilities were specified prior to agreeing to a marriage. In making out such contracts, the primary concern was often for the conditions and directions for property distribution. Today, although in most cases they are not legally binding, marriage contracts are being used in lieu of a marriage license. Most contracts are drawn up by the two parties involved as a matter of mutual agreement. A typical contract often includes such topics as what names will be used after the marriage, what type of birth control, if any, will be used, what child-rearing practices will be employed, where the couple will live, how child care and household chores will be distributed, what type of financial arrangement will be used, and what sexual rights and freedoms each might enjoy.

"LIVING TOGETHER" According to the U.S. Census Bureau, approximately 1 percent of the populace, or 2 million people, are presently cohabiting or "living together" without being married. There are many reasons for this practice, ranging from the economic problems of the elderly and poor, whereby they receive greater Social Security benefits than if they were married, to the cynicism of youth who have become disenchanted with the institution of marriage. Although unmarried couples lived together in the past, most of these arrangements were out of necessity rather than choice. In the old West, for example, preachers were few and far between. Thus, it was often necessary for a couple to set up housekeeping as husband and wife under common law until the marriage could be properly administered. Even today, there are around a dozen states that still recognize common law marriages. Most require a minimal time period to transpire (usually five to seven years) before the couple who have presented themselves as husband and wife in the community are legally recognized as being married.

However, in contrast to the old days, when the purpose of cohabitation was often to establish a marriage and family, most of today's "live-ins" do not intend to marry their roommates. One survey conducted by Arafat and Yorburg indicated that over 80 percent of the male respondents and 66 percent of the female respondents did not consider future marriage a primary reason for cohabiting. About 36 percent of the males in their survey indicated that their primary reason for living in with someone was because of the ease in obtaining sexual gratification.

Despite the growing popularity of living together, it does not seem to present itself as a viable alternative to marriage. Even though many of the people living together express their desire to avoid the restrictions, role playing, and hassles of marriage, they also avoid any of the advantages as well. Living together offers neither the securities nor the legal rights and privileges that marriage offers, and it is still not generally regarded as morally acceptable. For most parents, the discovery that their son or daughter is living with someone of the opposite sex will often generate a great deal of stress within the family unit.

SUMMARY

In this chapter, we have seen that the institutions of marriage and family are in transition. These institutions are not necessarily breaking down, but are under pressure to adapt to the social changes that are taking place. Divorce and marriage have taken on new roles and are more in keeping with the needs of the individual.

We have also explored the introduction of the dating process as a replacement for arranged marriages, the psychoanalytic, behavioristic, and existential explanations for why we select the mates we do, and what our chances are of having a successful marriage.

In addition, we have discussed what it means to be married, the variation in styles of marriage, and the degrees of responsibility shared in a marriage. In this discussion, we included some of the factors that can contribute to the success or failure of a marriage.

This chapter also dealt with the fact that not all marriages are successful, and that some will result in desertion, separation, or divorce.

Alternatives within a marriage and alternatives to a marriage were also dealt with, such as open marriages, group marriages, marriage contracts, and "living together."

DISCUSSION QUESTIONS

1   In what ways do you think that the family of today differs from the family of fifty years ago?

2   What do you believe to be the future of the institution of marriage? The institution of the family?

3   Do you believe today's dating process is an effective means of mate selection?

4   Do you agree with the psychoanalytic premise that we tend to marry people who are similar to our parents?

5   Do you believe that "love at first sight" is merely the result of generalization and classical conditioned responses, or that there really is a "certain someone" for each person?

6   What does "being married" mean to you?

7   What do you believe to be the main cause of marital failure?

8   Do you believe getting married and getting divorced should be made more difficult?

9   What are some of the primary disadvantages of "living together" instead of being married?

10   With regard to a marriage relationship, what does "living up to expectations" mean to you?

EXPERIENTIAL EXERCISES

1 Arrange to interview several couples who have been married for twenty-five to fifty years, and attempt to ascertain what factors were in these relationships that may have contributed to the durability of these marriages.

2 Visit a courtroom during the divorce proceedings. Write your general impressions of the proceedings, the couples involved, and the lawyers and judge.

3 Form a discussion group made up of students from foreign countries or from different ethnic or cultural backgrounds. Have the group discuss the dating or mate-selection procedures practiced within their particular cultures.

CHAPTER 12

PARENTS AND

CHILDREN

[Erika Stone.]

And a woman who held a babe against
her bosom said, Speak to us of Children.
And he said;

Your children are not your children.
They are the sons and daughters of Life's
longing for itself.
They come through you but not from
you,
And though they are with you yet they
belong not to you.

You may give them your love but not
your thoughts,
For they have their own thoughts.
You may house their bodies but not
their souls,
For their souls dwell in the house of tomorrow,
which you cannot visit, not even
in your dreams.

You may strive to be like them, but seek
not to make them like you.
For life goes not backward nor taries
with yesterday.
You are the bows from which your children
as living arrows are sent forth.

Kahlil Gibran
The Prophet

RAISING CHILDREN TODAY

No relationship is as unique, as predisposed to emotional extremes, and yet as enduring as the one between parent and child. For the parent, the relationship presents the opportunity to experience unconditional love, heart-rending sorrow, and a satisfying sense of fulfillment. For the children, there is the opportunity to experience a time to just be, to learn about disappointment, and to enjoy total acceptance.

This unique relationship, however, presents only the *opportunity* to experience such vitality; it is not a guarantee that such fulfillment will be realized. For some, parenthood is perceived as a cruel trick of fate that forces a person into adulthood while initiating the untimely and premature demise of their own childhood. The famous Scopes "monkey trial" lawyer, Clarence

Darrow (1857–1938), pessimistically noted that "the first half of our lives is ruined by our parents, and the second half by our children." Unfortunately, such pessimism is not without foundation. Studies conducted by social psychologist Urie Bronfenbrenner have indicated that "in terms of broken homes, working mothers and child abuse, the middle-class family of today is approaching the level of social disorganization that characterized the low-income family of the early 1960's."

Such social deterioration is, however, not universal, since in 1978 67 percent of all American children were living with their own two parents, who had married only once. Most of the parents in these families perceived their stewardship as an essential contribution to the welfare of the child, the family, and society. As Spencer W. Kimball admonished, "Society without basic family life is without foundation and will disintegrate into nothingness."

The traditional family concept of having children raised by two parents still prevails. The United States has 47 million families that contain both a husband and a wife, and these families have 23 million children under the age of thirteen. However, for over a million children, or about one in six, the family consists of only one parent, and for some, neither parent.

Divorce stands out as the leading cause of children being raised by only one parent. Illegitimacy and death are the other major causes. As most parents are aware, raising a child is a difficult enough task when there are two parents to share it. Attempting to accomplish this task alone presents an even greater challenge. In an effort to alleviate some of the burden, special parental guidance and support programs have been organized, such as Parents Anonymous and Parents without Partners. However, as supportive as these groups can be, the ultimate burden of responsibility for raising the child does not lie with the professional, but with the parent. Far too often, the parent is well aware of how alone one can feel while attempting to fulfill the parental role.

The Traditional Family

Many of the traditional values held by American society came under severe scrutiny during the late sixties and early seventies. As a result, many of these values were discarded or modified. New emphasis was placed on individual fulfillment. For many women, this meant a career. Simultaneously, the institutions of marriage and family were questioned, and respect for parenthood as a career declined.

Traditionally, the challenge of raising a family was often met through the mutual support and cooperation of relatives and neighbors. In the twenties and thirties, census reports indicate, about 50 percent of the families had at least one extra adult living with them. In contrast, less than 5 percent of the families are now so constituted. Such support has been reduced in part by the social mobility of today's society; the average family relocates about every five years.

Frequent relocating also presents the parents with the problem of frequent readjustment to different standards, opinions, and attitudes toward child-rearing practices. In an effort to cope, many parents have turned to specialists. Rather than continuously trying to readapt, they have forfeited many of their responsibilities to the state. Such might be the situation where the parents have turned the responsibility for sex education, training in ethics, and moral development over to the schools or other state institutions.

Economics has also hit hard at the traditional family. More and more mothers are being forced to leave the home in order to supplement the family income. It is gradually becoming more and more difficult to purchase the traditional family home. In many cases, it is impossible to purchase a home without combining the incomes of both the mother and father. Education too has been affected by economics, and an ever-increasing number of parents find themselves unable to adequately provide for their children's education on a single income.

However, even if they must raise their children alone, face the constant struggle of readjustment, and do extra work, most parents find that the rewards and satisfactions of raising children far outweigh the problems associated with child rearing. Therefore, the traditional family has endured and will continue to endure.

The Working Mother

In 1890, only about 15 percent of the white women and about 38 percent of the nonwhite women worked. Today nearly 50 percent of all women work (U.S. Bureau of the Census). Approximately 39 percent of all mothers with children under six years of age work. This figure increases to 51 percent if one considers only mothers with school-age children. Many working mothers are actually trying to hold down *two jobs*—one job outside the home and the other job inside. This is primarily because the women's liberation movement, thus far, has been mostly *unidirectional*. An ever-increasing number of women have been assuming traditionally male jobs, but only a very small number of men have attempted to assume jobs considered to be traditionally held by females.

This situation has resulted in an outflow of mothers from home to factory, but a compensatory movement of fathers from factory to home has failed to materialize. As a result, the parental vacuum in many homes has not been filled. Thus, many children find themselves coming home from school to an empty house, where parental guidance is communicated through notes on the kitchen table: "Dear Ralph, you'll find cookies on the counter. Don't drink all the milk. Clean up after yourself, and don't forget to leave a note telling me where you'll be when I get home. Love, Mom." For many mothers, parenting by proxy creates a burden of tremendous emotional tension, a sense of inadequacy, and feelings of guilt. In many cases, these feelings of self-doubt can generalize to the point where the mother feels that she is failing in *all* her endeavors.

In the more democratic families, work loads and responsibilities are often distributed as equally as possible among all members. In such situations, tasks are assigned primarily in accordance with skills and abilities, rather than sex. Should it become necessary for the mother to work outside the home, her more traditional tasks would be absorbed by the other members of the family. In this manner, the *quality* of the time shared with each other can be maintained, even though the *quantity* of shared time may decrease. With such appreciation and

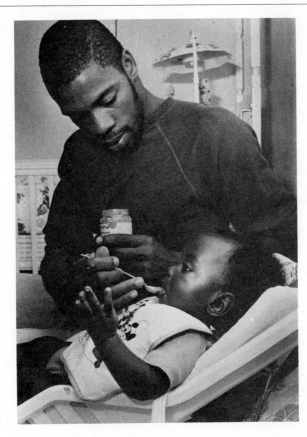

Due to the ever-increasing need
for mothers to work, the role of
the father has expanded and is
perhaps more vital today than at
any other time in our history.
[*Kenneth Karp.*]

FIGURE 12.1

support, the mother is often able to realize her own potentials, satisfy her
creative needs, and fulfill her part as a contributing family member without
jeopardizing her position as mother.

In 1974, psychologist Lois Hoffman and sociologist F. Ivan Nye wrote in
their book *Working Mothers:* "The working mother who obtains personal
satisfaction from employment, does not have excessive guilt, and has
adequate household arrangements is likely to perform as well as the
nonworking mother or better." In other words, Hoffman and Nye found that the
mother's emotional state is of primary importance. Children appeared to suffer
the most in tests of self-esteem and adjustment if their mothers were not
working but wanted to, or worked and were beset by strain and harassment.

The Single Parent

Although the working mother in a traditional family has a difficult challenge, the
father, in most cases, will provide some degree of support. For example, when
one parent disciplines a child, the child can go to the other for comfort and
reassurance even though the other parent supports the disciplinary action.
However, in the case of the single parent, there is usually no one else for the

child to turn to. This situation often presents the single parent with severe conflicts of an approach-avoidance nature. On the one hand, the parent wishes to reach out and console the saddened child, but on the other hand, the parent wishes to impress on the child the consequences of misbehaving. It is not uncommon to find that most single parents fear becoming a "bad" parent and engage in an almost constant struggle between being "too" permissive and being "too" authoritarian.

Most often, however, these doubts about being a bad parent are aimed primarily at the fear of being too neglectful, since many of the children of single parents are placed in day-care centers. In actuality, since 85 percent of all single parents are mothers, most of whom have to work for a living, the issue of neglect is usually reduced to fears of what the consequences will be for the child whose mother is absent a great deal of the time.

A 1976 report to the American Association for the Advancement of Science, presented by Jerome Kagan, concluded that "even if the substitute care was started as early as three months of age, the differences (in the children studied) were insignificant between a full-time mother, a helper in the home, and day care." In the report given by Kagan, the children used in the comparisons were matched by sex, age, social class, and ethnic background. Comparisons were made in the areas of intellectual, social, and language development.

In the Kagan report, as in similar reports, the crucial factor again seems to be associated with the *quality* of the maternal contact rather than the *quantity*. If the mother feels fulfilled and happy, whether in the home or out of the home, this vitality is shared with and reflected by the children. Oscar Wilde (1859–1900) once said "The best way to make children good is to make them happy." A happy parent is more likely to be able to accomplish this.

However, for a single parent, achieving such fulfillment can be, and often is, more difficult than it would be for a parent who is aided by a supportive partner. One of the difficulties faced by the single parent is finding a supportive partner, and this often requires the resumption of dating.

Many single parents find dating to be awkward and prefer to have a common sharing experience. The difference is that in traditional dating each person tends to assume personal responsibility for the happiness of the other, whereas in a common sharing experience each person is doing what makes him or her happy, and the happiness is there to be shared with the other. Sharing, for many single parents, can become a way of life: sharing by necessity with their child, and sharing because of need with others. Many single parents find themselves craving the companionship of adults of either sex to engage in adult conversation. Finding the time and place to engage in such conversations can often present a problem because children do not always respect the parent's need for privacy.

Privacy can also become a factor with regard to morals. This occurs because, with renewed dating, the single parent must not only *talk* about moral conduct but must *demonstrate* such conduct and set the standards through *example*.

In almost all cases of single parenting, the relationship between the parent and child tends to be more *intense*. In some cases, the bond of affection can

Child abuse hurts everybody

National Committee for Prevention of Child Abuse. A Public Service of Outdoor Advertising and The Advertising Council.

Write: Box 2866, Chicago Ill. 60690

FIGURE 12.2 Although physical abuse will often leave external scars, the psychological and emotional abuse of a child may leave internal scars that can create deep, enduring pain that is far less obvious to the outside world. [*The Advertising Council.*]

become almost smothering. In other cases, the perpetual venting of hostile feelings left over from the trauma of separation can lead to severe cases of child abuse. For some, possessive feelings for the child can become dictatorial. For others, however, an attitude of "everyone for himself" can become dominant, and parental control over the child becomes almost nonexistent. The most important factor in relationships between single parents and children seems to be the avoidance of letting their relationship become a substitute for all other relationships.

The Dysfunctioning Parent

The noted anthropologist Margaret Mead believes that "we have become a society of people who neglect our children, are afraid of our children, find children a surplus instead of the *raison d'être* of living" (Mead, 1975, p. 179). Unfortunately, there is ample evidence to substantiate her beliefs.

Interest in parental neglect, mistreatment, and abuse began to develop in the late fifties. In 1962, C. Henry Kempe of the University of Colorado School of Medicine conducted a survey of seventy-one hospitals across the nation in an attempt to discover the extent of the occurrence of child abuse. The results showed that *every* hospital had handled cases of child abuse during the past year. The reason it was necessary for Kempe to conduct a special survey was because until 1963, when New York passed the first law requiring physicians to report cases of child abuse to police and social agencies, there were no laws prohibiting mistreatment of children. In fact, the first child abuse case ever brought before a court in America was tried under regulations prohibiting cruelty to animals. The New York Society for the Prevention of Cruelty to Animals argued that Mary Ellen, who had been chained and starved, was a "human animal" and thus could not be so treated.

Although the exact number of cases of child abuse may never be known, at least 60,000 cases are reported each year. Margo Gritz, the director of training at Parents Anonymous, a national self-help organization of parents with child abuse problems, estimates that more children under the age of five die at the hands of their own parents than are killed by tuberculosis, whooping cough, polio, measles, diabetes, rheumatic fever, and hepatitis combined.

There are several theories why some parents abuse their children. Keith Spiegel of California State College at Northridge links some cases of abuse with the oppression of women in American society. In such cases, the women feel trapped and are unable to fight back or escape because of their husbands. As a result, some turn their anger and frustration on their children. Other observers look to learning theory principles, such as those put forth by Bandura, suggesting that the parents have learned to abuse their children from having been abused by their own parents. Some sociologists attribute child abuse to American society's tolerance for physical punishment and the belief that hitting children is the natural way to raise them.

Physical abuse is, however, not the most frequent form of mistreatment children must cope with. The number of reported cases of sexual molestation of children by a parent is more than double that of those who are physically assaulted.

The frequency of cases of psychological abuse is thought to be incalculable. It ranges from the use of "double-binding" (a situation wherein a person ends up being wrong regardless of which choice is made) to maladaptive training by psychotic parents. This became evident in Theodore Lidz's study, in 1965, of the families of seventeen schizophrenic patients. Lidz found pervasive psychopathology in *every* family. He found mothers unstable, fathers aggressive and paranoid, and other members passive and ineffectual. In 60 percent of the cases, at least one parent was considered psychotic; in the majority of cases, the marriages were considered to be severely disturbed.

As a rule of thumb, children raised by parents who are adjusted as individuals and adjusted as partners will tend to grow up to be normal. Children raised by parents who are adjusted as individuals, but maladjusted as partners or vice versa, tend to grow up to be neurotic. Children raised by parents who are maladjusted as individuals and also maladjusted as partners have the distinct possibility of developing a psychosis. With regard to the consequences of parenting, Oscar Wilde wrote in *The Picture of Dorian Gray,* "Children begin by loving their parents; as they grow older they judge them; sometimes they forgive them."

A child who feels *secure* and *valued* as a human being develops positive feelings of self-esteem and a sense of well-being. Most of these feelings stem from parental assurance that the child is *unique, loved,* and *irreplaceable.*

Since each child is unique, one child cannot validly be compared to any other. As Fritz Perls admonished, "You are not here to live up to my expectations, and I am not here to live up to yours." In other words, each child is here to live up to his or her greatest potential. In the words of L. Tom Perry, "One of the gifts of a loving family is the encouragement and confidence we receive to magnify ourselves."

The individual uniqueness of children is threatened when their abilities are critically compared and one child is found to be not as fast, smart, or artistic as someone else. The same threat exists when physical attributes are compared and a child is found to be not as pretty, strong, or tall as someone else. Such comparisons tend to encourage *competition* rather than *cooperation* within the family unit.

It must be recognized that each child makes a unique contribution to the family unit, and that all contributions have *value*. No child should ever be taken for granted. No member of a family should ever feel less important than another. Nor should a member of a family ever feel more important than another. However, all members of a family should always feel that they are *important* parts of the family.

PARENTAL ATTITUDES AND THEIR INFLUENCE

Many people find themselves somewhat fearful of the responsibilities associated with parenthood. Perhaps some of this anxiety stems from their awareness of the importance of parenting to the future of their children. Some of it, though, seems to result from not having been taught to "parent" by their own parents. According to the director of a family agency coordinating center in Chicago, "The people we service have no sense of parenting because they weren't parented themselves." This problem is compounded in today's world by a lack of consensus as to what parenting is, let alone what good parenting is. Some sociologists believe that because of the vast sociological changes taking place, people no longer have common experiences to fall back on in order to solve parenting problems. As a result, more and more parents are turning to professionals for help. However, even among the professionals, there is a lack of consensus in defining good parenting. With regard to this problem, the author of *The Common Sense Book of Baby and Child Care,* Dr. Benjamin Spock, points out:

> The more people have studied different methods of bringing up children the more they have come to the conclusion that what good mothers and fathers instinctively feel like doing for their babies is the best after all. (1968, p. 4)

However, it is often difficult to rely on one's instincts when struggling with such conflicts as permissiveness versus authoritarianism, competitiveness versus cooperation, or hostility versus warmth. This is especially true when the concerned parents are aware of the tremendous influence their particular orientation and attitude toward child rearing will have on their children. Even in biblical times, parents were aware of the consequences:

> Train up a child in the way he should go;
> and when he is old he will not depart from it. (Proverbs 22:6)

Dimensions of Parental Relationships

The number of variables able to influence the development of a child's personality appears to be almost infinite. Genetic factors, physical health, predisposition, and even diet can all play a part. Environmental factors, such as interaction with siblings and peer groups, traumatic events, and the process of socialization, can also make substantial contributions to development of personality. Numerous attempts to quantify the relative importance of each contribution have yielded mixed, and sometimes contradictory, results. Still, two factors consistently appear as among the most influential elements affecting the child's development: (1) the nature of the parents, and (2) the quality of the relationship the child has with them.

The importance of these factors was pointed out by Thomas Harris, author of *I'm OK-You're OK* (1973). He stated that the "emphasis in Transactional Analysis is on what the *parents* can achieve so that the nature of the transactions between parent and child will change. When this happens, the change in the child will soon follow" (p. 174). Harris believes that children will model their own ego states after those of the parents. Therefore the parent ego state will be based on the kind of parenting done by the parents; the adult ego state will be based on the examples of mature judgment and logical reasoning exhibited by the parents; and the child ego state will be based on early childhood experiences and "internal" events.

In many cases, a child's world may be dominated by parents who function and communicate only through their parent ego states, with the parent state of one spouse constantly in conflict with that of the other, or the parent of one spouse dominating the child ego state of the other. In such situations, there is little opportunity for the child's adult ego state to develop. As a consequence, the child's parent ego state will tend to become the dominating influence in the personality when adulthood is reached.

In an attempt to study some of the dimensions of parent-child relationships, E. S. Schaefer (1959) developed a two-dimensional model which can be used to determine the type of atmosphere a child is raised in. The two dimensions selected by Schaefer were *love versus hostility,* which deals with the *emotional relationship* between parent and child, and *control versus autonomy,* which deals with the *disciplinary relationship* between parent and child. (See Figure 12.3.)

LOVE VERSUS HOSTILITY   The love aspect of these dimensions refers to the warmth the parent demonstrates toward the child. This dimension includes frequent use of reason and explanation when disciplining, and all but excludes use of physical punishment as a means of disciplining. A loving parent is an approving parent, who concentrates primarily on the child's accomplishments rather than failures. Such a parent will often apply the principle of "equal time." For every minute used to tell the child what he or she did wrong, an equal amount of time is devoted to telling the child what he or she did right. If a child's report card has four good grades and one poor grade, and the parent devotes five minutes to the poor grade, an additional five minutes must be devoted to each of the four good grades so as to place the child's accomplishments and failures in proper perspective. This is in contrast to the hostility aspect of Shaefer's dimensions, in which the parent is disapproving and concentrates on the child's shortcomings. In our example the entire conference session would have been devoted solely to the poor grade. The hostile parent is usually negative, cold, and often uses excessive physical punishment.

Learning that there is someone
to turn to in times of
need . . . being taught how to
care by someone who cares.
[*Ken Heyman.*]

FIGURE 12.3

Generally speaking, the love-oriented parent is more child-centered, whereas the hostile parent is more self-centered. The loving parent can more easily identify with the child and, as a consequence, will attempt to acquaint the child with the reasoning behind certain rules of disciplinary action. Thus the child is enabled to internalize a benevolent concept of justice. In addition, a loving parent is less likely to resort to physical punishment because of the child's responsiveness to any possibility of parental disapproval or withdrawal of love.

CONTROL VERSUS AUTONOMY   The elements of control and autonomy refer to the positions the parents take on restriction, dependent behavior, and consistency and flexibility of rule enforcement.

Schaefer considers parents as *control-oriented* if they tend to favor strict enforcement of demands, are inflexible with regard to setting limits and restrictions, and assume an authoritarian relationship with their child. Parents are considered *autonomy-oriented* if they tend to tolerate disobedience, establish few limits or restrictions, and assume a laissez faire relationship with their child.

In a study conducted by D. Baumrind (1967), it was determined that extremes in either control or autonomy could lead to deficiencies in personality development. Baumrind recommended that parents take a more moderate position—that is, be *authoritative* rather than *authoritarian.* By being authoritative, the parents assume the responsibility for the general welfare of the child and therefore impose certain reasonable limits on the child. However, the child is allowed the freedom to explore his or her physical and intellectual environment, express his or her creativity, and assert his or her individuality within these limits. Under such conditions, most children will develop high self-esteem, self-confidence, and self-control.

INTERACTION AMONG THE DIMENSIONS   Although each of the dimensions Schaefer selected is independent of each other, they can interact in a variety of different combinations in order to create a pervasive atmosphere in which the child may be raised. For example, a combination of love and control can create an atmosphere of *overprotection,* whereas a combination of love and autonomy can create an atmosphere of *cooperation* (Figure 12.4).

Perhaps one of the most unhealthy atmospheres in which to raise a child is one of severe *hostility* and *control* (restrictive). In such a situation, the parent is usually rejecting, restrictive, demanding, and physically punitive. Living under such abusive conditions, the child will often develop *counterhostility,* but due to the oppressive nature of the parents, will usually not express this anger and resentment directly. In such cases, the child will often develop antisocial behavior, fail to develop self-confidence, and be self-destructive.

In contrast, a child raised in an atmosphere of *hostility* and *autonomy* (permissive) often develops a tendency to be other-destructive, impulsive, and rebellious. Parents of such children often resent the children and perceive them as a nuisance. As a consequence, the children are usually left on their own as long as they don't cause the parents any direct problems. These children are often "raised in the streets" and tend to stay away from their parents as much as possible. Sometimes they view home as merely a boarding house, where the price of a room is putting up with the parents.

A home in which the parents use both *love* and *control* tends to develop greater dependence among the children than do some of the other combinations. Such children tend to be obedient, conforming, and submissive due to the overprotective, overindulgent attitude of the parents, who regard almost everything as "for the child's own good."

Although children raised in a warm-restrictive atmosphere may be considered ideal by some parents and teachers because of their tendency to be good, children of parents demonstrating *love* and *autonomy* are thought to be among the healthiest by many child-rearing specialists. Children raised in an atmosphere that combines acceptance and love with the freedom to be themselves within the standards of conduct set for the entire family are likely to be independent yet able to follow orders, friendly yet socially assertive, and creative yet able to accept the more traditional ways of doing things.

Dominant Parental Attitudes

An attitude can be defined as "an enduring system of perceptive evaluations, emotional predispositions, and action tendencies." A parental attitude is usually one which serves as a basis for most parent-child interactions—

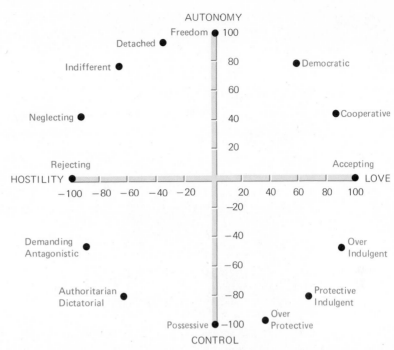

AUTONOMY

Freedom ● 100

Detached ●

80

Indifferent ●

60

Neglecting ●

40

20

Rejecting

Accepting

HOSTILITY ●————————————————●　LOVE

−100　−80　−60　−40　−20　　20　40　60　80　100

−20

Demanding
Antagonistic ●

−40

● Over
Indulgent

−60

Authoritarian
Dictatorial ●

−80

● Protective
Indulgent

Possessive ● −100

● Over
Protective

CONTROL

● Democratic

● Cooperative

FIGURE 12.4   The "atmosphere" in a child's environment is often a combination of love and hostility, control and autonomy. Where would you judge your parents to be on this chart? If you are a parent, where would you place your own attitudes? [*From E. S. Schaefer, "A Circumplex, Model for Maternal Behavior," J. abnorm. soc. Psychol., 1959,* **59:***232. Copyright 1959 by the American Psychological Association. Used by permission.*]

regardless of its appropriateness or inappropriateness with regard to the circumstances. As a consequence, inflexible parental attitudes can distort reality, interfere with personality development, and, in some cases, provide an unhealthy environment for adequate emotional maturation.

Within each family unit, more than just one parental attitude is usually present at any one time. However, there is often one attitude that is more pervasive than the others. This is referred to as the "dominant" parental attitude. Some of the more common *pathogenic* parental attitudes and their possible consequences are adopted far more frequently than one might suspect. Among these attitudes are permissiveness, perfectionism, overprotectiveness, and overindulgence.

PERMISSIVENESS   Largely due to the popularity of Dr. Benjamin Spock's book *Baby and Child Care,* permissive child rearing became the dominant parental attitude during the 1950s. Spock's advocacy of permissiveness was based on the work of several previous theorists. Dewey and Kilpatrick had conducted educational research on the importance of the child's *readiness* to progress and the *suitability* of the subject. Freudian theory discussed the unhealthy effects of strict toilet training and frightening a child about sex on the development of personality, and the possibility that a neurosis might result in consequence. Research done by McLendon and Simsarion dealt with "self-

FIGURE 12.5 Parents who value material things give material things, and their children grow to value material things. Parents who value their relationship with their children give of themselves, and the family grows to value each other. [*Sybil Shelton, Peter Arnold.*]

demand" feeding schedules for infants. The family histories of criminals and delinquents contained an unusually high incidence of harsh punishment.

The wide acceptance of permissive views led many parents to fear that they might stunt the intellectual growth of their children, and cause them to become neurotic, or force them to turn to a life of crime. As a result, many parents become *overly permissive*. Often, almost *all* restraints, restrictions, and parental control over the children were withdrawn. Children were allowed to express themselves in whatever way they wished without the interference of parents. Imagine being a dinner guest in a home where permissiveness was the dominant parental attitude. One of the children might climb onto the table and begin to play in your mashed potatoes and gravy. Stunned, you might look inquisitively at the parents and hear: "Junior likes the feel of squishing mashed potatoes. His are probably too cold, but he seems to like yours just fine. We don't want to discourage him from artistic expression or prevent him from having a sensual experience." Even Spock did not propose such extremes of permissiveness, but rather *moderation* in both strictness and permissiveness. More recently, greater emphasis has been placed on the parents' expression of their feelings in relation to the child's expression of feelings. For example, today a parent might say, "I'm not angry about you wanting to color. I'm angry about the fact that you colored on the wall." Such statements tend to emphasize the fact that the child is still loved, and that it is the child's behavior that is being rejected, not the child. In the past, a permissive parent might have *suppressed* such anger out of fear of discouraging "artistic growth." In many cases, the parent might have felt *guilty* for even feeling such anger. With reference to this dilemma, Spock remarked:

> When parents get unhappy results from too much permissiveness, it is not so much because they demand too little, though this is part of it. It is more because they are timid or guilty about what they ask or because they are unconsciously encouraging the child to rule the roost. (1968, p. 49)

Children raised with a dominant parental attitude of permissiveness often show little respect or consideration for either parents or other authorities. A study conducted by Sears (1961) showed that twelve-year-old children raised under such an attitude demonstrated a high degree of antisocial, aggressive behavior as well as a high level of insecurity. Baumrind (1967) found that children who were the most dependent, least inquisitive, and least self-controlled (impulsive and aggressive) were raised by permissive parents. In most cases, overpermissiveness results in the creation of what is commonly referred to as the "spoiled" child. B. F. Skinner, the noted behaviorist, takes the position that "permissiveness is not . . . a policy; it is the abandonment of policy, and its apparent advantages are illusory. To refuse control is to leave control not to the person himself, but to other parts of the society and nonsocial environments" (1971. p. 84).

PERFECTIONISM   Parents who develop a perfectionistic attitude toward child rearing often do so out of personal frustration. They themselves were often raised by perfectionistic parents and failed to achieve the desired criteria. As a result, they have become intent on seeing that their own children achieve the desired state of perfection. Such parents will sometimes comment, "I never became accomplished at playing the piano, and the main reason was my not practicing enough. My parents warned me that I needed more practice, but I didn't listen to them. I'm not going to let my children make the same mistake. They're going to practice until they get it down perfect."

To such parents, unhappiness is often equated with imperfection. Therefore, if a person is unhappy, it is most likely due to some imperfection—usually an imperfection in someone else. "What's the use of me trying to save money for your education if you don't try to get better grades?"

To those with a perfectionistic attitude, five As and a B are "very disappointing," being second on the honor roll is tantamount to failing, and graduating from college with a 3.99 grade point average can be "justifiable" provocation for attempting suicide. It is important to understand that children raised under a perfectionistic parental attitude have had only their errors reinforced, only the faults, inadequacies, and imperfections. Such constant emphasis on the negative aspects of one's life is thought to be a contributing factor to the increase in suicide among today's youth. Suicide has become the second leading cause of death among Americans between the ages of fifteen and twenty-four.

The tragedy of this particular attitude is that the child, however talented or gifted, will never know success. There will always be room for improvement, and accomplishment will always be short of perfection. Thus, the child will often develop a sense of *inadequacy,* due to having failed at almost everything that has ever been tried, and a sense of unworthiness, having failed to ever gain full parental approval.

OVERPROTECTIVE DOMINATION   The need to dominate plays an important part in an overprotective parental attitude. In order to adequately protect the child, the parent feels it necessary to maintain control over the child and the child's environment, friends, activities, and interests. The purpose is to prevent the child from being exposed to life's disappointments. In order to accomplish this, parental dependence must be established, and independent behavior must be inhibited, if not eliminated altogether.

The enforcement of such practices will usually result in a lack of self-reliance, feelings of inadequacy, and passive-dependent behavior. For example, if other children at a playground are playing on a slide, the overprotective, domineering parent may hold his or her child back, cautioning, "I don't think you should play on that slide. You might get hurt, besides, you shouldn't play too much until you start feeling better." The reference to the child's state of health is common with such parents, for their children are ill twice as often and undergo three times as many operations as do other children. Often such children are told that their poor health is at least partially due to not having been obedient to the parent's wishes, the trouble that the children have gotten into is because they didn't listen to what the parent said, and mistakes are the result of not having consulted the parent first.

Such children will usually develop feelings of inadequacy and become passive. They are destined merely to react to life rather than act on life, to become timid, shy, and reclusive, and to cling tenaciously to anyone who is willing to assume the responsibility for their lives.

OVERINDULGENCE   Parents who are uncomfortable with their emotions—in particular with emotional traumas—will often assume an *overindulgent* parental attitude in an attempt to reduce or avoid arguments, conflicts, or undesirable incidences. This attitude often translates into "Whatever the kid wants, give it to him, but I want this fighting to stop." "Anything to get some peace and quiet." "Okay, okay, but I don't want to see any more of these temper tantrums." However, such parents are usually uncomfortable not just with the negative emotions, but with *all* emotions, including love and other feelings of emotional intimacy. As a means of coping with such discomfort, many of these parents will tend to substitute material things for interpersonal involvement. As a consequence of such emotional and materialistic pampering, the overindulged child will often become very demanding of other people's attention, time, and resources; in the extreme, the child becomes a tyrant.

Since such children have been given whatever they want upon demand, they will usually have a very low tolerance for frustration. They will often become selfish, have little or no experience with patience or delayed gratification, and will usually be very intolerant of others. The overindulged child will tend to become exploitative of others, perceiving people as merely objects to be used in the same way the parents were used—to satisfy the child's needs. If someone fails or refuses to satisfy the child's needs, that person is discarded with such statements as "You're not the only fish in the sea, you know. If you don't want to, I'll get someone else who will."

To such children, people and things are replaceable, and there is a lack of appreciation for either. Since the only effort they have ever had to expend in order to get what they wanted was a simple demand, discriminatory value systems often fail to develop. A child raised by parents who are not overindulgent must put forth varying degrees of effort in order to achieve different goals. Based on the amount of effort put forth, the individual develops a discriminatory value system; that is, the child knows it takes more effort to save money to buy a bicycle than to buy a toy glider, and, therefore, the bicycle has a greater value than the glider. Lacking such a system, the overindulged child often lacks a sense of appreciation for things and, as a consequence, takes little responsibility for their care or maintenance. The child also lacks a sense of respect for people and, as a consequence, is often disobedient, insensitive, and rude.

Such children often have the attitude that the world owes them a living, and that they can do no wrong. This sense of impunity often stems from the fact that the parents seldom, if ever, reprimanded or punished the child for misbehaving. Consequently, the child will often fail to exhibit appropriate responsibility for his or her actions or for the consequences of his or her behavior and may even develop sociopathic tendencies.

REJECTION   Following World War II, many infants were left orphans and were placed in institutions. It soon became apparent, however, that despite the excellent physical care provided, many of them failed to develop normally. Many showed signs of deep depression, and some eventually died. Such institutional wasting away and death is referred to as "marasmus." As late as 1919, about one-half of the mortality among institutionalized infants under one year of age was attributed to marasmus. In an effort to analyze the cause of such degeneration, Rene Spitz compared the development of babies raised in penal institutions, where their mothers were able to fondle and care for them, and babies raised in foundling homes, where they received only minimal care. Spitz's conclusion was that the degeneration was due to a lack of "mothering." His conclusions were supported by such people as Margaret Ribble, in her book *The Rights of Infants,* and John Bowlby, whose report to the World Health Organization stated that depriving a child of maternal care during the first three years of life can cause maturational, emotional, and/or intellectual retardation.

A series of experiments conducted by Harry Harlow and his associates during the late fifties and early sixties provided laboratory data supporting the hypothesis that mothering provides an important contribution to an infant's development. Harlow used Rhesus monkeys as subjects in his research. In one phase of his research, in an effort to obtain greater control over experimental variables, Harlow attempted to reduce the effects of differences in the quality of mothering by providing surrogate mothers. In one such effort, Harlow provided newborn infants with two surrogate mothers, one made of bare wire mesh and another made of wire mesh covered with terry cloth. The "mother" made of bare wire mesh was fitted with a nipple and was the infant monkey's sole source of nutrition. The results of such exposure were somewhat surprising. The infants, when given a choice, preferred to spend more time with the nonfeeding, terry cloth mother than with the food-providing wire mother. It appears that the terry cloth mother provided *tactile* satisfaction and a sense of security through the ability of the infant to cling to the surrogate mother covered with the cloth. A longitudinal study of such infants, however, indicated that although their physical needs could be taken care of by such mothers, certain emotional, social, and maturational needs were not being provided. As adults, monkeys raised by surrogate mothers were often overly aggressive, unsocial, and sexually inadequate. They also tended to be inadequate as mothers, often exhibiting hostile behavior toward their offspring, rejecting their infants, or abandoning their infants completely.

Research such as that conducted by Harlow and others points out the importance of parent-child relationships for healthy development. As with the Rhesus monkeys, child abandonment occurs in our society, although actual *physical rejection* of a child is more likely to take place through such situations as having the child sent to live with relatives or friends, to a foster home, or to a boarding school. Physical rejection can also take place when one or both of the parents leave the child by going away on business, work late or on weekends, separate or divorce, are sick for an extended period of time, or, by the ultimate rejection, die. As common as physical rejection is, however, *emotional rejection* occurs far more frequently.

Emotional rejection is usually a much more subtle experience, but the effects can be equally devastating. Emotional rejection refers to the situation in which the parent is physically present but emotionally distant. In many such cases, the child is the result of an unwanted pregnancy. The parents may be unmarried, unprepared financially, or in an early stage of education or career. The reason the child is unwanted is often irrelevant. What seems to be crucial is that the child is often blamed for having interfered with the parents' plans, and is therefore perceived as a burden, handicap, or nuisance. Immature parents will often make statements like: "If it hadn't been for that kid, I would have finished my education." "I could have had a successful career by now, if I hadn't gotten pregnant." "Things were fine between you and me until that kid came along."

A parent may also reject a child emotionally because the child is the wrong sex. This can result in the child believing, "I've known since I was little that Daddy resented that I wasn't born a boy." A child may also be rejected because of being perceived as physically or intellectually inferior: "Pat has got to be one of the dumbest kids on the block. Dumb, scrawny kid takes after your side of the family, certainly not a Harrison."

A child raised with a parental attitude of rejection will usually develop a

Harry Harlow's work with "terry cloth mothers" was among the first to show just how essential mothering actually is to an infant's development. [*Sponholz, Monkmeyer Press Photo Service.*]

FIGURE 12.6

sense of inadequacy and unworthiness and will have a low self-esteem. More often than not, such children will assume personal responsibility for being rejected, blaming the rejection on the way they have behaved. Initially, the child may attempt to please the parents in order to ward off further rejection. Unfortunately, the parents will often view such behavior as further interference with their lives, resulting in additional episodes of rejection. "That scatter-brained kid put the dishes away again without asking me first. We won't be able to find anything for a week. Honestly, that kid causes more trouble. . . ." As a consequence of being raised with such an attitude, the child will often grow more and more insecure and apprehensive, never knowing if that next response will bring about further rejection or the elusive parental approval so desperately sought after.

Since the responses designed to bring about approval and acceptance often result in further rejection, most children will soon stop making them. These responses may be replaced by *withdrawal* and *apathy* or *attention-seeking* behavior motivated by hostility. Withdrawal or apathy usually occurs when children become convinced that their parents are right, that, in truth, they are unlovable. Such children will often assume the attitude of "why even try," since more trouble and more rejection are the usual results. Being as inconspicuous as possible seems to be the only thing that the parents approve of, so these children will often withdraw, both physically and emotionally, as far as possible from the social world. They become apathetic so as to reduce the frequency and intensity of further disappointment.

Other children raised with rejection will refuse to resign themselves to a life of anonymity and will aggressively seek out attention. Such children have responded with anger as well as hurt to their being rejected. In most cases, such children have dedicated their "all" in attempts to gain parental acceptance. The parents' continued rejection of these efforts and lack of reciprocation tend to generate a great deal of anger and hostility within the child. However, the child is often afraid of expressing these feelings directly toward the parents out of fear of further rejection. As a consequence, this hostility is usually expressed *indirectly*—being irresponsible, getting in trouble at school, destroying property, deliberately hurting other people or animals, or by other demonstrations of delinquent behavior. Any of these means of expression can be used to obtain the attention the child seeks. Attention under *any* circumstances seems to be preferred to being ignored.

In some cases, the attention-seeking behavior may manifest itself in a less destructive manner. In many instances, *humor* will be used as a means of disguising hostility, for example, the use of ethnic, racist, or sexist jokes. Some individuals will become the classroom or office clown as a means of getting accepted by others. By becoming clowns, these individuals reduce their chances of being rejected and simultaneously create a false front, and this acts as a protective barrier against further hurt. In this manner, should rejection come, it is the clown who is rejected, not the person's real self.

Another means of protecting oneself from being hurt by rejection, while still expressing pent-up resentment and hostility, is to *reject first*. Rejected children usually learn this method quite early, and often become dedicated to the idea of never allowing themselves to be emotionally vulnerable again. They will often espouse this dedication through such statements as: "I'll never let anyone get that close to me again." "Only a fool falls in love." "In the future, if there's any rejecting to be done, I'll be the one who does it." Later in life, they will often see relationships as games in which each person sees how deeply he or she can get others to commit themselves without having to become personally involved. The master stroke of the game is to anticipate the other person's rejection and to reject first. As an added precaution, this kind of person will often maintain a back-up relationship, so as not to be left alone following any rejection within the primary relationship. Unfortunately, such emotional hedging within relationships often becomes a contributing factor to their consistent failure.

STRENGTHENING PARENT-CHILD RELATIONSHIPS

The famous American Congregational minister Henry Ward Beecher (1813–1887) once said, "There is no friendship, no love, like that of the parent for the child." The expression of that love is one of the most important factors in strengthening parent-child relationships. No child should ever have to experience a sense of being unloved or prolonged feelings of loneliness.

Loneliness is not merely a by-product of the presence or absence of the parents. A child can be lonely while physically with the parents, if that child is seldom listened to, seldom praised, seldom payed attention to, or seldom told he or she is loved.

Parents, too, should never have to experience a sense of being unloved or lonely. However, a mother can be lonely while among family members, if she is taken for granted, unappreciated, or neglected. A father can feel lonely if he is seen only as a meal ticket, if he must carry alone the worry about debts and the future costs of raising a family, or if he is unable to share his hopes and aspirations of what he might have been or what he will yet be.

The means by which love is communicated may vary from parent to parent. Some means of expression may not always be fully understood by the child at the time they are expressed. Other expressions of love leave no doubt whatsoever in the child's mind. In either case, the challenge of communicating love as often and as clearly as possible is an unceasing one—a challenge that is far too often neglected.

In an attempt at meeting this challenge, Dr. Leo Folsom, in his book *Parent Awareness* (1974), presents some of the most common parental communication patterns and the consequences of using them. Folsom also deals with the issue of questions between parent and child, along with the effects various responses can have on communication. It is Folsom's belief that through the proper selection and application of communication patterns, a habit of thoughtful *talking* and *listening* between parent and child can be established. With the parent acting as a model and setting the example for effective communication, the child can be expected to:

1 Move closer to the parent with greater understanding of both the parent in the role of parent and the parent as a person
2 Relate better to other people, both children and adults
3 Develop language usage to express what he or she experiences, thinks, and feels
4 Think more clearly and make better decisions
5 Develop self-assurance

Parental Patterns of Communication

Folsom believes that parents develop a habitual pattern in talking to their children. These patterns are thought to develop subtly over a long period of time, and therefore most parents are unaware of the particular pattern they use to communicate with their children.

The particular pattern a parent uses, however, has a tremendous influence on determining the pattern of communication the child uses. For example, if a parent's pattern of communication includes *not listening* to the child, then the child will most likely pick up this pattern and tend to *not listen* to the parent. Such would be the situation where a parent is scolding a child and shouting, "I don't want to hear any of your excuses. If you'd learn to listen to me, you wouldn't get yourself in so much trouble. Now, I don't want to hear another word out of you until this mess is cleaned up. Honestly, when will that child ever learn to listen?" In such a situation, the parent is exhorting the child to listen while telling the child that the parent doesn't want to listen.

The results of using a particular communication pattern can be positive if the pattern is one which demonstrates warmth and closeness. In this case, family life will tend to flow in a creative fulfilling manner. However, should the parents select a communication pattern that demonstrates hostility and distance, the family life will often become chaotic and full of stress and tension.

Folsom believes that most parental patterns of communication fall into eight categories: (1) reward/support; (2) sharing; (3) explaining; (4) questioning; (5) ordering; (6) redirecting; (7) disciplining; and (8) rejecting.

REWARD/SUPPORT When parents select a pattern of communication that demonstrates *love, acceptance,* and *emotional support* when communicating with their children, the parents are using a pattern of *reward/support.* Such parents will frequently say things like "I sure love you," or "I knew you could do it." These parents will tend to express their approval of their child's behavior or accomplishments, viewing any minor transgression or ineptness as a natural consequence of the learning process and growing up.

Rewarding and supportive parents are interested and concerned about their child's progress. They tend to reassure the child in meeting new challenges, rather than merely view the child's life in retrospect, criticizing what the child has or has not accomplished. Supportive parents are likely to say, "We never doubted your ability to see it through." Critical parents are likely to remark, "Is that as well as you can play after all those lessons?" Supportive parents appreciate not only what the child does, but also what the child *tries* to do.

SHARING Closely related to reward and support is the category of *sharing.* Parents who *trust* their children tend to share themselves with their child. For example, they may share their *feelings* through such statements as "I'm really going to miss you." "Now, I'm really mad," or "You sure have brought a lot of happiness into my life." These parents will also want to share their *ideas* and *thoughts* with their children by spontaneously offering suggestions like "I was just thinking. You know, it's been a long time since we, . . ." "I've got an idea. Let's, . . ." or "You know, watching you just then reminded me of when I was your age, and. . . ." The sharing of personal experiences can be especially helpful to a child who is in the process of humanizing the parents. When parents share amusing mistakes, their own childhood misconceptions, and anecdotal stories with their children, the parents tend to become less remote and thereby more easy to identify with. The children often become more self-accepting once they realize that no one is perfect. For instance, a confused child may be reassured when a parent tells about the first time he or she changed oil in a car and drained the transmission by mistake.

Sharing parents usually take the initiative in revealing something about themselves. By opening up first, the parents allow themselves to become vulnerable, and thus they appear less threatening to the child. Such opening up is often used as a means of showing interest, reducing tension, or adding merit to the parent's empathy by sharing the fact that he or she has "been there before."

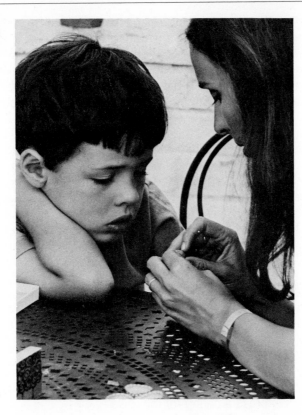

By sharing, a parent becomes
more human, more easily
identified with, and often more
loveable. [*Myron Wood, Photo
Researchers.*]

FIGURE 12.7

EXPLAINING   Much of the responsibility of parenting involves *teaching* the
child. Therefore, it is not surprising that a great deal of the communication
between parent and child takes the form of *explaining*. A parent who is
involved with explaining things to a child tends to deal more with facts than with
emotions. The intent of such instruction is to enable the child to acquire new
skills and knowledge. For example, the parent may give directions on how to
get from one place to another. "Go down to Elm Street, turn left, and it's the
second white house on the left." The parent may also give directions on how to
perform a task or how to operate some device. "First, you have to turn the knob
until it stops. Then, you. . . ." The important fact to keep in mind while teaching
is that the purpose of the instruction is to impart knowledge and not to criticize
ignorance.

QUESTIONING   Explaining can often represent only the sending part of a
communication attempt. The receiving part usually takes the form of a
question. Questions are an excellent way of getting others involved, especially
children. When questions are properly constructed, they can encourage a
conversation. However, when improperly asked, they can just as easily put an
end to a conversation.

Questions that tend to lead to a dead end are referred to as "short-answer" questions. There are questions that can be answered "Yes," "No," or "I don't know." An example of a short-answer question would be "Did you have a nice day at school?" A long-answer question would be "What sort of things happened at school today?" The short-answer question often expresses only a limited interest ("I just want a brief synopsis. I'm not interested in details"). In contrast, a long-answer question often demonstrates a sincere interest in the child, and can provide the child with a sense of importance.

Although many questions can be stimulating and create an atmosphere of closeness and sharing, some questions can generate feelings of hostility, mistrust, and distance. When parental questions create such negative responses in a child, it is usually because the parent is being insensitive to the child's need for privacy and is attempting to pry into the child's life through the use of accusations and interrogation. For example, authoritarian parents might bombard their child with such questions as "Where were you last night?" "What time did you get home?" "Who were you with?" More sensitive parents might ask questions like, "Where did you go with your date last night?" "How do you feel about the time you got home last night?" "What's your opinion of the people you were with?" "How would you judge your conduct?" In this illustration, the insensitive parents were asking only for *information*, whereas the sensitive parents asked not only for information but for *feelings, opinions, and judgments*.

Questions that ask for an expression of feelings show a concern for the physical, mental, and emotional well-being of the child. Feeling questions are usually more intimate and personal than information or opinion questions and they tend to express a caring for the child.

Questions that ask for an opinion or judgment show a respect for what the child *thinks*. Such questions let children know that their ideas are considered to be important. Asking for a child's opinion provides an opportunity for the child to consider alternatives and possible consequences, and to reevaluate standards. Asking for a child's judgment gives the child an opportunity to develop a concept of fairness and justice and enhances the maturation of moral reasoning.

The most important factor for the parent to remember with regard to questions, however, is to *listen to the answer*. The parent must first decide on the *nature* of the response desired—that is, is the parent seeking information, an opinion, or a feeling—and then listen carefully to be sure that that is the nature of the answer given.

ORDERING   In order for family unit to function smoothly and efficiently, parents must maintain a position of authority. Such a position is not one of oppressive power, but that of a respected leader. As leaders, parents have the authority and responsibility to give orders to their children. The orders may be given as a means of assigning a task ("I want you to clean up your room") or delegating responsibility ("I want you to watch this until I get back"). In both cases, the parent is expressing confidence in the child by letting the child know the parent believes him or her capable of carrying out the order.

In order to attain a sense of independence, children must have a sense of control. Children must be aware of what they can and cannot do. Although it is important for children to be aware of their capabilities and limitations, it is also important that they know that others are aware of these characteristics. When parents are unfamiliar with their child's limitations, they may order the child to do a task that is beyond the child's capabilities. When this happens, the child not only experiences the disappointment of failure and the accompanying sense of inadequacy, but also the feelings of self-devaluation that come from the awareness that the parents don't really know their own child.

Parental sensitivity or insensitivity to a child is most often reflected in the manner in which the order is given, especially in the *tone* in which the order is given. It is suggested that a tone of respect and dignity accompany each order so as to encourage the child to experience a sense of cooperation and equality. Talking down to the child, maintaining an air of superiority, or remaining detached and impersonal can lead to rebellion, defiance, and feelings of resentment and hostility on the part of the child.

REDIRECTING   When a parent attempts to stop a child's current behavior by shifting the child's attention to an alternative, more acceptable, form of behavior, that parent is using the communication pattern of *redirection*. Unfortunately, redirection is often used more by those who are not the child's parents than by the parents. Teachers, nursery school assistants, and babysitters often do not have the authority to use severe discipline in response to the child's behavior, nor do they necessarily enjoy a position of being unconditionally loved by the child. As a result, they will often rely heavily upon the use of redirection.

Redirection is sometimes seen as a combination of explaining and ordering. Often, it encompasses only limited disapproval. For example, the behavior might be acceptable, but not the time or place in which the behavior is taking place. To illustrate, a parent might redirect by saying, "Jimmy, I don't want anything spilled on my clean floor, so do your bubble making outside or down in the basement." As shown in this example, redirection often provides a means of presenting the child with alternatives. By allowing the child to choose between alternatives, the parent can give the child a sense of having a direct involvement with the decision-making process.

Generally, the more redirection a parent uses, the less discipline is necessary. It is suggested that redirection be used as frequently as possible. However, should the child reject the alternatives given, defy the parental attempts to stop the undesired behavior, or stubbornly persist with the original behavior, then the parent may resort to the use of discipline.

DISCIPLINING   When a parent inflicts punishment as a means of correcting a child's conduct, the parent is communicating through discipline. Through the use of discipline, the parent attempts to enforce rules and regulations, control behavior, and remind the child of standards of conduct expected of the family members.

Whenever a parent administers discipline, it is imperative that (1) the child know the reason for the punishment, and (2) the severity of the punishment be appropriate to the transgression. In this way, the discipline can be used to teach the child personal responsibility as well as a concept of justice.

It is important that parents make every attempt to avoid administering discipline in anger, carelessly, or unfairly. Discipline should be used sparingly and should not be too harsh. Discipline should never be used as a weapon or a means of gaining revenge or retaliation. Nor should discipline ever be used as a means of venting pent-up emotions. Discipline administered through such motivation will usually result in the child acquiring a sense of rejection. Whenever a parent uses discipline, it should always be clear to the child that it is the *behavior* that is being rejected, not the child. The parent should make every effort to communicate "I don't like what you are doing," rather than "I don't like you."

REJECTING Whenever parents demonstrate their disapproval of a child, ignore a child, or send a child away, the parents are communicating through *rejection*. The rejection can be quite obvious, through statements like: "How can you be so stupid?" "I haven't got time now," or "Didn't I tell you to stay out of here until I'm finished?" However, the parental rejection can also be more subtle, through such means as simply ignoring the child, using sarcasm, or casually shutting the door.

According to Folsom, most parental rejection will take the form of what he refers to as a "close-out." A close-out is any response or behavior that stops a child from talking. Some examples of close-outs would be: "Be quiet, I don't want to talk about it." "Enough already. Don't you have an 'off' button?" Parents can also close-out a child in nonverbal ways, such as by physically turning away or by turning their attention to another child.

Maintaining Conversations

The children of parents who consistently use rejection as a pattern of communication and persist in using close-out techniques as a means of controlling the conversation will gradually stop depending on their parents for personal and emotional support. Eventually, they will begin to close-out the parents. In contrast, warm, sensitive parents will tend to maintain a close, symbiotic relationship with their children through such conversation-maintaining techniques as *rewarding, sustaining, extending,* and *waiting.*

REWARDING A parent can maintain a conversation by encouraging a child to talk through *reward*. A reward is any response that expresses love and acceptance for the child and an interest in what the child is involved with. Some common reward statements are "That was great!" "Nice going!" "Keep it up."

SUSTAINING A parent can *sustain* a conversation—that is, keep the conversation going—by asking a question of interest ("And then what happened?"), offering encouragement ("Yes . . . go on."), or by requesting greater detail ("Why don't you start at the beginning?").

EXTENDING A parent can *extend* a conversation—that is, encourage exploration into new but related areas—by supplementing the child's knowledge with additional information. A parent may attempt to relate the subject in an

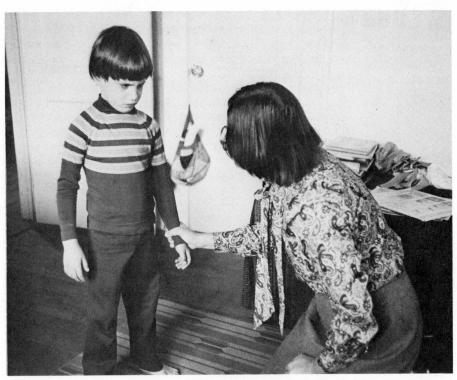

FIGURE 12.8   No one, not even a child, can be wrong all the time. [*Michael Kagan, Monkmeyer Press Photo Service.*]

unorthodox manner in order to encourage originality and stimulate creativity. They would be the case when a parent makes a statement like "Come to think of it, flying is a lot like swimming, only in a lighter medium. Have you looked into the aerodynamic potential?"

WAITING   Perhaps the simplest and most courteous means of maintaining a conversation, however, is for the parent to merely *wait,* pausing for a moment in order to allow the child time to collect his or her thoughts. Such waiting is also conducive to the development of good listening. It indicates that the parent is willing to be patient. Above all, it lets the child know that the child's time is *as important as* the parent's time, and that the conversation is between equals.

SUMMARY

In this chapter, some of the problems of raising children in today's society were explored. It was found that the traditional family unit is being challenged both socially and economically. An ever-increasing number of mothers are being required to work outside the home, and the problems of the working mother are especially acute with regard to the single parent. The problems generated by the dysfunctioning parent were discussed, primarily with regard to the problem of child abuse.

This chapter has also explored the effects various parent-child relationships can have on the creation of a home atmosphere with regard to the dimensions of *control* and *autonomy* and/or *love* and *hostility*. In addition, there was a presentation of the effects of various parental attitudes on the child's personality development, concentrating on perfectionism, permissiveness, overprotectiveness and domination, overindulgence, and rejection (both physical and emotional).

Next the chapter dealt with the effects of various patterns of communication commonly established between parent and child. Some of the major patterns discussed were those involving sharing, explaining, rewarding, disciplining, supporting, and rejecting. Special emphasis was given to the category of questioning a child. A distinction was made with regard to asking for information, feelings, opinions, or judgments. Additional emphasis was given to the problem of sustaining and extending conversations between parent and child.

DISCUSSION QUESTIONS

1 What do you think is the future of the family?
2 Do you believe that mothers should work outside the home?
3 What do you think would be the most difficult task in being a single parent?
4 What was the general atmosphere in your home while you were being raised (cooperative, restrictive, permissive, etc.)?
5 What do you think the dominant parental attitude was in your home while you were growing up (perfectionistic, overprotective, rejecting, etc.)?
6 Which of Folsom's patterns of communication was most prevalent between you and your parents (reward/support, sharing, explaining, orders, etc.)?
7 Do you believe your parents value your opinions or judgment? What makes you think so?
8 What qualities do you think a good parent should have?
9 In your opinion, when is discipline no longer appropriate punishment but so severe as to constitute child abuse?
10 What does a child owe, if anything, to his or her parents?

EXPERIENTIAL EXERCISES

1 Perform a simple survey, by asking members of your class to indicate on a piece of paper whether they were raised by their natural parents, stepparents, foster parents, or a single parent. Those volunteering to participate should remain anonymous. However, the results may surprise you.

2 As an experiment, for one day attempt to formulate only "long answer" questions. Be sure to check the responses you receive for accuracy, making sure that the nature of the response matches the nature of the question. For example, a "feeling" question should get a "feeling" answer. Similar matching should occur with regard to opinions, thoughts, information, and judgments.

3 Explore being a parent to your parents; that is, view your own parents as if they were your children. How would you handle teaching, expectations, discipline, orders, etc.?

CHAPTER 13

VOCATIONAL AND

RECREATIONAL ADJUSTMENT

Work . . . in technological society . . . requires a dissociation of feeling, a subordination of passion, impulse, fantasy, and idealism before cognitive problems and tasks. As breadwinners, most Americans neither find nor even seek "fulfillment" in their jobs. Work, split away from "living" by convention and tradition, becomes instrumental, a dissociated part of life that makes possible, yet often vitiates, the rest of a "living."

Kenneth Keniston
The Uncommitted: Alienated Youth in American Society

THE IMPORTANCE OF WORK

For many individuals, it is not enough to merely "be." Significance for them comes only through accomplishments. As a consequence, they dedicate a good part of their lives to "the expenditure of physical and mental energy in order to accomplish a specific task." In other words, the lives of such persons are dedicated to *work*. The degree of dedication each individual allocates to work varies, but for most people, between one-third and one-half of their lives is involved with work.

"Proper" recognition and external reward for one's efforts, however, are not guaranteed. Therefore, most individuals must rely heavily on self-satisfaction as a primary source of reward. Such satisfaction is most often experienced by the person who has worked alone and can therefore see the end product as a personal achievement. However, much of the work performed throughout history has been achieved through group efforts, wherein individual recognition and personal satisfaction occur less frequently.

Whether an individual works as part of a group or alone, the importance of performing meaningful work with regard to its impact on the individual's mental and physical health should not be underestimated, for it is often one of the major sources of personal identity, self-esteem, and social significance.

Meaningfulness: Achievement and Recognition

Some of us perceive work as a means of achieving our "daily bread." Others see work as a means of achieving "immortality." Some see work as meaningful and relevant, while others see their work as being purposeless and inconsequential. However, almost all of us, at one time or another, see work as an opportunity to leave a mark, to make an impression—to contribute *something* during our lifetime.

In most cases, the degree to which this opportunity is realized depends on the amount of effort we are willing to put forth, the amount of ingenuity we can demonstrate, and the amount of faithfulness to duty each of us can generate with regard to working toward a particular goal. The vocation through which these efforts are directed can often be an individual's most important source of personal identity, self-esteem, and social significance. Some people even believe that it is the only reason for their existence.

PERSONAL IDENTITY AND SELF-EXPRESSION   Quite often at social gatherings an inquiry is made as to the identity of a particular person. The answer, rather than merely giving the person's name, will include the person's occupation: "That's Pat, the druggist." Or, "That's Jan, the town's only librarian." Sometimes the name is left out altogether, and identity rests solely with the person's occupation. For example, a person may be identified as "the cop next door" or "the architect from across the street." The tendency to combine *who* someone is with *what* someone does seem to be commonplace in today's society. This practice is not necessarily a modern innovation, however.

Historically, personal identity was usually associated with family bloodlines. In a sense, it was inherited rather than developed, especially in situations wherein royal bloodlines were involved. In the past, using a person's occupation as a means of identification was not much different from using a bloodline, for vocational selection was a matter not so much of choice and abilities as of birth. In most cases, the son assumed the same occupation as the father. James Lowell (1819–1891) wrote, "No man is born into the world whose work is not born with him."

During the Middle Ages, however, economic and social groups of people in the same business or craft began organizing into *guilds.* Membership in a guild was determined by profession rather than class. The guild consisted of masters, apprentices, and journeymen. The masters owned the shops and trained the apprentices, who were bound to them. Journeymen were workers who had finished training but, because of limitations on the number of masters permitted, were unable to assume that rank. As the name implies, journeymen would travel from place to place seeking employment. In many instances, people became known by their specific trade rather than by their given names. Hence the present-day existence of such surnames as Carpenter, Cooper, Weaver, and Smith.

Even with the advent of guilds, however, the variety of vocational choices was still limited by such factors as geographical conditions and climate. For instance, most silversmith apprenticeships would be found near mineral deposits, and weaving jobs near where sheepherding was possible. As a consequence, during the early years of vocational diversification, personal aptitudes, innate talents, and unique personality characteristics were not given too much consideration; availability was the primary concern. Gradually, through the combined effects of urbanization and greater social mobility, a relationship began to emerge between occupational choice and the uniqueness of an individual's personality. People began to select vocations which tended to "suit" their personalies. By the twentieth century, the personal needs of the individual had come to be a primary concern with regard to the selection of an occupation.

An extensive study of such "occupational matching" between vocation

FIGURE 13.1 During the early days of the guilds, a person's occupation was his or her "identity" and not merely another identifying characteristic of personality. [*The Bettmann Archive.*]

and personality was conducted by M. Rosenberg (1957). Rosenberg's findings were based on the responses made by nearly 9000 college students to questionnaires which dealt primarily with personal values and wants. In one segment of the study, some of the students were provided with a list of wants and values and asked, "Consider to what extent a job career would have to satisfy each of these requirements before you could consider it *ideal.*" The want or value selected from the list as being the most important was "Uses my special abilities or aptitudes" (78 percent). The second most important factor was "Provides a stable, secure future" (61 percent), followed by "Permits creativity and originality" (48 percent). Such findings seem to substantiate the tremendous emphasis career-oriented individuals place on self-realization through their occupation.

The attitude that self-realization may be attained through one's occupation seems to be found chiefly among middle-class workers. They more often perceive "work" as a means of enhancing their prestige, realizing their potentials, or expressing themselves. In contrast, among lower-class workers, "work" usually means a necessary but unpleasant means of obtaining food and shelter and is, in most cases, neither interesting nor desirable. Friedman and Havighurst (1954), in a study of over 600 industrial workers, concluded that "workers of the lower skill and socio-economic levels regard their work more frequently as merely a way to earn a living and in general recognize fewer extra-financial meanings in their work than do workers of high skill and socio-economic levels."

Rosenberg's study also attempted to investigate the effect interpersonal response traits might have on occupational choice. Using Karen Horney's trait theory of personality as a basis, Rosenberg classified his subjects as being compliant, aggressive, or detached, depending upon how they responded to certain items on his questionnaire.

Horney's trait theory classified individuals into three categories: (1) those who move toward people; (2) those who move against people; and (3) those who move away from people. The person who moves toward people tends to need affection and approval from others and to be wanted, appreciated, and accepted. Students who demonstrated such characteristics while responding to his questionnaire were classified by Rosenberg as being *compliant*.

Horney defined people who move against other people as being highly exploitive, competitive, and with an excessive need to excel. Rosenberg classified his subjects with these characteristics as being *aggressive*.

Horney's third category of personality traits is made up of individuals who tend to move away from people. They are defined as being rather independent, socially withdrawn, and resistant to any attempts at coercion or undue influence by others. Rosenberg classified students demonstrating such characteristics as being *detached*.

When Rosenberg matched the students' interpersonal response traits with their occupational choices, he found that 43 percent of those classified as

FIGURE 13.2   Those who are people-oriented often find the greatest vocational satisfaction in occupations such as teaching or social work. [*Ken Heyman.*]

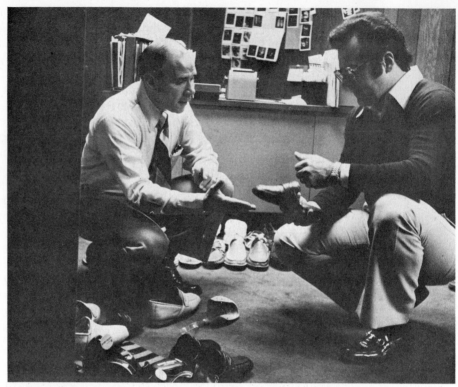

FIGURE 13.3   People who tend to be aggressive often feel quite comfortable in highly competitive occupations such as sales or business. [*Sybil Shelton, Monkmeyer Press Photo Service.*]

being *compliant* chose "people-oriented" occupations, such as medicine, teaching, social work, social science, and personnel. Thirty-two percent of the people classified as *aggressive* tended to select such "financially exploitive" occupations as sales, advertising, business, law, and real estate. Thirty percent of those students whom Rosenberg classified as *detached* chose such "self-directing" occupations as architecture, drama, art, and natural science. The high correlation between personality type and occupational choice found in Rosenberg's study strongly supports the belief that certain people are more suited for a particular occupation than others, and that strong consideration should be given to such matching.

Matching specific personality traits with specific vocational opportunities is one of the oldest approaches to vocational counseling (Parsons, 1909). One of the most widely used tests employed in such a counseling approach is the Strong Vocational Interest Blank (SVIB), first published in 1927 and revised in 1974 to become the Strong-Campbell Interest Inventory. This test attempts to match the interest patterns of individuals trying to decide on a career with the interest patterns of successful members of various occupations. Another trait-oriented test used for vocational counseling is the Kuder Preference Record. This test is based on trait descriptions associated with ten clusters of interests: mechanical, computational, artistic, clerical, outdoor, scientific, persuasive, literary, musical, and social service.

As important as the determination and classification of an individual's personality might appear, however, it must be remembered that such psychometric findings do not represent the "totality" of an individual's existence. Moreover, the findings may represent the individual's personality only at the time of the testing, and may be invalid by the time the individual has completed the educational requirements and/or training necessary to launch a career. Equally important is the reciprocal effect that an occupation can have on the individual's personality. Not only do certain types of personalities seem to select particular occupations, but certain occupations appear to have a particular effect on individual personalities. Thorstein Veblen pointed out that the "kind of work by which men live and particularly the kind of technique which that work involves . . . is the influence which shapes men's thoughts, their relations with one another, their culture and their institutions of control" (MacIver, 1937).

The tremendous potential that a job has for affecting an individual's personality is dramatically illustrated in the development of such manifestations as the "peace officer syndrome." This term refers to the process whereby a once eager rookie becomes callous, cynical, and emotionally insulated. Another example is the "bureaucratic blues," an overconcern for rules and regulations, and a tendency to remove the human element from the organizational aspects of the company or institution and replace it with an endless number of forms and statistics.

An even more dramatic illustration of the effects an occupation can have on personality is the relatively high suicide rate among lawyers, doctors, psychiatrists, and people in the creative arts. All of these are fields where there is often a discrepancy between levels of aspiration and actual achievement. The epidemic of Wall Street suicides that followed the stock market crash of 1929 also reflects the tendency to interrelate one's personal worth with one's financial worth, occupational expertise, and social expectations.

SOCIAL SIGNIFICANCE   An individual's choice of occupation involves not only the selection of a way to make a living, but also the selection of a way of living. The acquisition of a trade is often crucial in the determination of the amount of education one will seek, the socioeconomic class to which one will belong, and how much prestige one will be allotted. The relationship between occupation and social status is, however, a reciprocal one. Occupation helps to determine one's social status, but one's social status can often determine which occupation one will select. In many instances, certain occupations recruit their members selectively, often in accordance with patterns of prejudice and discrimination.

In a 1949 study of the relationship between occupation and class conducted by Centers, 1100 subjects were asked to group 11 occupations with social classes. The results indicated that middle-class occupations were seen as being represented primarily by businessmen, doctors, lawyers, and other white-collar workers. Working-class occupations were viewed as being more physical than mental, such as manual labor, factory work, some farm work, and restaurant or domestic service. A similar survey conducted by the National Opinion Research Center (Hodge, 1964) indicated that the high-prestige occupations generally receive the higher incomes. However, there are some exceptions, most notably where certain poorly paid positions are highly respected and carry a great deal of social prestige, such as clergy, diplomats, and college professors. (See Table 13.1.)

Generally speaking, there are three ways in which the middle-class occupations typically differ from the working-class occupations. One is that the middle-class occupations tend to deal more with the manipulation of interpersonal relations, ideas, and symbols, while working-class occupations are likely to deal more with the manipulation of things. The second difference is that the middle-class occupations are more subject to self-direction, while the working-class occupations are often subject to standardized rules and direct supervision. The third difference is that getting ahead in the middle-class occupations is usually more dependent upon one's own actions and assertiveness, while in the working-class occupations advancement is more dependent upon collective action, especially within unionized industries.

Although much of the status of an occupation is determined by the "degree of specialization" associated with it, in today's society all occupations, or at least all work, tends to be respected by at least some part of the community.

THE WORK ETHIC   The association of value and work, an integral part of American society since the time of the New England Puritans, is referred to as the "Protestant work ethic." The Protestant work ethic advocates diligence in work, pride in craftsmanship, and the will to persevere as the only manner in which anything of any true value can be rightfully obtained. In conjunction with this work code is the implication of a thrift code, which advocates thrift, conservation, and often the need to delay gratification. In other words, people are believed able to accomplish just about anything if they work hard enough for it. The social incorporation of this work ethic in the United States is almost universal. Thus one's personal worth is closely associated with (1) how much one's labor contributes to the community; (2) how ambitious and industrious one is perceived to be; and (3) how self-reliant and self-sufficient one becomes. Thomas Edison once admonished, "There is no substitute for hard work. Genius is one percent inspiration and ninety-nine percent perspiration."

As a consequence of this work ethic, those who are unemployed or on some form of welfare are often looked upon with disdain. They are perceived as lazy or unambitious, or as social parasites living off the labors of the more industrious members of society. A 1972 study by the Brookings Institution, however, demonstrated that the "work orientation" of the poor is quite similar to that of more prosperous Americans with regard to employment incentive and the attainment of rewards. Statistics support these findings, showing that 7 percent of the heads of families who work full time earn incomes that are below the poverty level, and fully 30 percent of the single workers who are fully employed are poor. In fact, one-third of the 2.4 million impoverished families in

TABLE 13.1 OCCUPATIONAL PRESTIGE RATINGS, 1963 AND 1947

OCCUPATION	1963 SCORE	1947 SCORE	OCCUPATION	1963 SCORE	1947 SCORE
U.S. Supreme Court Justice	94	96	Newspaper columnist	73	74
Physician	93	93	Policeman	72	67
Nuclear physicist	92	86	Reporter on a daily newspaper	71	71
Scientist	92	89	Radio announcer	70	75
Government scientist	91	88	Bookkeeper	70	68
State governor	91	93	Tenant farmer (owns livestock and		
Cabinet member in federal government	90	92	machinery and manages the farm)	69	68
College professor	90	89	Insurance agent	69	68
U.S. Representative in Congress	90	89	Carpenter	68	65
Chemist	89	86	Manager of a small store in a city	67	69
Lawyer	89	86	A local official of a labor union	67	62
Diplomat in U.S. Foreign Service	89	92	Mail carrier	66	66
Dentist	88	86	Railroad conductor	66	67
Architect	88	86	Traveling salesman for a wholesale		
Country judge	88	87	concern	66	68
Psychologist	87	85	Plumber	65	63
Minister	87	87	Automobile repairman	64	63
Member of board of directors of a large			Playground director	63	67
corporation	87	86	Barber	63	59
Mayor of a large city	87	90	Machine operator in a factory	63	60
Priest	86	86	Owner-operator of a lunch stand	63	62
Head of a department in state			Corporal in the regular army	62	60
government	86	87	Garage mechanic	62	62
Civil engineer	86	84	Truck driver	59	54
Airline pilot	86	83	Fisherman who owns his own boat	58	58
Banker	85	88	Clerk in a store	56	58
Biologist	85	81	Milk route man	56	54
Sociologist	83	82	Streetcar motorman	56	58
Instructor in public schools	82	79	Lumberjack	55	53
Captain in the regular army	82	80	Restaurant cook	55	54
Accountant for a large business	81	81	Singer in a nightclub	54	52
Public school teacher	81	78	Filling station attendant	51	52
Owner of a factory with about 100			Dockworker	50	47
employees	80	82	Railroad section hand	50	48
Building contractor	80	79	Night watchman	50	47
Artist who paints pictures exhibited in			Coal miner	50	49
galleries	78	83	Restaurant waiter	49	48
Musician in a symphony orchestra	78	81	Taxi driver	49	49
Author of novels	78	80	Farm hand	48	50
Economist	78	79	Janitor	48	44
Official of an international labor union	77	75	Bartender	48	44
Railroad engineer	76	76	Clothes presser in a laundry	45	46
Electrician	76	73	Soda fountain clerk	44	45
County agricultural agent	76	77	Share-cropper (owns no livestock or		
Owner-operator of a printing shop	75	74	equipment and does not manage farm)	42	40
Trained machinist	75	73	Garbage collector	39	35
Farm owner and operator	74	76	Street sweeper	36	34
Undertaker	74	72	Shoe shiner	34	33
Welfare worker for a city government	74	73	Average	71	70

Source: Hodge, Siegel, and Rossi, 1964.

1967 were headed by a fully employed person. There is also statistical evidence with regard to people's being on welfare that tends to dispel some of the derogatory myths associated with the poor. For example, a survey of low-income families in Detroit in 1965 showed that of those families that were eligible, 43 percent were not on the welfare rolls. And in a similar 1968 investigation of 150,000 New York City families that were eligible for wage subsidies, only about 15,000 were filing claims. In spite of such contradictory evidence, however, the Protestant work ethic still contributes heavily to the myth that certain minority groups have a lower standard of living because they do not *want* to work, rather than because their pay is low or jobs are not available.

Self-Esteem: A Sense of Relevance

Self-acceptance has been a natural part of the development of some people. For others, attaining a favorable opinion of themselves has always been difficult. The ease with which individuals acquire positive feelings toward themselves often depends heavily upon how their parents responded to them in the past. An individual who experiences "unconditional" love as a child, being loved just for being, will tend to acquire a sense of worth just by reason of being alive. Children who experience a greater degree of praise than criticism during the process of learning and developing skills are likely to develop a self-confidence based on their potentials. If children have been adequately rewarded for their personal accomplishments, their self-esteem will often be based on their capabilities.

Self-esteem is a matter of attitude: one's attitude toward oneself as a person, toward one's potentials, and toward one's accomplishments. Everett Shostrom, author of *Man the Manipulator* (1972), proposes that development of self-esteem is achieved through sequential steps. These steps represent the degree to which we have developed our individual talents and skills. The steps progress from a state of being *inadequate,* to being *adequate,* to being *capable,* then to being *worthwhile,* and finally to being *important.*

BEING INADEQUATE   Far too often people confuse being *inadequate* with being *inferior.* The two words are not synonymous. Being inferior implies that one person is less important or valuable than another, and therefore can be accorded a lower station or rank and treated with less dignity or respect. Being inadequate, however, merely suggests that a person may be imperfect— untrained in a particular skill, for instance, or lacking sufficient knowledge of a particular subject. However, being inadequate implies nothing with regard to a person's potentials or capabilities. Academically, a college professor may perceive a first-year student's knowledge of a certain subject to be inadequate, and therefore select a graduate student as an assistant. The first-year student, however, is not inferior, but merely unqualified, a distinction that many a young person fails to perceive.

Being inadequate is part of being human. It is the acknowledgment that one cannot be all things to all people in all situations. It is the acknowledgment

Self-directed individuals seem to work best in the arts or natural sciences. [*C. C. Kleinsorge, Editorial Photocolor Archives.*]

FIGURE 13.4

that one may not be able to do everything, be everything, or know everything. For many people, being inadequate creates an obsession to overcome a particular failing in order to become "perfect," but others more appropriately perceive inadequacy as merely an opportunity to learn rather than an obligation to learn.

Often, a feeling of inadequacy is due to repeated attempts to operate outside of one's *range of challenge*. A range of challenge is that area of performance in which a person tends to function comfortably and yet is still able to experience a sense of accomplishment from what is achieved. Our range of challenge is determined by the degree of competence we have realized with regard to a particular talent or skill as compared with our *expectations* of what can be achieved, given these attributes. If our expectations are *too high,* frequent failure will usually be experienced. When we attempt to function at a level that is beyond our capabilities, it is often necessary to deceive others by guile, or to bluff through with such a statement as, "Sure, I know how to operate one of these, I've had lots of experience with these. Only, it has been a while, and I notice that the controls are in a slightly different configuration from the one I'm used to. Perhaps you could run through the operation a couple of times just to reacquaint me." One of the disadvantages of such tactics is that, even though others may be temporarily fooled by the bluff, the "phony" is always aware of being a phony and self-esteem suffers because of this awareness.

Others maintain a feeling of inadequacy by persisting in placing their expectations *too low.* The individual whose expectations are set too low will usually not experience any sense of accomplishment when completing a job, and may mumble something like, "Well, there's another 300 widgits put together; I wonder how many a monkey could have completed." People who consistently operate at a level that is below their capabilities tend to become depressed, apathetic, and chronically frustrated.

Individuals who habitually choose demeaning or degrading jobs often do so because they are familiar with feeling inadequate. It may be an uncomfortable feeling, but it is a familiar one that the person is used to coping with. Some theorists attempt to explain such self-defeating behavior as being due to a lack of narcissistic love, or self-love. A lack of narcissistic love is often the result of having had perfectionistic parents who concentrated their efforts on the errors rather than the efforts of their child.

BEING ADEQUATE The most important premise behind being adequate is self-acceptance. It is imperative that we be able to accept ourselves "as is" and not expect to be "superpersons." The term "self-acceptance" refers to realistic awareness of our potentials, capabilities, and limitations, and does not necessarily imply that we will have positive feelings or like what we accept.

Being adequate is experienced most frequently at the beginning of a learning process. At this point, an individual recognizes the presence of the potential to master a particular task or skill but, for the time being, lacks sufficient knowledge or training. By being able to accept oneself at this preparatory state of transition, one is able to embark on an attempt at self-improvement from a positive position. On the other hand, individuals who cannot accept themselves in their present state of ignorance or incompetence will often become even more self-rejecting should they fail in their attempts at self-improvement. Such persons usually have problems with patience, wanting to *know* without having to *learn.*

Being adequate means having only a rudimentary knowledge of a particular skill. For some, this is as far as they desire to progress. They are willing to become a "jack of all trades but master of none." For others, having a minimal skill or knowledge in some areas is quite sufficient, but in a few specific areas, they have a need for a greater realization of their potentials and seek additional practice, training, and study so that they may become more capable of carrying out their jobs.

BEING CAPABLE Being capable means that most of the challenges associated with a particular vocation are well within the limitations of our abilities. Through continued improvement of existing talents and skills, we achieve a certain degree of expertise, and with this mastery comes a sense of self-confidence.

People who have confidence in their ability are able to be relaxed and are often able, therefore, to be more spontaneous and creative. This potential is in contrast with the anxiety and trepidation usually experienced by the beginner or the person new on the job.

Being capable usually implies the acquisition of a trade through having earned a journeyman's rating, a postgraduate degree, or a professional license. By having developed a skill, an individual is capable of earning a living and is thereby able to experience a greater feeling of independence than is the unskilled worker. Along with this sense of freedom, people who feel capable of doing a job well often find tremendous personal satisfaction and a sense of pride in what they have done. As a result, they are more likely to make such statements as "I'm one of the best," "I'll compare my work with anyone else's," or "Now, that's the way it's supposed to be done."

BEING WORTHWHILE   From the ranks of those who are capable and have mastered the fundmentals of their trade will emerge the craftworker, the artisan, and the expert. These are the people who have developed to a stage of perceiving themselves and what they do as being worthwhile. Such individuals are able to add a little of themselves to what they do. They have developed an individualized style, a distinctive characteristic, which acts as a personal signature to their contribution. This uniqueness of style tends to separate their contributions from the contributions of others and to become their *trademark*. The work of a particular artist, composer, or architect represents a distinctive style that can be easily identified with that individual. Just as the distinctive work of a cabinetmaker, chef, or glassblower can become identifiable, so too can the skill of an exceptional athlete, the style of an author, or the technique of a gifted surgeon. The more distinctive the style becomes, the more it reflects the realization of a specific talent and the more *irreplaceable* its possessor becomes.

It is through the awareness of one's irreplaceability that a personal sense of worth is promoted. Often the person who says, "Nothing I do seems worthwhile," really means "Anyone can do what I'm doing." Such might be the case of the individuals who find themselves "overeducated" or "overqualified" for the job they currently hold, and as a consequence have low self-esteem (Kasl and Cobb, 1970). In contrast, a person who has individualized his or her capabilities is able to say, "Without me, this would not be." With this realization comes a sense of significance, a realization that one's existence matters, and that one's death would have an impact. There is the recognition that "What I do is worthwhile, what I say is worthwhile, and what I think and what I feel are worthwhile." With such awareness, individuals are more likely to think of themselves as a "thou" rather than a "thing." Perhaps this was what the English novelist Joseph Conrad (1857–1924) had in mind when he wrote in *Heart of Darkness* (1902): "I don't like work—no man does—but I like what is in work—the chance to find yourself. Your own reality—for yourself, not for others—what no other man can ever know."

Feeling worthwhile, however, does not necessarily mean that one's significance and irreplaceability are recognized by others. Therefore, such feelings should be independent of the evaluations of others. They may not understand or appreciate one's uniqueness or fully comprehend the significance of one's contributions, but the worth is still there. Those who do appreciate another's work may also resent its quality because of their own inability to duplicate what the other person has done. As a result of such envy, these individuals may make such comments as "I don't know how she does it. She must not be sharing the whole recipe," "Aw, the Beatles weren't so hot," or "I could outfly Baron von Richthofen and Eddie Rickenbacker, if I had a better plane."

When an individual does receive recognition and appreciation from others, the importance of the work may become more fully understood. Not only does the work seem important to others, but the person performing the work is also perceived as being important.

BEING IMPORTANT   A sense of dignity and self-respect is an integral part of feeling important. It is imperative, however, not to confuse being important with being conceited. Being important is synonymous with being *essential,* and not necessarily with being powerful, famous, or wealthy. A person can feel essential to a job without necessarily having the feeling of being *better* than the other workers. Being important is being *vital*—a parent, a president, and a pilot are all vital and important.

Having a sense of importance can often add a sense of urgency to a project and a critical element to the need to complete a task. Often, completion of a task can generate a feeling of self-fulfillment and the self-satisfaction of having completed one's mission. A person who has a sense of being important often perceives work as a medium of self-expression, rather than merely as a laborious effort in futility, and as a result the end product of the work often becomes a "labor of love." The love of work that one experiences when doing work that is considered important will usually become manifest in one of three forms: eros, philos, or narcissism. Eros is the type of love that results from perceiving the excellence in what has been accomplished. Philos is experienced as a result of commitment and identification with the accomplishment. Narcissistic love is experienced as a result of pride and self-respect in having accomplished what one has set out to accomplish.

Vocational Choice

People select careers on the basis of the prospect of attaining both immediate satisfaction and long-range goals. They choose their careers for both the external and internal rewards that can be accrued (status, prestige, and wealth) as well as the altruistic and personal satisfaction that can be experienced. These goals, however, are usually attainable only when a person has been fortunate enough to have made a wise occupational choice. Since at least one out of every five workers is unhappy in his or her life's work, it is apparent that a wise choice is not always made. Therefore, serious research, study, and analysis should play an important part in any consideration given to the selection of a particular vocation.

TRADITIONAL VOCATIONAL SELECTION AND MEN   The colloquial phrase "like father, like son" used to imply much more than merely the similarity that might exist between a child's behavior and value system and those of the father. It also referred to skills associated with an occupation. Historically, the identification of a boy with his father usually included the father's occupation. Mimicry, imitation, and training associated with the occupational role began at a very early age.

In an agrarian society, the boy would work in the fields beside his father and learn farming skills so as to be able to take over the same piece of land when his father became too old to work. Most communities were small, and it was assumed that the blacksmith's son would become a blacksmith, the cobbler's son a cobbler, the farmer's son a farmer, and so on. When a family had more sons than could support themselves by working at its traditional occupation, some of them would have to leave home to find a livelihood. In some cases they would colonize new areas or study as apprentices under skilled craftsmen. Even then, however, an individual's status in life was more a factor of acceptance and resignation than of choice.

By the sixteenth century and the Protestant Reformation, however, the selection of an occupation had gained a much greater level of importance. Martin Luther (1483–1546) argued that since *vocation* literally means one's calling, then not only is the ordained priest called, but:

> . . . a cobbler, a smith, a peasant, every man has the office and function of his calling. . . . All alike are consecrated priests and bishops, and every man should in his office or function be useful and beneficial to the rest, so that various kinds of work may all be united for furtherance of body and soul, just as the members of the body all serve one another. (Fosdick, 1952, pp. 99–100)

Martin Luther's concept of vocations, however, was to come under severe criticism with the advent of the Industrial Revolution (1750s to 1800s) and the subsequent reduction of the status of workers to factory "hands"—"necessary extensions of the machine." Soon the choice of occupation became dependent on geographical location and socioeconomic necessity; coal-mining communities produced miners, textile factory company towns produced textile workers, and steel foundries drew their workers from the surrounding mill towns. In most cases, one's occupation was determined by the coincidence of a "job opening." For many, this coincidence occurred before a person reached adolescence.

Working conditions became insufferable, wages were inadequate, and human dignity faltered. Then trade unions gradually began to form in an attempt to improve the workers' plight. Just such conditions as these prompted the revolutionist Karl Marx (1818–1883) to declare, "The workers have nothing to lose but their chains. They have a world to win. Workers of the world, unite!"

Through the combined efforts of labor unions and legislation such as the Fair Labor Standards Act (1938), which set a sixteen-year minimum age for employing children, working conditions improved and vocational choice began to take on new meaning. For instance, a significant number of people

FIGURE 13.5 Whether with the slave, the serf, or the worker, whenever profit has been valued above human dignity, exploitation of the individual has become the accepted practice. [*Culver Pictures.*]

began basing their choices on interpersonal identification with "greats" in a given profession. Erik Erikson notes that "the adolescent looks most fervently for men and ideas to have *faith* in, which also means men and ideas in whose service it would seem worthwhile to prove oneself trustworthy."

Such transfer of identification from the traditional father model is also evident in research reported by Beardslee and O'Dowd (1962). Their report deals with surveys conducted with students just entering college. The results of these surveys revealed that most of the students' occupational preferences represented a significant rise above their fathers' occupational attainments. However, the data from these surveys also point out that although the students aspired to higher levels of accomplishment, for the most part they still preferred to enter the vocational fields in which the fathers worked. For instance, the sons of executive-level business and industrial personnel tended to select business careers, whereas the sons of professional men (doctors, lawyers, etc.) rarely selected business careers. This indicates that in general, the father-son tradition may still be in effect. However, most studies indicate that probably fewer than 10 percent of boys choose the *same* occupation as their fathers (Duncan and Hodge, 1963).

VOCATIONAL SELECTION AND WOMEN One of the best-known and most frequently used themes of martyrdom is the couplet:

Man may work from sun to sun,
But woman's work is never done.

Unfortunately, the implied suffering depicted in this verse may be truer today than ever before. Although women have worked, and worked hard, throughout history, traditionally their work has been within the family rather than outside the home. Today, however, many women hold jobs in both spheres simultaneously.

During the times when infant mortality approached 50 percent and life expectancy was only thirty or forty years, mere maintenance of the population required a woman's full time and devotion to child rearing. Her vocational choice thus was limited to motherhood. In addition to this primary duty, she was often required to assist her husband with the farming, cleaning game, guarding the herd, or preserving food. As difficult as these jobs were, however, the wife-mother did not work alone, but enjoyed the cooperation and closeness of an extended family. She was often admired for her domestic skills and appreciated as a vital force in the survival of the family unit.

With the advent of the Industrial Revolution, and, later, the need for factory workers during World War II, women began to work outside the home. Simultaneously, modern medicine drastically reduced the birth rate. As a consequence of these social and economic changes, the average woman began to enter the national labor force. Almost immediately she became "isolated." She was isolated from her traditional source of fulfillment, and simultaneously was denied full acceptance into the working world, often being employed only as a "token."

In order to win greater acceptance, many working women readopted some of the more "traditional" roles. An investigation conducted by Kanter (1976) was able to identify some of these adoptive roles. For instance, in the role of "mother," the woman provides cookies for the department and mends clothing when necessary, simultaneously comforting the man and providing a sympathetic ear. Another role is the "sex object," in which the woman's seductive talents are employed in such a way as to promote competition among the male employees for her attention. If neither of these two roles is comfortable, the woman often assumes the role of "pet" or kid sister, who can encourage the men and act as a confidante without threatening them. If the token woman is unable to play any of these roles, Kanter found, she is likely to be looked upon with suspicion and hostility, and to be perceived as an "iron maiden" and a militant "women's libber."

All of these roles are perceived as degrading by the working women who assume them. More often than not, however, the resentment is directed toward the social or personal situation that requires them to work rather than toward the injustice and prejudice of their work situations. In fact, in some cases, women who have successfully reached the top have been found to discriminate against other women in order to exclude the competition and maintain the status of being someone special. They try to convey the impression that they are the "exceptions to the rule."

In spite of the extensive efforts of the women's liberation movement to "equalize" the working woman, a cultural lag seems to persist which resists the transfer of the source of a woman's fulfillment from the family to a non–family-oriented career. One study, conducted by Garai and Scheinfeld (1968), concluded:

> To attain masculine sex identity, boys need identification with a vocational goal, preferably one that is characterized by a meaningful or prestige-conferring activity. Girls, on the other hand, tend to attain their feminine sex identity primarily through intimacy in interpersonal relationships, i.e., success in marriage—whereas identification with a vocational goal appears to play a secondary role in their quest for identity. (pp. 260–261)

These findings are further supported by O. E. Thompson (1968). His survey of adolescence indicated that boys, more frequently than girls, rate as important the opportunity to be a leader, to be boss, to receive high pay, and to gain fame. Girls more often value jobs which would allow them to express their abilities to help other people. Even in elite women's colleges, many students consider any pressure to plan seriously for a career an unwanted distraction from the main emotional concern—to get married and have children.

In an attempt to determine the long-term effects on college-educated women who avoid a career in preference for a traditional family life, Judith Bernbaum (1975) conducted a comparative study of women who had graduated with honors from the University of Michigan. In this study, twenty-nine of the subjects had gotten married, had children, and sought no further education or employment. For comparison, twenty-five married women with children and twenty-seven single women with Ph.D.'s or M.D.'s were selected from the University of Michigan's faculty. The comparison indicated that the housewives had lower self-esteem and poorer emotional health than did the professionals. Interestingly enough, this finding is just the opposite of the findings of a survey conducted by Alice Rossi in the early 1960s. The contrast indicates that there has been a substantial shift in social attitudes since the sixties, when the life of the wife-mother was envied by the professional. In the seventies, the professional woman is often envied by the nonprofessional woman.

Today, with nine out of ten women working sometime during their lives, the question is no longer one of whether a woman should work, but how she can achieve fulfillment in her work. In order to increase the probability of women's attaining personal satisfaction through their vocation, certain social adjustments must continue to evolve to a level where:

1 Social institutions (including the family unit) are developed to support and encourage those women who have to work or want to work.
2 Women's conceptions of their potentials are upgraded.
3 Equal pay and equal opportunity are afforded.

4   The vestiges of masculine oppression are replaced with mutual respect and cooperation.
5   The importance and status of those women who do choose a family-oriented vocation are reaffirmed.

OCCUPATIONAL ADJUSTMENT

The English author and critic John Ruskin (1819–1900) believed that "In order that people may be happy in their work, these three things are needed: They must be fit for it. They must not do too much of it. And they must have a sense of success in it." The difficulty in attaining the first of Ruskin's requirements is that a person's commitment toward becoming "fit" for a particular occupation often has irreversible consequences. For example, the decision to become a schoolteacher may forfeit any chance of becoming a prima ballerina. With regard to Ruskin's caution on working too much, the difficulty usually lies in attaining a balance between the work a person *has* to do and the work a person *wants* to do. Far too often, the "too much of it" seems to be associated with work of a compulsory nature. Ruskin's acknowledgment of the need to experience "a sense of success" in one's work is almost universally accepted as an integral part of successful occupational adjustment. However, in a modern industrial society, feelings of personal accomplishment can often be elusive, and a sense of success can be difficult to attain.

Aptitude and Selection

Louis L. Thurstone (1887–1955) believed that "if something exists, it exists in some amount, and therefore can be measured." For years, psychometrists and theorists in the field of vocational aptitudes have been attempting to fulfill Thurstone's statement. Tests have been designed to measure mechanical aptitude, clerical aptitude, motor skills, artistic and musical talent, intelligence, and personality. The purpose of these tests is to identify an appreciable number of special abilities and discover how much of each ability is required for success in a particular occupation.

Although these tests have facilitated vocational counseling, aptitudes have been found to be more complex and more dependent on previous experiences than was first suspected. Therefore, the ability to "scientifically" select occupations has failed to materialize.

One of the factors contributing to this problem is that many individuals who demonstrate an aptitude for a certain field do not have an interest in that field. Technological developments have also confounded vocational testing. Many young people being tested today will eventually be employed in jobs that didn't even exist at the time of the testing.

In spite of these obstacles, vocational testing does afford an opportunity for self-appraisal. Vocational researchers such as Donald Super and David

FIGURE 13.6   For some people, there is an overwhelming feeling that they were always meant to be in the vocation they have chosen. [*Lilo Raymond, Woodfin Camp.*]

Hershenson propose that "the individual must have a view of himself before he can determine what his strengths and limitations are, and he must determine these before he can select vocational goals for himself."

MENTAL ABILITIES   Most studies of the relationship between IQ and occupation indicate that persons with higher measured intelligence tend to be found in occupations considered to be high in status and prestige. It is important to note, however, that IQ is only a good predictor of how well a person will *train* for a job and not how well a person will actually perform on a job.

In an attempt to analyze general intelligence and its possible effects on performance, L. L. Thurstone administered a series of sixty tests to students in college, high school, and elementary school. He then computed the intercorrelations between the scores on all the tests. Through exhaustive statistical analysis, the process yielded seven "primary abilities" which Thurstone felt determine general intelligence. He identified them as the verbal, quantitative or numerical, spacial, perceptual, memory, reasoning, and word fluency abilities.

Although Thurstone's view of mental abilities is thought by many to be an oversimplification, there is evidence that people in different occupations do differ from one another in their special abilities. One source of such evidence is the study performed by Robert Thorndike and Elizabeth Hagen (1959) and reported in their book *10,000 Careers*. They located more than 10,000 individuals who had taken the Air Force battery of tests in 1943 and then compared the test results with actual job selections and performance twelve years later (1955). The results of the comparisons confirmed that occupational groups do indeed differ in patterns of abilities. For example, the patterns of abilities for office clerks are substantially different from those of garage mechanics. However, the study also indicated that the degree of success a person will attain within an occupation cannot be predicted from these test scores.

APTITUDE   The purpose of aptitude tests is to measure special capacities required for meeting practical situations, and then, using the results of these tests as a basis, to determine the suitability of an individual for training in a specific area. Aptitude tests fall into three categories: (1) tests for business and industry, which include the testing of hearing, vision, motor skills, and mechanical and clerical abilities; (2) tests for aesthetic areas like art, music, and literature; and (3) tests for the professions, such as medicine, law, teaching, and engineering.

An all-encompassing aptitude test, called the General Aptitude Test Battery (GATB), can compare an individual's profile with each of 22 occupational ability patterns, which have been identified through research and cover more than 500 jobs. This test was developed and is used by the United States Employment Service. The GATB provides not only a profile, but also a minimum score for each area. This score enables a participant to become aware of having *more* than the minimum amount of some special ability in a field that has not been considered as well as of having *less* than the minimum amount of an ability apparently required in a type of work that is being considered.

VOCATIONAL INTERESTS   Aptitude tests are validated by comparing the scores of people already in the field with those of people aspiring to enter the field. Interest tests are validated in the same manner. In the case of the Strong Vocational Interest Blank (SVIB), E. K. Strong and others noticed in their study of occupational differences that different groups of professional people showed consistent differences in their likes and dislikes. Such findings suggested that a profession may represent a way of life as well as a way of earning a living. Norms were established over the years by administering tests to various people in different occupations. These norms are compared with the test results indicating the interests of an individual attempting to decide on a career.

The Kuder Preference Record is another interest-oriented test used extensively in vocational counseling. The Kuder test scores generate a profile that emphasizes an individual's "leanings" toward a particular occupational category, such as "scientific-social service" or "persuasive-literary."

For those with a limited vocational potential, the Brainard Occupational Preference Inventory is often used. This inventory attempts to categorize the individual into such areas as commercial, mechanical, scientific, and agricultural. This test is similar to the Minnesota Vocational Interest Inventory, which also attempts to classify participants in occupational categories that do not require a college education.

It is important to keep in mind that the profiles, percentile scores, and categorizations that are based on the test results from ability tests, aptitude

FIGURE 13.7 Testing for aptitude and interest is one of many aids available in choosing a satisfying vocation. [*Herman Emmet, Photo Researchers.*]

tests, and interest tests usually describe the "average" person found in various occupations. The individual "extremes" within these occupations have often been eliminated, but are nonetheless a representative part of the field. Therefore, it is suggested that these tests be used only as supplementary tools in the decision-making process and not as the sole basis for selecting a vocation.

VOCATIONAL DEVELOPMENT Many current theories focus on vocational selection and development as a continuous coping process. It begins with childhood chores, neighborhood jobs, menial tasks for pay, trial apprenticeships, and eventual mastery of a trade. A longitudinal study by Moss and Kagan (1961) found that the striving level of activity demonstrated by a child in elementary school provides a reasonably good indicator of achievement behavior in adolescence and adulthood.

Donald Super proposed that the early childhood development of self-concepts and occupational concepts would be highly influential in the later determination of vocational choice and satisfaction. Robert Havighurst (1964) also recognized the importance of childhood experiences in the determination of career choices. However, he believes that vocational development is not restricted solely to a period in one's youth—vocational development is a lifelong process.

Havighurst divides this process into six stages reaching from childhood through old age (see Table 13.2). The *first stage* occurs between the ages of five and ten years. During this stage, children will form an identification with a parent or other significant person, and will incorporate this image into their "ego ideal." Using the examples set by the model, children will begin to develop a concept of what "working" is all about. The *second stage* (ages ten through fifteen) is characterized by the acquisition of the basic habits of industry. During this stage, children develop work habits that will tend to persist throughout their lives. For example, a child who learns to do slipshod work as a youth will do work as an adult that is typified by the same low level of performance and shoddy workmanship. This period is also a time in which children learn to manage their time and establish priorities. The *third stage* (ages fifteen through twenty-five) is concerned primarily with acquiring "occupational identity"; that is, actually selecting an occupation and beginning the necessary preparations for entering that occupation. During this stage, the individual will attempt to satisfy the educational or training requirements for a given vocation, and will tend to select jobs that will provide work experience associated with the chosen profession.

TABLE 13.2 VOCATIONAL DEVELOPMENT: A LIFELONG PROCESS

STAGES OF VOCATIONAL DEVELOPMENT	AGE
I *Identification with a worker* Father, mother, other signigicant persons. The concept of working becomes an essential part of the ego-ideal.	5–10
II *Acquiring the basic habits of industry* Learning to organize one's time and energy to get a piece of work done. School work, chores. Learning to put work ahead of play in appropriate situations.	10–15
III *Acquiring identity as a worker in the occupational structure* Choosing and preparing for an occupation. Getting work experience as a basis for occupational choice and for assurance of economic independence.	15–25
IV *Becoming a productive person* Mastering the skills of one's occupation. Moving up the ladder within one's occupation.	25–40
V *Maintaining a productive society* Emphasis shifts toward the societal and away from the individual aspect of the worker's role. The individual sees himself as a responsible citizen in a productive society. He pays attention to the civic responsibility attached to his job. He is at the peak of his occupational career and has time and energy to adorn it with broader types of activity. He pays attention to inducting younger people into stages III and IV.	40–70
VI *Contemplating a productive and responsible life* This person is retired from his work or is in process of withdrawing from the worker's role. He looks back over his work life with satisfaction, sees that he has made his social contribution, and is pleased with it. While he may not have achieved all of his ambitions, he accepts his life and believes in himself as a productive person.	70+

Source: Robert Havighurst, 1964, p. 190.

Once the necessary apprenticeship for the chosen vocation has been fulfilled, the individual is ready to enter the *fourth stage* of vocational development (ages twenty-five through forty). Productivity is perhaps the most representative factor associated with this stage. It is in this period that most individuals will make their greatest vocational advancements. Mastery of the skills needed in the profession is acquired and a person's "style" is developed. It is also during this period that an individual is most likely to progress to higher levels of responsibility. During the *fifth stage* of development (ages forty through seventy), emphasis shifts from maintaining one's career to maintaining civic duties and continuing as a responsible citizen. Such productivity prepares the individual for the *sixth stage* (ages seventy and beyond), which involves retirement from work and a critical review of one's life of work.

Workers' Discontent

As the Industrial Revolution progressed, the composition of the national work force began to change. In 1820, 70 percent of all workers were farmers. By 1900, the proportion of farm workers had dropped to 37 percent, and in 1976, only 3.3 percent of the labor force consisted of farmers.

Paradoxically, there has not been a corresponding increase within the ranks of workers involved in manufacturing. The proportion of blue-collar workers—around 35 percent—has remained relatively unchanged since the turn of the century. The major shift in proportions has occurred among the white-collar workers: from approximately 17 percent in 1900 to over 50 percent in 1976. According to Canial Bell (1973), this shift represents a change from a manufacturing, *machine-centered* labor force to a service-oriented, *information-centered* postindustrial society.

In spite of what appears to be a shift in emphasis from the importance of the machine to the importance of the individual, many workers today complain of "dehumanization by a technological society." In many instances, they believe that their time is, or has been wasted, on educational requirements that increasingly exceed what employers can use, that their talents are being frustrated through the growing use of computerization, and that their hopes and dreams are being crushed through the demoralizing drudgery of unfulfilling work. As an indication of the consequences of such discontent, a 1972 Gallup poll revealed that 57 percent of the total public admitted that they could produce more if they tried. This figure rose to 70 percent when only professionals were considered, and 72 percent when people eighteen to twenty-nine years of age were included. Kenneth Keniston (1965), having conducted extensive research among American workers, concluded:

> Work . . . in technological society . . . requires a dissociation of feeling, a subordination of passion, impulse, fantasy, and idealism before cognitive problems and tasks. As breadwinners, most Americans neither find nor even seek "fulfillment" in their jobs. Work, split away from "living" by convention and tradition, becomes instrumental, a dissociated part of life that makes possible, yet often vitiates, the rest of a "living." (p. 267)

MORALE Perhaps one of the most influential factors affecting occupational adjustment is *worker morale*. In most situations, worker morale depends on a combination of factors, such as feelings of personal worth, value of the work being performed, enthusiasm, and interpersonal relationships with fellow employees. Generally, it has been found that an employee with high morale tends to work harder, has a lower absentee rate and fewer accidents, and stays on the job longer than an employee with low morale.

The recognition of the importance of worker morale and motivation stems primarily from the studies conducted by the Western Electric Company at its Hawthorne plant in New Jersey. The studies were originally designed to assess the effects that changing the physical working conditions and work schedules might have on productivity. The results of these studies showed that as these conditions improved, productivity went up. For example, if illumination in a work area was improved, productivity in that area increased. However, it was also discovered that productivity rose when the conditions were returned to their original state. Follow-up studies revealed that one of the main reasons for the increases in productivity was the higher worker morale generated when the workers felt they were important enough for the company to care about adjusting their working conditions. This phenomenon came to be known as the "Hawthorne effect." It eventually led to the introduction of the *human relations* element in industry.

Human relations programs are designed primarily to deal with such morale-oriented factors as employee attitudes, job satisfaction, supervisory practices, communication, and job design. Research has indicated that employee attitudes are favorably affected when workers are allowed to voice their views through unstructured interviews or confidential questionnaires. This is especially true with concern to such topics as changes in policy, procedures, or working conditions.

Studies carried out by Herzberg (1959) indicated that job satisfaction depends a great deal on opportunities for personal growth and self-actualization, recognition of achievement, and possibility of advancement. It was found that these factors have a great deal of influence on the attitudes of workers and whether or not they like their jobs. With regard to a worker's attitude and liking of a job, Douglas Jerrold (1803–1857), in *Wit and Opinions of Douglas Jerrold* (1859), optimistically wrote: "The ugliest of trades have their moments of pleasure. Now, if I were a grave-digger, or even a hangman, there are some people I could work for with a great deal of enjoyment."

Herzberg also found that job dissatisfaction is strongly affected by the context in which the job is performed, objectionable company policies, poor working conditions, and incompetent supervisors. Likert (1961) found that supervisors of high-producing units are usually employee-centered. Concerned about the workers and friendly, they apply only general supervisory control. Supervisors of low-producing units were found to be job-centered. They were concerned chiefly about production, and were aloof and rigid in their supervisory control over the workers.

MONOTONY One of the most frequently mentioned contributors to job dissatisfaction and low worker morale is *monotony*. As automation and

FIGURE 13.8   Along with the monotony associated with many assembly-line jobs is the gnawing realization that your job exists only because you're cheaper than a machine, or that a machine has not been developed to replace you, yet. [*Western Electric.*]

assembly-line techniques have developed, greater emphasis has been placed on single-task specialization in order to reduce costs. Studies conducted by Walker and Guest (1952) showed that 67 percent of the workers found single-operation jobs boring, 56 percent were bored with jobs involving two to four operations, and only 30 percent were bored with jobs of five or more operations.

A typical work curve representing the productivity of an employee working at a monotonous job often demonstrates a drop in efficiency. A normal working curve is composed of (1) a *warm-up*, showing a steady increase in production as the worker gets organized, (2) a *beginning spurt*, indicating an initial vigor and a period of peak production, followed by (3) a gradual *downward trend*, and (4) an *end spurt*, which is characteristically a sharp rise in production near completion of the project. This is in contrast with a monotonous job curve, which tends to show large fluctuations in output throughout the work period as the worker's concentration wanes and lapses of attention are experienced, followed by an end spurt as the worker attempts to compensate for the earlier below-normal output.

In order to counteract the monotonous effects of certain jobs, employers have introduced such techniques as job rotation, job expansion, and worker participation in job structuring and planning. The English essayist Walter Pater (1839–1894), in *Marius the Epicurean* (1885), noted:

> We need some imaginative stimulus, some not impossible ideal such as may shape vague hope, and transform it into effective desire, to carry us year after year, without disgust, through the routine work which is so large a part of life.

RETRAINING AND RETIREMENT   As the general quality of health and the length of the life span of the average worker continue to increase, the probability of having a "second chance" at life also rises. As a consequence, more and more people are taking up a second career. One 1967 study reported that about 5½ million Americans employed in 1966 had changed to different occupations in the previous year, and 40 percent of these changes were made by workers over thirty-five years of age. In 1969, an average of 800,000 workers a month were changing jobs (Snelling, 1969), and a 1978 survey, conducted by *Psychology Today,* concluded that today's workers "do not have the strong commitment to working for a particular organization or in a particular occupation. . . . They appear to be willing to change jobs if they can better themselves" (May 1978, p. 65). In addition, a special labor force report (Byrne, 1975) indicated that 8.7 percent of all workers changed occupations between January 1972 and January 1973. Out of a labor force of 69 million, over 5 million had changed occupations, and 70 percent of these changes were made by workers under thirty-five years of age.

Some assume a second career upon retiring from their first career. Others voluntarily choose to switch careers before retirement, and still others are forced to change careers because their previous jobs have gone out of existence. The rapid changes in technology seem to be a major contributing factor to the present level of today's vocational mobility. Much of the mobility is either a shift from blue-collar to white-collar jobs (Johnson and Stern, 1969) or a result of technological relocation, such as the reassignment of some 55,000 aerospace engineers at the completion of the moon exploration program (August 1971). Still other contributing factors to greater vocational mobility are a general resistance to retirement and an unwillingness to become idle in retirement.

The resistance to retirement appears to be a growing trend, with the recent enactment of federal laws extending the mandatory retirement age from sixty-five to seventy being a prime example. Another indication of this resistance is the fact that only about half the production workers employed by the "Big Three" auto makers retire before reaching sixty-five, although employees over fifty-eight with thirty years of service are eligible for retirement.

In addition, a number of agencies, such as Retire to Action (Arthur, 1969), Service Corps of Retired Executives (SCORE), and the University of California's Hastings College, where all full-time faculty members must be sixty-five or over, are being organized in order to aid retired individuals in getting established in a new career. For the optimistic older worker, Berton Braley's poem "No Chance" (quoted in Henry, 1952, p. 315) seems to carry fresh meaning.

The best verse hasn't been rhymed
yet,
The best house hasn't been
planned,
The highest peak hasn't been
climbed yet,
The mightiest rivers aren't
spanned;
Don't worry and fret, faint-hearted,
The chances have just begun
For the best jobs haven't been
started
The best work hasn't been done.

THE IMPORTANCE OF PLAY

In contrast with those whose lives are dedicated to work, a portion of the population have dedicated their lives to avoiding work. Viewed through the perspective of the Protestant work ethic, such people are often seen as "operators," hustlers, or con artists. They are frequently considered to be nonproductive, noncontributing, exploitive elements of society, to be shunned and avoided whenever possible. As a consequence, many individuals go to extremes in order not to be accidentally mistaken for "shirkers." One way in which such an image may be avoided is to work incessantly; another is not to engage in play. Both methods have the potential of jeopardizing a person's physical and mental health.

Others avoid playing unless they have "earned" the privilege to do so. Still others avoid playing merely because they have never learned how. However, in order to achieve a balanced lifestyle, experience sufficient diversity, and maintain a high level of physical, emotional, and social well-being, some form of play must be included as an integral part of one's way of life. The Canadian physician-historian William Osler (1849–1919) once noted:

> No man is really happy or safe without a hobby, and it makes precious little difference what the outside interest may be—botany, beetles or butterflies, roses, tulips or irises; fishing, mountaineering or antiquities—anything will do so long as he straddles a hobby and rides it hard. (Cushing, 1940, p. 871)

Play: A Continuous Process

The term "play" has different connotations for different people. For the infant, shaking a rattle is play. For a young child, it may be kicking a ball. For an adolescent, it may involve a team sport. For an adult, it may mean bowling or a card game, and for the elderly, perhaps a friendly game of chess.

Play is also experienced by many through exercise of the imagination and exploration of the world of fantasy, both of which are thought to stimulate a child's creative ability. Carl Jung (1875–1961) noted:

> The dynamic principle of fantasy is play, which belongs also to the child, and as such it appears to be inconsistent with the principle of serious work. But without this playing with fantasy no creative work has ever yet come to birth. The debt we owe to the play of imagination is incalculable. (1953, p. 82)

One generally accepted definition of play is "a self-motivated activity that is engaged in for the sake of the activity alone and results in a feeling of pleasure" (Berlyne, 1960). This statement is in contrast to the definition of work as "an activity engaged in order to attain a goal that lies beyond the activity itself and does not necessarily result in feelings of pleasure."

Owing to physical, cognitive, and social changes that take place as we mature and grow older, the nature of the activities engaged in may vary, but the need to engage in some type of play activity seems to persist throughout our lifetime.

INFANCY   Brian Sutton-Smith (1971) pointed out that "the pleasure in play is the pleasure of mastery; the functional becomes fun." For an infant, the whole world waits to be mastered—to be explored, analyzed, and controlled. Even the baby who is as young as two or three months is able to draw a connection between his or her actions and their effect on the environment. Normally, this cause-and-effect relationship is established as a by-product of interpersonal relationships—for instance, the baby's exploration of a parent's mouth will often result in the parent's making comical sounds and tickling the child. However, John Watson (1972) demonstrated that a baby will exhibit the same kind of play response (smiling and cooing) when seeing a mobile turning above the crib in response to the baby's movements; here, the baby's play is not totally dependent upon an interpersonal relationship.

As a baby matures, play continues to share an important role in the child's cognitive development. According to Jean Piaget (1896–   ), "Play is an assimilation of reality into the self." Piaget sees play as developing in qualitatively different stages as the child matures. He refers to the first stage as *practice play,* a period in which simple motor skills are explored, such as staring at a finger, mouthing objects, and banging things. The second stage is called *symbolic play* and represents the introduction of "make-believe." Piaget's third stage, called *cooperative play,* is distinguished by a reduction in the egocentric nature of the child's thinking and a greater interest and emphasis on "playing by the rules." Successful advancement to this third stage of development seems to be crucial to achieving adequate socialization.

The importance of play as a social function cannot be overemphasized. Play facilitates the development of language skills through the child's need to ask questions, give directions, and solve problems. Play also helps the child achieve a balance between independence and dependence as he or she establishes friendships and interacts with peer groups. Partin (1932) suggests that there are six different levels of play and peer interaction: *unoccupied*

The wonderful world of make-believe allows the child to easily manipulate a world that is otherwise very resistant to change. [*Erika Stone.*]

FIGURE 13.9

(random, nonspecific behavior); *solitary* (playing alone); *onlooker* (watching others playing but not participating); *parallel* (playing near, but not with, another child); *associative* (interacting, sharing, and taking turns); and *cooperative* (working and playing together with other children toward a common goal).

CHILDHOOD   The socializing aspect of play takes on a new characteristic, that of *interpersonal comparison,* as the child reaches school age. Play becomes a means of answering the questions "Who can run the fastest, jump the farthest, and climb the highest?" It is during this period that a child's motor proficiency and coordination commence to influence leadership selection (L. M. Jack, 1934), and the child's athletic abilities begin to be recognized as an important factor in the selection of playmates.

The selection of playmates is also heavily influenced by the child's sex (Helgerson, 1943), with most boys of preschool age preferring to play with other boys and most girls preferring to play with other girls. This same-sex preference among children tends to persist until adolescence and is strongly associated with a certain amount of sex typing of particular play activities. For example, playing with trucks was generally seen by seven- and eight-year-olds as a boys' game, while playing with doll carriages was a girls' game (Hardesty, 1964). It has been shown that the social assignment of "sex appropriateness" to otherwise neutral play activities has caused sixth-grade boys to perform best at "masculine" activities and sixth-grade girls to perform best at "feminine" activities. Both sexes performed their "worst" at "opposite sex" activities (Stein, Pohly, and Mueller, 1971). The results of such studies indicate that most children regard their play activities as an important source of feedback with regard to sex-role development and identification. Attitudes developed from such play activities tend to persist into adulthood.

ADOLESCENCE   The "sexual" connotations of play become more manifest as the child reaches adolescence and the competitive nature of play tends to increase. As a consequence, a great deal of adolescent "play" activity is often directed toward sports, strategy games, and dating.

Harry Stack Sullivan (1892–1949) divided adolescence into three major periods: preadolescence, early adolescence, and late adolescence. During *preadolescence,* the individual has a need for interpersonal intimacy; that is, a close, one-to-one relationship. This is in contrast with the earlier juvenile period in which groups of playmates are usually preferred. Freud called this preadolescence period the "homosexual" phase because the intimacy Sullivan referred to is usually developed between members of the same sex. The intimacy of this stage is, however, *nonsexual* and implies a best-friend relationship rather than a lover relationship. Most play activity during this period is with one's best friend.

Sullivan's *adolescence* phase is characterized by the introduction of sexual desires and the start of a gradual integration process wherein the upper-status members of a unisexual group will begin to form heterosexual relationships (Dunphy, 1963). During this phase, "play" becomes more oriented toward the opposite sex. This trend continues into *late adolescence,* when play activities become dominated by dating and courting activities.

ADULTHOOD   As an individual reaches adulthood, the importance of the peer group diminishes, the importance of selecting a mate increases, and "play" tends to be taken more seriously. Premarital playing often takes on the air of entertaining, and the motivation behind playing centers more on impressing others. As a consequence, the "toys" (cars, boats, skies, etc.) become more expensive, and the games (cards, racing, skydiving, etc.) become more other-oriented.

After marriage, play will often gravitate toward organized activities which are participated in on a routine basis; for instance, bowling on Friday nights or going to the annual picnic on the Fourth of July. Such activities are usually shared with close friends, and friendships are usually limited to two close friends who live in the same neighborhood (Babchuck, 1965). In most cases, the friends will be of the same sex rather than of the opposite sex.

Once a married couple have had children, their play activities are most often determined by the play-activity needs of the children. In most cases, this approach is mutually agreed upon and accepted as being compatible with promoting family unity and cohesiveness. In fact, after the children have been reared, many parents look back on such play activities as among the most satisfying times in their lives.

Once the children have left home, the parents once again begin to develop their own circle of friends and renew their interest in extrafamilial activities. With twice as many free hours as most people had in 1900, an individual's personal responsibility for the use of leisure time has become more and more important. Advancement in age and general state of health also have to be taken into consideration. As an acknowledgment of the importance of play with relation to health, an ever increasing number of middle-aged individuals are beginning to include more physically active recreation in their play rather than merely become sedentary spectators (De Vries, 1970). However, the type and amount of physical exertion must be kept appropriate to the unique characteristics and abilities of each individual.

Contrary to popular belief, the elderly need not, and most do not, stop

A youth-oriented society often has a tendency to disregard the recreational needs of the elderly, and their need to "play." [*F. Grunsweig, Photo Researchers.*]

FIGURE 13.10

playing. This is especially true for those who have maintained outside interests and activities during middle age (Zborowski, 1962). Since there are now almost 20 million Americans over sixty-five, and their numbers are increasing by 1600 every day (U.S. Census Bureau), meeting the recreational needs of the elderly is straining the resources of many communities. Thus, many private "senior citizen" and "golden years" organizations and clubs, as well as adult educational community college programs, have become popular supplements. Other older people convert their avocations or hobbies into second careers which serve the dual roles of satisfying the need to work and the need to play. Thus they support the claim of the English humorist and playwright Jerome K. Jerome (1859–1927) that "It is impossible to enjoy idling thoroughly unless one has plenty of work to do."

SUMMARY

In this chapter, the necessity for meaningfulness and significance has been discussed with regard to work. It was shown that occupation can influence one's personal identity, individual worth, and social status.

In addition, one's work skill can influence one's feelings of self-esteem. There is a relationship between the level of mastery of a particular skill and the level of esteem. This relationship provides for a progression of esteem from a state of being inadequate to a state of being important.

The traditional means by which men and women have chosen vocations, or have been forced into vocations, provide greater understanding of the problem of occupational adjustment. The problems of adjustment were investigated from the standpoint of individual aptitudes, mental abilities, and interests.

The stages of vocational development were also presented. In conjunction we explored the sources of worker discontent, such as morale, working conditions, and effects of supervisory attitudes. Where adjustment is improbable, retraining plays a role in achieving vocational satisfaction.

To emphasize the need for a balanced lifestyle, the importance of play and individual development and adjustment has also been considered here. We emphasized the concept that play must become an integral part of one's life from infancy to old age, and is not to be considered a unique dominion of childhood.

DISCUSSION QUESTIONS

1 What is it that would make your work meaningful?
2 What do you believe the difference is between what a person "does" and what a person "is"?
3 Do you believe that the Protestant work ethic, which advocates hard work, pride in craftsmanship, and perseverence, is as influential on workers as it once was?
4 What skills have you already mastered or do you hope to master? Include in your answer your work skills, play skills, and expressive art skills.
5 What sort of work gives you the greatest sense of satisfaction? Why?
6 Do you believe that women have equal opportunity in today's labor market?
7 For what kind of work do you think you possess a natural aptitude?
8 Do you believe that there should be a mandatory retirement age?
9 How important is "playing" in your parents lives? In your life? In the lives of children?
10 Do you believe that the use of leisure time is becoming a major problem among today's workers?

EXPERIENTIAL EXERCISES

1 As a class project, the students may draw up a list of ten occupations. Then they can be asked to rank-order these occupations in accordance with their estimation of which ones are the *most* prestigious. The frequency of each selection can then be tabulated. What occupations do you think seem to be the most universally prestigious? What gives each occupation its degree of prestige?
2 Arrange to spend some time at your community's unemployment office. Observe the composition of those seeking employment with regard to race, age, sex, or national heritage. Talk to a few of the applicants in an attempt to determine their attitudes toward being unemployed.
3 Turn off the TV for a night. Provide a variety of games to play (Monopoly, Scrabble, Chinese checkers, chess, etc.), and invite a group of friends to "play for the fun of it." Observe those who participate in the games. Are there some who seem to be unable to have fun, but tend to take the game too seriously? Ask the group to discuss what determines when a game is fun and when it is work.

PART FOUR

THE INDIVIDUAL

AS A GROWING BEING

CHAPTER 14

INTELLECTUAL AND

EMOTIONAL ADJUSTMENT

Intellect is a vital force in history, but it can also be a dissolvent and destructive power. Out of every hundred new ideas ninety-nine or more will probably be inferior to the traditional responses which they propose to replace. No one man, however brilliant or well-informed, can come in one lifetime to such fullness of understanding as to safely judge and dismiss the customs or institutions of his society, for these are the wisdom of generations after centuries of experiment in the laboratory of history.

Will and Ariel Durant
Lessons of History

The interrelationship between intellectual and emotional adjustment is very close indeed. Without knowledge there is ignorance, and where there is ignorance there is often fear and sometimes hatred. For example, a stranger may evoke feelings of fear and suspicion until you become acquainted. With greater knowledge such feelings may be replaced by acceptance and affection. Similarly, the desire for friendship may quickly disappear once you find that qualities you first admired in a new acquaintance are only superficial.

Emotional adjustment relies upon such intellectual factors as reason, logic, and continuity. When intellectual and emotional faculties work together, one is better equipped to evaluate and appraise the behavior and motives of others, the appropriateness of certain emotions, or the consequences of a particular event. For some, it is not enough to know what others are doing without also knowing their motivation; nor is it enough to evaluate the outcome of a decision without also considering the possible effects the decision may have on one's emotional future: that is, whether one can reasonably anticipate a future filled with loneliness and grief or with happiness.

Achieving a sense of harmony between intellectual capabilities and emotional capacities is essential to becoming a well-adjusted individual. Intellectual adjustment allows an individual to acquire not only knowledge but the ability to use it effectively, and emotional adjustment allows a person to accept a variety of emotional experiences and to share them appropriately.

INTELLECTUAL ADJUSTMENT

A great deal of what is referred to as "intellectual adjustment" is dependent on such concepts as intellectual *competence* and *flexibility*. Intellectual competence implies the ability to understand, to reason, and to solve problems effectively. Intellectual flexibility implies the capability to interpret the environment from more than just one perspective, to think creatively, and to develop a number of alternative plans concerning one's aspirations or goals.

However, intellectual adjustment also refers to the ability to learn about oneself, and thereby to develop a feeling of self-confidence with regard to one's potentials and a sense of acceptance toward one's limitations.

The Quest for Knowledge

The quest for knowledge is often synonymous with the quest to *understand;* to know the why and how of things. It can also include the quest for *information* upon which decisions can be based. But perhaps the quest for knowledge, more than anything else, is an integral part of the need to satisfy one's *curiosity:* the need to explore, to invent, and to discover. In this regard, knowledge is seen as an end in itself. However, for many, knowledge is seen as a means to an end, a tool to be used as a means of achieving some other measure of success.

THE NEED TO UNDERSTAND   Aristotle, in his *Metaphysics,* stated that "all men by nature desire knowledge." This early acknowledgment of the innateness of the "curiosity motive"—the need to know "why," the need to investigate the elements of cause and effect, novelty, and change—appears to be well supported in modern research. According to Alamshah (1963), the need to understand is an integral part of this basic need and "consists of tensions which motivate the self to identify the causes and the purposes of things."

From the need to identify the cause, we generate hypotheses, theoretical formulations, which, when confirmed, tend to satisfy our need to live in a *rational world.* These scientific theories are devised in an attempt to systematize our knowledge and to provide broader guidelines for our assumptions. Even with such guidelines, however, there is often a tendency to "overidentify" with the subjects of our scientific investigation, and, consequently, a tendency to anthropomorphize (ascribe human characteristics to something). In order to restrain such a tendency within the realm of psychological research, Conway Morgan (1852–1936) presented what is called "Morgan's canon" in his book entitled *Introduction to Comparative Psychology* (1895). In it he states: "In no case may we interpret an action as the outcome of the exercise of a higher psychical faculty, if it can be interpreted as the outcome of the exercise of one which stands lower in the psychological scale."

Scientific knowledge and the discovery of the relationship between cause and effect do not necessarily eliminate the tension of curiosity. There is often an additional component of such tension, which urges us also to discover the *purpose* of something, and it is to this end that we are led to seek a philosophical or theological understanding. Through these endeavors, we engage in the process of seeking *"truth,"* a process which Allport associates with what he refers to as *propriate striving;* that is, striving to reach one's full potential.

Propriate striving confers unity upon personality, but it is never the unity of fulfillment, of repose, or of reduced tension. The devoted parent never loses concern for his child; the devotee of democracy adopts a lifelong assignment in his human relationships. The scientist, by the very nature of his commitment, creates more and more questions, never fewer. Indeed the measure of our intellectual maturity, one philosopher suggests, is our capacity to feel less and less satisfied with our answers to better and better problems. (1955, p. 67)

For Allport, the great tasks of life, such as finding truth in art, science, and religion, are by their very nature never to be completed. Consequently, there will always be motivation in these areas. For Alamshah, "truth" is made up of a combination of both *knowledge* and *belief* that results in the formation of an ideal. As an ideal, we have knowledge of the potential for its existence; however, because of our own imperfections, we are able to recognize that there is much of "truth" that we may never understand. Yet, rather than becoming a source of continuous frustration, these unknowns often generate renewed interest and motivate even greater scientific efforts.

Murray (Kukhohn and Murray, 1953) also talks of the limitations of human understanding with regard to what is "knowable" about a person and what must remain "unknowable." In the statement, "Every man is in certain respects *(a)* like all other men, *(b)* like some other men, and *(c)* like no other man," Murray contends that, through the scientific efforts of anthropology, sociology, and psychology, *(a)* and *(b)* are "knowables." However, owing to the unique idiosyncracies of each individual—each person has some characteristic that is different from those of any other person—an element of each individual will always remain "unknowable."

DECISION MAKING   We are not necessarily responsible for everything that happens to us, but, according to such theorists as Viktor Frankl (1965) and William Glasser (1965), we are responsible for how we cope with what happens, or is likely to happen, to us. Each of us is free to choose what precautionary measures we are to take in our lives. For example, we have the freedom to decide whether to immunize ourselves against disease, exercise regularly, or get annual medical checkups; to open savings accounts or buy bonds; or to maintain our car on a regular basis, check on road conditions, or carry snow chains when heading into the mountains.

Frankl argues that not only are we free to make such choices, but also that we are *responsible* for the choices we make. He admonishes us, "Live as if you were living for the second time and had acted as wrongly the first time as you are about to act now" (1965, p. 64). What Frankl is telling us is to act as our own experienced advisor, one who has previously acted in an irresponsible manner and has had to pay the consequences. For example, imagine that what you are about to do (take a company car without permission, leave work early, drink on the job, etc.) resulted in your being fired the last time you did it. Would you advise you to do it this time?

Glasser believes that responsibility is a learned characteristic and must be taught as early as possible. In his book *Reality Therapy* (1965), he suggests:

Children ordinarily learn by means of a loving relationship with responsible parents, an involvement which implies parental teaching and parental example. In

Tests in themselves represent merely one appraisal of how much a student knows. That appraisal is symbolized by a grade, a grade that may or may not reflect the true dimensions of the student's knowledge. [*Mimi Forsyth, Monkmeyer Press.*]

FIGURE 14.1

addition, responsibility is taught by responsible relatives, teachers, ministers, and friends with whom they become involved. The responsible parent creates the necessary involvement with his child and teaches him responsibility through the proper combination of love and discipline. (p. 16)

INTELLECTUAL GOALS Each individual is personally responsible for determining what he or she wishes to achieve in life. In making plans for the future, one often must establish a set of priorities as to what is to be achieved first. Another important consideration is the need to decide on what particular type of success may be most satisfying. In this way, the relative importance of a certain goal or achievement can often be seen more clearly, and the risks involved, the amount of commitment required, and the price a person must pay for success can be put in their perspectives.

These points seem to be especially applicable to the setting of intellectual goals. Gerald Gladstein, author of *Individualized Study* (1967), explores the setting of intellectual goals from a college student's point of view. He makes a distinction between six types of intellectual achievement: academic, artistic, social, athletic, economic, or occupational success. In regard to *academic success*, Gladstein further distinguishes between the student who bases academic success on a high scholastic average and the one who equates success with a high level of scholastic learning. In the first situation, the student has often been rewarded for good grades rather than for good thinking and has therefore come to value the grade received more than the knowledge acquired. Typically, the consequences of such a value system are that the individual may be able to remember factual knowledge, but will often be unable to apply the knowledge effectively or creatively.

The type of success known as *artistic success* depends on a combination of inherent talents and acquired skills. It can be measured subjectively through the experience of having feelings of self-satisfaction and fulfillment, or objectively through the recognition the artist's work receives in the form of praise, awards, or financial gain. In many cases, the collegiate challenge comes from the need to master the artistic media which are to be used as a means of self-expression; that is, to become familiar with the tools, mechanics, and styles available. However, artistic advancement is often a relative measure of one's self-improvement, the gradual emerging of untapped talents, and the realization of one's full potential for expression.

A third type of success is labeled *social success*. Social success is often a matter of being accepted by others and of being able to function well in social situations. In most cases, the attainment of such goals is motivated by a sincere desire to belong to, and identify with, a particular group, such as a clique, club, fraternity, or sorority. However, in some cases, social success is actually a function of "status seeking" for the purpose of bolstering one's ego or of attaining a position which offers an advantage for future exploitation.

A similar division of motives is often found with regard to *athletic success*. In most cases, athletic success will incorporate such factors as being accepted as a member of a team, winning recognition of one's excellence by peers or coaches, or receiving letters or other symbols of achievement. However, for a few, athletic success may be measured only with regard to being "number one," winning, or being the best, and anything less than this status is considered to be failure.

Many students attend college with the goal of *economic success* as a primary motivation. However, owing to an overabundance of college graduates in many fields, the opportunities to secure high-paying jobs are often limited. In addition, many students with economic gain the only motivating force behind attending college often find the length of time they must wait before receiving any significant economic rewards unacceptable. As a consequence, they may leave college in quest of more immediate financial gratification.

Similarly, *occupational success* is often dependent upon the student's motive for wanting to enter a particular vocation. Some individuals value the attainment of the skills and knowledge necessary in order to make a meaningful contribution within a chosen profession. Others, however, tend to look primarily at the social prestige, financial gain, or job security associated with a certain profession.

From a very early age, much of what we learn is *discovered* through experience. [*Mary M. Thacher, Photo Researchers, Inc.*]

FIGURE 14.2

Gaining Knowledge

The premise that, at birth, a person's mind is a *tabula rasa,* or blank state, was proposed as far back as Aristotle. However, the formulation of this concept is credited to the efforts of the British philosopher John Locke. In his *Essay Concerning Human Understanding* (1690), Locke insisted that all knowledge is acquired through *experience.* The tabula rasa concept was later accepted by such behaviorists as Watson and Skinner as a complementary part of their theories concerning the acquisition of knowledge, or *learning.* To the behaviorists, learning is "a relatively permanent change in behavior due to some experience." The rate of change, the amount of change, and the nature of the change are dependent upon a combination of an individual's inherent abilities, motivation, and the quality of the environment.

John Phillips, in *The Origins of Intellect: Piaget's Theory* (1975), discriminates among various forms of learning according to *how* the knowledge is acquired:

Knowledge gained via logico-mathematical experience (e.g., conservation, classification, law of floating bodies) is *invented.* Knowledge gained via physical experience is *discovered* (rubber objects bounce, iron objects do not; round things roll, square ones do not; thin rods bend or break, thick ones do not). Knowledge gained through social transmission is merely *accepted* (this is a cow; we wash our hands before we eat; "he" is singular, "they" plural). (p. 141)

ABILITY VERSUS CAPABILITY   The term *ability* carries with it a number of connotations, such as inherent traits, physical or mental limits, and the current level of mastery associated with a particular task. As a consequence, most ability tests are designed to measure performance: performance of "familiar" tasks, as in a driving test, or "unfamiliar" tasks, as might be encountered in coordination testing. Many ability tests attempt to measure *maximum levels of performance,* and most "intelligence tests" would fall into this category.

It is important to keep in mind, however, that an IQ score usually represents a measure of one's *general mental ability,* which may be made up of a composite of "special" or *primary abilities*. Individuals may therefore have the same IQ scores yet vary markedly with regard to specific abilities. In one attempt to identify these primary abilities, Thurstone (1938, 1947) gave a series of tests to college students and concluded that there were six primary abilities: verbal (V), number (N), spatial (S), word fluency (W), memory (M), and reasoning (R).

This view of specific mental abilities, however, is not held by all theorists. Cattell (1963, 1971) proposed that general intelligence is a combination of *fluid intelligence* and *crystallized intelligence.* Fluid intelligence refers to those intellectual abilities, such as brightness and adaptability, that exist in a person independent of experience or education. On the other hand, crystallized intelligence is the cumulative result of socialization, training, and education. Other theorists tend to disregard any separation of intellectual functions and view intelligence as a unitary phenomenon (Spearman, 1927; Jensen, 1969).

Regardless of what an individual's intellectual abilities may be, however, definitions of intelligence often include not only the ability to acquire knowledge, but also the ability to *apply* the knowledge that has been acquired. Tests designed to measure how effectively a person is able to apply knowledge are known as "proficiency tests" or "achievement tests," and most college exams would fall into this category. While achievement tests evaluate how well a person *does* perform, they do not necessarily measure how well a person *can* perform. Tests which tend to predict future performance, or to measure a person's *capacity* to learn, are called "aptitude tests." The Differential Aptitude Tests (DAT) and General Aptitude Test Battery (GATB), along with many college entrance exams (ACT or SCAT), are examples of tests with strong predictive value as to future performance.

Having the aptitude, or capability, to do something, however, does not inevitably mean that a person will be motivated toward actually accomplishing a particular task or have the desire to master a particular skill. Jerome Kagan (1971) proposed that the motivation of *mastery* is more closely linked to probability than to certainty; that is, according to Kagan, the desire for mastery is not generated if either success or failure is "guaranteed." The probability of success is highly dependent on a realistic appraisal of one's capabilities so that one can sustain a hope of eventual success while not becoming bored with the ease at which it is attained. Mastery involves growth, and growth is often a by-product of having overcome challenges; therefore, a desire for mastery is often synonymous with a desire for personal growth.

PERCEPTION AND THINKING   The term "perception" refers to the process of *interpreting* sensory experiences, a process which allows people great latitude insofar as how they individually choose to define reality. Such freedom of choice allows for others to arrive at their own realities, which may or may not coincide with one's own impressions. For example, the four words presented below provide a sensory experience. In this situation, an individual's "reality" is the way he or she chooses to perceive the group of words; that is, the individual arrives at "reality" by determining which of the four words does not belong in the group. The words are "prayer," "temple," "church," and "skyscraper."

Many will perceive the words "prayer," "temple," and "church" as being religiously oriented, and therefore the word "skyscraper" is perceived as not belonging to the group. However, others will choose to perceive the words "temple," "church," and "skyscraper" as being buildings, and therefore the word "prayer" is judged as not belonging to the group.

There is no right or wrong answer to this example. Each person is free to choose either interpretation, just as anyone is free to interpret which person does not belong with a particular group of people, which college provides the best architectural program, or which candidate is best suited for an office.

The particular way a person perceives the world can be strongly influenced by learning experiences. For instance, the perceptual effects that language and the socialization process can have on an individual can be gross, as in the selection of verbal symbols, or words, used to represent various objects, or subtle, such as the use of specific gestures while conversing. However, some sociologists and linguists believe that the influence of socialization on language goes far beyond merely the selection of words and gestures.

Edward Sapir (1934) and Benjamin Whorf (1956) proposed a hypothesis that the way people *perceive* the world, their *conception of space and time,* and the very *nature of their thinking* are affected by their cultural experiences and the acquisition of their native language. In support of this hypothesis, examples of linguistic differences among cultures are pointed out, such as the Eskimo's use of about thirty different words referring to snow and ice, with three words (quali, kimoagruk, and pukak) for snow alone (Whorf, 1940); the ability of the Hanunoo tribe, in the Philippines, to refer to ninety-two varieties of rice (Brown, 1965); or the reported existence of some 6000 Arabic words for camel. According to Whorf, not only are objects "seen" differently from culture to culture, but time is also experienced differently. For example, the Hopi language has one grammatical category for "temporary" events and another for long-term events, plus the view that past, present, and future events are all experienced in the "now." Therefore, the language does not carry the same implications of past and future tenses as those that occur in the English language.

Those who are in opposition to the Sapir-Whorf hypothesis argue that such discriminatory differences in languages are a result of *cultural need* rather than *perceptual ability;* that is, the Eskimos and Arabs have a need to discriminate among different kinds of snows or camels, whereas most English-speaking cultures do not have this need. However, should such a need arise, the perceptual abilities of the English-speaking population would be equal to those of the Eskimo or Arab.

Although Sapir and Whorf arrived at their hypothesis on "linguistic determinism" independently in the late twenties and thirties, proof of their hypothesis has been evasive. As a consequence, the controversial hypothesis has been modified to propose that language does not necessarily have the profound effect on thinking that it was once thought to have, but that it does provide the *conceptual categories* that influence how experiences are encoded and stored in memory. Support for this revision is provided by research such as that conducted by Miller and McNeal (1969), which substantiated their prediction that since the language of the Zuni Indians had only one word for both the colors of yellow and orange, they would have difficulty with memory tests involving these two colors, but not in perceiving these colors.

LEARNING AND MEMORY   During the process of growing up, each person seems to be the subject of continuous evaluation and to be exposed to an almost constant bombardment of appraisals from others. It is not uncommon to hear statements such as "My, you're tall for your age," "The child is gifted [retarded]," or "The child is a fast [slow] learner." The problem with such statements, especially those concerning mental abilities, is that they are usually generalizations which are being presented as though they were absolutes. In addition, one can develop problems with one's self-esteem should one come to believe such statements.

For instance, being labeled a "slow learner" implies that the individual has difficulty with all forms of learning, which is usually not the case. Therefore, it is important to realize that, depending on the particular type of learning involved, individual performance can vary. Some persons tend to have difficulty with regard to *trial-and-error* learning, while others seem to thrive on it. Trial-and-error learning involves the ability to "profit by one's mistakes," so that responses that do not lead to the desired consequences are discarded (Thorndike, 1911). Going through a ring of keys until the key that opens the lock is found is an example of the trial-and-error learning process. As one might expect, the personality characteristics of *patience* and *persistence* are essential to the success of this type of learning. Thomas Edison, for example, tried literally hundreds of different materials before discovering a practical filament for the light bulb.

For most students, *rote learning* is the form of learning most frequently used. Rote learning involves the tedious task of repeatedly going over material until it is mastered. Often this task can be eased if the learning is managed properly. For instance, a student with a list of items, such as names, dates, or formulas, to learn has the option of using the *whole method* or the *part method* when attempting to memorize the material. When using the whole method, the student will run through the entire list each practice session. When using the part method, the student concentrates on only a portion of the list at a time. When one portion is mastered, the student then progresses to another portion, and so on until the entire list is learned.

With regard to studying, the student also has the option of using a *massed practice* or *distributed practice* method of learning. When using the massed practice method, the student will read through a chapter, or section, of material, and upon completion, immediately start through the material again without inserting a rest period between sessions. In contrast, when the distributed practice method is used, a rest period is inserted between each study session.

In most cases, the part method in combination with a distributed practice approach to studying will be the most effective means of learning the material. Theoretically, one of the reasons for this combination's effectiveness is the limitation on the brain's "holding" capacity; that is, the brain's ability to store bits of information while in the process of transforming this information into a permanent memory (McGaugh, 1963, 1970). Therefore, by limiting the amount of information one places in a "holding pattern" (the part method) and allowing the brain time to transform information into a permanent form (the rest period in distributed practice), one enhances the learning procedure. Besides, should someone comment on the fact that the student appears to be "taking a break" instead of studying, the student can reply, "Don't harass me; I'm in the process of building a permanent memory."

Just as some students may have doubts concerning their ability to learn, an even greater number seem to be uncertain about their ability to remember. Often these doubts are expressed by such statements as "I can't believe it. I just finished reading that chapter not more than an hour ago, and I doubt if I can remember half of what I read." Actually, the student's estimation of his or her recall is probably quite accurate, for, in most cases, this would be the expected level of recall.

Ebbinghaus (1964), one of the first to measure the *rate of forgetting,* found that, initially, there is a rapid loss of recently learned information; following this initial drop in the amount of information retained, there is a gradual reduction in the rate of loss until the stability of a permanent memory is achieved. It is important for a student to be aware of this loss rate in order to avoid the disappointment that often comes from having crammed for an exam a few hours before the test is given. Ebbinghaus found that twenty minutes after the information had been memorized, 47 percent had been lost; after one hour, 55 percent had been lost, and after twenty-four hours, 62 percent had been lost. But after two days, there was relatively little additional loss of information. With this in mind, one can see the advantage of studying well in advance of the time when the information may need to be retrieved.

FIGURE 14.3
There is often a high degree of impulsiveness associated with emotions, and in extreme states of arousal our problem-solving capacities tend to diminish. [*Ellen Levine, Editorial Photocolor Archives.*]

EMOTIONAL ADJUSTMENT

Although we are born with the capacity to experience emotions, the exact thing that generates, or triggers, a particular emotion is learned. In addition, the specific manner of expressing emotions is also learned and, perhaps even more important, our *attitudes* toward certain emotions are also subject to cultural and social influences (Averill, 1976). As a consequence, some emotions are perceived as being "bad," while others are to be sought after.

Such attitudes tend to perpetuate the belief that people should maintain control over their emotions; that is, that when "undesirable" emotions cannot be avoided altogether, one should demonstrate restraint toward their expression. Even where "desirable" emotions are concerned, impulsive, unrestricted expression is discouraged in preference to expression that is considered to be appropriate for the circumstances.

In most cases, it is the person's attitude toward a particular emotion, rather than the emotion itself, that causes problems with adjustment. It is the fear of being considered weak that usually restrains a person from crying openly, a sense of guilt that often prevents a person from acknowledging anger, or feelings of hurt and resentment that frequently cause a person to withhold feelings of love. As a consequence, an individual is not given sufficient opportunity to become familiar with certain emotions to develop a sense of confidence toward their expression.

In contrast, emotional adjustment requires (1) an acceptance of the naturalness of *all* emotions, (2) the development of acceptable emotional expression, and (3) the development of emotional expression that is truly representative of the person's real feelings.

What Are Emotions?

Emotions can be defined as the state of increased arousal experienced in response to physiological changes which prepare a person to move away from, toward, or against a source of stress. Emotions are primarily the feelings associated with a particular experience. In fact, for many, emotions *are* the experience; that is, it is the emotions which provide the vitality and essence of an experience. For example, reading that a number of auto accidents occurred over the weekend can be informative, but reading that a close friend was among the fatalities can be a highly emotional experience. In the process of remembering that specific event, people will most likely remember the way they felt, rather than what they thought.

Emotions are also looked upon as *energizers,* or the activating force behind motivation (Leeper, 1970). For this reason, in most instances when we ask someone to get more involved with what is going on, we are actually asking the person to become more emotionally involved. The amount of effort a person puts forth is often directly proportional to the intensity of the emotional involvement. There are a number of theories as to why a particular emotion may be generated and why the level of intensity may vary. A few of these theories are presented in the following sections.

JAMES-LANGE THEORY OF EMOTION   William James (1842–1910), the noted American psychologist, was one of the first to perceive a link between emotions and physiological changes. In his book *Principles of Psychology* (1890), James presented his hypothesis that, with regard to an emotional response, physiological changes take place in the body first, to be followed by the experience of an emotion.

James's theory was supported by the Danish physiologist Carl Lange (1895), and it then became known as the James-Lange theory of emotion. For almost forty years, it remained virtually unchallenged; many people attempted to control their emotions by controlling their behavior, while others believed that if they did not express any emotions, they would not feel any emotions.

CANNON-BARD THEORY OF EMOTION   Walter Cannon (1871–1945) was also interested in the connection between physiological changes and emotions. Through subsequent investigations, he was able to demonstrate how the sympathetic nervous system, along with adrenal secretions, would prepare the body for "flight or fight." Cannon presented his findings in his book *Bodily Changes in Pain, Hunger, Fear, and Rage* (1915). Through continued research, however, he gradually shifted his proposed center for emotional experiences to the mid-brain area, especially the thalamus and hypothalamus.

In 1927, Cannon challenged the James-Lange theory and proposed that it is the thalamus that really determines the nature of emotions, and that they are not merely the result of monitoring physical changes in the body. He believed that sensory experiences are simultaneously relayed to both the brain and the body, and that the "emotional experience" takes place in the brain, regardless of what physiological changes occur. Cannon, working closely with his pupil Philip Bard, conducted extensive research in order to provide support to this theory. As a result, the theory became known as the Cannon-Bard theory of emotion. Their research pointed out several discrepancies in the James-Lange theory, such as (1) that cats whose spines had been severed (thereby preventing an awareness of any physical changes that might take place) were still able to experience emotions; (2) that, although the physiological changes associated with fear and anger differ somewhat, similar discriminating differences do not appear with regard to other emotional response; and (3) that many physiological changes take place too slowly to be an effective influence on rapidly occurring emotional reactions.

COGNITIVE THEORY OF EMOTION   More recent research (Schacter and Singer, 1962) has led to a theory of emotions that incorporates elements of both the James-Lange and the Cannon-Bard theories. Known as the *cognitive theory of emotions,* this theory proposes that emotional experiences are dependent upon both the physiological changes taking place and the nature of the situation. In Schacter's words, "Given a state of physiological arousal for which an individual has no immediate explanation, he will label this state and describe his feelings in terms of the cognitions available to him" (1962, p. 398).

As an illustration of this theory, imagine a couple of students waiting for the instructor to read off some exam scores. One of the students might share with the other the fact that he feels weak, his palms are sweating, and he is afraid that he might throw up (physiological changes). The other student may sympathize with the first by relating that she has felt the same way—once when she had to tell how she managed to wreck her father's car, and once when she fell in love with her physical ed teacher (nature of the situation).

Aggression

Since we seem to live in a society that has come to accept aggression and violence as integral parts of our way of life, it is not too surprising to find that a great deal of study and research is being devoted to achieving a greater understanding of the nature of aggression. Owing to a diversity of approaches and philosophical biases, there are a number of competing hypotheses as to what aggression really is, where it originates, and whether it is instinctual or learned, a product of frustration or imitation, or merely generated out of boredom.

INSTINCTUAL OR LEARNED?   Along with his concept of a "life instinct" (eros), which included such survival-oriented drives as hunger, thirst, and sex, Sigmund Freud, in his book *Beyond the Pleasure Principle* (1920), introduced another concept called the "death instinct" (thanatos) as an explanation for aggression, destructiveness, and such neurotic manifestations as sadism and masochism. Freud argued that when the aggressive energy generated by the death instinct is directed inward, a person will become suicidal, masochistic, and self-destructive.

Such masochistic tendencies were thought to be *unconscious* means of inflicting self-punishment through *indirect aggression*. A person may accomplish this goal by such methods as becoming accident-prone, setting himself or herself up to fail, or developing psychosomatic illnesses. However, when the aggression is directed outward, Freud believed that a person will become homicidal, sadistic, and other-destructive.

The release of this aggression can take an active or a passive form, and can be expressed directly or displaced. *Active aggression* is expressed through overt physical or verbal means, such as fighting or cursing. *Passive aggression* is often expressed covertly or through omission, such as "being late for an appointment" or failing to remind a fellow employee that he is leaving for labor negotiations without the contract that is on his desk. If the aggression is expressed directly at the source of the feeling, it is called *direct aggression,* such as when a roommate borrows clothing without permission and is "chewed out" for having taken such a liberty. When aggression is redirected to a source other than the original cause of the feeling, it is regarded as *displaced aggression,* such as when a person kicks a desk after receiving a rejection notice from a highly desirable college.

Another prominent theorist who advocated an instinctual explanation for aggression was Konrad Lorenz, a well-known ethologist (one who studies the relationships between animals and their natural habitat). He believed that aggression is instinctual in *all* social animals, including humans. Lorenz presented this theory in his controversial book *On Aggression* (1966). Almost simultaneously, Robert Ardrey, in his book *The Territorial Imperative* (1966), also argued in favor of an instinctual explanation of aggression. However, Ardrey links aggression with territorial invasion. He believes that animals, including humans, "stake out" particular territories, and aggressive behavior is a result of an outsider's trespassing, or intruding, on that territory; the deeper the intrusion, the more violent the attack.

Although the "instinctual" theories on aggression put forth by Freud, Lorenz, and Ardrey have been generally rejected by the academic community, many sociologists accept the concept of "individual territory" or "personal space," which is an informally declared area considered to be "owned," and therefore inviolate. The size of this space varies from culture to culture, and generally, it decreases as the intimacy of a relationship increases.

FRUSTRATION OR IMITATION? Another "instinctually" related theory on aggression is that proposed by John Dollard and Neal Miller (1939), and later modified by Leonard Berkowitz (1965). Originally, Dollard and Miller proposed that aggression is an *instinctual response to frustration*. Frustration was seen as the result of having "goal-directed behavior blocked by a physical obstacle,

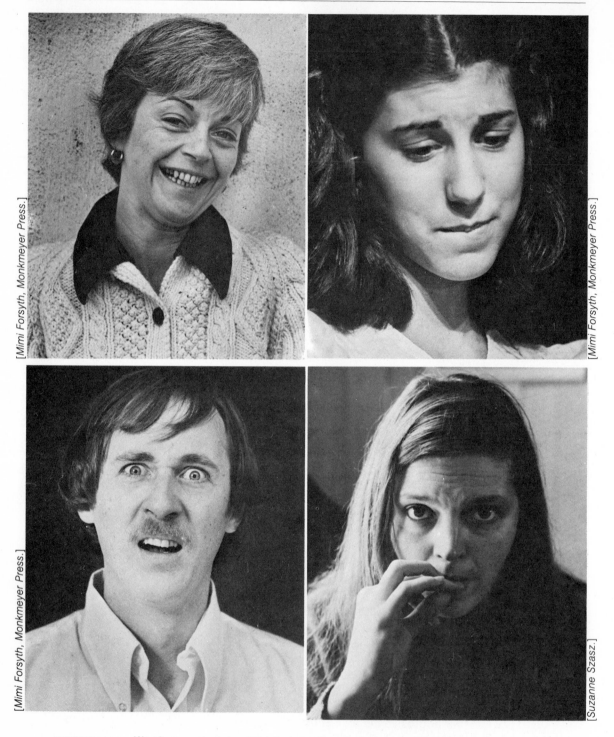

FIGURE 14.4   We often reveal what we think by how we talk and what we feel by how we look.

deficiency, or conflict." The resulting aggression can take the form of *primary aggression* or *secondary aggression*. Primary aggression is distinguished by the appropriateness of the reaction to the frustrating situation. Becoming irate and complaining to the maître d'hôtel when a previously reserved table is given to someone else is an example of primary aggression. Beating up the busboy and smashing the wine racks because another person's party is seated before one's own would be an example of secondary aggression; it is often unrelated to the current situation, but is, rather, an opportunity to vent pent-up hostility.

Further research, however, indicated that aggression can occur in the absence of observable frustration, and that aggression is not the only response which can result from experiencing frustration. It was found that, depending on previous experience, the response to frustration can be one of apathy, avoidance, denial, rationalization, or any number of alternate behavior patterns. As a consequence of these findings, frustration was seen as merely an *instigation* to aggression. Berkowitz further revised the Dollard and Miller theory to include *environmental cues* as influential factors in determining whether or not frustration will lead to aggressive behavior.

Albert Bandura, through his social learning theory, rejects the concept that aggression is a product of instincts. He theorizes that aggressive behavior results from having observed aggressive behavior in others and having imitated that behavior. Consequently, if children are reared by aggressive parents, exposed to overt aggression between parents or siblings, or the victims of harsh and abusive disciplinary techniques, they are likely to become aggressive and abusive adults. Those who are reared in a democratic atmosphere which emphasizes cooperation and consideration are likely to be less aggressive as adults (Bandura and R. H. Walters, 1963; Walters and Llewellyn Thomas, 1963).

BOREDOM   Erich Fromm, author of *The Heart of Man* (1964) and *The Anatomy of Human Destructiveness* (1973), wrote in an article:

> Probably the most important source of aggression and destructive rage is found in the *bored character.* Boredom, in this sense, is not conditioned by external circumstances, not by the lack of stimulation, for example, as in the experiments in which sensual perceptions are shut out, or as in the isolation cell of a prison. It is a *subjective factor in man himself,* an incapacity to enter into a real interest in things and people in his environment. (Quoted in Reif, 1975, p. 22)

Fromm believes that boredom is a product of the modern industrialized societies in which a person is often perceived as an instrument or as an extension of a machine. Under such circumstances, Fromm believes, life loses its meaning and many individuals lose hope and fall into a state of despair, developing what Nietzsche called a "resentment" toward life. Fromm postulates that this resentment can generate anger and even hate within a person.

He hates life because he is aware of what he is missing. He hates life because he experiences his loneliness, his isolation, and cannot attempt anything against it. He hates life because he cannot master it in any other sense, namely, in the sense of joy in living, in the sense of loving, understanding behavior, the sense of solidarity, of interest in people, in the sense of joy in the creation. (Reif, 1975, p. 22)

According to Fromm, aggression is the natural consequence of such feelings and may result in acts of violence. The aggressive action may appear in the form of *revengeful violence,* an attempt to "hurt back," or, when a person is no longer able to accept such a state of powerlessness, the action may take the form of *compensatory violence* "as a substitute for productive activity in an impotent person."

Dealing with Emotional Paradoxes

On the surface, the hedonistic principles of seeking pleasure and avoiding pain seem practical enough. However, in reality, pleasure cannot always be found and emotional pain cannot always be avoided. On the contrary, in some instances, just the reverse seems to be true; that is, some individuals appear deliberately to attempt to avoid happiness and to seek pain. The exact reasons behind such paradoxical behavior may vary; however, in many cases, the behavior becomes habitual and the consequences will be all too familiar.

THE FEAR OF HAPPINESS   Many times, through either frequent reinforcement, selective choice, or unconscious motivation, some people will come to believe that "happiness is evil" and should therefore be avoided whenever possible. Therefore, many individuals will seek out relationships in which they can most easily avoid being happy.

Such a notion is usually acquired indirectly from the teachings of our parents and society. For example, our parents might have remarked, "That Mrs. Harding is such a good woman. My land, the way she suffers and sacrifices with never so much as a cross word! She's not at all like Mrs. Alton, spending her hard-earned money on such foolishness as dancing, yoga, and the like." Sometimes, however, the teaching of the view that happiness is evil is more direct. For instance, a parent might say, "Mark my words, you're going to have to pay the piper." Or one may have been taught that one must pay for some indiscretion "in the morning," or merely "sooner or later." It doesn't seem to matter who the debtor was or when the debt was due, so long as the point got across that "nothing is free in life"; and because a person has enjoyed something or has been happy, that person is then indebted, and the debt must be paid. As a result, many people will attempt to "work off" this debt in a relationship, with an attitude of "I've had my fun. Now I'm going to have to pay for it."

A supporting attitude that can also be very detrimental to a relationship is

Interpreting the outward
expression of an emotion is not
always easy, for there are tears
of happiness as well as tears of
sorrow and rage. [*Suzanne
Szasz.*]

FIGURE 14.5

the belief that "nothing good lasts forever." As a consequence of such an attitude, many people will become uneasy when a relationship has been going *too* well for *too* long. They will often make such statements as "I don't know—things have been going too well lately. Something bad is bound to happen soon." Or, "My luck can't hold out forever. Someday she's going to take a real good look at me, and it's going to be all over." Such pessimism often leads to "self-fulfilling prophecy," wherein a person will deliberately do something to destroy the relationship. Such a person may even take advantage of an innocent situation and manage to break up the relationship over something that he or she did not do. Outside observers may ask, "Why didn't you tell her [or him] it wasn't you?" And the accused will often reply, "Listen, if I haven't developed more trust than that by this time, then I deserve whatever's coming to me."

THE FEAR OF SUCCESS   It's quite common to perceive our failures as being someone else's fault or due to circumstances beyond our control. Often we prefer not to consider the possibility that our failure might be mostly our responsibility, that our actions might have, in some way, expedited our failure. Consciously, one would think that the frustration, depression, and feelings of inadequacy which frequently accompany failure would make it something to avoid at all costs. Yet, many times, we may find ourselves doing little or nothing in order to avoid failing. At such times, it may seem as if we were deliberately setting ourselves up to fail. Such self-defeating behavior, however, is often the result of an unconscious motivation to set oneself up to fail out of a fear of success.

Women appear to possess a fear of success that is also unconsciously linked with their sexuality, their femininity. However, according to Martina Horner (1969), the cause of this fear is more likely to be social than instinctual. Horner's research centered on her theory regarding the motive to avoid success and the attitudes our society holds toward successful professional women. Although they have yet to be scientifically validated, her preliminary findings indicate that professional success is associated with a loss of femininity, social rejection, and personal or societal destruction. Horner's findings further suggest that regardless of the lip service being given to "women's liberation," the majority of both males and females in our society still believe that true feminine fulfillment is to be found in marriage and having a family. Such expectations and pressures are not so great during a girl's early academic life, and therefore a higher percentage of girls tend to achieve excellent grades during their elementary school education. However, social pressure gradually increases as the child grows older, and as a consequence, a lesser proportion go on to achieve academic excellence in high school and college. The implication is that females in our culture are programmed by society to fear success.

THE FEAR OF AUTHENTIC LOVE Although their theoretical approaches are widely separated, both Harlow (1959) and Maslow (1970), as well as many other theorists, agree that in order to develop into a well-adjusted individual, a person requires a certain amount of love. Yet, many people not only do not receive enough love, but also often actively avoid, or escape from, opportunities in which they might experience a satisfying love relationship.

In most instances, such avoidance is the result of past misfortunes and is motivated by a fear of being hurt again. Having been naive and vulnerable in the past and, as a result, exploited, many individuals become suspicious and defensive with regard to any new relationships. Such an individual will often want the other person in a relationship to reveal inner thoughts and feelings without benefit of any reciprocal effort at "self-disclosure." As a consequence, the sense of intimacy which is so desperately sought after becomes almost impossible to achieve. When one refuses to commit oneself to a relationship, authentic love cannot develop.

Others avoid authentic love by maintaining the belief that they are "unworthy" of being loved, fearing that they will be incapable of loving back in kind. However, Hodge, in *Your Fear of Love* (1967), believed:

> If we postponed the experience and expression of love until we no longer feared it, we would postpone it forever. Some people do appear to use their fear of love as a perpetual excuse for stalemated living—loving and trembling seem to go together. If we desire love we must learn to love in spite of our fears. (pp. 267–268)

Some individuals fear love because of a low level of self-esteem and a poor self-image, often believing that they are "unlovable." Yet, even with such attitudes, the desire for love is not eliminated, and therefore each source of love is guarded jealously.

In such cases, in place of an authentic love relationship based on mutual respect, freedom, and dignity, an individual who is desperate for love will often develop a parasitic relationship based on mistrust, oppression, and irreverence. Control within the relationship becomes paramount. The other person in the relationship is usually viewed as a possession that is to be molded and changed so as to become a more effective means of satisfying the needs of the oppressor. In such a relationship, there is little opportunity to grow to truly know another individual, nor is there room for individual freedom and personal growth.

GETTING REJECTED   Unfortunately, there seem to be a great many people who demonstrate an incredible persistence, dedication, and consistency in their pattern of setting themselves up to get rejected. The failure pattern of such individuals often becomes quite familiar to those around them, but rarely are any attempts at counseling ever successful. This lack of success usually occurs because the "counselors" are seldom aware of just how much such people may really want a relationship to fail.

People who really want a relationship to fail will often assume a very negative attitude toward everything and everyone, as if to set the mood by rejecting first. They will often reject invitations to attend parties, clubs, social, or sporting events, or any other functions that might enable them to enjoy themselves—that might present an opportunity for them to share experiences. They may also reject all opportunities to develop such skills as dancing, doing well in sports, or using artistic talents.

If such attempts at anonymity fail, then the negativism may be focused directly on why the individuals in the relationship are unsuited for each other. The person wanting to be rejected may point out the faults of the other by saying, for example, "I don't think I've ever met anyone as clumsy as you," or "Your lack of education really shows." Often, however, it is sufficient merely to remark that the other person is of a different age, nationality, religion, education, family background, etc.

Differences can also be used in the development of the "noblest" of all reasons for being rejected, one's *unworthiness;* that is, not being good enough for the other person. Often people who think they are unworthy will say that they are not smart enough, rich enough, or attractive enough. This type of person may also emphasize that he or she is not much fun on a date, does not know how to do anything, and cannot seem to keep friends. In addition, if such individuals are truly dedicated to getting themselves rejected, they may even volunteer potentially harmful information, such as rumors of insanity in their family, their friendship with inmates of Sing Sing, or their having been fired from their last three jobs.

GETTING HURT   Some people are not satisfied with just setting themselves up to be rejected. They want to assure that they get hurt as well. It often seems as if the people who "want" to get hurt are able to demonstrate an almost supernatural ability for detecting and selecting that certain someone who will satisfy their need to be hurt. Intuition appears to play an important part in this process, but past experience is often helpful. They will usually stay with, or return to, someone who has hurt them before. This masochistic tendency frequently bewilders concerned onlookers, but they usually explain the behavior away by saying, "It must be love." Unfortunately, it usually is not love, but merely a desire to set oneself up to be hurt.

People who get themselves hurt consistently tend to select the people who may hurt them from among those about whom they have been warned. Statements like "Stay away from that one—you'll just end up getting yourself hurt" seem merely to increase their appetites. Such people seem to prefer the "hurting" type. The insensitive sociopath may say, "I don't know what it is that attracts me to him. Maybe it's the way he looks at me after he has beaten his dog, or the way he sweats just before he steals something." They also tend to choose someone who is presently in the process of hurting someone else: "Sure she knows I'm with you. All torn up about it, too, but right now you're all that matters." In fact, one of the most efficient methods for setting themselves up to be hurt is to select someone who is already deeply committed to another person. In this way, they can better assure themselves that the relationship will (1) be with someone who is untrustworthy, (2) probably not last, and (3) most likely end up in their getting hurt.

THE PAIN OF DIVORCE   There is little doubt that the termination of a marriage is an event filled with misery. Holmes and Rahe (1967) developed a social readjustment scale which places a comparative value on how much stress a specific event will normally inflict on an individual. In the development of their scale, they found that the most stressful event in a person's life is the death of a spouse (100 points), followed by divorce (73 points) and marital separation (65 points). Fourth on the list is a jail term (63 points).

The misery seems to be almost universal, with both the husband and the wife experiencing their fair share. In order to reduce some of the pain, many turn to food and/or alcohol, often developing problems with obesity or drinking. Others will turn to sex or their work, developing problems with promiscuity or workaholism. In a survey of 425 divorced women, William Goode found that only 37 percent had not suffered seriously after divorce.

The life of divorced people is often loaded with demands for readjustment. The familiar world they once knew suddenly becomes unfamiliar, and it is filled with uncertainties. Friends of the family often become distant or take the other partner's side. Divorced males and females are often seen as potential threats by other spouses. Male friends, acquaintances, and associates often view the newly divorced wife as "sex-starved," and she may be inundated with sexual overtures. The question of how to be a good single parent arises (81 percent of divorced mothers work), and the individual is often torn between the desire to be "free at last" and the desire to be a "dutiful parent."

The stress resulting from the termination of a marriage, however, is not limited to the two adults involved. It can often have a major impact on the children as well. Many children will assume partial responsibility for the death of a parent or a divorce, believing that their behavior or wishes, expressed or unexpressed, somehow contributed to the death or the parents' split. In most cases, the child is faced with the crisis of being left by at least one parent. The Population Reference Bureau points out that two of every five children born in this decade will live in single-parent homes for at least part of their youth; 16 percent will live with their mothers only; 1 percent with their fathers only; 3 percent with custodians; and 13 percent with remarried parents. In addition, the children are often used by the parents as a means of getting back at one another or of proving to each other which parent the children love the most. Such emotional manipulation can be expected to exact a toll on the emotional and social adjustment of the children. Surveys indicate that children from broken homes are more likely to become delinquent than those coming from unbroken homes, and that the rate of delinquency is highest among those who have lost a parent through death.

It may or may not be true that "misery loves company," but divorced people show a tendency to seek out other divorced people, and surviving spouses tend to seek out other widows or widowers as companions. Perhaps the Roman poet Syrus expressed their plight best in his maxim, "It is a consolation to the wretched to have companions in misery."

SUMMARY

In this chapter, the basic principles of intellectual and emotional adjustment were discussed. The quest for knowledge was explored from the standpoint of the need to understand the world one lives in and the part effective decision making plays in the development of an adaptive lifestyle. There are various types of success, including academic, artistic, social, athletic, economic, and occupational success. In conjunction with intellectual goal setting, the need to realistically appraise one's abilities is important. Biases may affect one's perception of the environment. The effects of preferences for learning or remembering techniques were also explored.

The problems associated with emotional adjustment were investigated from the standpoint of various theoretical explanations for emotions, including the James-Lange, Cannon-Bard, and cognitive theories of emotions. The derivation and expression of aggression were also investigated, with special emphasis on instincts, frustration, and boredom.

Also included was a discussion of the problems which arise when dealing with emotional paradoxes, such as wanting to be successful but fearing success, and wanting to be happy but fearing happiness. Perhaps the most important of all paradoxes, however, is the desire to have an authentic love relationship but fearing love, and often finding that one has set oneself up to be rejected or hurt repeatedly.

DISCUSSION QUESTIONS

1   Do you believe that science can provide ultimate truths or only knowledge in its current state?
2   Do your intellectual goals lie primarily in attaining good grades or in acquiring knowledge?
3   Do you believe that a person's IQ is mostly a product of heredity, environment, or both?
4   Do you think that students with IQs above 132 should be categorized as gifted and placed in special programs or treated the same as the other students?
5   Which emotion are you most uncomfortable with? For example, are you most uncomfortable when you feel anger, anxiety, embarrassment, affection, or some other emotion?
6   Are you ever aware of others trespassing on your territorial space? For example, entering your room, going into your desk or closet, sitting on your bed or desk, or reading your books or notes?
7   What is most likely to frustrate you? Under what conditions are you most likely to get bored?
8   Do you become a little anxious when things have been going "too well for too long," for fear that something bad is about to happen?
9   What are some of the ways you have seen people set themselves up to fail?
10 How do you deal with rejection or the fear of being rejected?

EXPERIENTIAL EXERCISES

1   Arrange with a local school district for a group of students to visit classes for gifted children and classes for the educationally handicapped. Investigate the student-teacher ratios, cost per student, criteria for selecting the students, etc. Have the members of the group share their experiences and acquired information with the rest of the class.
2   Arrange for graduate students to speak to the class on the stresses associated with graduate school. Ask them to discuss what their recommendations would be for the undergraduate with regard to preparing for a master's or Ph.D. program. What do they consider to be some major mistakes that undergraduates should try to avoid?
3   Arrange to have representatives of Parents Without Partners, or of a community center which helps battered wives or children, appear as guest speakers. Ask them to discuss how different people attempt to cope with rejection, abandonment, divorce, or being physically or emotionally abused.

CHAPTER 15

PSYCHOLOGICAL

RESOURCES

Let me, finally, say a word about the encounter in the therapeutic relationship. To be able to sit in a real relationship with another human being who is going through profound anxiety or guilt or the experience of imminent tragedy taxes the best of the humanity in all of us. . . . In this encounter I have to be able, to some extent, to experience what the patient is experiencing. My job as a therapist is to be open to his world. He brings his world with him and therein we live for fifty minutes.

Our chief concern in therapy is with the potentiality of the human being. The goal of therapy is to help the patient actualize his potentialities. . . . The goal of therapy is not the absence of anxiety, but rather the changing of neurotic anxiety into normal anxiety. The patient after therapy may well bear more anxiety than he had before, but it will be conscious anxiety and he will be able to use it constructively. Nor is the goal the absence of guilt feeling, but rather the transformation of neurotic guilt into normal guilt, together with the development of the capacity to use this normal guilt creatively.

Rollo May
Psychology and the Human Dilemma

USING PSYCHOLOGICAL RESOURCES

Although the title *The Agony and the Ecstasy* (1961) identifies Irving Stone's novel about the life of Michelangelo, in many cases, it could easily describe a typical student's experience with college. For one's college years can be a time of intense feelings of alienation and loneliness, as well as of the deepest feelings of love and belonging. It can also be a period of humiliating failures as well as unqualified successes. The years spent attending college often require a person to cope with emotional extremes, a multitude of personal doubts, and severe social stress with only the very minimum of life's experiences from which to draw. As a consequence, living with anxiety often becomes commonplace, and bouts with depression can be frequent and intense. However, college can also be a time for "finding" oneself and for personal growth, a time for expanding one's self-awareness and recognizing untapped potentials.

In either case, the agony or the ecstasy, psychological resources can be of tremendous assistance by providing a means of gaining personal insight, emotional support, or increased motivation and new direction. In other words, although a person may require some psychological assistance as a result of stress, there is no longer a need to be "crazy" in order to go to a "shrink."

FIGURE 15.1   Psychological counseling should not be limited to improvement of mental health but should be applied to educational, vocational, and personal guidance and development as well. [*Sybil Shelton, Monkmeyer Press.*]

Today, there are a variety of psychological resources available, and not all of them deal solely with mental illness or "what can go wrong"; many resources are concentrating more and more on mental growth, or "what can go right."

When to Seek Psychological Counseling

For a number of reasons, many people are still somewhat reluctant to seek psychological counseling. For some, it is the element of *privacy* that makes them hesitant; they believe that family problems should be kept in the family, or that one just doesn't talk to strangers about sex problems. Others are still fearful of the "stigma" associated with seeing a therapist, believing that they might become social outcasts or be labled "crazy" because of their having sought therapeutic help. Still others, finding themselves caught up in the Western tradition of self-reliance and independence, prefer to solve their own problems in their own way. As a result of such attitudes, few people will seek professional assistance until a situation has deteriorated to such a degree that disastrous consequences are difficult to avoid. For example, depressions are often allowed to reach suicidal levels, marital discord is often allowed to escalate to the point where divorce appears to be the only solution, and drinking problems are permitted to compound themselves into chronic alcoholism.

Similarly, some people find themselves merely treading water as they go through life. But the time to seek out a means of reactivating or rejuvenating their lifestyles is before too many years have passed so as not to be faced with the frustration of "what might have been."

The key to successful psychological counseling is similar to the key to beneficial medical or legal assistance; that is, to seek help *early!* Ideally, some form of counseling should be undertaken as soon as the consequences of habitual behavior patterns become consistently unacceptable, when the neurotic symptoms of anxiety or depression first progress to a point at which they are interfering with an individual's daily life, or when a person is no longer willing to accept mediocrity and prefers to expand the significance and meaning of life and realize the greatest potentials possible.

INEFFECTIVE LIFESTYLE   As we pass through life, we each leave a record of our effectiveness, a legacy of reality reflecting what we are doing with our lives that can be far more revealing than what we intended to do. If an individual's history is one of inefficiency, that is, of consistent inability to satisfy personal needs, then psychological counseling may be helpful.

William Glasser, author of *Reality Therapy* (1965), believes that the only way a person can become motivated is "to look honestly at his own behavior to determine whether or not it contributes to fulfilling his needs" (p. 11). For Glasser, the pertinent question is, *What* is the person doing? not, *Why* is a person doing it? If a person is constantly getting fired from jobs, consistently being rejected by those whose friendship is desired, or repeatedly receiving a passing grade in class, but then failing to turn in the projects and flunking the finals, then the person's need to feel worthwhile, loved, and responsible is most likely not being fulfilled.

A more efficient lifestyle, one that is more able to satisfy one's needs, is often possible if one seeks appropriate counseling and is able to (1) face reality and realize how irrational one's past behavior has been, (2) reject irresponsible behavior patterns, and (3) learn more effective ways of fulfilling one's needs (Glasser, 1965).

NEUROTIC SYMPTOMS   The presence of chronically *high anxiety* is analogous to having a persistently high fever—something is wrong, psychologically or biologically, and corrective measures need to be taken in order to bring things back to normal. Anxiety that is so intense as to incapacitate a student during an exam, cause a severe loss in appetite, insomnia, and nightmares, or lead to an excessive use of alcohol or drugs is an anxiety that warrants the attention of therapeutic counseling.

Such anxiety is usually the result of internal conflicts, and therefore, some form of *insight therapy* can often be beneficial. The purpose of insight therapy is to bring about a conscious awareness of the source of internal motivations and the capacity to see oneself as one really is. Carl Rogers (1959), founder of client-centered therapy, points out that a person whose self-concept is grossly distorted, incomplete, or out of tune with the rest of his or her personality is in a state of *incongruence,* and as a result, will experience persistent feelings of frustration and conflict. Rogers believes that through the process of "reflecting" a person's thoughts and feelings back to the individual, attention can be called to what is really being experienced. As a result of such clarification, the person is provided with greater insight concerning the source of the conflicts.

Similarly, *depression* must not be allowed to continue beyond the point at which a person is no longer able to function or carry out routine activities. It is important to realize that severe depression often precipitates attempts at committing suicide. Eight out of ten people give warning of their suicidal intent, yet only about 5 percent sincerely want to die. The vast majority of would-be suicides are actually crying out for help (Schneidman et al., 1965; Rudestam, 1971).

In an attempt to make such help as readily available as possible, many communities have established "suicide prevention centers" or some form of "crisis center." These centers usually provide counseling over the telephone 24 hours a day, and are attended by professionals and paraprofessional volunteers. However, should such professional help not be available to someone who is contemplating suicide, don't hesitate to get involved. In such a situation, try to accept the feelings being expressed as being genuine. Do not attempt to belittle the reasons for these feelings or to provide superficial reassurance that everything is going to be all right. In addition, confront the possibility of suicide directly; do not attempt to avoid the issue or play it down (Lester, 1971).

In the case of phobic reactions, the inconvenience of such fears need not be endured. Many people tend merely to accept the phobia as a part of their character, a facet of their personality that, although it is undesirable, cannot be changed. On the contrary, the principles of desensitization and counterconditioning employed by therapists using behavior modification techniques have a remarkable degree of success with regard to ridding individuals of phobic fears (Wolpe, 1969).

PSYCHOPHYSIOLOGICAL ILLNESSES The relationship between stress and illness has been fairly well substantiated (Selye, 1974; Friedman and Rosenman, 1974). Therefore, it is not uncommon for some form of psychotherapy to be recommended for individuals with a history of ulcers, hypertension, heart condition, allergy, or migraine. Therapy seems especially suited to those cases in which the illnesses follow a specific pattern, such as occurring only during the holiday season, in the presence of a particular person such as a boss or a certain relative, or in the absence of such biological causes as the use of an allergy-causing agent. In such cases, the therapy can often determine the nature of the "secondary payoff," or the real purpose for developing the illness, such as gaining attention, sympathy, or control over others, avoiding responsibilities, or displacing hostile feelings.

Biofeedback is a new technique by which an individual can learn to control such internal processes as alpha rhythms in the brain, heart rhythms, and respiration rhythms. It holds promise as a therapeutic means of reducing psychological tension, enhancing physiological health, and increasing self-awareness. [*Ray Ellis, Rapho/Photo Researchers, Inc.*]

FIGURE 15.2

SEXUAL DYSFUNCTIONS   The personal agony suffered by individuals who fail to live up to their own sexual expectations or those of their partners can, in many cases, be overwhelming. Entire lifestyles can be developed around this one facet, this "flaw" in an individual's personality. For some, it means avoiding interpersonal relationships, destroying a marriage, or enduring life with the belief that one is not a "whole" person.

Rather than merely accept sexual dysfunctions, such as impotency, premature ejaculation, or frigidity, along with the emotional side effects which often accompany these problems, it is important to realize that sex problems are almost always psychologically caused (Jacobs and Whiteley, 1975). It is also helful to know that the rate of success in treating sexual dysfunctions is quite high. For example, using some of the methods developed by Masters and Johnson (1970), almost 70 percent of all the cases of secondary impotence (the inability to achieve an erection in one out of every four attempts at intercourse), 97 percent of the cases of premature ejaculation, and 82 percent of the cases of primary orgasmic dysfunction (a situation in which the woman has never experienced an orgasm) have had the dysfunction corrected.

With such encouraging results, it would seem unnecessary to endure the disappointment, humiliation, and bitterness which are often associated with sexual problems. However, it is imperative that counseling be sought at the earliest possible opportunity, before too many traumatic experiences occur and maladaptive, self-defeating behavior patterns become self-perpetuating.

SUPPORT AND MAINTENANCE   The institutions of marriage and the family are under tremendous stress in today's society. For instance, economic pressures often require both husband and wife to work outside the home, and being separated or divorced has gained greater acceptance. In addition, social, moral, and ethical standards frequently vary dramatically from community to community or from generation to generation, thereby making interpersonal communication difficult and ineffective.

Another factor contributing to poor communication is the high mobility of members of today's society, thereby presenting a greater opportunity for people to marry someone with a different cultural background; the couple then attempts to raise a family in the absence of the traditional support and experience of members of an extended family.

As a consequence of such factors, some theorists believe that many couples fail to achieve true intimacy and tend to substitute a life of "games" for an authentic relationship. For instance, Eric Berne, author of *Games People Play* (1969), believes that many married couples develop destructive "marital games," which he calls "If It Weren't for You," "Look How Hard I've Tried", or "Courtroom." Such games are usually designed to punish, or get back at, the partner, and they often prevent the development of effective communication patterns.

The goal of most marital therapies is to establish effective communication, eliminate destructive personal habits, and develop a mutually beneficial means of satisfying individual needs. In an effort to determine the relative effectiveness of marriage counseling, Gurman and Kniskern (1976) found that about two-thirds of the relationships between couples receiving treatment through nonbehavioral approaches to marital therapy were significantly improved.

Not all marital counseling, however, is successful, and many relationships end in divorce. Divorce is one of the most stressful situations a person can experience, second in severity only to the death of a spouse (Holmes and Rahe, 1967). Therefore, should a divorce or separation appear to be exceptionally difficult, some form of supportive therapy can often prevent a person's being emotionally overwhelmed.

In such cases, an existentially oriented therapy frequently can supplement and enhance an individual's inner reserves of strength. Much of this strength becomes available as one begins to recognize that one is *free to choose* the direction and purpose of one's life, and that one is *independently responsible* for the decisions that are made (Boss, 1963). The thrust of existential therapy is to put individuals "at the center" of life and to enable them to cope effectively with what *does* happen rather than to worry ineffectively about what *might* happen.

Similar individualized support is often needed in situations where a person is attempting to overcome destructive habits such as compulsive gambling, drug abuse, chronic obesity, and excessive drinking. Such individualized attention is an integral part of organizations like Alcoholic Anonymous (founded in 1939), perhaps the most famous of the organizations formed on the concept that "it takes one to help one." The members of AA are organized so that former drinkers who are alcoholics act as "sponsors," or personal guides and examples, for others who are attempting to stop drinking. This organization, with a membership of over one million (1976), is based on such principles as the need for members to admit that they are alcoholics and, therefore, powerless to control their drinking; that a power greater than themselves (God) is to be the prime means of overcoming their drinking problem; and that they must take personal inventories in order to admit where they have gone wrong (Alcoholics Anonymous, 1976).

PERSONAL GROWTH In a society that values and rewards conformity, it is often difficult not to go along with the crowd, to do what one is supposed to do, and to be what one is expected to be. However, for many of those who have successfully accomplished these objectives, a growing sense of emptiness often begins to dominate their perception of life. Life is frequently perceived as meaningless and purposeless, and everything and everyone seem irrelevant or pointless.

Salvatore Maddi (1967) suggests that such a person has developed a *premorbid personality* and is experiencing what he calls an *existential neurosis*. An existential neurosis is a condition characterized by a general loss of interest, apathy accompanied by feelings of pessimism, low self-esteem, and futility. Such symptoms are not uncommon among college students, especially among those who are attending college because their parents wanted them to or because it was always just assumed that they would go. These symptoms are also prevalent among those who are striving to be doctors, lawyers, architects, etc., only because these vocations are considered to have high prestige and not because they represent an opportunity for self-expression or the ability to do what one really wants to do in life. For many such students, life is perceived as a role to be played and not as an experience to be lived to its fullest.

One of the most effective ways of overcoming such a condition is through the implementation of one of the "growth" therapies. Existential therapy, for instance, emphasizes the need to discover meaning in life, the importance of living in the here and now, and the necessity for becoming more fully aware of one's feelings, attitudes, and goals (May, Angel, and Ellenberger, 1958).

In a similar vein, *gestalt therapy* can also be a very effective means of alleviating the symptoms of existential neurosis. Frederick Perls (1971) was instrumental in the development of this form of therapy and points out how gestalt therapy tends to focus on the elimination of obstacles that stand in the way of self-actualization by attempting to integrate the various fragments of a client's thoughts and perceptions. This type of therapy is likely to concentrate on the potential for growth and self-actualizing which are thought to exist in each individual.

What Assistance Is Available?

When everything that can go wrong has gone wrong, and when every obvious way to get out of the present dilemma has been tried, most people will finally reach out for help. However, during a crisis, or when an individual is in the midst of being overwhelmed by emotions, it is often very difficult to think clearly or rationally. As a consequence, trying to decide where to turn for help can often be as traumatic as the original feelings of distress. For instance, during such times, a person will often feel very fragile and vulnerable, afraid of being pushed even nearer the brink by someone who chooses to exploit anyone who is temporarily defenseless and weak.

Under such circumstances, it is understandably imperative that a person seeking counseling should carefully consider the selection of the counselor. Attention should also be given to the nature of the therapeutic techniques to be used and to the availability of various counseling and mental health resources within a given community.

FAMILY AND FRIENDS   With only one psychiatrist for every 10,000 people in the United States, it is not surprising that the vast majority of individuals who seek psychological assistance will find it with someone other than a psychiatrist. For most people, the most readily accessible source of counseling, and one of the most effective, is with a member of the family or a close friend.

Members of the immediate family and long-term friends have the inherent advantage of knowing a great deal about the background of the person who is having difficulties. Their knowledge may include firsthand information about the person's childhood and previous relationships, as well as subtle details concerning various characteristics of the individual's personality. As a result, these people often are the first to recognize that a person may be having trouble, and they may be able to link "cause-and-effect" variables accurately and quickly. However, there is also the distinct possibility that these people may be too close, too personally involved and biased, to be able to counsel objectively.

In order to be as effective as possible while attempting to counsel a family member or close friend, it is imperative that a *confidential relationship* be established; that is, a relationship in which what is said between the two people involved is not revealed to others. Only through the maintenance of such confidentiality can a sense of trust be developed. It is also important that the counselor be an *active listener,* that is, one who really pays attention to what is being communicated. Carl Rogers (1951) found that his clients would often report feeling better even though he had offered no directives or advice, but had merely listened attentively in a warm, permissive manner. Being an active listener also means paying attention to the nonverbal messages being expressed as well as to the verbal communications. A person's "body language," as well as the emotional quality and tone of the speaker's voice, can often reveal contradictions and confirm realities in what is being said.

In any attempts to identify the source of the stress, it is essential to respond with *understanding* and *empathy* whenever possible. Try not to act as a judge or present an air of superiority. For example, when someone is depressed because of having recently broken up a relationship, avoid making statements such as "You were an idiot for pairing up with that turkey in the first place. I told you from the beginning that it was a mistake. I would have dumped that fool a long time ago."

In such a situation, it is recommended that the listener respond to the person's feeling of depression with a feeling (sorrow, anger, empathy, etc.) rather than with an evaluation (appraisal, criticism, or judgment). Where appropriate, share a personal experience that is similar to the one currently being experienced by the person seeking counsel. However, one should keep in mind that one of the major problems with being a good listener is the compulsion to express oneself without really listening to the other person because one is too busy thinking of what one will say next (Rogers, 1951). Gerard Egan, in his book *You & Me* (1977), which deals with communication skills, suggests that a person should avoid using the following responses, which he considers "poor substitutes" for dealing and understanding:

1 *Clichés.*   They are phony and create distance between communicators.
2 *Parroting.*   Repetition of what has been said as if the listener were a tape recorder.
3 *Inadequate responses.*   Saying "uh-huh" or just nodding.
4 *Pretending to understand.*   Saying something like, "Oh, now I understand what you're getting at" (when you don't).
5 *Ignoring what a person says.*   Making no response, or changing the subject.
6 *Being long-winded.*   Using five minutes to say what could be said in thirty seconds.
7 *Questions.*   Rather than responding with a self-disclosing statement, putting the other person through the "third degree" with a series of penetrating questions.
8 *Judgments.*   Being critical and opinionated.
9 *Advice giving.*   Placing oneself in an "all-knowing" position.
10 *Patronizing.*   Responding to the other person in a condescending or disrespectful manner. (pp. 156–166)

PARAPROFESSIONALS AND PROFESSIONALS   In 1963, Congress passed the Community Health Centers Act, which provided that one mental health center be created for every 50,000 people in a community. The purpose of these mental health centers is to provide immediate access to psychological assistance for members of the local community. This objective is to be achieved by providing such resources as (1) *outpatient services,* including individual and group therapy, family and marital counseling, and supportive services for those who have formerly been in mental hospitals; (2) *emergency services,* in order to accommodate the needs of those who attempt suicide, have problems with alcohol or drug abuse, or suffer from the effects of transient situational disturbances due to natural or economic disasters; (3) *consultation* for teachers, the clergy, and law enforcement personnel; and (4) *training* for paraprofessionals (Jones, 1953).

The consultation services and paraprofessional training provided by these centers have been particularly beneficial to the communities. Clergy and teachers have traditionally been sought out in times of trouble. However, until recently, many of these people were ill-prepared to provide effective therapeutic counseling. As a consequence, many who sought their assistance received little or no support when trying to deal with the disruptions in their lifestyles or marriages. With the consultation available through today's community health centers, however, such counseling can become far more effective and supportive.

In addition, the use of lay members of the community or paraprofessionals has, in many instances, proven to be as effective as when professionals are used (Brown, 1974). Paraprofessionals often have A.A. or B.A. degrees, or are currently involved in graduate work. However, many are merely local residents who have received intense, supervised training. A classic example of such efforts was illustrated by Margaret Rioch (1967), who found that carefully selected housewives, after being given two years of intense training, performed as effectively as professional therapists.

It is important to realize that the term "therapist" can refer to professionals with a wide range of credentials, degrees, and training. To use terminology that is more specific, a *psychiatrist* is a medical doctor (M.D.) who has received at least three years of supervised training in the field of psychiatry. As medical doctors, psychiatrists are qualified to employ *somatotherapy* techniques (physiological treatment), such as prescribing drugs, administering electroshock treatments, and conducting biophysical therapies. Although psychiatrists will also employ psychotherapy (psychological treatment), they often have a strong biological perspective toward mental health. Psychiatrists who specialize, in both their training and their practice, in the therapeutic tehniques developed by Sigmund Freud are referred to as *psychoanalysts.*

In contrast, a *clinical psychologist* has earned a Ph.D. in psychology. However, a psychologist, who is anyone with a Ph.D. in psychology, is quite different from a clinical psychologist, who has completed one to two years' internship involving supervised training in individual and group therapy techniques. Similarly, a *counseling psychologist* may have earned a Ph.D. or an Ed.D. with specialized training in educational, vocational, or personal counseling, rather than in counseling clients who have been diagnosed as having more severe mental health problems.

A large proportion of the therapeutic counseling that takes place in the United States, however, is conducted by *psychiatric social workers* who hold an M.S.W. (master of social work) degree, or by *marriage, family, and child counselors,* who often hold an M.A. degree or a Ph.D. These professionals have usually received extensive training in dealing with problems relating to interpersonal communication, sex, and parent-child relationships. In most states they must be licensed before they are allowed to enter into private practice.

CHOOSING A THERAPIST   The first step in choosing a therapist is to *personally* decide that a therapist is needed, for there is often a lack of commitment found among those who are taken, or sent, to a therapist when they don't sincerely want to go or don't think a therapist is really needed.

Once the decision is made, a choice of therapists can be found by looking in the "yellow pages" of a telephone book under "Psychologists" or "Marriage and family counseling"; by seeking recommendations from the family doctor, school counselors, instructors, or a community mental health center; or by contacting such agencies as the National Association of Mental Health, the American Psychiatric Association, the American Psychological Association, the Association of Humanistic Psychology, or the Association for Women in Psychology.

Often such contacts will provide the names of two or three professionals from which to select a therapist. In order to facilitate the selection, a short "diagnostic consultation" is recommended. During this first session, it is important for the prospective client to evaluate the therapist, as well as the therapeutic techniques to be used. The therapist's background, training, and experience are often as informative as the number and nature of the degrees the therapist may have. Such information, however, does not guarantee effective psychotherapy. Jacob Swartz of the Boston University Medical Center takes this position:

> At the very least, professional training tells you there has been some sort of systematic study of the problem involved. Professional credentials are not a guarantee, but at least you know the therapist has had some exposure to what is going on in his field and has some idea of what sort of treatment is applicable. (Quoted in Katz, 1972, p. 9)

As a practical matter, the fees involved and how they are to be paid must also be considered. Generally, a psychiatrist's fee will be $50 to $60 or more per hour, while the fees of psychologists will average around $30 to $40 per hour. These fees may seem exorbitant. However, when one considers the extent of the therapist's education and training, or what the average medical practitioner earns per hour, the charges may appear quite reasonable. Much more important than what the therapist may charge, however, is what maladaptive or neurotic behavior costs the client in substitutive behavior, such as buying expensive cars, houses, or other luxury items in order to counteract feelings of inadequacy or low self-esteem. Similarly, the monthly bill of an alcoholic or drug abuser is often three or four times what therapy might cost.

In the selection of a therapist, the most important factor to consider is the quality and nature of the rapport that is experienced between the client and the therapist; that is, the degree of trust and confidence the client is able to experience, based on the warmth, integrity, and sincerity perceived in the therapist (Frank, 1973). David Viscott, author of *The Making of a Psychiatrist* (1972), points out:

More important than whether a person is a psychiatrist or a psychologist, is whether he can identify with the healthy side of the patient and make that side more and more important. A good therapist is tolerant and understanding and open. And these qualities don't come from a medical school any more than they come from a Ph.D. program. They come from life. (Quoted in Katz, 1972, p. 9)

TERMINATION OF THERAPY   Regardless of the expertise or personality of the therapist, the techniques may prove to be ineffective or the personalities of the client and the therapist may be incompatible. In such cases, termination of the counseling may be advisable. In some instances, however, a desire to terminate therapy may be due to the individual's wish to avoid dealing with certain undesirable aspects of his or her personality. In such cases, the client may be considered to be "resisting" (deliberately avoiding threatening areas), and termination of therapy may be considered to be "premature." In order to avoid terminating therapy prematurely, Otto and Miriam Ehrenberg, authors of *The Psychotherapy Maze: A Consumer's Guide* (1977), suggest that full consideration be given to the following conditions:

1   When everything in the therapy was going fine but then suddenly it seemed to turn sour;
2   When you've been with several therapists and find yourself repeatedly coming up with the same kinds of dissatisfaction;
3   When the dissatisfactions with the therapist are similar to those with other important people in your life;
4   When sudden attitude changes occur toward things affecting the therapy, such as finding the therapy is costing you too much time or money, or becoming convinced that therapy really doesn't work;
5   Perhaps most telling of all, when there's nothing specific you dislike about your therapist but you just have an overwhelming impulse to flee. (pp. 153–154)

If the desire to terminate therapy occurs in conjunction with any of the preceding conditions, the likelihood is that the client is experiencing some degree of resistance and additional therapy may be warranted. However, the Ehrenbergs further suggest that if a client encounters some of the following situations, the fault may lie with the therapist or with the therapeutic techniques. In such cases, termination of therapy may be warranted. The client should be wary of situations such as the following:

1   When the personalities of the client and therapist are totally incompatible.
2   When there is a conflict of values, ethics, or life styles.
3   When the therapist is more involved with his or her own ego than with the ego of the client.
4   When the therapist becomes "personally" involved rather than "professionally" involved with the client.
5   When the therapy fails to make any progress over a reasonable period of time.
6   When the client feels that he or she must live up to the expectations of the therapist rather than being who he or she really is.
7   When the client and therapist both act in destructive ways.

8   When the therapist is inconsiderate, undependable, or inflexible.
9   When the therapist will not discuss the client's doubts about the progress, or lack of progress, being made in therapy. (1977, pp. 154–155)

THE MAJOR PSYCHOTHERAPEUTIC APPROACHES

During the Middle Ages, mental illness was thought to be the result of possession by demons. Treatment was limited primarily to *exorcism,* a ritualistic effort to drive out the demons (Rosen, 1968). If exorcism failed, whipping, immersion, imprisonment, and burning at the stake were commonly used as alternative forms of treatment.

Many asylums for the mentally disturbed were little more than prisons where those who were interned were often locked in cages, chained to walls, and put on display for the curious. In 1792, Philippe Pinel (1745–1826) advocated more humane treatment of the insane, removed their restraints, regarded them as "patients," and began treating them with kindness and compassion. Gradually, through the efforts of psychiatrists such as Wilhelm Griesinger and Emil Kraeplin, the medical perspective gained dominance over the belief in demonic possession. Soon neurologists, including Jean-Martin Charcot, Josef Breuer, and Sigmund Freud, noted the influence that hypnosis had with regard to mental disturbances, especially hysteria. It seemed that the severity of the hysterical symptoms would often diminish if, after being hypnotized, the patient was encouraged to talk about personal conflicts and frustrations (Jones, 1963). Freud soon observed that hypnosis was not really necessary; that the patients' mental state would often improve merely by talking about the things that troubled them. With this discovery, the principle of *psychoanalysis* and the concept of *psychotherapy* were introduced to the field of psychology.

Today, there are literally hundreds of variations of psychotherapy available (Harper, 1959, 1975). Some are still based on the psychodynamic approach founded by Freud, but many have discarded such treatment as being "unscientific" and have opted for the more modern behavior modification techniques developed by the behaviorists. Still others, preferring the humanistic approach, seek to explore the uniqueness, dignity, and significance of the individual, rather than dwell on the more primitive levels of functioning. The humanistic therapists concentrate on the "positive" aspects of an individual's personality and potential for self-actualization.

Regardless of the approach, however, the goals of most therapies are usually quite similar: to increase insight, resolve conflicts, enhance one's sense of identity, improve interpersonal relationships, modify inaccurate assumptions, and/or get rid of "bad habits" or other self-defeating behavior patterns. Each approach attempts to provide an explanation for why a person is the way he or she is; a rationale for the development of particular attitudes, beliefs, emotional reactions, and behavior; and therapeutic techniques designed to correct undesired personality characteristics or behavior patterns.

FIGURE 15.3   "Classic psychoanalysis," in which the therapist assumes a relatively passive role, has lost much of its popularity to newer approaches that require the therapist to be an active participant in the therapeutic process. [*Jan Lukas, Rapho/Photo Researchers, Inc.*]

Dynamic Therapies

The psychodynamic therapies tend to concentrate on the identification and resolution of *inner conflicts;* the basic premise is that such conflicts are a result of faulty development, and special emphasis is therefore placed on early childhood experiences. Treatment focuses primarily on "talking things through" in the hope of providing the client with personal insight, better integration of the various components of the client's personality, and greater emotional maturity.

SIGMUND FREUD   It is important to keep in mind that Freud was a medical doctor, and consequently his interest in psychology centered on pathology, particularly on the treatment of hysteria. Much of his theory, therefore, was heavily influenced by other physicians, among them Charcot (hypnosis), Breuer (the "talking" cure, catharsis, and abreaction), and Bruke (the influence of sexuality). It is also relevant to note that Freud was living during much of the Victorian era, and inevitably his attempts to bring *sexuality* out into the open generated controversy. In fact, many psychoanalysts today still believe that a major cause of people's difficulties in achieving adjustment stems directly from the influence that the sexual ethics of the Victorian era have had upon today's society.

THE GOAL OF THERAPY   To Freud, therapy was a means of undoing the harm inflicted in childhood by fixating the patient's attention at an early stage of development and "artificially" taking him or her through the process of successful resolution of subsequent stages. Thus, with the successful resolution of the psychosexual stages, the patient becomes an *emotionally mature* person. By "emotionally mature," Freud meant a person who is "capable of engaging in productive work and loving."

In order to succeed in either, Freud believed, a state of "harmony" must exist between one's ego (the part of an individual's psyche that deals with the real world), superego (the conscience), and id (the instinctive animal part of the human being). In other words, there must be a minimum of conflict between what one desires and how one satisfies those desires. Such conflicts are usually at a minimum when one's ego self (how one actually turned out) and ego ideal (how one wanted to turn out) are as similar as possible. The greater the resemblance is between these two images, the less opportunity there is for conflict to exist between them. The closest degree of similarity seems to occur when a person has had an acceptable parental model upon which to based her or his concept of an ideal self.

The intent of Freudian therapy is to provide the client with a means of encountering repressed inner conflict so that it no longer has to be contained and the resultant anxiety no longer needs to be converted into physical disturbances. In order to accomplish this, Freudian analysts use several methods of revealing repressed material. One method is the use of *free association,* in which the client is encouraged to talk freely of whatever comes to mind. A similar method is *word association,* in which the client is asked to say the first word that comes to mind in response to a word that is given by the analyst. These two methods are usually used in conjunction with *dream analysis,* in which the meaning of the dream is interpreted from the symbolic content of the dream as told by the client. Employing these methods, the analyst will encourage the client to explore areas in which resistance is demonstrated; that is, the areas the client is rather reluctant to explore. The assumption is that a highly threatening area will be heavily defended. During the course of therapy, the defenses are weakened, resulting in a rather dramatic increase in anxiety. When final breakthrough of the defenses is achieved, a correspondingly dramatic decrease in the level of anxiety will occur. Such a breakthrough, and subsequent "talking through" the once repressed material, is called *catharsis.* Or, if it is experienced as an emotional "reliving" of the material, it is called *abreaction.*

A significant feature of the psychoanalytic method is the development of a phenomenon called *transference.* The process of transference involves the "ventilation" of unresolved feelings and conflicts stemming from childhood. These feelings are transferred to the therapist, who acts as a substitute for those who originally generated the feelings (usually the client's parents).

Freud, speaking of the goals of therapy, stated:

Our aim will not be to rub off every peculiarity of human character for the sake of a schematic "normality," nor yet to demand that the person who has been

Film or video tape can be an important therapeutic tool, providing clients the opportunity to see themselves as others see them. [*James H. Karales, Peter Arnold.*]

"thoroughly analyzed" should feel no passions and develop no internal conflicts. The business of the analysis is to secure the best possible psychological conditions for the functions of the ego; with that it has discharged its task. (Quoted in Roazen, 1974, p. 113)

THE NEO-FREUDIANS   Almost from the very inception of classical psychoanalysis, various facets of it, if not the entire concept, have generated some degree of dissension among Freud's followers. The main areas of disagreement tend to revolve around the emphasis on sex, the dynamics of the unconscious processes, and the importance of early childhood experiences. The length of time devoted to psychoanalysis (two to three sessions per week for five or more years) has also been questioned, with many neo-Freudian therapists developing shorter, more economical, forms of therapy.

Many of the "descendants" of Freud placed greater emphasis on the importance of interpersonal relationships than on "instinctual drives." For instance, Harry Stack Sullivan (1953) stressed the influence of *communication,* especially with regard to *"significant others,"* such as parents, teachers, and girl or boy friends. Sullivan believed that, based on the anxiety resulting from such interactions, a self-concept emerges which is divided into a "good me," a "bad me," and a "not me." However, should one of these divisions become dominant, neurotic or psychotic behavior may result.

Karen Horney (1939) also stressed the importance of interpersonal relationships. However, she emphasized the role of repressed hostility in the development of personality orientations. As examples, she cited people who move *toward* others in order not to produce feelings of hostility, those who move *away* from others in order to avoid feelings of hostility, and those who move *against* others in order to act out feelings of hostility. Personality disturbances are believed to occur when one of these three orientations becomes dominant to the exclusion of the others. The aim of therapy is to resolve the inner conflict between the "real" self and the "idealized self-image" which is based on the individual's dominant orientation toward others.

Erich Fromm (1947) also talked of the development of the individual within a social context, pointing out that each person is first a "social being" and that rejection, a lack of love, and/or a lack of encouragement from others, especially parents, can have a major impact on personality development. Fromm talked of the development of a nonproductive "social character," such as a *marketing, hoarding, receptive, or exploitive* type of personality. For him, the goal of therapy is to bolster the individual's capacity for self-reliance and the development of a "productive" lifestyle, not merely the achievement of a level of conformity.

Behavioral Therapies

The therapeutic techniques employed by behavioral therapists have been derived from extensive research and laboratory studies. The behavioral techniques are founded on learning theory and are designed to eliminate maladaptive behavior, and/or develop new behavior patterns that are effective and adaptive.

The behavioral therapists have little concern for the client's past experiences or childhood, and no concern for what are referred to as "unconscious processes." They deal with overt behavior. For the behavioral therapist, *the symptom is the problem;* that is, the psychological disturbance is eliminated when the symptom is eliminated. In order to accomplish this task, the therapist will (1) set specific goals, (2) establish specific procedures, and (3) arrange for an objective assessment of the client's progress and the ultimate results of the therapy.

DESENSITIZATION AND COUNTERCONDITIONING   In the treatment of many neurotic reactions, the behaviorists will often attempt to weaken or eliminate undesirable stimulus-response associations through the process of *extinction*. In the classic situation where Albert developed a fear of rats (Watson and Raynor, 1920), extinction would have taken place by repeatedly presenting the conditioned stimulus (the white rat) without ever pairing it with the unconditioned stimulus (the loud noise) until the fear response to the rat no longer occurred.

Another therapeutic technique used to disrupt inappropriate stimulus-response connections is *counterconditioning*. Counterconditioning is merely the process of classically conditioning a new, more appropriate, response to an old stimulus. In the classic case of Peter, who had a phobic fear of rabbits, a stimulus such as ice cream was presented in the company of the rabbit so as to create a pleasurable, rather than a fear, response (Jones, 1924). A special type of counterconditioning is called *desensitization*. The process of desensitization involves a graduated progression of associations beginning with the

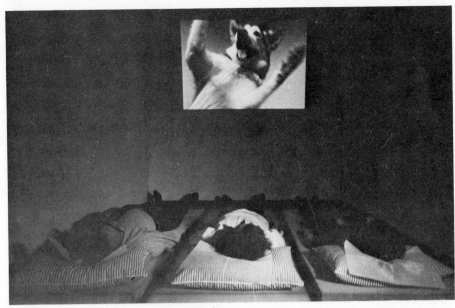

FIGURE 15.5 Learning to relax in the presence of certain kinds of stimuli is vital to the desensitization process used in behavioral therapy. [*The New York Times.*]

least arousing and progressing to the *most* arousing stimulus; an individual learns to relax in the presence of what was formerly an anxiety-provoking stimulus (Wolpe, 1958).

AVERSION THERAPY   Many problems of adjustment stem from the inappropriate use of *reward* (reinforcement through the presentation of something that is *desired*) and *punishment* (reinforcement through the presentation of something *undesired*). In practice, reward will tend to *increase* the probability of the behavior's reoccurrence, while punishment tends to *decrease* the probability of the behavior's being repeated. Unfortunately, individuals will inadvertently reward undesired behavior and thereby increase the probability of the undesired behavior's reappearance. For example, O. I. Lovass, a pioneer in the use of behavior modification techniques in the treatment of autistic children, found that in many cases, their self-destructive behavior, such as biting, hitting, or other self-mutilating acts, was being rewarded by the staff members of many institutions. It seemed that the only time an autistic child would be presented with attention and signs of affection and care (rewards) was when he or she was engaging in self-destructive behavior. As a consequence of such rewards, the self-destructive behavior would continue and even increase. In such cases, "love" did more harm than good.

Punishment, on the other hand, is often seen as "bad." However, in many situations, punishment can serve a very useful purpose. In one particularly difficult case of self-mutilation, Lovaas (1965) employed the use of punishment in the form of a cattle prod as a means of eliminating self-destructive behavior.

Each time the child began to engage in self-destructive behavior, a shock would be applied. After only a few such pairings, the self-destructive behavior stopped.

Aversion therapy has also been used successfully in the elimination of stuttering (Goldiamond, 1965) and bed-wetting (Wickes, 1958). One must bear in mind, however, that punishment merely suppresses undesired behavior; it does little or nothing in the way of teaching desired behavior. The primary reason for using punishment is to eliminate behavior that produces an even greater punishment. Whenever possible, one should employ positive reinforcement in order to modify behavior.

TOKEN ECONOMIES AND SECONDARY REINFORCEMENT   One of the most successful uses of positive reinforcement as a means of treating the mentally ill has been the introduction of *token economies*. A token economy is based on the principle of *chaining.* Chaining means the process by which "one response may produce the stimulus for the next." A rat, for example, will pull a string in order to lift a shield; this permits the rat to get to a food pellet. Since the shield is associated with the food, the shield becomes "valued" and the rat will perform some task in order to gain access to the shield. The shield's acquisition of value makes it a *secondary reinforcer.* In a token economy, a patient will exhibit some form of desired behavior in order to get a "token," which can then be exchanged for food, material rewards, or privileges.

Early research with token economies began in the late thirties with chimpanzees (Wolge, 1936; Cowles, 1937). However, it was not until Skinner's work in the area of shaping, and the application of these techniques to psychotic patients by Ogden Lindsley in 1954, that the therapeutic benefits of the token economy approach began to be fully realized. Today, token economies have been successfully used in hospitals, classrooms, reform schools, and other institutions (Ayllon and Azrin, 1968). In a less conspicuous manner, these economies have been successfully utilized by various socioeconomic systems for centuries in the form of money.

WARNING CUES AND SECONDARY NEGATIVE REINFORCERS   A secondary reinforcer, however, does not always possess the "positive" qualities of reward; through association with negative reinforcement, a stimulus can become a *secondary negative reinforcer.* In 1916, John Watson (1878–1958), one of the founders of American behaviorism, adopted a conditioning technique developed by the Russian reflexologist Vladimir Bekhterev (1857–1927). Using this technique, the researcher would pair an electric shock (unconditioned stimulus) with a tone (neutral stimulus), and as a result, the experimental animal would demonstrate a reflexive withdrawal response to the presentation of the tone even in the absence of the shock.

In later experimentation, it was noticed that the subjects could learn to make a withdrawal response in order to avoid receiving the electric shock (Brogden, Lipman, and Culler, 1938). In such experiments, the subjects would be provided with a *discriminative cue,* or "warning cue," such as a buzzing sound just before the shock was administered. The subjects would then learn that if they made a particular response, such as pressing a bar, running in a cage, or leaping from a distinctive cage, they could avoid getting a shock (Mower and Lamoreaux, 1942; Solomon and Wynne, 1954). Such avoidance conditioning has an extremely high resistance to extinction even though a subject may never be reinforced again.

Mower (1947) developed a two-factor theory of explanation for such resistance. In this theory, Mower argues that the subject is first conditioned to fear a given stimulus, which results in an involuntary *emotional response* such as fear. The second factor involves making an instrumental or voluntary response, such as escaping, which reduces or removes the emotion of fear. Thus the subject learns to respond to the warning cue rather than to the actual event that originally caused the fear response.

A great deal of neurotic behavior is due to misperceiving warning cues. Avoidance behavior requires external warning cues in order to be effective. A rat, for example, may be trained to flee from a cage within ten seconds after a light comes on, in order to avoid an electric shock. The light serves as a warning cue. In real life, a child may learn that from the time the front door slams, he or she has only ten seconds to get out of the kitchen with a cookie, in order to avoid being punished. Unfortunately, an individual may also learn that once a person hears someone say, "I love you," he or she has only a short time to get out of the relationship, in order to avoid being hurt again.

SELF-MANAGEMENT   The behaviorists (Skinner, 1971) refer to this self-management, or ego control, as "self-control" or "self-management." Self-management refers generally to one's assumption of personal responsibility for modifying one's own behavior. It involves getting rid of undesirable habits as well as establishing desirable habits. For instance, if a person finds that through association with a particular individual, sexual dysfunctioning occurs, she or he may select to avoid further association with that individual so as not to have the sexual dysfunction become a habitual stimulus-response consequence.

Self-management also involves the removal of irrational fears, especially those that interfere with satisfying interpersonal relationships, by either engaging in desensitization programs or by developing assertiveness in order to override old responses. For example, it has been found that socially inhibited individuals who engage in a program of expressing their feelings of resentment or appreciation in a graded fashion tend to experience a gradual reduction in the level of their anxiety (McFall and Marston, 1970).

With regard to establishing desirable habits, Watson and Tharp, in their book *Self-Directed Behavior* (1977), point out that behavior is a function of environment, and that the way a person behaves in a particular situation is influenced by previous experiences in similar situations. "The effect of the environment, then, is to evoke behavior already learned and to teach new behaviors. . . . Therefore, in the process of self-modification, you set out to produce new learning for yourself in specific situations" (p. 10).

Although there are a variety of sequences available in self-directed programs, Watson and Tharp (1977) recommend the following steps:

1 Select a goal.
2 Specify the behaviors you need to change, called *target behaviors,* in order to reach the goal.
3 Make observations about the target behaviors; keep a diary describing those behaviors count how often you engage in them, discover the events that stimulate your acts and the things that reward them.
4 Work out a plan for change, gradually replace an unwanted action with a desirable one.
5 Readjust your plans as you learn more about yourself. (p. 15)

Sex Therapies

The determination of what is sexually healthy and what is sexually unhealthy is an extremely difficult undertaking, with many believing that any such attempt would be nothing more than an exercise in futility. Some reasons for this difficulty are these: (1) Often the issue is not so much *what* is healthy, but *how much* is healthy; (2) the circumstances under which an act takes place, and with whom it takes place, can also be contributing factors; and (3) the moral or social acceptability of a particular act may vary not only from culture to culture, but from one time period to another within a culture. Because of such difficulties, there seems to have been more agreement in determining what is no longer considered sexually unhealthy than in deciding what is sexually healthy. For instance, one no longer needs to fear insanity or hairy palms as the penalty for masturbation; the ancient biblical emphasis (Genesis 38:9) on the preservation of one's "precious body fluids" is no longer a major concern of the male population; and the old fears of *vagina dentata* (a vagina with teeth) have all but disappeared.

However, there are still many sexual areas that can cause emotional or marital problems. As a result, one may wish to seek treatment for such difficulties. When treatment for sexual problems is desired, there are a number of theoretical orientations available, such as psychoanalysis and behavior modification, each of which has the potential of improving the quality and degree of one's sexual satisfaction.

SEXUAL DYSFUNCTION Although Freudian psychologists and behaviorists may disagree on the specific cause of sexual dysfunctions, they usually do concur that the experience itself is often a very traumatic one. A period of sexual intimacy is usually an unguarded one, and an individual can be extremely vulnerable to criticism, including self-criticism as well. Therefore, any inability to fully express oneself sexually can be personally devastating. Most often, the person experiencing "sexual inadequacy" will become filled with doubts, feelings of worthlessness, and self-ridicule. Feelings of rejection may occur in both partners, and unfortunately, the partner who is otherwise

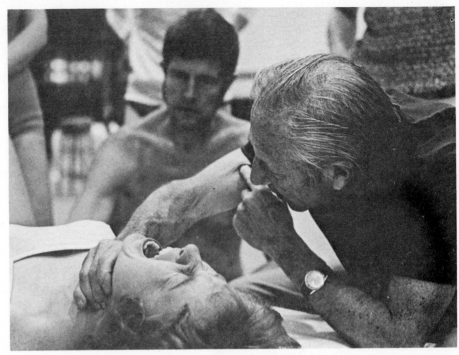

FIGURE 15.6   The bioenergetic approach to therapy is designed to gain access to a client's emotions through the body. Therapists using this approach concentrate on identifying sources of muscular tension created by "negative emotions" and provide a means of releasing such tensions to permit emotions of a more positive nature to be experienced. [*Hella Hammid, Rapho/Photo Researchers, Inc.*]

functioning satisfactorily will often attempt to assume responsibility for the other partner's failure.

Although, in most cases, sexual dysfunction in one partner is not the "fault" of the other partner, many sexologists adhere to the principle that sexual dysfunctions are a mutual problem and often require the cooperation of both partners in order to overcome the difficulty (Masters and Johnson, 1970), provided that one or both of the sex partners agree that a problem actually exists. Sometimes, however, a sexual problem is seen merely as one of sexual orientation, or preference, for which treatment may not be required or even sought.

PSYCHOANALYTIC APPROACH   Since most sexual dysfunctions are considered to be psychosomatic disorders (physical disturbances in which emotional factors play a causative role), Freud's psychoanalytic therapy possessed an inherent advantage in having been an outgrowth of the treatment of hysteria. For Freud, psychosomatic disorders were the physical manifestation of psychological conflict: an internal conflict between the primitive urges of the id and the moralistic inhibitions of the superego. Through the use of repression and other defense mechanisms, we tend to push these urges from consciousness and attempt to contain them in our unconscious. Such containment is never totally successful, and therefore, some of this contained energy may escape. The threat of this escape is experienced as anxiety, and when an attempt is made to reduce this anxiety, some of it may be converted into psychosomatic disorders such as sexual dysfunctions.

Once the repressed material has been exposed to consciousness (through the use of free association, dream interpretation, and catharsis), the forces can be consciously directed in order to find a more acceptable expression. Then the unconscious need to render oneself impotent or to experience premature ejaculation, frigidity, or other forms of sexual dysfunctioning will no longer exist. Perhaps as a means of reducing the frequency of severity of sexual problems, Freud proposed:

> A place must be created in public opinion for the discussion of the problems of sexual life. It will have to become possible to talk about these things without being stamped as a trouble-maker or as a person who makes capital out of the lower instincts. And so here, too, there is enough work left to do for the next hundred years—in which our civilization will have to learn to come to terms with the claims of our sexuality. (Quoted in Roazen, 1974, p. 103)

BEHAVIORAL THERAPY   Generally, the behaviorists are in agreement with the connection Freud drew between a lack of sexual enlightenment and its association with negative feelings later in life. However, behavioral theories of sexual dysfunction are based primarily on early childhood conditioning, in which sexual feelings are paired with traumatic experiences, resulting in feelings of guilt, shame, disgust, and fear. An unrealistically moral parent, for example, may yell at the son who is watching his five-year-old sister undress, "Don't look at her, Johnny! Shut your eyes quick! If you see a naked person, your eyes will fall out!" A few statements like these, in addition to horrified screams of "Don't touch yourself there! Nasty! Dirty!" and the boy will become fairly well conditioned to respond with fear and anxiety to most sexual situations he may encounter as an adult. Such fear responses cause an automatic "switching" to take place in an individual's autonomic (involuntary) nervous system. As a result of this switching, normal sexual responsiveness becomes physically inhibited or impossible. Thus, failure to perform adequately is paired with sexual situations, and, as a consequence, the individual becomes fearful of failing again in future sexual situations. This fear, unfortunately, causes the switching to occur again and the individual to fail again, thus creating a vicious repetitive cycle of fear and failure. The therapeutic goal of the behaviorist, therefore, is to eliminate the fear response, usually through the process of systematic desensitization.

MASTERS AND JOHNSON   Using a modified version of desensitization, Masters and Johnson (1970; Kaplan, 1974) have developed a remarkably successful program for treatment of sexual dysfunctions. Their methods of treatment are based on two assumptions. The first is that sexual dysfunction is not an

FIGURE 15.7 Primal therapy, developed by Arthur Janov, is based on the premise that pain is generated by the failure to have basic emotional, or "primal," needs satisfied during childhood. The pain, repressed in later years, must be experienced openly as part of the therapeutic process if the person is to become a well-adjusted individual. [*Hella Hammid, Photo Researchers, Inc.*]

individual problem, but a *mutual* problem involving both sexual partners. The second assumption is that the sexual dysfunction is caused primarily by *performance anxiety*, fear of being sexually inadequate, and that this anxiety must be removed.

In order to determine the cause of this anxiety more accurately, treatment begins with in-depth interviews of each partner, first by a therapist of the same sex, then by a therapist of the opposite sex. Finally, both partners are interviewed in a joint conference in which both therapists are included. Having developed some well-defined channels of communication, the couple is introduced to the next phase of therapy, that of the *sensuous exercises*. During the sensuous exercise phase, the couple is forbidden to indulge in intercourse. This imposed abstinence seems to be very effective in reducing performance anxiety. The next phase of therapy includes specific "pleasure-enhancing" instructions. And eventually, through graduated, nondemanding exercises, the couple culminates the therapeutic process with successful intercourse. Satisfying intercourse acts as a positive reinforcement and serves as an incentive to continue with the therapeutic program. Skinner once wrote, "Operant conditioning shapes behavior as a sculptor shapes a lump of clay." If the lump of clay wants the reinforcer badly enough, there is virtually no limit to how it can be shaped by an experimenter with a food pellet, a mother with a smile, or, as in the Masters and Johnson program, a sexual partner with satisfying sex.

SEXUAL THERAPY AND HOMOSEXUALITY   Freud believed that an individual's selection of sexual partners of the same sex is a direct outgrowth of the Oedipal complex. However, he did not consider homosexuality necessarily neurotic. He considered it neurotic only when the individual was overly disturbed, anxious, or unduly ashamed of his sexual preference. A letter from Freud to the mother of a homosexual (quoted in Jones, 1963, p. 140) is quite descriptive of his views on homosexuality:

April 9, 1935

Dear Mrs._____

I gather from your letter that your son is a homosexual. I am most impressed by the fact that you do not mention this term yourself in your information about him. May I question you, why you avoid it? Homosexuality is assuredly no advantage, but it is nothing to be ashamed of, no vice, no degradation, it cannot be classified as an illness; we consider it to be a variation of the sexual function produced by a certain arrest of sexual development. Many highly respectable individuals of ancient and modern times have been homosexuals, several of the greatest among them (Plato, Michelangelo, Leonardo da Vinci, etc.). It is a great injustice to persecute homosexuality as a crime, and cruelty, too. If you do not believe me, read the books of Havelock Ellis.

By asking me if I can help, you mean, I suppose, if I can abolish homosexuality and make normal heterosexuality take its place. The answer is, in a general way, we cannot promise to achieve it. In a certain number of cases we succeed in developing the blighted germs of heterosexual tendencies which are present in every homosexual; in the majority of cases it is no more possible. It is a question of the quality and the age of the individual. The result of treatment cannot be predicted.

What analysis can do for your son runs in a different line. If he is unhappy, neurotic, torn by conflicts, inhibited in his social life, analysis may bring him harmony, peace of mind, full efficiency, whether he remains a homosexual or gets changed. If you make up your mind, he should have analysis with me!! I don't expect you will!! He has to come to Vienna. I have no intention of leaving here. However, don't neglect to give me your answer.

Sincerely yours with kind wishes,

Freud

The American Psychiatric Association, in December 1973, found itself in agreement with Freud's views and voted to eliminate *homosexuality per se* as a mental disorder, substituting the new category of "sexual orientation disturbance." The *Diagnostic and Statistical Manual of Mental Disorders II* now reads:

302.0   Sexual orientation disturbance (homosexuality)
This is for individuals whose sexual interests are directed primarily toward people

of the same sex and who are either disturbed by, in conflict with, or wish to change their sexual orientation. This diagnostic category is distinguished from homosexuality, which by itself does not constitute a psychiatric disorder. Homosexuality *per se* is one form of sexual behavior, and with other forms of sexual behavior which are not by themselves psychiatric disorders, are not listed in this nomenclature. (p. 44)

Kinsey (1948) too had trouble classifying homosexuality and resorted to a concept of classification based on *degrees*. This classification ranged from "0" (entirely heterosexual) to "6" (entirely homosexual), with the degrees in between, categories "1" through "5," regarded as bisexual. Kinsey's chart appeared as follows:

0 Entirely heterosexual
1 Largely heterosexual, but with incidental homosexual activities or responses
2 Largely heterosexual, but with distinct homosexual activities or responses
3 Equally heterosexual and homosexual
4 Largely homosexual, but with distinct heterosexual activities or responses
5 Largely homosexual, but with incidental heterosexual activities or responses
6 Entirely homosexual (p. 638)

Each of these views places emphasis on the presence or absence of a sexual preference for members of the same sex, rather than on a person's attitude toward such a preference. For some individuals, however, an inclination toward homosexuality can be a source of great anxiety, internal conflict, and a devalued self-image. Many of those who become sufficiently disturbed about their sexual preferences have turned to psychotherapy for help. The prognosis for successful conversion to heterosexual behavior, however, has been consistently poor, no matter which therapeutic treatment has been employed. For instance, the psychoanalytic method has met with only limited success, with only about one-fourth of the homosexuals undergoing psychoanalysis for two years becoming heterosexual (Bieber et al., 1962).

For the most part, the behaviorist approach to the treatment of homosexuals concentrates on the development of effective heterosexual behavior, as well as the elimination of the homosexual behavior. Such training emphasizes the use of positive reinforcement for behavior considered to be heterosexual. This training often takes place in a controlled environment in which heterosexual modeling of the behavior is provided. Desensitization of any fear or hostility associated with the opposite sex is also an effective treatment. The desensitization procedure usually employs the use of photographs of females in conjunction with relaxation training (Stevenson and Wolpe, 1960). The use of photographs of homosexual behavior, in conjunction with electric shock to the penis, has also been used as a means of achieving an aversion to homosexual behavior (Wilson and Davison, 1974).

Existential-Humanistic Therapies

The philosophical basis for the existential-humanistic approaches to therapy is founded on the contributions of such thinkers as Kierkegaard, Nietzsche, and

Sartre. The psychotherapeutic application of such thinking, however, is primarily the result of the efforts of two Austrian psychiatrists, Ludwig Binswanger (1958) and Medard Boss (1963). Binswanger (1963) viewed abnormal behavior as the consequences of an *existential weakness:*

> By existential weakness we mean that a person does not stand autonomously in his world, that he blocks himself off from the ground of his existence, that he does not take his existence upon himself but trusts himself to alien powers, that he makes alien powers "responsible" for his fate instead of himself. (p. 290)

The goal of therapy, therefore, is to develop a more *mature outlook,* in which one is aware of one's *freedom to choose* and of one's being *independently responsible* for one's fate.

ROLLO MAY   Through the efforts of Rollo May (in his presentation at the Annual Convention of the American Psychological Association, 1959), the existential approach was brought to the United States. In *Existential Psychology* (1967), May reemphasized Kierkegaard's position that "truth exists for the individual only as he himself produces it in action" (p. 12). In other words, our world is our own creation, based on how we perceive it, experience it, and relate to it. In addition, May believed that each person is constantly undergoing change, constantly in the process of learning, evolving, and moving toward the realization of potentials. When this process is interfered with, that is, when the natural tendency toward self-actualizing is frustrated, disturbances in the personality will occur.

According to May, it is the task of the therapist is to attempt to understand the client's problem from the client's subjective point of view. The therapist must attempt to perceive reality as the client perceives it. Having achieved this perspective, the therapist can assist clients more effectively in their struggle between being and non-being, between self-acceptance and rejection, in order to achieve greater awareness of their full potentials.

VIKTOR FRANKL   As one of the few survivors of the Nazi concentration camps, Viktor Frankl (1955) was able to report firsthand on what he refers to as the "human predicament." By this he means the sense of meaninglessness that is left when traditional values break down and are not replaced with new ones that are acceptable. This distinctly human problem stems from each person's inherent need to find meaning in life, what Frankl calls a *"will to meaning."* Resolution of the "human predicament" comes when a person is able to find satisfying purpose, value, and meaning in life. Satisfying meaning, according to Frankl, goes beyond self-gratification to include socially constructive achievements.

Frankl (1955) developed *logotherapy,* a relatively unstructured approach to therapy. Included in logotherapy are such techniques as *confrontation,* in which people attempt to deal objectively with their perceptions of reality. Frankl stressed this point because he believed that *obsessional neurosis* is due to a

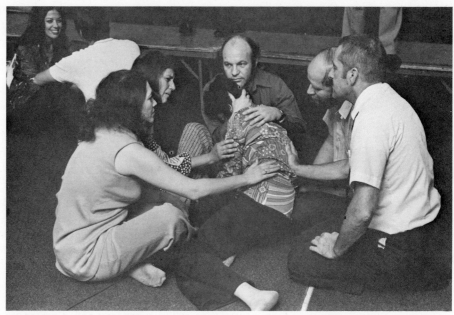

FIGURE 15.8   Sensitivity training is designed to help people gain a greater awareness of their own feelings and those of others, and thereby to become more sensitive and effective while interacting with others. [*Richard Kalvar, Magnum Photo Library.*]

person's inability to endure the discrepancy between the "real" and the "ideal." As a consequence, the individual becomes obsessed with the dream of someday living in a "perfect" world.

Logotherapy also incorporates the use of the *encounter,* in which the person is encouraged to experience an intense, authentic interaction with others, and *paradoxical intent,* in which the person achieves control over undesirable responses by attempting to exaggerate rather than prevent or escape the response. For example, someone who tends to perspire excessively when giving a talk in front of a large group should not try to keep from perspiring, but should concentrate on sweating as much as possible—quarts or gallons instead of just a few drops. Paradoxically, according to Frankl, the greater the effort to perspire, the less this person actually perspires.

CARL ROGERS   One of the best known of the humanistic approaches to therapy is that developed by Carl Rogers (1942), called *client-centered therapy.* Rogers developed this approach as a protest to what he viewed as a dehumanizing attitude held by the behaviorists, and also as a means of providing a viable alternative to psychoanalysis, which he felt was too pessimistic and deterministic.

Client-centered therapy is considered to be a growth therapy in that it is directed toward self-growth, or self-actualization. It is an optimistic approach that is based on the belief that people are basically good, have an innate desire to realize their greatest potential, and are capable of solving their own problems and of making sound decisions.

The goal of this type of therapy is to assist clients in gaining an awareness of their behavior, true feelings, and basic attitudes. Having achieved such awareness, it is believed, clients are more likely to accept the responsibility of being "themselves" and eventually of realizing their full potential. In order that this goal may be achieved, the therapist, following the same line of reasoning that was formulated by Rollo May, must be genuine, warm, and empathetic while maintaining unconditional acceptance and respect for the client. Rogers referred to this attitude toward the client as "unconditional positive regard" and considered it to be essential to successful therapy.

This form of therapy is considered *nondirective* in that the therapist does not attempt to judge, interpret, or advise the client. In client-centered therapy, an environment of trust is established in which the therapist merely reflects the client's emotional state and feelings. Rogers found that through the use of such reflective techniques, clients would often gain insight into their true motivations and feelings and, as a result, would develop a greater willingness to be more authentic persons.

ABRAHAM MASLOW   One of the most dedicated advocates of the humanistic approach to psychology was Abraham Maslow (1908–1970). He, like Rollo May, held the optimistic view that people are basically good and that they must be considered as being dynamic (constantly undergoing change) and creative (effective in solving problems). As a result, Maslow perceived pathology not so much from the standpoint of its being an illness or an inherent defect, but rather from the perspective that pathology is the result of being frustrated in one's attempt to become self-actualizing.

Maslow developed a hierarchy of needs, a stratification of motivational adjustment, in which a person must satisfy the needs of a lower level before attempting to move up to a higher level. The determination of what is required to satisfy each need level is up to each individual. However, if a person is unable to achieve satisfaction at a particular level, then efforts toward self-actualizing will be blocked and abnormal behavior, or personality disturbances, will often develop.

Maslow (1965) noted that many people who are already living reasonably effective lives have been attracted to the humanistic movement in order to enhance their effectiveness and to facilitate their efforts toward self-actualization. While many of these people have turned to sensitivity training or encounter groups, others have sought individual *actualization therapy*. Everett Shostrom (1967) proposes that there are ten recognized therapeutic approaches associated with actualization therapy:

1   *Caring.*   The therapist's attitude of loving regard for the individual, expressed by unconditional warmth or aggressive, critical caring.

2 *Ego strengthening.*   The therapist's development of thinking, feeling, and perceptive ability in the patient to help him or her cope more effectively with life.

3 *Encountering.*   The active encounter between patient and therapist, both of whom are *being* and *expressing* their real feelings.

4 *Feeling.*   The therapist's provision for the client's experiencing a psychologically safe relationship of feelings which heretofore have been found too threatening to experience freely.

5 *Interpersonal analysis.*   The analysis of the manipulative games people play on one another.

6 *Pattern analysis.*   The analysis of the patient's unworkable patterns of functioning, and assistance in the development of adaptive patterns of functioning.

7 *Reinforcing.*   Rewarding behaviors which are growth-enhancing and punishing behaviors which are self-defeating.

8 *Self-disclosing.*   The therapist's exposure of his or her own defensive patterns of living and encouragement of the patient to do the same.

9 *Value reorienting.*   The reevaluation of the patient's loosely formulated values, assumptions, and attitudes.

) *Reexperiencing.*   The patient's reexperiencing of past influential learning and the desensitizing of any pathological effects. (pp. 148–155)

Many of the approaches associated with actualization therapy are also found in other forms of existential-humanistic therapies, and can therefore be considered as parts of a unifying theme. It is possible to find the element of "caring," considered essential to therapist effectiveness in Rollo May's existential therapy; "value reorienting," a fundamental step in identifying one's "will to meaning" in Frankl's logotherapy; the "feeling" of Carl Rogers's client-centered therapy, for establishing a psychologically safe environment for the client; and the "ego strengthening" which is the basis for development of the self-reliance that enables a person to become what Abraham Maslow refers to as self-actualizing.

SUMMARY

In this chapter, the effective use of psychological resources was explored. One of the major areas of discussion was the problem of deciding when someone should seek psychological counseling. It was suggested that counseling may be warranted when a person's lifestyle appears to be self-defeating and unfulfilling, when neurotic behavior or psychosomatic symptoms occur, or when a person is disturbed by sexual dysfunctions. It was also pointed out that a person may wish to seek counseling during times of severe stress, such as during a divorce, after losing a job, or, from a more positive standpoint, for the purpose of achieving greater personal growth.

The availability and variety of psychological resources were also explored, with special emphasis being given to the effectiveness of friends, relatives, and paraprofessionals. Consideration was also given to the problems associated with selecting a therapist and, when necessary, of terminating therapy.

Four major psychotherapeutic approaches to therapy were discussed: (1) the dynamic therapies used by psychoanalysts and the neo-Freudians; (2) the behavioral therapies using such techniques as extinction, aversion, and reinforcement; (3) the sex therapies designed to eliminate sexual dysfunctions and enhance interpersonal relationships; and (4) the existential-humanistic therapies which stress the uniqueness of the individual and his or her potential to become a self-actualizing person.

DISCUSSION QUESTIONS

1 What do you think are some of the main reasons people might be reluctant to seek psychological counseling?
2 What do you believe are some of the major contributing factors behind the rise in the number of attempted suicides among today's youth?
3 Do you have a confidential relationship with a member of your family? If so, how did the relationship come about, and if not, why not?
4 If you were to select a therapeutic approach in counseling, which of the theoretical schools would you prefer: the psychoanalytic, behavioristic, or existential-humanistic?
5 What mental health centers are available in your community?
6 Harry Stack Sullivan emphasized how a person can be heavily influenced by a "significant other." Who do you think has been most influential in your development?
7 Is there anything in particular that you are afraid of (insects, snakes, crowds, etc.)? Would you like to go through a desensitization program in order to eliminate this fear?
8 Do you believe that the current attitudes toward sex are causing more or fewer problems than the more traditional attitudes? In what ways?
9 Do you agree or disagree with Frankl's contention that most people in today's world have lost contact with traditional values and have found little of significance with which to replace them?
10 Do you think that your lifestyle could be improved through one of the growth therapies? In what ways?

EXPERIENTIAL EXERCISES

1 Arrange to have professionals and/or paraprofessionals from a local mental health clinic or hospital appear as guest speakers. Ask them to discuss some of the services that are available, and what it is like to work in the mental health field.
2 Arrange for a group of students to visit a variety of mental health facilities in the community. Arrange for the group to report their their experiences to the class.

3 For a better understanding of the existential-humanistic approach to therapy, ask a number of students to present reports on such books as:

Existential Psychology, by Rollo May
Love and Will, by Rollo May
Toward a Psychology of Being, by Abraham Maslow
Counseling and Psychotherapy, by Carl Rogers

CHAPTER 16

AUTHENTICITY

Unless we have faith in the persistence of our self, our feeling of identity is threatened and we become dependent on other people whose approval then becomes the basis for our feeling of identity. Only the person who has faith in himself is able to be faithful to others, because only he can be sure that he will be the same at a future time as he is today and, therefore, that he will feel and act as he now expects to. Faith in oneself is a condition of our ability to promise, and since, as Nietzsche said, man can be defined by his capacity to promise, faith is one of the conditions of human existence. What matters in relation to love is the faith in one's own love; in its ability to produce love in others, and in its reliability.

Erich Fromm
The Art of Loving

BECOMING AUTHENTIC

Those for whom authenticity is a goal recognize the value of what they already have, and, as well, clearly understand what is enough, what is sufficient, and what is excessive. They are well aware of the price associated with the attainment of certain goals and have set limits on the sacrifices they are willing to make to achieve "success." Many times, they find that the price of "success" is too high with regard to self-respect, time afforded to loved ones, and peace of mind.

Self-Acceptance

Alfred Adler (1939) proposed that in order to avoid a neurotic lifestyle, it is necessary to seek *self-acceptance* rather than high esteem. We must stop comparing ourselves with others and start concentrating on *self-improvement*. If we are to develop a healthy personality, we must disregard the myth of becoming a "perfect" person and learn to appreciate being "good" without having to be "best."

OVERCOMING INADEQUACIES   Adler (1930) believed that the prime motivating force behind all human endeavors is the desire to overcome feelings of inferiority. His premise was that each person begins life as a dependent, insecure infant whose initial existence is one of inadequacy and inferiority. The process of growing up is primarily one of overcoming this state of inferiority. The child strives to learn things others know, to do things others can do, and eventually to be what others are perceived to be—*superior*.

During the course of this transition from inferiority to superiority, there is a tendency to become involved in wishful thinking and fantasy. For some, such involvement can lead to the development of unrealistic expectations, false beliefs, and unfulfilling lifestyles. For example, some individuals may become preoccupied with thoughts of becoming rich, indulging in frequent day-dreaming about what life will be like when they are wealthy. As a consequence, their expectations of how much money they will earn are often unrealistic. Such individuals tend to spend money as if they already had it, thereby often incurring heavy indebtedness. However, rather than face up to the reality of the situation, they will usually develop elaborate, and often complicated, manipulative techniques in order to maintain a certain economic front. Similarly, individuals with unrealistic expectations will tend to underestimate the amount of time and effort required to "reach the top" and will want to be the president of the company six weeks after they have been hired.

Adler believed that goals should be organized so that whatever is necessary and sufficient has first priority. Whatever one "needs" should be acquired before one seeks what one "wants." Physical and intellectual development should be aligned with a "useful lifestyle" wherein successes occur frequently enough to maintain an optimistic attitude toward life. Acquiring a college education prior to entering the field of business management, for example, is necessary in order to be adequately qualified when promotional opportunities arise. In this manner, the adage that "good luck is merely when preparation meets opportunity" tends to hold true, and the stresses associated with having been unrealistic, unprepared, or unqualified can be reduced to a minimum.

PERSONAL RESPONSIBILITY   Gordon Allport (1961) proposed that a sense of personal responsibility does not fully develop until a person's value system has progressed from the level of a "must" conscience to that of an "ought" conscience. According to Allport, the values of a "must" conscience are set by others and are administered, or enforced, by an authoritarian form of thinking. A person with a "must" conscience is motivated primarily by fear, as might be represented by such statements as "Dad would kill me if he ever caught me doing something like that," or "If I don't do it, I'll lose my job."

In contrast, an "ought" conscience is guided by a more humanistic type of thinking. A person with an "ought" conscience is more concerned with the *beneficial consequences* resulting from behaving responsibly than with the detrimental effects of behaving irresponsibly. Such a person would most likely make statements like "I think I'd be able to enjoy myself much more this weekend if I had this work completed," or "Once I have everything organized, things will be easier to find." The difference between the two types is clear. The person with the "must" conscience tends to submit reluctantly to life's demands, doing only what is required. The person with the "ought" conscience is apt to be more autonomous and self-motivating. The "must" conscience "has to do"; the "ought" conscience "prefers to do."

Self-Actualizing

In recent years, there has been a growing tendency to move away from a belief in the existence of inborn personality characteristics. However, Maslow (1955) proposed that an innate drive toward *self-actualization* exists in every individual; that is, one has a need to realize one's greatest potential. Maslow believed that the realization of these potentials is achieved by passing through a sequence of need levels, beginning with the lower *deficit needs* (physiological needs, safety needs, and love and belonging needs) and progressing to the *growth needs* (esteem needs and self-actualizing). In this process, each person must determine what is required in order to satisfy a particular need level; there are no set amounts, and sufficiency is relative to the individual. However, a person must satisfy the lower needs prior to attempting to become seriously involved with a higher level, and must adhere to the sequence of this hierarchy.

PHYSIOLOGICAL NEEDS   Level 1 of Maslow's hierarchy deals primarily with *survival* needs such as hunger, thirst, and sex. Maslow considers these needs to be among the most basic and, consequently, they will take precedence over all other needs should they become deficient. For example, if a person is starving or dying of thirst, the obtainment of food or drink will take priority over concern for safety needs such as passing an exam, or love and belonging needs such as being accepted into a fraternity. A street urchin in Hong Kong who must, by necessity, spend the entire day in search of food allocates little concern to where he will sleep that night.

In the vast majority of cases, however, the plight of an individual is less critical than the extremes thus far illustrated. In most instances, the biological needs in terms of quantity and nutrition can be satisfied, with the exact amounts differing from individual to individual. Insufficiency, therefore, is usually a consequence of not having satisfied the *psychological overtones* associated with satisfying the physiological needs. For instance, the need to have food prepared and served in an affectionate and attractive manner is extremely important to many people. This need is in contrast with that of a person who survives on a diet of TV dinners. The satisfaction of one's thirst can also involve ritualistic toasting and camaraderie that satisfy more than just the physiological requirement of getting something to drink.

SAFETY NEEDS   The second level of Maslow's hierarchy deals with the issue of *security,* both physical and psychological safety. Each individual must determine both the nature of that which poses a threat and the degree of protection that can reasonably be obtained in order to remove or diminish that threat. Protection from the elements, protection from violent acts, and the security of loved ones and possessions all require consideration at this level. However, in many cases, the greatest threats do not originate from the external world, but stem from internal sources. It is vital, therefore, that we attain psychological safety prior to becoming involved with the process of satisfying our love and belonging needs.

LOVE AND BELONGING NEEDS   Achieving sufficiency at this level is highly dependent upon the degree of intensity with which we are able to commit ourselves in relationships with others. Belonging needs are satisfied by befriending, caring for, and loving others. The stronger the commitment, the greater the sense of belonging. Ralph Waldo Emerson (1803–1882), in *Of Friendship,* wrote, "The only way to have a friend is to be one."

In order to attain sufficiency in one's love needs, a person must first feel safe enough to love without demanding reciprocation. If an individual loves someone, and that person rejects this love or fails to love back, that person has—tragically—missed an opportunity to experience being loved. In our trip through life, such opportunities are often rare, and to miss being loved by someone who offers such love is a loss that may never be recovered.

ESTEEM NEEDS   While attempting to achieve sufficiency at this level, it is necessary to consider both the need for *self-esteem* and the need to be held in high *esteem by others.* A person will achieve sufficiency in self-esteem through the development of her or his potentials. By developing these talents, a person becomes capable of making contributions, however large or small they may be, and thus is able to gain a sense of self-worth and self-respect. Another's appreciation of one's own contributions will often provide the recognition needed to attain sufficiency with regard to the need for esteem from others.

SELF-ACTUALIZING   To Maslow, self-actualizing persons are not necessarily "super-persons," but rather, persons who are expressing their individuality as fully as possible. A self-actualizing person's perception is often more efficient that that of others. Consequently, such a person is able to see the world as it really is and to accept the reality of self-awareness for what it really is. Self-actualizing persons are more able to accept not only *who* they are, but also *when* they are living. Therefore, these people are more likely to be spontaneous because of a tendency to live in the here and now rather than in the past or future.

A self-actualizing person is capable of forming strong, binding relationships, but usually only with a very select few. One of the reasons for such selectivity is that, although the self-actualizing person tends to accept others in a very democratic way, this type of person also tends to seek solitude and places a high value on privacy.

The self-actualizing individual is autonomous, self-sufficient, and self-reliant. However, such a person seeks out not only various means of *self-expression,* but also various emotions and ways of experiencing and expressing them as well. In this manner, a freshness of appreciation is able to be maintained, and a person need not require each successive experience to outdo the preceding one in order to be enjoyed.

The self-actualizing person can be in a crowd and still preserve identity.

FIGURE 16.1 *(Top)* Much of the bond of friendship comes from a willingness to share just about everything. [*Laimute E. Druskis, Editorial Photocolor Archives, Inc.*] *(Bottom)* Being "just friends" can often form the basis for an intimate relationship that outlasts many more intense encounters. [*Ginger Chih, Peter Arnold.*]

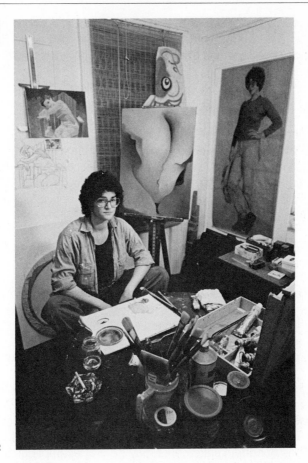

The need to develop a means of self-expression is a major characteristic of the self-actualizing person. [*Timothy Eagan, Woodfin Camp and Associates.*]

FIGURE 16.2

Such an individual does not succumb to mass beliefs, prejudice, or stereotyping, but tends to operate on a personal value system, appraising each situation, event, or person independently. By preserving one's own individuality, one is more likely to accept the individuality of others. By realizing one's own potentials one is more likely to appreciate the potential in others.

Rather than separate oneself from humanity and attempt to change the world, as a self-actualizer one can identify with humanity and try to set an example as to how one would prefer the world to be. One does not, as a self-actualizing individual, assume responsibility for the whole human race, but recognizes in a very deep sense that one is still a very essential part of it.

BEING AUTHENTIC WITH OTHERS

In order for growth to take place within an interpersonal relationship, a proper environment—one that is nutritive, supportive, and forgiving—must be maintained. One's commitment to the relationship must be seen as an opportunity, rather than as an obligation. And, although a deep emotional investment exists, one's resources must be perceived as a contribution rather than as a sacrifice. One must be willing to dedicate oneself to the preservation and perpetuation of the relationship, and to perceive the opportunity to expend such efforts with humility and gratitude.

Growth Relationships

Vital to the continued growth of a relationship is the ability to accurately perceive the effect one's actions and words may have on another—to be able mentally to enter the world of other persons and to identify with what their eyes may be seeing, what their ears may be hearing, or what their hearts may be feeling. Empathy requires *effective perception, active listening,* and *constant vigilance.*

EFFECTIVE PERCEPTION   According to Fritz Perls (1973), effective perception includes being able to experience things in the here and now; that is, to be able to appreciate a situation as though it were being experienced for the first time, as is often the case with the one with whom the situation is being shared. Effective perception includes experiencing people as individuals rather than perceiving them through the distortion of stereotyping and prejudice. It also means being able to understand and appreciate the differences in opinions and impressions arising from differences in age, sex, or cultural backgrounds.

ACTIVE LISTENING   Active listening is a process by which one provides constant feedback to the person attempting to communicate. An active listener *never assumes.* An active listener is constantly performing "reality checks," that is, reaffirming the accuracy of his or her perception and what the implications of certain statements may be. For example, if an active listener is told, "Emmie Lou and I have broken off our engagement," the listener will not make broad, generalizing assumptions, but will inquire, "Does that mean that the two of you won't be dating each other anymore?" The listener may then be told, "Oh, no. We're still going to date each other. We just thought that we weren't quite ready to be planning a marriage."

VIGILANCE   The need for vigilance stems from the need to be constantly aware of the *fluidity* of a relationship. Growth usually means change, and change often means adaptation. By being vigilant, one is more able to take certain precautions in order to prevent or reduce the negative consequences of an impending change. For example, if one of two partners is soon to be left alone at night, certain precautionary measures may be taken. "Since I'll be going to night school this fall, I thought it would be a good idea to install a phone. I'll feel a lot better knowing you can get in touch with someone in case of an emergency."

Vigilance also implies being *alert* within the relationship—noticing subtle changes early, being observant of any deviations from the normal patterns of behavior, and especially, being attentive to nonverbal communication. A person who remains vigilant within a relationship is often more aware of its

FIGURE 16.3 The unconditional trust developed between members of a close, loving family is often the basis for maintaining faith, hope, and unshakable optimism throughout their lives. [*Suzanne Szasz.*]

importance and the significance of the other person, and is less likely to take the relationship, or the other person, for granted.

TRUST   The word "trust" originally came from the Scandinavian language and meant "to comfort," "to console," or "to confide in." It had nothing to do with estimating another's behavior. In fact, even today, the allocation of trust is often independent of another's behavior. For, in one situation, a person may be double-crossed a number of times, and yet decide to trust the double-crosser "one more time." In another situation, a person may decide not to trust someone who has performed with the utmost integrity. "I know he hasn't done anything wrong yet, but there's something about him that I just don't trust."

Trust is being comfortable while at the same time being *vulnerable*. Being vulnerable is absolutely essential in maintaining a growing relationship, for only by being vulnerable can one grow to trust the other person. The greater the risk involved in being vulnerable, the greater the opportunity for developing intimacy. The individual who will not risk sharing a sensitive area with another is acknowledging a lack of trust in that person. Once a person shares a sensitive area, the person who is trusted has the potential of using such information to hurt or to protect the one who trusts. When a person discovers that someone has betrayed a confidence, trust may be withdrawn and the person may choose not to be vulnerable again. "What I told you was in the strictest confidence, and not to be spread all over school or thrown in my face every time you get upset with me." However, should the confidence not be betrayed, then the potential for growing to know one another becomes unlimited. "Yes, Marge knows about it. She's known about it for over twenty-two years, and has never once brought it up or used it against me. I've shared a lot more than just that with her." If the partners are willing to be vulnerable and learn to trust, the true quality of a relationship will be recognized and the true potential of a relationship can be realized.

Confronting Others

Unfortunately, many people associate confronting with attacking, aggression, and assault. However, confronting can also mean coming face to face with the various components of a dilemma or creating an opportunity to examine any discrepancies or distortions of the facts that are being analyzed. For example, a wife may confront her husband with the "realities" of the budget, or an instructor may confront a student with the possibility of failure in a course unless there is an improvement in future test scores.

With regard to being authentic with others, confrontation is often used as a means of challenging the importance, accuracy, or significance of the stressful material within a relationship. Shostrom (1968) believes that the most effective means of presenting such a challenge is through the process of *expressing* and *asserting.*

EXPRESSING   The process of expressing involves confronting others with the way we feel, think, or believe. Along with the expression of feelings, however, it is imperative that we assume personal responsibility for our feelings and not attempt to blame others for our emotional state. For example, a person might say something like "I really let myself get upset over her dating someone else." Such a statement can be contrasted with that of someone who does not assume personal responsibility for his or her emotions and makes a statement like "He makes me so mad when he does that!"

Keep in mind, however, that when expressing an emotion, one is expressing a feeling, not an evaluation. One should, therefore, avoid indiscriminate mixing of emotions and thoughts when attempting to communicate. For example, the expression of an emotion would be on the order of "I feel *excited* about the Ferrari's winning!" rather than "I feel that the Ferrari will always win." Generally, feelings can be expressed in one or two words, whereas an evaluation involves a cognitive process—thinking—and will usually, therefore, require an extended explanation.

When expressing one's thoughts, it is important to remember that the objective is to *express,* not to *impress* the listener. For example, when asked to provide "expert" guidance for another individual, one should give counsel rather than advice. Counseling proffers information and alternatives based on personal experience, and the listener is free to accept or reject the counsel. In this manner, the listener retains personal responsibility for the ensuing decisions or actions. In contrast, the provision of advice merely tells the listener what to do or not to do and, in effect, relieves the individual of any personal responsibility. In other words, the "expressor" thinks *with* others rather than *for* others.

A similar assumption of responsibility takes place with regard to the expression of one's convictions, that is, the sharing of one's beliefs, attitudes, or opinions. When making such disclosures, we are more likely to create a successful confrontation if we use the pronoun "I" rather than "they," "you," or abstract terms like "society" or "everybody." For example, "I disapprove . . . ," rather than "society disapproves," or "I believe . . . ," rather than "everybody believes. . . ."

By maintaining personal responsibility for experiencing and expressing our own thoughts and feelings when confronting someone, we are more likely to trust others to accept personal responsibility for coping with their own lives and feelings. When such trust is mutually expressed, the confrontation has the potential for developing a greater sense of respect and closeness between the participants.

ASSERTING   By asserting ourselves, we are being aggressive without being suppressive. The distinguishing characteristic is that the rights of others are respected. That is, the assertor's goal is not to be achieved "at any cost," but within the confines of her or his ethical standards.

In addition, the assertor is motivated by *desire* rather than by *envy*. The primary difference between the two motivational forces is the absence of the intent to mistreat another person, in the case of desire. By desiring something, the assertor may wish to obtain an object or goal which another may or may not have obtained, but not at the expense of denying the other person the benefits of his or her achievement. Such is not usually the case with envy, which often includes the emotions of jealousy, revenge, and hostility.

Engaging Others

The process of *engaging* means to attract and occupy the attention or efforts of others, as when one engages in a conversation or a project. It also implies the elements of mutual respect, cooperation, and a sense of equality. In order to satisfy these implications, Shostrom believes, engaging can be most effective-ly achieved through *leading* and *respecting*.

LEADING   One of the fundamental differences between leading and dictating is the element of *consent*. The leader consents to accept the responsibility of domination and is more likely to be concerned about the welfare and feelings of those who consent to follow. A dictator, on the other hand, takes charge with or without the consent of others. Generally, the element of mutual consent found in relationships with a leader tends to encourage authenticity, whereas the element of oppression found in a dictatorial relationship is apt to encourage pseudoaccommodation (the pretense of being supportive).

In the process of leading, authority may be allocated to others, but not responsibility. The leader is responsible for selecting the person who is to perform a given task. Should that person turn out to be inept or incapable of fulfilling the assignment, the responsibility for failure in that task is that of the leader who selected the individual.

The person selected by a leader is often aware of this standard of conduct, and is therefore usually more willing to expend the greatest effort possible, knowing that it is the leader who will assume the blame should the project fail. Similarly, the leader will demand good work and maximum effort from those who choose to follow. However, being aware of the limitations and competencies, adequacies, and inadequacies of others, a good leader is willing to accept human error and has an understanding of human frailty.

RESPECTING   Crucial to the process of respecting is the concept of dignity. The concept of dignity involves the perception of another's worthiness, the acknowledgment of another's nobility, and the recognition of another's excellence. A person who respects others is able to find something to respect in everyone—even in enemies. Such respect, for example, is often exhibited on the battlefield between "worthy" foes, such as when British Field Marshal Bernard Montgomery and German Field Marshal Erwin Rommel (the "Desert Fox") struggled for supremacy over North Africa during World War II. The point is that the respecter recognizing the fact that each person is unique and irreplaceable, treats each person as a "thou" rather than as a "thing."

In addition, the respecter recognizes that within each individual there exists a potential—a talent, skill, or quality—through which that individual can develop a means of self-actualization. It is through the development of these potentials that people are able to make contributions that have significance, thereby providing meaning and relevance to their lives. The objective of the respecter is to use his or her intellectual abilities in order to assist others in discovering their potentials. In other words, the respecter strives to guide others to insight, rather than to exploit or outwit them.

Contacting Others

In order to cope with the stresses associated with alienation and aloneness, it is absolutely vital for an individual to be able to establish *meaningful contact* with another person. Usually, this can be accomplished only if a person abandons the use of "manipulative games" and attempts to establish a relationship based on honesty, self-disclosure, and trust.

Contacting can take place at a physical, intellectual, or emotional level. Regardless of the manner in which contacting occurs, understanding is essential to its success. Shostrom proposed that such understanding could be most effectively achieved through *appreciation* and *empathy*.

APPRECIATION   Of the several meanings that can be conveyed by the word "appreciation," perhaps the most important connotation, especially in regard to being authentic, is that of placing a sufficiently high estimate on the importance, or gravity, of a situation, and then to *care* about the possible consequences. Far too often, our lack of appreciation for how important a particular event, person, or object is to another individual causes that individual to experience the stress of feeling irrelevant and unappreciated. Such is the case when little acts of thoughtfulness go unnoticed, or when someone's extra effort goes unpraised.

Intimate relationships are based, in part, on sensitivity and thoughtfulness. These, in turn, are dependent upon the ability to detect, evaluate, and realize the relative worth and importance another person has attached to something. One of the most effective methods of accomplishing this, of course, is to talk openly about matters of significance. However, close observation of an individual's behavior and top priorities can also provide clues to what that person considers significant.

Appreciation also encompasses an adequate recognition of the separateness of the other individual. As Kahlil Gibran warns in *The Prophet* (1964):

. . . let there be spaces in your togetherness,
And let the winds of the heavens dance between you.

Fill each other's cup but drink not from
one cup.

Given one another of your bread but eat
not from the same loaf. (p. 15)

People have a need for privacy and must therefore be afforded opportunities not only to be alone, but also to disclose only that which they freely choose to disclose.

Appreciation for an individual's separateness also includes the recognition of each person's ability to change, to grow, and to be receptive to new experiences. Unfortunately, a great deal of stress is generated through attempts to prevent another person from growing, or from being overly possessive and therefore jealous of all experiences outside the relationship. Such possessiveness usually implies the absence of equality and/or role flexibility within the relationship, and thus can often be a prime source of stress.

EMPATHY   Much of what is termed *empathy* is the ability of one individual to enter emotionally into the "spirit" of what another person is experiencing. Empathy requires sensitivity, compassion, and above all, understanding. Usually, such depth of understanding is possible only through having personally experienced the same or a similar situation before.

Empathy involves a sensitivity to the familiar burdens of life and a sincere attempt at sharing those burdens. It involves patience, tolerance, and the need to be nonjudgmental. Empathy allows one to recognize social injustice, economic inequity, and political insensitivity. Between two people sharing an intimate relationship, empathy offers an opportunity to inspire one another, to instill hope, and to demonstrate concern, as well as requiring active involvement in the other person's life.

Empathetic support can do wonders toward the alleviation of anxiety and doubt, the development of one's self-confidence, and the realization of one's

FIGURE 16.4 "Baring one's soul" can be an extremely intimate moment when a person expresses how he or she really thinks or feels, and it is usually an honor to be the listener. [*Erika Stone, Peter Arnold.*]

potential for self-reliance. Between people who are close, the experience of empathy is often intuitive—a sense of being in tune with one another. It is often expressed through nonverbal means of communication that transmit a sense of "knowing" and "oneness." Empathy lets the other person know that "You are not alone. We're in this together."

AUTHENTICITY

The word "personality" originates from the Latin term for mask—*persona*—and the word is often quite fitting when used to describe the façade behind which people sometimes hide while interacting with one another. However, in order to encourage growth within a relationship, one must be willing to come out from behind the "mask" and disclose one's true nature. The honesty to be oneself is essential to a successful relationship. There is little or no merit in having a phony self loved while living in constant fear that one's true self may some day be uncovered. However, in order to achieve authenticity, individuals must first be willing to be honest with themselves. They must have the courage to be *honest* in their convictions, *open* with their emotions, and *objective* in their perceptions.

People who are being honest are demonstrating a positive attitude toward their convictions and can be opinionated without being dogmatic. Being honest makes it possible to maintain a sense of dignity and self-worth. How much merit would there be in the statement "What you believe in is as important as what I believe in," if individuals thought that their opinions and beliefs were worthless?

Individuals who are open with their emotions are able to share their feelings as well as their thoughts. "I think our decision to have a baby was the right one, but the thought of parenthood still frightens me." It is important to keep in mind, however, that we must be aware of what our feelings really are before we can effectively share them. We must be able to ascertain whether we are feeling angry or hurt, appreciative or envious, or more resentful than annoyed.

Being open also encompasses the sharing of opinions rather than the mere making of judgments. By sharing opinions, we divulge something about ourselves. When making judgments, we are merely pointing out the frailties of others.

The ability to be objective in our perceptions of the world around us renders us more able to leave room for doubt, for the opinions of others, and the possibility that we may be wrong. Objectivity enables us to more readily accept the fact that each person's view of the world is unique. The recognition of this uniqueness often prompts people to set up *authenticity* as their goal. By attempting to become authentic, we are attempting to become *genuine* in personal appearance, mannerisms, and the experiencing and expressing of feelings. People who are authentic attempt to be *truthful* when sharing thoughts and opinions, and to be *responsible* for the results of their behavior. Attempts are made to establish *honest* relationships that allow for individual freedom and permit others to be "themselves" within the relationship. Rainer Maria Rilke (1875–1926) stated:

> Once the realizatign is accepted that even between the *closest* human beings infinite distances continue to exist, a wonderful livifg side by side can grow up, if they succeed in lgvifg the distance between them which makes it possible for each to see the other whole against the sky. (Rilke, 1948, pp. 57–58)

Goals and Self-Concepts

Alfred Adler (1870–1937), in his theory of personality called *individual psychology,* emphasized the importance of social influence and goal striving. He believed that many individuals strive to overcome or overcompensate for real or imagined *inferiorities.* In his view, when such striving becomes obsessive, the person is considered to be neurotic. However, Adler also believed that everyone possesses a "creative self." This "active principle of life" is in many ways similar to the concept of a soul. In *Understanding Human Nature* (1954), Adler wrote:

> It seems hardly possible to recognize in the psychic organ, the soul, anything but a force acting toward a goal, and Individual Psychology considers all the manifestations of the human soul as though they were directed toward a goal. (p. 9)

ASPIRATIONS   According to the behavioral learning theory put forth by John Dollard and Neal Miller (1950), goals are essentially *cue-producing responses* which are generalized into the future. When a child is trained to be future-oriented by stressing the importance of careful planning (seemingly an essential part of successful living), then the plans themselves can become reinforcing, and the feelings associated with such plans are often referred to as *aspirations* or *hopes*.

The level of aspiration for each individual is often heavily influenced by the nature of a person's self-concept, social pressures, and experience. Generally, the person with a healthy self-concept will tend to set goals somewhat higher than she or he actually anticipates attaining. Such a tendency reflects not only the elements of self-confidence, but also a realistic appraisal of one's capabilities and limitations. A person with an unhealthy self-concept will often generate unrealistic levels of aspirations, too high or too low, which will usually result in failure, frustration, and a lack of any sense of accomplishment.

In many instances, parents can be highly instrumental in the development of an unrealistic self-image in their child. This is especially true among parents who attempt to achieve vicariously through their child, often with complete disregard for the child's true abilities, that which they themselves were unable to achieve through their own efforts. The parent who was unable to go to college may push his or her child into a scholastic program which is far beyond the child's capabilities; or, the parent whose athletic ambitions were thwarted by the realities of raising a family may force his or her children into physical challenges that they are incapable of meeting. Unfortunately, children reared by such parents will often experience far more failures in their lives than successes. What is even more important, such children are often rejected by their parents for having failed to live up to their expectations.

Generally, the more experience a person has with success, the higher will be that person's level of aspiration; the more experience a person has with failure, the lower will be that person's level of aspiration. In addition, individuals tend to remember completed tasks which have ended in failure more readily than uncompleted tasks (Rosenzweig, 1943; Glixman, 1949). In fact, the more a person is threatened by failure (that is, the more *ego-involved* an individual is with his or her performance), the more likely that person will be to recall past failure.

On the other hand, the more ego-involved we are with our performance or with the completion of a task, the more effort, devotion, and sacrifice we are willing to put forth. This is a principle which many large companies and institutions are presently emphasizing in attempts to increase employee productivity. Ego involvement also seems to be vital to the achievement of a sense of meaningfulness and importance. Only when one becomes *personally* involved does an event, object, idea, or person take on any real significance.

THE SEARCH FOR MEANING   With a life goal of authenticity in mind, a person is likely to be concerned with the *meaningfulness* of an experience and how it may tend to contribute to growth and maturity, enhance the opportunity for self-expression, or complement his or her "purpose" in life. For such a person, it is not just the attainment of a goal that matters, but also all the things that are encountered along the way.

Friedrich Nietzsche (1844–1900) believed that "He who has a *why* to live can bear with almost any *how*." As long as one is able to perceive meaning in one's existence, purpose in one's behavior, and relevance in one's goals, there will exist a will to live.

Viktor Frankl, founder of logotherapy, narrowed this drive for life, this will to live, to the *will to meaning.* He traced some forms of neurosis to the "failure of the sufferer to find meaning and a sense of responsibility in his existence." Often, as a means of determining what had meaning for his patients, Frankl would ask, "Why do you not commit suicide?" Some would answer, "Because I want to see my children grow up," "Because I have an unused talent," or "Because I want to go to heaven." The reasons varied, but all of the patients have a goal, a purpose, an answer to the "why" of life. Bertrand Russell (1872–1970), in *Why Men Fight* (1915), wrote:

> The world has need of philosophy, or a religion, which will promote life. But in order to promote life it is necessary to value something other than mere life. Life devoted only to life is animal without any real human value, incapable of preserving men permanently from weariness and the feeling that all is vanity. If life is to be fully human it must serve some end which seems, in some sense, outside human life, some end which is impersonal and above mankind, such as God, or truth, or beauty. (p. 268)

One of the greatest difficulties a person faces today is the problem of *recognizing* such ends. Many are unable to recognize what they *really* want and will therefore devote much of their energy toward the attainment of what they are *supposed* to want. For example, many individuals may really want a close, loving relationship, but peer group pressure convinces them that they are supposed to want to "play the field." As a consequence, they will often substitute sex for intimacy and confuse passion with love.

REPLACEABLES VERSUS IRREPLACEABLES   Others have difficulty with the area of *priorities,* often devoting enormous resources toward the attainment of *replaceables* rather than toward the preservation of that which is *irreplaceable.* When individuals center their desires on that which is replaceable, they often fail to recognize the intrinsic value therein and the potential to achieve a satisfying sense of identification. That which is replaceable is often perceived as having utilitarian value only. As a consequence, it is desired and valued only so long as it serves some purpose. Almost all material quests, all "things" that

FIGURE 16.5

While all else is in turmoil or in the process of change, a sense of security often comes from being in the presence of something that is familiar and cherished, something for which there can be no substitute. [*Ken Heyman.*]

are not one of a kind, can fall into the category of the replaceable. Chevrolet fenders, screen doors, most jobs, and money are replaceable; Michelangelo's ceiling of the Sistine Chapel, Da Vinci's *Mona Lisa,* and Beethoven's Fifth Symphony, along with other artistic originals, are irreplaceable. Most toys are replaceable; however, favorite blankets, dolls, or teddy bears are often irreplaceables. Most jewelry is replaceable, but great-grandmother's wedding ring is irreplaceable. Most things built or created by others are likely to be replaceable, while that which is built or created by one's own hands can often become irreplaceable; carrots abound in the supermarket, but those eaten by the gopher after the gardener's plowing, planting, and weeding, and watering them are irreplaceable. It is important to note, however, that since each person is one of a kind, people by this definition should *never* be considered replaceable.

Adjusting Levels of Aspiration

Since of us is unique, and is therefore "blessed" or "cursed" with capabilities and limitations that may change with time or situation, it is often necessary to go through a period of reassessment. During such self-appraisals, task-oriented people are able to evaluate more clearly just what they are or are not capable of accomplishing. For instance, a person who is thirty-four years old may have had the goal of being a millionaire by the age of thirty-five. In such a situation, a realistic evaluation might very well warrant an adjustment in the level of aspiration.

Gordon Allport (1955) proposed that many of the goals to which the healthy person aspires are, in the final analysis, *unattainable.* With each success, the potential for even greater success comes within the realm of realistic possibility, resulting in a continuous elevation of one's level of aspiration. For example, after receiving a high school diploma, a student may perceive college as a possibility. After receiving the B.A., the student sees graduate school as a more viable alternative, and later, the still higher goals of earning a master's degree and a Ph.D. Allport (1955) wrote: "Salvation comes only to him who ceaselessly bestirs himself in the pursuit of objectives that in the end are not fully attained" (p. 67).

Adjustment in one's level of aspiration may also involve a certain degree of accommodation or compromise. In such cases, people are often willing to settle for *part* of what they had originally set out to get. This is often true in regard to negotiations between labor and management, parent and child, or husband and wife. Ideally, by adjusting the levels of aspiration, in many instances both parties will be able to realize a portion of their demands. When this is possible, *mutual accommodation* has been achieved.

When neither adjustment of the levels of aspirations nor compromise seems to provide sufficient satisfaction, most individuals will become willing to accept an alternative, or substitute, goal. This aspect of adjustment is often seen as a last resort because of the social implication that a substitute is inferior to the original. For the ego-oriented personality, alternative goals are often seen as "settling for less than the best." Such an attitude can prevail after having married someone other than the person's first choice or after having taken a job with a company other than the one really preferred.

This attitude can be contrasted with the attitude of the task-oriented person whose perception toward alternative goals is often one of general acceptance and with the more positive attitude that the substitute is "better than nothing." For example, a person may wish to own a Ferrari, but, unable to afford one, buys a modestly priced sports car and has fun anyway. The primary difference then, is that, in comparison with the task-oriented person, the ego-oriented person shows the lack of a positive attitude, and perhaps even more important, the lack of appreciation.

Learning to Achieve Our Potentials

Kurt Goldstein (1879–1965) developed a theory of personality based on a holistic approach, which advocated the need to understand the "total" person in order to truly comprehend what motivates that person. The theory is known as the *organismic theory.* It is founded on the premise that human beings are basically good and have a natural motivation toward self-realization. Goldstein (1939) called this natural motivation the *"master-motive."* He believed that it governs all behavior directed toward *"replenishment"* or *"self-fulfillment."*

Maslow (1955) agreed with Goldstein's concept of a master motive, but referred to it as the need to *self-actualize.* What Goldstein referred to as the acts of replenishing, he regarded as a need to satisfy *deficiency* needs. He viewed behavior oriented toward self-fulfillment as the expression of one's *growth* needs.

In both perspectives, however, the criterion for satisfaction is arbitrary. Each person must *learn* what is needed in order to feel replenished and to achieve a feeling of fulfillment. The neurotic person often fails to learn what is sufficient. The neurotic, unfortunately, will often quit college short of a degree or become obsessed with the thought of attaining ever higher degrees with little sense of accomplishment for prior achievements.

William Alamshah (1963) proposes that such ineffectual behavior is often due to a lack of *unity* in a person's motives and a failure to take *"cultural needs"* into account. The cultural needs he has in mind are (1) the need to be charitable, and (2) the need for beauty.

THE NEED TO BE CHARITABLE   Alamshah (1963) defines the need to be charitable as "the urge to exercise feelings of gentleness, compassion, the higher levels of sympathy, and tenderness . . . a kind of tension which motivates the self to identify with other beings." Such a definition is similar to Henry Murray's (1938) concept of *n Nurturance,* which emphasizes the needs to provide assistance to the weak, to express "maternal" impulses, and to express other forms of caring, compassion, or tenderness. However, Alamshah perceived the need to be charitable as characterized by "an overflow (rather than a deficiency) . . . of energy or feeling which must somehow be used creatively."

Alamshah states that, based on the belief in the principle of similarity, that is, the belief that all people possess the same inherent needs, "empathy enables us to know or to sense the feelings or intentions of the other." With this knowledge, one is able to act or react appropriately: that is, to relate in a sensitive and caring manner, and to identify with the consequences of one's own behavior. It is this ability to identify with one's own influence on others that enables one to experience *philos,* or brotherly love, and to develop a strong sense of responsibility within a relationship. Once a mature person has assumed responsibility for his or her behavior, charitable behavior occurs "expectedly and consistently," whereas, in an immature and irresponsible person, charitable behavior tends to occur "unexpectedly and sporadically."

The element of *commitment* is an integral part of assuming personal responsibility within a relationship. Such a commitment includes a resolution to serve not only one's own needs, but the needs of others as well. It also requires a person to recognize that her or his ultimate well-being is intimately involved with the well-being of others. There is little comfort in being physically satiated whide watching loved ones starve, and very rarely can one expect to materialize one's intellectual hopes when surrounded by ignorance.

Another requirement of charity is to remain *detached* and *nonpossessive.* An act of charity is not intended to promote a return of like for like. William Alamshah, in *The Pursuit of Excellence* (1963), states:

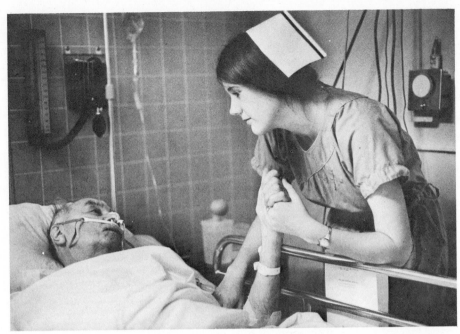

FIGURE 16.6   The need to be charitable is often motivated out of the awareness that one's own sense of well-being is intimately involved with the well-being of others. [*Sherry Suris, Photo Researchers, Inc.*]

The lover, in giving of his or her love, is concerned with only two things: first, to love, since this is perceived as inherent in one's being; second, to love because the other has feed of it. Charity, thus, asks no return for love given. For charity is aware that in the act of loving one has already received one's full cmmpensation: to love is to gratify the need to be charitable. (p. 51)

THE NEED FOR BEAUTY   Alamshah defines the need for beauty as "a kind of tension which motivates the self to experience aesthetic impressions . . . to turn these impressions into expressions, and ultimately to express the *universal in the particular.*" It is Alamshah's belief that just such a tension stimulates the creation of a civilized society rather than merely a collection of members organized for their mutual advantage and protection.

Aesthetic impressions begin with the perception of *form,* which has the potential of generating interest, pleasure, and satisfaction. While experiencing a given form, one may develop an appreciation for its excellence, or for the harmonious relationship the parts of the form have with the total image. When a person has learned how to organize several parts into a harmonious whole, she or he is described as having "good taste."

When the harmonious quality of the form is recognized as representing the "universal in the particular," the form is perceived as having beauty. For example, the smile of the *Mona Lisa* is a particular smile which represents, to many, the smile of all women. Similarly, the Taj Mahal seems to represent the potential of all architectural efforts. Since such representations are difficult to achieve, people are often motivated to preserve and cherish those examples which do occur. Because of the elusive, and often subliminal, nature of the universal aspect of art, be it painting, poetry, or music, it is often necessary to learn of the skills required and of the demanding nature of a medium before one can fully appreciate how difficult a task it is to represent an ideal truthfully and thus create beauty. Willa Cather (1876–1947) wrote, in *The Song of the Lark* (1915), "Artistic growth is, more than it is anything else, a refining of the sense of truthfulness. The stupid believe that to be truthful is easy; only the artist, the great artist, knows how difficult it is" (p. 477).

When we attempt to represent our impressions in order to share them more easily, we will usually try to express them symbolically. The function of symbolic representation is to recreate the experience of the original impression or to *generate* a similar impression in others. However, one of the most direct means of accomplishing such a task is through the process of *imitation*. Alamshah (1963) states that "an imitative expression is an effort to reproduce, with little or no alteration or interpretation." In this vein, we will often attempt to mimic another's mannerisms, copy another's style, or generate an "authentic reproduction" of the original.

The need for beauty appears to be inherent in all human beings, either as creators or appreciators of beauty, or both. Each of us, however, is faced with the responsibility for recognizing our particular needs for expression, for developing our own skills of expression, and for learning how to satisfy our need for understanding, charity, and beauty. Aristotle, in *On Man in the Universe* (1963), stated: "The end toward which men strive in life is happiness. Happiness for each creature is found in the best possible performance of the function for which he is peculiarly adapted" (p. 86).

THE NEED TO BELIEVE IN SOMETHING OR SOMEONE   Along with the socially oriented needs to belong, love, and be important, human beings also have the need to believe in something or someone "as a dependable source for the gratification of security needs" (physiological and psychological safety needs) (Alamshah, 1963).

Alamshah suggests several reasons for the development of such a need. One such reason is the lengthy state of dependency children experience with their parents; they must believe in the *permanency* of this dependent relationship. Another reason for needing to believe in something or someone is based on our ability to contemplate the continuity of the past, present, and future—the ability to believe in the prior existence of something before our awareness, as well as the continued existence of something after our own existence terminates. The last reason lies within our awareness of the transient (temporary) nature of objects and people—our acknowledgement that although they exist now, they may not exist at some point in the future.

Many of us become preoccupied with attempts to gain a sense of security through the acquisition of material possessions, i.e., land, money, and other "things." Others of us will seek security by attempting to perpetuate a particular social, economical, or political system, or by attempting to prolong a particular way of life. In each case, we are trying to achieve a sense of permanence and security. However, since land can be lost, money stolen, and systems overthrown, the feelings of insecurity usually persist. Such anxiety continues unless we undergo the experience that William James called *"metanoia,"* "turning soul to light." Abraham Maslow referred to this as a "peak experience," and many Christians describe it as the "experience of conversion."

After experiencing metanoia, a person tends to seek a sense of security and permanence through *understanding* and the acquisition of *wisdom* rather than through possessiveness and the acquisition of things. After such an experience, a person recognizes that the need to believe in something or someone is a need for *faith*. Before such a conversion, "faith" is usually based on prior experience (having succeeded in doing a particular task before, one has "faith" that one can do it again). However, after experiencing metanoia, faith is often based on *ideals*—scientific "laws," religious doctrine, or an intuitive faith in oneself. Permanence is found through satisfying *spiritual* needs rather than physical needs.

SUMMARY

One of the major topics discussed in this chapter was the process by which a person can attempt to become more authentic. Included in this discussion was the need for self-acceptance, whereby a person concentrates on overcoming inadequacies through self-improvement rather than through competition with others. Major emphasis was placed on Maslow's hierarchy of needs—physiological, safety, love and belonging, esteem, and self-actualizing.

Being authentic with others was also discussed. Special consideration was given to the need to empathize with another person, "listening" attentively to both verbal and nonverbal attempts to communicate, and staying alert to any changes that may take place within a relationship. In addition, the discussion covered the importance of confronting another person with how one truly feels and thinks, as well as letting others know what it is that one appreciates about them, and the problems associated with being a leader within a relationship, while still maintaining the respect of those who choose to follow.

The chapter concluded with a general description of the goals and aspirations that are characteristic of an authentic person. Included was the need to temper one's various levels of aspiration with a realistic appraisal of one's limitations and capabilities. It was suggested that the primary goal of an authentic person is to find meaning and purpose in life, along with the fulfillment of the need to be charitable, the need to perceive beauty, and the need to believe in someone or something.

DISCUSSION QUESTIONS

1 As you were growing up, was there someone that you consistently felt inferior to and secretly wished to become superior to someday? Do you still feel that way?
2 Do you believe that you have sufficiently satisfied the deficiency needs (physiologi-

cal, safety, and love and belonging) in Maslow's hierarchy of needs? If not, which level do you think is most deficient?

3 While being vigilant in a relationship, what sorts of things do you look for as signs that something may be upsetting the other person?

4 What do you consider the advantages of immediately telling a person that something is bothering you rather than postponing the confrontation? Do you tend to do this? If not, why?

5 Can you think of an individual whom you would consider to be a leader; someone whom you would consider to be a dictator? What are the primary differences between these two individuals?

6 Have you experienced a relationship with a person who was overly possessive? In what ways did this person attempt to keep you from growing?

7 Is there someone with whom you have a confidential relationship in which you can be honest and open about how you really think and feel? What is it about this person that enables you to be so vulnerable?

8 How have your goals and aspirations changed over the years? Have they been elevated or reduced? Have they become more realistic? If so, in what way?

9 What is it that gives your life the greatest meaning or sense of purpose?

10 Whom or what do you believe in as being enduring and dependable? That is, in whom or what do you have faith?

EXPERIENTIAL EXERCISES

1 Make arrangements with your friends and family to "correct" you each time you use pronouns such as "they," "we," and "you" or collective terms such as "society," "everyone," "everybody," and "people" instead of a responsible "I." For example, have the others correct you if you make statements such as "We thought you meant . . . " rather than "I thought you meant . . . " or "Everyone thinks he would make a good canditate" rather than "I think he would make a good candidate." The objective of this exercise is to make you more aware of, and thus more responsible for, your statements. Try it for one week and then share any insight that may have occurred.

2 Select a number of students in the class to read *The Velveteen Rabbit,* by Margery Williams, and to present a report on their impressions of the book.

3 Have the students in the class write a two-page essay on what being an authentic person means to them. Select some of the papers as examples to be shared with the entire class.

GLOSSARY

abreaction the process of totally eliminating or reducing the anxiety associated with emotionally threatening conflicts or repressed material. This is possible by reliving or imagining the incident that was the original cause of the conflict.

accommodation a situation where individuals know their status or roles and are willing to adjust their differences in order to work together.

acquaintanceship the progression of a relationship to the level of both interest and concern; passive involvement with an associate.

acrophobia fear of high places. As with most *phobias,* the acrophobic person feels that the reason for the fear is irrational.

active aggression aggression that is expressed through overt physical or verbal means, such as using abusive language or fighting.

active involvement a relationship which includes the emotion of concern and involves personal commitment.

addiction recurring use of a natural or synthetic drug, because of the psychic and/or physical dependence on the effects produced by the drug.

adjustment the ability to select appropriate and effective means of coping with the stresses and demands of the environment without feeling overwhelmed.

aggressive mob a group that releases hostility indiscriminately in the form of destructive behavior.

aggressive people individuals who consistently move against other people. They generally tend to be highly exploitive and competitive, with an excessive need to excel.

agoraphobia fear of open places. Like most other *phobias,* the fear seems unwarranted to the person suffering it.

anaclitic depression the mental, emotional, and physiological retardation in the development of an infant who is deprived of sufficient, effective mothering.

anal stage the second of the *psychosexual stages,* occurring between the ages of two and four. During this stage the individual resists enculturation by resisting attempts at toilet training. Overly strict toilet training was thought by Freud to result in the development of an anal-retentive personality, characteristic of an individual who is extremely self-controlled. Overly permissive toilet training may lead to the development of an anal-repulsive personality pattern of impulsivity and disorganization.

anima, animus anima is Jung's term for the feminine part of one's personality, and the animus is his term for its masculine part. He believed that everyone has these parts to his or her personality, both of which need to be accepted.

anorexia nervosa a psychological disturbance which results in an inability or refusal to eat.

anthropomorphize to ascribe human characteristics to a nonhuman object or animal.

antisocial personality a personality disorder that causes an individual to be constantly in trouble with society. It manifests itself through lack of identification with authority figures.

aptitude test a test which aids in assessing a person's capacity to learn or the quality of his or her future performance.

artist level of adjustment Otto Rank's highest level of personal *adjustment,* achieved through the resolution of conflict between life and death fears by accepting the reality of separateness and acknowledging that everyone is indeed unique.

attitude an enduring system of perceptive evaluation, emotional predisposition, and action tendencies.

authenticity the honesty to be oneself that is essential to a successful relationship.

autonomy-oriented parents parents who tend to tolerate disobedience, establish few limits or restrictions, and assume a laissez faire relationship with their children.

average man level of adjustment Otto Rank's lowest level of adjustment. An individual's belief, fostered by an intense life fear, that what the group wants is what the individual wants. Therefore, adjustment is the same as conforming.

basic anxiety an insidiously increasing, all-pervading feeling of being lonely and helpless in a hostile world.

behavioral sink a condition where an extreme level of pathological behavior occurs, primarily because of overpopulation pressures.

behaviorism a school of psychology that is based on the learning and unlearning of overt behavior. It focuses primarily on that which is observable.

biological clock an unexplainable internal mechanism by which metabolic processes are regulated. For example, some people are able to know the approximate time of day with few external cues.

body image one's internalized image of one's physical characteristics and one's feelings about these qualities.

bulimia pathological overeating.

Cannon-Bard theory of emotions the theory that sensory experiences are simultaneously relayed to both the body and the brain and that the emotional experience takes place in the brain, regardless of the nature of the physiological changes that occur. Furthermore, it is the thalamus that alerts both the cortex and *hypothalamus,* which are individually responsible for the particular emotion. Emotions are not simply the outgrowth of physical changes in the body.

catalogic thinking Suicidal thought processes that are characterized by extreme *depression,* feelings of despair, and hopelessness.

chaining   the process by which one response may produce the stimulus for the next.

classical conditioning   the pairing of an involuntary response (e.g., jerking back from an electric shock) with a neutral stimulus (e.g., light), so that the stimulus alone can cause the response. Explored by Ivan Pavlov.

claustrophobia   the fear of small, closed places.

client-centered therapy   a type of therapy developed by Carl Rogers which emphasizes the individual's ability to find his or her own potential when in an atmosphere of *unconditional positive regard*.

clinical psychologist   one who holds a Ph.D. in psychology plus one to two years of internship that involved supervised training in the individual and group therapy techniques.

cloning   the reproduction of a "twin" from a single cell of the "parent individual" without the employment of sexual reproduction.

cognitive dissonance   stress caused through either the incompatibility of behavior with beliefs or the acceptance of two incompatible ideas.

cognitive theory of emotion   the theory that emotional experiences are the outgrowth of one's *appraisal* of both the physiological changes taking place and the nature of a given situation.

collective unconscious   Jung's concept of universal mental images and symbols that are derived from the common ancestral roots of all human beings and are shared by them.

compensation   an attempt to make up for, or cover over, some weakness by emphasizing one's strong points.

compensatory violence   the substitution of violence for productive activity in an impotent or ineffective person.

compliant person   a person who moves toward others to gain affection, approval, and a feeling of acceptance.

concrete operation, stage of   the stage, between the ages of seven to eleven, when a child is able to think logically about certain physical properties, but is still not able to use sophisticated abstract thinking.

conditional positive regard   the approval of only some aspects of an individual.

conflict   the presentation of two or more mutually exclusive goals which results in difficulty in deciding on a course of action.

conformity   the result of bowing to group or peer pressure to behave or believe in accordance with group expectations.

connotative meaning of a word   emotional or personal overtones that a word implies to a particular individual.

contact comfort   the basic need for affection and physical contact that is essential for normal development.

contaminated thinking   suicidal thinking colored by strong religious or cultural beliefs; death is perceived as a transition to another life or spiritual level, or as a means of saving face.

control-oriented parents   parents who are inflexible in setting limits and restrictions, and who assume an authoritarian relationship with their children.

cost of maintaining a relationship   the weighing of both the positive and negative aspects of a relationship.

counseling psychologist   a psychologist who has a Ph.D., an Ed.D., an M.S.W., or an M.A., with specialized training in education, vocational, or personal counseling.

counterconditioning   the substitution of a new, more appropriate response to an old stimulus through *classical conditioning*.

crystallized intelligence   the combined result of an individual's training, education, and socialization.

cultural need   William Alamshah's term for the need to understand, to be charitable, and to experience beauty.

cultural relativity   the measure of an individual's behavior as appropriate or inappropriate according to the norms and values of a particular culture.

culture shock   the stress experienced by anyone undergoing any kind of change (social, geographic, economic, cultural, etc.) in lifestyle.

day-patient care   a therapeutic program, usually at a hospital or out-patient clinic, where out-patients spend the day in socialization and occupational activities.

death fear   Rank's term for a person's fear of loss of individuality through conforming.

defense mechanism   a cognitive or behavioral pattern which protects a person from anxiety or guilt. *Rationalization,* denial, and repression are examples of this mechanism.

defensive identity   an attempt to increase one's sense of self-worth by identifying with another person or by affiliating or associating with a group.

denotative meaning of a word   the dictionary, or explicit, definition of a word.

depressant   an agent, primarily a barbiturate, that acts to reduce the body's functional activity.

depression   any emotional state keynoted by an inability to react appropriately to stimuli, or certain kinds of stimuli, and a pervasive feeling of helplessness and gloom.

deprived environment   a milieu in which an individual has few alternative choices or one in which there is relatively little stimulation.

desensitization   a therapeutic technique which teaches a person to relax when presented with a series of associations that progress from the least arousing to the most arousing stimulus. A fearful individual thus learns to relax in the presence of an anxiety-provoking stimulus.

detached person   a person who moves away from others and is independent and socially withdrawn.

developmental aphasia   an inability to understand or express oneself verbally because of *minimal brain dysfunction.*

direct aggression   aggression that is expressed directly at the person or object producing frustration.

discrimination   the ability to perceive the differences among similar stimuli; the ability to associate new information with old information.

discriminative cue   a warning cue which signals a subsequent action; often associated with conditioning but not directly involved.

displaced aggression   aggression that is redirected to a person or object other than the one originally causing the frustration. This aggression may be disguised.

dominant parental attitude   an attitude that is more pervasive than other parental stances.

double-bind   a situation in which all possible solutions fail to lead to a successful resolution, and may lead to increased anxiety; two conflicting "messages" sent simultaneously.

drive   the desire or state of arousal that is experienced after having been deprived of something needed or wanted. The motivating force behind behavior.

drive-reduction theory   Hull's theory that learning can occur only when drive-reducing *reinforcement,* such as food or water, modifies an organism's internal state.

dyad a relationship formed by two members that is usually stable and positive in attitude.

dyscalculia the inability to manipulate numbers because of *minimal brain dysfunction*.

dysgraphia the inability to write because of *minimal brain dysfunction*.

dyslexia the inability to read because of improper visual perception (usually reversal) of letters and words.

ectomorph Sheldon's term for the lean person who tends to be self-conscious and intellectual.

ego in Freud's scheme of the psyche, that part which mediates between the impulses of the *id*, the punitiveness of the *superego*, and the demands of the real environment. The ego operates according to the *reality principle*. It may also be defined as a person's self-perception, which is influenced both by one's own and by others' evaluations.

ego integrity the ability to reflect on life with the perspective and accumulated knowledge of a full life without experiencing a sense of having been cheated.

Electra complex the female's conflict, most prominent during the *phallic stage*, between her love for her father and competition with her mother for his love. Resolution of this conflict results from the girl's identification with her mother.

elicited response in *classical conditioning*, behavior that would normally be elicited by an unconditioned stimulus or has been trained to occur upon the presentation of a once neutral stimulus that has been paired with an unconditioned stimulus.

emotion a feeling associated with a particular experience.

empathy the ability to mentally enter another person's world and to identify with what she or he is experiencing.

endogenous depression *depression* that results from internal sources. The symptoms include loss of appetite, apathy, and lowered self-esteem.

endomorph Sheldon's term for the rotund person who enjoys people and physical comforts.

enriched environment a setting in which an individual has many alternative choices, or one which offers a great deal of stimulation.

escape or avoidance behavior behavior which prevents, avoids, or removes the possibility of experiencing a painful or unpleasant stimulus.

ethologist a scientist who studies the relationships between animals and their natural habitats.

existential belief the premise that each person has freedom of choice based on individual perception, and that each person is solely responsible for the way he or she chooses to feel. The belief stresses self-reliance, self-direction, and self-acceptance.

existential neurosis a condition characterized by a dispirited approach to everyday living. The person senses no purpose or significance to life.

exogenous depression a *depression* that results from external *stress*. Reactions generally include oversleeping, overeating, and a sense of dejection.

expedient conformity compliance merely for the sake of propriety and not because of any deep inward conviction.

expressing revealing to others what one feels, thinks, or believes.

expressive mob characteristically, a nonaggressive group which concentrates its efforts on attaining a particular end.

extinction the unlearning of a previously learned response by withholding the original stimulus or reward.

fear of success   avoidance of success for fear that negative social consequences will result.

fixation   failure to successfully pass through one of Freud's *psychosexual stages*, which results in one's personality being dominated by exaggerated forms of the characteristics of that stage.

fixed interval schedule   a schedule of reinforcement in which an individual is given *reinforcement* after a fixed amount of time has passed.

fixed ratio schedule   a schedule of reinforcement in which an individual is given *reinforcement* after making a predetermined number of responses.

fluid intelligence   an individual's intellectual abilities (e.g., brightness and adaptability) regardless of experience or education.

formal group   a group characterized by clearly defined lines of authority and well-established channels of communication.

free association   a therapeutic technique, developed by Freud, in which a client follows whatever thoughts come to mind in order to discover the unconscious connections between certain feelings and thoughts and a given stimulus.

friendship   a relationship that includes a perception of excellence, a feeling of appreciation, and interest and concern for another individual.

frustration   a feeling that arises when goal-directed behavior is blocked by a physical obstacle, deficiency, or conflict.

functional fixedness   an inability to transfer learning from one specific situation to another.

general adaptation syndrome   similarity of physical distress symptoms that occur when the body, faced with a *stress*-provoking incident, mobilizes all its adoptive resources to deal with that incident.

generalization   the process of responding to stimuli that are similar to the one which an individual has learned to associate with certain feelings or behavior. Primary generalization is a response to stimuli that are physically similar to the original stimulus. Secondary generalization involves responses to stimuli that have the same meaning rather than the same physical properties as the original stimulus.

generativity   concern for the welfare of others and of future generations.

genital stage   Freud's final *psychosexual stage*, which he defined as beginning at the onset of puberty and continuing into adulthood. It has two phases: homosexual and heterosexual. The first phase, the "gang" phase, is the homosexual one which involves deep emotional, but nonsexual, intimacy with a same-sexed friend. Later, the heterosexual phase is possible. It involves the unity of sexual and emotional intimacy with a member of the opposite sex.

gestalt theory   the concept that a response to a situation can be considered only as a part of a whole response to a whole situation. The parts of a response represent salient figures rather than distinct elements. This theory disagrees with the premise that the response to a given situation can be understood by merely investigating each element in a situation separately and then adding one's observations together.

group   an association of two or more people.

group loyalty   a relationship which renders group members reluctant to question group behavior, since doing so might threaten group uniformity and cohesiveness.

group think   a deterioration of mental efficiency, reality testing, and moral judgment resulting from group pressure to carry out the plans of the group regardless of the consequences.

habit   a tendency to give a response, mental or physical, which is usually performed when a particular stimulus is present.

halfway house a residence in the community where a person who has been institutionalized can live and gradually learn skills needed for independent living. Halfway houses usually serve small groups of individuals who are supervised but are given much freedom and are self-governing.

hallucinogen a substance, such as hashish, peyote, or LSD, that induces hallucinations—or makes the individual unable to distinguish reality.

halo effect the judgment, based on the consideration and generalization of irrelevant characteristics, to form an overall favorable impression of an individual.

hedonism the theory that the avoidance of pain and the search for pleasure govern all human behavior.

holistic attaining a total picture of a particular situation through processing diverse information about it.

homeostasis an internal balance between the body's nutritional, temperature, and water needs that is achieved through a complex system of self-regulation.

humanistic psychology a school of psychological thought which focuses on an individual's quest for identity, meaning, and the fulfillment of his or her potential.

hypersomnia oversleeping, sometimes a result of *stress* or *depression.*

hypochondriacal neurosis a condition characterized by a constant preoccupation with, or concern about, one's own physical condition despite good physical health.

hypothalamus the part of the brain located in the forebrain. It is believed to be the control center for the regulation of hunger, thirst, sleep, and temperature.

hysteria a type of neurotic disturbance that is characterized by physical symptoms that have no organic basis.

id in Freud's scheme of the psyche, the id is the part containing the primitive innate urges of fear, rage, and lust. The id is not rational or moral and therefore tends to press for immediate gratification.

ideal self each individual's conception of the type of person he or she would like to be. One's ideal self is a composite of parental wishes and attributes of models that one hopes to emulate.

identity crisis a head-on confrontation between society's demands and the individual's personal needs.

imitation an exact reproduction of observed behavior.

incentive and motivational process the process of receiving rewards or punishment as a result of imitating another's behavior, emotional responses, and/or attitudes.

incongruency Carl Rogers's term for an individual's experience of his or her behavior as inconsistent with that person's self-concept.

informal group a group generally based on cliques, the "grapevine," or friendships. Such a group often takes the place of inefficient or unsatisfactory formal groups.

insight therapy a form of therapy that brings to conscious awareness the source of one's motivations and the ability to view oneself as one really is.

insomnia the inability to sleep adequately, sometimes resulting from anxiety or depression.

intellectual competence the ability to understand, to reason, and to solve problems effectively.

intellectual flexibility the ability to interpret one's environment from a variety of perspectives. It also includes the abilities to think creatively and to develop alternatives to one's plans or goals.

intelligence often seen as the ability to handle new situations quickly and successfully.

interlocutory separation an agreement stipulating provisional obligations and restrictions to which a married couple must adhere prior to being granted a final divorce decree.

internalization   the process by which one adopts the attitudes and behavior of important people in one's life, thereby making these qualities part of one's own personality.

interpersonal theory   Harry Stack Sullivan's theory of personality which is based on the importance of interactions with other people, especially one's parents.

inter-role conflict   the phenomenon that occurs when an individual tries to satisfy two incompatible roles.

James-Lange theory of emotion   a theory that, first, physiological changes take place in the body, and are then followed by the experience of an emotion.

kinesics   the analysis of nonverbal expression, particularly body posture and movement, as it relates to communication.

latency stage   one of Freud's *psychosexual stages*, occurring between the ages of eight and twelve, during which a child concentrates on playing and learning; sexual conflicts are not prominent at this time.

learning disability   difficulty in acquiring knowledge because of neurological or emotional problems, or both.

legal separation   a formal agreement providing for many of the responsibilities of marriage while each spouse sets up separate residences.

libido   Freud's term for the primitive source of energy that motivates pleasure-seeking and goal-seeking behavior.

life fear   Rank's term for the fear of being separate and alone.

life space   the psychological environment that one experiences subjectively; one's personal perception of the internal and external world.

logotherapy   a form of therapy, developed by Victor Frankl, stressing the need to find meaning and purpose in life. It emphasizes the need for taking personal responsibility for one's existence.

love relationship   a meaningful relationship with the addition of devotion to the emotions of caring, appreciation, concern, and interest.

maladjustment   the inability to select appropriate and effective means of coping with the stresses and demands of the environment without feeling overwhelmed.

manic depressive reaction   a psychotic reaction characterized by spontaneously occurring mood disturbances.

marasmus   a "wasting away" by a child, due to lack of physical contact and love.

marginal person   an individual whose life is divided between two antagonistic cultures, neither of which offers full acceptance of the person as a member of the group.

masculine protest   a needless domineering attitude by either sex toward the opposite sex.

master motive   an individual's natural inclination toward self-discovery and actualization.

meaningful relationship   a friendship that includes the additional feeling of caring; it is often based on identification, empathy, compassion, and the recognition that the other person is as important as oneself.

mesomorph   Sheldon's term for the muscular, athletic person who tends to be aggressive and energetic.

milieu therapy   one form of therapy where clients live in a structured, supportive community with the purpose of effecting behavioral and psychological changes in all the participants.

minimal brain dysfunction   impairment in learning resulting from faulty functioning of the central nervous system.

modeling or no-trial learning   the acquisition of a new behavior pattern by merely observing how a model performs it.

motivation   the energy activating a behavior.

mutual predictability   the ability of each member of a group to predict with uncanny accuracy how other group members will behave.

mysophobia   the fear of dirt and germs.

nature-nurture conflict   the unresolved debate by psychologists concerning the relative influence of heredity and environmental conditions on the growth and development of individuals.

need for achievement   the desire to meet an internalized standard of excellence.

negative reinforcement   the avoidance or removal of an undesired stimulus after a desired response is performed. It serves to increase the probability of the reinforced response occurring in the future.

neurotic   characterized by erratic, excessively emotional behavior. The neurotic person is driven by anxieties and compulsions for which there are no "logical" explanations.

neurotic level of adjustment   Otto Rank's second level of adjustment, characterized by an intense inner struggle to avoid both life fear and death fear.

nondirective therapy   a form of therapy wherein the therapist attempts to neither judge, interpret, nor advise the client, but merely to accept and reflect the client's emotions.

nonproductive personality   Erich Fromm's classification of a person who lacks individuality, creativeness, and a desire to contribute to the general welfare. For example, a hoarding, exploitive, receptive, or marketing type of person.

nonverbal communication   communication that is expressed by silence, gestures, posture, or personal mannerisms that telegraph a person's feelings, attitudes, or interests.

nyctophobia   the fear of darkness.

observational learning   the type of learning experience that advances the theory that human behavior develops as the direct result of the individual's perception of prior social-learning events.

obsessive/compulsive personality   an individual whose preoccupation with unwanted ideas causes extreme anxiety and persistent impulses to commit certain behavior again and again.

ochlophobia   the fear of crowds.

Oedipal complex   the male's conflict, most prominent during the *phallic stage*, between his love for his mother and competition with his father for her love. Resolution of this conflict results from the boy's identification with his father.

operant conditioning   a method of teaching an animal or individual by reinforcing or punishing a voluntary response in order to increase or decrease the frequency of its occurrence.

opiates   narcotics derived from opium and its derivatives—heroin, morphine, and codeine.

optimum group size   according to studies, a group containing about five members.

oral stage   the first of Freud's *psychosexual stages,* spanning the period from birth to about one and one-half or two years of age. During this stage the mouth is the focus of all sexual and aggressive feelings. If *fixation* occurs during this time, the individual may develop an oral-receptive or oral-aggressive personality. The oral-receptive personality is thought to develop from overgratification during the oral stage, leading to an overly dependent person. The oral-aggressive personality results from oral deprivation and leads to an individual who is excessively independent and who uses words to manipulate and hurt.

organismic theory a theory emphasizing the necessity of understanding the components of the total person in order to comprehend the individual's motivations.

paleologic thinking a thought pattern that, due to hallucinations and/or delusions, causes the individual to feel compelled to end his or her life as a means of atoning for imaginary misdeeds, or "inherent" evilness.

paradoxical intent an individual's effort at controlling less-than-desirable responses by attempting to exaggerate those responses. The harder you try to blush, sweat, etc., the less likely the response will occur.

paranoid personality an individual who is extraordinarily sensitive to perceived slights or injuries, prone to exhibit projection, and often suspicious, envious, and stubborn.

partial reinforcement *reinforcement* which occurs on the basis either of different ratios of responses to reinforcement or of different intervals of time between a response and the presentation of the reinforcement. See also *fixed ratio schedule, variable ratio schedule, fixed interval schedule*, and *variable interval schedule.*

passive aggression aggression expressed covertly or through omission.

passive-aggressive personality an individual who lacks the ability to be independent and consequently reacts to difficulty by confusion, clinging to others for assistance, or misdirected destructiveness or obstructionism.

passive involvement vague interest in another person, activity, or thing.

penis envy phenomenon whereby the female, during childhood, associates the male's possession of a penis with power and dominance and subsequently equates her lack of a penis with a lack of power and dominance.

perception the interpretation of sensory experience.

perceptual constancy a principle of *perception* whereby an individual is able to perceive objects correctly despite changing retinal images. See *size constancy* and *shape constancy.*

persona Jung's term for the social mask that one presents to the world.

personal identity one's subjective perceptions and feelings about oneself as well as others' evaluation of oneself.

personification the internalized image of a person who has been personally important in one's life.

personology Henry Murray's term for the study of the "totality of motivational forces" which influence human behavior.

perspective the ability to see a relationship for what it really is and to establish a hierarchy of interpersonal relationships; a point of view.

phallic stage the *psychosexual stage* between the ages of five and seven when the male child faces the problem of transferring identification to the father and the female child of maintaining identity with the mother.

phantom limb a very common phenomenon experienced by an amputee who feels that the missing limb is still there.

philos love for humanity; "brotherly love." (Derived from the Greek word *philos*, meaning "loving, dear.")

phobia an excessive fear of a particular object or situation. This fear is viewed as persistent and without an acceptable basis by the individual who has the phobia.

placebo effect the positive effect of pills that have no medicinal value ("sugar pills").

positive reinforcement anything which increases the probability, frequency, or magnitude of the preceding response.

presses Henry Murray's term for external pressures which do something *to* or *for* a person; i.e., have an effect on the person.

primary aggression aggression distinguished by the appropriateness of the reaction to the *frustration* stimulus.

primary drive an unlearned, basic need, such as hunger, thirst, pain avoidance, sex, etc.

productive-type personality Fromm's characterization of a person who is dedicated to the attainment of knowledge and love.

propriate striving Gordon Allport's concept of the attempt to reach one's full potential.

Protestant work ethic the concept that diligence in work, pride in craftsmanship, and the will to persevere are the only means of rightfully obtaining anything of true value.

proxemus analysis of expression and interpretation of nonverbal communication as it deals with relative position and distance between people.

psychiatrist a medical doctor who has received at least three years of supervised training in the field of psychology.

psychoactive drug a drug capable of altering a person's mood, emotional state, or thinking processes.

psychological dependence a fairly high degree of psychological compulsion, but not physiological *addiction,* associated with a behavior. Once such dependence is established, stopping the behavior can be very difficult.

psychological regularities similar attitudes and behaviors that are culturally determined and stabilize the social system.

psychologist a person with a Ph.D. in psychology (not necessarily a therapist).

psychosexual stages Freud's scheme of normal child development, which states that a child passes through successive stages (oral, anal, phallic, latency, and genital) in which the phases of personality development and the accompanying tensions are centered on different body areas and fantasies.

psychosis a personality disorder characterized by an inability to distinguish reality from fantasy. The victim often cannot relate effectively to other people, and mental functioning is so impaired that the ability to meet the demands of everyday life is lost. The major forms of this disorder are manic depression, *schizophrenia,* and paranoia.

psychosomatic disorders physical disorders where emotional factors have played a causative role.

punishment the presentation of an undesired stimulus or the withholding of a desired stimulus in response to a particular behavior.

racism the attitude that one race of people is superior to another and is therefore entitled to special rights and privileges.

rationalization a *defense mechanism* by which a person devises plausible explanations for the purpose of justifying an action to him- or herself and/or others.

reaction formation the mechanism whereby an individual acts in a manner that is the antithesis of his or her unacceptable desires.

real danger an external threat directed toward an individual.

reality principle mature awareness of the demands of the external world and the ability to act in a rational, effective way.

reference group the group of individuals against whom a person competes and with whom he or she compares himself or herself.

reflex an involuntary, purely physical response.

regression the return to patterns of an earlier *psychosexual stage* during periods of stress or overwhelming anxiety.

reinforcement anything which changes the probability of a response occurring again.

role diffusion an unclear division between where one social role ends and another begins.

role expectations assumptions that dictate the function and behavior of an individual in a given position within a particular society.

rote learning the process of continually repeating given material until it has been memorized.

scapegoating the practice of displacing aggression or blame onto a particular person or group.

schizophrenia a form of *psychosis* characterized by a severe distortion of thinking and affect, bizarre behavior, delusions, hallucinations, and social withdrawal. It often becomes manifest during early adulthood.

secondary aggression the discharge of pent-up hostility that is often unrelated to the current situation.

secondary drives acquired social drives, such as affiliation, aggression, and cooperation.

secondary reinforcer an object or behavior which is not reinforcing in itself but which leads to either *positive reinforcement* or *negative reinforcement.*

selective inattention a process by which a person may ''notice'' something, yet remains consciously unaware of it because it would threaten his or her self-esteem.

self-actualizing person Maslow's term for a person who has fulfilled all the basic needs and has reached a state of self-acceptance and fulfillment of his or her potentialities.

self-administered reinforcement a self-inflicted reward or punishment.

self-concept a person's evaluation, concepts, or beliefs about him- or herself.

self-consistency the tendency to resist experiences that are not consistent with one's value-structure in order to maintain one's personal integrity.

self-management the recognition that one is personally responsible for altering one's own behavior.

sensory deprivation the lack of any type of visual, auditory, tactile, or olfactory stimulation.

serial polygamy a form of polygamy wherein an individual will experience more than one wife or husband sequentially rather than simultaneously.

sex role standards a culture's standards of masculinity and femininity; its stereotyped expectations for how men and women ought to behave.

sexual identity one's sense of oneself as male or female.

shadow Jung's term for that part of one's personality which is seen as unacceptable.

shape constancy a phenomenon of *perception* that enables an individual to correctly perceive the shape of an object despite its changing image on the retina.

shaping the reinforcing of successive approximations of the desired behavior.

size constancy a phenomenon of *perception* by which the perceived size of an object remains constant regardless of the changes in the size of the retinal image.

social exchange interaction between people in which feelings of superiority and inferiority are manipulated.

social facilitation the bolstering of feelings and the increasing of energy output resulting from having others around.

social-genetic hypothesis a theory which holds that the behavior of individuals and groups is genetically determined so as to ensure the passage of one's genes on to the next generation.

social interference the impeding of one's performance by the presence of others.

socialization   the transmission of the norms and values of one generation to another. This process occurs through the influence of *modeling* and the *reinforcement* of accepted societal behavior.

social role   accepted or approved standards of performance for any particular end.

somatopsychology   the investigation and treatment of the psychological effects of prolonged physical illness and disability.

specific hunger   the need for a dietary component, such as vitamins, calcium, or salt, that is detected by the body's regulatory system.

spontaneous recovery   the sudden reappearance of a learned response after it appeared to have undergone *extinction*.

stimulant   an agent, such as cocaine or an amphetamine, that produces a sudden, temporary burst of functional activity or efficiency in an individual.

stimulus reinforcer   in *operant conditioning*, the consequence (either positive or negative) following a response.

stress   a powerful force capable of placing the system under duress, or in general, a response to anything that imposes a demand for *adjustment*.

sublimation   a *defense mechanism* that rechannels the energies associated with unconscious desires that cannot be realized into a nonsexual, socially acceptable activity.

superego   in Freud's schema, the part of the psyche that contains one's set of values, moral conscience, and *ideal self*.

"symbolic" models   models of behavior found in books, magazines, movies, and on television.

synergy   combined cooperative action of two individuals working in concert; when one person grows, the other person is stimulated to grow as well.

tabula rasa   the premise that at birth one's mind is a blank slate (tabula rasa) and, therefore, that all knowledge is a result of experience.

thema   Henry Murray's term for a need that is dependent on both the individual's motivational state and the nature of the stimulus. This need-press combination determines the thema.

token economies   a form of behavior modification in which a person who exhibits some form of desired behavior is given a "token" which can then be exchanged for food, material rewards, or privileges.

traits   consistent behavioral attributes which characterize an individual.

transaction   a communication between people.

transactional stimulus   the event which initiates communication between people. Often, a distinction is made between communication attempts that reflect the characteristics of parents, of children, and of adults.

transient situational disturbances   the acute reactions to overwhelming environmental *stress* that occur in individuals with no apparent underlying mental disorder. These are generally transient in nature despite varying degrees of severity (including those of psychotic proportions).

triad   a group formed by three people. It is usually unstable and tends to evolve into a *dyad* plus an "outsider."

trust   a relationship in which one is comfortable and, at the same time, vulnerable.

two-sided cooperation   a mutually beneficial relationship in which all group members receive some gratification.

unconditional positive regard   unqualified appreciation, respect, and concern for an individual just because he or she exists.

unconditional stimulus   a stimulus which normally elicits a response (innate) without the necessity of training.

unconscious Freud's conceptualization of that part of the mind which remains unknown to the individual except through the exploration of dreams, *free association,* and common slips of the tongue.

undoing an activity that involves symbolic acts or rituals designed to abolish or atone for past "misadventures."

variable interval schedule a reinforcement schedule in which an individual is given *reinforcement* after intervals of time that vary from trial to trial.

variable ratio schedule a reinforcement schedule in which an individual is given *reinforcement* after a predetermined number of responses have been made. The number of responses required varies from reinforcement to reinforcement.

will to power Alfred Adler's theory that people are driven to attain "power" and "superiority," and not to establish *homeostasis* or equilibrium.

womb envy the male's feelings of envy of the female's procreative ability.

word association the connections established between certain words and objects, events, or people.

Yerkes-Dodson law the assumption that *stress,* in tolerable amounts, can be helpful to the learning of simple tasks, but that as the tasks become more difficult, stress adversely affects the ability to perform them.

BIBLIOGRAPHY

Adler, A., *The Practice and Theory of Individual Psychology*. New York: Harcourt, Brace & World, 1927.

———, "Individual Psychology," in C. Murchison (ed.), *Psychologies of 1930*. Worcester, Mass.: Clark University Press, 1930.

———, *Understanding Human Nature*. New York: Fawcett, 1954.

Ainsworth, M. D., "Object Relations, Dependency, and Attachment: A Theoretical Review of the Infant-Mother Relationship," *Child Development*, **40**:969–1025, 1969.

Alamshah, William, *The Pursuit of Excellence*, unpublished essay. Fullerton, Calif.: Orange State College, 1963.

Alcoholics Anonymous, "Is AA for You: Twelve Questions Only You Can Answer," *Alcoholics Anonymous*. New York: Alcoholics Anonymous Publishing, Inc., 1954.

———, *Alcoholics Anonymous*. New York: Alcoholics Anonymous World Service, Inc., 1976.

Alexander, Tom, "Psychologists Are Rediscovering the Mind," *Fortune*, **82**:108–111, November 1970.

Allport, G. W., *Becoming: Basic Consideration for a Psychology of Personality*. New Haven, Conn.: Yale University Press, 1955.

———, *Pattern and Growth in Personality*. New York: Holt, Rinehart, 1961.

American Psychiatric Association, *Diagnostic and Statistical Manual of Mental Disorders (DSM-II)* (2d ed.). Washington: American Psychiatric Association, 1968.

———, Draft Task Force of Nomenclature and Statistics, *Diagnostic Criteria* (DSM III). Washington: American Psychiatric Association, 1978.

Amundsen, K., *The Silenced Majority*. Englewood Cliffs, N.J.: Prentice-Hall, 1971.

Angyal, A., *Foundations for a Science of Personality*. New York: Commonwealth Fund, 1941.

Arafat, Ibithaj, and Betty Yorburg, "On Living Together without Marriage," *Journal of Sex Research*, **9**(2):97–106, 1973.

Ardrey, R., *The Territorial Imperative: A Personal Inquiry into the Animal Origins of Property and Nations*. New York: Atheneum, 1966.

Aristotle, in Louise Loomis (ed.), *On Man in the Universe*. Roslyn, N.Y.: Walter J. Black, Inc., 1943.

———, "Politics," in Renford Bambrough (ed.), *The Philosophy of Aristotle*. New York: New American Library, 1963.

Asch, S. E., "Studies of Independence and Conformity: A Minority of One against a Unanimous Majority," *Psychological Monographs*, **70**,(416), 1956.

Aun, Emil Michael, "New Horizons for Aerospace Engineers," *Manpower*, January 1971, pp. 8–13.

———, "Senior Aides: Fighting Stereotypes," *Manpower*, February 1972, pp. 7–12.

Averill, J. R., "Emotion and Anxiety: Social, Cultural, Biological and Psychological Determinants," in M. Zuckerman and C. Spielberger (eds.), *Emotion and Anxiety*. Hillsdale, N.J.: L. Erlbaum Associates, 1976, pp. 87–130.

Ayllon, T., and N. Azrin, *The Token Economy: A Motivational System for Therapy and Rehabilitation*. New York: Appleton-Century-Crofts, 1968.

Babchuk, N., "Primary Friends and Kin: A Study of the Associations of Middle Class Couples," *Social Forces*, **43**(5):483–493, 1965.

Bach, George, and P. Wyden, *The Intimate Enemy: How to Fight Fair in Love and Marriage*. New York: Morrow, 1969.

Bakke, E. W., *The Unemployed Worker*. New Haven, Conn.: Yale University Press, 1940.

Bakwin, H., "Loneliness in Infants," *American Journal of Diseases of Children*, **63**(1):30–40, 1942.

Bandura, A., *Principles of Behavior Modification*. New York: Holt, Rinehart, 1969.

———, D. Ross, and S. A. Ross, "Transmission of Aggression through Imitation of Aggressive Models," *Journal of Abnormal and Social Psychology*, **63**(3):575–582, 1961.

———,———, and———, "Imitation of Film—Mediated Aggressive Models," *Journal of Abnormal and Social Psychology*, **66**(1):3–11, 1963.

———,———, and———, "A Comparative Test of the Status Envy, Social Power, and Secondary Reinforcement Theories of Identification Learning," *Journal of Abnormal and Social Psychology*, **67**(6):527–534, 1963.

———,———, and———, "Imitation of Film-Mediated Aggressive Models," in M. Wertheimer (ed.), *Confrontation: Psychology and the Problems of Today*. Glenview, Ill.: Scott, Foresman, 1970.

———, and R. H. Walters, *Social Learning and Personality Development*. New York: Holt, Rinehart, 1963.

Bardwick, J., "Evolution and Parenting," *Journal of Social Issues*, **30**(4):39–62, 1974.

Barker, R. G., and B. A. Wright, "Disablement: The Sematopsychological Problems," in E. Wiltkower and R. Cleghorn (eds.), *Recent Developments in Psychosomatic Medicine*. Philadelphia: Lippincott, 1954.

Barraclough, B. M., B. Nelson, J. Bunch, and P. Sainsbury, "The Diagnostic Classification and Psychiatric Treatment of 100 Suicides," in *Proceedings of the Fifth International Conference for Suicide Prevention*, London, 1969.

Barron, Frank, "Motivational Patterns in LSD Usage," in R. C. DeBold and R. C. Leaf (eds.), *LSD: Man and Society*. Middletown, Conn.: Wesleyan University Press, 1968.

Barry, H., M. K. Bacon, and I. L. Child, "A Cross-Cultural Survey of Some Sex Differences in Socialization," *Journal of Abnormal and Social Psychology*, **55**(3):331–334, 1957.

Bateson, G., "Minimal Requirements for a Theory of Schizophrenia," *Archives of General Psychiatry*, **2**:477–491, 1960.

Bayer, E., "Betrage Zur Zweikomponenten-theorie des Hungers," *Zeitschrift fur Psychologie*, **112**:1–54, 1929.

Bayh, B., *U.S. Senate: Hearings on the Abuse of Barbiturates*. Opening statement, Dec. 15, 1971.

Bayley, N., "Mental Growth during the First Three Years," *Genetic Psychological Monographs*, **14**(1):1–92, 1933.

Beardslee, David, and Donald O'Dowd, "Students and the Occupational World," *The American College*. New York: Wiley, 1962.

Beauvoir, Simone de, *The Coming of Age* (trans. by Patrick O'Brian), New York: Putnam, 1972.

Bechrach, A. J., J. W. Erwin, and J. P. Mohr, "The Control of Eating Behavior in an Anorexic by Operant Conditioning Techniques," in L. P. Ullman and L. Krasner (eds.), *Case Studies in Behavior Modification*. New York: Holt, Rinehart, 1965.

Beck, A. T., *Depression: Clinical, Experimental, and Theoretical Aspects*. New York: Harper & Row, 1967.

———, "The Meaning of Depression," *Science News*, **96**(24):554, 1969.

Becker, W. C., "Consequences of Different Kinds of Parental Discipline," in M. L. Hoffman and L. W. Hoffman (eds.), *Review of Child Development*, vol. 1. New York: Russell Sage, 1964.

Beels, C. Christian, "The Case of the Vanishing Mommy," *The New York Times*, July 4, 1976.

Beier, Ernst, *The Silent Language of Psychotherapy*. Chicago: Aldine, 1967.

Bem, Sandra I., and Daryl J. Bem, "Training the Woman to Know Her Place: The Social Antecedents of Women in the World of Work." Harrisburg: Pennsylvania Department of Public Instruction, 1971.

Bendix, R., and F. Howton, "Social Mobility and the American Business Elite," in R. Bendix and S. Lysset (eds.), *Social Mobility in Industrial Society*. Berkeley: University of California Press, 1959.

Benedict, R., *Patterns of Culture*. Boston: Houghton Mifflin, 1934.

Berg, Ivar, *They Won't Work*. New York: The Columbia Forum, vol. II, no. 1, Columbia University, 1973.

Berger, Arthur A., "Sex and the Serpent on Madison Avenue," *Human Behavior*, June 1973, p. 72+.

Berkowitz, L., *Roots of Aggression: A Re-examination of the Frustration-Aggression Hypothesis*. New York: Atherton, 1968.

———, *Social Psychology*. Glenview, Ill.: Scott, Foresman, 1972.

Berlyne, D. C., *Conflict, Arousal, and Curiosity*. New York: McGraw-Hill, 1960.

———, "Laughter, Humor, and Play," in G. Lindzey and E. Aronson (eds.), *Handbook of Social Psychology*, vol. 3. Reading, Mass.: Addison-Wesley, 1969, pp. 795–852.

Bernard, Harold, and Wesley Huckins, *Dynamics of Personal Adjustment*. Boston: Holbrook Press, 1975.

Bernbaum, Judith, in Martha Shuck Mednick et al. (eds.), *Women and Achievement: Social and Motivational Analyses*. New York: Halsted Press, 1975.

Berne, Erich, *Games People Play* (2d ed.). New York: Grove Press, 1964

Berrett, William E., *The Restored Church*. Salt Lake City: Deseret Book Company, 1961.

Berscheid, Ellen, and Elaine Walsler, "Beauty and the Best," *Psychology Today*, March 1972, p. 42+.

———, ———, and George Bohrnstedt, "The Happy American Body: A Survey Report," *Psychology Today*, November 1973, p. 119+.

Bettelheim, B., "Individual and Mass Behavior in Extreme Situations," in E. E. Maccoby, T. Newcomb, and E. Hartley (eds.), *Readings in Social Psychology*. New York: Holt, Rinehart, 1958.

———, *The Informed Heart*. Glencoe, Ill.: Free Press, 1960.

———, and M. Janowitz, *Dynamics of Prejudice: A Psychological and Sociological Study of Veterans*. New York: Harper & Row, 1950.

Bieber, I., "Homosexuality," in A. M. Friedman, H. I. Kaplan, and H. S. Kaplan (eds.), *Comprehensive Textbook of Psychiatry*. Baltimore: Williams & Wilkin, 1967, pp. 963–976.

Binswanger, L., *Sigmund Freud: Reminiscences of a Friendship*. New York: Grune & Stratton, 1957.

———, "The Existential Analysis School of Thought: Insanity as Life-Historical Phenomenon and as Mental Disease," in R. May, E. Angel, and H. Ellenberger (eds.), *Existence*. New York: Basic Books, 1958, pp. 191–236.

———, *Being in-the-World*. New York: Basic Books, 1963.

Birch, H. G., "Sources of Order in the Maternal Behavior of Animals," *American Journal of Orthopsychiatry*, **26**(2):279–284, 1956.

Birdwhistell, Ray L., *Kinesics and Context*. Philadelphia: University of Pennsylvania Press, 1970.

Birren, J. E., *The Psychology of Aging*. Englewood Cliffs, N.J.: Prentice-Hall, 1964.

Bliss, E. W., and C. H. Branch, *Anorexia Nervosa: Its History, Psychology, and Biology*. New York: Hoeber Medical Books, 1960.

Bloomquist, E. R., *Marijuana*. New York: Glencoe Press, 1968.

Blum, G. S., *Psychoanalytic Theories of Personality*. New York: McGraw-Hill, 1953.

Bogardus, E. S., "Measuring Social Distance," *Journal of Applied Sociology*, **9**:216–226, January–February 1925.

Boll, E. S., "The Role of Pre-School Playmates: A Situational Approach," *Child Development*, **28**(3):327–342, 1957.

Boss, M., *Psychoanalysis and Daseinsanalysis*. New York: Basic Books, 1963.

Bossard, J. H. S., and E. S. Boll, *The Sociology of Child Development*. New York: Harper & Row, 1960.

Bowlby, J., "Maternal Care and Mental Health," WHO Monograph Series, no. 2. Geneva, Switzerland: World Health Organization, 1951.

———, "Grief and Mourning in Infancy and Early Childhood," *Psychoanalytic Study of the Child*, **75**(1):9–52, 1960.

Brecher, Ruth, and E. Brecher, "The Happiest Creatures on Earth?" *Harper's*, **222**(4):85–90, 1961.

Brogden, W. J., E. A. Lipman, and E. A. Culler, "The Role of Incentive in Conditioning and Extinction," *American Journal of Psychology*, **51**(1):109–117, 1938.

Brown, R., and D. McNeill, "The 'Tip of the Tongue' Phenomenon," *Journal of Verbal Learning and Verbal Behavior*, **5**(4):325–337, 1966.

Brown, W. F., "Effectiveness of Paraprofessionals: The Evidence," *Personnel and Guidance Journal*, **53**(4):257–263, 1974.

Bruch, H., *The Importance of Overweight*. New York: Norton, 1957.

Bruner, J. S., and L. Postman, "Tension and Tension-Release as Organizing Factors in Perception," *Journal of Personality*, **15**(4):300–308, 1947.

———, and———, "Emotional Selectivity in Perception and Reaction," *Journal of Personality*, **16**(1):69–77, 1947.

Bryan, J., "How Adults Teach Hypocrisy," *Psychology Today*, December 1969, pp. 50–52.

Buber, Martin, *I and Thou*. New York: Scribner, 1970.

Buchout, Robert B., *Youth and the Hazards of Affluence*. New York: Harper & Row, 1967.

Buhler, C., "Loneliness in Maturity," *Journal of Humanistic Psychology*, **9**(2):167–181, 1969.

Burgess, E. W., and L. S. Cottrell, *Predicting Success or Failure in Marriage*. Englewood Cliffs, N.J.: Prentice-Hall, 1939.

———, and Paul Wallin, *Engagement and Marriage*. Philadelphia: Lippincott, 1953.

Business Week, "The High Cost of Divorce," Feb. 10, 1975, pp. 83–86+.

Butcher, J. N., *Abnormal Psychology*. Belmont, Calif.: Brooks/Cole, 1971.

Butler, J. M., and G. V. Haigh, "Changes in the Relation between Self-Concepts and Ideal Concepts Consequent upon Client-Centered Counseling," in C. R. Rogers and R. F. Daymond (eds.), *Psychotherapy and Personality Change*. Chicago: University of Chicago Press, 1954, pp. 55–75.

Butler, R. A., and H. M. Alexander, "Daily Patterns of Visual Exploratory Behavior in the Monkies," *Journal of Comparative and Physiological Psychology*, **48**(4):247–249, 1955.

Cadwallader, Mervyn, "Marriage as a Wretched Institution," *The Atlantic Monthly*, **218**(11):62–66, 1966.

Calhoun, J. B., "A Behavioral Sink," in E. Bliss (ed.), *Roots of Behavior*. New York: Harper & Row, 1962.

Cameron, N., "The Paranoid Pseudocommunity Revisited." *American Journal of Sociology*, 1959, **65**(1):52–58.

Campbell, Angus, "The American Way of Mating," *Psychology Today*, May 1975, p. 37+.

Campbell, B. A., "The Reinforcement Difference Limen (RDL) Function for Shock Reduction," *Journal of Experimental Psychology*, **52**(4):258–262, 1956.

Cannon, W. B., *Bodily Change in Pain, Hunger, Fear and Rage* (2d ed.). New York: Appleton-Century-Crofts, 1929.

———, *The Wisdom of the Body*. New York: Norton, 1939.

———, "Voodoo Death," *American Anthropologist*, **44**(2):169–181, 1942.

Carmichael, Stokely, and Charles Hamilton, *Black Power: The Politics of Liberation in America*. New York: Random House, 1967.

Carmon, A., and I. Nachshon, "Effect of Unilateral Brain Damage on Perception of Temporal Order," *Cortex*, **7**(4):410–418, 1971.

Carter, Hugh, and Paul C. Glick, *Marriage and Divorce: A Social and Economic Study*. Cambridge, Mass.: Harvard University Press, 1970.

Casler, L., "The Effects of Extra Tactile Stimulation on a Group of Institutionalized Infants," *Genetic Psychology Monographs*, **71**:131–175, 1965.

Cather, Willa, *The Song of the Lark*. Boston: Houghton Mifflin, 1915.

Cattell, R. B., "Theory of Fluid and Crystallized Intelligence: A Critical Experiment," *Journal of Educational Psychology*, **54**(1):1–22, 1963.

———, *Abilities: Their Structure, Growth, and Action*. Boston: Houghton Mifflin, 1971.

Centers, R., *The Psychology of Social Classes*. Princeton, N.J.: Princeton University Press, 1949.

Cleckley, H., *The Mask of Sanity* (4th ed.). St. Louis, Mo.: Mosby, 1964.

Clements, S. D., "Minimal Brain Dysfunction in Children," *National Institute of Neurological Diseases and Blindness*, no. 3. Washington: U.S. Department of Health, Education, and Welfare, 1966.

Coale, Ansley, and E. Hoover, *Population Growth and Economic Development in Low-Income Countries*. Princeton, N.J.: Princeton University Press, 1958.

Collier, James, "The Procreation Myth," in Robert Leaver (ed.), *Focus: Human Sexuality*. Guilford, Conn.: The Dushkin Publishing Group, Inc., 1976, pp. 81–84.

Colson, C., "An Objective Analytic Approach to the Classification of Suicidal Motivation," *Acta Psychiatrica Scandinavica*, **49**(2):105–113, 1973.

Cooley, C. H., *Human Nature and the Social Order*. New York: Scribner, 1902.

Corey, Gerald, *I Never Knew I Had a Choice*. Monterey, Calif.: Brooks/Cole, 1978.

Cowles, J. T., "Food-Tokens as Incentives for Learning by Chimpanzees." *Comparative Psychological Monographs*, **14**(5):1–95, 1937.

Crowley, Joan E., Teresa E. Levitin, and Robert P. Quinn, "Seven Deadly Half-Truths about Women," *Psychology Today*, March 1973, pp. 94–101.

Cuber, John, and Peggy B. Harroff, *Significant Americans: A Study of Sexual Behavior among the Affluent*. New York: Appleton-Century-Crofts, 1965.

Cushing, Harvey, *The Life of Sir William Osler*. London: Oxford University Press, 1940.

D'Andrade, R. G., "Sex Differences and Cultural Institutions," in E. E. Maccoby (ed.), *The Development of Sex Differences*. Stanford, Calif.: Stanford University Press, 1966, pp. 174–203.

Daniels, Victor, and Laurence Horowitz, *Being and Caring*. Palo Alto, Calif.: Mayfield Publishing Co., 1976.

Davis, C. M., "Self-Selection of Diet by Newly Weaned Infants," *American Journal of the Diseases of Children*, 1928.

Dawkins, Richard, *The Selfish Gene*. New York: Oxford University Press, 1976.

Deese, James, *The Psychology of Learning*. New York: McGraw-Hill, 1958.

De Mause, Lloyd, "Our Forebearers Made Childhood a Nightmare," *Psychology Today*, April 1975, pp. 85–88.

Dement, W., "The Effect of Dream Deprivation," *Science*, **131**(3415):1705–1707, 1960.

———, and N. Kleitman, "The Relation of Eye Movements during Sleep to Dream Activity: An Objective Method for the Study of Dreaming," *Journal of Experimental Psychology*, **53**(5):339–346, 1957.

Dennis, W., "Causes of Retardation among Institutional Children: Iran," *Journal of Genetic Psychology*, **96**(3):47–59, 1960.

Denton, D. A., "Salt Appetite," in C. F. Cook (ed.), *Handbook of Physiology: Alimentary Canal*, vol. 1. Washington: American Physiological Society, 1967, pp. 433–459.

De Vries, H., "Physiological Effects of an Exercise Regime upon Men Ages 52 to 88," *Journal of Gerontology*, **25**(4):325–336, 1970.

Di Caprio, Nicholas, *Personality Theories: Guides to Living*. Philadelphia: Saunders, 1974.

Dion, Karen, E. Bersheid, and E. Walster, "What Is Beautiful Is Good," *Journal of Personality and Social Psychology*, **24**(3):285–290, 1972.

Dohrenwend, B. P., and B. S. Dohrenwend, "Social and Cultural Influences on Psychopathology," in M. R. Rosenzweig and L. W. Porter (eds.), *Annual Review of Psychology*. Palo Alto, Calif.: Annual Reviews, 1974, pp. 417–452.

Dollard, J., L. Doob, N. Miller, D. Mourer, and R. Sears, *Frustration and Aggression*. New Haven, Conn.: Yale University Press, 1939.

———, and N. E. Miller, *Personality and Psychotherapy: An Analysis in Terms of Learning, Thinking, and Culture*. New York: McGraw-Hill, 1950.

Dreiser, Theodore, *Sister Carrie*. New York: The Modern Library, 1900.

Du Bois, William, *The Souls of Black Folk*. New York: Dodd, Mead, 1961.

Dunbar, H. F., *Emotions and Bodily Changes* (4th ed.). New York: Columbia University Press, 1954.

———, *Mind and Body: Psychosomatic Medicine* (rev. ed.). New York: Random House, 1955.

Duncan, O. D., and R. W. Hodge, "Education and Occupational Mobility: A Regression Analysis," *American Journal of Sociology*, **68**(6):629–644, 1963.

Dunham, H. W., "Epidemeology of Psychiatric Disorders as a Contribution to Medical Ecology," *Archives of General Psychiatry*, **14**(1):1–19, 1966.

Dunphy, D. C., "The Social Structure of Urban Adolescent Peer Groups," *Sociometry*, **26**(2):230–246, 1963.

DuPont, R. L., and M. H. Greene, "The Dynamics of a Heroin Addiction Epidemic," *Science*, **181**(4101):716–722, 1973.

Durant, Will, and Ariel Durant, *The Lessons of History*. New York: Simon and Schuster, 1968.

Ebbinghaus, H., *On Memory*. New York: Dover, 1964.

Eberstadt, Nick, "Myths of the Food Crisis," *New York Review*, Feb. 19, 1976, pp. 32–37.

Egan, Gerard, *You and Me*. Monterey, Calif.: Brooks/Cole, 1977.

Ehrenberg, O., and M. Ehrenberg, *The Psychotherapy Maze*. New York: Holt, Rinehart and Winston, 1977.

Ehrlich, Annette, "The Adaptable Primates," *Human Behavior*, November 1976, pp. 24–30.

Ehrmann, Max, *Desiderata*. Los Angeles: Brooke House, 1972.

Elkind, David, *Children and Adolescence*. New York: Oxford University Press, 1974.

Elsarrag, M. E., "Psychiatry in the Northern Sudan: A Study in Comparative Psychiatry," *British Journal of Psychiatry*, **114**(8):945–948, 1968.

Epstein, S., "The Self-Concept Revisited," *American Psychologist*, **28**(5):404–416, 1973.

Eriksen, C. W., "Psychological Defenses and 'Ego Strength' in the Recall of Completed and Incompleted Tasks," *Journal of Abnormal and Social Psychology*, **49**(1):45–50, 1954.

Erikson, E. H., *Childhood and Society*. New York: Norton, 1950.

Erikson, Erik, *Identity and the Life Cycle*. New York: International Universities Press, 1959.

———, *Identity: Youth and Crisis*. New York: Norton, 1968.

Fabum, Don, *Children of Change*. Beverly Hills, Calif.: Glencoe Press, 1969.

Fairbairn, W. R., *Object-Relations Theory of the Personality*. New York: Basic Books, 1954.

Fantino, E., "Immediate Reward Followed by Extinction vs. Later Reward without Extinction," *Psychonomic Science*, **6**(5):233–234, 1966.

Fantz, R. L., "Visual Perception from Birth as Shown by Pattern Selectivity," *Annals of the New York Academy of Sciences*, **118**:793–814, 1965.

Farberow, N. L., and T. L. McEvoy, "Suicide among Patients with Diagnoses of Anxiety Reaction or Depressive Reaction in General Medical and Surgical Hospitals," *Journal of Abnormal Psychology*, **71**(4):287–299, 1966.

Fast, Julius, *Body Language*. New York: Pocket Books, 1970.

Fenichel, O., *The Psychoanalytic Theory of Neurosis*. New York: Norton, 1945.

Ferster, C. B., and K. Hammer, "Variables Determining the Effects of Delay in Reinforcement," *Journal of Experimental Analysis and Behavior*, **8**(4):243–254, 1965.

Festinger, L., "Wish, Expectation and Group Performance as Factors Influencing

Level of Aspiration," *Journal of Abnormal and Social Psychology*, **37**(2): 184–200, 1942.

————, "A Theory of Social Comparison Process," *Human Relations*, **7**(2):117–140, 1954.

————, *A Theory of Cognitive Dissonance*. Stanford, Calif.: Stanford University Press, 1957.

Field, M. J., *The Search for Security*, Evanston, Ill.: Northwestern University Press, 1960.

Fischer, William, *Theories of Anxiety*. New York: Harper & Row, 1970.

Fisher, Seymour, "Experiencing Your Body: You Are What You Feel," *Saturday Review/World*, July 1972, pp. 27–32.

Fitzgerald, H., and D. McKinney, *Developmental Psychology*. Homewood, Ill.: Dorsey, 1977.

Folsom, Leo, *Parent Awareness*. Studio City, Calif.: Prismatica International, 1974.

Fosdick, Harry F., *Great Voices of the Reformation*, Martin Luther's "Address to the Christian Nobility of the German Nation." New York: Random House, 1952.

Frank, J. D., "The Demoralized Mind," *Psychology Today*, April 1973, p. 22+

Frankl, V., *Man's Search for Meaning: An Introduction to Logotherapy*. Boston: Beacon Press, 1962.

————, *The Doctor and the Soul*. New York: Knopf, 1965 (2d ed.).

French, E., and F. Thomas, "The Relation of Achievement Motivation to Problem-Solving Effectiveness," *Journal of Abnormal and Social Psychology*, **56**(1):45–48, 1958.

Freud, Anna, *The Ego and the Mechanisms of Defense*. London: Hogarth, 1937.

Freud, Ernst (ed.), *Letters of Sigmund Freud* (trans. by Tania and James Stern). New York: Basic Books, 1960, pp. 423–424.

Freud, Sigmud, *The Complete Psychological Works of Sigmund Freud* (standard ed.), 33 vols. London: Hogarth, 1955–1975. See especially: *An Autobiographical Study, Inhibitions, Symptoms and Anxiety, The Question of Lay Analysis, and Other Works* (vol. 20), 1959; "Analysis of a Phobia in a Five-Year-Old Boy" (vol. 10), 1955; "Civilisation and Its Discontents" (vol. 21), 1961; "The Future of an Illusion" (vol. 21), 1961; "Group Psychology and the Analysis of the Ego" (vol. 18), 1957; "Inhibitions, Symptoms and Anxiety" (vol. 16), 1963; "The Interpretation of Dreams (vol. 4), 1964; "New Introductory Lectures on Psychoanalysis" (vol. 22), 1964.

————, *A General Introduction to Psychoanalysis*. New York: Liveright, 1935.

————, *Jokes and Their Relation to the Unconscious*. New York: Norton, 1960.

————, *The Problem of Anxiety*. New York: Norton, 1936.

————, *The Psychopathology of Everyday Life*. New York: Macmillan, 1917. (First published, 1904.)

Friedman, E., and R. J. Havighurst, *The Meaning of Work and Retirement*. Chicago: University of Chicago Press, 1954.

Friedman, Meyer, and Ray Rosenman, *Type A Behavior and Your Heart*. New York: Knopf, 1974.

Fromm, Erich, *The Sane Society*. New York; Holt, Rinehart, 1955.

————, *The Heart of Man: Its Genius for Good and Evil*. New York: Harper & Row, 1964.

————, Lecture to the American Orthopsychiatric Association, April 13, 1966. Reported in *The New York Times*, April 14, 1964.

————, *Man for Himself*. New York: Holt, Rinehart, 1966 (18th ed.).

————, *The Art of Loving*. New York: Harper & Row, 1970.

————, *The Crisis of Psychoanalysis*. New York: Holt, Rinehart, 1970.

————, *The Anatomy of Human Destructiveness*. New York: Holt, Rinehart, 1973.

————, "Erich Fromm on Human Aggression," *Human Behavior*, April 1975, pp. 16–23.

Frosch, W. A., E. S. Robbins, and M. Stern, "Untoward Reactions to Lysergic Acid

Diethylamide (LSD) Resulting in Hospitalization," *New England Journal of Medicine,* **273**(23):1235–1238, 1965.

Galenson, Marjorie, *Women and Work: An International Comparison.* Ithaca, N.Y.: Cornell University, School of Industrial and Labor Relations, 1973.

Gallop, G. G., "Mirror-Image Simulation," *Psychological Bulletin,* **70**(6):782–783, 1968.

Gantt, W. H., *Experimental Basis for Neurotic Behavior.* New York: Hoeber, 1944.

Garai, Josef, and Amram Scheinfeld, "Sex Differences in Mental and Behavioral Traits," *Genetic Psychology Monographs,* **77**(5):169–299, 1968.

Gardner, G., and G. Tarjan, and J. B. Richmond, *Mental Retardation: A Handbook for the Primary Physician.* Chicago: American Medical Association, 1965.

Gardner, R. A., and B. J. Gardner, "Teaching Sign Language to a Chimpanzee," *Science,* **165**(3894):664–672, August 1969.

Gardner, W. I., *Reactions of Intellectually Normal and Retarded Boys after Experimentally Induced Failure: A Social Learning Theory Interpretation.* Doctoral dissertation, George Peabody College. Ann Arbor, Mich.: University Microfilms, 1958.

Garfield, S. L., Abnormal Behavior and Mental Deficiency, in N. R. Ellis (ed.), *Handbook of Mental Deficiency.* New York: McGraw-Hill, 1963.

Gibran, Kahlil, *Sand and Foam.* New York: Alfred Knopf, 1926.

———, *The Prophet.* New York: Knopf, 1964.

Ginott, Haim, G., *Between Parent and Child.* New York: Avon, 1969.

Gladstein, Gerald, *Individualized Study.* Chicago, Ill.: Rand McNally, 1967.

Glass, A., "Problem of Stress in the Combat Zone," in *Symposium on Stress.* Washington: National Research Council and Walter Reed Army Medical Center, 1953, pp. 90–102.

Glasser, William, *Reality Therapy.* New York: Harper & Row, 1965.

Glick, Paul, *American Families,* New York: Wiley, 1957.

Glixman, A. F., "Recall of Completed and Incompleted Activities under Varying Degrees of Stress," *Journal of Experimental Psychology,* **39**(3):281–295, 1949.

Goldenson, Robert M. *The Encyclopedia of Human Behavior.* Garden City, N. Y.: Doubleday, 1970.

Goldhamer, H., and A. Marshall, *Psychoses and Civilization.* Glencoe, Ill.: Free Press, 1949.

Goldiamond, I., "Fluent and Non-Fluent Speech (Stuttering): Analysis and Operant Techniques for Control," in L. Krasner and L. P. Ullman (eds.), *Research in Behavior Modification.* New York: Holt, Rinehart, 1965.

Goldstein, K., *The Organism.* New York: American Book Co., 1939.

Goodall, J., *Primate Behavior: Field Studies of Monkies and Apes* (I. De Vore, ed.). New York: Harper & Row, 1965.

Goode, William, *World Revolution and Family Patterns.* New York: Free Press, 1963.

———, *The Family.* New York: Prentice-Hall, 1964.

———, "Has the Family Circle Come Full Circle?" *Realities,* July 1966, pp. 38–41.

Goodenough, Florence L., "The Use of Free Association in the Objective Measurement of Personality," in *Studies in Personality Contributed in Honor of Lewis M. Terman.* New York: McGraw-Hill, 1942, pp. 87–104.

Gould, R., "An Experimental Analysis of 'Levels of Aspiration'," *Genetic Psychology Monograph,* **21**:3–115, 1939.

Gove, Walter R., and Jeannette F. Tudor, "Adult Sex Roles and Mental Illness," *American Journal of Sociology,* **78**(4):812–835, 1973.

Graham, D. T., R. M. Lundy, L. S. Benjamin, and F. K. Kabler, "Some Specific Attitudes in Initial Interviews with Patients Having Different 'Psychosomatic' Diseases," *Psychosomatic Medicine,* **29**:257–266, 1962.

Green, Hannah, *I Never Promised You a Rose Garden*. New York: Signet Holt, Rinehart, 1964.

Green, J., *Los Angeles Statistical Data*, 1972–1973. Los Angeles: Suicide Prevention Center, 1041 Menlo Park, Los Angeles, Calif.

Greer, Germaine, *The Female Eunuch*. New York: McGraw-Hill, 1971.

Grinker, R. R., *Men Under Stress*. Philadelphia: Blakiston, 1945b.

———, and J. P. Spiegel, *War Neuroses*. Philadelphia: Blakiston, 1945a.

Grossek, George, Henry Wecholer, and Milton Greenblatt (eds.), *The Threat of Impending Disaster*. Cambridge, Mass.: MIT Press, 1964.

Gurman, A. S., and D. P. Kniskern, "Research on Marital and Family Therapy," in S. L. Garfield and D. E. Bergin (eds.), *Handbook of Psychotherapy and Behavior Change*. New York: Wiley, 1976.

Gutmann, D., "Parenthood: A Key to the Comparative Study of the Life Cycle," in N. Datan and L. H. Ginsberg (eds.), *Life Span Developmental Psychology: Normative Life Crisis*. New York: Academic, 1975.

Guttentag, Marcia, and Helen Bray, *Undoing Sex Stereotypes*. New York: McGraw-Hill, 1976.

Haley, J., "An Interactional Description of Schizophrenia," *Psychiatry*, **22**(4):321–332, 1959.

Hall, Edward T., "A System for the Notation of Proxemic Behavior," *American Anthropologist*, **65**(5):1003–1026, 1963.

Hamarskjöld, Dag, *Markings*. New York: Alfred Knopf, 1964.

Hamilton, C. L., "Food and Temperature," in C. F. Code (ed.), *Handbook of Physiology: Alimentary Canal*, vol. 1, sec. 6. Washington: American Physiological Society, 1967, pp. 303–318.

Hare, A. P., "A Study of Interaction and Consensus in Different Sized Groups," *American Sociological Review*, **17**(3):261–267, 1952.

Harlow, Harry F., "The Effects of Rearing Conditions on Behavior," *Bulletin of the Menninger Clinic*, **25**:213–226, 1962.

———, "The Heterosexual Affectional System in Monkies," *American Psychologist*, **17**(1):1–9, 1962.

———, and R. R. Zimmerman, "The Development of Affectional Responses in Infant Monkies," in *Proceedings of the American Philosophical Society*, **102**:501–509, 1958.

———, and———, "Affectional Responses in the Infant Monkey," *Science*, **130**(3373):421–432, 1959.

Harper, R., *Psychoanalysis and Psychotherapy*. Englewood Cliffs, N.J.: Prentice-Hall, 1959.

———, *The New Psychotherapies*. Englewood Cliffs, N.J.: Prentice-Hall, 1975.

Harris, Thomas, *I'm OK, You're OK*. New York: Avon Books, 1973.

Harrison, Randall, "Non-verbal Behavior: An Approach to Human Communications," in Richard W. Budd and Brent Ruben (eds.), *Approaches to Human Communication*. New York: Spartan Books, 1972.

Hartford, Thomas, "Patterns of Alcohol Use among Adolescents," *Psychiatric Opinion*, **12**(3):17, 1975.

Hartley, R. E., and F. P. Hardesky, "Children's Perception of Sex Roles in Childhood," *Journal of Genetic Psychology*, **105**(9);43–52, 1964.

Havighurst, R. J., *Human Development and Education*. New York: Longmans, 1953.

———, "Youth in Exploration and Man Emergent," in H. Borow (ed.), *Man in a World at Work*. Boston: Houghton Mifflin, 1964.

Hawthorne, Nathaniel, *The Blithedale Romance*. New York: W. W. Norton, 1958.

Hayes, C. *The Ape In Our House*. New York: Harper & Row, 1951.

Heber, R., H. Garber, C. Hoffman, and S. Harrington, "Preventing Mental Retardation through Family Rehabilitation," *Technical Assistance Delivery System Infant Education Monograph*. Chapel Hill, N.C.: TADS, 1976.

Heider, Fritz, *The Psychology of Interpersonal Relationships*. New York: Wiley, 1957.

Helgerson, E., "The Relative Significance of Race and Sex and Facial Expression in Choice of Playmate by the Preschool Child," *Journal of Negro Education*, **12**(4):617–622, 1943.

Hemingway, Ernest, *A Farwell to Arms*. New York: Scribner, 1957.

Henley, William E., Quoted in Stanley Honer and Thomas Hunt, *Philosophy*. Belmont, Calif.: Wadsworth, 1978, p. 206.

Henry, Lewis, *5000 Quotations for All Occasions*. Garden City, N. Y.: Garden City Books, 1952.

Heron, W., "The Pathology of Boredom," *Scientific American*, January 1957, pp. 52–56.

———, "Cognition and Physiological Effects of Perceptual Isolation," in P. Solomon et al., (eds.), *Sensory Deprivation*. Cambridge, Mass.: Harvard University Press, 1961, pp. 6–33.

Hershenson, David, and William Langbauer, "Sequencing of Intra-psychic Stages of Vocational Development," *Journal of Counseling Psychology*, **20**(6):519–521, 1973.

Herzberg, F., "Motivation, Morale, and Money," *Psychology Today*, March 1968, pp. 42–45.

Hetherington, E. Mavis, and Ross D. Parke, *Child Psychology*. New York: McGraw-Hill, 1975.

Hilgard, E. R., "Human Motives and the Concept of the Self," *American Psychologist*, **4**(9):374–382, 1949.

Hiroto, P. S., "Locus of Control and Learned Helplessness," *Journal of Experimental Psychology*, **102**(2):187–193, 1974.

Hjelle, Larry A., and Daniel J. Ziegler, *Personality*. New York: McGraw-Hill, 1976.

Hoagland, H., "The Physiological Control of Judgments of Duration: Evidence for a Chemical Clock," *Journal of General Psychology*, **9**(2):267–287, 1932.

Hodapp, V., G. Weyer, and J. Becker, "Situational Stereotyping in Essential Hypertension Patients," *Journal of Psychosomatic Research*, **19**(2):113–121, 1975.

Hodge, M., *Your Fear of Love*. Garden City, N.Y.: Doubleday, 1967.

Hodge, R., P. Siegel, and P. Rossi, "Occupational Prestige in the United States, 1925–1963," *American Journal of Sociology*, **70**(11):286–302, 1964.

Hoffman, Lois, and F. Ivan Nye, *Working Mothers*. San Francisco: Jossey-Bass Publishing, 1974.

Holmes, T. H., and M. Masuda, "Psychosomatic Syndrome," *Psychology Today*, April 1972, p. 71+.

———, and R. H. Rahe, "The Social Readjustment Rating Scale," *Journal of Psychosomatic Research*, **11**(2):213–218, 1967.

Honer, M., "A Bright Woman Is Caught in a Doublebind," *Psychology Today*, November 1969, pp. 36–38.

Honer, S., and T. Hunt, *Invitation to Philosophy*. Belmont, Calif.: Wadsworth, 1978.

Horn, Patrice, "The Effects of Crowding on Children, Adults, and !Kung," *Psychology Today*, April 1974, p. 22+.

Horney, Karen, *The Neurotic Personality of Our Time*. New York: Norton, 1937.

———, *New Ways in Psychoanalysis*. New York: Norton, 1939.

———, *Our Inner Conflicts*. New York: Norton, 1945.

———, *Feminine Psychology*. New York: Norton, 1967.

————, "On the Genesis of the Castration Complex in Women," in Jean B. Miller (ed.), *Psychoanalysis and Women*. New York: Brunner/Mazel, 1973. First published, 1922.

Hornick, Edward, and L. Myles, "Teenage Drinking," *Psychiatric Opinion*, 1975.

Hull, Clark L., *Principles of Behavior*. New York: Appleton-Century-Crofts, 1943.

Hunt, M., *Sexual Behavior in the Seventies*. Chicago: Playboy Press, 1974.

————, "In the News," *Medical Aspects in Human Sexuality,* **15**(5):114, 1970.

"Interest Tests" in Robert Goldenson (ed.), *Encyclopedia of Human Behavior*. Garden City, N.Y.: Doubleday, 1970, pp.638–640.

Huston, Ted L., Gilbert Geis, and Richard Wright, "The Angry Samaritans," *Psychology Today,* June 1976, pp. 61–64.

Izard, C. E., *The Face of Emotion*. New York: Appleton-Century-Crofts, 1971.

Jacobs, M., and J. M. Whiteley, "Approaches to Sexual Counseling." *Counseling Psychologist*, **5**(1):3–8, 1975.

Jacobson, Edith, "On Normal and Pathological Moods," in R. S. Eissler et al. (eds.), *The Psychoanalytic Study of the Child*, vol. 12. New York: International Universities Press, 1957, pp. 73–113.

James, W., *The Principles of Psychology*, vols. 1, 2. New York: Holt, 1890.

————, *The Letters of William James*. Boston: Harvard University Press, 1920.

————, *The Will To Believe*. New York: Dover, 1956.

Janis, I. L., "Psychodynamic Aspects of Stress Tolerance," in S. A. Klausner (ed.), *The Quest for Self-Control*. New York: Free Press, 1965.

————, *Stress and Frustration*. New York: Harcourt Brace, 1971.

————, *Victims of Groupthink: A Psychological Study of Foreign Policy Discussions and Fiascoes*. Boston: Houghton Mifflin, 1973.

————, "Groupthink," *Yale Alumni Magazine*, January 1973.

————, D. Chapman, J. Gillin, and J. Spiegel, *The Problem of Panic*. Washington: Federal Civil Defense Administration, Bulletin TB-19-2, 1955.

Janov, Arthur, *The Primal Scream*. New York: Putman, 1970.

Jellinek, E. M., "Phases of Alcohol Addiction," in G. D. Shean (ed.), *Studies in Abnormal Behavior*. Chicago: Rand McNally, 1971, pp. 86–98.

Jensen, A. R., "How Much Can We Boost IQ and Scholastic Achievement?" *Harvard Educational Review*, **39**(2):1–124, 1969.

Jones, E., *Sigmund Freud*, vol. II. New York: Basic Books, 1955.

————, *The Life and Work of Sigmund Freud*. L. Trilling and S. Marcus (eds.). New York: Doubleday Anchor, 1963.

Jones, M., *The Therapeutic Community: A New Treatment Method in Psychiatry*. New York: Basic Books, 1953.

Jones, M. C., "A Laboratory Study of Fear: The Case of Peter," *Pedagogical Seminary and Journal of Genetic Psychology*, **31**(4):308–315, 1924.

Jung, C. G., *Collected Papers on Analytical Psychology*. New York: Moffat, Yard, 1917.

————, *Contributions to Analytical Psychology*. London: Kegan Paul, Trench, Trubner & Co., Ltd., 1928.

————, *Modern Man in Search of a Soul*. New York: Harcourt, Brace, 1933.

————, "Psychology of the Unconscious," in H. Read, M. Fordham, and G. Adler (eds.), *The Collected Works of C. G. Jung,* vol. 7. New York: Pantheon, 1953, pp. 3–19.

————, "The Archetypes and the Collective Unconscious," in *Collected Works*, vol. 7, part I. (trans. by H. Read, M. Fordham, and G. Adler) New York: Pantheon, 1959, pp. 90–113.

————, *Civilization in Transition, in Collected Works*, vol. 10 (trans. by R. F. C. Hull). New York: Pantheon, 1964, p. 170.

Kagan, J., "Acquisition and Significance of Sex Typing and Sex Role Identity," in M. Hoffman and L. Hoffman (eds.), *Review of Child Development Research*, vol. 1. New York: Russell Sage Foundation, 1964.

——, *Understanding Children: Behavior, Motives, and Thought*. New York: Harcourt, Brace, 1971.

——, An Address to the American Association for the Advancement of Science, 1974.

——, and M. Berkun, "The Reward Value of Running Activity," *Journal of Comparative Physiological Psychology*, **47**(2):108, 1954.

——, and R. Klein, "Cross-Cultural Perspectives on Early Development," *American Psychologist*, **28**(11):947–961, 1973.

Kahn, E. J., *The American People*. New York: Weybright and Talley, 1974.

Kangas, J. A., and G. F. Solomon, *The Psychology of Strength*. Englewood Cliffs, N.J.: Prentice-Hall, 1975.

Kanter, Rosabeth Moss, in Alice Sargent (ed.), *Beyond Sex Roles*. St. Paul, Minn.: West, 1976.

Kantor, R. E., and W. G. Herron, *Reactive and Process Schizophrenia*. Palo Alto, Calif.: Science and Behavior Books, 1966.

Kaplan, H. S., *The New Sex Therapy: Active Treatment of Sexual Dysfunctions*. New York: Quadrangle, 1974.

Kase, S., and S. Cobb, Blood Pressure Changes in Men Undergoing Job Loss: A Preliminary Report, *Psychosomatic Medicine*, **32**(1):19–38, 1970.

Katz, B. J., "Finding Psychiatric Help Can Be Traumatic Itself," *The National Observer*, Dec. 16, 1972, p. 9.

Keller, Fred, *Learning Reinforcement Theory*. New York: Random House, 1954.

Keller, Suzanne, "The Social Origins and Career Lines of Three Generations of American Business Leaders," Ph.D. dissertation, Columbia University, 1953.

Kendell, R. E., "The Classification of Depressive Illnesses." *Maudsley Monograph*, no. 18. London: Oxford University Press, 1968.

Keniston, Ellen, and Kenneth Keniston, "An American Anachronism: The Image of Women and Work," *The American Scholar*, no. 4, Summer 1965, p. 628.

Keniston, Kenneth, *The Uncommitted: Alienated Youth in American Society*. New York: Harcourt, Brace, 1965.

Kephart, William M., *The Family, Society and the Individual*. Boston: Houghton Miffin, 1961.

Kierkegaard, Soren, *The Point of View* (trans. by W. Lowrie). London: Oxford University Press, 1939.

——, *Kierkegaard's Concluding Unscientific Postscript* (trans. by D. F. Swenson). Princeton, N.J.: Princeton University Press, 1941.

——, *The Concept of Dread* (trans. with introduction by Walter Lowrie). Princeton, N.J.: Princeton University Press, 1944. (First published, 1844.)

——, *Concluding Unscientific Postscript* (trans. by D. F. Swenson). Princeton, N.J.: Princeton University Press, 1944.

Kiloh, L. G., and R. F. Garside, "The Independence of Neurotic and Endogenous Depression," *British Journal of Psychiatry*, **109**(461):451–463, 1963.

Kimball, Spencer W., *Marriage and Divorce*. Salt Lake City: Deseret Book Company, 1976.

Kinsey, A. C., W. B. Pomeroy, and C. E. Martin, *Sexual Behavior in the Human Male* (2d ed.). Philadelphia: Saunders, 1953.

Klein, P. C., and M. E. P. Seligman, "Reversal of Performance Deficits and Perceptual Deficits in Learned Helplessness and Depression," *Journal of Abnormal Psychology*, **85**(1):11–26, 1976.

Kluckhorn, C., and H. Murray, "Personality Formation: The Determinants," in C. Kluckhorn, H. Murray, and D. Schneider (eds.), *Personality in Nature, Society, and Culture*. New York: Knopf, 1953.

Koch, H. L., "The Relation of Certain Formal Attributes of Siblings to Attitudes Held toward Each Other and toward Their Parents." *Monograph of the Society for Research in Child Development*, **25**(4), 1960.

Koestenbaum, Peter, *Existential Sexuality*. Englewood Cliffs, N.J.: Prentice-Hall, 1974.

Kogen, N., and F. C. Shelton, "Beliefs about Old People: A Comparative Study of Older and Younger Samples," *Journal of Genetic Psychology*, **100**(3):93–112, 1962.

Kohlberg, L., "The Development of Children's Orientations toward a Moral Order: I. Sequence in the Development of Moral Thought." *Vita Humana*, **6**:11–33, 1963.

———, "Stage and Sequence: The Cognitive-Developmental Approach to Socialization," in D. A. Goslin (ed.), *Handbook of Socialization Theory and Research*. Chicago: Rand McNally, 1969, pp. 374–480.

Koller, G., "Der Nestbae der weissen Maus und seine hormonale Auslösung," *Verlag deutsche zoologesche Gesellschaft*. Freiburg, W. Germany, 1952, pp. 160–168.

Konner, I. N., "Hope as a Method of Coping," *Journal of Counseling and Clinical Psychology*, 1970.

Koppitz, E. M., "Relationships between Some Background Factors and Children's Interpersonal Attitudes," *Journal of Genetic Psychology*, **91**(9):119–130, 1957.

Krech, D., R. S. Crutchfield, and E. L. Ballachey, *Individual in Society*. New York: McGraw-Hill, 1962.

———, M. Rosenzweig, and E. Bennett, "Relations between Brain Chemistry and Problem Solving among Rats Raised in Enriched and Impoverished Environments," *Journal of Comparative and Physiological Psychology*, **55**(5):801–807, 1962.

Kübler-Ross, Elisabeth, *On Death and Dying*. New York: Macmillan, 1969.

Lacey, J. I., "Somatic Response Patterning and Stress: Some Revisions of Activation Theory," in M. H. Appleby and R. Trumbull (eds.), *Psychological Stress*. New York: McGraw-Hill, 1967, pp. 14–36.

Laing, R. D., "Is Schizophrenia a Disease?" *International Journal of Social Psychiatry*, **10**(3):184–193, 1964.

———, and A. Esterson, *Sanity, Madness, and the Family*. London: Tavistock, 1964.

Lane, R. E., *Political Ideology: Why the American Common Man Believes What He Does*. New York: Free Press, 1962.

Lange, A. J., and P. Jakubowski, *Responsible Assertive Behavior*. Champaign, Ill.: Research Press, 1976.

Langer, Jonas, *Theories of Development*. New York: Holt, Rinehart, 1969.

Latane, Bibb, and John M. Darley, "Group Inhibition of Bystander Intervention in Emergencies," *Journal of Personality and Social Psychology*, **10**(3):215–221, 1968.

Lazakus, Richard, Psychological Stress and the Coping Process. New York: McGraw-Hill, 1966.

Lecky, Prescott, *Self-Consistency: A Theory of Personality*. New York: Island Press, 1945.

Leeper, R. W., "The Motivational and Perceptual Properties of Emotions as Indicating Their Fundamental Character and Role," in M. B. Arnold (ed.), *Feelings and Emotions: The Loyola Symposium*. New York: Academic, 1970, pp. 151–168.

Lehrman, N., *Masters and Johnson Explained*. Chicago: Playboy Press, 1970.

Leonard, C. V., "Depression and Suicidality," *Journal of Consulting and Clinical Psychology*, **42**(1):98–104, 1974.

LeSham, L., "An Emotional Life-History Pattern Associated with Neoplastic Disease," *Annals of the New York Academy of Science*, January 1966.

519

BIBLIOGRAPHY

Lessing, G. E., quoted in John H. Randall, Jr., *The Making of the Modern Mind*. Cambridge, Mass.: Riverside Press, 1940.

Lester, D., "Relationship of Mental Disorders to Suicidal Behavior," *New York State Journal of Medicine*, **71**:1503–1505, 1971.

Levin, Malinda Jo, *Psychology: A Biographical Approach*. New York: McGraw-Hill, 1978.

Levin, R. J., "The Redbook Report on Premarital and Extramarital Sex," *Redbook*, October 1975, pp. 38–44, 190.

———, and A. A. Levin, "Sexual Pleasure," *Redbook* report. *Redbook*, September 1975, pp. 51–58.

Lewin, K., *A Dynamic Theory of Personality*. New York: McGraw-Hill, 1935.

———, *Principles of Topological Psychology*. New York: McGraw-Hill, 1936.

Lewis, M., "Behavior Resulting from Calcium Deprivation in Parathyroid-Ectomized Rats." *Journal of Comparative Physiological Psychology*, **57**(3):348–352, 1964.

Liddell, H. S., "Conditioned Reflex Method and Experimental Neurosis," in d. M. V. Hunt (ed.), *Personality and Behavior Disorders*, vol. 1. New York: Ronald, 1944, pp. 389–412.

Lidz, T., *The Origins and Treatment of Schizophrenic Disorders*. New York: Basic Books, 1973.

———, S. Fleck, and A. Cornelism, *Schizophrenia and the Family*. New York: International Universities Press, 1965.

Liebert, R. M., J. M. Neale, and E. S. Davidson, *The Early Window: Effects of Television on Children and Youth*. Elmsford, N.Y.: Pergamon, 1973.

Lilly, J. C., "Mental Effects of Reduction of Ordinary Levels of Physical Stimuli on Intact, Healthy Persons," *Psychiatric Research*, **5**:1–9, 1956.

Lindsley, O. R., *Studies in Behavior Therapy: Status Report III*. Waltham, Mass.: Metropolitan State Hospital, 1954.

———, and B. F. Skinner, "A Method for the Experimental Analysis of the Behavior of Psychotic Patients," *American Psychologist*, **9**(8):419–420, 1954.

Lipset, S. M., and R. Bendix, *Social Mobility in Industrial Society*. Berkeley: University of California Press, 1959.

Lobenz, Norman M., and Clark W. Blackburn, *How to Stay Married: A Modern Approach to Sex, Money, and Emotions in Marriage*. New York: Cowles, 1969.

Lorenz, Konrad, *On Aggression*. New York: Harcourt, Brace, 1966.

Lovaas, O. I., G. Freitag, V. Gold, and I. Kassorla, "Experimental Studies in Childhood Schizophrenia: Analysis of Self-Destructive Behavior," *Journal of Experimental Child Psychology*, **2**(1):67–84, 1965.

———, B. Schaeffer, and J. Simmons, "Building Social Behavior in Autistic Children by Use of Electric Shock," *Journal of Experimental Research in Personality*, **1**(1):99–109, 1965.

Luther, Martin, "Address to the Christian Nobility of the German Nation," in Harry E. Fosdick (ed.), *Great Voices of the Reformation*. New York: Random House, 1952, pp. 96–117.

Luttge, W. G., The Role of Gonadal Hormones in the Sexual Behavior of the Rhesus Monkey and Humans: A Literature Survey, *Archives of Sexual Behavior*, **1**:61–68, 1971.

Machover, K., *Personality Projection in the Drawing of the Human Figure*. Springfield, Ill.: Charles C Thomas, 1949.

MacIver, R. M., *Society, a Textbook of Sociology*. New York: Farrar & Rinehart, 1937.

Maddi, S. R., "The Existential Neurosis," *Journal of Abnormal Psychology*, **72**(4):311–325, 1967.

———, *Personality Theories*. Homewood, Ill.: Dorsey, 1972.

Maier, Henry W., *Three Theories of Child Development*. New York: Harper & Row, 1969.

Marin, P., and A. Y. Cohen, *Understanding Drug Use: An Adult's Guide to Drugs and the Young*. New York: Harper & Row, 1971.

Marquis, Donald R., "Pride," in *Archy Does His Part*. Garden City, N.Y.: Doubleday, Doran, 1935.

Martin, Barclay, *Abnormal Psychology*. New York: Holt, Rinehart, 1977.

Marx, Karl, *Karl Marx: Early Writings* (T. B. Bottsmore, ed. and trans.). New York: McGraw-Hill, 1964.

Maslow, A. H., "Deficiency Motivation and Growth Motivation," in M. R. Jones (ed.), *Nebraska Symposium on Motivation*. Lincoln: University of Nebraska Press, **3**:1–30, 1955.

———, "A Philosophy of Psychology: The Need for a Mature Science of Human Nature," in F. T. Severin (ed.), *Humanistic Viewpoint in Psychology*. New York: McGraw-Hill, 1965.

———, *Motivation and Personality* (2d ed.). New York: Harper & Row, 1970.

———, *The Farther Reaches of Human Nature*. New York: Viking, 1971.

Masters, W. H., and V. E. Johnson, *Human Sexual Inadequacy*. Boston: Little, Brown, 1970.

Masuda, M., and T. H. Holmes, "The Social Readjustment Rating Scale: A Cross-Cultural Study of Japanese and Americans," *Journal of Psychosomatic Research*, **11**(2):227–237, 1967.

May, Rollo, *Man's Search for Himself*. New York: Dell, 1953.

———, *Psychology and the Human Dilemma*. New York: Van Nostrand Reinhold, 1967.

———, "The Origins and Significance of the Existential Movement in Psychology," in R. May, E. Angel, and H. F. Ellenberger (eds.), *Existence: A New Dimension in Psychiatry and Psychology*. New York: Basic Books, 1958.

———, E. Angel, and H. Ellenberger, *Existence: A New Dimension in Psychiatry and Psychology*. New York: Basic Books, 1958.

Mayer, J., N. Marshall, J. Vitale, J. Christensen, M. Mashayekhi, and F. Stare, "Exercise, Food Intake and Body Weight in Normal Rats and Genetically Obese Adult Mice," *American Journal of Physiology*, **177**(3):544–548, 1954.

———, R. Roy, and K. Mitra, "Relation between Caloric Intake, Body Weight and Physical Work: Studies in Industrial Male Population in West Bengal," *American Journal of Clinical Nutrition*, **4**(2):169–175, 1956.

McCandless, Boyd R., and Robert J. Trotter, *Children: Behavior and Development*. New York: Holt, Rinehart, 1977.

McClelland, D. C., *Studies in Motivation*. New York: Appleton-Century-Crofts, 1955.

———, *The Achieving Society*. Princeton, N.J.: Van Nostrand, 1961.

———, and A. M. Liberman, "The Effect of Need for Achievement on Recognition of Need-Related Words," *Journal of Personality*, **18**(2):236–251, 1949.

———, and E. L. Lowell, *The Achievement Motive*. New York: Appleton-Century-Crofts, 1953.

———, and Robert Steele, *Human Motivation, A Book of Readings*. Morristown, N.J.: General Learning Press, 1973.

McConnell, J. V., *Understanding Human Behavior* (2d ed.). New York: Holt, Rinehart, 1977.

McDougall, W., *An Introduction to Social Psychology*. London: Methuen, 1908.

McFall, R. M., and A. R. Marston, "An Experimental Investigation of Behavior Rehearsal in Assertive Training," *Journal of Abnormal Psychology*, **76**(2):295–303, 1970.

McGaugh, James, *Psychobiology: The Biological Cases of Behavior*. San Francisco: Freeman, 1967.

———, "Time-Dependent Processes in Memory Storage," in K. McGaugh and M. J.

Herz (eds.), *Controversial Issues in Consolidation of the Memory Trace*. New York: Atherton, 1970.

McGinnies, E., "Emotionality and Perceptoral Defense," *Psychological Review*, **56**(5):244–251, 1949.

McGovern, L. P., Jan L. Detzian, and Stuart P. Taylor, "Sex and Perceptions of Dependency in a Helping Situation," *Bulletin of the Psychonomic Society*, **5**(4):336–339, 1975.

McGuire, R. J., "Classification and the Problems of Diagnosis," in H. J. Eysenck (ed.), *Handbook of Abnormal Psychology*. New York: Basic Books, 1961, pp. 3–33.

McNeil, E. B., *The Psychoses*. Englewood Cliffs, N.J.: Prentice-Hall, 1970.

Mead, George, *Mind, Self, and Society*. Chicago: University of Chicago Press, 1934.

Mead, Margaret, "Introduction," in Winston Ehrmann, *Premarital Dating Behavior*. New York: Holt, 1959.

———, "A Cultural Anthropologist's Approach to Maternal Deprivation," *Public Health Papers*, **14**:45–62, 1962.

———, "Socialization and Enculturation," *Current Anthropology*, **4**(4):184–188, 1963.

———, "Future Family," *Transaction*, **8**:11, 1971.

———, "Parent Gap," *Newsweek*, Sept. 22, 1975, pp. 48–50+.

Meanick, S. A., "A Learning Theory of Schizophrenia: Thirteen Years Later," in M. Hammer, K. Salginger, and S. Sutton (eds.), *Psychopathology: Contributions from the Social, Behavioral, and Biological Sciences*. New York: Wiley, 1973.

———, and F. Schulsinger, "Some Premorbid Characteristics Related to Breakdown in Children with Schizophrenic Mothers," in D. Rosenthal and S. S. Ketry (eds.), *The Transmission of Schizophrenia*. New York: Pergamon, 1968.

Mehrabian, Albert, "Inference of Attitudes from Posture, Orientation, and Distance of a Communicator," *Journal of Consulting and Clinical Psychology*, 1968, **32**(3):296–308.

Mikulas, William, *Behavior Modifications: An Overview*. New York: Harper & Row, 1972.

Milgram, S., "Some Conditions of Obedience and Disobedience to Authority," *Human Relations*, **18**(1):57–76, 1965.

Miller, G. A., and D. McNeill, "Psycholinguistics," in G. Lindzey and E. Aronson (eds.), *Handbook of Social Psychology*, vol. 3. Reading, Mass.: Addison-Wesley, 1969.

Miller, Neal, "The Frustration Aggression Hypothesis," *Psychological Review*, **48**(4):337–342, 1941.

Millon, T., *Modern Psychopathology*. Philadelphia: Saunders, 1969.

———, and Renée Millon, *Abnormal Behavior and Personality*. Philadelphia: Saunders, 1974.

Mischel, W., and R. Metzner, "Preference for Delayed Reward as a Function of Age, Intelligence, and Length of Delay Interval," *Journal of Abnormal and Social Psychology*, **64**(6):425–431, 1962.

Missildino, W. Hugh, *Your Inner Child of the Past*. New York: Simon & Schuster, 1963.

Morgan, D. T., and R. A. King, *Introduction to Psychology*. New York: McGraw-Hill, 1966.

Morgan, H. H., "An Analysis of Certain Structured and Unstructured Test Results of Achieving and Non-Achieving High Ability College Students." Unpublished Ph.D. dissertation, University of Michigan, 1951.

Morgan, Richard, *Psychology: An Individualized Course*. Unit on "Social Problems," Palo Alto, Calif.: Westinghouse Learning Press, 1972.

Mosher, L. R., "Psychiatric Heretics and Extra-Medical Treatment of Schizophrenia," in R. Cancro, N. Fox, and L. Shapiro (eds.), *Strategic Intervention in Schizophrenia: Current Developments in Treatment*. New York: Behavioral Publications, 1974.

Moss, H. A., and Jerome Kagan, "Stability of Achievement and Recognition Seeking

Behavior from Early Childhood through Adulthood," *Journal of Abnormal and Social Psychology*, **63**(3):629–635, 1961.

Mousseau, Jacques, "The Family, Prison of Love," *Psychology Today*, August 1975, pp. 52–54.

Mower, O. H., "On the Dual Nature of Learning—A Reinterpretation of 'Conditioning' and 'Problem Solving'," *Harvard Educational Review*, **17**:102–148, 1947.

———, and R. R. Lamoreaux, "Avoidance Conditioning and Signal Duration: A Study of Secondary Motivation and Reward." *Psychological Monograph*, **54**, (247), 1942.

———, and A. P. Ullman, "Time as a Determinant in Integrative Learning," *Psychological Review*, **52**(2):61–90, 1945.

Murphy, Gardner, *Historical Introduction to Modern Psychology*. New York: Harcourt, Brace, 1949.

Murray, Edward, *Motivation and Emotion*. Englewood Cliffs, N.J.: Prentice-Hall, 1964.

Murray, H. A., *Explorations in Personality*. New York: Oxford University Press, 1938.

Murray, J. P., "Television and Violence: Implications of the Surgeon General's Research Program," *American Psychologist*, **28**(6):472–478, 1973.

Mussen, P. H., and A. Parker, "Mother Nurturance and Girls' Incidental Initiative Learning," *Journal of Personality and Social Psychology*, **2**(1):94–97, 1965.

National Commission on Marijuana and Drug Abuse, *Marijuana: A Signal of Misunderstanding*. New York: New American Library, 1972.

National Institute of Alcohol Abuse and Alcoholism, *Facts about Alcohol and Alcoholism*. Washington: U.S. Department of Health, Education, and Welfare, pub. no. ADM 75–81, 1974.

National Opinion Research Center, "Jobs and Occupations: A Popular Evaluation," *Opinion News*, Sept. 1, 1947.

Newcomb, T. M., R. H. Turner, and P. E. Converse, *Social Psychology*. New York: Holt, Rinehart, 1965.

Nietzsche, Friedrich, *Joyful Wisdom*. New York: Ungar, 1960.

Norwalk, C. A., "Does Youthfulness Equal Attractiveness?" in L. E. Troll, J. Israel, and K. Israel (eds.), *Looking Ahead: A Woman's Guide to the Problems and Joys of Growing Older*. Englewood Cliffs, N.J.: Prentice-Hall, 1977.

Noyes, A. P., and L. C. Kolb, *Modern Clinical Psychiatry*. Philadelphia: Saunders, 1963.

O'Neill, Nena, and George O'Neill, *Open Marriage*. New York: M. Evans, 1972.

Ornstein, Robert, *The Psychology of Consciousness*. New York: Harcourt, Brace, 1977.

Orton, S., *Reading, Writing, and Speech Problems in Children*. New York: Norton, 1932.

Ostow, M., "The Death Instincts," *International Journal of Psycho-Analysis*, **39**:5–16, January–February 1958.

Ott, Herbert, *The Family in Search of a Future*. Englewood Cliffs, N.J.: Prentice-Hall, 1970.

Ottenberg, Donald, "Teenage Alcohol Abuse: Focusing Our Concern." *Psychiatric Opinion*, **12**(3):3, 1975.

Overmier, J. B., and M. E. Seligmann, "Effects of Inescapable Shock upon Subsequent Escape and Avoidance Learning," *Journal of Comparative Physiological Psychology*, **63**(1):28–33, 1967.

Packard, Vance, *The Hidden Persuaders*. New York: McKay, 1957.

———, *The Sexual Wilderness: The Contemporary Upheaval in Male-Female Relationships*. New York: Holt, 1968.

Page, J., and C. Landis, "Trends in Mental Disease," *Journal of Abnormal and Social Psychology*, **38**(4):518–524, 1943.

Parsons, F., *Choosing a Vocation*. Cambridge: Riverside Press, 1909.

Parten, M. B., "Social Participation among Preschool Children," *Journal of Abnormal and Social Psychology*, **27**(3):243, 1932.

Pavlov, I. P., *Lectures on Conditioned Reflexes* (W. H. Gantt, trans.). New York: International Publishers, 1928.

Payne, D. E., and P. H. Mussen, "Parent-Child Relations and Father Identification among Adolescent Boys," *Journal of Abnormal and Social Psychology,* **52**(3):358–362, 1956.

Perls, F. S., *Gestalt Therapy Verbatim.* Maob, Utah: Real People Press, 1969.

———, *The Gestalt Therapy and Ex-Witness to Therapy.* Palo Alto, Calif.: Science and Behavior Books, 1973.

———, Ralph Hefferline, and Paul Goodman, *Gestalt Therapy.* New York: The Julian Press, Inc., 1971.

Phillips, John, *The Origins of Intellect: Piaget's Theory.* San Francisco: Freeman, 1975.

Piaget, J., *Judgment and Reasoning in the Child.* Peterson, N.J.: Littlefield, Adams, 1959.

———, *Science of Education and the Psychology of the Child* (trans. by Derek Coltman). New York: Orion, 1970.

Pietropinto, Anthony, "Hite-ing Back." *Time,* Dec. 12, 1977, p. 106.

Poduska, Bernard E., *You Can Cope.* Englewood Cliffs, N.J.: Prentice-Hall, 1976.

Pokorny, A. D., "Suicide Rates in Various Psychiatric Disorders," *Journal of Nervous and Mental Diseases,* **139**(6):499–506, 1964.

Polansky, N. A., R. D. Borgman, and C. De Said, *Roots of Futility.* San Francisco: Jossey-Bass, 1972.

Pollard, J., L. Doob, N. Miller, O. Mowrer, and R. Sears, *Frustration and Aggression.* New Haven, Conn.: Yale University Press, 1939.

Popenoe, Paul, and Donna Wicks, "Marital Happiness in Two Generations," *Mental Hygiene,* **21**(2):218–223, 1937.

Postman, L., J. S. Bruner, and E. McGinnies, "Personal Values as Selective Factors in Perception," *Journal of Abnormal and Social Psychology,* **43**(2):142–154, 1948.

Poussaint, Ann A., "Are Second Marriages Better?" *Ebony,* March 1975, pp. 55–56+.

Powell, Marvin, and Allen Fredrichs, *Readings in Adolescent Psychology.* Minneapolis: Burgess, 1971.

Premack, Ann J., and David Premack, "Teaching Language to an Ape," *Scientific American,* October 1972, pp. 92–99.

President's Committee on Mental Retardation, MR67: *A First Report to the President on the Nation's Progress and Remaining Great Needs in the Campaign to Combat Mental Retardation.* Washington: U.S. Government Printing Offices, 1967.

———, and Bureau of Education of the Handicapped, *The Six-Hour Retarded Child.* Washington: U.S. Government Printing Office, 1969.

President's Panel on Mental Retardation, *Report to the President: A Proposed Program for National Action to Combat Mental Retardation.* Washington: U.S. Government Printing Office, 1962.

Prugh, P. G., and R. G. Harlow, "Marked Deprivation in Infants and Young Children," in *Deprivation of Maternal Care: A Reassessment of Its Effects.* Geneva, Switzerland: World Health Organization, 1962, pp. 9–29.

Rachman, S., and J. Teasdale, *Aversion Therapy and Behavior Disorders: An Analysis.* Coral Gables, Fla.: University of Miami Press, 1969.

Raker, J. W., A. F. Wallace, and J. F. Raymer, *Emergency Medical Care in Disasters: A Summary of Recorded Experiences,* Disaster Study No. 6. Washington: National Academy of Sciences, National Research Council, pub. no. 457, 1956.

Ramey, C. T., L. Hieger, and D. Klisz, "Synchronous Reinforcement of Vocal Responses in Failure-To-Thrive Infants," *Child Development,* **43**:1449–1455, 1972.

Randall, John H., *The Making of the Modern Mind.* Cambridge, Mass.: Riverside Press, 1940.

Rank, Otto, *The Trauma of Birth*. New York: Bruner, 1952.

Rebelsky, Freda, *Life, the Continuous Process*. New York: Knopf, 1975.

Rees, L., "The Importance of Psychological, Allergic, and Infective Factors in Childhood Asthma," *Journal of Psychosomatic Research*, **7**(4):253–262, 1964.

Reif, Adelbert, "Erick Fromm on Human Aggression," *Human Behavior*, April 1975, pp. 16–23.

Reiss, I. L., *Premarital Sexual Standards in America*. Glencoe, Ill.: Free Press, 1960.

———, "Adolescent Sexuality," in W. W. Oaks, G. A. Melchiode, and J. Ficher (eds.), *Sex and the Life Cycle*. New York: Grune & Stratton, 1976.

Rheingold, H. L., and C. O. Eckerman, "The Infant Separates Himself from His Mother," *Science*, **168**:78–83, April 3, 1970.

Ricciuti, H., and D. Schultz, *Level of Aspiration Measured and Self Estimates of Personality in Relation to Achievement Motivation*. Princeton, N.J.: Educational Testing Service Contract, 1958.

Richter, Curt, in D. Colligan, "That Helpless Feeling: The Dangers of Stress," *New York Magazine*, July 14, 1975, pp. 28–32.

Richter, C. P., "On the Phenomenon of Sudden Death in Animals and Man." *Psychosomatic Medicine,* **19**(3):191–198, 1957.

———, and S. Helfreck, "Decreased Phosphorus Appetite of Parathyroidectomized Rats," *Endocrinology*, **33**(5):349–352, 1943.

Richards, L. G., and E. E. Carroll, "Illicit Drug Use and Addiction in the United States: Review of Available Statistics." *Public Health Reports*, **85**:1035–1041, 1970.

Rilke, Rainer, *Letters of Rainer Maria Rilke,* vol. 1 (trans. by Jane Bannard Greene and M. D. Herter Norton). New York: Norton, 1948.

Ringness, Thomas, *Mental Health in the Schools*. New York: Random House, 1969.

Rioch, M. J., "Pilot Projects in Training Mental Health Counselors, in E. L. Cowen, E. A. Gardner, and M. Zax (eds.), *Emerging Approaches to Mental Health Problems*. New York: Appleton-Century-Crofts, 1967.

Roazen, Paul, *Freud and His Followers*. New York: Meridian–New American Library, 1974.

Robertson, J., *Young Children in Hospital*. London: Tavistock Publications, 1958.

Robertson, Wyndham, "The Ten Highest-Ranking Women in Big Business," *Fortune*, April 1973, pp. 80–89.

Robins, E., J. Gassner, J. Hayes, R. Wilkinson, and G. Murphy, "The Communication of Suicidal Intent: A Study of 134 Successful (Completed) Suicides," *American Journal of Psychiatry*, **115**(8):724–733, 1959.

Robins, N. L., *Deviant Children Grow Up*. Baltimore: Williams & Wilkins, 1966.

Roe, A., B. Burks, and B. Mittelmann, "Adult Adjustment of Foster Children of Alcoholic and Psychotic Parentage and the Influence of the Foster Home." *Mem. Section on Alcoholic Studies*, no. 3. New Haven: Yale University Press, 1945.

Roethlisberger, F. J., and W. J. Dickson, *Management and the Worker*. Cambridge, Mass.: Harvard University Press, 1939.

Rogers, C. R., *Counseling and Psychotherapy: New Concepts in Practice*. Boston: Houghton Mifflin, 1942.

———, "Psychometric Tests and Client-Centered Counseling," *Educational and Psychological Measurement*, **6**(1):139–144, 1946.

———, "A Theory of Therapy, Personality, and Interpersonal Relationships as Developed in the Client-Centered Framework," in S. Koch (ed.), *Psychology: A Study of Science*, vol. 3. New York: McGraw-Hill, 1959.

———, *On Becoming a Person*. Boston: Houghton Mifflin, 1961.

———, *Client-Centered Therapy* (2d ed.). Boston: Houghton Mifflin, 1969.

Rosen, G., *Madness in Society*. Chicago: University of Chicago Press, 1968.

Rosenberg, C. M., "Personality and Obsessional Neurosis," *British Journal of Psychiatry,* **113**(498):471–477, 1967.

Rosenberg, M., *Occupations and Values.* Glencoe, Ill.: Free Press, 1957.

Rosenthal, Robert, and Lenore Jacobson, *Pygmalion in the Classroom: Teacher Expectations and Pupils' Intellectual Development.* New York: Holt, Rinehart, 1968.

Rosenzweig, M. R., E. L. Bennett, and M. C. Diamond, "Brain Changes in Reponse to Experience," *Scientific American,* **226**(2):22–29, 1972.

Rosenzweig, S., "An Experimental Study of 'Repression' with Special Reference to Need-Persistive and Ego-Defensive Reactions to Frustration," *Journal of Experimental Psychology,* **32**(1):64–74, 1943.

Roszak, Theodore, *The Making of a Counterculture.* Garden City, N.Y.: Doubleday, 1969.

Rudestam, K. E., "Stockholm and Los Angeles: A Cross-Cultural Study of the Communication of Suicidal Intent," *Journal of Consulting and Clinical Psychology,* **36**(1):82–90, 1971.

Rush, Diane, "Where No Science Exists," *Business and Economic Dimensions,* May 1971.

Rychlak, Joseph F., *Introduction to Personality and Psychotherapy.* Boston: Houghton Mifflin Co., 1973.

Saben, Samuel, "Occupational Mobility of Employed Workers," *Monthly Labor Review,* June 1967, pp. 31–38.

Sage, Wayne, "Violence in the Children's Room," *Human Behavior,* July 1975, pp. 40–47.

Salter, Andrew, *Conditioned Reflex Therapy.* New York: Creative Age, 1949.

Sapir, Edward, "The Emergence of the Concept of Personality in a Study of Culture," *Journal of Social Psychology.* **5**(1):408–415, 1934.

Sartre, J. P., *L'Etre et Le Néant.* Paris: Librairie Gallimard, 1943.

———, *Existentialism.* New York: Philosophical Library, 1947.

———, *Existentialism and Human Emotions.* New York: Philosophical Library, 1957.

———, *Being and Nothingness.* New York: Citadell, 1971.

Satir, V., *Conjoint Family Therapy: A Guide to Theory and Technique.* Palo Alto, Calif.: Science and Behavior Books, 1964.

Saxton, Lloyd, *The Individual, Marriage, and the Family.* Belmont, Calif.: Wadsworth, 1972, p. 191.

Schachter, S., and J. E. Singer, "Cognitive, Social and Physiological Determinants of Emotional State," *Psychological Review,* **69**(5):379–399, 1962.

Schaefer, E. S., "A Circumplex Model for Maternal Behavior," *Journal of Abnormal and Social Psychology,* **59**(2):226, 1959.

Schanche, Don, "The Emotional Aftermath of 'The Largest Tornado Ever'," in Rudolf Moor (ed.), *Human Adaptation: Coping with Life Crises.* Lexington, Mass.: Heath, 1976, pp. 385–393.

Scheff, T. J., "Schizophrenia as Ideology," *Schizophrenia Bulletin,* **1**(2):15–19, 1970.

Schilder, P., *The Image and Appearance of the Human Body.* New York: International Universities Press, 1950.

Schneidman, E. S. (ed.), *Suicidology: Contemporary Developments.* New York: Grune & Stratton, 1976.

———, and N. L. Farberow, "The Logic of Suicide," in E. S. Schneidman, N. L. Farberow, and R. E. Litman (eds.), *The Psychology of Suicide.* New York: Science House, 1970.

———,———, and L. Cabista, *Some Facts about Suicide Causes and Prevention.* Washington: Government Printing Office, 1965.

Schopler, J., and N. Bateson, "The Power of Dependence," *Journal of Personality and Social Psychology*, **2**(2):247–254, 1965.

Schultz, Duane, *Growth Psychology: Models of the Healthy Personality*. New York: Van Nostrand, 1977.

Sears, R. R., E. E. Maccoby, and H. Levin, *Patterns of Child Rearing*. Evanston, Ill.: Row, Peterson, 1957.

Seashore, S. E., *Group Cohesiveness in the Industrial Work Group*. Ann Arbor: University of Michigan, Institute for Social Research, Survey Research Center, 1954.

Segal, Julius, "How Much Sleep Do You Need?" in J. Kravitz and W. Hillabrant (eds.), *The Future Is Now*. Itasca, Ill.: F. E. Peacock Publishers, 1977.

Seidman, D., S. Bensen, I. Miller, and T. Meeland, "Influence of a Partner on Tolerance for a Self-Administered Electric Shock," *Journal of Abnormal and Social Psychology*, **54**(2):210–212, 1957.

Seligman, M., and J. Geer, "The Alleviation of Learned Helplessness in the Dog," *Journal of Abnormal and Social Psychology*, **73**(3):256–262, 1968.

———, and S. Maier, "Failure to Escape Traumatic Shock," *Journal of Experimental Psychology*, **74**:1–9, 1967.

Selye, Hans, *The Stress of Life*. New York: McGraw-Hill, 1956.

———, *Stress Without Distress*. Philadelphia: Lippincott, 1974.

Severin, F. T., *Humanistic Viewpoints in Psychology*. New York: McGraw-Hill, 1965.

Sewell, W. H., "Inequality of Opportunity for Higher Education," *American Sociological Review*, October 1971, pp. 793–809.

Sheldrake, P., M. Cormack, and J. McGuire, "Psychosomatic Illness, Birth Order, and Intellectual Preference," *Journal of Psychosomatic Research*, **20**(1)37–44, 1976.

Sherif, M., and C. W. Sherif, *An Outline of Social Psychology*. New York: Harper, 1956.

Shostrom, Everett, *Man, the Manipulator*. New York: Bantam, 1972.

Silverman, Samuel, *How Will You Feel Tomorrow?* New York: Stein and Day, 1975.

Simeons, A. T., *Man's Presumptuous Brain: An Evolutionary Interpretation of Psychosomatic Disease*. New York: Dutton, 1961.

Skeels, H. M., and H. B. Dye, "A Study of the Effect of Differential Stimulation on Mentally Retarded Children." American Association on Mental Defenciencies:*Proceedings*, **44**:114–136, 1938–1939.

Skinner, B. F., "The Measurement of 'Spontaneous Activity'," *Journal of Genetic Psychology*, **9**(1):3–23, 1933.

———, *The Behavior of Organisms*. New York: Appleton-Century-Crofts, 1938.

———, *Walden Two*. New York: MacMillan, 1948.

———, *Science and Human Behavior*. New York: Macmillan, 1953.

———, "Operant Behavior," *American Psychologist*, **18**(8):503–515, 1963.

———, *Beyond Freedom and Dignity*. New York: Knopf, 1971.

Slater, P. E., "Contrasting Correlates of Group Size," *Sociometry*, **21**(2):129–139, 1958.

———, *The Pursuit of Loneliness*. Boston: Beacon Press, 1970.

Slobin, D. I., "Developmental Psycholinguistics," in W. O. Dingwall (ed.), *A Survey of Linguistic Science*. College Park: University of Maryland, Linguistics Program, 1971.

Smith, M. B., "Combat Motivations among Ground Troops," in S. A. Stouffer, A. A. Lumsdaine, R. Williams, M. Smith, J. Janis, S. Star, and L. Cottrell (eds.), *The American Soldier*, vol. 2: *Combat and Its Aftermath*. Princeton, N.J.: Princeton University Press, 1949.

Smith, Manuel, *When I Say No, I Feel Guilty*. New York: Dial, 1975.

Solomon, P., et al., *Sensory Deprivation*. Cambridge, Mass.: Harvard University Press, 1961.

Solomon, R. I., and L. C. Wynne, "Traumatic Avoidance Learning: The Principles of Anxiety Conservation and Partial Irreversibility." *Psychological Review*, **61**(6):353–385, 1954.

Spearman, C., *The Abilities of Man*. New York: Macmillan, 1927.

Spinoza, B., "Origin and Nature of the Emotions," in *Spinoza's Ethics*. London: Everyman Edition, 1910, pp. 84–139.

Spitz, R. A., "Hospitalism: An Inquiry into the Genesis of Psychiatric Conditions in Early Childhood," *Psychoanalytic Study of the Child*. New York: International Universities Press, 1945.

———, "The Role of Ecological Factors in Emotional Development in Infancy," *Child Development*, **20**(3):145–156, 1949.

———, and K. M. Wolf, "Analytic Depression: An Inquiry into the Genesis of Psychiatric Conditions in Early Childhood. II," in A. Freud et al. (eds.), *Psychoanalytic Study of the Child*. New York: International Universities Press, 1946.

Spitzer, R. L., J. Endicott, and E. Robins, "Clinical Criteria for Psychiatric Diagnosis and DSM-III," *American Journal of Psychiatry*, **132**(11):1187–1192, 1975.

Spock, Benjamin, *Baby and Child Care*. New York: Pocket Books, 1968.

Staines, Graham, Carol Tavris, and Toby Eptein Jayaratne, "The Queen Bee Syndrome," *Psychology Today*, January 1974, 55–60.

Steen, Edwin B., and James H. Price, *Human Sex and Sexuality*. New York: Wiley, 1977.

Stein, A. H., S. R. Pohly, and E. Mueller, "The Influence of Masculine, Feminine, and Neutral Tasks on Children's Achievement Behavior, Expectancies of Success, and Attainment Values," *Child Development*, **42**(1):195–207, 1971.

Steinmetz, Suzanne K., and Murray A. Straus, *Violence in the Family*. New York: Dodd, Mead, 1974.

Stephenson, William, *The Study of Behavior*. Chicago: University of Chicago Press, 1953.

Stevenson, I., and J. Wolpe, "Recovery from Sexual Deviations through Overcoming Non-Sexual Neurotic Responses," *American Journal of Psychiatry*, **116**(8):737–742, 1960.

Stonequist, E. V., *The Marginal Man*. New York: Scribner, 1937.

Stouffer, S., E. Suchman, L. De Vinney, S. Star, and R. Williams, *The American Soldier*, vol. 1: *Adjustment during Army Life*. Princeton, N.J.: Princeton University Press, 1949.

Strong, Edward K., Jr., "Interpretation of Interest Profiles," in Edward Strong (ed.), *Vocational Interests of Men and Women*. Stanford, Calif.: Stanford University Press, 1943, pp. 412–456.

Stuart, Richard, in Richard Trotter, "Obesity and Behavior," *Science News*, **106**(5):76, 1974.

Suchman, E. A., "The Hang-Loose Ethic and the Spirit of Drug Use," in Michael Wertheimer (ed.), *Confrontation: Psychology and the Problems of Today*. Glenview, Ill.: Scott, Foresman, 1970.

Suelzle, Marijean, "Women in Labor," in M. E. Adelstein and J. G. Pivel (eds.), *Women's Liberation*. New York: St. Martin's, 1972.

Sullivan, H. S. *The Interpersonal Theory of Psychiatry* (H. S. Perry and M. L. Gawel, eds.). New York: Norton, 1953.

———, *Clinical Studies in Psychiatry* (H. S. Perry, M. L. Gawel, and M. Gibbon, eds.). New York: Norton, 1956.

———, *Schizophrenia as a Human Process*. New York: Norton, 1962.

———, *The Fusion of Psychiatry and Social Science*. New York: Norton, 1964.

Swift, Pamela, "Youth Notes," *Parade*, July 5, 1970.

Talkington, L. W., S. Hall, and R. Altman, "Communication Deficits and Aggression in the Mentally Retarded," *American Journal of Mental Deficiency*, **76**(2):235–237, 1971.

Tallent, Norman, *Psychology of Adjustment*. New York: Van Nostrand, 1978.

Tanner, Ira J., *Loneliness: The Fears of Love*. New York: Harper & Row, 1973.

Terman, Lewis M., et al., *Psychological Factors in Marriage Happiness*. New York: McGraw-Hill, 1938.

Thompson, O. E., "Student Values in Transition," *California Journal of Educational Research*, **19**(3):77–86, 1968.

Thorndike, E. L., *Animal Intelligence*. New York: Macmillan, 1911.

Thorndike, R. L., and Elizabeth Hagan, *10,000 Careers*. New York: Wiley, 1959.

Thurstone, L. L., "Primary Mental Abilities," *Psychometric Monograph*, no. 32, 1938.

——, *Multiple-Factor Analysis*. Chicago: University of Chicago Press, 1947.

Tilghen, A., *Work: What It Has Meant to Men through the Ages*. New York: Harcourt, 1930.

Toker, E., "Mental Illness in the White and Bantu Population of the Republic of South Africa," *American Journal of Psychiatry*, **123**(7):55–65, 1966.

Tresemer, David, "Fear of Success: Popular, but Unproven,"*Psychology Today,* March 1974, pp. 82–85.

Trotter, Robert J., "Sexism Is Depressing," *Science News*, **108**(11):173–174, 1975.

——, "Intensive Intervention Program Prevents Retardation," *American Psychological Association Monitor,* September/October 1976.

Turner, L. H., and R. L. Solomon, "Human Traumatic Avoidance Learning: Theory and Experiments on the Operant Respondent Distinction and Failure to Learn," *Psychological Monograph*, **76**, no. 40, 1962.

Tyler, L. E., *The Psychology of Human Differences*. New York: Appleton-Century-Crofts, 1965.

U.S. Bureau of the Census, Bureau of Labor Statistics, *Statistical Abstract of the United States* (annual). Washington: Government Printing Office, 1976; 1977, p. 65; 1978.

——, *Statistical History of the United States*. Washington: Government Printing Office, 1965.

U.S. Department of Health, Education, and Welfare, *Alcohol and Health. Second Special Report to the U.S. Congress*. Washington: Government Printing Office, 1964.

——, *Work in America: Report of a Special Task Force to the Secretary of Health, Education, and Welfare*. Cambridge, Mass.: MIT Press, 1973.

U.S. Department of Labor, *Handbook of Labor Statistics*. Washington: The Department, 1976, pp. 32–33.

U.S. News & World Report, "The American Family: Can It Survive Today's Shocks?" Oct. 27, 1975, pp. 30–32.

Vaillant, George, *Adaptations to Life*. Boston: Little, Brown, 1977.

van den Berghe, Pierre, *Race and Racism: A Comparative Perspective*. New York: Wiley, 1967.

Veblen, Thorstein, *The Theory of the Leisure Class*. Boston: Houghton Mifflin, 1973.

Verner, A. M., and G. S. Stewart, "More Teenagers Sexually Active in Michigan Study," in J. H. Gagnon (ed.), *Human Sexuality in Today's World*. Boston: Little, Brown, 1977.

Vernon, J., *Inside the Black Room*. New York: Ronald, 1961.

Virginia Slims, "American Women's Opinion Poll," *Ebony*, September 1975, pp. 144–146+.

Viscott, David, *The Making of a Psychiatrist*. New York: Arbor House, 1972.

Udry, J. R., *The Social Context of Marriage*. Philadelphia: Lippincott, 1966.

Ullman, L. P.,and L. Krasner, *A Psychological Approach to Abnormal Behavior* (2d ed.). Englewood Cliffs, N.J.: Prentice-Hall, 1975.

Wallace, A., *Tornado in Worcester*. Washington: National Academy of Science—National Research Council, Committee on Disaster Studies, 1956.

———, "Mazeway Disintegration: The Individual's Perception of Socio-Cultural Disorganization," *Human Organization*, **16**(2):23–27, 1957.

Walter, R. H., and Llewellyn Thomas, "Enhancement of Punitiveness by Visual and Audiovisual Displays," *Journal of Psychology*, 1963.

Warren, H. C. (ed.), *Dictionary of Psychology*. Cambridge, Mass.: Houghton Mifflin, 1962.

Watson, D. L., and R. G. Tharp, *Self-directed Behavior: Self Modification for Personal Adjustment*. Monterey, Calif.: Brooks/Cole, 1977.

———, ———, and J. Krisberg, "Case Study of Self-Modification: Suppression of Inflammatory Scratching while Awake and Asleep," *Journal of Behavior Therapy and Experimental Psychiatry*, **3**(3):213–215, 1972.

Watson, J. B., "Psychology as the Behaviorist Views It," *Psychological Review*, **20**(3):158–177, 1913.

———, *Behavior: An Introduction to Comparative Psychology*. New York: Holt, 1914.

———, *Behaviorism*. New York: Norton, 1924.

———, and R. Rayner, "Conditioning Emotional Responses," *Journal of Experimental Psychology*, **3**(2):1–14, 1920.

Watson, J. S., "Smiling, Cooing and 'the Game'," *Merrill-Palmer Quarterly*, **18**(4):323–340, 1972.

Watzlawick, Paul, Janet Beavin, and Don Jackson, *The Pragmatics of Human Communication*. New York: Norton, 1967.

Weber, Max, *The Protestant Ethic and the Spirit of Capitalism*. New York: Scribner, 1930.

Weiss, E., and O. S. English, *Psychosomatic Medicine*. Philadelphia: Saunders, 1949.

Werner, H., "The Concept of Development from a Comparative and Organismic Point of View," in D. B. Harris (ed.), *The Concept of Development: An Issue in the Study of Human Behavior*. Minneapolis: University of Minnesota Press, 1957.

Wernick, Robert, *The Family*. New York: Time-Life, 1974.

White, B. L., and R. Held, "Plasticity of Sensorimotor Development in the Human Infant," in J. F. Rosenblith and W. Allensmith (eds.), *The Causes of Behavior*, vol. 1 (2d ed.). Boston: Allyn & Bacon, 1966.

Whitehead, Alfred, *Science and the Modern World*. New York: New American Library (Mentor Book), 1948.

———, *Dialogues of Alfred Whitehead*. Westport, Conn.: Greenwood Press, 1953.

Whitney, Eleanor, and May Hamilton, *Understanding Nutrition*. St. Paul, Minn.: West, 1977.

Whorf, B. L., "Science and Linguistics," *Technology Review*, 1940.

———, in J. B. Carroll, (ed.), *Language, Thought and Reality*. New York: Wiley, 1956.

Wickes, I. G., "Treatment of Persistent Enuresis with the Electric Buzzer," *Archives of Diseases in Childhood*, **33**(168):160–164, 1958.

Wiesner, B. P., and N. M. Sheard, "Sex Behavior in Hypophysectomized Male Rats," *Nature* (London), **132**(3338):641, 1933.

Wilkins, L., and I. Richter, "A Great Craving for Salt by a Child with Cortico-Adrenal Insufficiency," *Journal of the American Medical Association*, **114**(10):866–868, 1940.

Wilson, Edward, *Sociobiology: The New Synthesis*. Cambridge, Mass.: Harvard University Press, 1975.

Wilson G. T., and G. C. Davison, "Behavior Therapy and Homosexuality: A Critical Perspective," *Behavior Therapy*, **5**(1):16–28, 1974.

Wolfe, J. B., "Effectiveness of Token-Rewards for Chimpanzees," *Comparative Psychology Monograph*, **12**, no. 60, 1936.

Wolpe, J., *Psychotherapy by Reciprocal Inhibition*. Stanford, Calif.: Stanford University Press, 1958.

———, *The Practice of Behavior Therapy*. Elmsford, N.Y.: Pergamon, 1969.

Woodward, K. L., and P. Malmud, "The Parent Gap," *Newsweek,* Sept. 22, 1975, pp. 48–50+.

World Almanac. New York: Newspaper Enterprise Association, 1978.

World Health Organization, *World Health Statistics Annual*. Geneva, Switzerland, 1965.

Yanklovich, Skelly, and White Research Firm, "The New Morality," *Time*, Nov. 21, 1977, pp. 111–112+.

Yerkes, R. M., and J. D. Dodson, "The Relation of Strength of Stimulus to Rapidity of Habit-Formation," *Journal of Comparative Neurological Psychology*, **18**:459–482, 1908.

Young, Patrick, in "Cancer and Personality: Can They Be Connected?" *The National Observer*, April 3, 1976, p. 1+.

Zimbardo, Philip G., Paul A. Pilkomis, and Robert M. Norwood, "The Social Disease Called Shyness," *Psychology Today*, May 1975, pp. 68–72.

Zuckerman, M., "Sexual Behavior of College Students," in G. A. Melchiode, I. Ficher, and W. W. Oaks, (eds.), *Sex and the Life Cycle*. New York: Grune & Stratton, 1976.

ACKNOWLEDGEMENTS

532
ACKNOWLEDGE-
MENTS

Page 52. From *Psychology and the Human Dilemma,* by Rollo May, Litton Educational Publishing, Inc., 1967, pp. 17–18. Reprinted by permission of D. Van Nostrand Company.

Chapter 3

Page 73. Excerpts from *Archy Does His Part,* by Don Marquis. Copyright 1935 by Doubleday and Company, Inc. Reprinted by permission of the publisher.

Chapter 5

Page 124. From *I Never Promised You a Rose Garden,* by Hannah Green. Copyright © 1964 by Hannah Green. Reprinted by permission of Holt, Rinehart and Winston, Publishers.

Pages 125 and 150. *Stress without Distress,* by Hans Selye (J. B. Lippincott). Copyright © 1974 by Hans Selye, M.D. Reprinted by permission of Harper & Row, Publishers, Inc.

Page 140. *The Concept of Dread,* by Søren Kierkegaard, translated by Walter Lowrie. Copyright 1944, © 1957, by Princeton University Press. Reprinted by permission of Princeton University Press.

Page 141. From *Man for Himself,* by Eric Fromm. Copyright 1947, © 1975, by Eric Fromm. Reprinted by permission of Holt, Rinehart and Winston, Publishers.

Page 149. "The Social Readjustment Rating Scale," by T. H. Holmes and R. H. Rahe. Reprinted by permission from the *Journal of Psychosomatic Research, vol. 11, no. 2, 1967. Copyright* © 1967 by Pergamon Press, Ltd.

Chapter 6

Page 167. From *Client-Centered Therapy,* by Carl R. Rogers. Copyright © 1951 by Carl R. Rogers. Reprinted by permission of Houghton Mifflin Company.

Page 169. *Stress without Distress,* by Hans Selye (J. B. Lippincott). Copyright © 1974 by Hans Selye, M.D. Reprinted by permission of Harper & Row, Publishers, Inc.

Page 170. From *Growth Psychology: Models of the Healthy Personality,* by Duane P. Schultz. Copyright © 1977 by Litton Educational Publishing, Inc. Reprinted by permission of D. Van Nostrand Company.

Chapter 7

Page 203. From "Is AA for You?" Copyright © 1954 by Alcoholics Anonymous World Services, Inc. Reprinted by permission of Alcoholics Anonymous World Services, Inc.

Chapter 10

Pages 282 to 284. Reprinted by permission from the February 1974 GOOD HOUSE-KEEPING MAGAZINE. © 1979 by the Hearst Corporation.

533

ACKNOWLEDGE-
MENTS

Chapter 11

Page 317. "Future Family" by Margaret Meade, from TRANSACTION, vol. 8, no. 11, p. 53. Copyright ©1971 by Transaction, Inc. Published by permission.

Page 331. From *Man the Manipulator,* by Everett Shoftrom. Copyright © 1967 by Abingdon Press. Adapted from George Bach, *The Marital Fight Game,* 1963.

Pages 337 to 339. Table 11.1: "What Divorce Laws Say Coast to Coast." Reprinted from the February 10 issue of *Business Week* by special permission. Copyright © 1975 by McGraw-Hill Inc, New York. All rights reserved.

Chapter 12

Page 357. Figure 12.4, showing dimensions of autonomy-control and hostility-love, by Earl S. Schaefer. Copyright © 1954 by the American Psychological Association. Reprinted by permission.

Chapter 13

Page 397. From *Man in a World of Work,* edited by Henry L. Borow. Copyright © 1964 by Houghton-Mifflin Company. Reprinted by permission of the publisher.

Page 402. From "No Chance," by Berton Braley, in *5,000 Quotations for All Occasions,* edited by Lewis C. Henry. Copyright 1945 by Blakiston Co. Reprinted by permission of Doubleday and Company, Inc.

Chapter 14

Page 428. From "Erich Fromm on Human Aggression," by Adebert Reif, *Human Behavior Magazine,* April 1975. COpyright © 1975 by Human Behavior Magazine. Reprinted by permission.

Page 431. Excerpts from *Your Fear of Love,* by Marshall Bryant Hodge. Copyright © 1967 by Marshall Bryant Hodge. Reprinted by permission of Doubleday and Company, Inc.

Chapter 15

Page 438. From *Psychology and the Human Dilemma,* by Rollo May, pp. 108–109. Copyright © 1967 by Litton Educational Publishers, Inc. Reprinted by permission of D. Van Nostrand Company.

Page 446. From *Man the Manipulator,* by Everett Shoftrom. Copyright © 1967 by Abingdon Press. Adapted from George Bach, *The Marital Fight Game, 1963.*

Page 462. From *The Life and Work of Sigmund Freud,* by Ernest Jones, edited and abridged by Lionel Trilling and Stephen Marcus. Copyright © 1961 by Basic Book Publishing, Inc., New York.

Page 463. From *Sexual Behavior in the Human Male,* by A. C. Kinsey, W. B. Pomeroy, and C. E. Martin. W. B. Saunders, 1948. Reprinted by permission of the Institute for Sex Research, Inc.

Chapter 16

Page 486. From *Understanding Human Nature,* by Alfred Adler. Copyright © 1954 by Alfred Adler. Reprinted by permission of Fawcett World Library.

INDEX

Orgasm:
  failure to attain, 284
  unchanged frequency and incidence of, 283
Origins of Intellect, The: Piaget's Theory (Phillips), 413
Other-directed behavior toward mirror image, 66
Other-esteem, 133
"Ought" conscience, "must" conscience vs., 469
Outpatient services in community health centers, 442
Overcrowding, effects of, 137
Overindulgence, 357–358
Overpopulation as source of stress, 137–139
Overprotectiveness, 352, 356

Packard, Vance, 89, 322
Pain, reactions to, 96
Pairing of stimuli, 43
Paleologic thinking of suicidal individuals, 197
Panic:
  neurotic anxiety and, 123–124
  (*See also* Fear)
Paradoxical intent technique, 461
Parallel play, 400
Paranoia, 210
  paranoid tendencies of authoritarian personalities, 235
  reality distortion and, 185–186
Paranoid schizophrenia, defined, 209
Paraprofessionals, counseling by, 442–443
Parent-child relationships, 360–369
  historical, 307–310
  strengthening, 360–367
    by maintaining conversation, 366–367
    parental patterns of communication and, 360–366
Parent Communications (Folsom), 361
Parent ego state, 251–252
Parental attitudes, 349–360
  apathy-futility type of, 21
  dimensions of, 349–352
  dominant, 353–360
Parents:
  and development of self, 72–73
  as models, 109
  (*See also* Child rearing; Children; Divorce; Marriage; Mothers; Parent-child relationships; Parental attitudes)
Parents Anonymous, 343, 348
Parsons, F., 330, 376
Passive aggression, 421
  reality distortion and, 184–185
Passive-congenial marriage, defined, 323

Pathogenic parental attitudes, 353
  (*See also* Overindulgence; Overprotectiveness; Perfectionism; Permissiveness)
Pathogens, direct and indirect, 146
Pathological depressive reactions to loss, 151
Pattern analysis in actualization therapy, 463
Pavlov, Ivan, 10, 18, 88, 192
PCP (angel dust), 204
Peace officer syndrome, 377
Peers, influence of, on development of self, 73–74
Penis envy, 286
Perception:
  effective, needed for growth of relationships, 474
  of excellence, friendships and, 264
  of form, aesthetic impressions and, 487
  of others, interpersonal relationships and, 246, 247
  of past social-learning events, behavior based on, 296
  primary and secondary qualities of, 17
  psychological needs generated through, 89
  thinking and, 415–416
Perceptual constancies, stability and, 19
Perfectionist parents, 355–356
  and sexual identification, 295
Performance anxiety, sexual dysfunctions and, 457
Peripheral husband, marriage to, 322–323
Perls, Fritz S., 22, 348, 474
Permanence, sense of, 488
Permissiveness, 353–355
  leading to anal-expulsive personality, 40
Persona:
  conflict between shadow and, 77
  defined, 480
Personal growth therapies, 440
Personal responsibility:
  authenticity and, 477, 481
  choice and, 82, 84, 410, 411
  in existential model, 51, 52, 460
  for self and others in interpersonal relationships, 255–262
  self-acceptance and, 469
Personality:
  disease and, 144–147
    and resistance to disease, 146–147
  as hypothetical entity, 75
  origin of term, 480
  (*See also specific theories and types of personality*)
Personality disorders:
  defined, 183
  and distortion of reality, 184
  (*See also specific personality disorders*)
Personification, role of, 72
Personology, 100
Pentamic Army, 217

Phallic stage of psychosexual development, 41, 286–288, 294
  resolution of, 287–288, 290, 291
Phantom limb phenomenon, 68
Philos, 266, 486
Phobia, 193, 437
Physical abuse:
  battered wives, 328
  of children, 347–348
Physical appearance, 61–68
  deficiencies in, as source of frustration, 131–132
  disfigurement and, 67–68
  norms and attitudes toward, 62–65
    ideal weights for men and women, table, 64
  self-concept, body image and, 65–67
Physical disorders:
  defined, 183
  [*See also* Disease(s)]
Physical loneliness, stress of, 127
Physical obstacles as sources of frustration, 310–131
Physical rejection, 358
Physical violence (see Violence)
Physiological demands made by stress, 121–122
Physiological needs (see Survival needs)
Physiological reactions to stress, 143–146
  social readjustment scale, table, 145
Physiology, 10
Piaget, Jean, 399
Peitropinto, Anthony, 275, 283
Pill, the, 276
  other contraceptive methods compared with, table, 278–279
Pinel, Philippe, 446
Play as continuous process, 398–402
Plea for a Psychology as a Natural Science, A (James), 42
Political Ideology (Lane), 140
Politics (Aristotle), 228
Polygamy, serial, defined, 306
Positive regard, conditional and unconditional, 54–55
Positive reinforcement, 46–47
  (*See also* Reward)
Positive view of man, 34–35
  (*See also* Existentialism; Humanistic psychology)
Practice play in infancy, 399
Preadolescent play, 401
Prealcoholic phase of alcoholism, 200–201
Pregnancy (see Procreation)
Prejudice, 234–238
  as source of stress, 139–140
Premarital sex, 275, 282, 283
Premature ejaculation, 284
Premoral level of moral reasoning, 240
Premorbid personality, existential neurosis and, 440